HANDBOOK OF INTERNATIONAL ECONOMICS
VOLUME I

HANDBOOKS IN ECONOMICS

3

Series Editors

KENNETH J. ARROW
MICHAEL D. INTRILIGATOR

NORTH-HOLLAND
AMSTERDAM · NEW YORK · OXFORD · TOKYO

HANDBOOK OF INTERNATIONAL ECONOMICS

VOLUME I
INTERNATIONAL TRADE

Edited by

RONALD W. JONES
University of Rochester

and

PETER B. KENEN
Princeton University

NORTH-HOLLAND
AMSTERDAM · NEW YORK · OXFORD · TOKYO

© ELSEVIER SCIENCE PUBLISHERS B.V., 1984

ISBN for this volume: 0 444 70422 1

First edition 1984
Second printing (paperback) 1988

Published by:
ELSEVIER SCIENCE PUBLISHERS B.V.
P.O. Box 1991
1000 BZ Amsterdam
The Netherlands

Sole distributors for the U.S.A. and Canada
ELSEVIER SCIENCE PUBLISHING COMPANY, INC.
52 Vanderbilt Avenue
New York, NY 10017
U.S.A.

PRINTED IN THE NETHERLANDS

INTRODUCTION TO THE SERIES

The aim of the *Handbooks in Economics* series is to produce Handbooks for various branches of economics, each of which is a definitive source, reference, and teaching supplement for use by professional researchers and advanced graduate students. Each Handbook provides self-contained surveys of the current state of a branch of economics in the form of chapters prepared by leading specialists on various aspects of this branch of economics. These surveys summarize not only received results but also newer developments, from recent journal articles and discussion papers. Some original material is also included, but the main goal is to provide comprehensive and accessible surveys. The Handbooks are intended to provide not only useful reference volumes for professional collections but also possible supplementary readings for advanced courses for graduate students in economics.

CONTENTS OF THE HANDBOOK

VOLUME I

Chapter 1
The Positive Theory of International Trade
RONALD W. JONES and J. PETER NEARY

Chapter 2
The Normative Theory of International Trade
W. MAX CORDEN

Chapter 3
Higher Dimensional Issues in Trade Theory
WILFRED J. ETHIER

Chapter 4
Growth and Development in Trade Models
RONALD FINDLAY

Chapter 5
International Factor Movements
ROY J. RUFFIN

Chapter 6
Capital Theory and Trade Theory
ALASDAIR SMITH

Chapter 7
Increasing Returns, Imperfect Markets, and Trade Theory
ELHANAN HELPMAN

Chapter 8
The Role of Natural Resources in Trade Models
MURRAY C. KEMP and NGO VAN LONG

Chapter 9
Uncertainty in Trade Models
JOHN POMERY

Chapter 10
Testing Trade Theories and Predicting Trade Flows
ALAN V. DEARDORFF

Chapter 11
Trade Policies in Developing Countries
ANNE O. KRUEGER

Chapter 12
Trade Policies in Developed Countries
ROBERT E. BALDWIN

VOLUME II

Chapter 13
Macroeconomic Analysis and Policy in the Insular Economy
PETER B. KENEN and RONALD I. McKINNON

Chapter 14
Asset Markets, Exchange Rates, and the Balance of Payments: The Reformulation of Doctrine
JACOB A. FRENKEL and MICHAEL L. MUSSA

Chapter 15
The Specification and Influence of Asset Markets
WILLIAM H. BRANSON and DALE W. HENDERSON

Chapter 16
The Specification of Goods and Factor Markets in Open Economy Macroeconomic Models
NEIL BRUCE and DOUGLAS PURVIS

Chapter 17
Stabilization Policies in Open Economies
RICHARD C. MARSTON

Chapter 18
Exchange Rate Dynamics
MAURICE OBSTFELD and ALAN STOCKMAN

Chapter 19
Empirical Studies of Exchange Rates: Price Behavior, Rate Determination and Market Efficiency
RICHARD M. LEVICH

Chapter 20

Income and Price Effects in Foreign Trade
MORRIS GOLDSTEIN and MOHSIN S. KHAN

Chapter 21

Empirical Studies of Macroeconomic Interdependence
JOHN F. HELLIWELL and TIM PADMORE

Chapter 22

International Reserves and the International Monetary System
STANLEY W. BLACK

Chapter 23

Interdependence, Consistency, and Policy Coordination
RICHARD N. COOPER

PREFACE TO THE HANDBOOK

The scope of the Handbook

Very few economic problems can be analyzed completely without asking whether and to what degree an economy is open. Many problems are, of course, too intricate to analyze completely, and the implications of openness are therefore ignored to make room for other complications. But the international aspects of "domestic" problems are treated with increasing frequency and thoroughness in theoretical, empirical, and policy studies. In the United States, *The Annual Report of the Council of Economic Advisers* has almost always had an international chapter, but it was usually the last; in 1983, however, it moved from the back to the middle of the book.

Those of us who call ourselves international economists rejoice in the increasing importance attached to our subject; it is rewarding intellectually and may even have employment-creating effects. When it comes time to define our specialty, however, the trend is a bit perplexing. We cannot claim that our subject is coextensive with the whole of economics, but it is hard to draw defensible boundaries. Which problems should we claim as being intrinsically international? Which ones should we cede as being basically domestic? To organize this Handbook, we had first to define our subject carefully.

We have not included every subject and problem that has international aspects or ramifications. Instead, we have adopted a traditional definition of our subject, focusing primarily on the explanation of international transactions in goods, services, and assets, and on the main domestic effects of those transactions. We have done so for reasons of manageability, and for two other reasons as well. First, we believe that a traditional definition is least likely to disappoint or surprise those readers of this Handbook who approach it with expectations based on that sort of definition. Second, we expect other Handbooks to deal extensively with the international dimensions and ramifications of their own subjects.

The first volume of the Handbook deals with the "real side" of international economics. It is concerned with the explanation of trade and factor flows, with their main effects on goods and factor prices, on the allocation of resources and income distribution and on economic welfare, and with the effects of national policies designed explicitly to influence trade and factor flows. In other words, it deals chiefly with microeconomic issues and methods. The second volume deals with the "monetary side" of the subject. It is concerned with the balance-of-payments adjustment process under fixed exchange rates, with exchange-rate determination under flexible exchange rates, and with the domestic ramifications of these phenomena. Accordingly, it deals mainly with macroeconomic issues, although microeconomic methods are frequently utilized, especially in work on expectations, asset markets, and exchange-rate behavior.

Organization and objectives

Each volume of the Handbook is introduced by a pair of chapters which survey broadly the subjects covered by that volume. The chapters that follow supplement the introductions in one or more ways. Some chapters examine in detail subjects discussed briefly in the introduction; some chapters focus on new issues and approaches; some chapters complement the analytical surveys by reviewing empirical work. All of the chapters, however, attempt to integrate the results of recent research and to identify problems that call for more research.

The two chapters that introduce the first volume of the Handbook divide up their task analytically. In the first chapter, Jones and Neary present the "positive theory" of international trade, paying particular attention to the contributions and limitations of the Heckscher–Ohlin model that has been at the core of analytical work for about four decades. In the second chapter, Corden presents the "normative theory" of international trade, looking at the gains from trade and factor movements and at the various reasons for interfering with them. Subsequent chapters extend these surveys by looking more closely at trade and growth, international factor movements, trade in resource products, and other analytical issues. Other chapters review empirical work on the testing of trade models and on trade policies in developed and developing countries.

The two chapters that introduce the second volume of the Handbook divide up their task historically. In the first chapter, Kenen traces the evolution of international monetary theory through the three decades following the Second World War, paying particular attention to the Meade–Fleming–Mundell model, which played a role on the monetary side as important as that of the Heckscher–Ohlin model on the real side. In the second chapter, Frenkel and Mussa review more recent developments by assessing the contributions of monetary and asset-market models. Subsequent chapters examine in detail the modelling of asset markets and goods markets, the behavior and efficiency of foreign-exchange markets, aspects of policy interdependence, and the roles of reserves and reserve assets.

Some topics have fallen between the cracks, even though we have deliberately limited the scope of this Handbook. The activities of multinational firms are discussed in two chapters, but there is no comprehensive survey of research on their behavior or the broad economic implications of their activities. International capital movements are discussed extensively, but there is not much said about the Euromarkets, international bank lending, or the many issues related to them. More generally, the chapters in the first volume of the Handbook fit together fairly well, but those in the second are not as well integrated. This testifies, however, to the state of the art rather than the success or failure of the editors and authors. The real side of trade theory is more cohesive than the monetary side, which reflects all too well the disintegration of professional consensus on macroeconomic theory and policy.

Acknowledgements

We are deeply grateful to the authors of this volume for the care they took in preparing their chapters, the time they took to read and comment on others authors' drafts, and the attention they paid to the instructions and advice with which we assaulted them. We want also to thank the International Finance Section at Princeton University for sponsoring two conferences at which the authors presented first drafts of their papers, dealt with gaps and duplication, and gave the editors useful advice about the enterprise as a whole. Without those meetings, the Handbook would have taken longer to complete, and it would have had many more defects.

RONALD W. JONES
University of Rochester

PETER B. KENEN
Princeton University

CONTENTS OF VOLUME I

Introduction to the series   v

Contents of the Handbook   vii

Preface to the Handbook   xi

Chapter 1
The Positive Theory of International Trade   1
RONALD W. JONES and J. PETER NEARY

  1. Introduction   2
  2. Models of trade   4
     2.1. The exchange model   7
     2.2. The Ricardian model   10
     2.3. The Heckscher–Ohlin model   14
     2.4. The specific-factors model   21
     2.5. Extensions   27
  3. Multi-level trade   31
     3.1. Trade in intermediates and natural resources   31
     3.2. Trade in factors   37
     3.3. Trade in technology   42
     3.4. Trade in securities   43
  4. Multi-behavioral trade   45
     4.1. Market distortions   45
     4.2. Increasing returns   48
     4.3. Imperfect competition   50
  5. Concluding remarks   53
  References   53

Chapter 2
The Normative Theory of International Trade   63
W.M. CORDEN

  1. Introduction   65
  2. Normative economics: Some general remarks   66
  3. The gains from trade   69
     3.1. The basic gains from trade propositions: Samuelson and Kemp   69
     3.2. Perspective   72
     3.3. Gains from trade: Recent extensions   73
     3.4. Increasing returns with Marshallian assumptions   75

3.5.	Given commodity taxes and the gains from trade	76
3.6.	Product differentiation and increasing returns	76
4.	**The devices of trade intervention**	77
4.1.	The effect of a tariff	77
4.2.	The symmetry between import and export taxes	78
4.3.	Consumption and production taxes	79
4.4.	The equivalence between import quotas and tariffs	79
4.5.	Balance of payments effects	81
4.6.	Theory of tariff structure	82
5.	**The terms of trade argument and optimal tariff theory**	82
6.	**The theory of domestic distortions**	86
6.1.	Domestic distortions theory: Introduction	86
6.2.	The hierarchy of policies and by-product distortions	88
6.3.	Wage rigidity, marginal product differential and unemployment	89
6.4.	The infant industry argument	91
6.5.	Trade distortions	92
6.6.	Non-economic objectives and fixed targets	94
6.7.	Mixed cases	94
7.	**Distortions, the budget constraint and optimal tax theory**	96
7.1.	The limitations of domestic distortions theory	96
7.2.	Revenue limits and income distribution effects of correcting a distortion: The Anand–Joshi qualification	97
7.3.	Optimal tax theory and domestic distortions	98
7.4.	Trade taxes for revenue: Small and large country case	100
8.	**The cost of protection**	101
9.	**Cost–benefit analysis for the open economy**	105
9.1.	Non-tradeables	107
9.2.	Import quotas	107
9.3.	Terms of trade effects	108
9.4.	Budget constraint	108
9.5.	Factor proportions variable	110
10.	**The political economy of protectionism**	111
11.	**Customs union theory**	112
11.1.	Introduction	112
11.2.	Two assumptions	113
11.3.	The two-good model	114
11.4.	The three-good Meade model	115
11.5.	Broadening the model, and intra-union terms of trade effects	117
11.6.	The common external tariff	118
11.7.	External terms of trade effects	119
11.8.	Can a customs union be optimal?	120
11.9.	Economies of scale	123
11.10.	Other aspects of customs unions	123
	References	124

Chapter 3

Higher Dimensional Issues in Trade Theory   131
WILFRED J. ETHIER

1. Basic concepts   133
2. The law of comparative advantage   135
3. The basic propositions of the modern theory   140
4. Many goods   141
    4.1. Factor-price equalization   142
    4.2. Stolper–Samuelson   144
    4.3. Rybczynski   145
    4.4. The Heckscher–Ohlin theorem   145
5. Many factors   147
    5.1. The basic propositions   147
    5.2. The specific-factors model   148
6. Strong results in even technologies   149
    6.1. Global univalence   150
    6.2. Stolper–Samuelson and Rybczynski   152
    6.3. The Heckscher–Ohlin theorems   160
7. General results   161
    7.1. Factor-price equalization   162
    7.2. Stolper–Samuelson   163
    7.3. Rybczynski   167
    7.4. General results   169
    7.5. The Heckscher–Ohlin theorems   173
8. Odd or even: Does it matter?   178
9. Concluding remarks   181
References   181

Chapter 4

Growth and Development in Trade Models   185
RONALD FINDLAY

1. Ricardian theory   187
    1.1. A dynamic Ricardian model   187
    1.2. Lewis on the terms of trade   191
    1.3. Unequal exchange   192
2. Neoclassical theory   194
    2.1. Comparative statics of growth and trade   194
    2.3. "Immiserizing" growth and foreign investment   198
    2.3. Steady state growth in the open economy   203
3. Development and asymmetrical interdependence   212
    3.1. Wage differentials and infant industry protection   212
    3.2. Two-gap models and export-led growth   215

3.3.   The open dual economy   218
3.4.   North–South models   221
References   232

Chapter 5
International Factor Movements   237
ROY J. RUFFIN

1.   Some statistics on labor and capital movements   238
    1.1.   Labor   238
    1.2.   Capital movements   240
    1.3.   Direct investment   245
2.   The concept of international capital movements   246
    2.1.   The transfer problem   246
    2.2.   Cross-hauling and direct foreign investment   247
3.   Factor mobility and the national advantage   249
    3.1.   Private versus social interests   249
    3.2.   The gains from factor mobility   255
    3.3.   Optimal restrictions on capital versus optimal restrictions on labor   258
4.   International factor movements and income distribution   259
    4.1.   The MacDougall–Kemp model   259
    4.2.   The general case of a small open economy   261
5.   Trade and capital movements   265
    5.1.   The Heckscher–Ohlin model   266
    5.2.   The Kemp–Jones model   269
References   286

Chapter 6
Capital Theory and Trade Theory   289
ALASDAIR SMITH

1.   Introduction   290
2.   A general intertemporal model of production and trade   290
    2.1.   Comparative statics and comparative dynamics   290
    2.2.   The intertemporal welfare economics of trade   293
3.   Capital and growth in non-steady-state models   297
    3.1.   The Heckscher–Ohlin–Samuelson model   297
    3.2.   Trade in capital assets   307
    3.3.   Two-period models   309
    3.4.   A footnote   310
4.   Steady-state models with many capital goods   311
    4.1.   Comparative dynamics of prices   311
    4.2.   Comparative dynamics of quantities   316
    4.3.   An alternative theory of trade?   318

5.   Conclusion   320
References   321

Chapter 7
Increasing Returns, Imperfect Markets, and Trade Theory   325
ELHANAN HELPMAN

1.   Introduction   326
2.   Types of economies of scale   327
3.   Types of competition   330
4.   Homogeneous products   332
5.   International returns to scale   337
6.   National returns to scale   341
7.   Limited entry and market segmentation   348
8.   Differentiated products   355
References   363

Chapter 8
The Role of Natural Resources in Trade Models   367
MURRAY C. KEMP and NGO VAN LONG

1.   The need for new theories   368
2.   Anti-Heckscher–Ohlin theory   370
3.   Generalized Heckscher–Ohlin theory   377
4.   Generalized anti-Heckscher–Ohlin theory   388
5.   Hybrid theory   388
6.   Resource-renewal and resource-replacement   395
     6.1.   Resource-renewal   395
     6.2.   Resource-replacement   397
7.   Cartels – introduction   405
8.   Cartels – the case of binding contracts   406
9.   Cartels – no binding contracts   411
10. The formation of cartels   412
11. Bibliographical notes   413
References   415

Chapter 9
Uncertainty in Trade Models   419
JOHN POMERY

1.   Some preliminaries   420
2.   Walrasian-international models: Pure exchange   426
3.   Walrasian-international models: Production   435
4.   Welfare and government intervention   449
5.   Miscellany   457

    6.   Concluding remarks   461
    References   461

Chapter 10

Testing Trade Theories and Predicting Trade Flows   467
ALAN V. DEARDORFF

    1.   Introduction   468
    2.   How do you test a trade theory?   469
    3.   Tests of the Ricardian model   475
    4.   Tests of the Heckscher–Ohlin model   478
         4.1. Leontief-type analysis of the factor content of trade   480
         4.2. Regression analysis of the commodity composition of trade   485
         4.3. Tests of the Heckscher–Ohlin theorem   492
    5.   Tests of technology theories of trade   493
    6.   Other patterns of trade and theories to explain them   499
         6.1. Empirical regularities   500
         6.2. Gravity-type models of bilateral trade flows   503
         6.3. The Linder hypothesis   504
         6.4. Homogeneous-product explanations of intra-industry trade   506
         6.5. Product differentiation   507
         6.6. Scale economies and country size   510
    7.   Conclusion   511
    References   513

Chapter 11

Trade Policies in Developing Countries   519
ANNE O. KRUEGER

    1.   Trade policy, industrialization and growth   520
         1.1. Optimality of free trade   520
         1.2. Objections to free trade   521
    2.   Analysis of trade policies in developing countries   527
         2.1. Export promotion and import substitution   527
         2.2. Tariffs, quotas, and exchange rate overvaluation   531
    3.   Measures of protection and its effects   538
         3.1. ERPs versus DRCs   539
         3.2. Negative international value added   540
         3.3. Protection of what?   541
         3.4. Magnitude of protection   542
         3.5. The cost of protection   543
    4.   Interaction with domestic distortions   548
         4.1. Behavior under distortions   548
         4.2. Analysis of policies under distortions   551
         4.3. Empirical evidence on distortions and their effects   555

5. Terms of trade changes and export instability 557
    5.1. Secular deterioration in the terms of trade? 558
    5.2. Instability 560
    5.3. Empirical evidence on instability 564
6. Concluding remarks 566
References 566

Chapter 12
Trade Policies in Developed Countries 571
ROBERT E. BALDWIN

1. The political economy of protection 572
    1.1. The nature of the political decision-making process 573
    1.2. Alternative models and key industry characteristics 574
    1.3. Empirical tests: Results and appraisal 580
2. Analyses of the effects of trade liberalization 582
    2.1. General liberalization 582
    2.2. Sectoral studies 590
3. Adjusting to increased imports 590
    3.1. The concept of social adjustment costs 591
    3.2. Estimates of adjustment costs 593
    3.3. The effectiveness of trade adjustment assistance programs 594
4. Estimating the impact of foreign trade on employment 595
5. Customs unions and other preferential trading arrangements 597
    5.1. Customs unions 597
    5.2. Tariff preferences and other trade policies affecting the LDCs 598
6. Specific non-tariff trade measures 600
    6.1. Quantitative restrictions (QRs) 600
    6.2. Preferential government purchasing policies 602
    6.3. Export and domestic subsidies 604
    6.4. Dumping 605
    6.5. Border tax adjustments 607
    6.6. Offshore assembly provisions (OAPs) and domestic content protection 608
7. Current and prospective trade-policy issues 608
    7.1. Selectivity, reciprocity, and graduation 609
    7.2. Trade in services and trade-related investment issues 610
    7.3. Institutional reforms 611
References 612
Index 621

Chapter 1

THE POSITIVE THEORY OF INTERNATIONAL TRADE

RONALD W. JONES

University of Rochester

and

J. PETER NEARY*

University College Dublin

Contents

1.	Introduction	2
2.	Models of trade	4
	2.1. The exchange model	7
	2.2. The Ricardian model	10
	2.3. The Heckscher–Ohlin model	14
	2.4. The specific-factors model	21
	2.5. Extensions	27
3.	Multi-level trade	31
	3.1. Trade in intermediates and natural resources	31
	3.2. Trade in factors	37
	3.3. Trade in technology	42
	3.4. Trade in securities	43
4.	Multi-behavioral trade	45
	4.1. Market distortions	45
	4.2. Increasing returns	48
	4.3. Imperfect competition	50
5.	Concluding remarks	53
	References	53

*This paper was begun while the authors were visitors at the International Institute for Applied Systems Analysis, Laxenburg, Austria. We are grateful to this Institute and to the national Science Foundation under grant no. SES-7806159 for support and to J.N. Bhagwati, A.V. Deardorff, A.K. Dixit, W. Ethier, M.C. Kemp, P.B. Kenen, F.P. Ruane, and L.P.F. Smith for helpful comments.

Handbook of International Economics, vol. I, Edited by R.W. Jones and P.B. Kenen
© *Elsevier Science Publishers B.V., 1984*

1. Introduction

The theory of international trade is one of the oldest subfields of economics and its central concerns remain those of Ricardo. Nevertheless, in recent years the field has not stood still, but has exhibited an expansion of the range of topics studied and of the analytical tools brought to bear on them. In this chapter we attempt to present an overview of the present state of positive trade theory, concentrating on developments since the surveys of Mundell (1960), Bhagwati (1964) and Chipman (1965–66) while at the same time drawing attention to the continuity in the development of the subject. We begin in this section by outlining the scope of the field as we see it and the criteria which have guided our selection of topics to be covered.

As the title of our chapter indicates, we confine our attention to the positive theory of international trade, leaving normative questions for Chapter 2. Although the distinction is somewhat arbitrary, a reasonably clear line of demarcation can be drawn. As a rough guideline, questions concerning the effect of exogenous or policy changes on the level of *aggregate* real income or dealing with the ranking of alternative policy instruments will be considered the province of normative trade theory. By contrast, questions concerning the effect of exogenous or policy changes on the *composition* of outputs, relative prices, trade flows, or on the domestic distribution of real income will be considered within the realm of positive trade theory.

While trade theory makes extensive use of general-equilibrium theory, with its concern for interactions among markets, the key feature which distinguishes it is its recognition that not all commodities and factors are equally mobile. This phenomenon of differential mobility can take many forms. From Ricardo onwards, much of trade theory has been conducted in terms of the Classical mobility assumptions: all final goods are tradeable between countries whereas primary inputs are non-tradeable, though fully mobile between different sectors of the domestic economy. However, a great deal of recent work has been concerned with examining the consequences of departures from these assumptions.

Another feature which characterizes international trade theory is its focus on applied questions, making it natural to conduct analysis in the context of relatively small-scale models. This is not to say that trade theory is wedded to any particular model. For example, despite its dominance in the 1960s, the Heckscher–Ohlin model has not supplanted the Ricardian model, nor has it in its turn been eclipsed by the recent revival of interest in the specific-factors model. Rather, positive trade theory uses a variety of models, each one suited to a limited but still important range of questions. While this eclectic approach is sometimes criticized, since it is easy to show that the propositions derived from any one model are not necessarily robust with respect to relaxations of that model's assumptions, it seems to be a more satisfactory way of yielding useful insights and suggesting hypotheses for empirical testing than the attempt to construct a general model which encompasses all others as special cases.[1]

Among the issues with which positive trade theory deals is the question of the determinants of the *pattern of trade*, to which the proximate answer usually given is still that of Ricardo: namely, the principle of comparative advantage, with its focus on a comparison among autarkic relative prices in different countries. In the case of two commodities and two countries the principle is both easy to formulate and incontrovertibly true:[2] each country will tend to export under free trade that commodity which has the lower relative price in autarky. However, with more than two commoities the appropriate way to generalize the principle is not immediately apparent. It is tempting, for example, to argue that if commodities are ranked by their relative price ratios in autarky in the two countries, demand conditions will determine a critical ratio such that, when trade is opened up, the home country will export all commodities whose autarky relative price is below this ratio and import all other commodities. This assertion is correct in the Ricardian case of constant costs, but as Drabicki and Takayama (1979) and Dixit and Norman (1980, pp. 95–96) have shown, it need not hold in less special cases. However, the more paradoxical aspects of their counter-examples rely on the presence of strong complementarity in demand. In any case, whatever the pattern of substitutability or complementarity, the principle of comparative advantage may be reformulated in terms of a *correlation* between differences in autarky price levels and net export volumes for different commodities, as Deardorff (1980) and Dixit and Norman (1980) have shown.

While the principle of comparative advantage may thus be defended as a basic explanation of trade patterns, it is not a primitive explanation, since it assumes rather than explains inter-country differences in autarkic relative prices. Much of trade theory is therefore concerned with investigating alternative sources of these differences, and each such source has implications in turn for the effect of the opening up of trade on the structure of production and on the domestic distribution of income. The same questions can also be posed not in terms of a comparison between autarky and free trade but in the context of disturbances to

---

[1] This viewpoint is not shared by all trade theorists. For example, Pearce (1970, p. 17) states "There is but one world and only one model is needed to describe it."

[2] Nevertheless, the principle, with its denial that absolute superiority in productive power determines the pattern of trade, remains suspiciously counterintuitive to most non-economists. Samuelson (1969) recalls the time he was challenged by the mathematician Stanislaw Ulam to "name me one proposition in all of the social sciences which is both true and non-trivial." Samuelson remarks that years later he thought of the appropriate answer: the Ricardian theory of comparative advantage. "That it is logically true need not be argued before a mathematician; that it is not trivial is attested by the thousands of important and intelligent men who have never been able to grasp the doctrine for themselves or to believe it after it was explained to them."

an initial trading equilibrium. In discussing these and other issues, our strategy is to present in Section 2 an overview of a number of alternative models, stressing the complementarity between them and the differences in the questions which each is well suited to answer. For the most part, this section stays within what we call the "Classical paradigm." This encompasses not only the Classical assumptions about goods and factor mobility already mentioned, but also neglects intermediate stages in the production hierarchy and assumes that all agents are atomistic, operating in an undistorted and competitive environment in which technology exhibits constant returns to scale. More recent work which relaxes these assumptions, allowing for trade at different levels of the production spectrum and for departures from competitive behavior, is reviewed in Sections 3 and 4 respectively.

Inevitably, throughout the chapter there is some overlap with other contributions to this volume (though not on empirical matters, which we leave to Chapter 10). In general, we go into less depth on individual topics than other contributors, attempting instead to fit recent extensions into an overall framework which provides a coherent view of the field. Moreover, a survey of a wide field such as this cannot hope to be anything other than highly selective. Without attempting to provide a comprehensive coverage, therefore, we hope to give the flavor of a subject which remains a vibrant and fruitful source of theoretical insight and testable hypotheses.

2. Models of trade

Although the theory of international trade combines elements of demand behavior with production structure in a general-equilibrium context, it is primarily variations in the specification of the production side that distinguish the basic models of trade. Section 2.1 describes the uses to which the "exchange model" has been put; this model can be interpreted as one in which each of two factors is used to produce a separate commodity so that no intersectoral factor mobility is allowed. Section 2.2 describes the Ricardian model, the polar opposite of the exchange model in that only one productive factor (labor) is employed, but this factor can be freely reallocated between sectors so as to maximize its earnings. Section 2.3 presents the basic propositions of the Heckscher–Ohlin model, the model most frequently used in positive trade theory, whereas Section 2.4 deals with the specific-factors model, which focusses on asymmetry in the degree of factor mobility between sectors. Finally, Section 2.5 extends these models to consider some properties of higher dimensional cases as well as the possibility of joint production.

The production structures of the basic trade models discussed in this section have many properties in common. For each country it is possible to relate the value of the national product, Y, to the vector of factor endowments, v, and the vector of final commodity prices, p, where competition ensures that the composition of output (shown by the vector, x) maximizes the value of Y at those prices.[3] Price-output responses are normal, in the sense that no commodity can fall in supply if its price rises (and all other prices and endowments remain constant). Similarly, an increase in the endowment of any factor of production cannot raise that factor's return if commodity prices and all remaining endowments are held constant. Furthermore, a basic relationship – that of *reciprocity* – equates the effect which an increase in the endowment of factor i[4] has on the output of commodity j (all commodity prices constant) to the effect which an increase in commodity j's price has on the return to factor i.

The models of trade described in Sections 2.1–2.4 differ from one another in the specification of the numbers of factors and commodities and the degree of intersectoral mobility of the factors. They all share, however, the requirement that the economy's demand for inputs to produce commodities not exceed the availability of factors in the endowment base, and the stipulation that in a competitive equilibrium the unit costs in any activity do not fall short of market price. Furthermore, we postpone our discussion of intermediate goods and joint production.[5] Throughout we generally assume that factor endowments are given. This rules out international trade in productive factors (see Section 3.2), the possibility that the local supply of factors may respond to changes in factor rewards,[6] or the possibility that current production affects future factor supplies.[7] If all final commodities are traded on world markets, the commodity price vector, p, as well the factor endowment vector, v, can be treated as exogenous for a small open economy. But often trade models allow a subset of commodities to enjoy only a national market; even for a small open economy the p_j's for non-traded goods thus depend endogenously upon local demand conditions.

The study of models with non-traded goods has expanded enormously in recent years, in part because of their relevance to macroeconomic policy in small open

---

[3] Formally, $Y = g(p, v) = \max_x[p'x: F(x, v) < 0]$, where the aggregate production possibilities set defined by the function $F(x, v)$ is convex. The national product function was introduced by Samuelson (1953) and its properties have been examined under a variety of assumptions by Chipman (1972), Diewert (1974), and Dixit and Norman (1980) among others.

[4] The reciprocity relationship is due to Samuelson (1953) and discussed, inter alia, by Jones and Scheinkman (1977). Referring to the previous footnote, outputs and factor prices are reflected in the partial derivatives of the national product function when these are well defined (as when the number of factors is at least as great as the number of commodities): $x = g_p$ and $w = g_v$. g is a concave function of v (implying g_{vv}, or $\partial w / \partial v$, is negative semi-definite) and a convex function of p (implying $\partial x / \partial p$ is positive semi-definite). Reciprocity follows from the symmetry of the matrix of second derivatives of g.

[5] Section 2.5 considers joint production, while Section 3.1 allows the existence of intermediate goods in the production spectrum as well as international trade in these goods.

[6] For a discussion of variable labor supply, see Walsh (1956), Kemp and Jones (1962), and Martin and Neary (1980).

[7] This latter possibility is made explicit in neo-classical growth models in which capital is one of the productive factors and is currently produced. See Oniki and Uzawa (1965) and the discussion of Findlay (1970) in Section 2.3.

economies.[8] Although the terms of trade (the relative price of exports to imports) are exogenous for such economies, domestic policy can nonetheless influence the level and composition of national income and (if the model is extended to incorporate a monetary sector) the trade balance if it can alter the real exchange rate (defined as the relative price of traded to non-traded goods). Any exogenous shock induces changes in the prices of non-traded goods and these effects are superimposed on the direct effects of the shock itself. For example, Ethier (1972b) and Jones (1977) show that an increase in the price of one traded good relative to other traded goods may lead to a fall in its output in the presence of a non-traded good. Moreover, the induced change in the price of non-traded goods may be in either direction. Consider, for example, the case examined by Jones (1974b) of an increase in the price of importables with the price of exportables held constant. To the extent that substitution effects between importables and non-tradeables are strong, the price of the non-traded good tends to rise, since demand is switched away from imports and resources are bid away by the import-competing sector. But the rise in the price of importables has a negative income effect, and if it dominates, then the demand for the non-traded good falls and its price'is likely to fall. Similar conflicts between income and substitution effects due to the presence of non-traded goods arise in the analyses by Burgess (1978) of foreign capital inflows and Corden and Neary (1982) of the "Dutch Disease."

Finally, although the general production framework described above holds for all the models in Sections 2.1–2.4, the response of commodity outputs to commodity prices is smooth and well defined only if the number of primary factors is at least as great as the number of final commodities.[9] If this condition is not met, the production possibilities frontier in output space consists of ruled surfaces, and output levels are indeterminate for price ratios coincident with the slopes of those surfaces.[10] The phenomenon of production indeterminacy is by no means a curiosum – it arises in the Ricardian model, for example – and when it obtains the actual production pattern chosen will be determined by considerations outside the particular model being studied, such as the time path by which the economy approaches its current equilibrium or demand conditions at home and abroad. Alternatively, production indeterminacy may be resolved if some

---

[8]The implications of non-traded goods for trade models have been considered by McDougall (1965), Komiya (1967), Ethier (1972b) and Jones (1974b). Their application to macroeconomic policy has been considered by many writers, including Salter (1959), Pearce (1961), Dornbusch (1974), Jones and Corden (1976), Helpman (1977), Noman and Jones (1979), Neary (1980c) and Neary and Purvis (1982).

[9]In models with joint production, the relevant comparison is between the number of primary factors and the number of productive *activities*, as Woodland (1977b) has pointed out. We return to this issue in Section 2.5 below.

[10]The consequences of more commodities than factors being produced were first noted by Samuelson (1953). Melvin (1968) studies the two-factor, three-commodity case in detail and Chang (1979) presents a comprehensive analysis of the general case.

goods are not traded on world markets so that their equilibrium prices are determined by the interaction of domestic supply and demand.

2.1. The exchange model

Many questions in trade theory involve the behavior of demand in a crucial way. To study these questions it proves useful to strip the production side of the model to a bare minimum. The resulting model, often referred to as the "exchange model," is here envisaged as a two-sector model in which each product is produced with a single factor specific to that sector and exogenously given in supply. The very sparseness of the production structure – outputs do not respond to price changes – makes the exchange model an ideal vehicle for studying problems in which demand behavior is important.

The first such problem is the question of stability of equilibrium. Given the non-negative relationship between prices and outputs noted earlier, production response always enhances stability. Hence the exchange model isolates the potential source of instability, namely, asymmetric income effects in demand. Of course this role of income effects has been well-known at least since Hicks (1939) but it tends to be obscured by the usual presentation of the Marshall–Lerner condition for stability.[11] Only when the elasticities in this condition are decomposed into income and substitution effects does it become clear that no threat to stability arises unless each country has a higher marginal propensity to consume its own export good; in that case, the income effect of a rise in the relative price of the home country's export good, which raises real income at home and lowers it abroad, tends to *increase* the world excess demand for the home country's export good. (Note an immediate implication: the Marshall–Lerner condition must be satisfied if tastes are the same in both countries.)

A second problem for which the exchange model is especially appropriate is the effect of international goods transfers on the equilibrium terms of trade. Since the answer to this question is found by examining the sign of world excess demand for either good at the initial terms of trade, it is perfectly legitimate in many circumstances to consider the issue in the exchange model because even when production is variable it does not actually change until after the terms of trade alter. It is this consideration which leads to the important result of Samuelson (1952) that the direction of change in the terms of trade depends solely on income

[11] The Marshall–Lerner condition referred to in the text is that the sum of the elasticities of the offer curves of the two countries (i.e. their general-equilibrium import demand elasticities) should exceed unity. This should be distinguished from the special case (corresponding to infinite supply elasticities in both countries) of the partial-equilibrium Bickerdike–Robinson–Metzler condition. Jones (1974b) and Dornbusch (1975) investigate the circumstances in which the latter may be given a general-equilibrium interpretation. The decomposition of the offer curve elasticity into income and substitution effects is given in Jones (1961a).

effects: specifically, in a two-country two-commodity free-trade world, the terms of trade of the donor country will worsen if and only if it has a higher marginal propensity to consume its own export good than has the recipient country. In such a case the transfer leads, at initial prices, to a net decline in world demand for the donor's exports, which must give rise to a worsening of its terms of trade. (Note that this criterion is exactly the same as that given above for the income effects of a change in the terms of trade to be destabilizing.)

Samuelson concluded from this result that no presumption could be established in favor of what he called the "orthodox" view that a donor country would suffer a "secondary burden" of a decline in its terms of trade (over and above the primary burden occasioned by the direct loss of purchasing power arising from the transfer itself).[12] This conclusion derives from the fact that economic theory places no restrictions on marginal propensities to consume, other than that they must lie between zero and one in the absence of inferior goods. However, as Jones (1970a) has pointed out, the marginal propensities to consume in question are for the good *exported* by the donor country and we would not in general expect taste differences between countries to be unrelated to trade patterns. On the contrary, the country with the larger marginal propensity to consume a given commodity is likely to be the country which *imports* that commodity. In a pure exchange model with equal initial endowments, this must be the outcome if marginal and average propensities are positively correlated. This line of reasoning therefore suggests an anti-orthodox presumption that the transfer is likely to raise world demand for the donor's exports, and so to improve its terms of trade.

While much can be said about the transfer problem using the exchange model, it cannot deal with situations where the transfer induces changes in production *before* the terms of trade alter. One obvious illustration of this is when the transfer is effected by means of productive factors rather than final goods. Another is when the transfer is effected via final goods, but either country also produces a non-traded good.[13] The issue of production changes is also relevant to the effects of a transfer on the real incomes of the countries involved. For example, if the anti-orthodox outcome ensues, can the secondary benefit arising from the improvement in the donor's terms of trade be so great as actually to raise its real income? In a two-country exchange model this paradox is impossible: the improvement in the donor's terms of trade just sufficient to keep the real income

---

[12]However, in a later paper [Samuelson (1954)] he showed that artificial impediments to trade (including tariffs though excluding transport costs which reflect the fact that international transportation consumes real resources) go some way towards salvaging the orthodox view.

[13]The transfer problem in the context of non-traded goods has been considered by Johnson (1956), McDougall (1965), Samuelson (1971a), Chipman (1974) and Jones (1975a). Samuelson considered the case where the non-traded commodity is leisure rather than a final good, but from a formal point of view the issues raised in the two cases are the same.

of both countries constant gives rise to substitution effects which raise world demand for the donor's import good. Hence the actual change in the equilibrium terms of trade must be *less* than that sufficient to redistribute world real income towards the donor.[14] However, if the transfer leads to output changes of tradeables at the initial terms of trade, this argument need not hold. Moreover, even remaining within the confines of the exchange model, it has recently been shown that the donor may gain if there is a third country engaged in trade, even if it is not a party to the transfer. The presence of the third country does not alter the Samuelsonian criterion for the direction of change in the terms of trade (since, at initial prices, the third country is unaffected by the transaction). However, if the terms of trade improve for the donor and taste patterns differ between the third country and the recipient (with the taste bias in the third country towards its export good), the redistribution of world income may encourage such a rise in the donor's export price that its real income rises.[15]

Moving on from the transfer problem we come next to the theory of tariffs, where once again the exchange model is the ideal vehicle for studying the qualitative effects on the international equilibrium of changes in tariff rates on final goods, since any induced production response would merely enhance the substitution effects in demand of price changes. While much of tariff theory is concerned with normative questions, we may mention one important positive issue with which it deals, namely, the effects of a tariff on world and domestic prices. The "normal" outcome in this case is that a tariff raises the domestic relative price of the home country's import good and lowers its relative price on world markets. In other words, the tariff is "protective" in that it encourages increased domestic production in the import-competing sector, while at the same time it improves the home country's terms of trade. However, either of these normal outcomes can be reversed if either country's demand for imports is price-inelastic, requiring a large change in prices to restore world markets to equilibrium. Thus, if home demand is highly inelastic and all the proceeds of the tariff revenue are spent on imports, the resulting increase in import demand may be sufficient to *worsen* the home country's terms of trade. Alternatively, if foreign demand is highly inelastic and all the tariff revenue is spent on exports, the terms of trade may improve to such an extent that the domestic relative price of imports

[14] This argument is presented in Caves and Jones (1981, pp. 64–65).

[15] This result was demonstrated in a numerical example by Gale (1974), although the logic of the argument for both donors and recipients was earlier discussed in Johnson (1960), and criteria in the Johnson framework derived by Komiya and Shizuki (1967). General criteria for this and related three-agent transfer paradoxes were derived by Yano (1981), who shows that they are consistent with Walrasian stability and with some degree of substitutability in demand. Some of these results were independently obtained by Chichilnisky (1980) and Brecher and Bhagwati (1981) in two-country models where one country consists of two groups with different taste patterns.

falls.[16] The first of these paradoxes admittedly requires some degree of asymmetry in the disposition of the tariff revenue: a deterioration in the terms of trade is impossible in a two-commodity model if tariff revenue is returned to the private sector in a lump-sum manner. However, the possibility of the tariff's being anti-protective survives the relaxation of this and other assumptions, requiring only that the foreign elasticity of demand for imports be less than the home marginal propensity to consume exportables.[17]

Finally, although the exchange model is a crude vehicle for considering questions of domestic income distribution, it permits an examination of the effects of exogenous shocks on the distribution of real income between countries. While this issue is closer to the concerns of normative theory, we mention one aspect which links with our earlier emphasis on the importance of import demand elasticities: namely the phenomenon of "immiserizing growth," first pointed out by Edgeworth (1894) and independently rediscovered by Johnson (1953, 1955) and further discussed by Bhagwati (1958). As with an international transfer, growth imposes a "secondary burden" on the growing country if it raises the excess demand for imports at the initial terms of trade. However, with no matching change in supply abroad, the resulting deterioration in the terms of trade can be significant enough to leave the growing country worse off as a result of growth, provided the elasticity of the rest of the world's demand for imports is sufficiently low.

2.2. The Ricardian model

In turning from the exchange model to the Ricardian model, the focus moves towards a model which predicts extreme shifts in production patterns when trade is opened up. The two models are polar opposites because the exchange model excludes completely the possibility of resource transfer, whereas the Ricardian model permits the maximum degree of internal factor mobility. Moreover, whereas the exchange model pins down the quantities of different goods which are available for trade, the Ricardian model pins down relative prices (at least, before trade is opened up) by its assumptions that production costs are independent of the level of output and that techniques of production are independent of factor prices and the composition of output. This makes it an extremely useful model for isolating the effects of intercountry differences in technology or in scale (where the latter are not confused with the effects of differences in the degree of scale,

---

[16] Both of these outcomes are illustrated in Figure 4 of Lerner (1936) although the second case was examined in greater depth by Metzler (1949) and has come to be associated with his name. The possibility of this "Metzler paradox" was disputed by Sodersten and Vind (1968), but their analysis was corrected by Jones (1969).

[17] Komiya (1967) and Jones (1974a) extend the Metzler paradox to models with intermediate and non-traded goods.

which we consider in Section 4.2 below). At the same time, the Ricardian model throws no light on questions related to the internal distribution of income, since it assumes either a single mobile factor or many mobile factors which are used in equal proportions in all sectors (so that they may be aggregated into a single Leontief composite factor).

Although mainly used by Ricardo to demonstrate the gains from trade, the major interest of this model stems from its positive application in providing a theory of trade and production patterns. The reasoning leading to this theory in the two-country, two-commodity case is straightforward. Since each sector uses a single factor, competition ensures that output prices are directly linked to wage rates: e.g. in the home country p_j equals $a_{Lj}w$ (where commodities are indexed by $j = 1, 2$, and a_{Lj} is the labor requirement per unit output in sector j). Internal labor mobility ensures that the same wage obtains in each sector, so that if a country produces both goods their relative price must equal the ratio of unit labor coefficients. The home country thus has a lower autarkic relative price of good 1, and so a comparative advantage in producing that good, if and only if:

$$\frac{a_{L1}}{a_{L2}} < \frac{a_{L1}^*}{a_{L2}^*}, \tag{2.1}$$

where an asterisk denotes variables relating to the foreign country. When barriers to trade are eliminated, competition therefore forces at least one country to specialize in the production of the commodity which it produces relatively more efficiently and trade patterns completely reflect comparative advantage.

The Ricardian model isolates differences in technology as the basis for trade, but it does not rule out a role for demands. For example, of the four possible equilibria in which at least one country specializes in production, the principle of comparative costs rules out only one: the inefficient case where both countries specialize according to comparative *disadvantage*. Depending on demand conditions, a free-trade equilibrium may occur at any of the other three points of complete specialization, or at intermediate points where one or the other country produces both goods.[18] Moreover, demand takes on a special role if equilibrium occurs at the point where countries specialize completely according to comparative advantage, since the equilibrium relative price ratio is then only bounded by relative production costs.[19] Finally, although it is comparative rather than abso-

---

[18] This argument may be illustrated using the world efficiency frontier, introduced by Whitin (1953). McKenzie (1954) showed that, irrespective of the number of countries and commodities, this frontier is defined by the set of linear combinations of all efficient specialization patterns.

[19] Graham (1923) was highly critical of Mill (1848) for focusing on such "limbo" price ratios, and argued that with many commodities and countries such outcomes were highly unlikely. However, the work of McKenzie and others has shown that there is no general presumption as to whether equilibrium will occur on a "flat" or at a corner of the world efficiency frontier.

lute advantage which determines efficient patterns of trade and specialization, there is still a role for absolute advantage in determining relative wage rates (or the "double-factoral" terms of trade). Since the price of any good cannot exceed its unit cost, whether the good is produced or not, it is easily shown that relative wage rates are bounded by the ratios of labor productivities for each commodity in the two countries, implying that:

$$\frac{a_{L1}^*}{a_{L1}} \geq \frac{w}{w^*} \geq \frac{a_{L2}^*}{a_{L2}} \tag{2.2}$$

with the wage ratio taking on its upper bound (where all the gains from trade accrue to the home country) when both countries produce good 1 and conversely when both produce good 2.

One of the attractive features of the Ricardian model is that its relatively simple production structure allows virtually all the results we have stated to be extended to many countries and many commodities. Some new features also emerge in higher dimensions. For example, with many commodities but only two countries, commodities can be ranked by comparative costs in a "chain" of decreasing relative labor costs:

$$\frac{a_{L1}^*}{a_{L1}} > \frac{a_{L2}^*}{a_{L2}} > \cdots > \frac{a_{Lj}^*}{a_{Lj}} > \cdots > \frac{a_{Ln}^*}{a_{Ln}}. \tag{2.3}$$

Demand conditions determine where the chain is broken, but the immutable cost ratios ensure that the home country must export all commodities to the left of the break and import all those to the right, with at most one commodity produced in common. When more than two countries are considered explicitly, no such neat criterion is available. Obviously, an efficient pattern of specialization must satisfy bilateral comparisons such as (2.1) for all possible pairings of commodities and countries. However, as McKenzie (1954) and Jones (1961b) have shown, this requirement is not sufficient to exclude inefficient production patterns. Regardless of the number of countries or commodities, a general criterion for efficient specialization is available which is the appropriate generalization of (2.1): the product of labor requirements in the efficient assignment of commodities to countries must be less than the corresponding product in all other possible assignments that allot the same number of countries to each commodity as does the efficient assignment.

More recently, Dornbusch, Fischer and Samuelson (1977) have shown how a two-country Ricardian model with an infinite number of commodities can be analyzed using elementary geometry and calculus. The key to this simplicity is the assumption that the ratio of unit labor requirements in the two countries varies continuously between commodities: i.e. if commodities are indexed by z, the ratio $a^*(z)/a(z)$ is a continuous and monotonically decreasing function of z. This function is thus the continuous analogue of the discrete chain (2.3), and the point at which it is broken by demand determines not only the pattern of trade but also, by extension of the reasoning which led to (2.2), the equilibrium double-factoral terms of trade. An additional strategic assumption is that demands take the Mill-Graham form (i.e. preferences can be represented by a monotonic transformation of a Cobb–Douglas utility function) with identical tastes in the two countries. This makes the fraction of world income spent on home-produced commodities an increasing function of the index of the borderline commodity, $\bar{z}$, and so the double-factoral terms of trade consistent with balanced trade is also increasing in $\bar{z}$. (The higher is $\bar{z}$, the greater the share of world income spent on the home country's goods and so the higher, relatively, must be the home wage.) Combining these two functions therefore provides a simple illustration of how the unique equilibrium value of the borderline commodity is determined, and a number of useful comparative statics results are easily derived by considering how various changes shift either of the curves.[20]

The tractability of the continuum model has led to its extension in a number of directions. Samuelson (1982) shows that the model easily accommodates general homothetic tastes which are the same in the two countries: the value of w/w^* consistent with balanced trade need no longer be an increasing function of z but it can never decrease at a faster rate than $a^*(z)/a(z)$. Hence equilibrium is still unique and most of the earlier comparative-statics results continue to hold. A more extensive generalization has been carried out by Wilson (1980) who allows for non-homothetic and non-uniform demands and an arbitrarily large (though finite) number of countries. Simple diagrammatic analysis is no longer possible: equilibria need not be unique nor is it true that each country produces only those commodities which lie along a single interval. However, Wilson simplifies the model considerably by expressing the demand for each country's products in terms of the derived demand for its labor and thus effectively reduces the model to a many-country exchange model where each country supplies only one good (i.e. its own labor). To deduce the consequences of any parameter change it is thus sufficient to consider in the first instance its effects on the equilibrium wage rate in each country, from which the implications for production and trade patterns can be inferred.

---

[20] Trade theory is sometimes criticized for neglecting transport costs (although it is unlikely that very much of substance hinges on this, and, in any case, they are just as important in domestic as in international trade). The continuum model lends itself well to their inclusion, for it permits small changes in demands or costs to alter endogenously the range of goods that are exported, not traded internationally, or imported. Similar results have been obtained in a simulation analysis of Heckscher–Ohlin-type models by Helpman (1976).

While the continuum approach clearly permits a tractable analysis of some issues, there remain a number of questions which it is not well-suited to answer. One of these concerns the effects of technological progress in a single sector.[21] This issue was first examined in a Ricardian model by Hicks (1953), who introduced the important distinction between "export-biased" and "import-biased" improvements in technology. The former lowers costs in export industries, so worsening the growing country's terms of trade and benefitting the rest of the world, whereas the latter has exactly opposite effects.[22] Jones (1979a) considers this question further, noting that the Ricardian model with a finite number of commodities is a convenient framework within which to isolate conditions which give rise to either of the two possible extreme outcomes: immiserization for the growing or the lagging country. This is so because in this model growth in one sector changes at most two relative prices: that of the growing sector's output relative to other home-produced commodities, and the double-factoral terms of trade which determine the relative price levels of commodities produced in the two countries.

2.3.   The Heckscher – Ohlin model

While the Ricardian model isolates differences in technology between countries as the basis for trade, the Heckscher–Ohlin model focuses instead on differences between countries in their relative factor endowments and on differences between commodities in the intensities with which they use these factors. Costs of production thus become endogenous and, in general, will differ between countries in autarky, even when all have access to the same technology for producing each good. This model therefore provides an alternative explanation of trading patterns and an explicit basis for conflict in internal income distribution.

Largely due to the work of Samuelson, this model dominated international trade theory for much of the post-war period, and its four main properties or "core propositions" came to be viewed as "the central body of international trade theory." [See Chang, Ethier and Kemp (1980).] We begin by stating these propositions for the standard (minimal-sized) case of two commodities using two internally mobile productive factors.[23]

---

[21] Dornbush, Fischer and Samuelson, Wilson, and Krugman (1982), consider the effects in the continuum model of technological progress which takes the form of either a uniform improvement in all sectors in a given country or a convergence between the $a(z)$ schedules of two countries (which may be viewed as reflecting the international diffusion of technological knowledge).

[22] Although Hicks explicitly used a Ricardian model, he did not specify the structure of trade and production in great detail, and most later formalizations of his approach adopted a Heckscher–Ohlin framework. (See footnote 35 below.)

[23] The original sources for these propositions are: Lerner (1952) and Samuelson (1948, 1949) for the factor-price equalization theorem; Stolper and Samuelson (1941) for the Stolper–Samuelson theorem;

(1) *Factor-price equalization theorem.* In its global form, this theorem states that, under certain conditions, free trade in final goods alone brings about complete international equalization of factor prices. In its local form, the theorem asserts that, at constant commodity prices, a small change in a country's factor endowments does not affect factor prices.

(2) *Stolper–Samuelson theorem.* An increase in the relative price of one commodity raises the real return of the factor used intensively in producing that commodity and lowers the real return of the other factor.

(3) *Rybczynski theorem.* If commodity prices are held fixed, an increase in the endowment of one factor causes a more than proportionate increase in the output of the commodity which uses that factor relatively intensively and an absolute decline in the output of the other commodity.

(4) *Heckscher–Ohlin theorem.* A country has a production bias towards, and hence tends to export, the commodity which uses intensively the factor with which it is relatively well endowed.

To illustrate these propositions, we turn first to the model's implications for the distribution of income, which are easily seen with the help of the unit cost curves, c_1 and c_2, in Figure 2.1.[24] Each curve shows the combinations of the wage rate w and the rental rate r which imply a unit cost of production equal to the output price of the sector in question. The coordinates of point A are thus the only values of w and r compatible with zero profits in both sectors. Provided such an equilibrium is consistent with the economy's factor endowment, factor prices are thus determined solely by the location of the curves c_1 and c_2, in other words, by technology and commodity prices. To understand the caveat about consistency with factor endowments we may note that the slope of the unit cost curve always equals the cost-minimizing capital–labor ratio in the sector in question. Moreover, for both factors to be fully employed, the economy's overall capital–labor ratio k must be a weighted average of the capital–labor ratios used in each sector:

$$k = \lambda_{L1}k_1 + \lambda_{L2}k_2, \tag{2.4}$$

where the weights, λ_{Lj}, denote the proportion of the total labor force employed in

---

Rybczynski (1955) for the Rybczynski theorem; and Heckscher (1919) and Ohlin (1933) for the Heckscher–Ohlin theorem. The term "core propositions" was introduced by Ethier (1974) who also presents a vigorous defense of their robustness.

[24] These curves were introduced by Samuelson (1962) and have been applied to trade problems by a number of authors, including Schweinberger (1975), Burgess (1976), Woodland (1977a) and Mussa (1979), their increased use [along with that of the national product function] reflecting the recent drift from primal towards dual techniques. For an economy with more than one sector, we prefer the term "unit cost curve" to "factor price frontier", since the latter usually refers to the locus of efficient factor prices for the economy as a whole. In Figure 2.1 the factor price frontier is the outer envelope of the individual sectors' unit cost curves (illustrated by a heavy line). Another popular diagram used to illustrate properties of the Heckscher–Ohlin model is known as the Harrod–Johnson diagram. See Harrod (1958), Johnson (1957), and earlier use by Samuelson (1949).

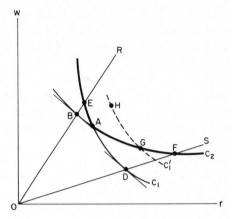

Figure 2.1.   Unit cost curves.

sector j. Hence, joining the origin O to the points B and D at which each sector's capital–labor ratio equals the endowment ratio gives rise to the cone ROS, which we may call a "cone of diversification."[25] Provided the intersection point A lies within this cone the economy produces both goods and factor prices are locally independent of endowments.

While the factor-price equalization theorem asserts that factor prices are independent of endowments, the Stolper–Samuelson theorem is concerned with the nature of their dependence on commodity prices. Specifically, it predicts what Jones (1965) has called a "magnification effect": a given proportional change in commodity prices gives rise to a greater proportional change in factor prices, such that one factor price unambiguously rises and the other falls relative to *both* commodity prices. This may be seen in Figure 2.1: the increase in the price of good 1 shifts c_1 to c'_1 and thus lowers the wage rate and raises the rental by a greater proportionate amount than the price increase (since the new equilibrium point G lies to the right of H which is on the same ray from the origin as A and so represents a situation where the relative rental increase just matches the increase in the price of good 1). More formally, the changes in the unit cost and hence in the price of each commodity must be a weighted average of the changes in the two factor prices (where the weights are the distributive shares of the two factors in the sector concerned and a circumflex denotes a proportional change: $\hat{w} \equiv$

[25] This concept was discussed by McKenzie (1955) in the context of the primal representation of technology whose geometric depiction in the two-sector case was developed by Lerner (1952) and Pearce (1952). See also Chipman (1965–66).

dw/w):[26]

$$\theta_{L1}\hat{w} + \theta_{K1}\hat{r} = \hat{p}_1, \qquad (2.5)$$

$$\theta_{L2}\hat{w} + \theta_{K2}\hat{r} = \hat{p}_2. \qquad (2.6)$$

Since each commodity price change is bounded by the changes in both factor prices, the Stolper–Samuelson theorem follows immediately, with its prediction of unambiguously conflicting changes in real factor rewards following a change in commodity prices.[27]

Corresponding to the magnification effect of the Stolper–Samuelson theorem is a similar relationship between endowment changes and output changes implied by the Rybczynski theorem, the duality between the two theorems reflecting the reciprocity relations discussed earlier. An increase in the capital–labor endowment ratio leaves the wage–rental ratio, and hence factor proportions in each sector, unaffected, provided relative commodity prices do not change and both goods continue to be produced. Equation (2.4) therefore implies that the fraction of the labor force employed in the less capital-intensive sector must fall and the fraction in the other sector must rise by a greater relative amount than the endowment change. With a constant capital–labor ratio in each sector, this in turn implies a similar pattern of output changes, which is the essence of the Rybczynski theorem. To see this more formally, we totally differentiate the two full-employment conditions for this model to obtain:

$$\lambda_{L1}\hat{x}_1 + \lambda_{L2}\hat{x}_2 = \hat{L}, \qquad (2.7)$$

$$\lambda_{K1}\hat{x}_1 + \lambda_{K2}\hat{x}_2 = \hat{K}. \qquad (2.8)$$

In a manner analogous to (2.5) and (2.6), these equations state that endowment changes are bounded by output changes and so the highly asymmetric response to endowment changes predicted by the Rybczynski theorem must apply.

The final core proposition is the Heckscher–Ohlin theorem itself, but this in fact is closely related to the Rybczynski theorem. Consider two countries with different relative factor endowments and the same technology for producing both

---

[26] These equations follow from totally differentiating the competitive profit conditions and invoking the envelope property of the unit cost function. Our algebraic development of this model follows the approach of Jones (1965).

[27] A stronger form of the Stolper–Samuelson theorem (as it was presented by its originators) is that protection must raise the real return to the factor used intensively in the import-competing sector. This requires the additional assumption that protection raises the domestic relative price of the import-competing good; in other words, that the conditions for the Metzler paradox outlined in Section 2.1 do not hold.

goods. If both countries face the same commodity prices then, by the Rybczynski theorem, the country with the greater relative endowment of capital will produce relatively more of the capital-intensive good. This may be seen by subtracting (2.8) from (2.7) to obtain:[28]

$$\hat{x}_1 - \hat{x}_2 = \frac{1}{|\lambda|}(\hat{L} - \hat{K}), \tag{2.9}$$

where $|\lambda|$ equals $(\lambda_{L1} - \lambda_{K1})$. Provided this production bias is not offset by a demand bias, the relatively capital-abundant country will export the relatively capital-intensive good. When it is expressed in terms of a physical definition of factor abundance, the Heckscher–Ohlin theorem is thus a simple corollary of the Rybczynski theorem, and no consideration of autarky production patterns is required. Alternatively, the concept of factor abundance may be formulated in terms of relative factor prices before trade takes place. When expressed in this way, the Heckscher–Ohlin theorem requires in addition that the relationship between relative commodity and factor prices predicted by the Stolper–Samuelson theorem hold. From equations (2.5) and (2.6):

$$\hat{w} - \hat{r} = \frac{1}{|\theta|}(\hat{p}_1 - \hat{p}_2), \tag{2.10}$$

where $|\theta|$, equal to $(\theta_{L1} - \theta_{L2})$, has the same sign as $|\lambda|$ in (2.9).[29] In the absence of trade, the relative scarcity of the labor-intensive good in the capital-abundant country is reflected in its relative price being higher than abroad which, from (2.10), implies that capital will be relatively cheap in the capital-abundant country. Thus relative factor abundance in either the physical or the value sense is the source of comparative advantage in this model.

This prediction about trade patterns is one of the central features of the Heckscher–Ohlin model and it has inspired extensive empirical testing, beginning with the famous study of U.S. trade patterns by Leontief (1953). We leave further consideration of these and other empirical matters to Chapter 10 below and concentrate here on some theoretical issues which have arisen in the process of extending the Heckscher–Ohlin model. One of these is the question of whether, when the number of commodities is increased but the number of factors and countries remains equal to two, it is possible to construct a "chain" of compara-

---

[28] The term $|\lambda|$ is the determinant of the matrix of factor-to-sector allocations, λ_{ij}, and is positive if and only if sector 1 is relatively labor-intensive (in the sense of having a lower capital–labor ratio than sector 2, i.e. $k_1 < k_2$).

[29] $|\theta|$ is the determinant of the matrix of factor shares and is positive if and only if sector 1 is relatively labor-intensive (in the sense that wages constitute a larger proportion of the value of its output than in sector 2).

tive advantage, similar to that which holds in the Ricardian model [eq. (2.3) above] but in terms of factor intensities rather than relative labor productivities.[30] Jones (1956) argued that ranking commodities by their capital-labor ratios (assuming that factor-intensity reversals do not take place) does indeed yield such a chain, with all commodities having capital-intensities higher than a certain level being exported by the more capital-abundant country and all others being imported; the location of the cut-off point in the chain is determined (as in the Ricardian model) by demand and by the relative sizes of the two countries. The validity of this proposition has been demonstrated explicitly by Deardorff (1979): provided factor prices in the two countries continue to differ after trade takes place, the capital-abundant country must have the higher wage-rental ratio and hence must specialize in and export the more capital-intensive goods (with at most one commodity being produced in common by both countries). However, the proviso that trade does not equalize factor prices is crucial here, as Melvin (1968) and Bhagwati (1972) have pointed out.[31] If factor prices are equalized by trade then the pattern of production in each country and hence the pattern of trade is indeterminate and so the "chain" proposition need not hold in general.[32]

As we would expect, when we consider a small country for which relative commodity prices are fixed, the case where many commodities are produced with only two factors is straightforward. As shown by Jones (1974c), such a country will locate along the "chain" at a point determined by its factor endowment, producing only those goods (one or two) whose factor intensities are "close" to its own endowment ratio. Even if technology is the same at home as in another similar small country, factor prices are unlikely to be equalized internationally in such a world since the mix of commodities produced is likely to differ between the two countries unless they have very "similar" endowments. Nevertheless, trade patterns in this world reflect the Heckscher–Ohlin theorem in the modified sense that the factor intensities of the small country's exports mirror its endowment ratio, while it imports goods which are both more and less capital-intensive than those it produces.

[30] We confine attention here to the case where the number of commodities is finite and so the "chain" is a discrete one. However, as with the Ricardian model, it is possible to assume instead that the number of commodities is infinite, with the capital–labor ratio of each commodity varying along a continuum. Such a model has been analyzed in detail by Dornbusch, Fischer and Samuelson (1980), although the pay-off to this extension is not as great as in the Ricardian case, since the discrete Heckscher–Ohlin model already allows considerable scope for substitution between factors.

[31] Travis (1964, ch. 2) and Dixit and Norman (1980, pp. 114–121) give a useful diagrammatic technique for determining which allocations of a given world factor endowment are consistent with factor-price equalization when there are two factors and three goods.

[32] In this case, both countries produce along the same ruled surface of their production possibility frontiers (except for differences in scale) and both produce strictly positive amounts of all goods (apart from boundary cases). (Recall our earlier discussion of ruled surfaces and the references given there.) An open question for research is whether the implied trade patterns conform with the predictions of the Heckscher–Ohlin theorem if the production indeterminancy is resolved by specifying an explicit dynamic adjustment mechanism for the transition from autarky to free trade.

The low dimensionality of the simple Heckscher–Ohlin model has attracted much attention and will be considered further in Section 2.5 and in Chapters 3 and 10. By contrast, a limitation of the model which is at least equally significant but has received rather less attention is its view of factor endowments as an exogenous determinant of trade patterns. In fact, endowments may not be "primitive" in this sense, but can be influenced by trade, both instantaneously (as when trade affects the choice between work and leisure) and over time (through changes in the rate of capital accumulation). Most attempts to examine the latter issue have considered open-economy extensions of the two-sector growth model of Uzawa (1961) in which the capital good is internationally traded. By contrast, Findlay (1970) presents a model which is closer in spirit to the Heckscher–Ohlin approach in that both traded goods are used for final consumption while additions to the capital stock are produced by a third, non-traded goods, sector.[33] The results he obtains are recognizably Heckscher–Ohlin in spirit but relate not to the effects of changes in endowments but of changes in the genuinely exogenous parameters of his model, the rates of population growth and of savings. A rise in the former lowers the economy's steady-state capital–labor ratio which (in a manner similar to that of the Rybczynski effect) lowers the relative quantity of the capital-intensive good produced. By contrast, a rise in the savings rate may raise or lower the relative output of the capital-intensive good in the short run, but must raise it in the long run. At least in this model, therefore, the spirit of the Heckscher–Ohlin theorem is preserved provided factor abundance is interpreted not in terms of exogenous physical endowments but of the rate of labor force growth and the propensity to accumulate capital.[34]

In conclusion, the relatively rich production structure of the Heckscher–Ohlin model has made it a source of fruitful hypotheses for empirical testing (whose usefulness is not diminished by the fact that in its simplest form – two goods, two factors and identical technology worldwide – the model's predictions are overwhelmingly rejected by the data) as well as a useful vehicle for the study of a wide range of theoretical issues.[35] Nevertheless, the very starkness of its predictions, and in particular its rigid linking of factor prices to commodity prices, has led

[33]With only two factors perfectly mobile between all three sectors, the fixity of traded goods prices pins down the price of the non-traded good as well as domestic factor prices, exactly as in the static models of Komiya (1967) and Ethier (1972b). A model with an identical formal structure has been used by Samuelson (1965) to demonstrate that free trade equalizes not only the rental on capital but also the real interest rate between countries, since the latter equals (in equilibrium) the rental divided by the price of (non-traded) machines. The properties of all these models are extremely sensitive to the assumption that both traded goods continue to be produced, and, as Ethier points out, this is more stringent than requiring non-specialization in an otherwise identical model with no non-traded goods. Deardorff (1974) shows that the production sector of Findlay's model becomes identical to that of Uzawa's closed-economy growth model if only one traded good is produced.

[34]For a related analysis, see Deardorff and Hanson (1978).

[35]To take just one example of the latter, the analysis of the post-World War II "dollar shortage" by Hicks (1953), mentioned in Section 2.2, suggested that technological progress in a country's export

many economists to question its generality. Partly for this reason, trade theory has recently seen a revival of interest in an older model, which abandons the assumption of complete intersectoral mobility of all factors and assumes instead that some are specific to particular sectors.

2.4. The specific-factors model

This model has its antecedents in the work of Cairnes and Bastable, and was used explicitly or otherwise in inter-war writings by Haberler and others who attempted to break out of the Ricardian straitjacket of constant costs. However, it was eclipsed by the rise of the Heckscher–Ohlin model and recent interest in it dates only from the work of Jones (1971c) and Samuelson (1971c).[36]

In its simplest two-sector form, the assumptions of this model differ from the basic Heckscher–Ohlin model in only one respect: only one factor is assumed to be intersectorally mobile. Nevertheless, the properties of this model contrast strongly with those of the Heckscher–Ohlin model. To illustrate these, we invoke Figure 2.2.[37] In the left-hand panel the horizontal axis measures the economy's labor force and, for given commodity prices, each sector's labor demand curve is drawn with respect to the appropriate origin (O_1 or O_2) as a downward-sloping function of the wage rate, the diminishing returns to labor reflecting the presence of a specific factor in each sector. The initial equilibrium wage rate, w_0, is thus determined at the point of intersection of the two curves, A, and since constant returns to scale prevail in each sector the returns to the specific factors may be read off the unit cost curves in the right-hand panel. These curves are identical to those introduced in Section 2.3 but the interpretation of the horizontal axis is very different: the stocks of "capital" in each sector are now distinct factors and so their returns, r_1 and r_2, are not commensurable. Although they are set equal to

---

sector would necessarily worsen the country's terms of trade. However, as Findlay and Grubert (1959) have demonstrated, consideration of this issue in a Heckscher–Ohlin context points up the crucial importance of the factor bias of the technological progress. In particular, if it is biased towards accentuating the difference in factor intensities between the two sectors (for example, if the capital-intensive export sector experiences a labor-saving improvement) the net outcome (at initial commodity prices) may be an *increase* in the output of the (non-progressing) import-competing sector, opening up the possibility of an *improvement* in the terms of trade.

[36] Caves (1960) documents many of the early contributions to what he calls the "neoclassical" model. Samuelson (1971c) suggests the term "Ricardo–Viner" for this model since it extends Ricardo's assumption of diminishing returns in agriculture to all sectors.

[37] Diagrams similar to the left-hand panel of Figure 2.2 were used by Jones (1971c) and Mussa (1974), while Schweinberger (1980) makes extensive use of the unit cost curve diagram in this context, noting that it can easily be harnessed to derive all the properties of the specific-factors model with many commodities. Dixit and Norman (1979, 1980) analyze this model with a different diagram which makes commodity prices endogenous and so is useful for studying trade patterns and the effect of trade on factor prices. Differences between the properties of the Heckscher–Ohlin and specific-factors model additional to those considered here are noted in Neary (1978a, Section 6).

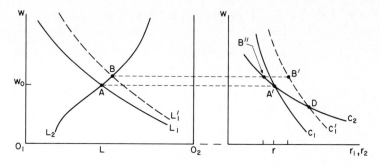

Figure 2.2. Effect of a price increase in the specific-factors model.

one another at the initial equilibrium A', this is just an arbitrary normalization and, for the present, has no substantive significance.

Consider first the effects of an increase in the relative price of good 1. Choosing good 2 as numeraire, this causes the labor demand curve for sector 1 in Figure 2.2 to shift upwards by the same proportionate amount as the price increase, from L_1 to L_1', giving rise to a new equilibrium at B. Since employment in the first industry has risen, the output of that sector must also increase. The wage rate must rise but by relatively less than the extent of the price increase. (This is clear from the geometric construction; in economic terms the real wage facing firms in sector 1 must fall if they are to expand output.) Thus there is no magnification effect of prices on wages in this model. By contrast, the returns to both specific factors must change by magnified amounts: the right-hand panel of Figure 2.2 shows that r_2 must fall absolutely (point B'') while r_1 rises by more than the increase in p_1 (point B'). This outcome is unaffected by the relative factor intensities of the two sectors: as the curves c_1 and c_2 are drawn, sector 2 is relatively labor-intensive (in the sense that the share of wages in the value of its output is greater than that in sector 1: $\theta_{L1} < \theta_{L2}$), but the same conclusion follows if this assumption is reversed.

By comparison with the Heckscher–Ohlin model, therefore, price changes lead to unambiguous changes in the real returns of the two specific factors, but the change in labor's real return cannot be predicted without a knowledge of taste patterns because the wage rate rises in terms of one good and falls in terms of the other. Does this mean that nothing can be said in this model about the Stolper–Samuelson question of the effect of protection on real wages? Ruffin and Jones (1977) have provided a partial resolution of this "neoclassical ambiguity" which applies in all competitive models but takes a particularly simple form in the specific-factors model. Consider the relationship between wage changes and changes in commodity prices and endowments, as derived by Jones (1971c) (we defer consideration of the expression in parentheses):

$$\hat{w} = \beta_1 \hat{p}_1 - \frac{1}{\gamma}\left(\hat{L} - \lambda_{L1}\hat{K}_1 - \lambda_{L2}\hat{K}_2 \right). \tag{2.11}$$

The coefficient β_1 measures the relative contribution of sector 1 to γ, the economy-wide elasticity of labor demand:

$$\beta_1 = \frac{1}{\gamma}\lambda_{L1}\gamma_1, \qquad \gamma \equiv \lambda_{L1}\gamma_1 + \lambda_{L2}\gamma_2, \tag{2.12}$$

where γ_j is the real-wage elasticity of demand for labor in sector j. At constant endowments, an increase in p_1 raises the wage relative to the numeraire by more, the larger the relative size of the first sector and the more elastic is its demand for labor relative to that of the second sector. However, to the extent that wage earners consume the first commodity, the price increase tends to reduce their welfare. The net effect on the real wage therefore depends on the sign of $\beta_1 - \alpha_1$, where α_1 is the share of good 1 in wage-earners' consumption. The Ruffin–Jones argument is that, if wage-earners' tastes are typical of those of the economy as a whole, α_1 equals the share of the first good in aggregate consumption which, since good 1 is the import good, must exceed its share in national production, which we denote by θ_1. Without detailed knowledge of the structure of the economy we cannot be sure whether this average production share is greater or less than the marginal response β_1. However, it can be shown that the two are equal if commodity 1 is "unbiased" with respect to labor, in the sense that an increase in p_1 brings about a proportionate increase in the wage equal to the average increase in all factor prices.[38] Thus there is a presumption that protection will reduce real wages in the specific-factors model, although the outcome is not unambiguous. (In the Heckscher–Ohlin model the parameter corresponding to β_1 must be either negative or greater than unity, depending on relative factor intensities, and the outcome is thus unambiguous.)

Turning next to changes in factor endowments, their effects on factor prices may be deduced by manipulating Figure 2.2 and are given explicitly by the term in parentheses in equation (2.11). Wages are reduced by growth in the labor force and increased by a rise in the endowment of either specific factor. Exactly the converse is true of the returns to the specific factors. Clearly, with more factors than commodities, international trade does not lead to factor-price equalization in

[38] It can be shown that $\beta_1 - \theta_1$ is proportional to $\theta_{L1}\gamma_1 - \theta_{L2}\gamma_2$. As eq. (2.13) below shows, when this expression is zero, an increase in the economy's labor endowment at constant commodity prices gives rise to "balanced growth" (an equal proportionate expansion of both sectors). A necessary though not sufficient condition for protection to raise real wages in this model is thus that commodity 1 be "biased" towards labor, which implies that the price-elasticity of supply in sector 1 ($\theta_{L1}\gamma_1$) exceeds that in sector 2 ($\theta_{L2}\gamma_2$).

this model even in the local sense. Samuelson (1971c) argued nonetheless that the transition from autarky to free trade would induce partial factor-price equalization in the sense of a reduction in factor-price differences between countries (as Ohlin had originally asserted in his 1933 book). However, this depends both on the commodity relative to which changes in factor prices are measured and, as Dixit and Norman (1979) show, on the nature of endowment differences between countries and technology differences between sectors.

Just as there is no basis for expecting partial, far less complete, factor-price equalization in this model, so the pattern of trade cannot be inferred from a knowledge of factor endowments and factor intensities alone. Nevertheless, both of these elements play a role. This is shown by the expression for the effects on relative outputs of changes in endowments at given commodity prices:[39]

$$\hat{x}_1 - \hat{x}_2 = (\hat{K}_1 - \hat{K}_2) + \frac{1}{\gamma}(\theta_{L1}\gamma_1 - \theta_{L2}\gamma_2)(\hat{L} - \lambda_{L1}\hat{K}_1 - \lambda_{L2}\hat{K}_2). \tag{2.13}$$

The term $\theta_{Lj}\gamma_j$ is the elasticity of supply of x_j with respect to p_j for a given wage. Hence an increase in the labor force lowers the wage rate, from (2.11), which brings about an increase in the output of both goods but a greater increase in the output of the good in more elastic supply. While relative supply elasticities thus play a role similar in this model to the role of relative factor intensities in the Heckscher–Ohlin model, it is also illuminating to consider separately the two components of these elasticities. Thus, if the two industries have equal labor demand elasticities γ_j (or equal elasticities of substitution σ_j), factor intensities have a similar effect on output patterns as in the Heckscher–Ohlin model: the more labor-intensive sector is encouraged to expand to a greater extent. Elasticities of substitution also matter, however, since they determine the extent to which each sector can increase its labor intensity and so expand output in response to a given fall in wages. Finally, eqs. (2.11) and (2.13) show that increases in the endowments of each of the sector-specific factors have similar effects on wages and hence on relative outputs, but they also have direct effects on outputs and it is easily shown that the latter must dominate. Not surprisingly, the country with the greater endowment of the factor specific to sector j will, other things equal, have a production bias towards that sector's output, and hence be more likely to export it.

One of the more attractive features of the specific-factors model is that all its properties generalize straightforwardly to the case where the number of sectors is arbitrarily large, each one using a specific factor and drawing on the common

---

[39] The determinants of comparative advantage in the specific-factors model have been examined by Amano (1977) and Dixit and Norman (1979). The breakdown provided by (2.13) is developed in Jones (1971c).

pool of labor.[40] Many of the responses of the general model exhibit a strong gross substitutability property: for example, a rise in the price of any good raises its output and increases the real return of the corresponding specific factor while lowering the output of all other sectors and the real returns of all other specific factors. Similarly, by reciprocity, an increase in the endowment of any specific factor at constant commodity prices raises the output of the corresponding good and lowers the output of all other goods. As for an increase in the labor force, it raises the output of all goods, with output changes ranked according to the position of each sector in the "chain" of increasing elasticity of supply. These properties make the specific-factors model a useful tool in contexts where a tractable multi-sectoral production model is desired, without the extreme implications for specialization patterns typical of the Ricardian model.[41]

Many other issues have been analyzed in the context of the specific-factors model. As Samuelson (1971b) has noted, it is a fully specified general-equilibrium model but its properties are consistent with a partial-equilibrium analysis of a single sector; for this reason it provides a rationalization for simple economic intuition without the potential for paradox which more complex general-equilibrium models introduce.[42] For example, the concept of a sector's "profitability" can be identified with the return to its specific factor but cannot be easily interpreted in a competitive model where all factors are intersectorally mobile. This makes it an obvious framework within which to study the phenomenon of the "Dutch Disease", whereby the profitability of one sector is squeezed as a result of a boom in other traded goods sectors.[43] A very different application of the model has been carried out by Dixit (1980) who reinterprets the two commodities as the same good in two different periods produced with period-specific labor and with capital and a natural resource, both of which are "mobile" between periods as a consequence of the endogeneity of savings and resource-use decisions. By exploiting the analogy between this model's formal structure and that of the specific-factors model and by making some other strategic simplifications, Dixit succeeds in deriving a number of interesting results concerning the determinants of and the relationship between trade in goods and trade in resources.

---

[40] The properties of the specific-factors model with many commodities have been investigated by Samuelson (1971c), Mussa (1974), Jones (1975b), Dixit and Norman (1980), and anticipated by Harrod (1958).

[41] See, for example, the application to effective protection by Jones (1975b), discussed in Section 3.1 below.

[42] This argument is developed further in Neary (1978a). Among the issues which were first considered in the more tractable specific-factors framework are the implications of rural–urban migration in response to expected wage differentials [see Harris and Todaro (1970) and Section 3.1 below] and the employment effects of capital subsidies [see Neary 1978c)].

[43] As Corden and Neary (1982) show, this squeeze is accentuated if the spending effect of the boom raises profitability in sectors producing non-traded goods. By contrast, the contraction of the non-booming traded goods sector may not take place if all factors are intersectorally mobile.

As we have seen, one of the basic features of the specific-factors model is its demonstration that the returns to factors which are trapped in particular sectors will reflect those sectors' fortunes to a magnified extent. These contrasting shifts in factor rewards suggest a strong incentive for market forces to bypass the barriers which enforce the factor specificity, and, if such barriers can be surmounted with the passage of time, we are led to a reinterpretation of the specific-factors model as a short-run model. The simplest way of modelling this process is to assume that the stocks of capital specific to each sector are not physically distinct factors, but rather are temporarily immobile and gradually move between sectors in response to intersectoral differences in rentals.[44] On this interpretation the specific-factors model depicts the short-run or momentary equilibrium of the Heckscher-Ohlin model, where the latter is assumed to apply to some medium-run horizon over which the economy's stock of capital is fixed in aggregate but perfectly mobile between sectors. Thus, in Figure 2.2, the initial equilibrium represented by A and A' is one where capital stocks have had time to adjust such that the same reward r is earned in both sectors. A disturbance to this equilibrium in the form of a once-and-for-all increase in the relative price of good 1 gives rise in the short run to the new equilibrium represented by B, B' and B'', as already discussed. However, the resulting rental differential means that this equilibrium cannot persist: as soon as capital mobility becomes possible, capital will be reallocated out of the low-rental sector into sector 1. It is at this point that the relative factor intensities of the two sectors play a role for the first time: the movement of capital out of the relatively labor-intensive sector into the relatively capital-intensive sector leads, at the initial wage rate, to excess supply of labor.[45] Hence the wage rate falls as the capital reallocation process continues, until the new "long-run" equilibrium at D is attained.

This "short-run capital specificity" assumption provides a convenient link between the specific-factors and Heckscher–Ohlin models, as well as a plausible hypothesis about the medium-run evolution of a competitive economy.[46] In its simplest form, however, it relies on an ad hoc specification of the rate of capital reallocation, which is assumed to respond myopically to current differences in quasi-rents rather than to the difference between the present values of locating a

[44] This model has been examined by Mayer (1974b), Mussa (1974), Jones (1975b), Neary (1978a) and Dixit and Norman (1979). See also Grossman (1981).

[45] The term "factor intensities" should be interpreted here in its "physical" sense, corresponding to the sign of $|\lambda|$ in eq. (2.9). As noted by Jones (1975b) and Dixit and Norman (1979), it is possible for the relative factor intensities of the two sectors in the "value" sense, corresponding to the sign of $|\theta|$ in equation (2.10), to be temporarily reversed during the adjustment process. However, this does not affect the attainment of the new long-run equilibrium, which is globally stable provided there are no permanent factor-market distortions (as discussed in Section 4.1 below). [See Jones and Neary (1979).]

[46] Kotlikoff, Leamer and Sachs (1981) extend this model to allow for sluggish international as well as intersectoral capital mobility, and argue that its predictions conform closely to post-World War II patterns of international trade and factor-price differences.

unit of capital in one of the other sectors. These deficiencies have been overcome by Mussa (1978), who models the reallocation process by combining an explicit adjustment-costs technology with the assumption of perfect foresight by capital owners. Mussa shows that the more sophisticated model implies a slower convergence towards long-run equilibrium (because the future diminution of the rental differential is foreseen, reducing the incentive to reallocate), but its positive properties are otherwise identical to those of the simple myopic model, provided there are no fixed costs to capital reallocation. The other assumption of the simple model, that labor is perfectly mobile between sectors, has also been relaxed by Mussa (1982) and Grossman and Shapiro (1982), who show how skill differences can restore some degree of coincidence between the interests of workers and the fortunes of the sector in which they are currently employed. Finally, mention should be made of a different mechanism whereby a specific-factors production structure can be transformed into a Heckscher–Ohlin model. If the specific factors are tradeable, their heterogeneity can be circumvented by exchanging them on world markets. If, in addition, these factors are the only commodities in which trade takes place (i.e. all final goods are non-traded) then the balance-of-trade equilibrium condition combined with the assumption of fixed world prices allows any number of specific factors to be aggregated into a single factor, "foreign exchange." In this fashion the specific-factors model can be transformed by trade rather than by time into a Heckscher–Ohlin model, as in the analysis of "middle products" by Sanyal and Jones (1982), to be discussed in Section 3.1 below.

2.5. Extensions

The models presented in previous sections are the basic building blocks of positive international trade theory and much of the theoretical work in the field can be categorized by the manner in which it has attempted to combine or extend them. For example, a number of writers have used elements from different models to throw light on specific issues.[47] Gruen and Corden (1970) graft a single sector producing textiles from labor and specific capital onto a Heckscher–Ohlin model in which land and labor produce wool and grain to illustrate how in a multi-good model a tariff may paradoxically worsen a country's terms of trade. If wool is the

---

[47]Of course, the most obvious way of combining models is to examine trade between two countries, each of whose production structures is characterised by a different model. However, this direction of research has not been extensively pursued, since there are rarely persuasive grounds for believing that the differences between two models correspond adequately to the differences between two particular countries. An exception to this general trend is the model of North–South growth and trade of Findlay (1980) which combines a Solow-type full-employment model for the developed country ("North") with a Lewis-type, labor-surplus capital-good-importing country ("South") to examine the interactions between growth and the North–South terms of trade. (See Chapter 4 below.)

only export and is land-intensive relative to grain, a uniform tariff at initial terms of trade causes manufacturing to draw labor out of agriculture, leading, via the Rybczynski effect, to an increase in the output of wool, making possible a worsening of the terms of trade. In a very different application, Falvey (1981) superimposes on a standard two-sector Heckscher–Ohlin structure a continuum of sector-specific capital goods, each combining with labor to produce a distinct good within the manufacturing sector. The result is a model which provides an explanation for the phenomenon of "intra-industry trade" without any of the departures from competitive assumptions to be considered in Section 4.3 below.

A different way of extending simple models is to use the insights they yield as a way of understanding and interpreting the properties of more complex models. We have already given one example of this: Wilson's reduction of a very general Ricardian model with many countries and a continuum of commodities to an exchange model as an intermediate step in analyzing the general model. Another example is the analysis of a two-good, three-mobile-factors model by Jones and Easton (1983), drawing on earlier work by Batra and Casas (1976) and Ruffin (1981). They show that this model combines elements of both the Heckscher–Ohlin and specific-factors models: the factor which is least specific to either sector (the "middle" factor) exhibits many of the properties of the mobile factor in the specific-factors model, the ease of substitutability between it and the other factors being a key determinant of output and factor-price responses. However, since both other factors are also mobile, the relative degree of substitutability between these factors and the difference between the distributive shares of the middle factor in the two sectors are also key characteristics helping to determine how changes in commodity prices affect the distribution of income. Another interpretative link between models has been noted by Jones (1970b, 1980) and Ferguson (1978): if capital is internationally mobile in a Heckscher–Ohlin model, trade patterns are determined primarily by comparative labor costs. If, in addition, technology differs between countries, patterns of trade and international capital flows will reflect comparative as well as absolute advantage; differences in technology play a role similar to the one they play in the simple Ricardian model. (This issue is discussed further in Chapter 5 below.)

While splicing models together or viewing one in the perspective of another constitute important directions for the development of the subject, the task of "extending" trade models has often been interpreted very differently; namely, as examining the robustness of the basic properties of simple models to relaxations of their assumptions. Particular attention has focused on one of the most widely criticized assumptions, their low dimensionality. Since this issue is covered at length in Chapter 3 below, we avoid going into detail here and merely note that at least three different approaches to this problem have been explored.

The first approach has concentrated on the case which is the most obvious generalization of the Heckscher–Ohlin model, the so-called "even" case where the numbers of goods and factors are equal. A variety of results have been derived, mostly in the form of relatively stringent conditions on the matrix of factor input–output coefficients which are sufficient to yield results such as the "strong" generalization of the Stolper–Samuelson condition: an increase in the relative price of each good raises the real return of one factor and lowers the real returns of all other factors.[48]

A second approach, largely initiated by Ethier (1974), has been to investigate what results may be derived when less severe restrictions are imposed on the technology of the economy. We have already noted some relatively weak but completely general properties which are satisfied by all competitive models. Ethier showed that considerably stronger results can be obtained in the model studied by exponents of the first approach (the generalized even Heckscher–Ohlin model) with no restrictions on the input–output matrix other than that all its elements be strictly positive (i.e. each factor is used to some extent in every sector). For example, a rise in the price of one good must raise the real return of at least one factor and lower the real return of at least one other.[49] Similar results were derived by Diewert and Woodland (1977), Jones and Scheinkman (1977) and Chang (1979) in more general models with any numbers of goods and factors where some of the former may be intermediate goods and some of the latter may be specific to certain sectors. All of these contributions have brought to the fore the significance of the comparison between the number of goods and factors, a model characteristic whose importance was first stressed by Samuelson (1953). The even model, with equal numbers of goods and factors, is the knife-edge dividing line between the case of more commodities than factors (where production indeterminacy must be resolved either by allowing specialization or by introducing considerations extraneous to the production side of the model in order to pin down some outputs) and that of more factors than commodities (where local factor-price equalization does not obtain and so the full-employment and price-equals-cost equations must be solved jointly for the effects of commodity prices on factor prices).[50]

Both of the approaches mentioned so far attempt to "generalize" the Heckscher–Ohlin model in the literal sense of deriving results analogous to those of the two-good two-factor model relating changes in individual endowments and commodity prices to induced changes in individual outputs and factor prices.

---

[48]See, for example, Chipman (1969), Kemp and Wegge (1969) and Inada (1971).

[49]See also Kemp and Ethier (1976).

[50]As noted by Inada (1971), Rodriguez (1975a) and Neary (1980b), the key distinction of relevance here is not really between goods and factors but between commodities whose prices are exogenous (including traded goods and traded factors) and those whose prices are free to fluctuate. As shown by Neary (1980b) for a given structure of technology, if the number of commodities in the latter category is progressively reduced, the prices of those factors which are still freely variable become progressively less responsive to changes in the endowments of non-traded factors; i.e. the economy moves steadily closer to a closer to a state of local factor-price equalization.

However, it is probably asking too much of general-equilibrium models to provide detailed predictions at such a high level of disaggregation without imposing extremely strong restrictions on the technology. A number of authors have therefore looked for general properties which do not necessarily apply to individual prices or quantities. One example of this approach is the work of Deardorff (1980) and Dixit and Norman (1980) mentioned in Section 1, which shows that the principle of comparative advantage as a basis for trade may be generalized not in terms of individual commodities but in terms of a *correlation* between autarkic price differentials and import volumes. Another example is the suggestion in Jones (1977) that general results may be derived for changes in the output of one good or the real reward of one factor relative to the changes in the average of all other outputs or rewards. This approach, of investigating limited questions in general models rather than the converse, is also pursued in Jones and Scheinkman (1977), Dixit and Norman (1980) and Neary (1979), where it is shown that if the exogenous shocks considered are restricted to those which concern comparisons between *dichotomous* groups of factors and commodities, it is possible to aggregate a general production model to a two-by-two form which exhibits many of the properties of the standard Heckscher–Ohlin model.

One more direction of extending the basic models which belongs in this rather than in subsequent sections concerns another key assumption, namely, the absence of joint production. It is this which gives rise to the phenomenon of magnification effects: irrespective of the detailed structure of production, if each good is produced with more than one factor in a distinct productive process, the price-equals-unit-cost equation for any activity can be totally differentiated as follows:

$$\sum \theta_{ij} \hat{w}_i = \hat{p}_j. \qquad (2.14)$$

Since each price change is thus a weighted average of factor price changes, some $\hat{w}_i$ must always exceed any $\hat{p}_j$ and so factor i's real reward must rise. However, if sector j produces more than one good, the right-hand side of (2.14) becomes itself a weighted average of the corresponding goods prices, and so magnification effects need not obtain. These considerations led Jones and Scheinkman (1977) to argue that in the presence of joint production the asymmetry between factors and commodities characteristic of the Heckscher–Ohlin model ceases to hold. Of course, it is still possible to interpret the left-hand side of (2.14) (as amended) as a measure of the change in the value of the activity in sector j and to rank factor-price changes relative to this change, and hence to rank them among themselves. This fact was exploited by Chang, Ethier and Kemp (1981) in a detailed analysis of the two-factor two-good model with joint production. Using an argument similar to that of Ruffin and Jones (1977) they note that if tastes are uniform and homothetic all that is needed for an increase in the real return of a factor is that its return rise relative to the average of other factors. Under this additional assumption, therefore, magnification effects are not necessary in order to pin down income distribution and so results of a Stolper–Samuelson kind can be derived even in the presence of joint production.

3. Multi-level trade

The Classical paradigm of international trade limits contact among countries to the exchange of commodities at the final level. Such a view of the nature of international trade was challenged over fifty years ago by Williams (1929), who stressed the historic importance of international labor and capital mobility in his criticism of the Ricardian view that commodities are internationally mobile and factors are not. In recent years renewed efforts have been made to escape the Classical paradigm by allowing links between countries at various stages of the production process, such as the exchange of intermediate products, the international mobility of capital and labor, or trade in technical knowledge.

In calling this section "multi-level" trade we intend to emphasize that much of this work is concerned with trade at more than one level instead of replacing trade in final goods by (say) trade in primary factors. Of course, the literature on trade theory has investigated topics that go beyond the types of trade we discuss here. In particular, the theory of customs unions and economic integration contemplates not only multi-level trade but the possibility of fiscal and monetary union and the harmonization of tax structures. Many important normative questions concerning the advisability of such regional groupings are not discussed below, but are dealt with in Chapter 2.

3.1. Trade in intermediates and natural resources

Once international trade in more than final consumer goods is allowed, basic notions of comparative advantage need to be re-examined. We have already discussed the limitations in a multi-commodity world of comparing autarky prices in two countries to predict item-by-item the pattern of trade; generally only correlations can be made except under additional assumptions. With trade in intermediates allowed, the problems in predicting trade in final goods become even greater. As McKenzie (1954) remarked in one of his classic papers on the Ricardian model, the familiar nineteenth century trade pattern in which Lancashire produced and exported cotton textiles would most probably not have

been observed if England had had to grow its own cotton.[51] We shall have
occasion both in this section and in Section 4 to revert to this theme: the pattern
of trade in final goods may not be readily deducible from a comparison of
pre-trade relative prices in these markets.

3.1.1. Effective protection

The past fifteen years have witnessed a flood of literature concerned with one
aspect of trade theory when final goods flows are accompanied by trade in
intermediates: how do interferences in such trade, especially by the use of tariffs,
affect the allocation of resources and the "effective protection" which such a
pattern of tariffs provides to various sectors and factors of production? The early
literature [(e.g. Corden (1966)] held out the hope that a structure of effective
protective rates, defined, for the sector producing commodity j, as

$$v_j \equiv \frac{t_j - \sum_i \theta_{ij} t_i}{1 - \sum_i \theta_{ij}} \tag{3.1}$$

would, more accurately than final nominal tariffs alone, indicate the effect of a
tariff structure on outputs. (Here t_j represents the tariff on final good j, t_i the tariff
on imports of intermediate product i, and θ_{ij} the distributive share of intermediate product i in the jth sector.) This hope was somewhat dashed even for a
model with only two final goods by a counter-example of Ramaswami and
Srinivasan (1971). For a given tariff structure they show how, in an economy with
one set of factor endowments, outputs and resources are pulled in a direction
opposite to that in another economy with a different set of factor endowments.[52]
   Subsequent work in the area attempted either to salvage something for the
concept of effective protection by imposing strong restrictions on the technology
(such as fixed coefficients or separability between primary factors and intermediate products in the production process),[53] or to suggest alternative formulae
for effective rates that would indeed predict gross output changes or resource

---

[51] In Jones (1980) a two-country Ricardian model is illustrated in which one commodity requires an
intermediate input and technologies differ between countries. The pattern of trade can be reversed as a
result of variations in the price of the traded intermediate.
   [52] This counter-example is also discussed in Appendix I of Jones (1971a).
   [53] References to the role of separability and the so-called "substitution problem" include Corden
(1971), Jones (1971a), Ethier (1972a), Bhagwati and Srinivasan (1973) and Khang (1973).

flows.[54] Furthermore, some models allowed local import-competing production of intermediates, whereas others did not.[55]

No doubt part of the frustration exhibited in this literature stems from the difficulty in multi-commodity models, even without intermediate products, of ranking output responses to correspond precisely with changes in relative prices. As is now clearly understood, one should expect no more of effective rates in a model with intermediate goods than one does of nominal tariff rates in a model without.[56] Nonetheless, two of the models discussed in Section 2 possess sufficient structure to make possible at least some predictions on the basis of effective rates. First, recall our interpretation of the model of exchange in Section 2.1 as a production model in which each sector employs primary factors fixed in total supply to that sector. In addition, let each sector require any number of imported intermediates. Effective tariff rates then accurately signal the changed return to the bundle of primary factors stuck in each sector.

The second model is the many-commodity version of the specific-factors model described in Section 2.4, extended to allow each sector to make use of imported intermediate products not produced locally. [See Jones (1975b).] Suppose there is a small change in the tariff structure. Then, by the competitive profit conditions, the effective rate of protection granted to the jth sector equals a positive weighted average of the changes in the wage rate and the return to the factor used only in sector j (where the weights are distributive shares in local value added). Thus, in every sector which receives effective protection to a greater extent than the change in the wage rate, the specific factor gains relative to labor. This result does not require separability or other such constraints on the technology. Without a separability assumption, however, output changes or resource flows are more difficult to pin down than are changes in income distribution, since labor flows are then dependent on the degree of substitutability between labor and all the intermediate products. But if separability is imposed, the change in employment in sector j is positively related to the extent to which sector j's effective rate of protection exceeds the change in the wage rate. Thus in the specific-factors model a ranking of industries by effective rates of protection is not necessarily the same as the ranking by domestic resource (labor) flows resulting from these rates, but it does (in the separable case) provide a ranking which is cut by the change in the

---

[54] Except in the simplest cases, these formulas require detailed knowledge of elasticities of substitution throughout the system as well as of the tariff structure, thus vitiating their usefulness as predictive devices. See Ethier (1971, 1972a, 1977).

[55] Ethier (1977) is particularly emphatic in arguing that models that do not allow local production of imported intermediates should not be expected in general to have output responses predictable from n (effective) tariff rates (where n equals the number of final commodities) when $n + m$ separate outputs and inputs are involved (where m equals the number of imported non-locally-produced intermediates).

[56] See the discussion and references in Ethier (1977), probably the most penetrating of the many articles on this subject.

wage rate, with labor flowing from all industries receiving less effective protection than the wage change to all industries receiving more effective protection.

3.1.2. The "Austrian" model

In Section 2 we had occasion to stress the role of differences in supply conditions between countries as determinants of trade patterns in basic models of trade. More recent work on trade in a dynamic context, with special emphasis on the time-phased nature of the production process, suggests that differences in time preference may also affect the pattern of trade. Here we bypass the interesting normative issues that such models pose and instead note some positive questions which arise in a model in which trade takes place in an intermediate good as well as in a final good, the "Austrian" model of trade developed by Findlay (1978b).

The intermediate good in Findlay's model is "wood," which, combined with labor, instantaneously produces a consumption good which can be traded. Wood is also traded, but is produced by a point-input, point-output process whereby labor is applied initially and the output of wood grows continuously with the passage of time, the period of production being determined by the rate of interest. The technology whereby wood and the final product are produced implies an inverse relationship between the interest rate and the level of per capita consumption that can be maintained in a steady-state equilibrium. Findlay assumes this relationship to be identical for the two countries. But if rates of time preference differ between countries, so also will autarkic relative prices and thus a basis is established for mutually profitable exchange. In particular, the more "impatient" country exports the final product in exchange for wood, since final output is labor-intensive compared with the intermediate product. The relative price of wood is lower in the country with the lower rate of interest. In Findlay's model a free-trade equilibrium can be established with incomplete specialization in each country leading to equalization of interest rates and wage rates as in the standard Heckscher–Ohlin case, but without the concept of homogeneous capital and fixed endowments traditionally found in such models. The "Austrian" flavor of the model links the concept of capital to the existence of a traded intermediate good, with the value of the capital stock dependent upon the rate of interest and the pattern of trade determined by differences in taste patterns (time preference) between countries.

3.1.3. Middle products

The phrase "middle products" was used by Sanyal and Jones (1982) to encompass what traditionally are referred to as intermediate goods, goods-in-process, and natural resources which have been extracted and prepared for trade on world markets. The core concept in their model is that of a productive spectrum whereby, at initial stages, natural resources and raw materials are processed and, in the final stages, goods-in-process and intermediate products are locally assembled for national consumption. International trade, according to this view, takes place in commodities somewhere in the "middle" of this productive spectrum, freeing up a nation's input requirements in the final stages of production from its output of tradeable middle products at earlier stages.

Such a view of the role of international trade suggests a natural division between that part of the economy which produces commodities (middle products) *for* the world market (including the local economy), called the Input Tier, and that section of the economy which makes use of internationally traded middle products as inputs along with local resources to produce non-traded goods for final consumption (the Output Tier). Ruled out by assumption in the simple version of this model is the notion that the "middle" stages of the productive spectrum might be "thick" in the sense that tradeable middle products might use other tradeable middle products as inputs. In addition, the production structure in each tier of the economy is assumed to resemble that of the specific-factors model discussed in Section 2.4. Labor is mobile both among sectors in each tier and between tiers. The balance of payments provides an additional link between the two tiers; if the trade account is balanced, the value of total output from the Input Tier of the economy is matched by the value of middle products used as inputs (along with labor) in the Output Tier.

Several types of questions have been raised in the context of this model, and of central concern in each case is the allocation of labor between tiers and the real wage. For example, a transfer payment which gives rise to a trade surplus requires labor to be reallocated to the Input Tier as consumption falls, and this serves unambiguously to reduce the real wage.

If domestic (and world) prices of traded middle products remain constant to the small country, all non-labor inputs in the Output Tier can be aggregated, à la Hicks, into a composite middle product input, which serves to convert the production structure in the Output Tier from an $(n+1)$-factor, n-commodity specific-factors model into a two-factor, many-commodity Heckscher–Ohlin model. We described in Section 2.4 how, with the passage of time, a specific-factors model may converge to a (long-run) Heckscher–Ohlin model as factors lose their occupational specificity. In the middle-products model it is the existence of a world market in which middle products can be exchanged for each other that permits such a conversion.

With prices of all final consumer goods dependent at least in part on local conditions (wage rates) as well as on world prices of middle products, the model seems naturally suited to analyze how consumer price levels in two small open economies might differ in response to a commonly faced change in the world price of a middle product. This question is pursued in Jones and Purvis (1982), who show how standard monetary assumptions appended to a middle-products model can yield simultaneous determination of wage rates and exchange rates. In particular, even if the rise in the world price of an imported middle product affects the two countries' price levels to the same extent, the more flexible country (in the sense of a greater elasticity of substitution between labor and middle products) can experience an appreciating currency and rising wages vis-à-vis the less flexible country, a result in conflict with standard predictions of the purchasing-power-parity doctrine.

The middle-products model allows countries and sectors to differ in the extent to which local value must be added to transform middle products into final commodities, and much depends upon this comparison. It does not, however, focus upon another question: in a vertical production structure with many stages, which goods-in-process or middle products does a country import and which does it export? Two recent papers have tackled this issue independently and with different models. Sanyal (1980) assumes that in each of two countries a commodity is produced in a *continuum* of stages, with different Ricardian labor-only input structures. Depending upon technological differences and relative country size, a cut-off point will be determined, with one country producing the commodity from raw material stage to some intermediate point, and then exporting this good-in-process to the other country where labor is applied to finish the production process. By contrast, Dixit and Grossman (1982) use a specific-factors model, with one of the commodities (manufacturing) produced in a continuum of stages using capital and labor (the other sector using land and labor).[57] These stages are arranged such that, as goods-in-process develop towards the final stage, more labor-intensive techniques are required. Thus with two countries, the labor-abundant country will tend to specialize in later stages of the productive spectrum.[58] They analyze how endowment changes alter the cut-off point, as well as investigating issues related to content protection.

3.1.4. Natural resources

As Chapter 8 in this volume discusses, the normative question of pricing natural resources (exhaustible or renewable) has received much attention in the literature of the past decade. The middle-products approach stresses that some activities, the extraction of natural resources, must take place locally although international trade then allows other countries access to these resources. Obviously, comparative advantage changes over time for countries engaged in exporting exhaustible resources. In an early work Vanek (1963) traced through the changing pattern of

---

[57]Both papers cite the use of the continuum concept in Dornbusch, Fischer, and Samuelson (1977).

[58]A limitation of both papers is the assumption that costs (or factor proportions) move monotonically from lower to higher stages of production. If not, trade may take place at many points in the productive spectrum in the absence of inhibiting transport costs.

United States trade in natural resources, and suggested that asymmetries in resource use and availability could account for the Leontief paradox.

In a context of multi-level trade, the costs of resource extraction in one country often depend on the availability of foreign capital. Kemp and Ohyama (1978) have presented a simple model of North–South trade in which South makes use of Northern capital to develop its resources and exports these resources to the North where they are used to produce final commodities.[59] They put their model to use in exploring the normative issue of different degrees of bargaining strength and ability to exploit via export taxes and tariffs in the two regions. But the model also stresses the involvement of capital flows in resource extraction. Schmitz and Helmberger (1979) argue strongly for complementarity between trade in resources and trade in capital, a point also stressed by Williams in his 1929 article. We turn to consider more generally, now, the interaction between trade in goods and trade in factors.

3.2. *Trade in factors*

Bertil Ohlin lent his name to the model of trade most frequently used to illustrate the Classical paradigm whereby trade in final commodities is allowed but trade in factors is not. And yet his basic treatise (1933) contains extensive discussions of international factor movements – of both capital and labor – and their relationship to the international exchange of commodities. Meade (1955) also explored some of the issues involved when factors of production can participate in international markets. Most modern analytical treatments of the relationship between capital mobility and trade, however, start their bibliographical references with the work of Mundell (1957).

In the Mundell analysis both countries are assumed to share a common technology and to be incompletely specialized in producing two commodities with internally mobile labor and capital – the standard Heckscher–Ohlin framework. Even in the absence of international factor mobility free trade in these circumstances results in factor-price equalization. Mundell examines the implications of a small tariff levied by the country which imports the capital-intensive good. By the Stolper–Samuelson argument such a tariff raises the domestic real return to capital. If capital now becomes internationally mobile, it will be attracted to the tariff-levying country, and local production of the capital-intensive import-competing industry will rise. Thus the induced capital flow tends to reduce commodity trade; this process continues until all commodity trade is wiped out. In Mundell's model trade and factor mobility are substitutes in the sense that impediments to trade encourage factor mobility.

---

[59] This model is described in simplified terms by Findlay (1979).

Continuing research in this area initially followed Mundell in retaining the Heckscher–Ohlin production structure, although dispensing with the assumption that countries have identical technologies. Kemp (1966) and Jones (1967) investigated the relationship between tariffs and taxes on capital flows for a country simultaneously engaged in trade and investment of some of its capital stock abroad. A central characteristic of these analyses refers to the links which technology or markets provide between commodity prices and the rate of return to capital. A tariff that improves a country's commodity terms of trade may nonetheless worsen its real income if, say, such a price change depresses the rate of return to capital and the tariff-levying country is heavily engaged in foreign investment.[60]

Is commodity trade a substitute (perhaps imperfect) for factor mobility? In the Heckscher–Ohlin model used by Mundell, the answer is in the affirmative. Purvis (1972), however, argues that if technology differs between countries (as it does in the analysis of Kemp and Jones), the possibility for capital to move internationally may enlarge, rather than reduce, the volume of trade. That is, trade and factor movements may be complements.[61] The issue has been analyzed in a more general context by Markusen (1983). He argues that if the basis for trade is differences in factor endowments, as in Mundell, trade and factor movements will tend to be substitutes. However, if the basis for trade resides in other characteristics, international factor mobility is likely to enhance commodity trade – trade and factor movements tend to be complements.

Markusen surveys several possible bases for trade other than factor proportions – returns to scale, taxes, and imperfect competition as well as Ricardian-type differences in technology (as in Purvis). In each case a standard technique is employed: countries are assumed to be identical in every respect (including factor proportions) except for the single basis for trade. For example, suppose the home country has an absolute technical advantage in producing the labor-intensive good so that, when trade in goods (only) is allowed, the home country exports this commodity. Since both face the same commodity prices, the presumed technical superiority of the home country in the labor-intensive good must result in a higher wage rate and a lower return to capital at home than in the foreign country. If capital mobility is now allowed, capital must flow abroad and by the Rybczynski theorem this must raise the output in each country of that country's exportable; factor mobility has caused a complementary expansion in commodity trade.

---

[60] Chapter 5 discusses normative aspects of this model, as well as the phenomenon of a flat on the world transformation surface when both countries are diversified in production.

[61] In our discussion of natural resources we cited the suggestions of Schmitz and Helmberger (1970) that international capital flows encourage development and trade in natural resources; trade and capital flows are again complements.

Once some degree of international factor mobility is allowed, the broad question that is addressed by these models concerns the effect of increased factor mobility on the overall *level* of commodity trade. But there remains the somewhat related question raised at the outset in connection with trade in intermediates: does the international mobility of factors cause the *pattern* of trade to depart from what it would be in the absence of such factor movements? This issue has been discussed in the context of capital mobility in a Heckscher–Ohlin model by Jones (1970b),[62] and by Ferguson (1978).[63]

In these models of international capital mobility it is typically the case that ownership of the capital good is unchanged so that no actual sales of capital take place. The signal for a movement of capital is a discrepancy between rates of return among countries. Other models, especially in a growth context, have emphasized capital mobility in the form of sales of capital goods. Thus Oniki and Uzawa (1965), Baldwin (1966), and Inada (1968) allow for current production of capital goods, and, as well, for prices (costs of production) of capital goods and savings behavior to link trade in capital goods with relative commodity prices. In a properly specified model in which interest rates are equalized between countries it makes little difference whether capital goods are sold or ownership retained. But if interest rates in the country wishing to obtain the services of foreign capital are higher than in the source country, that country may not be willing to purchase capital goods at current prices even if the local stream of returns is somewhat higher.[64] Here we direct our attention away from growth models and the rate at which capital is accumulated in favor of more static models concerned with the endogenous response of the location of existing capital goods, the allocation being guided by current rates of return.[65]

Economists interested in industrial organization have wanted to explain the role of the multinational firm, with its expertise in particular well-defined spheres of activity, and this concern led to the important contribution by Caves (1971a).[66] To imbed his discussion in a general-equilibrium context, Caves set aside the Heckscher–Ohlin view of capital as homogeneous and inter-sectorally mobile in favor of the specific-factors model, in which endogenous capital flows have a direct effect on factor returns quite aside from any influence on commodity

[62] In particular, if capital is internationally mobile and technology differs between countries it is shown that the Harrod measure of this difference at a given rate of profit is a better indicator of trade patterns than the Hicksian measure, which is more applicable if factors are internationally immobile.

[63] In the context of the specific-factors model, Jones (1979b) notes that the situation in which the pattern of trade with capital mobility differs from that without mobility parallels the later stages of Vernon's (1966) product cycle. See also the remarks in Jones (1970b).

[64] This issue is discussed in more detail in Berglas and Jones (1977).

[65] Models of trade and growth are discussed in Chapters 4 and 6, and dynamic models of foreign investment in Chapters 4 and 5.

[66] A more extensive treatment of multinationals is provided in Caves (1982). See also the interesting work by Hymer (1976).

markets and prices, even if countries are incompletely specialized.[67] The specific-factors model with capital mobility leads to some results in accord with earlier Heckscher–Ohlin models.[68] But other important results are different.

To return to the question of possible complementarity between goods and factor flows, recall that in the Heckscher–Ohlin model trade flows that reflect differences in endowment patterns tend to be substitutes for the international mobility of capital. This is less clearly the case in the specific-factors model. Adopt once again the Markusen (1983) technique of having two countries identical except for a single basis for trade. Suppose the home country has a larger labor force and that this causes it to export the first commodity in a two-commodity setting.[69] Under free trade the wage rate at home will be lower and the returns to both types of specific capital will be higher than abroad. Whether subsequent international capital mobility reduces or expands commodity trade depends upon which type of capital is mobile. If type-1 capital is mobile, the flow into the home country serves to expand commodity trade, whereas if type-2 capital is mobile, home exports of commodity 1 will fall, instead. Indeed, in the latter case the pattern of commodity trade can be reversed following the flow of type-2 capital into the home country.[70] Of course if labor is internationally mobile instead, an outward flow of labor from the home country will restore relative endowment balance between countries and all trade will vanish.[71]

The phenomenon of "cross-hauling" of international capital may appear in the specific-factors model. Caves (1971a) gives an example in which an exogenous inflow of type-1 capital into a country serves to cause an outflow of type-2 capital via the consequent reduction in returns to *both* types of sector-specific capital. A more complete account of the possibility of two-way flows of international capital would examine the consequences on the endogenous location of both types of capital of an exogenous change in some key variable other than one or other stock of capital. The influence of commercial policy or resource discoveries in causing

---

[67]This change in models has given rise to an extensive literature. See Amano (1977), Berglas and Jones (1977), Jones (1979b), Burgess (1980), Batra and Ramachandran (1980), Khandker (1981), Jones, Neary, and Ruane (1981), and Jones and Dei (1983). The same approach underlies the staples model of Canadian economic history. See especially Chambers and Gordon (1966), Caves (1971b), and Easton and Reed (1981).

[68]For example, many of the patterns of optimal taxes and tariffs are similar. See Jones (1979b).

[69]This implies that $\theta_{L1}\gamma_1 > \theta_{L2}\gamma_2$ so that the larger labor force raises output of commodity 1 at constant prices by relatively more than commodity 2. See Section 2.4 for details.

[70]This reversal of the trade pattern *must* occur if $\theta_{L1}\gamma_1$ is sufficiently close to (but greater than) $\theta_{L2}\gamma_2$ so that the initial trade flow is small relative to the difference between countries in labor supply and rates of return to capital.

[71]In this model trade in any factor will cause the difference between relative endowments in the two countries, as measured by $\{\hat{L} - (\lambda_{L1}\hat{K}_1 + \lambda_{L2}\hat{K}_2)\}$, to equal zero in a free-trade equilibrium, since only then will the return to the mobile factor be equated between countries. If the internationally mobile factor is the one which is initially in more ample supply in one country, factor movements will wipe out trade. But suppose, for example, that K_1 is exogenously in greater supply at home and that K_2 is endogenously mobile (internationally). Then K_2 must flow out of the home country and thus enlarge the basis for trade (since the home country exports the first commodity).

one type of capital to flow out of a country while another flows in is suggested in two alternative models by Jones, Neary, and Ruane (1981).[72] For example, suppose that new resource discoveries lead to expansion in one sector of the economy, aided by an inflow of capital specific to this sector but internationally mobile. This is the setting for the "Dutch Disease," whereby the return to capital in other sectors can be squeezed by the implied rise in wage rates. If this other capital is also mobile internationally, it may be able to avoid the consequences of such a squeeze by flowing to other countries not experiencing the resource boom.

International movements of labor have occasionally been pronounced. To the extent that the labor flow has primarily non-economic explanations, standard trade theory can analyze the consequences of such a movement on trade patterns, factor prices, etc.[73] Of more interest analytically are situations in which economic incentives provide the underlying rationale for labor mobility. The vast literature on the "brain drain" [e.g. Bhagwati and Hamada (1974)] attests to the important normative issues involved. We mention these only in passing, as well as the possible "buffer" use of international labor flows represented by the guest-worker system in Germany and other northern European countries (or the seasonal use of Mexican labor in the Southwestern region of the United States).[74] For some countries (Pakistan, Malawi, etc.) earnings of nationals abroad are so large that without such flows local wage rates and the volume of commodity trade would be much reduced.

Finally, note that in the Classical paradigm with no internationally mobile factors, trade is determined by positions of comparative advantage in which international differences between countries in political systems, degree of taxation, danger of expropriation, etc., have effects on the allocation of resources trapped within a nation's boundaries only to the extent that they affect each sector differently. However, once factors of production are mobile internationally, such inter-country differences can assume major importance in determining where factors of production choose to be employed. The doctrine of comparative advantage then yields in some respects to the doctrine of "relative attractiveness" – the relative capacity of countries to attract internationally footloose productive factors.[75]

---

[72] Not all shocks lead to cross-hauling. For example, local growth in the labor supply is likely to cause an endogenous inflow of both kinds of capital.

[73] Ohlin (1933) describes cases in which the flow of labor has substituted for trade – e.g. French Huguenots in the seventeenth century moving to Germany and Holland and setting up textile production that weakened the French export position. In a recent paper Engerman (1982) documents the nineteenth century British pattern in sugar production whereby international movements of British capital and Indian labor provided the factors required to combine with the natural resources and climate of third regions (Mauritius, Trinidad, Natal, etc.).

[74] Ethier (1981) presents an interesting analysis of the temporary flows of unskilled labor, in part motivated by considerations of dumping which he analyzes in Ethier (1982a).

[75] For further details see Jones (1980).

3.3. Trade in technology

International exchange of technological knowledge clearly takes place, and yet economists find the phenomenon somewhat difficult to incorporate into formal models. Recent attempts include those of Smith (1974), Rodriguez (1975b), Berglas and Jones (1977), Findlay (1978a), and Krugman (1979a). These models differ in the form which the trade in technology is assumed to take as well as in the characterization of those aspects of economies most likely to encourage such technology transfer.

None of the papers cited attempts to explain either the level or the rate of improvement of technology in the advanced country. The focus, instead, is on the transfer of technology from the advanced region to the less developed areas. The paper by Smith (1974) considers the sale of vintage capital equipment by advanced to developing areas. Thus second-hand machines find a market in relatively low-wage countries although their economic usefulness in advanced areas has been exhausted. Berglas and Jones (1977) also consider a model in which technology is embodied in capital equipment which is located (not sold) by the advanced in the developing region. The attraction is the lower wage rate, and a deterrent is provided by higher perceived risks. Like the Findlay (1978a) model, both advanced and relatively backward capital coexist in the developing region, with rates of return not necessarily equalized.

One feature of a model in which the transfer of technology implies the transfer of the capital good is that less is thereby available in the source country. This is not the case with licensing arrangements whereby technology can be adopted in foreign countries without restricting its use at home. Rodriguez (1975b) considers such a case and concludes that the owner of the technology behaves like a monopolist in the foreign market. Optimal behavior is analyzed, much as in the earlier Kemp (1966) and Jones (1967) models of optimal tax and tariff patterns in a Heckscher–Ohlin world of capital mobility, except that the export of technology does not impair its availability at home. The Berglas and Jones model also considers optimal commercial policy for the advanced country and compares this with the alternative whereby the government follows a hands-off policy but a multinational firm controls the export of technology (via capital exports) with an eye towards its own return. Technology exports may easily prove excessive compared with the level that is optimal for the country in this case.

Findlay's (1978a) paper delves more deeply into the determinants of the rate at which technology is transferred. The two key ingredients involve the Veblen–Gerschenkron idea that the rate of improvement in technology in the backward country is larger the greater the gap separating its technology from that in the advanced area, and, secondly, the "contagion" postulate whereby the greater the direct contact with advanced productive technology (in the form of advanced capital located in the backward country) the more rapid is the improvement in the less developed region. Findlay weaves these two postulates together to build a formal dynamic model of steady-state growth, foreign investment, and technology transfer.

A somewhat different explanation of the transfer of technology is given in Berglas and Jones (1977). Here the building-blocks are Arrow's (1962) concept of learning-by-doing (supplemented by the concept of "forgetting-by-not-doing") and the Atkinson and Stiglitz (1969) concept of the localization of technical progress.[76] The basic idea is that domestic factor prices determine not only the techniques a country uses, but also the regions in which its industries' isoquants tend to move in (with technical progress) or move out (where techniques not used are forgotten). Thus the effective isoquants of advanced (high-wage) countries do not dominate those of low-wage countries; instead, they lie closer to the capital axis and further from the (unskilled) labor axis. Such a view has a strong implication for trade in technology: countries relatively *close* to each other in stage of development (and so having similar factor price ratios) will experience a greater transfer of new technology than countries further apart. This view contrasts with the Veblen–Gerschenkron idea cited by Findlay. Furthermore, it provides an example (for technology trade) of a broader phenomenon: "similarity" between countries may enhance rather than discourage some kinds of trade. This is a theme to which we return in Section 4's discussion of monopolistic competition.[77]

Krugman's model postulates both a given rate of new goods (technology) introduced in the advanced region (the North) and a given lag before the less developed area (the South) can obtain the technology to produce these goods. With these two ingredients given exogenously, the Krugman model can in a simple fashion explore how North–South wage and real income relationships depend upon them both. The commodity composition of trade, of course, changes constantly; the North has a (monopoly-type) advantage in producing new goods, in a fashion described by Vernon's product cycle.

3.4. Trade in securities

The theory of international economics is often divided (as in these two volumes) into real and monetary sections. Most real trade theory, concerned as it is with question of composition (relative prices and outputs, internal and/or international distribution of income), finds it convenient to assume that a nation's aggregate spending matches its current income. This, of course, does not mean a

---

[76]See also the discussion in Jones (1970b).

[77]A recent paper by Feenstra and Judd (1982) discusses technology transfer in a framework of monopolistic competition. A fixed cost element is introduced by the assumption of an initial outlay on research and development that is centralized in one country.

barter economy. Instead, it implies either that asset accumulation does not take place or, if spending includes real investment, that capital goods are the only asset stocks that expand (as in some models of growth and trade). Precluded is a nation's use of its trading partners in an attempt to "live beyond its means" by issuing debt or to accumulate claims against foreigners' future production.

This assumption of balanced trade can be stoutly defended by pointing out that the qualitative answers to many compositional questions are not sensitive to the absence of trade deficits or surpluses. Nevertheless, for some questions the assumption needs to be removed. For example, Fischer and Frenkel (1974) provide a formal analysis of a small growing country engaged in commodity trade and able to trade securities with the rest of the world. With net trade in securities, various time paths of the balance of indebtedness are possible, and they correspond to less analytical discussions in development economics.

The recent surge of literature on the role of uncertainty in trade models, documented in detail in Chapter 9 below, suggests a somewhat different role for international trade in securities. Such trade may help countries share risks in much the same fashion as individuals do in the stock market.[78]

In Section 2 we discussed the "core propositions" associated with the Heckscher–Ohlin model. The earlier writings on uncertainty and trade often attacked these theorems as valid only in the absence of uncertainty. Helpman and Razin (1978) provide a way out of this situation by showing how a model may be specified that allows international trade in securities to validate once again these core propositions (with the exception of the Heckscher–Ohlin theorem itself). The trick is to identify real equities with the expected output in any industry of the inputs of labor and capital. Input decisions have to be made before uncertainty is resolved. In the first industry, for example, $f_1(L_1, K_1)$ denotes the expected output of the first commodity. Uncertainty, however, leads the value of realized output to equal $\theta_1(\alpha)f_1(L_1, K_1)$, where θ_1 is a positive random variable whose value depends on the state of nature (denoted by α). Trade in commodities takes place after the uncertainty is resolved, and, if θ_1 does not equal unity, factor payments need not be matched by commodity prices and the standard link between the two is thereby ruptured. However, trade in securities allows security prices to take on the role filled by commodity prices in deterministic models, so that, for example, the equality of security prices between countries implies, under the standard assumptions, equality of factor prices as well. Of course, the significance of Helpman and Razin's approach is not just that it "rescues" the

---

[78] The basic paper cited by Helpman and Razin (1978) as providing a suitable framework in which to analyze international trade in securities is that of Diamond (1967). Of the vast literature of the 1970s attempting to deal with uncertainty and trade, the contributions by Pomery (1976, 1979) and Helpman and Razin (1978) go furthest in focusing on the possibility of trade in some form of stocks or securities as well as commodities. For earlier work, however, see Kemp and Liviatan (1973).

core propositions but that it draws attention to the importance of specifying which markets are assumed to extend across national boundaries.

4. Multi-behavioral trade

Our use of the phrase "multi-behavioral" trade to capture the material discussed in this section needs explanation. Basically we are concerned with departures from purely competitive behavior, in some cases prompted by the existence of increasing returns to scale. But we also wish to discuss the consequences for positive trade theory of departures from the assumption that markets are "clean" – free of taxes or other distortions either at the goods or factor level. Just as in Section 3, this literature typically involves a *mixture* of elements – some clean competitive markets and some distorted or imperfectly competitive sectors.

4.1. Market distortions

The patterns of trade predicted in standard trade models can be altered if distortions to commodity and factor markets exist. To the extent that trade theory has been concerned with the analysis of tariffs, the focus has been on the appearance domestically of productive activities that are ruled out in the harsher climate of free trade rather than on a reversal of trade patterns.[79] By contrast, subsidies can in general alter the direction of trade. In addition, as is well documented in the normative literature on the subject, the welfare consequences are potentially severe: for example, when comparative advantage is based upon artificially low payments to a factor in a nation's export industry the misallocation of resources may (but need not) make free trade worse than autarky. [For an early analysis see Haberler (1950).][80]

As well as having implications for trade patterns, the existence of certain types of factor-market distortions has called into question several of the core propositions of the Heckscher–Ohlin model. Magee (1969, 1971), Bhagwati and Srinivasan (1971), Herberg and Kemp (1971), and Jones (1971b) all deal with the Heckscher–Ohlin model in which a factor in one sector (say capital in X) receives a fixed percentage premium over the return of the same factor in the other

---

[79] Deardorff (1980) describes as " natural" trade situations in which impediments such as tariffs do not artificially create new export industries.

[80] An even earlier example is the argument for protection on the basis of distortions in factor markets put forth by Manoilesco (1931). See also the critical reviews by Ohlin (1931) and Viner (1932), which anticipate many of the points made in the recent literature.

sector.[81] Potential paradoxes emerge: the output of X may fall as the relative price of X goes up or, alternatively, as the premium rises. Underlying these paradoxical results is the possibility that the factor-market distortion (whereby capital earns more in sector X than in sector Y) may cause the ranking of industries by distributive shares (the value-intensity ranking) to differ from the ranking by physical factor proportions. (For example X may be physically labor intensive but nonetheless pay capital a higher share than Y). The Stolper–Samuelson link between factor and commodity prices depends upon the value ranking, whereas the Rybczynski relationship asserts that at constant commodity prices an expansion in the labor force reduces output in the sector that is capital intensive in physical terms. Thus in the example above an increase in the relative price of X causes the wage rate to fall. At the intensive margin this leads both sectors to economize on capital. Outputs then adjust as they would at constant prices if the endowment of labor fell and capital rose, thus forcing a contraction of sector X since it is physically labor intensive.[82]

As shown by Neary (1978b), all the paradoxes which depend upon this divergence between factor-intensity rankings can be dismissed by invoking stability arguments. Under a class of adjustment processes which includes as a special case the "short-run capital-specificity" process discussed in Section 2.4, he investigates whether an economy will approach an equilibrium in which it is incompletely specialized and rates of return to capital are separated only by the amount of the distortion. The answer is that a small price-taking open economy does *not* approach such a long-run equilibrium if, at such a point, the physical and value intensity rankings diverge. Therefore, those paradoxes, such as an inverse relationship between price and output, which depend upon a divergence between the alternative factor-intensity rankings are associated with unstable equilibria and so will never be observed.[83]

A factor-market distortion that takes the form of a proportional premium earned by a factor in one sector is not the only kind which has received attention in the literature.[84] For example, Lefeber (1971), Brecher (1974) and Schweinberger (1978) have focused on the existence of economy-wide minimum wages. The use of the Heckscher–Ohlin model for this purpose presents difficul-

---

[81] Thus these models build upon the earlier analysis of the corporation income tax in Harberger (1962). See also the analysis of union wages in Johnson and Mieszkowski (1970).

[82] In terms of the notation introduced in Section 2.3, the reversal of physical and value rankings implies that the product $|\lambda| \, |\theta|$ is negative.

[83] Some debate has emerged on Neary's conclusions. See Herberg and Kemp (1980), and Neary's reply (1980a).

[84] Indeed, it may not be the appropriate way to represent certain distortions. For example, Jones (1971b), argues that the analysis of wage differentials caused by union activity, as in the analysis of

ties in that a small open economy facing world-determined terms of trade has at most one wage rate consistent with incomplete specialization. Should this rate fall short of the minimum wage, the country is driven to complete specialization and some labor may become unemployed.[85] A recent generalization of this kind of distortion is provided by Neary (1980b), who stresses the relationship between Heckscher–Ohlin models with minimum wages à la Brecher and the Mundell case discussed in Section 3.2 in which the rigid factor price reflects international factor mobility.

Minimum wage rates may not apply throughout the economy. One of the most interesting recent developments in trade and development theory concerned with factor-market distortions is the model developed by Harris and Todaro (1970). They distinguish between a rural (agricultural) sector and an urban sector. Only in the latter does a minimum wage prevail, at a higher level than exists in the rural sector. For labor-market equilibrium to obtain, the urban wage, scaled down by a fraction representing the ratio of urban employment to the total urban labor force (including unemployed job-seekers), must equal the rural wage. Krueger (1977) has an interesting discussion of the implications of such a model for positions of comparative advantage. Corden and Findlay (1975) alter the assumption, made by Harris and Todaro, that capital is sector-specific, and show that in a Heckscher–Ohlin setting an increase in the urban minimum wage may cause industrial output to expand. Further properties of the Harris–Todaro model with intersectoral capital mobility are developed in Khan (1980) and Neary (1981).

One persistent difficulty with this entire literature is the ad hoc character of the distortions.[86] An important departure from this view is the notion that economic resources are devoted to obtaining licenses or special treatment leading to enhanced rents or revenues. The locus classicus for this argument in a trade context is Krueger (1974), and related work has been carried out by Bhagwati and Srinivasan (1980) and Findlay and Wellisz (1982) in Heckscher–Ohlin and specific-factors models respectively. The phenomenon of rent-seeking raises important normative questions which we do not discuss here.

Johnson and Mieskowski (1970), might better be captured by a specific-factors model in which union labor earns a premium that depends *endogenously* on its control of union membership. By restricting entry the union would raise union wages but might raise non-union wages by a greater relative amount and thus lower its percentage premium. This kind of objection does not arise in Harberger's (1962) case of corporate income taxation where the discrepancy between returns to capital is caused by exogenous government behavior.

[85]A specific-factors model with (temporarily) sticky wages is analyzed in Noman and Jones (1979). In their model a (given) wage may coexist with unemployment, but the economy is nonetheless incompletely specialized.

[86]An exception is the work of Carruth and Oswald (1982), who examine in general equilibrium the effects of introducing a utility-maximizing trade union which simultaneously chooses the wage and employment level of its members.

4.2. Increasing returns

The assumption that technology exhibits constant returns to scale is almost universally adopted in general-equilibrium models, including those small-scale versions popular in the theory of international trade. The case of decreasing returns poses little analytical difficulty, but economists have typically been wary of modelling increasing returns. Part of the problem derives from a desire to preserve the assumption of perfectly competitive behavior. (Some forms of imperfect competition rest intimately on the existence of scale economies, and we discuss them in Section 4.3.) But a strand of the literature attempts to maintain the competitive framework by assuming that increasing returns are external to the firm and internal to the industry.

The effects of these increasing returns on the core propositions of the Heckscher–Ohlin model serve as the focus for the Jones (1968) discussion of variable returns to scale. The slope of the transformation schedule differs from the commodity price ratio to the extent that the degree of increasing returns differs between industries. The transformation schedule may not be bowed out everywhere, depending on the strength of returns to scale and the difference in factor intensities.[87] The effect of an increase in the labor endowment on outputs at constant commodity prices, the Rybczynski relationship, depends on the local shape of the transformation schedule, as does the Stolper–Samuelson theorem. The possibility that production functions are non-homothetic introduces an additional distinction between average and marginal factor intensities,[88] and this may affect the Stolper–Samuelson result as well.

The wide array of possible outcomes with increasing returns was questioned by Mayer (1974a) for the same reason that Neary (1978b) invoked later in connection with the literature on factor market distortions: a plausible set of stability conditions is inconsistent with incompletely specialized equilibria in which relative prices and outputs are inversely related. Such restrictions serve to reestablish the Rybczynski result and (if marginal and average factor intensity rankings coincide) the Stolper–Samuelson theorem as well.

A somewhat different approach to increasing returns is reflected in the early paper by Melvin (1969) and, more recently, by Markusen and Melvin (1981). They treat increasing returns as providing a basis for trade alternative to differences in factor endowments or productivity and examine the consequences for the gains from trade. Whereas the Melvin (1969) paper considered trade

---

[87]The question of the shape of the transformation schedule with increasing returns, especially near the axes, is discussed thoroughly in Herberg and Kemp (1969).

[88]Recent work by Panagariya (1980) simplifies the issue by assuming homotheticity in production but relaxing some other assumptions made in the Jones (1968) analysis, e.g. that the expansion of any industry at constant commodity (or factor) prices increases the demand for both productive factors.

between two identical countries in which both goods exhibit increasing returns, Markusen and Melvin introduce asymmetry in two key ways: only one commodity is produced under increasing returns, and although countries share identical factor proportions and tastes, they differ in absolute size. Economies of scale thus establish a comparative advantage for the large country in the production of the commodity which exhibits increasing returns to scale.[89]

In these papers scale economies are linked exclusively to national levels of output. A recent article by Ethier (1979) has zeroed in on the distinction between these "economies of scale in the traditional sense"[90] and increasing returns that are tied to the scale of world demand and output. As world output of a particular commodity increases, greater degrees of specialization are allowed, and this can give rise to increasing returns even if national output is unaltered. Each country produces two commodities (wheat, W and manufacturing, M) and a bowed-out production-possibilities curve connects output of wheat (the constant-returns sector) and the *scale* of manufacturing activity, m. But actual *output* of manufactures, M, equals some multiple, k, of m, where k captures the extent of increasing returns as linked to the scale of world output, $(m + m^*)$. [Thus k equals $(m + m^*)^{\alpha - 1}$, where α exceeds unity.] The relationship between m and W thus follows the standard Heckscher–Ohlin model, whereas that between outputs M and W also incorporates the extent of world increasing returns.[91] Ethier finds traditional offer curve analysis too cumbersome because of the dependence of each nation's output on the other nation's output and so introduces a new concept (the allocation curve) which incorporates this interdependence. With the aid of allocation curves, Ethier analyzes the stability of world equilibrium using the Marshallian conditions appropriate to the case of decreasing costs.

Perhaps Ethier's most interesting proposition concerns the effect in this model of having the underlying bowed-out curves between wheat and the scale of manufacturing production become more similar between countries. The volume of trade in manufactured goods (intra-industry trade) rises absolutely and relative to inter-industry trade. This is a theme he develops in more detail in Ethier (1982b), where he combines world increasing returns with more traditional national increasing returns.[92] Although Ethier's approach is different, his interest in the

---

[89] Both these articles also discuss the possible complementarity of goods trade and factor flows when increasing returns provide the basis for trade, along lines we discussed above in Section 3.2 in describing the recent paper by Markusen (1983).

[90] This is the phrase used by Balassa (1967) and cited in Ethier (1979).

[91] In discussing Graham's argument for protection, Ethier (1982c) switches away from an underlying Heckscher–Ohlin model to a Ricardian model with increasing returns of the national variety, since the production possibility schedule must then be bowed in. In a Heckscher–Ohlin model increasing returns promote a bowed-in schedule, but differences in factor intensities intensities support increasing opportunity costs.

[92] The core propositions of Heckscher–Ohlin theory are also analyzed in Ethier (1982b), and versions of these survive the introduction of increasing returns relatively intact.

contrast between inter-industry and intra-industry trade is shared by the recent burgeoning literature on monopolistic competition.

4.3. Imperfect competition

Free entry can rule out profits even if returns to scale are increasing. Similarly, the lack of free entry may encourage monopolistic or monopsonistic behavior even if returns to scale are constant. Alternatively, increasing returns may support monopolistic behavior or, if entry is free, markets characterized by monopolistic competition.

Like economies of scale, elements of monopoly behavior are typically absent from models attempting to use general-equilibrium techniques. [An exception for small-scale models is the 1973 article by Melvin and Warne.] In the presence of monopoly, production remains on the transformation schedule, but the price ratio is distorted away from its slope. To the extent that free trade dispels the firm's monopoly power, a country may gain from trade both for the usual reasons and because of the enforced change in market structure. As discussed by Caves (1974), if the import sector is monopolized, trade may serve to raise production of importables. If the export sector is monopolized, trade may lower the relative price of exportables. Both of these movements run counter to those found in traditional competitive markets.

The analysis of monopoly is extended by Markusen (1981) to a two-country setting with monopolies in the same sector in each country, each treating its rival's output as fixed. In a fashion made familiar in earlier articles by Melvin and by Markusen, the two countries are lined up before trade so that they have similar tastes, factor endowments, and constant-returns technology, but one country is larger than the other. This difference in size leads to trade in which the large country imports the product of the monopolized sector. The combination of monopoly and increasing returns leads to ambiguity in the trade pattern, since we have already seen in Section 4.2 that increasing returns alone has the opposite bias, encouraging the large country to *export* the good which is produced under economies of scale.[93]

These models highlight the potential effect of the increased competition in product markets resulting when free trade lessens a firm's monopoly power. However, even if monopoly power is completely eliminated, a large firm can still act as a monopsonist in domestic factor markets. This issue has been treated by

---

[93] The analysis in Markusen (1981) can be viewed as an attempt to deal with oligopoly in trade models. A less formal discussion is provided by Caves (1979). In more recent work Markusen (1982) has attempted to analyze one potential reason for the behavior and existence of multinational firms – the gains available to multi-plant operations when some activities, such as research and development, can be centralized in one location but made available to all plants.

Itoh (1978), Feenstra (1980), McCulloch and Yellen (1980), and Markusen and Robson (1980). Feenstra links his analysis to the literature on factor-market distortions discussed in Section 4.1; monopsonies provide a rationale for such distortions. The locus of a nation's outputs lies below the competitive transformation schedule (but above the hyperplane joining the end points) and, in addition, the slope of such a distorted locus may not equal the price ratio. Monopsony has the effect of making factor intensities systematically less dissimilar between the monopsonized sector and the competitive sector. All the authors cited share these results, while Markusen and Robson also illustrate how a monopsonist may raise output above the levels expected in a competitive sector. Itoh considers, as well, the joint existence of monopsony and foreign investment, thus moving away from the Classical paradigm in two different respects. A multinational firm may loom large in a small country's labor market and thus may distort wage rates to its advantage.

The introduction of scale economies to support Chamberlinian monopolistic competition in a general-equilibrium setting represents one of the most active recent areas of interest in trade theory. Although Negishi (1972) discussed the problem in general terms, it is the recent work of Krugman (1979b, 1980, 1981), Dixit and Norman (1980), Lancaster (1980) and Helpman (1981a) that has attracted most attention. The empirical phenomenon that inspires all these papers is the importance of intra-industry trade, a feature emphasized by Balassa (1967), Grubel (1970), and Grubel and Lloyd (1975), among others.

Krugman's models are particularly simple. He adopts the Dixit and Stiglitz (1977) model of monopolistic competition whereby a consumer's utility is positively related to the number of varieties of manufactured products and each variety is produced subject to the increasing returns to scale that result when an element of fixed costs is added to labor costs that are proportional to output. The 1979 article assumes that each economy produces many varieties of a single type of (manufactured) good, whereas elements of inter-sectoral trade are introduced in the 1981 article by letting each economy produce two kinds of products, with many varieties of each kind. The background production structure is an ingeniously simple blend of the exchange and Ricardian models: each type of product uses only one kind of labor, which is available to all varieties of that type but immobile between types. The trade pattern that emerges depends both on the difference between relative endowments of each kind of labor in the two countries and upon relative sizes of countries.

The model developed by Helpman (1981a) differs both in the specification of demand [consumers have preferred characteristics of products à la Lancaster (1979)] and in terms of the production structure. Each economy produces not only varieties of the manufactured good that are subject to increasing returns but also a commodity (food) exhibiting standard constant returns to scale. Moreover, both sectors use capital and labor which are perfectly mobile domestically.

Helpman's model allows both for traditional Heckscher–Ohlin-type trade involving two broad product categories (inter-industry trade) as a result of differences in factor endowments and for the exchange of different varieties of manufactured goods (intra-industry trade).

Two general types of questions are raised in this literature. First, is trade stimulated by differences between countries or by similarities? In the models satisfying the Classical paradigm it is differences between countries in factor endowments, technology, or tastes that encourage relatively large volumes of trade. The recent models that incorporate monopolistic competition suggest that intra-industry trade is likely to be more extensive between economies similar in size and factor proportions, although inter-industry trade is still encouraged by differences in underlying factor endowments.[94] Thus some kinds of trade are stimulated by similarities between countries.[95]

The second type of question, which we had occasion to raise in our earlier discussion of comparative advantage, concerns the power of autarkic prices to predict trade patterns. Because manufactures, say, are produced subject to increasing returns, they tend to be relatively cheap in large countries before trade. But suppose countries are identical in every respect except size; when trade is opened up there is no inter-sectoral (food for manufactures) trade. The reason pre-trade commodity prices cease to have trade-predictive powers is that certain key characteristics determining autarkic prices are utterly changed once trade becomes possible. In autarky, a large country tends to have low relative prices for goods subject to increasing returns since it is the extent of the *local* market that determines cost. Once trade takes place, prices in both large and small countries depend on the extent of the same *world* market. The problem is analogous to that discussed in Section 3; a country may export a final commodity that is relatively expensive in autarky if it requires as an input an intermediate good which becomes cheap only with trade.

Finally, both Krugman and Helpman discuss the role of factor prices in these models. Krugman (1981) emphasizes that if countries are roughly similar in their proportions of the two types of labor, not only will intra-industry trade tend to dominate, but trade could allow all factor returns to rise. By contrast, in

[94] Ethier (1982b) reaches similar conclusions with a different model (described in Section 4.2). A blend of the Ethier and Helpman (1981a) approaches is developed by Helpman (1981b), in which differentiated middle products instead of final consumption goods are subject to increasing returns. Falvey's recent model (1981), discussed in Section 2.5, illustrates how intra-industry trade can be explained without relying on increasing returns and monopolistic competition. In an analogous vein, Brander (1981) models intra-industry trade without requiring differentiated production.

[95] Linder (1961) presents an argument in which tastes are important in explaining trade. Unlike Classical models, however, it is similarity in taste patterns, as linked to per capita income levels, that encourages trade; countries produce commodities that are consumed not only locally but by other countries with roughly similar per capita levels of income. Recall, as well, our discussion of technology transfer in Section 3.3; such transfer is more likely to take place among countries at comparable stages of development.

traditional models trade tends to depress the return to the country's scarce factor. In discussing how pre-trade commodity prices may fail to predict trade patterns, Helpman points out that relative factor prices are a better predictor of inter-industry trade. And, with free trade between countries sharing the same technology, factor prices can once again be equalized even in the presence of increasing returns and monopolistic competition.

5. Concluding remarks

We have tried to indicate in this chapter recent developments in the positive theory of international trade, especially since it was last surveyed in the mid-1960s. As an organizing device we have treated the Classical paradigm as a set of assumptions under which trade is limited to final commodities and markets are undistorted and characterized by constant returns to scale and perfect competition. There is no doubt that the bulk of the older literature in trade theory abides by these assumptions, just as it is clear that much of the progress made in the field since it was last surveyed has involved departures from the Classical paradigm. This new work has in part been motivated by certain key features of real-world trade: the vast exchange of raw materials and commodities that require further processing before being consumed, the large volume of intra-industry trade, and the importance of the size of markets.

These extensions in analysis have generally been made without throwing away building blocks found in the earlier literature. For example, Helpman (1981a) discusses the importance of monopolistic competition by blending a Chamberlinian sector with a sector exhibiting Heckscher–Ohlin properties. Krugman (1982) adopts a continuum version of Ricardo to model trade with a Heckscher–Ohlin flavor: high-technology countries tend to have a comparative advantage in "technology-intensive" commodities. Furthermore, extensions of the simple models of production within the Classical paradigm have broken out of the traditional two-by-two mold to analyze the importance of joint production, complementarity between factors, and general properties in higher dimensions. Earlier work on simpler trade models has proved of value in all these extensions.

References

Amano, A. (1977), "Specific factors, comparative advantage and international investment", Economica, 44:131–144.

Arrow, K.J. (1962), "The economic implications of learning by doing", Review of Economic Studies, 29:155–173.

Atkinson, A.B. and J.E. Stiglitz (1969), "A new view of technological change", Economic Journal, 79:573–578.

Balassa, B. (1967), Trade liberalization among industrial countries (McGraw-Hill, New York).

Baldwin, R.E. (1966), "The role of capital-goods trade in the theory of international trade", American Economic Review, 56:841–848.
Batra, R. and F. Casas (1976), "A synthesis of the Heckscher–Ohlin and the neoclassical models of international trade", Journal of International Economics, 6:21–38.
Batra, R. and R. Ramachandran (1980), "Multinational firms and the theory of international trade and investment", American Economic Review, 70:278–290.
Berglas, E. and R.W. Jones (1977), "The export of technology", in: K. Brunner and A. Meltzer, eds., Optimal policies, control theory and technology exports, Carnegie-Rochester Conference on Public Policy, 7:159–202.
Bhagwati, J.N. (1958), "Immiserizing growth: A geometrical note", Review of Economic Studies, 25:201–205.
Bhagwati, J.N. (1964), "The pure theory of international trade: A survey", Economic Journal, 74:1–84.
Bhagwati, J.N. (1972), "The Heckscher–Ohlin theorem in the multi-commodity case", Journal of Political Economy, 80:1052–1055.
Bhagwati, J.N. and K. Hamada (1974), "The brain drain, international integration of markets for professionals and unemployment: A theoretical analysis", Journal of Development Economics, 1:19–42.
Bhagwati, J.N., R.W. Jones, R.A. Mundell and J. Vanek, eds. (1971), Trade, balance of payments, and growth: Essays in honor of Charles P. Kindleberger (North-Holland, Amsterdam).
Bhagwati, J.N. and T.N. Srinivasan (1971), "The theory of wage differentials: Production response and factor price equalization", Journal of International Economics, 1:19–35.
Bhagwati, J.N. and T.N. Srinivasan (1973), "The general equilibrium theory of effective protection and resource allocation", Journal of International Economics, 3:259–281.
Bhagwati, J.N. and T.N. Srinivasan (1980), "Revenue seeking: A generalization of the theory of tariffs", Journal of Political Economy, 88:1069–1087.
Brander, J.A. (1981), "Intra-industry trade in identical commodities", Journal of International Economics, 11:1–14.
Brecher, R. (1974), "Minimum wage rates and the pure theory of international trade", Quarterly Journal of Economics, 88:98–116.
Brecher, R. and J. Bhagwati (1981), "Foreign ownership and the theory of trade and welfare", Journal of Political Economy, 89:497–511.
Burgess, D.F. (1976), "Tariffs and income distribution: Some empirical evidence for the United States", Journal of Political Economy, 84:17–45.
Burgess, D.F. (1978), "On the distributional effects of direct foreign investment", International Economic Review, 19:647–664.
Burgess, D.F. (1980), "Protection, real wages, and the neoclassical ambiguity with interindustry flows", Journal of Political Economy, 88:783–802.
Carruth, A.A. and A.J. Oswald (1982), "The determination of union and non-union wage rates", European Economic Review, 16:285–302.
Caves, R.E. (1960), Trade and economic structure (Harvard University Press, Cambridge, MA).
Caves, R.E. (1971a), "International corporations: The industrial economics of foreign investment", Economica, 38:1–27.
Caves, R.E. (1971b), "Export-led growth and the new economic history", in: J.N. Bhagwati et al., eds. (1971) 403–442.
Caves, R.E. (1974), "International trade, international investment, and imperfect markets", Special Papers in International Economics, No. 10, International Finance Section, Princeton University.
Caves, R.E. (1979), "International cartels and monopolies in international trade", in: R. Dornbusch and J. Frenkel, eds., International economic policy (Johns Hopkins University Press, Baltimore).
Caves, R.E. (1982), Multinational enterprise and economic analysis (Cambridge University Press, Cambridge).
Caves, R.E. and R.W. Jones (1981), World trade and payments, 3rd edn. (Little Brown, Boston).
Chambers, E.J. and D.F. Gordon (1966), "Primary products and economic growth: An empirical measurement", Journal of Political Economy, 74:315–332.
Chang, W. (1979), "Some theorems of trade and general equilibrium with many goods and factors", Econometrica, 47:709–726.

Chang, W., W. Ethier and M. Kemp (1980), "The theorems of international trade with joint production", Journal of International Economics, 10:377–394.

Chichilnisky, G. (1980), "Basic goods, the effects of commodity transfers and the international economic order", Journal of Development Economics, 7:505–519.

Chipman, J.S. (1965–66), "A survey of the theory of international trade", Econometrica, 33:477–519, 33:685–760, 34:18–76.

Chipman, J.S. (1969), "Factor price equalization and the Stolper–Samuelson theorem", International Economic Review, 10:399–406.

Chipman, J.S. (1972), "The theory of exploitative trade and investment policies: A reformulation and synthesis", in: L.E. DiMarco, ed., International economics and development: Essays in honor of Raul Prebisch (Academic Press, New York) 881–916.

Chipman, J.S. (1974), "The transfer problem once again", in: G. Horwich and P.A. Samuelson, eds., Trade, stability, and macroeconomics: Essays in honor of Lloyd A. Metzler (Academic Press, New York) 19–78.

Corden, W.M. (1966), "The structure of a tariff system and the effective protective rate", Journal of Political Economy, 74:221–237.

Corden, W.M. (1971), "The substitution problem in the theory of effective protection", Journal of International Economics, 1:37–57.

Corden, W.M. and R. Findlay (1975), "Urban unemployment, intersectoral capital mobility and development policy", Economica, 42:59–78.

Corden, W.M. and J.P. Neary (1982), "Booming sector and de-industrialization in a small open economy", Economic Journal, 92:825–848.

Deardorff, A.V. (1974), "Factor proportions and comparative advantage in the long run: Comment", Journal of Political Economy, 82:829–833.

Deardorff, A.V. (1979), "Weak links in the chain of comparative advantage", Journal of International Economics, 9:197–209.

Deardorff, A.V. (1980), "The general validity of the law of comparative advantage", Journal of Political Economy, 88:941–957.

Deardorff, A.V. and J.A. Hanson (1978), "Accumulation and a long-run Heckscher–Ohlin theorem", Economic Inquiry, 16:288–292.

Diamond, P.A. (1967), "The role of a stock market in a general equilibrium model with technological uncertainty", American Economic Review, 57:759–776.

Diewert, E. (1974), "Applications of duality theory", in: M. Intriligator and D. Kendrick, eds., Frontiers of quantitative economics, Vol. II (North-Holland, Amsterdam).

Diewert, E. and A.D. Woodland (1977), "Frank Knight's theorem in linear programming revisited", Econometrica, 45:375–398.

Dixit, A.K. (1980), "A model of trade in natural resources and capital", mimeo.

Dixit, A.K. and G.M. Grossman (1982), "Trade and protection with multi-stage production", Review of Economic Studies, 49:583–594.

Dixit, A.K. and V.D. Norman (1979), "Notes on the Ricardo–Viner model", mimeo.

Dixit, A.K. and V.D. Norman, (1980), Theory of international trade (Cambridge University Press, Cambridge).

Dixit, A.K. and J.E. Stiglitz (1977), "Monopolistic competition and optimum product diversity", American Economic Review, 67:297–308.

Dornbusch, R. (1974), "Real and monetary aspects of the effects of exchange rate changes", in: R. Aliber, ed., National monetary policies and the international financial system (University of Chicago Press, Chicago), 64–81.

Dornbusch, R. (1975), "Exchange rates and fiscal policy in a popular model of international trade", American Economic Review, 65:859–871.

Dornbusch, R., S. Fischer and P.A. Samuelson (1977), "Comparative advantage, trade, and payments in a Ricardian model with a continuum of goods", American Economic Review, 67:823–839.

Dornbusch, R., S. Fischer and P.A. Samuelson (1980), "Heckscher–Ohlin trade theory with a continuum of goods", Quarterly Journal of Economics, 94:203–224.

Drabicki, J.Z. and A. Takayama (1979), "An antinomy in the theory of comparative advantage", Journal of International Economics, 9:211–223.

Easton, S.T. and C. Reed (1981), "The staple model", unpublished.

Engerman, S.L. (1984), "From servants to slaves to servants: Contract labor and European expansion", in: E. van den Boogaart and P.C. Emmer, eds., Colonialism and migration: Indentured labour before and after slavery (Martinus Nijhoof, Leiden University Press).

Ethier, W. (1971), "General equilibrium theory and the concept of the effective rate of protection", in: Grubel and Johnson, eds., Effective tariff protection (GATT and GIIS, Geneva) 17–44.

Ethier, W. (1972a), "Input substitution and the concept of the effective rate of protection", Journal of Political Economy, 80:34–47.

Ethier, W. (1972b), "Nontraded goods and the Heckscher–Ohlin model", International Economic Review, 13:132–147.

Ethier, W. (1974), "Some of the theorems of international trade with many goods and factors", Journal of International Economics, 4:199–206.

Ethier, W. (1977), "The theory of effective protection in general equilibrium: Effective-rate analogues of nominal rates", Canadian Journal of Economics, 10:233–245.

Ethier, W. (1979), "Internationally decreasing costs and world trade", Journal of International Economics, 9:1–24.

Ethier, W. (1981), "International trade and labor migration", unpublished.

Ethier, W. (1982a), "Dumping", Journal of Political Economy, 90:487–506.

Ethier, W. (1982b), "National and international returns to scale in the modern theory of international trade", American Economic Review, 72:389–405.

Ethier, W. (1982c), "Decreasing costs in international trade and Frank Graham's argument for protection", Econometrica, 50: 1243–1268.

Falvey, R.E. (1981), "Commercial policy and intra-industry trade", Journal of International Economics, II:495–511.

Feenstra, R.C. (1980), "Monopsony distortions in an open economy: A theoretical analysis", Journal of International Economics, 10:213–235.

Feenstra, R.C. and K. Judd (1982), "Tariffs, technology transfer, and welfare", Journal of Political Economy, 90:1142–1165.

Ferguson, D.G. (1978), "International capital mobility and comparative advantage", Journal of International Economics, 8:373–396.

Findlay, R. (1970), "Factor proportions and comparative advantage in the long run", Journal of Political Economy, 78:27–34.

Findlay, R. (1978a), "Relative backwardness, direct foreign investment, and the transfer of technology: A simple dynamic model", Quarterly Journal of Economics, 92:1–16.

Findlay, R. (1978b), "An 'Austrian' model of international trade and interest rate equalization", Journal of Political Economy, 86:989–1007.

Findlay, R. (1979), "Economic development and the theory of international trade", American Economic Review, Papers and Proceedings, 69:186–190.

Findlay, R. (1980), "The terms of trade and equilibrium growth in the world economy", American Economic Review, 70:291–299.

Findlay, R. and H. Grubert (1959), "Factor intensities, technological progress, and the terms of trade", Oxford Economic Papers, 11:111–121.

Findlay, R. and S. Wellisz (1982), "Rent-seeking, welfare and the political economy of trade restrictions", in: J. Bhagwati, ed., Import competition and response (University of Chicago Press, Chicago).

Fischer, S. and J. Frenkel (1974), "Economic growth and stages of the balance of payments", in: G. Horwich and P.A. Samuelson, eds., Trade, stability and macroeconomics: Essays in honor of Lloyd A. Metzler (Academic Press, New York) 503–521.

Gale, D. (1974), "Exchange equilibrium and coalitions", Journal of Mathematical Economics, 1:63–66.

Graham, F.D. (1923), "The theory of international values re-examined", Quarterly Journal of Economics, 38:54–86.

Grossman, G.M. (1981), "Partially mobile capital: A general approach to two-sector trade theory", mimeo.

Grossman, G.M. and C. Shapiro (1982), "A theory of factor mobility", Journal of Political Economy, 90: 1054–1069.

Grubel, H.G. (1970), "The theory of intra-industry trade", in: I.A. McDougall and R.H. Snape, eds.,

Studies in international economics: Monash conference papers (North-Holland, Amsterdam) 35–51.

Grubel, H.G. and P.J. Lloyd (1975), Intra-industry trade: The theory and measurement of international trade in differentiated products (Macmillan, London).

Gruen, F.H. and W.M. Corden (1970), "A tariff that worsens the terms of trade", in: I.A. McDougall and R.H. Snape, eds., Studies in international economics: Monash conference papers (North-Holland, Amsterdam) 55–58.

Haberler, G. (1950), "Some problems in the pure theory of international trade", Economic Journal, 60:223–240.

Harberger, A.C. (1962), "The incidence of the corporation income tax", Journal of Political Economy, 70:215–240.

Harris, J.R. and M.P. Todaro (1970), "Migration, unemployment and development: A two-sector analysis", American Economic Review, 60:126–142.

Harrod, R.F. (1958), "Factor price relations under free trade", Economic Journal, 68:245–255.

Heckscher, E. (1919), "The effect of foreign trade on the distribution of income", Ekonomisk Tidskrift, 497–512; reprinted as Chapter 13 in: A.E.A. Readings in the theory of international trade (Blakiston, Philadelphia, 1949) 272–300.

Helpman, E. (1976), "Solutions of general equilibrium problems for a trading world", Econometrica, 44:547–559.

Helpman, E. (1977), "Nontraded goods and macroeconomic policy under a fixed exchange rate", Quarterly Journal of Economics, 91:469–480.

Helpman, E. (1981a), "International trade in the presence of product differentiation, economies of scale and monopolistic competition: A Chamberlin–Heckscher–Ohlin approach", Journal of International Economics, 11:305–340.

Helpman, E. (1981b), "International trade in differentiated middle products", presented to International Economic Association conference on structural adjustment in trade-dependent advanced economies, Yxtaholm, Sweden, August 1982.

Helpman, E. and A. Razin (1978), A theory of international trade under uncertainty (Academic Press, New York). ·

Herberg, H. and M.C. Kemp (1969), "Some implications of variable returns to scale", Canadian Journal of Economics, 2:403–415.

Herberg, H. and M.C. Kemp (1971), "Factor market distortions, the shape of the locus of competitive outputs and the relation between product prices and equilibrium outputs", in: J. Bhagwati et al., eds. (1971) 22–48.

Herberg, H. and M.C. Kemp (1980), "In defense of some 'paradoxes' of trade theory", American Economic Review, 70:812–814.

Hicks, J.R. (1939), Value and capital (Oxford University Press, London).

Hicks, J.R. (1953), "An inaugural lecture: 2. The long-run dollar problem", Oxford Economic Papers, 5:121–135.

Hymer, S.H. (1976), The international operations of national firms: A study of direct foreign investment (M.I.T. Press, Cambridge).

Inada, K. (1968), "Free trade, capital accumulation and factor price equalization", Economic Record, 44:322–341.

Inada, K. (1971), "The production coefficient matrix and the Stolper–Samuelson condition", Econometrica, 39:219–240.

Itoh, M. (1978), "A theory of imperfect competition in international trade and investment", Ph.D. dissertation, University of Rochester.

Johnson, H.G. (1953), "Equilibrium growth in an international economy", The Canadian Journal of Economics and Political Science, 19:478–500.

Johnson, H.G. (1955), "Economic expansion and international trade", The Manchester School of Economic and Social Studies, 23:95–112.

Johnson, H.G. (1956), "The transfer problem and exchange stability", Journal of Political Economy, 64:212–225.

Johnson, H.G. (1957), "Factor endowments, international trade, and factor prices", Manchester School of Economic and Social Studies, 25:270–283.

Johnson, H.G. (1960), "A note on income distribution", Appendix to "Income distribution, the offer curve and the effects of tariffs", Manchester School of Economic and Social Studies, 28:215–242.

Johnson, H.G. and P.M. Mieszkowski (1970), "The effects of unionization on the distribution of income: A general equilibrium approach", Quarterly Journal of Economics, 84:539–561.

Jones, R.W. (1956), "Factor proportions and the Heckscher–Ohlin theorem", Review of Economic Studies, 24:1–10.

Jones, R.W. (1961a), "Stability conditions in international trade: A general equilibrium analysis", International Economic Review, 2:199–209.

Jones, R.W. (1961b), "Comparative advantage and the theory of tariffs: A multi-country, multi-commodity model", Review of Economic Studies, 28:161–175.

Jones, R.W. (1965), "The structure of simple general equilibrium models", Journal of Political Economy, 73:557–572.

Jones, R.W. (1967), "International capital movements and the theory of tariffs and trade", Quarterly Journal of Economics, 81:1–38.

Jones, R.W. (1968), "Variable returns to scale in general equilibrium theory", International Economic Review, 9:261–272.

Jones, R.W. (1969), "Tariffs and trade in general equilibrium: Comment", American Economic Review, 59:418–424.

Jones, R.W. (1970a), "The transfer problem revisited", Economica, 37:178–184.

Jones, R.W. (1970b), "The role of technology in the theory of international trade", in: R. Vernon, ed., The technology factor in international trade (NBER, New York) 73–92.

Jones, R.W. (1971a), "Effective protection and substitution", Journal of International Economics, 1:59–81.

Jones, R.W. (1971b), "Distortions in factor markets and the general equilibrium model of production", Journal of Political Economy, 79:437–459.

Jones, R.W. (1971c), "A three-factor model in theory, trade, and history", in: J.N. Bhagwati et al., eds. (1971) 3–21.

Jones, R.W. (1974a), "The Metzler tariff paradox: Extensions to nontraded and intermediate commodities", in: G. Horwich and P.A. Samuelson, eds., Trade, stability, and macroeconomics: Essays in honor of Lloyd A. Metzler (Academic Press, New York) 3–18.

Jones, R.W. (1974b), "Trade with non-traded goods: The anatomy of interconnected markets", Economica, 41:121–138.

Jones, R.W. (1974c), "The small country in a many-commodity world", Australian Economic Papers, 13:225–236.

Jones, R.W. (1975a), "Presumption and the transfer problem", Journal of International Economics, 5:263–274.

Jones, R.W. (1975b), "Income distribution and effective protection in a multicommodity trade model", Journal of Economic Theory, 11:1–15.

Jones, R.W. (1977), "Two-ness in trade theory: Costs and benefits", Special papers in International Economics, Princeton University, No. 12.

Jones, R.W. (1979a), "Technical progress and real incomes in a Ricardian trade model", Chapter 17 in: R. Jones, International trade: Essays in theory (North-Holland, Amsterdam) 279–286.

Jones, R.W. (1979b), "Trade and direct investment: A comment", in: R. Dornbusch and J. Frenkel, eds., International economic policy (Johns Hopkins University Press, Baltimore) 105–111.

Jones, R.W. (1980), "Comparative and absolute advantage", Schweizerische zeitschrift fur volkswirtschaft und statistik, No. 3, 235–260; also available as Reprint Series No. 153, Institute for International Economic Studies, University of Stockholm.

Jones, R.W. and W.M. Corden (1976), "Devaluation, non-flexible prices, and the trade balance for a small country", Canadian Journal of Economics, 9:150–161.

Jones, R.W. and F. Dei (1983), "International trade and foreign investment: A simple model", Economic Inquiry, forthcoming.

Jones, R.W. and S.T. Easton (1983), "Factor intensities and factor substitution in general equilibrium", Journal of International Economics, forthcoming.

Jones, R.W. and J.P. Neary (1979), "Temporal convergence and factor intensities", Economics Letters, 3:311–314.

Jones, R.W., J.P. Neary and F. Ruane (1981), "Two-way capital flows: Cross-hauling in models of foreign investment", unpublished.

Jones, R.W. and D.S. Purvis (1983), "International differences in response to common external shocks: The role of purchasing power parity", Chapter 2 in: E. Classen and P. Salin, eds., Recent issues in the theory of flexible exchange rates (North-Holland, Amsterdam).

Jones, R.W. and J. Scheinkman (1977), "The relevance of the two-sector production model in trade theory", Journal of Political Economy, 85:909–935.

Kemp, M.C. (1966), "The gain from international trade and investment: A neo-Heckscher–Ohlin approach", American Economic Review, 56:788–809.

Kemp, M.C. and W. Ethier (1976), "A note on joint production and the theory of international trade", Chapter 7 in: M.C. Kemp, Three topics in the theory of international trade (North-Holland, Amsterdam) 81–84.

Kemp, M.C. and K. Inada, (1969), "International capital movements and the theory of international trade", Quarterly Journal of Economics, 83:524–528.

Kemp, M.C. and R.W. Jones (1962), "Variable labor supply and theory of international trade", Journal of Political Economy, 70:30–36.

Kemp, M.C. and N. Liviatan (1973), "Production and trade patterns under uncertainty", Economic Record, 49:215–227.

Kemp, M.C. and M. Ohyama (1978), "On the sharing of trade gains by resource-poor and resource-rich countries", Journal of International Economics, 8:93–115.

Kemp, M.C. and L. Wegge (1969), "On the relation between commodity prices and factor rewards", International Economic Review, 10:407–413.

Khan, M.A. (1980), "The Harris–Todaro hypothesis and the Heckscher–Ohlin–Samuelson trade model: A synthesis", Journal of International Economics, 10:527–548.

Khandker, A.W. (1981), "Multinational firms and the theory of international trade and investment: A correction and a stronger conclusion", American Economic Review, 71:515–516.

Khang, C. (1973), "Factor substitution in the theory of effective protection: A general equilibrium analysis", Journal of International Economics, 3:227–243.

Komiya, R. (1967), "Non-traded goods and the pure theory of international trade", International Economic Review, 8:132–152.

Komiya, R. and T. Shizuki (1967), "Transfer payments and income distribution", Manchester School of Economic and Social Studies, 35:245–255.

Kotlikoff, L.J., E.E. Leamer, and J. Sachs (1981), "The international economics of transitional growth: The case of the United States", Working Paper No. 773, National Bureau of Economic Research, Cambridge, MA.

Krueger, A.O. (1974), "The political economy of the rent-seeking society", American Economic Review, 64:291–303.

Krueger, A.O. (1977), Growth, distortions, and patterns of trade among many countries, Princeton Studies in International Finance, No. 40.

Krugman, P.R. (1979a), "A model of innovation, technology transfer, and the world distribution of income", Journal of Political Economy, 87:253–266.

Krugman, P.R. (1979b), "Increasing returns, monopolistic competition and international trade", Journal of International Economics, 9:469–479.

Krugman, P.R. (1980), "Scale economies, product differentiation and the pattern of trade", American Economic Review, 70:950–959.

Krugman, P.R. (1981), "Intraindustry specialization and the gains from trade", Journal of Political Economy, 89:959–973.

Krugman, P.R. (1982), "A 'technology gap' model of international trade", presented to International Economic Association conference on structural adjustment in trade-dependent advanced economies, Yxtaholm, Sweden, August 1982.

Lancaster, K. (1979), Variety, equity, and efficiency (Columbia University Press, New York).

Lancaster, K. (1980), "Intra-industry trade under perfect monopolistic competition", Journal of International Economics, 10:151–175.

Lefeber, L. (1971), "Trade and minimum wage rates", in: J.N. Bhagwati et al., eds. (1971) 91–114.

Leontief, W.W. (1953), "Domestic production and foreign trade: The American capital position re-examined", Proceedings of the American Philosophical Society, 97:332–349.

Lerner, A.P. (1936), "The symmetry between import and export taxes", Economica, 3:306–313.

Lerner, A.P. (1952), "Factor prices and international trade", Economica, 19:1–15.

Linder, S.B. (1961), An essay on trade and transformation (John Wiley and Sons, New York).

McCulloch, R. and J. Yellen (1980), "Factor market monopsony and the allocation of resources", Journal of International Economics, 10:237–247.

McDougall, I. (1965), "Non-traded goods and the transfer problem", Review of Economic Studies, 32:67–84.

McKenzie, L.W. (1954), "Specialization and efficiency in world production", Review of Economic Studies, 21:165–180.

McKenzie, L.W. (1955), "Equality of factor prices in world trade", Econometrica, 23:239–257.

Magee, S.P. (1969), "Factor market distortions and the pure theory of international trade", Massachusetts Institute of Technology Ph.D. dissertation, Cambridge, MA.

Magee, S.P. (1971), "Factor market distortions, production, distribution and the pure theory of international trade", Quarterly Journal of Economics, 85:623–643.

Manoilesco, M. (1931), The theory of protection and international trade (P.S. King and Son, London).

Markusen, J.R. (1981), "Trade and the gains from trade with imperfect competition", Journal of International Economics, 11:531–551.

Markusen, J.R. (1983a) "Factor movements and commodity trade as complements", Journal of Integrational Economics, 43: 341–356.

Markusen, J.R. (1983b) "Multinationals, multi-plant economies and the gains from trade", Journal of International Economics, forthcoming.

Markusen, J.R. and J.R. Melvin (1981), "Trade, factor prices, and the gains from trade with increasing returns to scale", Canadian Journal of Economics, 14: 450–469.

Markusen, J.R. and A. Robson (1980), "Simple general equilibrium and trade with a monopsonized sector", Canadian Journal of Economics, 13:668–682.

Martin, J.P. and J.P. Neary (1980), "Variable labour supply and the pure theory of international trade: An empirical note", Journal of International Economics, 10:549–560.

Mayer, W. (1974a), "Variable returns to scale in general equilibrium theory: A comment", International Economic Review, 15:225–235.

Mayer, W. (1974b), "Short-run and long-run equilibrium for a small open economy", Journal of Political Economy, 82:955–967.

Meade, J. (1955), Trade and welfare (Oxford University Press, London).

Melvin, J.R. (1968), "Production and trade with two factors and three goods", American Economic Review, 58:1248–1268.

Melvin, J.R. (1969), "Increasing returns to scale as a determinant of trade", Canadian Journal of Economics, 3:389–402.

Melvin, J.R. and R.D. Warne (1973), "Monopoly and the theory of international trade", Journal of International Economics, 3:117–134.

Metzler, L. (1949), "Tariffs, the term of trade, and the distribution of national income", Journal of Political Economy, 57:1–29.

Mill, J.S. (1848), Principles of political economy (Parker & Co., London).

Mundell, R.A. (1957), "International trade and factor mobility", American Economic Review, 47:321–335.

Mundell, R.A. (1960), "The pure theory of international trade", American Economic Review, 50:67–110.

Mussa, M. (1974), "Tariffs and the distribution of income: The importance of factor specificity, substitutability, and intensity in the short and long run", Journal of Political Economy, 82:1191–1204.

Mussa, M. (1978), "Dynamic adjustment in the Heckscher–Ohlin model", Journal of Political Economy, 86:775–794.

Mussa, M. (1979), "The two-sector model in terms of its dual: A geometric exposition", Journal of International Economics, 9:513–526.

Mussa, M. (1982), "Imperfect factor mobility and the distribution of income", Journal of International Economics, 12:125–142.

Neary, J.P. (1978a), "Short-run capital specificity and the pure theory of international trade", Economic Journal, 88:488–510.

Neary, J.P. (1978b), "Dynamic stability and the theory of factor-market distortions", American Economic Review, 68:671–682.

Neary, J.P. (1978c), "Captial subsidies and employment in an open economy", Oxford Economic Papers, 30:334–356.

Neary, J.P. (1979), "Two-by-two international trade theory with many goods and factors", mimeo.

Neary, J.P. (1980a), "This side of paradox, or, in defense of the correspondence principle: A reply to Herberg and Kemp", American Economic Review, 70:815–818.

Neary, J.P. (1980b), "International factor mobility, minimum wage rates and factor price equalization: A synthesis", Seminar Paper No. 158, Institute for International Economic Studies, University of Stockholm.

Neary, J.P. (1980c), "Devaluation and the dynamics of the trade balance in a small open economy", mimeo.

Neary, J.P. (1981), "On the Harris–Todaro model with intersectoral capital mobility", Economica, 48:219–234.

Neary, J.P. and D.D. Purvis, (1982), "Sectoral shocks in a dependent economy: Long-run adjustment and short-run accomodation", Scandinavian Journal of Economics, 84:229–253.

Negishi, T. (1972), General equilibrium theory and international trade (North-Holland, Amsterdam).

Noman, K. and R.W. Jones (1979), "A model of trade and unemployment", in: J. Green and J. Scheinkman, eds., General equilibrium, growth, and trade: Essays in honor of Lionel McKenzie (Academic Press, New York) 297–322.

Ohlin, B. (1931), "Protection and non-competing groups", Weltwirtschaftliches Archiv., 33:30–45.

Ohlin, B. (1933), Interregional and international trade (Harvard University Press, Cambridge).

Oniki, H. and H. Uzawa (1965), "Patterns of trade and investment in a dynamic model of international trade", Review of Economic Studies, 32:15–38.

Panagariya, A. (1980), "Variable returns to scale in general equilibrium theory once again", Journal of International Economics, 10:499–526.

Pearce, I.F. (1952), "A note on Mr. Lerner's paper", Economica, 19:16–18.

Pearce, I.F. (1961), "The problem of the balance of payments", International Economic Review, 2:1–28.

Pearce, I.F. (1970), International trade (Norton, New York).

Pomery, J.G. (1976), "International trade and uncertainty: Simple general equilibrium models involving randomness", Ph.D. Dissertation, University of Rochester.

Pomery, J.G. (1979), "Uncertainty and international trade", Chapter 4 in: R. Dornbusch and J. Frenkel, eds., International economic policy: Theory and evidence (Johns Hopkins, Baltimore) 112–157.

Purvis, D.D. (1972), "Technology, trade and factor mobility", Economic Journal, 82:991–999.

Ramaswami, V.K. and T.N. Srinivasan (1971), "Tariff structure and resource allocation in the presence of substitution", in: J.N. Bhagwati et al., eds. (1971) 291–299.

Rodriguez, C. (1975a), "International factor mobility, nontraded goods, and the international equalization of prices of goods and factors", Econometrica, 43:115–124.

Rodriguez, C. (1975b), "Trade in technological knowledge and the national advantage", Journal of Political Economy, 83:121–135.

Ruffin, R.J. (1981), "Trade and factor movements with three factors and two goods", Economic Letters, 7:177–182.

Ruffin, R.J. and R.W. Jones (1977), "Protection and real wages: The neoclassical ambiguity", Journal of Economic Theory, 14:337–348.

Rybczynski, T. M. (1955), "Factor endowments and relative commodity prices", Economica, 22:336–341.

Salter, W.E.G. (1959), "Internal and external balance: The role of price and expenditure effects", Economic Record, 35:226–238.

Samuelson, P.A. (1948), "International trade and the equalisation of factor prices", Economic Journal, 58:163–184.

Samuelson, P.A. (1949), "International factor-price equalization once again", Economic Journal, 59:181–197.

Samuelson, P.A. (1952), "The transfer problem and transport costs: The terms of trade when impediments are absent", Economic Journal, 62:278–304.

Samuelson, P.A. (1953), "Prices of factors and goods in general equilibrium", Review of Economic Studies, 21:1–20.

Samuelson, P.A. (1954), "The transfer problem and transport costs, II: Analysis of effects of trade impediments", Economic Journal, 64:264–289.

Samuelson, P.A. (1962), "Parable and realism in capital theory: The surrogate production function",

Review of Economic Studies, 29:193–206.

Samuelson, P.A. (1965), "Equalization by trade of the interest rate along with the real wage", in: R.E. Baldwin et al., eds., Trade, growth, and the balance of payments: Essays in honor of Gottfried Haberler (Rand McNally, Chicago) 35–52.

Samuelson, P.A. (1969), "The way of an economist", in: P.A. Samuelson, ed., International economic relations, Proceedings of the Third Congress of the International Economic Association (Macmillan, London) 1–11.

Samuelson, P.A. (1971a), "On the trail of conventional beliefs about the transfer problem", in: J.N. Bhagwati et al., eds. (1971) 327–351.

Samuelson, P.A. (1971b), "An exact Hume–Ricardo–Marshall model of international trade", Journal of International Economics, 1:1–18.

Samuelson, P.A. (1971c), "Ohlin was right", Swedish Journal of Economics, 73:365–384.

Samuelson, P.A. (1982), "Two country Ricardian analysis for discrete goods and for a continuum of goods", Journal of International Economics, forthcoming.

Sanyal, K.K. (1980), "Stages of production: The role of international trade", Ph.D. dissertation, University of Rochester.

Sanyal, K.K. and R.W. Jones (1982), "The theory of trade in middle products", American Economic Review, 72:16–31.

Schmitz, A.P. and P. Helmberger (1970), "Factor mobility and international trade: The case of complementarity", American Economic Review, 60:761–767.

Schweinberger, A.G. (1975), "Intermediate products and comparative advantage", Economic Record, 51:671–682.

Schweinberger, A.G. (1978), "Employment subsidies and the theory of minimum wage rates in general equilibrium", Quarterly Journal of Economics, 92:361–374.

Schweinberger, A.G. (1980), "Medium run resource allocation and short run capital specificity", Economic Journal, 90:330–340.

Smith, M.A.M. (1974), "International trade in second-hand machines", Journal of Development Economics, 1:261–278.

Sodersten, B. and K. Vind (1968), "Tariffs and trade in general equilibrium", American Economic Review, 58:394–408.

Stolper, W. and P.A. Samuelson (1941), "Protection and real wages", Review of Economic Studies, 9:58–73.

Suzuki, K. (1983), "A synthesis of the Heckscher–Ohlin and the neoclassical models of international trade: A comment", Journal of International Economics, 14:141–144.

Travis, W.P. (1964), The theory of trade and protection (Harvard University Press, Cambridge).

Uzawa, H. (1961), "On a two-sector model of economic growth", Review of Economic Studies, 29:40–47.

Vanek, J. (1963), The natural resource content of United States foreign trade, 1870–1955 (M.I.T. Press, Cambridge).

Vernon, R. (1966), "International investment and international trade in the product cycle", Quarterly Journal of Economics, 80:190–207.

Viner, J. (1932), Review of: The theory of protection and international trade, by M. Manoilesco, Journal of Political Economy, 40:121–125.

Walsh, V. (1956), "Leisure and international trade", Economica, 23:253–260.

Whitin, T.M. (1953), "Classical theory, Graham's theory, and linear programming in international trade", Quarterly Journal of Economics, 67:520–544.

Williams, J.H. (1929), "The theory of international trade reconsidered", Economic Journal, 39:195–209.

Wilson, C. (1980), "On the general structure of Ricardian models with a continuum of goods: Applications to growth, tariff theory, and technical change", Econometrica, 48:1675–1702.

Woodland, A. (1977a), "A dual approach to equilibrium in the production sector in international trade theory", Canadian Journal of Economics, 10:50–68.

Woodland, A. (1977b), "Joint outputs, intermediate inputs and international trade theory", International Economic Review, 18:517–533.

Yano, M. (1981), "Welfare aspects in the transfer problem", Journal of International Economics, forthcoming.

Chapter 2

THE NORMATIVE THEORY OF INTERNATIONAL TRADE

W.M. CORDEN*

Australian National University

Contents

1. Introduction   65
2. Normative economics: Some general remarks   66
3. The gains from trade   69
    3.1. The basic gains from trade propositions: Samuelson and Kemp   69
    3.2. Perspective   72
    3.3. Gains from trade: Recent extensions   73
    3.4. Increasing returns with Marshallian assumptions   75
    3.5. Given commodity taxes and the gains from trade   76
    3.6. Product differentiation and increasing returns   76
4. The devices of trade intervention   77
    4.1. The effects of a tariff   77
    4.2. The symmetry between import and export taxes   78
    4.3. Consumption and production taxes   79
    4.4. The equivalence between import quotas and tariffs   79
    4.5. Balance of payments effects   81
    4.6. Theory of tariff structure   82
5. The terms of trade argument and optimal tariff theory   82
6. The theory of domestic distortions   86
    6.1. Domestic distortions theory: Introduction   86
    6.2. The hierarchy of policies and by-product distortions   88
    6.3. Wage rigidity, marginal product differential and unemployment   89
    6.4. The infant industry argument   91
    6.5. Trade distortions   92
    6.6. Non-economic objectives and fixed targets   94
    6.7. Mixed cases   94

*I am indebted to comments from Robert Baldwin, Carl Hamilton, Murray Kemp, Anne Krueger, Peter Neary, Frances Ruane and Amartya Sen, and to the Institute for International Studies, University of Stockholm and the Australian National University, where this work was done.

Handbook of International Economics, vol. I, Edited by R.W. Jones and P.B. Kenen
© *Elsevier Science Publishers B.V., 1984*

7.   Distortions, the budget constraint and optimal tax theory   96
       7.1.   The limitations of domestic distortions theory   96
       7.2.   Revenue limits and income distribution effects of correcting
               a distortion: The Anand–Joshi qualification   97
       7.3.   Optimal tax theory and domestic distortions   98
       7.4.   Trade taxes for revenue: Small and large country case   100
8.   The cost of protection   104
9.   Cost–benefit analysis for the open economy   105
       9.1.   Non-tradeables   107
       9.2.   Import quotas   107
       9.3.   Terms of trade effects   108
       9.4.   Budget constraint   108
       9.5.   Factor proportions variable   110
10.   The political economy of protectionism   111
11.   Customs union theory   112
       11.1.   Introduction   112
       11.2.   Two assumptions   113
       11.3.   The two-good model   114
       11.4.   The three-good Meade model   115
       11.5.   Broadening the model, and intra-union terms of trade effects 117
       11.6.   The common external tariff   118
       11.7.   External terms of trade effects   119
       11.8.   Can a customs union be optimal?   120
       11.9.   Economies of scale   123
       11.10. Other aspects of customs unions   123
References   124

1. Introduction

Normative economics is concerned with making welfare judgements about policies and economic events. Does a particular policy change represent a welfare improvement? How can a number of policies be ranked in terms of welfare? Is one first-best, another second-best, and so on? The particular policy that is "best" is usually described as "optimal".

While the focus is normally on government policies – and, in the case of trade theory, on commercial policy – normative economics also embraces the study of the welfare consequences of various events when policies are constant. For example, does an increased inflow of foreign capital with constant tax rates and inducements raise or lower national welfare? Similarly, does an increase in the domestically-owned capital stock or technical progress raise or lower welfare? But the present chapter will focus on policies.

The chapter aims to cover the main areas of normative trade theory, but not always fully. Apart from a discussion of the infant industry argument it does not deal with dynamic aspects, for example. There is some overlap with other chapters, especially Chapter 11, but some topics are left primarily to these other chapters.

The central parts of policy-orientated normative trade theory are covered in Section 5 on the terms of trade argument for protection and Section 6 on the theory of domestic distortions. These subjects are dealt with relatively briefly here because the author has surveyed them comprehensively in Corden (1974) and there have only been limited new developments since. Thus the relative length with which various topics are dealt with should not be interpreted as reflecting a judgement of the importance of the topics. Section 7 (on the budget constraint and optimal tax theory) and Section 9 (on cost–benefit analysis for the open economy) deal with interesting topics that have never been surveyed before and hence are done rather thoroughly. The longest section is Section 11, on customs union theory. This is a major branch of trade theory, and there is no overlap with other chapters.

Attention should be drawn at this point to some general references. Apart from articles and books referred to below as being seminal on particular subjects, the classic works in the field during the last fifty years or so are probably Haberler (1936) and Meade (1955a). A useful survey of several of the topics as perceived up to the early sixties is Bhagwati (1964). As just mentioned, the author's own survey and consolidation – with an emphasis on policy relevance – are in Corden (1974). Several of the key issues are dealt with very rigorously in Negishi (1972). Finally, a textbook that covers the whole field of this chapter quite fully (apart from the most recent developments and cost–benefit analysis), and that can be recommended for further exposition on many points, is Michaely (1977).

2. Normative economics: Some general remarks

One might begin by asking what is meant by "welfare". The answers to this are at the heart of modern welfare economics. But first there is a more basic question. What is the point of normative theory? Many people would suggest that the answer is just as obvious: the purpose is *prescriptive*. The usefulness of normative trade theory depends then on the readiness with which governments take the advice of economists who are trained in, and apply, this body of theory. The difficulty is that often the arguments of economists have "fallen on stony ground". In fact there is developing another body of theory – public choice theory – that is being applied to international economics and tries to explain *why* policies are as they are. In particular, it stresses that actual policies are the outcomes not of the pursuit by political decision-makers of maximum national (or international) "welfare" but rather of the interaction of interest groups engaged sometimes in expensive lobbying activities.

A modest answer to the problem might be that economists are simply observers who study the welfare effects of various policies and events, without expecting welfare ever to be maximised or that their views will carry any weight. The more hopeful answer is that economists provide an information input into the system and, on the assumption that decision-makers *are* concerned to some extent with "welfare", their analysis may, at times, still have some influence on outcomes. I shall return to this issue in Section 10.

We come now to the crucial question of "welfare". Consider Figure 2.1, where we are concerned with *national* welfare and suppose the nation to be made up of two persons, *X* and *Y*, who can, of course, be thought of as groups. The analysis can be generalised to many persons or groups. The axes indicate levels of utility

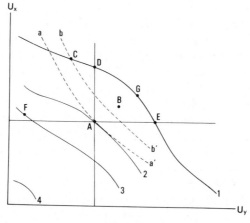

Figure 2.1

for each person. The approach is "individualistic" in the sense that national welfare depends, in some sense, on individual utilities. It is also assumed that utilities are not interdependent. The utility measures are *ordinal*: utility levels can be ranked but not measured, so that higher means better; but we cannot say how much better.

We start in position A. Suppose a policy change brings the two utilities to B. This means that both persons become better-off: the move represents a *Pareto-improvement*, which is any move that makes at least one person better off without lowering the utility of the other. This applies, for example, to movements from A to D or to E. Given the individualistic approach here, with no concern for relativities as such, and with no concern with the methods by which a change is obtained (unless it affects individual utilities), such changes represent unambiguous improvements in national welfare.

Next consider a movement from A to C. This is *not* a Pareto-improvement because person Y becomes worse off. But suppose that it were possible to redistribute the income at C, with the given policy at C, so that utility combinations along the utility possibility curve 1 could be attained. Thus positions D, G or E could be reached. It is not necessary that the same bundle of goods is consumed at D (say) as at C; as tastes of the two persons may be different they may choose to change the content of the bundle through trade. We can imagine that at the original position A there was also the possibility of redistribution, which could have brought the utility pairs to anywhere along curve 2. Similarly, another policy would initially have brought the persons to point F, and then redistribution possibilities would have opened up on all the points along curve 3. We thus envisage three possible policies in this case, represented by the three curves. The outcomes in the absence of associated redistributive policies are C, A and F respectively.

We now introduce the concept of "Pareto-efficiency". A point is Pareto-efficient if it is not possible to make one person better off without making another worse off. Pareto-inefficiency means that there is an unexploited possibility of an unambiguous welfare improvement. First, suppose that redistribution were technically not possible or, alternatively, that there is some political or institutional constraint that rules it out. Furthermore, the only choice is between the three policies, so that the only relevant points are C, A, and F. It is clear that F is Pareto-inefficient since a movement from F to C would make both persons better off. On the other hand C and A are both Pareto-efficient and, without comparing utilities, we cannot say which represents higher national welfare. Second, let us assume that redistribtion *can* take place; there are no technical or other obstacles. An initial movement from A to C can then be converted into a movement to D, G or E, for example. D is the special case of pure compensation, where the net gain goes wholly to the initial gainer. We can now say that only policy 1 is Pareto-efficient and the three policies are ranked as 1, 2, 3. A change from policy 2 to policy 1 with starting point at A can always bring the system to some point on line 1, from D to E, so that at least one person can be made better off.

The usual approach in normative trade theory is (1) to *assume* that redistribution does take place – i.e. that there is an independent income distribution policy which achieves the appropriate or best distribution given the policies and the various constraints, and (2) to use the Pareto-efficiency criterion.

It is usually supposed that redistribution takes place on the basis of some "social welfare function", and this is simply accepted. But the possibility must be allowed for that redistributive policies are not "the best" – e.g. that rich people control the government and do not redistribute appropriately to the poor, so that the final outcome may not be "optimal". For this reason a movement from A to C, followed by some movement along curve 1, is *efficient* rather than *optimal*. But there is a difficulty here. Should a policy change be regarded as leading even to a *potential* welfare improvement when it is known that the associated redistribution measures – while they *could* make everyone better off, or could lead, in some sense, to a national welfare improvement, in fact will, on all past experience, lead to a deterioration for some deserving people?

In any case, the essence of this whole approach is to focus on rankings in terms of Pareto-efficiency. Resource allocation and income distribution are treated as separate issues. This makes sense if one assumes that an independent income distribution policy is being followed and if one accepts the desirability or, at least, legitimacy of the income distribution judgements implied in this policy. But if it is known that redistributive policies are not being pursued, possibly because they are too costly, is there anything left of standard analysis? There would seem to be two ways out.

The first is owed to Hicks (1941). Any particular Pareto-efficient move is likely – in fact, is certain – to make someone worse off, and it must be conceded that no welfare judgement can be made about it in the absence of an explicit social welfare function. The argument goes that, if Pareto-efficient policies (or policy shifts in the direction of improved Pareto-efficient rankings) are being pursued consistently over a long period, the *chances* are that eventually – though not at every particular step – everyone will be better off. In terms of Figure 2.1, if such policies lead gradually from curve 4 to curve 1 there is a strong chance that finally both X and Y will be better off. Personally I find this view – which may be called the *Hicksian optimism* – a very convincing way of dealing with the negativism of the "new welfare economics" and of making a general case for the pursuit of Pareto-efficiency.

The second way out is to take income distribution effects directly into account in considering policies. The income distribution judgements can come out of some kind of social welfare function (SWF), which may be an expression of community value judgements or of the particular views of the observer. Possibly an analysis might be conducted allowing for various possible SWFs. In any case, taking a particular SWF, the two contours aa' and bb' represent national welfare contours, with *bb'* higher than *aa'*. It is clear that the movement from *A* to *C*, even if not associated with any redistribution, represents a welfare improvement, so that a judgement can now be made between *A* and *C*.

In the case actually drawn one can say that the movement from *A* to *C* can be decomposed into two elements: (1) there is a Pareto-efficiency improvement (the move from curve 2 to curve 1); and (2) the move leads to an undesirable income redistribution. (If income was redistributed back from *C* to *D*, for example, welfare would rise further.) The two effects have to be "traded off", and in this particular case *C*, on balance, comes out superior.

Much more could be said about these matters. There is an extensive literature on welfare criteria, much of it applied to trade theory. A thorough exposition, with extensive references to the literature, is in Takayama (1972, ch. 17). A general introduction is in Layard and Walters (1978). The issues are central to clear thinking in the area of normative economics, although it has not been possible here to spell out all the assumptions and qualifications.

It remains to note that the focus of normative trade theory has tended to be on *national* welfare, though this was considerably less so before the development of the theory of the optimal tariff, and Meade (1955a) made much use of the "cosmopolitan" criterion. In principle the theory can be applied to any defined group, whether a group within a nation, the whole nation, a group of nations making up a customs union, or the world. Normally a nation would be defined as including all those persons resident there, in which case net after-tax factor incomes received by foreign-owned factors of production would be excluded. It would also be necessary to classify permanent and temporarily resident foreign nationals appropriately. In any case, one might well regard the emphasis on national welfare in trade theory as excessive.

3. The gains from trade

3.1. *The basic gains from trade propositions: Samuelson and Kemp*

The central proposition of normative trade theory is that there are gains from trade and, more specifically, that given certain assumptions, not only is free trade Pareto-superior to autarky but it is also Pareto-efficient, being superior to various degrees of trade restriction.

The main idea is represented in Figure 3.1, which refers to the small country case (terms of trade given exogenously to the country concerned). A fuller exposition is in the classic article by Samuelson (1962).

There are two goods, *M* and *X*, and the production possibility curve is *PP'*. Full employment through factor price flexibility is assumed, as well as perfect competition. Autarky equilibrium is at *B*. The output pattern at this point yields a

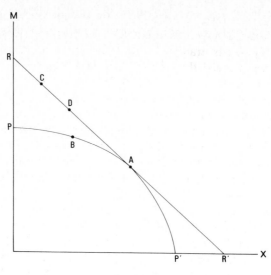

Figure 3.1

particular factoral income distribution, which in turn yields the demand pattern that leads to consumption at B. The autarky price ratio is represented by the slope of PP' at B. If income were redistributed by costless means (i.e. by lump-sum transfers) the equilibrium might move to some other point on PP'. In any case, for the nation the frontier of consumption (or absorption) possibilities under autarky is represented by PP'.

Given the world price ratio represented by the slope of RR', and given perfect competition – so that the marginal rate of transformation in production is equal to the marginal rate of transformation in foreign trade, output thus being at A – the free trade consumption possibilities are on RR'. Free trade thus expands the consumption possibility frontier and is Pareto-superior to autarky unless the autarky equilibrium at B happens to coincide with A – i.e. unless the two price ratios happened to be the same.

The actual free trade consumption point will result from the particular income distribution yielded by free trade, and may be, say, at C. This should not be directly compared with B. It would not necessarily be possible to redistribute the bundle of goods at C and make everyone better off than they were at B. Rather the comparison must be made between points representing the same income distribution. If free trade income were redistributed (again, by lump-sum transfers) such that it were the same as at B, a point like D might be reached, and D is superior to B. The move to free trade creates a potentially better *situation*, which allows a Pareto-improvement to take place.

The fundamental articles beginning the modern literature in this field were Samuelson (1939), Samuelson (1962) and Kemp (1962a). Samuelson (1939) showed that there were potential gains from trade to be derived in a small country model provided world prices diverged from autarky prices. This referred not only to a move from autarky to free trade but also to a move from autarky to restricted trade. He also hypothesised that the more these prices diverged, the more the gains. Essentially he made two contributions. Firstly, he proved the proposition in a very general model, with many commodities and factors, and with variable factor supplies. Secondly, he showed that the *potential* gains did not hinge on redistribution of particular bundles of commodities – e.g. the bundle that would be produced under free trade – but rather on the improved consumption possibilities that trade provided. All this was very clearly expounded in Samuelson (1962) in terms of the two-commodity model, and with use of utility possibility frontiers for the two-person case.

Apart from the greatly simplified exposition, the additional contribution in Samuelson (1962) was to extend the argument to the large country case by use of the "Baldwin envelope". This well-known construct from Baldwin (1948) shows consumption possibilities for a country that can influence its terms of trade. The envelope will be outside the autarky frontier at all but one point. The optimal point on the frontier for any given income distribution (and hence for any given aggregate demand pattern) will be reached by application of the optimal tariff (dealt with in Section 5 below). Thus the opportunity to trade makes a country better off potentially *both* in the small and in the large country case.

At this point one should note a distinction brought out in Bhagwati (1968a). In the small country case, the proposition that free trade is superior to autarky relates to a competitive price system. Thus under perfect competition free trade will cause the economy to attain the optimal production point, i.e. one which is Pareto-efficient. In the large country case this will result from trade with an optimal tariff. Quite distinct is the proposition that the *opportunity to trade* is superior to the autarky situation, since this applies regardless of the institutional situation; in particular it applies to a planned economy.

Kemp (1962a) showed that free trade is potentially superior to autarky even for the large country, hence extending Samuelson (1939). In this case, of course, free trade is not an optimal situation, so that the Samuelson (1962) line of argument about the economy choosing an optimal point on an open economy frontier does not apply. The proof is simple in the two-commodity fixed factor supply case, but Kemp proved it for the general case, with many commodities and factors, and with variable factor supplies. In addition Kemp (1962a) followed up the Samuelson (1939) hypothesis that the trade gain is greater the more prices deviate from the autarky state. His answer was a "heavily qualified yes", though it can, again, be easily shown in the two-commodity fixed factor supply case. He also showed that restricted trade is better than no trade. The implicit assumption was that trade was restricted by *trade* restrictions (not production or consumption taxes or subsidies). In all cases, of course, the gains are *potential*; they become actual only if compensation actually takes place, or if an explicit social welfare function is introduced (in which case an uncompensated move to free trade *may* yield a social gain, depending on the income distribution weights incorporated in the SWF). In addition Kemp showed that, in the small country case, various tariff levels could be ranked: the lower the tariff the greater the potential gain from trade.

Finally, it should be noted that these three articles all made a number of key assumptions, notably absence of increasing returns (i.e. they assumed convexity), no distorting domestic taxes, no externalities, the feasibility of lump-sum transfers, and flexible factor prices that ensure full employment of all factors.

3.2. *Perspective*

While the three articles by Samuelson and Kemp might be regarded as the foundations of the modern development of this subject, the recent literature should be seen in perspective. Essentially it represents the sorting-out and culmination of a very long discussion in which most of the leading figures of international trade theory participated. The debates and points of view are summarised in two long chapters in Viner (1955) and more concisely in Caves (1960). There was a debate about the "real cost" versus "opportunity cost" approach, with Viner advancing the former and Haberler the latter. The opportunity cost approach is now central to modern thinking. On this matter Caves (1960) is an excellent reference. The stress in Samuelson (1939) that the simple gains-from-trade proposition generalises to a model with variable factor inputs (something proven more rigorously in various later papers) is explained by an attempt to incorporate the central issue in this debate. The extensive literature on welfare criteria is also relevant, the application of these to trade theory having been discussed in Baldwin (1952). Also to be noted is the classic article by Haberler (1950) which pioneered the focus on "domestic distortions" in the comparison between autarky and free trade.

For perspective it is also well to remember that the divergence between autarky and free trade prices is only a proximate explanation of the gains from trade: the underlying explanation must derive from all those factors that lie behind the sources of comparative advantage, differences which give rise to the divergences between autarky and free trade prices. In other words, first one explains the causes of trade (Ricardian, Heckscher–Ohlin, etc.) and then one explains the gains, given these causes.

The post-1962 literature in this field is very extensive. To some extent it has been devoted to generalising and making more rigorous the Samuelson–Kemp results. It appears that, provided the principal assumptions of convexity and no domestic distortions (including monopoly, externalities, factor market distortions, and commodity taxes) are maintained, the results seem to generalise very well. In particular, Ohyama (1972) has provided a unified treatment of the issues in a model with trade in final consumption goods, intermediate goods and factor services, and with non-tradeables.

3.3. Gains from trade: Recent extensions

The next step has been to remove some of the key assumptions, whether explicit or implicit. Here one can make the broad distinction between those results which suggest that the main message of orthodox gains-from-trade theory is confirmed in spite of the removal of certain assumptions, and those results which lead to serious complications, a great deal falling apart. I begin with those results that can be regarded as, broadly, upholding the main conclusions, even though there are, inevitably some complications.

Buried in Dixit and Norman (1980, pp. 79–80) is a proof that it is *not* necessary to have the possibility of lump-sum transfers for the main Samuelson–Kemp propositions to hold up. Factor taxes (including income tax) will do. This must surely be regarded as an important result in the light of Samuelson's stress on the "feasibility" issue. To quote the second last sentence of Samuelson (1962), "If ideal lump-sum reallocations of income are not feasible the above conclusions need serious modification and qualification".

The basic idea can be explained as follows. One is really concerned with comparing three situations: the first is the autarky situation, which yields a particular income distribution; the second is the free trade situation which yields a different income distribution; and the third is the free trade situation combined with redistribution designed to ensure that, at the minimum, all losers from the move to free trade are fully compensated. In the absence of lump-sum transfers the move from the second to the third situation involves a cost, which may be thought of as the familiar disincentive effects of income taxes and subsidies. The Dixit–Norman "trick" is to by-pass the second situation, and compare the first and third situations directly. Suppose that everyone's income were restored exactly in the third situation to where it was in the first situation. Then no one will have any reason to substitute for or against leisure, so that there are no disincentive effects. But, in addition to this, there will be some gainers, for whom effort yields a higher real return than before, their real income gains being the standard gains from trade.

Ohyama (1972) allows for trade (import and export) subsidies. Clearly "over-trading", resulting from trade subsidies when these are associated with the opening-up of trade, might lead to a potential welfare level below that of autarky, and this possibility has led others to rule out such subsidies. Ohyama's more comprehensive result allows for such subsidies in a multi-commodity model, along with tariffs. He compares welfare under autarky with welfare under a distorted trade situation, i.e. where there are tariffs and trade subsidies. The condition for a welfare gain from such a move to distorted trade is that *net* revenue from taxes and subsidies on trade (i.e. tariff revenue minus the cost of subsidies) is positive. Thus his generalisation of the Kemp result is that trade under self-financing subsidies is better than autarky.

Krueger and Sonnenschein (1967) confirmed rigorously what Samuelson conjectured, that the greater the price divergence between autarky and free trade the greater the gains from trade, their contribution being to prove this for the multi-commodity case. But they also showed that an exogenous improvement in the terms of trade need not necessarily lead to an increase in the gains from trade in a model with more than two goods. This is shown in a three-commodity counter-example where a terms of trade improvement can lead to a welfare deterioration.

The gains from trade analysis has also been extended by Helpman and Razin (1978) to allow for uncertainty. This matter is discussed more fully in Chapter 9, but here the principal result should be noted. Even though trade may generate uncertainty, nevertheless free trade will remain superior to autarky, so that the fundamental gains from trade proposition is unaffected. Profit and utility maximising agents will adjust to uncertainty appropriately, and even though uncertainty may generate costs, it remains true that trade presents more opportunities than autarky. The introduction of uncertainty has the same sort of effect as an adverse movement in the terms of trade: in both cases the gains from trade are reduced, but it remains true that there *are* gains from trade.

Uncertainty can be reduced by international trade in securities, which itself yields the usual gains from trade; but for any degree of trade in securities that is permitted, there will remain gains from trade in goods and services. This result is important because there had earlier been suggestions in the literature that the gains from trade proposition might be weakened when trade uncertainty is allowed for.

Finally, the gains from trade analysis has been extended to growing economies. This is discussed more fully in Chapters 4 and 6. It has been shown by Deardorff (1973) that, with a constant savings propensity, the opening of trade may reduce the steady state level of consumption per head. But writers in the trade theory field (like Deardorff) have realised that this does not negate the usual gains from trade propositions. The fixed savings propensity is unlikely to be optimal, and (irrespective of whether the propensity is fixed) lower consumption in the steady state may be offset by higher consumption in the earlier period, as the steady state is approached. Neo-Ricardian theorists have reasoned erroneously that there are losses from opening up trade when the net result happens to lead to lower steady state consumption. The matter has been fully clarified in Smith (1979) who shows (given the usual assumptions) that there are intertemporal gains from trade exactly for the same reasons that there are static gains, and with the same qualifications.

3.4.   Increasing returns with Marshallian assumptions

Let me now turn to the various attempts to remove key assumptions of the original models and yet obtain coherent results even though the original simplicities disappear. There is a very extensive literature here, but perhaps the main contribution has come from Kemp and Negishi (1970). I begin with models that allow for increasing returns. Here a whole sub-literature has developed.

The modern discussion of the gains from trade with increasing returns opens with Kemp (1969a, pp. 270–275), where the crucial assumption is made that the increasing returns are Marshallian – i.e. external to the firm and internal to the industry. While the results seem to be fatal to any sweeping conclusions, nevertheless, an important proposition is developed (p. 274), which has been later extended in the literature. It is that, when industry 1 has increasing returns and industry 2 has constant returns, if the opening of trade leads to the expansion of industry 1, the small country will gain from trade.

While it may seem rather obvious, this provided a basis for a more general result in Kemp and Negishi (1970), applying to a many-commodity model. There will be a gain, or at least no loss, from opening-up trade provided increasing returns industries do not contract and decreasing returns industries do not expand. This is still rather limited, so they also put forward a highly plausible conjecture stating (essentially) that if all industries with relatively high increasing returns expand while those with relatively low increasing returns contract, there should certainly be a gain. Unfortunately they conclude that this conjecture is probably false, since there will be efficiency losses in the case of the contracting industries. Hence, nothing is certain unless the contracting industries have constant or decreasing returns. But Eaton and Panagariya (1979) generalise their main result, showing that, for infinitesimal changes, the conjecture is correct.

Markusen and Melvin (1980) take up this matter in a two-good model – thus not being concerned with the multi-commodity problems of Kemp and Negishi (1970) and Eaton and Panagariya (1979). They focus on the effects in both countries of a two-country trading world, while the others looked at one country only. They note that both Kemp (1969a) and Melvin (1969) had shown that one country could lose from the opening of trade if there are increasing returns of the Marshallian kind in one industry and constant returns in the other. The essential cause of the possibility of loss is that there is an externality – i.e. a distortion. Markusen and Melvin (1980) develop a model with a small and a large country and show that in certain plausible conditions only the small country can lose, and, in any case it is more likely to be the loser. But one country must always gain. If the production frontiers of both countries are strictly concave in the relevant region, the large country *must* gain.

In this sub-set of the literature the search for reasonably firm general and simple principles has not been very fruitful – at least beyond the very first proposition in Kemp (1969a) mentioned earlier. One also feels uncomfortable with the unrealistic Marshallian assumption, which is, of course, designed to maintain perfect competition while having increasing returns. The more recent developments to which I come below, which allow for monopolistic competition, are thus very important.

3.5. Given commodity taxes and the gains from trade

Kemp and Negishi (1970) and Eaton and Panagariya (1979) have also considered the effects on the various gains from trade propositions of various other given distortions, including factor market distortions, always within a multi-commodity model. Here let us briefly note the effects of given commodity taxes.

What happens when there are given production or consumption taxes, the rates staying constant as the country moves from autarky to free trade? The main result from Kemp and Negishi (1970) is that there cannot be a loss from trade if net tax revenue calculated at prices after the change does not contract. In the case of production taxes this condition will obtain when, as a result of opening-up trade, all industries subject to positive taxation do not contract output while subsidised industries do not expand. In the two-product model this applies when the taxed industry is the exportable – i.e. is the industry that expands. For consumption taxes the requirements are similar: the necessary tax revenue condition obtains when the consumption of all taxed commodities does not fall and that of all subsidised commodities does not rise.

Perhaps I should give a flavor of these results (which are hard to summarise briefly). The condition 5.1 in Eaton and Panagariya (1979) is that: "There exists a commodity, commodity 0, such that the consumption of every commodity subject to a higher rate of consumption taxation does not contract and the consumption of every commodity subject to a lower rate of taxation does not expand." If this condition "obtains at every price vector between autarky and free trade then a movement from autarky to free trade is non-harmful".

Before leaving the matter of commodity taxes, consider the case where a country moves from autarky without commodity taxes to free trade with commodity taxes. Bhagwati (1968a) showed that in such a case some trade is not necessarily better than autarky and suggested that this negated the general proposition that some trade is always better than no trade. But Kemp (1968) pointed out that this result in no way negates the proposition. Rather, there are two simultaneous changes going on: a movement from autarky to free trade, and the imposition of commodity taxes, which is a new distortion.

3.6. Product differentiation and increasing returns

Finally, the most important recent development in this field is the rapidly growing literature on product differentiation, monopolistic competition and increasing returns. This is more fully discussed in Chapter 7. It clearly has important implications for the gains from trade questions. Key papers are Melvin and Warne (1973), Krugman (1979, 1981), Markusen (1981) and Markusen and Melvin (1982). The search for simple general principles and for clear results that do not depend on very special cases is still under way, but this whole literature is likely to move the subject sharply in the direction of the real world.

Perhaps two simple propositions can be extracted. Firstly, if the opening-up of trade reduces or eliminates monopoly power there will be gains from trade additional to the usual ones. Secondly, if firms with decreasing costs produce differentiated products, this being inevitably associated with imperfect competition of some kind, trade will allow the production of more types of goods. This will lead to gains from trade even for countries with identical factor endowments and technologies.

Markusen and Melvin (1982) have attempted to develop a unified approach to the gains from trade issue in a model with economies of scale and monopolistic competition. Essentially they find that there are two elements in the problem: first, there can be gains or losses owing to prices not being equal to marginal costs (non-fulfilment of the "tangency conditions"), this being a familiar domestic distortion associated with absence of perfect competion; and secondly there are complications associated with the existence of economies of scale (the "convexity conditions") these being the complications that Kemp and others struggled with in their models where there were economies of scale but competition was perfect.

4. The devices of trade intervention

4.1. The effects of a tariff

Before going on with normative analysis it is necessary to have a brief positive interlude. Something must be said about the various policy devices of intervention and, above all, their "equivalences". The issues and concepts are fundamental to much of what follows.

Consider the familiar diagram of Figure 4.1, referring to a small country, with importables (M) on the vertical axis and exportables (X) on the horizontal. The domestic transformation curve is QQ', the given world price ratio is represented by the slope of RPS, and both continuous full employment and balance of trade equilibrium are assumed. Free trade equilibrium production is at P and the country can trade along RPS. The free trade consumption (or absorption) pattern is on the income-consumption line OZ (determined by the world price ratio). Hence free trade consumption is at C, where OZ intersects RPS. At this stage perfect competition, no "distortions" of any kind, and no taxes, subsidies, etc. are assumed. The domestic rate of transformation (DRT) and the domestic rate of substitution (DRS) are both equal to the given foreign rate of transformation (FRT).

Let a tariff be imposed on *M*, with the revenue remitted to consumers and spent by them. The domestic price of *M* in terms of *X* facing both consumers and producers will rise relative to the given foreign price. Production shifts to *P'*, the country must now trade along *R'P'S'*, and the pattern of consumption shifts to the income–consumption line *OZ'*, so that actual consumption will be at *E*. In this tariff situation, DRT = DRS but both diverge from FRT. The volume of trade measured at the world price ratio has declined both because of the production and the consumption shift (measured in terms of *X*, from *VP* to *V'P'*).

4.2. *The symmetry between import and export taxes*

The most important equivalence is with an export tax. As Lerner (1936) showed in a classic contribution, a tariff and an export tax are completely symmetrical in a two-good "real" model, i.e. one where balance of trade equilibrium is assumed. Like a tariff, an export tax lowers the domestic price of *X* relative to *M* and so (if at the appropriate rate) has the same effect on production and consumption as a tariff. Figure 4.1 could thus represent the effects of an export tax when, as in the case of the tariff, the revenue is remitted to consumers. Everything, including the trade restriction effect, will be the same.

The Lerner symmetry proposition can be extended to a multi-good framework [McKinnon (1966), Corden (1971, pp. 119–22)]. Consider a particular structure of

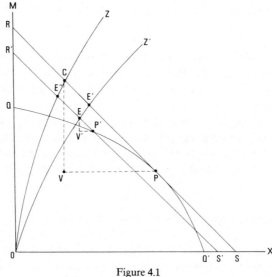

Figure 4.1

tariffs and export taxes yielding a set of domestic relative prices facing producers and consumers. In this "real" model only relative prices matter. Therefore, all the absolute tariff rates could be increased appropriately, and with it export tax rates would be reduced, and possibly even converted into export subsidies, such that domestic price relationships did not change. The new structure would be symmetrical with the old, yielding the same production and consumption outcomes. For example, if there is one importable (M) and two exportables $(X_1$ and $X_2)$, a structure consisting of a 25 percent tariff, a zero export tax or subsidy for X_1 and a 20 percent export tax for X_2 (the tax being calculated as a proportion of the untaxed price), would be symmetrical with a structure consisting of a zero tariff, a 20% export tax for X_1 and a 36% export tax for X_2. If a non-tradeable were introduced into the model with a given nominal price, for each structure there would be a particular nominal (and hence real) exchange rate. In the above example, the move to the structure with the lower tariff would require appropriate depreciation.

4.3. Consumption and production taxes

There are more equivalences and part-equivalences once we allow for consumption and production taxes and subsidies. In Figure 4.1, a tax on consumption of M, if at the same rate as the tariff, would leave production at P and bring consumption to E', i.e. DRS ≠ DRT = FRT. This is equivalent to a subsidy on consumption of X. The assumption is that in the first case the revenue is distributed back to consumers in lump-sum fashion, while in the second case the subsidy is financed by a lump-sum tax. Furthermore, a subsidy on production of M (if at the same rate as the tariff) would bring production to P' and consumption to E''. This is equivalent to a tax on production of X. In both these cases DRT ≠ DRS = FRT.

The important equivalence then follows that a consumption tax on M combined with a production subsidy for M, if they are at the same rate, are equivalent to a tariff. Exactly the same result can be obtained by combining an appropriate consumption tax (subsidy) on one product with a production tax (subsidy) on the other product. The initial revenue effects of the various policy packages differ, but here it is assumed that revenue can be and will be costlessly raised or remitted. It should be noted that all the devices affect the volume of trade; for example, both a consumption tax on M and a production subsidy to M are trade-reducing.

4.4. The equivalence between import quotas and tariffs

Given the assumption of perfect competition an import quota is equivalent to a tariff or an export tax. In Figure 4.1 the quantity of imports, or the value in terms of foreign prices, is fixed first at (say) EV', and then domestic production and consumption adjust, yielding, again, DRT = DRS ≠ FRT. If the scarcity rents from the quota were auctioned or taxed away, and the revenue redistributed in the same way as tariff revenue would have been, the final result would be exactly the same. But if the rents went to particular people, with the net result that the income distribution were different than in the case of the tariff, the final demand pattern might be different, yielding a different income-consumption curve OZ' and thus a different consumption point E. Leaving this aside, one can say that, given perfect competition, an import quota is equivalent to a tariff. The same applies to an export quota.

Non-equivalences between tariffs and quotas arise when there is some element of actual or potential monopoly – whether in domestic import-competing production, in trading (on the part of the recipients of the import licences) or of foreign suppliers. In that case a quota that has the same effect on imports as a tariff may not have the same effect on domestic production or on the domestic price. Considering these three aspects – import volume, domestic production and domestic price – one can set a quota to have the same effect as a tariff in any one of these respects and then find that the effects will differ with respect to the other two effects. This analysis was pioneered by Bhagwati (1965), with many subsequent contributions, including Shibata (1968) and Bhagwati (1968b). The effects of quotas in the large country case, and with domestic monopoly, have been analysed in a general equilibrium model by Panagariya (1981).

The main "non-equivalence" point can be seen by considering a particular case. There is a single domestic import-competing producer and the country is small, so that he faces initially a given price for his product. Thus he has no monopoly power at this stage. A non-prohibitive tariff would not alter this situation, though it would raise the price he faces, domestic output would go up and imports would fall. By contrast, while a quota will also lead to a fall in imports (assuming the quota is set sufficiently low), it will give the domestic producer monopoly power and he might now reduce his output [Corden (1971)]. Thus in this case there is clearly not equivalence, both devices reducing imports but one raising and the other possibly lowering domestic output.

An interesting contribution on the equivalence between tariffs and quotas under domestic monopoly has come from Sweeney, Tower and Willett (1977). They assume that the aim of policy is for imports to capture a given fraction of the domestic market. The domestic monopolist takes into account in his behavior the intention of the government. This is a "rational expectations" situation, and the outcome will be the same irrespective of whether a tariff or a quota is used. Given the demand curve for imports and home production combined, the monopolist will be faced with a net demand curve which shows how much he will be allowed to sell at various prices facing consumers. He will then choose that price-output combination that maximises his profits. The government will then impose either a tariff or a quota to make this a domestic market equilibrium.

Apart from these positive comparisons of tariffs and quotas, there are normative implications, since the cost of protection may differ between the two. This is dealt with in Section 8 below. It should also be noted that recently a literature has grown up which compares tariffs and quotas when there is uncertainty about movements in the demand and supply curves. This is discussed in Chapter 9. Finally, Falvey (1975) has shown that if a tariff actually leads to an increase in imports through general equilibrium effects [this being the Metzler (1949) paradox, possible only in the large country case], its effects cannot be replicated by a quota.

4.5. Balance of payments effects

It goes a little against the grain for all balance of payments effects of these devices to disappear in the kind of model usually used in trade theory. How can a tariff and an export tax have the same effect when it may seem obvious that the first must improve and the latter (in the small country case) worsen the balance of payments?

There are three alternative packages of assumptions behind real models where balance of trade equilibrium and full employment are always maintained. (1) The nominal exchange rate is fixed, the money supply is allowed to vary to maintain external balance (as in Hume's specie flow mechanism) and factor price flexibility maintains internal balance. (2) Average nominal factor prices (or just the nominal wage) are rigid or sluggish, the money supply is targeted on internal balance and the exchange rate on external balance. (3) The nominal money supply is fixed, the exchange rate maintains external balance and factor price flexibility internal balance.

The balance of payments can change if no instrument is targeted (by policy or through an automatic mechanism) on external balance. A frequent, and intuitively appealing, assumption is for the nominal exchange rate to be fixed, for the average nominal factor price or the nominal price of non-tradeables to be rigid, and for monetary policy to be targeted on internal balance. In the small country case, with revenue remitted as before, a tariff will then improve the balance of payments and an export tax worsen it. The various different tariff-export tax structures described above will no longer have identical effects.

An alternative assumption – which seems less realistic but comes out of the monetary theory of the balance of payments [Mussa (1976)] – is to hold domestic credit creation as well as the nominal exchange rate fixed, and allow a changed demand for money to be satisfied through the current account of the balance of payments. A tariff is likely to increase the demand for money (by raising the domestic price-level), and thus to lead to a *temporary* balance of payments surplus. In this model internal balance is maintained by factor price flexibility.

4.6.   *Theory of tariff structure*

Before leaving this brief review of the devices of intervention, attention should be drawn to the theory of tariff structure – which has been generalized to include all trade taxes and subsidies as well as taxes and subsidies on consumption and production of traded goods. A key element in this theory is the concept of the *effective rate of protection* (*ERP*). The theory, with an emphasis on the positive effects on resource allocation of an interventionist system, has been fully expounded in Corden (1971). It is essentially concerned with the interrelationships between different tariffs, export taxes, subsidies, and so on, and thus is general equilibrium in its essence, though elements of it can usefully be expounded in partial equilibrium terms. It takes into account the input–output structure of the economy, as well as horizontal relationships between activities. It puts much emphasis on the role of non-tradeables both as inputs into tradeable production and as alternative users of factors, this depending essentially on the relative price of non-tradeables to tradeables, i.e. the real exchange rate. This real exchange rate may be required to change as a result of changes in the tariff structure.

This body of theory has provided the basis for an immense amount of empirical and policy-orientated work, though there are inevitably problems associated with particular measures, especially the measure of *ERP* – and, as always, any simple conclusions coming out of "pure" models can be shown not to hold in general. It will not be referred to further in this survey, except briefly in connection with the cost of protection. It has been one of the main developments in the theory of international trade in the sixties, at least from the point of view of practical relevance, though from the point of view of the long-term development of the normative theory – and perhaps eventually, practical implications also – the theory of domestic distortions, to be dealt with below, must be given pride of place.

5.   The terms of trade argument and optimal tariff theory

Until the 1950s the normative theory of international trade was dominated by the terms of trade argument for protection, yielding the so-called theory of the optimal tariff. The very term "optimal tariff" implies that the elements in this model are the only considerations determining tariff optimality. We shall see later that optimal tariff theory involves much more than terms of trade considerations, so that this traditional concept will generally be called the *orthodox* optimal tariff here.

The basic idea is that a country concerned solely with the national interest should restrict its trade so as to exploit its potential monopoly or monopsony power. Hence the country is now assumed to be "large" – to be able to influence world prices. The optimal tariff and export tax rates are the inverse of the relevant foreign elasticities. In the two-good model the optimal export tax rate is thus the inverse of the elasticity of the foreign demand for exports in terms of imports. This is just an application of standard monopoly theory. Bearing in mind the Lerner symmetry theorem, in the two-good model either a tariff or an export tax will do the job, while in the multi-good model there will be an optimal trade-tax structure. It is required that DRS = DRT = FRT so that, while consumption or production taxes or subsidies can bring about restrictions of trade that improve the terms of trade, these will not be first-best devices as they would generate the inequality DRS ≠ DRT.

This theory was fully developed by the end of the nineteen fifties. It goes back to Bickerdike (1906), and even further back in its main idea, to Torrens, Mill and Sidgwick. Major contributions have come from Lerner (1934, 1944), Kaldor (1940), Scitovsky (1942), Kahn (1947), Graaff (1949), and Johnson (1951, 1954). A summary of this theory in all its aspects is in Corden (1974) and its exposition in terms of two-good geometry and offer curves can be found in every textbook. So we can be brief here, and just draw attention to some features and assumptions that are sometimes overlooked.

One key assumption is that the concern is with national, not world, welfare. As trade is restricted towards the optimum, world welfare in the Pareto-efficiency sense falls owing to less of the gains from trade being obtained, but the trade-restricting country's welfare improves. Another key assumption is that domestic importers and exporters are perfectly competitive. If there were some degree of monopsony in importing or monopoly in exporting private firms would already be exploiting the country's monopsony or monopoly power, and government intervention would not be needed, or not to the extent indicated by the formal theory. In effect, the theory suggests that a government should do what a cartel might also achieve.

Going back to the competitive case it needs to be noted that the theory of the optimal tariff assumes that an independent income distribution policy is being followed: it is concerned with Pareto efficiency from a national point of view. Nevertheless, income distribution is relevant, and this has been the source of many of the complications in the theory. It is related to the fairly subtle point that, while the optimal tariff (or export tax) *rate* must be equal to the inverse of the relevant foreign elasticity, this elasticity does not just "determine" the optimal rate. Domestic demand and supply conditions influence not only the quantitative outcomes of a particular tariff rate, but also influence the level of the optimal rate.

Consider Figure 5.1. The foreign elasticity of export demand is on the vertical axis and the tax rate on the horizontal. JJ' is the relationship derived from the optimal tax formula ($t_x = 1/e_x$). QQ' shows how the foreign elasticity changes as the tax is raised. It is assumed, plausibly, that the elasticity rises as trade is restricted, though the slope need not be consistently positive. The optimal tax rate is ON, with elasticity OL.

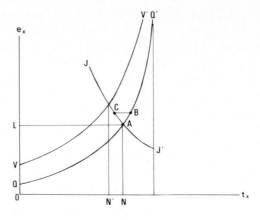

Figure 5.1

A change in domestic demand conditions would shift QQ' and hence change the optimal tax. For example, suppose that owing to a change in tastes, domestic demand shifted towards the country's exportable product. For a given rate of tariff or export tax, trade would be reduced, and the foreign elasticity would therefore rise. Thus QQ' would shift upwards to VV' and the optimal tax rate would fall. The same result would come about if income were redistributed towards people who, for given relative prices, would purchase more exportables relative to importables than the community in general. Thus, assuming that tastes differ among members of the community (or, more precisely, that marginal propensities to consume different goods differ), for every income distribution there will be a different rate of optimal tax and a different quantitative equilibrium.

A new development in orthodox optimal tariff theory, owed to Katrak (1977) and Svedberg (1979), concerns the appropriate tariff on imports from a foreign firm that has a monopoly in a particular product in the importing country. In this case the optimal tariff may be positive even though the country is small, the point being that profits of the foreign monopoly can be squeezed. A tariff will yield a consumers' surplus loss to the importing country, but a tariff revenue gain (up to a point); the optimal tariff trades off these two effects. They also allow for given rates of tax on profits in both countries. A tariff that is sufficiently high (called by Svedberg the *switchover tariff*) may then induce the foreign monopolist to transfer production to the previously-importing country, so that the latter loses the tariff revenue gain but gains profits tax revenue instead. Various parameters determine whether this would maximise its welfare and what is the *ultra-optimal tariff*, taking this possibility of a tariff-induced shift in the location of production into account.

In recent years import quotas as well as voluntary export restraints (*VER*s) have been growing in importance relative to tariffs. Hence their terms of trade aspects should be noted. Import quotas can improve the terms of trade of the quota-imposing country, just like a tariff. This will be so when the foreign suppliers are competitive and the import licences go to domestic traders or producers or are auctioned. But quotas will worsen a country's terms of trade when the licences go to foreign suppliers or to their subsidiary trading firms. In the latter case, profits of foreign-owned but domestically-located firms should be included in the true cost of imports to the country.

*VER*s are imposed by exporting countries on pressure from importing countries, with the implied threat that in the absence of such restraint the importing country will impose import quotas. A *VER* is certain to improve the terms of trade of the exporting country, though the degree of trade restriction it leads to may turn out to be above the optimum in relation to an alternative where the importing country imposes no restrictions. But if the real alternative consists of import quotas designed to achieve the same trade-restrictive result, then *VER*s are preferable for the exporting country.

So far nothing has been said about the possibility of foreign retaliation. Clearly more than one can play the nationalistic game implied in orthodox optimal tariff theory. Awareness of this actually inhibits some countries in imposing or raising trade restrictions. Probably game theory is most appropriate in this field. But the principal analyses in trade theory – by Scitovsky (1942) and Johnson (1954) – are based on a different approach: they assume that if the home country does not impose a tariff the foreign country will not do so either, but that the adoption of orthodox optimal tariff policy by the home country will then lead to the same policy by the foreign country. There is then an element of retaliation, the foreign country retaliating by initiating an optimal tariff policy. It seems highly probable that both countries would lose from this process but Johnson has shown that one country *could* nevertheless gain relative to free trade, in spite of the other country's optimal tariff policy. An element of myopia is implicit in this approach, as discussed in Corden (1974).

Finally, the extension of orthodox optimal tariff theory to capital movements has been an important contribution of the nineteen sixties. If a country is "buying" or "selling" capital competitively in a foreign market, unexploited monopsony and monopoly power may exist, as in the case of goods and services. This insight is owed to Kemp (1962b) and suggests that there is an optimal tax on the import and export of capital provided the expected rates of return are not given to the country by the world market. With many different types of capital (especially with "sector-specific capital") there will be a structure of optimal taxes. For a country that is trading in both goods and capital (the latter in the forms of bonds and equities), there will be an optimal structure of trade and capital taxes. Of course, there are various practical obstacles to imposing such a structure, and many other considerations, so that this hardly leads to a recommendation which can be applied directly.

The main developments in this field come from three papers – by Kemp (1966), Jones (1967) and Gehrels (1971) – which have explored rigorously the relationship between the two types of optimal taxes. They allow for the likelihood that the prices of traded goods in the foreign country (in a two country world) are affected by the cost of capital, so that the rates of optimal tax will be related and, more important, the actual formulae need to be adjusted. For example, the trade tax may benefit not only the terms of trade but also the terms of foreign borrowing, while the tax on foreign capital may benefit not only the terms of foreign borrowing but also the terms of trade. In these cases the first-best optimal tax rates will be higher than when the interrelationships are not taken into account.

Jones (1967) and Gehrels (1971) also analyse the second-best cases where only one instrument is available: for example, it may be possible to tax trade but not the import of capital appropriately. Clearly the trade tax must then be adjusted to take into account indirect effects on the terms of foreign borrowing. As is usual in second-best analysis, there are many possible cases here. Consider one case. Suppose that the only policy instrument available is a tariff. It is desired to "squeeze" foreign capital somewhat, but a tax on the import of capital cannot be imposed or increased. If the country is a capital importer and it imports the capital-intensive product a tariff will increase the returns to foreign capital domestically. In this case the tariff should be reduced below its first-best optimal level, and its second-best optimum might even be negative.

6. The theory of domestic distortions

6.1. Domestic distortions theory: Introduction

We come now to the major development in the normative theory of international trade in the post-war period. This is the theory of domestic distortions. In view of the extensive literature in this field a formal exposition will not be given here. A major result has been to downgrade the role of trade policy and thus to rehabilitate the case for free trade, at least aside from the orthodox optimal tariff argument. Most arguments for protection – other than the terms of trade argument – turn out to originate in some market failure in the domestic economy – some *domestic* divergence between prices and marginal costs, and so on. The first-best policy is then to deal with this divergence directly. For example, if some external economy attaches to import-competing domestic production of particular products, first-best policy is to provide production subsidies, not tariffs. In the presence of numerous domestic divergences there may be a case for many kinds of policy interventions, but this will not destroy the case for free trade for the small country, or for free trade modified by the orthodox optimal tariff for the large country.

Free trade is defined here as the absence of all *trade* taxes, subsidies and regulations, but still allowing non-trade interventions – e.g. taxes and subsidies on particular forms of domestic production or consumption which may still *incidentally* affect trade. Thus the case for free trade and the case for laissez-faire are divorced. Of course trade interventions may still be better than nothing in the absence of first-best domestic policy interventions.

The central theme is that any intervention should be as close as possible to the source of the relevant divergence or distortion. Thus a production subsidy should deal with a production distortion, a consumption tax with a consumption distortion, a factor subsidy or tax with a particular factor-market distortion, and so on. In terms of the simple trade model, the aim is to establish the equalities DRS = DRT = FRT, and, in addition, to ensure that production is on the transformation curve.

The principal contributions in this field have come from Haberler (1950), Meade (1955a), Corden (1957a), Hagen (1958), Bhagwati and Ramaswami (1963) and Johnson (1965a). The theory, with many examples and extensive discussion of qualifications, is expounded in Corden (1974), which also gives a brief history. A neat consolidation – but with less emphasis on limitations – is in Bhagwati (1971). There is also an exposition in Hazari (1978). While Haberler and Meade must be regarded as the pioneers, especially the latter, the most influential modern contributions have been the papers by Bhagwati and Ramaswami and by Johnson.

Right from the beginning it must be pointed out that a crucial assumption in much of this literature is (1) that lump-sum (non-distorting) taxes are available to finance the various required subsidies as well as to bring about appropriate after-tax income distribution, and (2) that a redistribution policy is actually being carried out continuously.

With regard to assumption (1) – which will be reconsidered more fully in the next section – it could be reinterpreted as involving two assumptions, namely (a) that the elasticity of supply of labor (effort) is zero and (b) that, after taxes and subsidies to deal with distortions have been imposed, all further government revenue needs are met, or excessive collections disposed of, either by income taxes or subsidies, or by uniform (and hence non-distorting) taxes or subsidies on the consumption of goods and services. As for assumption (2), it means that income distribution effects are ignored and the concern is purely with Pareto-efficiency. If one does not believe that such a policy is actually taking place, even though it would be costless, or cannot take place without considerable costs, then the only justification for ignoring income distribution effects when making policy recommendations based directly on this body of theory is what has earlier been called the *Hicksian optimisim*. Otherwise, it is necessary to take income distribution effects into account on the basis of some kind of social welfare function. The Pareto-efficiency considerations discussed here must then be traded off against income distribution effects. The analysis that follows can then only be regarded as a first step in a more comprehensive analysis.

The various distortions or divergences (the latter being Meade's more neutral term) are, of course, *marginal*, and can be classified in various ways. In particular, one needs to distinguish *policy-imposed distortions* from *endogenous distortions* [Bhagwati (1971)]. The first (for which the term distortions is very appropriate) are created by government policies, and are assumed not to be directly removable. They include distorting taxes, as well as regulations which create situations that allow monopolies to be formed. The second do not result from government policies, and would include certain rigidities in the labor market and those that result from non-convexities (economies of scale, etc.) in the system. Of course, the distinction between the two may often be hard to make. As we shall see below, to this categorisation will have to be added *by-product distortions*.

6.2.   *The hierarchy of policies and by-product distortions*

This is only a beginning, and focuses on first-best policies. The next step is to rank policies, to determine the principles on which the level of a second-best (or worse) policy instrument should be fixed, and to assess the gains and losses from inferior policies. We know that countries continue to use trade policies on the basis of arguments for protection which suggest that these policies are not first-best instruments to achieve the objectives. Apart from advocacy of first-best policies, the economist can then analyse the costs and gains resulting from such trade policies and compare these with the gains from first-best policies. The early emphasis of the literature – notably in Bhagwati and Ramaswami (1963) and in Johnson (1965a) – was decidedly negative, with an emphasis on the losses that might result from failure to choose first-best policies, but it is possible to be somewhat more positive, at least in a qualitative way. This involves ranking the policies for any particular distortion to form a *hierarchy of policies*. The main ideas are best explained with an example.

Suppose that the private cost of labor to manufacturing industry (assumed to produce importables only) exceeds its social opportunity cost. First-best policy then requires a subsidy to labor cost in manufacturing. Now suppose that the government actually prefers to subsidise manufacturing production. This will impose the *by-product distortion* of over-encouraging the use of non-labor factors in manufacturing. A *by-product distortion* is the undesirable result of seeking to offset an original (endogenous or policy-imposed) distortion. Bhagwati and Ramaswami (1963) and Johnson (1965a) stressed that if the subsidy were actually sufficient to offset the original distortion, the by-product distortion might be so large that there would be a net loss in welfare.

At this point one must introduce the concept of the *second-best optimal subsidy* (or tax, tariff, and so on). The gain from offsetting the original distortion can be traded off against the loss from the by-product distortion, and normally welfare will be maximised by such a second-best subsidy when it does not fully offset the original distortion. This important point actually was in Meade (1955a), but was rediscovered by Kemp and Negishi (1969) in a critique of Bhagwati and Ramaswami (1963). Furthermore, the welfare level attainable from the second-best optimal subsidy will be less than that obtainable from the first-best optimal subsidy (on labor use in manufacturing).

If a tariff is the actual instrument of protection policy the additional by-product distortion of a consumption distortion will be imposed. There will thus be two by-product distortions in this example. There will be a *second-best optimal tariff rate* that trades off the costs of these two against the benefit of partially offsetting the original labor market distortion, and the welfare level attained by this tariff rate will be below that obtained from the second-best optimal production subsidy. Needless to say, if the tariff is higher it will offset more of the original distortion, but a net welfare loss might result.

This example indicates the general principle. One can have cases where the *hierarchy of policies* which emerges is much longer, with many more by-product distortions. For example, if some manufactures are potentially or actually exportable, the use of a tariff without an associated export subsidy will lead to the by-product distortion of *home-market bias* (i.e. out of any given output, too much manufactured output is sold at home relative to sales on the world market). The hierarchy of policies would thus go: subsidy on labor use (first-best), subsidy to output, tariff with export subsidy, tariff alone.

Let us now turn to two broad categories of "arguments for protection", both of which can be analysed in terms of domestic distortions theory. In the exposition of both cases the small country assumption will be made. In the large country case optimal policy would require the orthodox optimal tariff to be superimposed.

6.3. Wage rigidity, marginal product differential and unemployment

Some much-analysed arguments for protection rest on market failure in the labor market. There are three main cases to consider.

First, suppose there is a *generalised rigid real wage* in the economy at a level too high to yield full employment with free trade and no taxes or subsidies. First-best policy calls then for a uniform employment subsidy. Haberler (1950) first showed that real wage rigidity may cause the opening-up of trade to lead to a loss of output. Brecher (1974) has explored this real wage rigidity case in detail, starting in free trade with unemployment, and comparing the effects of various policy instruments. If the importable is labor-intensive a tariff would increase employment and output (by raising the full employment real wage along Stolper–Samuelson lines), but it would not be first-best: capital and labor would be drawn excessively into the protected industry, and in addition there would be a by-product consumption distortion.

Secondly, suppose that there is an *inter-sectoral marginal product differential*. In a model with an advanced sector and a subsistence sector the former has to pay a wage rate in excess of the opportunity cost of labor – i.e. in excess of the marginal product of labor in the subsistence sector. This has been much analysed as the basis for an argument for protection, and also in all its positive implications. Some of the principal policy insights can be found in Ohlin (1931), and the modern revival of this case is owed to Hagen (1958), while the literature is surveyed in Magee (1973).

There are two sub-cases here. In the first case, originally analysed by Lewis (1954), the wage in both sectors is the same, but in the subsistence sector labor is paid its average rather than its marginal product. Thus there is *income-sharing*; in the extreme case the marginal product in this sector may be zero. In the second case labor may be paid its marginal product in both sectors but there is a *wage differential*, with the wage higher in the advanced than in the subsistence sector. Furthermore, this differential may be fixed (proportionately or absolutely); or there may be a rigid real wage in the advanced sector, so that a rise in the wage in the subsistence sector induced by a movement of labor out of that sector would lower the differential.

But all these distinctions do not matter much for the basic normative analysis. In all cases there is a *marginal product differential*, which causes employment in the advanced sector to be too low and first-best policy is to subsidise employment of labor in that sector. (The financing question is particularly important here and will be discussed later, while income distribution effects should surely not be ignored.) As Ohlin, Hagen and others have pointed out, all other methods are second-best or worse, as shown in the earlier example of a hierarchy of policies.

Thirdly, we come to the "urban unemployment" case originating with Harris and Todaro (1970), the policy implications of which have been worked out in detail in Corden and Findlay (1975). The labor force is divided between the urban (manufacturing) sector, the rural (agricultural) sector, and the unemployment pool. There is a wage differential in the form of a sector-specific rigid real wage in the urban sector (as in the previous wage differential case), but there is also an urban unemployment pool, the size of which is related to this differential and to the probability of an unemployed person getting an urban job.

This well-known model cannot be spelt out here. In a sense it is a special case of the second sub-case above, but the policy implications differ. This time (as in the generalised real wage rigidity case) the first-best policy is a general employment subsidy – i.e. not just for one sector – though this must again be subject to the financing problem to be discussed later. A subsidy to agriculture is not first-best but is sure to improve employment and output. A subsidy to manufacturing employment may lead to a rise in output, but it could also lead to a fall, essentially because a rise in urban employment may be more than offset by an increase in the urban unemployment pool. But the optimal manufacturing subsidy will be positive.

6.4. The infant industry argument

One of the oldest, as well as most popular, arguments for protection – the infant industry argument – can be analysed fruitfully in terms of the theory of domestic distortions. It is obvious that a protectionist argument that is concerned with the development of an industry – or perhaps the whole sector of an economy – will not justify a trade policy device as the first-best instrument. A tariff, compared with a production subsidy, would lead to a by-product consumption distortion; therefore, if there is any justification for the argument, and only these two instruments were available, a production subsidy would be preferable. But in recent years the argument has been analysed more deeply, and this suggests that – insofar as it has any sound basis at all – a production subsidy is also unlikely to be first-best. Important post-war contributions in this field have come from Meade (1955a), Kemp (1964, ch. 12), Johnson (1965a, 1970) and Baldwin (1969).

The essence of the infant industry argument is that it is an argument for temporary protection. Therefore, (1) *time* must enter the argument in some essential way, and (2) there must be some market failure – some imperfection or externality – somewhere. For the present discussion the main concern needs to be with the nature of this market failure. In fact there are a number of different bases for the infant industry argument, and only three of the most popular will be discussed here.

An "infant" firm or group of firms (industry) may need to go through an initial learning experience involving an investment in human capital. This is a case of *dynamic internal economies*, the learning benefits staying wholly within the firm. Imperfection of the capital market may make the financing of such investment difficult or too expensive – the capital market being biased against "invisible" investment, or perhaps the rate of interest for all long-term investment being too high owing to private myopia. If this is indeed so, first-best policy is to improve the capital market directly (perhaps by providing special financing agencies); a subsidy to that element of factor input or output which gives rise primarily to learning would be second-best or worse, while further down the hierarchy would be a general output subsidy to the industry, and then a tariff or export subsidy.

A second argument involves *dynamic external economies*. It is concerned with labor training by firms, when firms cannot necessarily retain the workers they have trained. In a perfect market situation, where new knowledge becomes embodied in mobile workers, the effects would be internalised: the workers would accept low wages during the learning stage, financing themselves by borrowing. But, again, if the capital market is imperfect, or if there are rigidities in wage determination, this may not be possible; firms will then not be rewarded for the training taking place during the "infant" or any later stage.

First-best policy is to improve the capital market, second-best policy is to provide finance for, or subsidise, labor training, while a third-best policy might be to subsidise the employment of labor by those firms or industries that contribute more than average to the pool of trained labor available to firms other than themselves. Subsidising the firms' outputs might be fourth-best.

A third argument (also a case of a *dynamic external economy*, but not involving a factor market imperfection) is concerned with knowledge diffusion. Knowledge spreads from firm to firm, especially in the infancy stage, though it will be in the interests of a firm to prevent this diffusion even when the marginal social cost of diffusion is low or zero. Once knowledge is created it is really a public good which ought to be freely available.

Baldwin (1969) pointed out that protection provides no incentive for a firm to acquire more knowledge than it would have otherwise, even though the social gains exceed the private gains; all protection can do is to favor firms which are known to be knowledge creators and diffusors. A subsidy related in some way to knowledge creation and diffusion would be first-best. Johnson (1970) stressed the public good aspect of knowledge creation and the need to encourage its diffusion.

6.5. *Trade distortions*

Apart from domestic distortions there can also be *trade distortions*, which can also be endogenous or policy-induced. Thus there is really a "generalised theory of distortions and welfare" [Bhagwati (1971)], of which domestic distortions theory is only a part. The principal endogenous trade distortion from a national point of view is the non-exploitation of potential national monopoly power by a competitive economy. On the other hand, a tariff in the small economy may be a policy-induced trade distortion. To analyse trade distortions further, for the moment let us assume *no* domestic distortions.

In the case of a large country, if there is no tariff (or other equivalent device) one can say there is a *trade distortion* from a national point of view resulting from a failure to apply the orthodox optimal tariff, the volume of trade being too great.

Even if there is a tariff it may not be at the optimal level. Without a tariff, DRS = DRT ≠ FRT, and the optimal tariff will create the necessary equality DRS = DRT = FRT. Any non-trade device designed to reduce the volume of trade, such as a production subsidy to an importable, will create a by-product distortion in the form of generating the inequality DRS ≠ DRT. First-best policy for a trade distortion is to use a trade policy device, in this case a tariff or an export tax, or a structure of them, as required by orthodox optimal tariff theory.

In the small open economy *given* tariffs or other trade taxes or subsidies are policy-induced trade distortions. We assume here that there are no externalities or public good effects connected with trade, and also assume away domestic distortions. First-best policy is to remove such distortions directly. If there is an institutional rigidity, they can be removed just as effectively indirectly. For example, in a two-good model a given tariff can be supplemented by an export subsidy that fully offsets the tariff (since an export subsidy is symmetrical with a negative tariff). In a model with two imports, where one has an irremovable tariff, the effects would be fully offset by a tariff at an equal rate on the second import, combined with a uniform export subsidy at that rate.

An extensive literature analyses second-best policies in the presence of such trade distortions. The standard case from Lipsey and Lancaster (1956) assumes, in a three-good model, that there is a fixed positive tariff on one importable, (M_1) and that no tax or subsidy can be provided for the exportable. What, then, is the second-best optimal tariff for the remaining importable (M_2)? The general answer is that, if the three goods are net substitutes in consumption and production, it will be positive but less than the fixed tariff on M_1. The higher the variable tariff up to the fixed tariff level, the more the trade distortion is being offset but, on the other hand, the greater is the by-product distortion resulting from the domestic price relationship with the exportable being changed; as in the domestic distortions theory, the second-best optimal tariff trades off these two effects. Once the possibility of complementarity is allowed for, the second-best optimal tariff could be either negative or higher than the fixed tariff. An unexpected result, owed to Findlay and Wellisz (1976), is that, while first-best policy will consist of removing or fully offsetting the trade distortion, factor taxes or subsidies may actually lead to higher welfare levels than *second-best* trade policies. This point will be taken up again later.

Much of the literature on these trade distortions has gone in a different direction of second-best analysis. It has asked: what rules of piece-meal tariff changes can ensure some welfare improvement? Broadly, two simple rules have emerged. Firstly, *radial reductions* – reductions of every tariff by the same percentage – will improve welfare at every stage [Bruno (1972a)]. Secondly, there is the *concertina method* [Bertrand and Vanek (1971), Corden (1974)]: the high tariffs are squeezed down to medium level at the first stage, then these and the existing medium tariffs are lowered, and so on; if at every stage the highest tariffs are reduced to the next level, distortions are being continually lowered, with no by-product distortions being created, and there is a welfare gain at every stage of such a process of gradual tariff reform. This principle can, of course, also be applied to other distorting taxes.

This subject of second-best tariff-making and piece-meal reform has been explored in detail in many papers; the pioneers were Meade (1955a) and Lipsey and Lancaster (1956), there is a survey and consolidation in Lloyd (1974), and other relevant papers include Foster and Sonnenschein (1970) and Hatta (1977). The latter presents a rigorous analysis of the conditions required for the two simple rules above to ensure welfare improvement at every stage. Vanek (1964) applied a world welfare criterion and showed that particular unilateral tariff reductions may not raise world welfare in some rather special conditions. But Hatta and Fukushima (1979) show that the two rules can be applied to piece-meal tariff reductions by different countries when such a cosmopolitan criterion applies.

6.6. *Non-economic objectives and fixed targets*

Distortions theory can be applied to the pursuit of non-economic objectives [Bhagwati and Srinivasan (1969)]. For example, if the non-economic objective has to do with domestic production a production subsidy or tax will be first-best. A tariff would create a by-product distortion. If the non-economic objective is the nationalistic one of making the country less dependent on trade, a uniform tariff or export tax will be first-best, unless the concern is really with instability, in which case more direct measures, such as the accumulation of foreign exchange reserves or of buffer stocks may be better. Furthermore, there will be a trade-off between the economic cost and the benefits of coming closer to the non-economic objective. A non-economic objective must be distinguished from a *fixed target*, which rules out the possibility of a trade-off.

6.7. *Mixed Cases*

The journals are filled with special cases and paradoxes in this field, usually resulting from mixed cases with more than one distortion, and with limitation on instruments that can be used. It is always important to focus on the basic underlying principles, in which case paradoxes disappear.

There may be two distortions. First-best policy then requires the simultaneous application of two policies, each aimed directly at one distortion. But the levels of the two policies – e.g. a tariff rate and a subsidy rate – may be related.

If only one policy instrument is available to be used its optimal setting in such a second-best situation will clearly not be the same as when both instruments can be set optimally – i.e. when a first-best policy package is applied. The sign, and not just the size, of the required change in this instrument may even differ between the first-best and the second-best situations. An example of such a two-distortion case may be given, adapted from Corden (1957a).

There is a domestic production distortion requiring the subsidisation of import-competing production. As this distortion increases, the subsidy will need to increase and the volume of trade will decline. If the country is large an orthodox optimal tariff must be imposed at the same time. In the absence of this tariff, there is initially a trade distortion. The rate of required tariff (export tax) will be the inverse of the foreign elasticity of supply (demand), and this elasticity may fall as the volume of trade rises. This is represented by the positive slope of QQ' in Figure 5.1. The production subsidy shifts the curve upwards, to VV'. (It causes the volume of trade to fall and hence the elasticity to rise.) The decline in the volume of trade brought about by the production subsidy leads then to a fall in the required rate of tariff from ON to ON'. There is the seeming paradox that an increase in import-competing production has been associated with a fall in the optimal tariff rate.

This only seems a paradox because one usually envisages a second-best situation with the tariff as the only instrument of a protection policy, so that an increase in import-competing production normally requires an increase in the tariff rate.

Next, one can assume that the tariff *is* the only instrument of policy. We have here a typical example where one instrument has to deal with two distortions. First, the tariff should be imposed at the orthodox optimal level (ON in Figure 5.1), leaving the production distortion. To deal with this production distortion the tariff should then be increased further until a point such as B is reached where the volume of trade has not been reduced as much as in the first-best solution. A by-product trade distortion will have been created by this further move, with $DRS \neq FRT$. This will have been traded off against the reduced production distortion. Note that the move from A in Figure 5.1 (where the tariff is at its orthodox optimal level but the production distortion is ignored) to the second-best optimal tariff at B involves a decline in the level of the orthodox optimal tariff, as represented by C.

An exogenous increase in the domestic production distortion has thus called for an increase in the tariff in this second-best case, even though it required a decrease in the first-best case earlier.

This is just one example. Many other combinations of distortions and combinations of instruments can be analysed. A good example from the literature concerns the Jones (1967) – Gehrels (1971) interaction, discussed earlier, between optimal trade taxes and optimal taxes on foreign borrowing and lending. The first-best package includes two sets of instruments, and "paradoxes" emerge when one instrument (or set of instruments) has to produce a second-best optimum that takes both distortions into account.

A detailed analysis of tariffs as second-best taxes or subsidies on foreign capital, taking into account many complications, such as double tax arrangements, externalities, indivisibilities, and the possibility of indirectly improving the terms of foreign borrowing (when the tax on foreign borrowing is below the optimum), is in Corden (1967). Bhagwati and Brecher (1980) have explored a rather special case of the Jones second-best problem. The country has foreign-owned factors of production which are in completely inelastic supply. From the national point of view first-best policy, of course, would require the rents of the foreign factors to be taxed away, and in the absence of any other distortions (and with the small country assumption) this should be combined with free trade. But they assume zero taxes on foreign capital and show that a move from autarky to free trade may lower national welfare.

An interesting mixed case, particularly relevant to developing countries, is when there is both a labor market imperfection in the form of a wage differential that reduces manufacturing employment and a capital market imperfection that favors manufacturing, the cost of similar capital being generally lower for firms in manufacturing than for the rural sector. First-best policy will consist of subsidising labor in manufacturing while subsidising capital in agriculture; an output subsidy to either sector would be second-best or worse (and a trade tax or subsidy even more so); in fact, it would not be at all clear which sector would have to be subsidised for a Pareto-efficient improvement to be assured.

A final example concerns optimal competition policy for a large country. Auquier and Caves (1979) have considered the case where competition policy can vary the degree of monopoly in an industry which both sells at home and exports. First-best policy from a narrow national point of view would require anti-monopoly policy to make the industry competitive while imposing the orthodox optimal export tax, to ensure that the country's international monopoly power is exploited. They then assume, realistically, that an export tax cannot be imposed (perhaps because of the possibility of retaliation) so that a second-best optimal degree of monopoly – achieved by competition policy alone – will involve trading off the social losses from monopolistic sales at home against the gain from exploiting monopoly power relative to foreigners.

7. Distortions, the budget constraint and optimal tax theory

7.1. The limitations of domestic distortions theory

A striking feature of the standard theory of domestic distortions is the assumption that lump-sum taxes are available and will be used to finance subsidies, or alternatively, that the elasticity of supply of effort is zero, so that it is possible to raise non-lump-sum taxes without creating a distortion relative to leisure. This assumption also underlies the normal habit of ignoring income distribution effects of the various policies advocated. Related to this is the tendency to ignore the role of tariffs as sources of government revenue (a role that is particularly important in developing countries); usually it is assumed that the revenue is remitted to consumers in lump-sum fashion. In addition, the main body of the theory fails to note that there may be limits to the revenue that can be raised, even if lump-sum taxes are available.

A whole range of important issues has thus stayed in recent years outside the mainstream of trade theory. At the same time there have been discussions of these matters, and I propose to bring some of this material, not all of it recent, together. This involves relating optimal tax theory to trade theory.

7.2.   Revenue limits and income distribution effects of correcting a distortion: The Anand – Joshi qualification

The first issue involves the elementary point that there must be limits to the revenue that can be raised. It is relevant when there is a factor market distortion in the form of a rigid real wage, either throughout the economy, as in Brecher (1974), or in one sector, this generating unemployment. It must surely be assumed that the wage rigidity is in post-tax terms, though this is not always specified. Taxes to finance the wage subsidies that are needed to achieve Pareto-efficiency must then be collected from other factors, presumably profits and rents.

The financing problem in the Harris–Todaro case is discussed in Corden (1974) and McCool (1982). The first-best policy, ignoring this financing complication, is a uniform employment subsidy for both sectors; an appropriate subsidy only in manufacturing, or alternatively any subsidy in agriculture, would also yield an improvement in total output, though neither would be first-best. But in both cases the subsidy must not be financed by a tax on wages in the other sector. It must come out of profits and rents. In this case, as in the Brecher model where there is a uniform rigid real wage at too high a level throughout the economy, it is obvious that a financing problem is likely. Even if all profits and rents were taxed away the revenue may be insufficient to finance a subsidy that fully offsets the factor-market distortion.

This possibility that a Pareto-efficient outcome cannot be attained with the usual subsidies even when lump-sum taxes are available has been stressed by Anand and Joshi (1979), and has very general applicability. But the main point in Anand and Joshi (1979) is more subtle. Suppose that enough revenue *could* be raised to finance the wage subsidy needed for the first-best Pareto-efficiency solution. This revenue is then *not* available for redistributive purposes.

Consider a standard model with an urban and a rural sector, a rigid post-tax real wage in the urban sector that keeps employment there below the Pareto-efficiency level, a low-income rural sector and no Harris-Todaro unemployment. If employment in manufacturing is subsidised a proportion of people previously in agriculture may obtain a large rise in income; if the same revenue, derived from taxes on urban profits, were used to subsidise the rural poor directly or indirectly, the income distribution effects would be more favorable, even though the efficiency effects might be adverse. Possibly the taxes would have to be partly raised from the rural sector (urban profits not being enough), and the income distribution may then move in an adverse direction.

Thus income distribution effects cannot be divorced from efficiency effects even though taxes may be lump-sum and would be willingly used for redistribution. This type of argument – more carefully spelt out in Anand and Joshi (1979) – must apply whenever the domestic distortion consists of a rigid factor price that is maintained in post-tax terms. The attempt to move towards Pareto-efficiency by subsidising employment has inevitable income distribution implications, a consideration that standard factor-market-distortions theory has overlooked.

7.3. *Optimal tax theory and domestic distortions*

Optimal tax theory as recently developed – and as pioneered by Ramsey (1927) and popularised by Pigou (1947) – is primarily concerned with the optimal structure of commodity and income taxes when some sectors or activities (notably leisure) are not taxable, so that there are inevitable distortions as a result of taxation. It is highly relevant for international economics. This is obviously not the place to expound it; there is a vast literature which, like the theory of domestic distortions, is somewhat repetitive and contains much overlap. Useful expositions are Dixit (1970), Sandmo (1976) Mirrlees (1976, 1979) and Atkinson and Stiglitz (1980).

The only two papers that are in the mainstream of this new literature and also deal with the open economy seem to be Boadway et al (1973) and Dasgupta and Stiglitz (1974). Also to be noted is Dixit and Norman (1980, ch. 6). I have dealt at length with many of these matters in Corden (1974), which is much indebted to Meade (1955a). But the results are more rigorously supported in the recent optimal-tax literature.

Let us begin with the small country case, so that orthodox optimal tariffs and export taxes are zero. Furthermore, assume away tax collection and subsidy disbursement costs. The important negative result then is that an optimal tax structure designed to raise revenue will not include trade taxes.

Let us also for the moment make the crucial simplifying assumption of a one-consumer economy, so that, in effect, income distribution considerations are assumed away. There will then be an optimal commodity tax structure consisting of non-uniform consumption taxes designed to attain the now-standard Ramsey result. This ensures that reductions in quantities purchased of all taxable goods are of the same proportion, at least provided income elasticities of demand are the same or the tax changes are so small that income effects can be ignored. If demand curves were independent this result would be attained by a structure of "inverse elasticity" taxes – relatively higher taxes for low-elasticity goods. There would be no production taxes. The basic idea is that goods and services which are relatively close substitutes for untaxable goods (a category that may only include leisure, but in some countries would include much more) should be taxed at a lower rate than those which are not close substitutes, or even complements. The aim is to minimise the inevitable distortions resulting from any tax system when some goods cannot be taxed.

Now we come to the aspect relevant to domestic distortions theory. In the optimal tax-subsidy structure there will be (1) taxes to offset external diseconomies and other endogenous domestic distortions on Pigovian lines, just as taught by the theory of domestic distortions, and (2) an optimal tax structure along Ramsey lines to bring revenue required to the desired level. These two tax structures will be added together. This "additivity property" is proven formally in Sandmo (1975).

The matter is a little more complicated when domestic distortions call for subsidies rather than taxes. The general principle is the same, but [as shown in Meade (1955a)], since the revenue effect is negative, and thus higher distorting consumption taxes are needed, the level of the offsetting subsidies may need to be incomplete; the distortions not offset are traded off against the new distortions created as a result of financing the subsidies. The qualitative implications of the theory of domestic distortions are thus not affected: it is first-best to deal with distortions by appropriate subsidies and taxes; but the level of the offsetting may need to be incomplete.

Once income distribution considerations are allowed for, matters become more complicated, as shown in Mirrlees (1976, 1979) and Atkinson and Stiglitz (1980). Non-proportional income taxes would now be combined with non-uniform consumption taxes to raise given revenue and the commodity tax structure must take into account income distribution effects through demand pattern differences between people of different initial endowments. But there are no clear implications for trade or distortions policy other than the considerations raised in Anand and Joshi (1979) which have yet to be systematically built into optimal tax theory.

One more point, from Corden (1974), needs to be added. Trade taxes can actually become first-best devices for dealing with certain domestic distortions if subsidy disbursement costs are sufficiently high.

7.4.   Trade taxes for revenue: Small and large country case

Let us now consider the role of trade taxes for revenue, first for the small and then the large country case. One approach is to set a revenue target, assume no distortions (including income and commodity taxes), ignore income distribution effects (i.e. have a one-consumer model), and then consider the optimal structure of trade taxes, as in Dasgupta and Stiglitz (1974) and Corden (1974). It is interesting that (in the small country case) the full Ramsey analysis is applicable, and the results are essentially the same. The optimal tariff and export structure will be non-uniform. In a model with one exportable and two importables, and with the supply of effort variable, if the import demand curves are independent the "marginal cost of raising revenue" will be equalised on the basis of the inverse elasticity formula: a higher tariff on the lower-elasticity good.

Is it possible to build a model where trade taxes become part of a first-best revenue tax package? This seems at least as important an issue as the optimal structure of a trade tax system given that such taxes are to be used. Here the crucial ingredient must be collection costs – i.e. costs that are relatively higher for income and commodity taxes than for trade taxes. This is surely a realistic assumption for many developing countries. I have suggested in Corden (1974) that relatively low collection costs for trade taxes are the essential requirement for some trade taxes to be first-best revenue-raising devices in the small country model; but a formal model with different collection costs for different types of taxes has yet to be built.

Finally, the role of trade taxes in raising revenue must be considered for the large country case. Here the key article is Boadway, et al (1973). First the orthodox optimal trade tax structure should be imposed. This will yield a given amount of revenue and is costless because it removes a distortion. Additional revenue needs should then be raised by the usual optimal tax structure. They assume away income distribution considerations, so that a Ramsey commodity-tax structure must then be added to the tariff-export tax structure. In a sense the two policies are independent; the tariff and commodity tax formulae are quite distinct, each following from a different body of theory. Nevertheless the actual tariff and tax rates are related. The optimal tariff rates depend on the foreign demand and supply elasticities, which are likely to change with the volume of trade, a volume which in turn depends on the commodity taxes; while the actual commodity tax rates depend, for a given revenue target, on how much revenue is raised by the trade taxes. Boadway et al. (1973) also make public goods supply (and hence revenue needs) endogenous, and in addition they also explore the case where only trade taxes are used for revenue.

8. The cost of protection

How should the welfare cost of protection be measured? This is a complex subject on which there is a large literature, and which cannot be expounded here in detail. But the brevity of the discussion should not be interpreted to mean that the subject is not important. This is the point at which trade theory provides a basis for a vast amount of empirical work.

The cost of protection refers to the efficiency losses imposed by all policy-induced distortions affecting the tradeables-producing sectors directly. The reference point is usually free trade, an existing situation with tariffs, quotas, export taxes, and so on, being compared with a situation where these are all absent. But other reference points are possible: for example, the state of the economy in the absence of particular instruments (e.g. some tariffs set at zero), while others stay at positive levels; or, alternatively, the state of the economy with an optimal setting of all the instruments.

If there are terms of trade effects to be exploited and free trade is the reference point, the cost of protection may turn out to be negative. In the subsequent discussion in this section we shall make the small country assumption, so that there are no terms of trade benefits to be reaped from protection. The costs of protection are then normally decomposed into a *production cost* and a *consumption cost*, referring to the two types of distortion that can be clearly separated in the small country case.

It is worth noting that a cardinal approach underlies these calculations, since it is not really welfare that is being measured but rather [to quote Michaely (1977) with regard to the loss from tariff protection] "the value of the goods (in terms of one of them) which could be taken away from the community when it pursues a free trade policy and still leave it as well off as it is under tariff protection."

The early papers on the cost of protection are Corden (1957b) and Johnson (1960). Of the numerous applications of the theory, an outstanding example is Magee (1972), which calculates the cost of protection for the United States, and is notable for taking into account import quotas, voluntary export restraints and adjustment costs. There is a survey in Corden (1975) – which refers extensively to empirical work – and a careful exposition of all the key theoretical issues in this field is in Michaely (1977). Aspects of this subject are discussed more fully in Chapter 11. On effective rates of protection (ERP) see Corden (1971) and on domestic resource cost (DRC) Krueger (1966) and Bruno (1972b). Recent developments have been mainly concerned with cost-benefit analysis, a closely related (if not the same) field, which is discussed in Section 9.

Four key distinctions are relevant for understanding the concept of the cost of protection, and how it relates to other measurement concepts: firstly, the distinction between the average tariff and tariff dispersion, secondly, the distinction between marginal and total costs; thirdly, the distinction between partial and general equilibrium; and fourthly, the distinction between effective protection and domestic resource costs.

When there are many imports, and hence many tariff rates, the cost of a tariff system is related not just to the level of the average tariff – a concept that raises various measurement issues expounded in Michaely (1977) – but also to the dispersion of tariff rates. Distortion costs result from the non-uniformity of nominal and effective tariff structures, these giving rise to the largest part of the total cost of protection when domestic export supply and exportable demand elasticities are low relative to the elasticities of substitution in demand and supply between different importables.

Effective rates of protection (ERPs) and domestic resource cost rate (DRCs) – the distinction between which will be discussed below – normally refer to marginal or incremental costs, not total costs. Thus calculations of *rates* of protection and of rates of divergence between private and social cost are ingredients in cost of protection calculations, as well as being of interest as guides to understanding resource allocation effects ex-ante and ex-post. But the distortion or total costs are areas – usually "triangles" – which depend on the amount of protected output as well as on the divergence for each marginal unit of output between private and social cost.

Turning to the distinction between partial and general equilibrium, in the early stages of development of this subject there were many partial equilibrium calculations. But if the cost of protection is calculated for just one product something must be assumed about protection elsewhere. The partial equilibrium approach is really only legitimate if it is assumed that there is no (or little) protection elsewhere. With regard to general equilibrium calculations, firstly this requires account to be taken of a real exchange rate adjustment that would be associated with a removal or reduction of tariffs and other devices. Secondly, it requires focus on *relative* ERPs (or DRCs).

The importance of *relative* (rather than absolute) ERPs needs particular stress. Assume a small country model and complete absence of all distortions, whether policy-induced or endogenous, other than tariffs and other trade taxes and subsidies, all these being taken into account in ERP calculations. Furthermore, focus only on production effects. There will be a scale of ERPs referring to all tradeables, whether importables or exportables, and a cost of protection will result if there is some non-uniformity in this scale. In a two-product model the cost will be greater the more the two ERPs diverge. Thus absolute levels of ERPs are not of interest in themselves – they give no indication of possible costs of protection – but are only of interest as ingredients in the total picture, where relative rates matter. The marginal cost of protection will be measured essentially by the difference between the rates, though in a multi-good model, this is not a simple idea. Furthermore, as stressed above, cost is a total not a marginal concept, so account must also be taken of the size of the resource allocation effects.

Finally, there is the distinction between ERPs and DRCs, both being the potential ingredients in the total production-distortion cost calculations. This question of the relationship between ERPs and DRCs has given rise to an extensive discussion, starting with Balassa and Schydlowsky (1968) and followed by Bruno (1972b), Krueger (1972), Balassa and Schydlowsky (1972), Findlay (1973, ch. 9), Michaely (1977), Srinivasan and Bhagwati (1978) and Bhagwati and Srinivasan (1979). See also Chapter 11.

ERPs normally take into account all policy-induced distortions affecting the tradeables sector directly, notably tariffs, export taxes and subsidies, import quotas, and perhaps consumption taxes and subsidies on inputs as well as production taxes and subsidies. If there are no other distortions a DRC calculation will yield the same result. But if there *are* other distortions, whether policy-induced or endogenous (such as a divergence between the social and the private cost of labor and capital, or a failure to tax foreign-owned factors of production at optimal levels) the DRC concept takes these into account. Thus the latter is clearly a more complete – in fact, the correct – concept to use for normative analysis, even though, in practice, comprehensive DRC calculations are difficult. In countries where the main distortions are policy-induced ones in the tradeable sector, ERP calculations may provide some guide not only to resource allocation effects of these particular distortions but also to welfare effects.

Let us now turn to some further developments in the cost-of-protection area, beginning with a comparison between tariffs and quotas, and then looking at some other costs, notably costs of smuggling and of "rent-seeking".

The cost of protection may differ, depending on whether a tariff or a quota is used. This comparison has several aspects. One is concerned with the production and consumption-distortion costs created by the two devices when there is a single import-competing producer, the tariff and quota being set to achieve the same target. This has been analysed in McCulloch (1973) in a partial equilibrium model, this paper being part of the "equivalence literature" discussed earlier.

She considers four possible targets or "equivalences", namely a domestic price target, a domestic profit target, an output target, and an import target. In the case of the common price target the quota imposes a lower cost; this is because it allows the domestic consumer to be exploited more (by raising the price) without imports having to be cut so much. With a common profit target the answer is ambiguous, but in the two most interesting cases – common output and common import level – the welfare cost of the quota is greater. Considering the last case, the point is that, for a given level of imports, the quota creates a domestic monopoly situation and so leads to a higher price and lower output. Thus the extra cost of the quota is the standard cost of monopoly.

The various protective devices have some other costs, not yet noted. Firstly, there are the collection costs (which should be called administration costs in the case of quotas) mentioned earlier. In many developing countries the prime motive for tariffs is revenue-raising, and this reflects the fact that collection costs for tariffs are usually much lower than for alternative taxes, such as income tax. Secondly, there are tariff and quota evasions costs, i.e. the real resource costs of smuggling. These have been analysed in detail, and fitted into a general equilibrium framework, by several authors, notably Bhagwati and Hansen (1973) and Sheikh (1974).

Thirdly there are the "rent-seeking" costs resulting from an import or export quota. As Krueger (1974) has pointed out in a celebrated article, real resources will be expended to obtain import licences and, at the limit, the whole of the potential monopoly profits from these licences could be dissipated in such costs, assuming competition among potential licence recipients. This is, of course, only a limiting case, the actual outcome depending on the precise licence dispensing arrangements. Some part of the expenditure by potential recipients may consist of bribes, direct and indirect, to licence dispensers, in which case there is simply an income redistribution effect.

Fourthly, there are the costs of lobbying to get particular tariffs or quotas imposed. Both tariffs and quotas generate rents for the protected producers (at least the intra-marginal ones), so that this type of rent-seeking is concerned not with obtaining licences from a given quota but rather with getting the benefits of protection. The extent of these costs depends on the political and institutional arrangements. Some countries have an implicit policy of providing tariffs, quotas or subsidies that are "made to measure" so as to minimise rents for any given protection objective [Corden (1974)]. This policy usually leads to complex tariff and subsidy structures, with frequent variations, and requires a considerable information input – information being required about costs of domestic producers, as well as about present and prospective import prices. Because of the large element of discretion that such a system inevitably involves, it is likely to generate a great deal of lobbying.

Finally, it might be noted that these costs of collection, smuggling, rent-seeking and lobbying could, conceivably, not be true "costs". Normally one would expect the resources that are used in these various activities, and hence are withdrawn from other uses, to have had some positive value elsewhere, so that there is a genuine output loss resulting from these "directly unproductive activities". When there are distortions in the system their shadow prices may, of course, diverge from their market prices. Bhagwati (1982) has stressed the extreme possibility that a shadow price may be negative so that, paradoxically, a social gain results from the withdrawal of resources into "directly-unproductive activities". As usual, this is a paradox resulting from a second-best situation, namely one where distortions have not been removed or appropriately offset by policy.

9. Cost–benefit analysis for the open economy

Social cost benefit analysis or project appraisal takes various distortions in the economy as given and makes recommendations for optimal decisions with regard to particular projects. The problem is thus a typical second-best one. It differs from the traditional trade theory approach in the following way. In trade theory we tend to ask (for example): what is the optimal tariff level for one industry when the tariff structure elsewhere is given. For example, in a three-good model, with one exportable (X) and two importables (M_1 and M_2), if the export tax (subsidy) is fixed at zero, and there is a given tariff on M_1, what is the optimal tariff for M_2? The implication is that, once the second-best optimal tariff (or subsidy) for M_2 is imposed, quantity adjustments follow. We set the price signals right and then expect the various decentralised decision-makers to decide whether it pays them to establish or not establish a project (i.e. expand an industry). By contrast, in cost-benefit analysis, an all-or-nothing quantity recommendation is made on the basis of shadow prices, and then the price policy required to implement the recommendation – i.e. a subsidy to cover losses, tax to absorb profits, or a tariff – follows by implication. But this implication has not been fully spelt out.

Additionally, in cost–benefit analysis investment in one project in a large economy is considered, and other policy instruments are held constant. The approach is, more or less, partial equilibrium and, if not marginal, at least incremental. In trade theory we also have such analyses, but mostly we focus on general equilibrium and the broader economy – for example, on one importable out of two in a three-good model. In ERP theory and related areas the concern is with the whole structure of a complex tariff system.

The basic structure of the problems posed in the theory of domestic distortions and the theory of second-best tariff-making is the same as in social cost-benefit analysis: optimise subject to specific constraints, which include some policy-imposed distortions. The fundamental question-mark about this sort of approach is also identical. Why should one expect a government to follow an optimal policy in one part of the system when it pursues non-optimal policies elsewhere? This is particularly true when, as is usual in the cases considered, the second-best optimal policies pursued in one part help to modify the effects of the other policies. Is someone being fooled? Or is one thinking of independent agencies of government? These questions have not been asked much by writers on second-best tariff-making, but they have been asked with regard to cost–benefit analysis, notably by Sen (1972), Joshi (1972) and Bertrand (1974).

The literature on cost–benefit analysis in the open economy started with Little and Mirrlees (1969). They produced an improved version with Little and Mirrlees (1974). This highly innovative but somewhat unclear OECD-sponsored "Manual" brought the project appraisal ship straight into the trade theory pond. It recommended that f.o.b. export and c.i.f. import prices (i.e. "border prices") should provide the basis for shadow-pricing all goods, and all factors used to make these goods, directly and indirectly – including non-tradeables that are inputs in tradeables. Domestic market prices distorted by tariffs and other interventions should be by-passed. The simple version of this approach makes the small country assumption, so that its strategic simplification is the same as that of ERP theory. Hence all the same issues have come to the fore – notably how to treat non-tradeable inputs, how to value non-tradeables consumed at home, and the question of the real exchange rate. A rival UNIDO-sponsored manual – Dasgupta et al. (1972) – was produced a little later, with a good deal of overlap with the OECD Manual, but as this put somewhat less emphasis on the foreign trade side I give it less attention here.

Numerous papers have been produced aiming to clarify the two manuals and to relate them. People unfamiliar with trade theory produced these two manuals, and yet to a great extent – especially in the Little–Mirrlees case – they were concerned with the issues which trade theorists had been sorting out, whether in the theory of domestic distortions and second-best tariff-making or in ERP theory. A trade theory take-over was thus inevitable.

The pioneering article in this respect was Joshi (1972), followed by Lal (1974), Corden (1974, Chapter 14) and various contributions to an *Oxford Economic Papers* Symposium, namely Balassa (1974a, 1974b), Scott (1974), Bertrand (1974) and Batra and Guisinger (1974). These papers, all written by authors familiar with trade theory, clarified a great deal and made many of the points which later authors were to emphasise or spell out more rigorously. The fullest treatment was in Lal (1974). Joshi (1972) made the key point that commodities must be "fully-traded" – and not just tradeable – if the Little–Mirrless method of valuing everything at border prices was to apply. Any change in demand for a fully-traded good must be wholly reflected in extra imports of it or fewer exports at constant prices, and any change in supply must also be reflected wholly in foreign trade, not domestic demand.

At this early stage a very common misunderstanding was cleared away: some people believed that valuing goods at their prices free of tariffs, etc. was to assume that such tariffs did not or would not exist. Thus it was thought that the Little–Mirrlees method used a first-best reference point. It was made clear in several of these papers that the great attraction of the Little–Mirrlees method was that it accepted existing distortions and sought to optimise subject to them.

The special role of Findlay and Wellisz (1976) was to present the first fully specified trade theory model that dealt with some of the central issues. In particular, they worked out the shadow prices of factors with trade distortions. With this article the marriage of cost-benefit analysis and trade theory was consummated. This was then followed by Srinivasan and Bhagwati (1978), who built upon Findlay and Wellisz (1976), though without much concern for the earlier literature. In several papers Warr (1977a, 1977b, 1982) has presented fully-specified models which sort out the issue of welfare-maximising shadow-pricing rules with tax and tariff constraints. Also very relevant is Boadway (1978), while Dasgupta and Stiglitz (1974) might also be noted.

While it is not possible here to give a systematic exposition of the whole subject, I shall go through some of the issues that have been discussed.

9.1. Non-tradeables

A project may use non-tradeables (i.e. goods not fully traded) as inputs, or it may draw labor out of the production of such commodities. This presents problems for the simple Little–Mirrlees approach, just as non-tradeable inputs do for the ERP theory. Little and Mirrlees underplayed the significance of goods that are not fully traded. The shadow-pricing rules for non-tradeables have been clearly set out in Warr (1982), though the various difficulties – which Little and Mirrlees tended to skate over – were already noted in several early papers.

There is no real problem when non-tradeables are only inputs into tradeables, whether direct or indirect; they can then be valued at border prices in terms of tradeables output forgone. The complication arises when there is domestic consumption of them. Consumers' surplus analysis (or measurement of "willingness to pay" as Dasgupta et al. (1972) put it) comes then into play. At the margin, that part of non-tradeable inputs which is drawn from domestic consumption of non-tradeables should be valued at prices facing consumers – which will be the market prices facing the project if there are no taxes on these goods. These domestic prices must then be converted into border prices by use of a "conversion factor", which is essentially the inverse of a shadow exchange rate.

9.2. Import quotas

It has been stressed that goods must be "fully-traded" if they are to be legitimately valued at border prices. But if there are fixed import quotas the whole impact of a change on domestic output will fall on domestic demand. In fact, goods with fixed quotas are just like non-traded goods, and should be treated as such, as Joshi (1972) and Lal (1974) have shown.

Thus "tradeables" are not necessarily fully traded. This is a major qualification to the usefulness of the Little-Mirrlees method because in most developing countries – notably India, which so many contributors to this literature have in mind – intervention in trade is principally through quantitative restrictions, not tariffs or other taxes and subsidies. The importance of this matter cannot be over-estimated. A country may have a thoroughly distorted economy as a result of quotas and yet it will be appropriate to value tradeable inputs, for example, at market prices rather than at border prices; *implicit* tariff rates should not be taken into account when calculating shadow wages and prices. On the other hand, if the quotas are not fixed it is necessary to see what the logic of quota determination is. Market pricing may then no longer be correct.

9.3. Terms of trade effects

Removing the small country assumption creates difficulties for the simple version of the Little–Mirrlees approach, just as it does in ERP theory. Ignoring for the moment effects on domestic production and consumption, a change in exports (for example) must be valued in terms of its *marginal* social value, taking into account terms of trade effects.

A fall in exports of a product because a new project has increased domestic demand for it will raise the price of intra-marginal exports and thus yield a gain which is rather like an external economy. The principle is quite simple [Scott (1974)]. But no longer will domestic prices of tradeables stay unchanged as a result of the project. In this example the price of the exportable rises, and so domestic demand falls and production rises. This effect has to be analysed just as if the exportable were a non-tradeable in our earlier analysis [Corden (1974)]. The fall in consumption would be valued in terms of willingness to pay, while the rise in production would be broken down into various elements of cost, principally output of tradeables forgone valued at border prices.

9.4. Budget constraint

An important issue is that of the budget constraint or the "implementation problem". There has been lack of clarity on this in some contributions, including Corden (1974) and Srinivasan and Bhagwati (1978). Suppose a project in the import-competing sector just breaks even at shadow prices and thus should be started, but would make a loss at market prices when it has to sell its product without tariff protection. One possibility would be to cover its loss out of the budget. (The other is to provide a tariff.) I shall now consider this case. Must the distortion costs of raising the revenue to finance this loss – or alternatively the implications of the government reducing its spending appropriately – be taken into account in the shadow-pricing exercise?

In answering this one must make a sharp distinction between two possible causes of why shadow prices and wages diverge from market prices, and hence why the project may break even socially though making a loss at market prices. Essentially the distinction is between non-tax and tax distortions.

(1) Suppose there is a factor-market distortion, such as a rigid real wage or a wage differential, making the market wage higher than the shadow wage. There are no tax or tariff distortions. In that case there will be a budgetary problem: extra income to labor will have to be traded off against reduced income in the hands of the government. Little and Mirrlees (1969, 1974) took this into account, and chose to give a higher weight to income in the hands of the government than to that of labor on the grounds that the former income will be saved and invested, and the latter consumed. This consideration thus led them to raise the shadow wage, reducing the likelihood that a project is viable at shadow prices.

An alternative assumption is that government revenue can be maintained by increasing taxes, but that taxes are distortionary. The shadow wage must then again be adjusted upwards for the distortion cost, again reducing the likelihood that a project is viable at shadow prices. If these adjustments are made to the shadow wage it is, of course, not necessary to make any further adjustments for the budget constraint. The main point is that the Little–Mirrlees approach incorporates the budget constraint problem. It might be added that if a protective tariff were provided for the project output, so that it breaks even at market prices, the consumption-distortion effects of the tariff would have to be incorporated in the calculation.

(2) Suppose now that there are given distorting tariffs and taxes, but no factor market or other distortions. Here an important point has been brought out by Warr (1977b, 1979). When the project just breaks even at shadow prices, and these diverge from market prices only because of taxes, subsidies and tariffs at given ad valorem rates, the loss of the project will be exactly offset by gains in revenue elsewhere. For example, if the project draws labor out of a tariff-protected industry *X*, so that the shadow wage is below the market wage on that account, the reduced output of *X* will lead to an equivalent increase in imports of *X*, and hence to extra tariff revenue. The same argument can be shown to apply to taxes on non-tradeables: if the project draws resources from non-tradeables the indirect revenue effects there will offset the profits or losses of the project.

The key point is that when these indirect effects are taken into account and there are no non-tax distortions, there is no budgetary problem. Hence there is no need to allow for any distortionary effects of extra taxes.

Another approach, yielding the same answers, is provided by Boadway (1978). When the only distortions are tax and tariff distortions, the net effect of the project on the budget indicates the gain from the project. If it just breaks even in terms of shadow prices then, presumably, it is a marginal project. In that case, also, there is no budgetary effect. If it is socially profitable there will also be a gain to the budget. Thus Boadway (1978) suggests that inputs and outputs might as well be priced at market prices, the net revenue effect being added on top to yield social benefits or costs.

9.5. *Factor proportions variable*

Consider again the case where the only distortion is a trade tax distortion. We wish to compare the cost-benefit approach with the trade theory approach. Let there be two existing industries, M and X, the former with a given tariff. The proposed project draws resources out of these two industries. First, assume that there is only one mobile factor, labor (or, alternatively, several, but employed in fixed proportions in the project). Each industry has, in addition, a specific factor. The shadow wage facing the project will now be below the market wage, because the tariff for M has over-priced the market wage. In the absence of a tariff for this new activity it could be optimal even if it makes a pre-subsidy loss.

Now let us put the problem in traditional trade theory terms. Rather than deciding first on the project by shadow-pricing procedures and then providing the necessary subsidy or tariff to make it privately viable (or finance its losses if it is a public project), we provide a second-best optimal subsidy or tariff. Ignoring consumption distortion effects for the purpose of this discussion, a second-best tariff, an output subsidy or a subsidy to labor input can all equally do the job, the second-best optimal rates of subsidy being (along Lipsey–Lancaster lines) positive but less than the given tariff for M, assuming that labor is drawn both from M and from X. Standard second-best trade theory leads thus to the same result as simple project analysis theory. This point, with this sort of example, was made in Corden (1974).

The advance made by Findlay and Wellisz (1976) was to consider this issue for the standard Heckscher–Ohlin case with *two* mobile factors employed in each industry in variable proportions. The tariff for M will then have altered the factor price ratio. There will be a separate shadow price for each factor. In parallel, second-best optimal subsidy-tax policy will then require factor subsidies (and possibly taxes) at different rates, while an output subsidy or a tariff would be an inferior device. The project needs to employ the factors in proportions different from those for which the distorted market prices provide an inducement. The factor in which M is intensive will tend to be over-priced and the other factor under-priced. It is a curious result that when a policy-created trade distortion cannot be removed (first-best policy being to remove or offset it directly) the optimal second-best policy is not a trade but a factor-market device.

Srinivasan and Bhagwati (1978) supplemented Findlay and Wellisz (1976) firstly by a very clear exposition of the issue in trade theoretic terms, and secondly by noting that the shadow price for one factor could actually be negative. In the latter case, withdrawal of the factor from the M-cum-X economy actually raises aggregate real output valued at world prices there. This is a case of negative growth yielding a *gain* at world prices, which is the Johnson (1967) story of tariff-induced immiserising growth in reverse.

To complete this discussion, let me note a few other issues that have come up in this literature. It has been much concerned with working out the implications of labor market distortions, this being built into the Little–Mirrlees and the UNIDO shadow wage concepts. All the same issues arise as in the trade theory literature. A rigorous analysis of appropriate shadow wage determination in a trade theory model under various labor market rigidities is in Srinivasan and Bhagwati (1978). The early literature sorted out the question of the "numeraire". Little and Mirrlees proposed foreign exchange as the numeraire with "conversion coefficients" (possibly one standard one) for non-tradeables, including wages. The UNIDO authors proposed domestic market prices, with a shadow exchange rate to convert foreign exchange values. If properly specified these must come to the same thing. This was shown by several of the 1974 authors.

Finally, there is the comparison of the first-best solution – with no trade distortions, and perhaps no other distortions – and the second-best optimal policy with given distortions. The use of a shadow exchange rate based on the first-best solution was recommended in a well-known paper by Bacha and Taylor (1971). It was necessary first for people to see that first-best differed from second-best, and then to compare project calculation outcomes for the two cases. A comparison of results from the two cases is in Findlay and Wellisz (1976).

10. The political economy of protectionism

A major development in the study of trade policy has been the analysis of why tariffs and other interventions are as they are and, in particular, what the role of political factors, of the lobbying process and, more broadly, of political institutions are in determining trade policy. It has involved the application of public choice theory to international trade issues. A standard reference is Caves (1976), an excellent survey of this new branch of international economics is in Baldwin (1982), while the analysis is applied to the study of U.S. policy in Baldwin (1983). As this subject is dealt with in Chapter 12, one question only will be addressed here, namely how the "political economy" issues relate to normative international trade theory.

The main issues can be brought out by referring to the elegant model of Findlay and Wellisz (1982). They present a two-sector, general equilibrium specific factors small country model where two interest groups lobby for and against protection, incurring costs in doing so, the tariff level thus being determined endogenously by a resource – using political process. From a national efficiency point of view two costs are being incurred, first the cost of a non-optimal intervention point being attained – which in this particular model is any departure from free trade – and second the resource costs of lobbying.

If it is correct to say that tariffs and other intervention policies are actually determined endogenously by a lobbying process – or perhaps by some more complex political process taking into account, for example, bureaucratic interests – one might ask whether any role remains for standard normative trade theory. This question was already raised earlier. It is true that normative theory can compare the outcome of the lobbying process with a hypothetical alternative that might be imposed by an efficiency-minded dictator who incurs no information or by-product political costs in attaining his objective. Findlay and Wellisz have done this. But if the lobbying process is inevitable there seems little point in engaging in the usual normative analysis which is concerned with the "national interest". Of course economists can still fulfil a servicing function for the lobbies, generating information or analysis to help the latter attain their ends better. In practice this is an activity that earns many economists a good crust.

Nevertheless, three reasons can be suggested why there may still be some role for standard normative analysis even though trade policies are, apparently, endogenous. Firstly, persons and groups concerned with the national, and not just sectional, interests (and motivated by a variety of considerations) may be part of the lobbying process, and normative analysis provides the information basis for their work. Secondly, normative analysis can show that the lobbies may not be efficient in pursuit of their own interests, since they could all be better off if they followed the efficiency-plus-compensation prescriptions that come out of normative theory. The problem then is to influence the lobbies, so that a politically collusive process replaces a competitive one. Thirdly, normative analysis may show the social inefficiency of the whole competitive political process – which would seem to be an implication of the Findlay and Wellisz (1982) paper – so that it suggests the desirability of a change in institutions to produce a better decision-making process.

Normative theory then provides one reference point for judging institutional arrangements. In other words, lobbying – or the extent of lobbying – need not be taken as given. Of course it needs to be remembered that alternative institutional arrangements will also have costs and need not ensure an optimal outcome.

11. Customs union theory

11.1. Introduction

Finally we come to a large subject, namely customs union theory – and, more generally, the theory of preferential trading arrangements, of which customs union theory is a part. This is a substantial part of international trade theory, with a vast literature, much of it inspired in the nineteen fifties and sixties by the establishment of the European Economic Community.

I shall not go into the early history of the subject, and especially into the discussion of the meaning of trade creation and trade diversion (what I shall call the two "Vinerian effects"). There was some excitement about a pseudo-paradox, namely that a "trade-diverting union" could be welfare-improving because of consumption effects. This was sorted out, primarily by Johnson. It is surely sensible to allow trade creation to embrace both production and consumption effects.

The first important contributions came from Viner (1950), Meade (1955b), Lipsey (1957, 1960), and Lipsey and Lancaster (1956). Johnson (1962) provided a standard exposition at a simple level. Underlying the Lipsey papers was his thesis, published later as Lipsey (1970). I shall refer specifically to later literature below, but here note that, in my view, the most important single contribution after 1960 has come from Vanek (1965). Some of the early debates and the literature up to 1972 are surveyed in Krauss (1972). Recent surveys or expositions are Michaely (1977) and El-Agraa and Jones (1981). A careful analysis of the pioneering contribution of Viner's is in Michaely (1976). Also a major work is Kemp (1969b) which, in the main, is a development and improved exposition of Vanek (1965).

Once one goes beyond very simple models, how is one to sort out this complex subject? Some authors have complained about the taxonomy, about the numerous special cases and "all things are possible" results, and have then added more special models and peculiar results of their own. Thus one must go in search of general propositions that will shed some light on possible outcomes in more than special cases. But it has to be accepted as inevitable that simplifying assumptions have to be made if anything is to be said clearly, and different assumptions may be appropriate for the analysis of different real-world situations. I propose to discuss at some length the distinctions between different models.

11.2. Two assumptions

Running through much of the literature – and in sections of the main books – are two assumptions, which I shall call the *non-optimality assumption* and the *small union assumption*. The first assumption means that it is assumed that the partners of the union start in a non-optimal tariff-distorted situation and establish a union (or preferential area of some kind) which also has a set of tariffs relative to the outside world that may be non-optimal. Thus, as has been recognised so often, customs union theory (of this orthodox kind) represents an application – in fact, one of the first – of second-best theory. This non-optimality assumption is by no means unreasonable: it is plausible to suppose that governments impose tariffs and form unions for non-economic reasons, or possibly on the basis of bad economic analysis, and economists simply analyse the welfare effects of policy decisions, however unsatisfactory they may seem if only Pareto-efficiency criteria are taken into account. Later I shall review the literature that removes this assumption; but to start with, I shall accept it.

The small union assumption is that the partners (usually assumed to be *two* partners – countries A and B) face a Large Outsider – country C – which presents them with given terms of trade. This is a special case of the small country assumption which trade theorists have found so useful in other fields, such as ERP theory. This assumption is a major simplification; obviously, it must be removed in due course. There is an extensive literature analysing terms of trade effects of a union with respect to outsiders. But, again, it seems a useful starting point to make that assumption.

11.3. *The two-good model*

Early expositions of the main elements of customs union theory – trade creation and trade diversion effects, and the distinction between the domestic production and consumption elements of trade creation – were presented from the point of view of one of the partner countries alone (country A). It imports one product, which is obtainable from either country B or country C at a given price (in terms of A's export) from each source, C being initially the cheaper source. Country A exports the other product to both B and C. This has been represented both in a partial equilibrium form by Johnson (1962) and in a general equilibrium model by Michaely (1965).

This popular model is a special case of the more general two-product model but has, at least, two limitations: first, it implies that there is no trade between B and C, so that there is an asymmetry in the potential union; secondly, because it makes not only C but also B a large country presenting A with a given price ratio, it leads to "sudden-death" effects: either A imports all of the product from C or it imports it all from B, and thus, only if there is such a complete switch of source will there be any trade diversion effects of the union.

The next big step was taken by Vanek (1965), and further expounded and developed in Kemp (1969b), with an explicit three-country two-good model, where neither of the partners is large relative to each other and effects for each are shown explicitly.

As Vanek made very clear, there are then two distinct possibilities: either the two partners don't trade with each other but export the same product to country C (in which case they are *similar*) or they trade with each other and only one of them trades with C (they are *dissimilar*). In a two-good model it is not possible for the partners to trade with each other and at the same time for both to trade with C. If they are similar, and if they keep their tariffs on imports from C constant, the formation of a free trade area will have no effects; there is neither trade creation nor trade diversion. The only aspect of the union that matters is the nature of the common external tariff and how it compares with their initial tariffs. Vinerian effects thus disappear. This is therefore an interesting case only if one wishes to focus on the common external tariff.

If the partners are dissimilar – and if A is the country that trades with C – some surprising and asymmetrical results emerge. The removal (or reduction) of A's tariff on imports from B will have no effect on prices within A (which are given by trade with C) and thus will have *no* trade creation effects. But there will be a trade diversion effect, the cost of which is borne by A. In addition A will lose its tariff revenue on imports from B, and the intra-union terms of trade will shift against A. As for B's tariff reduction on imports from A, this will further increase trade between A and B at the expense of trade with C, and yield a further gain to B and loss to A. Thus in this very special case the establishment of a free trade area yields a gain to B, the country that does not trade with the outsider, and a loss to A.

While some insights can be derived from such a model – which has been so thoroughly explored by Vanek and Kemp – it does not seem to be an ideal paradigm when it yields such extreme and asymmetrical results. It will surely not be suggested as a possible generalisation that countries that trade with outsiders always lose from the establishment of a customs union. Incidentally, the results stated here depend on a number of assumptions, notably that neither good is inferior, and that flows of trade do not cease or are not reversed. Furthermore, both Vanek (1965) and Kemp (1969b) explore at length the cases where the terms of trade relative to C are variable. But, for the moment, I shall continue to adhere to the small-union assumption.

11.4. The three-good Meade model

An alternative paradigm, which has also been presented in the literature, is completely symmetrical, with three countries and *three* goods. This seems to provide a better basis for expounding the main customs union issues. Each country exports one product and imports two. Each country can be assumed to produce all three products, although this is not essential. I shall call this the Meade Model, since it originates in Meade (1955b, ch. 3), though at that point Meade assumed each country only produced one good, so only consumption effects were allowed for. The model (with each country only producing one good) can also be found in the Appendix of Vanek (1965) and in Lipsey (1970). It has recently been given a thorough and rigorous exposition by McMillan and McCann (1981). A useful comparison of several three-good customs union models is in Lloyd (1982).

In this Meade Model, given that C trades in all three products and the small-union assumption is made, the duty-free prices of all three goods are given by C. This assumes, of course, that C's own tariffs are given. Hence the terms of trade are completely fixed for each partner: the establishment of the union leads neither to terms of trade changes relative to C nor to intra-union terms of trade changes. This, in turn, means that when A reduces its tariff on imports from B all the effects are felt by A, and vice versa for a tariff reduction by B. In effect C is a sponge that absorbs all external effects.

There is an important *additivity implication* of this constant-terms-of-trade assumption. If A obtains a net welfare gain as a result of joining the union, this will also be its contribution to the gain for the union as a whole and for the world as a whole. The union and world gains will consist of two parts: the gain (or loss) from A reducing its tariffs on imports from B, and the gain (or loss) from B reducing its tariffs on imports from A. One can thus present a welfare analysis for one of the partners only, as if it were a small country, and the result can be regarded as an ingredient in the union and world effects. The same type of analysis also applies to the other partner. The additivity implication is that for the union and the world effects one just adds up the separate partner effects.

Before briefly putting the Meade Model to work, two limitations of it should be noted. First (unlike the two-good model), there are no intra-union terms of trade effects; these can be introduced with some variation, as I shall suggest later. Secondly, there is no "orthodox" trade diversion effect since no country has the potential of importing an identical product from more than one source. The equivalent of the trade diversion effect is a shift in the pattern of imports away from the good produced by C towards the *different* good produced by the partner. The "import pattern effect" replaces "orthodox trade diversion".

Discussion of the common external tariff can be postponed for the moment. Thus, like early customs union theory, it will be assumed at this stage that the partners keep unchanged their respective tariffs on imports from C. This implies that, unless their tariffs happened to be the same initially, a free trade area rather than a customs union is being established and that there are appropriate natural obstacles (through transport costs) or legal obstacles to *trade deflection* – i.e. to goods from C being imported through that partner country which has the lower external tariff for final absorption in the other partner.

We now consider any one partner country, say country A. Two more key assumptions have to be made to get some traditional results. The first is the *substitution assumption*. The three goods must be net substitutes in that country. If it only produces one product, that is a straightforward concept; but if it both consumes and produces all three, the assumption means that they are net substitutes in consumption *and* production: when the price of product 1 rises relative to that of 2 and 3, consumption of 2 and 3 rises (quite apart from any income effect) and production of both falls. Thus imports go up or exports fall of these two goods. Secondly, it is assumed at this stage that, before the union is established, country A has the same tariff on both of its imports, i.e. *initial tariff uniformity* is assumed.

In this model, given these assumptions, many familiar results emerge. The main point is that there will be a trade diversion (or "import pattern") effect, yielding a welfare loss, and a trade creation effect, through more total trade, yielding a welfare gain. Extra imports by A from B will have both a trade diversion and a trade creation component. Clearly the extent of welfare effects depends, among other things, on the sizes of substitution elasticities on the production and consumption side. All this applies also to preferential tariff reduction that does not go so far as to establish complete free trade between the partners.

The two assumptions that I have just mentioned can then be removed.

What happens when the three goods are *not* all net substitutes for each other in A? If two goods are zero net substitutes ("independent") then one of the two effects – either trade creation or trade diversion – will disappear. For example, if A's export product and the product imported by A from B were zero net substitutes, there would be no trade creation, so there would have to be a loss from the establishment of the union as long as the products imported from B and C are substitutes. If the product imported from B is a complement of A's export product there can be no trade creation gain, and in fact there will be trade contraction as a result of the union. If the product imported from B is complementary with that imported from C there will be no trade diversion loss. A focus on these complementarity possibilities is in McMillan and McCann (1981).

Removing the assumption of initial tariff uniformity means that a change in the import pattern resulting from the union may lead to a gain. This is shown in Corden (1976). Suppose we eliminate the trade creation effect by assuming that A's export product and the product it imports from B are zero net substitutes, so that the volume of trade will not change as a result of A reducing its tariff on B's product. If the initial tariff on the product coming from B was higher than that from C, reducing it will raise welfare until it is equal to the tariff on C's product, and further reductions will lower welfare again. On balance, welfare may rise as a result of the shift in the import pattern; there is an element of "trade re-diversion". There can thus be a gain even though trade creation is assumed away.

11.5. Broadening the model, and intra-union terms of trade effects

Each of the two paradigms has something of value. The two-good model allows for orthodox trade diversion and for intra-union terms of trade effects. On the other hand it is quite asymmetrical. Its greatest limitation is that one cannot simultaneously have Vinerian trade creation/diversion effects and also have trade by both partners with the Outsider. The three-good Meade Model has the opposite virtues. It is then natural to consider various amalgams. A discussion of some of these issues of appropriate choice of models is in Collier (1979).

Berglas (1979) has presented the most comprehensive customs union model since Kemp (1969b). His three-good model *is* something of a compromise between the two original paradigms. Country A imports good 1 from both B and C – the key feature of the two-good model – so that Berglas gets the various results associated with that model – and country B imports good 2 from A and good 3 from C, so that there can be an import pattern effect (trade diversion) as a result of B's tariff reduction on good 2. But the model is not symmetrical.

As already pointed out, the Meade Model does not have any *intra-union terms of trade effects*, while in the two-good model there is such an effect, but it is not symmetrical. It is possible to construct a four-good model which does produce such effects symmetrically as a by-product of orthodox trade diversion. But one might prefer to display intra-union terms of trade effects *not* as a by-product of orthodox trade diversion, but rather to separate them out.

Suppose that there were two goods traded between the partners that were not traded at all with C – i.e. that from the point of view of the union as a whole, two goods were "non-traded". Mutual tariff reduction on these goods would then lead to an intra-union terms of trade change, which could favor A or B. To isolate this completely we could assume that A and B exported the identical good to C, and also imported the same good. Thus the partners would be "similar", and the prices in trade with each other would not be set by C. (In this case A exports 1 to B, B exports 2 to A, both export 4 to C, and C exports 3 to both.) There would be no orthodox trade diversion, but there would be an import pattern effect. The model that Collier (1979) proposes is rather like this.

11.6. *The common external tariff*

The early literature ignored the effects of establishing a common external tariff (CET), and was, in fact, analysing a free trade area. In practice the choice of a formula for the CET is a major aspect of the establishment of a customs union. In general, the CET could be established on any basis, but usually some kind of averaging procedure is used. Some tariffs on imports from C will then go up and some down.

Working within the Meade Model, if country A was initially the higher tariff country with regard to imports from C, its tariff will be reduced, while B's will be increased. We can imagine these adjustments to take place after a free trade area has been established, and for the CET effects to be superimposed on the usual trade creation and trade diversion effects. For A there will be *trade expansion* as a result, leading to a welfare gain, and for B there will be *trade contraction*. These are standard gains-from-trade or cost-of-protection effects.

Let us look at the trade expansion effect in more detail. When A reduces its tariff on C this expands trade with C partly by leading to more total trade for *A* and partly by reducing its trade with B, in the latter case, in effect, moderating the trade diversion effect yielded by the free trade area. Both responses yield a welfare gain, and it seems best to separate the combined "trade expansion (with C) effect" of the CET from the Vinerian effects of the free trade area. The same argument applies symmetrically with respect to B's increase in its tariff on imports from C, in which case there is trade contraction, leading to a welfare loss.

The CET could be established on various other principles, such as fixing it at the level of A's or at B's initial tariff. Of course, given the small-union assumption, it would be optimal to bring it down to zero, but this raises the optimality issues to which I come later.

An important concept introduced by Vanek (1965) is the *compensating common tariff*. He defines this as that CET "which would keep the rest of the world as well off as it was before the union". Since we are still working within the small-union model, the rest of the world is not affected by the establishment of the union, and the concept has to be re-interpreted here. It can be defined as the CET that keeps the volume of trade with C constant: trade expansion (resulting from the CET being lower than the initial tariffs on imports from C) will thus offset exactly the trade diversion effect. The union is then left with the trade creation gain.

One other aspect of the CET must be mentioned, namely the disposition of the tariff revenue. This is a most important matter, as all observers of the European Economic Community know, but there has not been much theory about it. The models all assume that the revenue is redistributed to the partners in proportion to their absorption of C's imports. But, of course, in the absence of such full automatic redistribution, the welfare effects on the partners separately cannot be analysed without adding the effects that follow from formulae for use and distribution of the tariff revenue.

11.7. External terms of trade effects

Let us now remove the small-union assumption and allow for external terms of trade changes of a customs union, as pioneered in Mundell (1964), and discussed in Vanek (1965), Kemp (1969b), Michaely (1977), Berglas (1979), and Riezman (1979). First we hold external tariffs constant, and then we introduce the CET.

There is some presumption that the terms of trade would turn against C because of the trade diversion effect. This is clearly so in the two-good model. A favorable terms of trade effect for the union must then be added to the trade creation and diversion effects.

If more than two goods are traded with C the direction of the terms of trade effect is not quite so certain: one may get the paradoxical outcome that the

Outsider's terms of trade actually improve relative to the union. If C imports 1 and 2 from the union, and the relative prices of 1 and 2 change, the terms of trade measured in terms of good 3 (C's export) might improve in terms of 1 but worsen in terms of 2. Because of intra-union terms of trade changes (i.e. changes in the ratio of the price of good 1 to the price of good 2) C's terms of trade could thus improve.

Coming back to the normal case, where the union's terms of trade improve, it is to be noted that this favorable effect is essentially a result of trade diversion, which – with constant external terms of trade – would lead, of course, to a welfare loss. We have then the same trade-off as in the case of the orthodox optimal tariff, and presumably there is a degree of trade diversion that will maximise the union's welfare gain (or minimise the loss). If the original tariff levels happened to be at the optimal tariff level from the point of view of the union as a whole, then the establishment of the union (really a free trade area at this stage) would have to lead to a welfare gain, essentially because of trade creation. In other cases the welfare effect seems unclear, though one can construct special cases.

So far we have not introduced the CET. One can use Vanek's concept of the compensating common tariff (CCT) as an intermediate step in the analysis. First we can imagine that the union adjusts its external tariffs so as to establish the CCT. This will require external tariff cuts, yielding trade expansion, which will offset trade diversion, so that the external terms of trade stay unchanged. Only trade creation remains, so that a gain for the union is assured. Next we consider the movement from this CCT to the CET, the latter being based on some formula or negotiations, and involving increases or decreases in tariffs. Whether this further move raises or lowers welfare depends on whether it is a move towards or away from the union's orthodox optimal tariff (and, when more than one good is traded with C, optimal tariff *structure*).

One complication must still be introduced. So far we have (implicitly) held constant the tariffs of the Outsider, C. But the union may have stronger bargaining power relative to C than the separate partners, so that it may succeed in getting C's tariffs reduced, possibly in return for some modification in its CET. Clearly, the lower C's tariffs the better the union's terms of trade (given its own CET). This issue has been fully explored by Arndt (1968, 1969).

11.8. Can a customs union be optimal?

Let us now remove the non-optimality assumption. There are many aspects of the optimality issue. Why are customs unions formed? Is unilateral tariff reduction as good as, or better than, forming a union? This particular issue has recently been reopened by Wonnacott and Wonnacott (1981). Why not establish an optimal tariff? Essentially the literature is concerned with the search for "economically rational" customs unions. To some extent it has been successful, but one might also hold the view that it is not necessary to show that forming a customs union is first-best in particular circumstances: in the main, unions are formed for non-economic reasons – often as a by-product of nation building – so that the role of the economist is simply to analyse the incidental economic effects. Similarly there is some interest in considering the possible economic effects of national disintegration when this is being considered for non-economic reasons. While the stimulus to the development of customs union theory has been the European Economic Community, its current relevance might be in considering the effects of national *dis*integration, whether in the actual case of Pakistan/Bangladesh or the possible case (for example) of Canada.

Cooper and Massell (1965a) made the simple point that for a small country unilateral tariff reduction was always preferable to joining a customs union, since it was obviously better to get trade creation alone rather than trade creation combined with trade diversion. In effect they were just rediscovering Viner's central proposition that the customs union was a second-best (or worse) policy, to be explained, as I have stressed, by non-economic motivations. But the crucial feature of the Cooper-Massell model was the the terms of trade were given (which would follow, for example, from the small-union assumption combined with the Meade Model).

The simplicity of the Cooper-Massell argument is destroyed once intra-union terms of trade effects are allowed for, even though the small-union assumption is still maintained. If A unilaterally reduced its tariffs, rather than forming a union, it would avoid the trade diversion loss, but would also forgo the gain to it from B reducing its tariffs. When they reciprocally reduce tariffs the intra-union terms of trade may turn in favor of A and, in spite of the trade diversion loss, joining a union may then be better for A than unilateral tariff reduction by it. But it will still be true for B that unilateral tariff reduction is preferable to joining the union. Furthermore, for A and B combined intra-union terms of trade effects must cancel out, so that for union as a whole (and for each separately *if there is compensation*) a movement to free trade will be preferable to forming a customs union with a positive external tariff.

This leads directly into a more general model, owed to Vanek (1965) and Kemp and Wan (1976). We now allow for external terms of trade effects. Any group of countries can form a union and improve joint welfare provided the common external tariff is adjusted appropriately. If it is fixed at the orthodox optimal level joint union welfare will be maximised, while if it is fixed at the compensating common tariff level some improvement for the union members will be ensured and no loss for outsiders. The crucial emphasis is on *joint* welfare: unless inter-country compensation actually takes place, an improvement for each individual partner is not assured. Assuming that none of the usual arguments for protection apply other than the terms of trade argument, it would then seem to be rational for countries to seek out partners with whom they can form a union, and, above all, agree on compensation arrangements. Kemp and Wan (1976) suggest that "an incentive to form and enlarge customs unions persists until the world becomes one big customs union, that is, until world free trade prevails".

More can be said about the optimality of customs unions, at least from the point of view of the welfare of the partners. Two aspects were already mentioned by Viner (1950) and have been developed by Arndt (1968, 1969). Firstly, countries that are competitive in their trade flows may gain from oligopolistic collusion. If country A raises its tariff on imports from C (or taxes exports to C) this improves not only its own terms of trade, but in this case will also improve B's terms of trade; and the same applies to B. Each generates an externality for the other at the expense of C, so that they would mutually benefit by colluding. Of course, they do not need to form a customs union for this; a cartel would do. But the process is likely to be easier when there is a common commercial policy. Secondly, as has already been mentioned, a larger country or group has stronger bargaining power relative to outsiders, and so will get an outsider's tariffs down more for any given offer of a home-country tariff reduction.

It has to be remembered that the customs union is only a special case of a reciprocal preferential tariff arrangement. The degree of intra-group tariff reduction and of harmonisation of the external tariffs can vary, and, above all, there is flexibility in the choice of partners. The question arises how a collusive preferential arrangement, of which the customs union is an example, compares with the outcome of tariff warfare, as well as with unilateral free trade. And, in addition, there is the question of the optimal choice of partners. The literature on tariff bargaining is relevant here – notably the pioneering paper by Johnson (1965b), and more recently Caves (1974) and Mayer (1981). Caves relates the theory of preferential trading to the theory of monopolistic discrimination. Mayer, in an elegant paper that should lend itself to further exploration, presents a theory of tariff negotiations, asking to what extent countries benefit from tariff negotiations instead of engaging in tariff warfare.

Two influential papers – Cooper and Massel (1965b) and Johnson (1965b) – have explored the theory of customs unions for developing countries. The small union assumption is made, and it is taken as given that a tariff must be used to protect manufacturing industry as a whole, though not any particular sector of it. Production or export subsidies are ruled out. Similarly free trade is ruled out because of the need for protection. Trade with the Outsider is held constant, so that there is no trade diversion. It is then shown that a customs union is more efficient for the union as a whole than separate tariffs because of "market-swapping". Each country specialises in the particular manufactured products in which, within the union, it has a comparative advantage. This is really just the trade creation effect, worked out in detail for a special, but important, case. If there are economies of scale there will also be a "cost-reduction effect" (on which see below).

11.9. Economies of scale

Economies of scale do not find a place in orthodox customs union theory, but have been introduced in partial equilibrium terms (with some attempt at general equilibrium) in Corden (1972), though there were already references in Viner (1950). The exploitation of scale economies is an important motive for customs unions – or proposals for unions – in developing countries, and the theory has been applied to an African case in Pearson and Ingram (1980).

While there can be the usual trade creation and trade diversion effects, there can also be two additional effects. The first is the *cost reduction effect*: as one partner expands its market into the other for a particular product its average costs go down and a gain may be obtained as a result by its home consumers (though, if prices to consumers are given by C's prices, the gain will be in profits). The partner will obtain the usual trade creation gain. But there is also the possibility of a loss from the *trade supression effect*. Suppose there is a given tariff on a product but this was not initially sufficient to protect the relevant industry in A. When the union is formed the potential market is expanded to include that of B, so potential costs fall and production in A begins, replacing imports into both partners from C. For A this is trade suppression and for B trade diversion.

11.10. Other aspects of customs unions

Customs union theory is a branch of protection theory, so that all the issues that can provide arguments for intervention, whether second-best or worse, can be introduced into customs union theory. For example, in the presence of domestic distortions, whether policy-induced or endogenous, a union may turn out to be superior to free trade, even with the small-union assumption, and even though there are trade diversion effects. Much hinges on whether compensation of losers would take place within a country and between countries within a union. If it would not, a careful distinction must be made between welfare effects on various sections within a country, and on the various partners within a union. In fact, the analyses should really allow for various degrees of *compensation probability*.

Account has been taken of effects on X-efficiency – on which see Corden (1970) and Martin (1978), who interpret this as referring to "intensity of managerial effort" – but while these matters attracted particular attention in analyses of the effects of the European Economic Community and in particular in the debates about whether Britain would or would not gain by joining, they do not have any aspects that are special to preferential arrangements.

An interesting recent development concerns the theory of "duty-free zones" or "free economic zones", which are becoming quite common. Several of the concepts of customs union theory seem to be relevant here, though they have not yet been fully applied. Hamada (1974) and Hamilton and Svennson (1982) consider the gain from such a zone when it is designed to attract foreign investment, and show that there is a possibility of welfare loss. Grubel (1982) brings out the very wide applicability of the concept of the free economic zone – well beyond ordinary goods trade – and notes the possibility of "locational trade diversion."

Finally, a recent paper by Tironi (1982) might also be noted. He shows that if there are foreign firms (the profits of which are not included in the welfare maximand) the effects of a union on foreign profits must be introduced explicitly into the welfare calculus (as also with domestic resource cost calculations, and in cost–benefit analysis). He assumes that the supply of foreign capital is held constant. He distinguishes foreign profit creation and diversion effects. Like the Bhagwati and Brecher (1980) model mentioned earlier, this is a case where there is a distortion, namely the failure to tax foreign profits adequately. If it were really true that the foreign capital is in fixed supply then first-best policy would be to tax away all foreign rents. In the realistic case, where the foreign capital supply elasticity is positive but less than infinite, the national interest calls for an optimal rate of tax, as shown by Kemp (1962b).

References

Anand, S. and V. Joshi (1979), "Domestic distortions, income distribution and the theory of optimum subsidy", Economic Journal, 89:336–352.

Arndt, S.W. (1968), "On discriminatory vs. non-preferential tariff policies", Economic Journal, 78:971–979.

Arndt, S.W. (1969), "Customs union and the theory of tariffs", American Economic Review, 59:108–118.

Atkinson, A.B. and J.E. Stiglitz (1980), Lectures on public economics (McGraw-Hill, Maidenhead, Berkshire).

Auquier, A. and R.E. Caves (1979), "Monopolistic export industries, trade taxes, and optimal competition policy", Economic Journal, 89:559–581.

Bacha, E. and L. Taylor (1971), "Foreign exchange shadow prices: A critical review of current theories", Quarterly Journal of Economics, 85:197–222.

Balassa, B. (1974a), "Estimating the shadow price of foreign exchange in project appraisal", Oxford Economic Papers, 26:147–168.

Balassa, B. (1974b), "New approaches to the estimation of the shadow exchange rate: A comment", Oxford Economic Papers, 26:208–211.

Balassa, B. and D.M. Schydlowsky (1968), "Effective tariffs, domestic cost of foreign exchange, and the equilibrium exchange rate", Journal of Political Economy, 76:348–360.

Balassa, B. and D.M. Schydlowsky (1972), "Domestic resource costs and effective protection once again", Journal of Political Economy, 80:63–69.

Baldwin, R.E. (1948), "Equilibrium in international trade: A diagrammatic analysis", Quarterly Journal of Economics, 62:748–762.

Baldwin, R.E. (1952), "The new welfare economics and gains in international trade", Quarterly Journal of Economics, 65:91–101.

Baldwin, R.E. (1969), "The case against infant-industry tariff protection", Journal of Political Economy, 77:295–305.

Baldwin, R.E. (1982), "The political economy of protectionism", in: J.N. Bhagwati, ed., Import competition and response: National Bureau of Economic Research conference report (University of Chicago Press, Chicago and London) 263–292.

Baldwin, R.E. (1983), The political economy of U.S. import policy (forthcoming).

Batra, R.N. and S. Guisinger (1974), "A new approach to the estimation of the shadow exchange rate in evaluating development projects in less developed countries", Oxford Economic Papers, 26:192–207.

Berglas, E. (1979), "Preferential trading theory: The n commodity case", Journal of Political Economy, 87:315–331.

Bertrand, T.J. (1974), "The shadow exchange rate in an economy with trade restrictions", Oxford Economic Papers, 26:185–191.

Bertrand, T.J. and J. Vanek (1971), "The theory of tariffs, taxes and subsidies: Some aspects of the second best", American Economic Review, 61:925–931.

Bhagwati, J.N. (1964), "The pure theory of international trade: A survey", Economic Journal, 74:1–81.

Bhagwati, J.N. (1965), "On the equivalence of tariffs and quotas", in: R.E. Baldwin et al., Trade, growth, and the balance of payments: Essays in honor of Gottfried Haberler (Rand McNally, Chicago, and North-Holland Amsterdam) 53–67.

Bhagwati, J.N. (1968a), "The gains from trade once again", Oxford Economic Papers, 20:137–148.

Bhagwati, J.N. (1968b), "More on the equivalence of tariffs and quotas", American Economic Review, 58:142–146.

Bhagwati, J.N. (1971), "The generalized theory of distortions and welfare", in: J. Bhagwati, R.W. Jones, R.A. Mundell and J. Vanek, eds., Trade, balance of payments and growth: Papers in international economics in honor of Charles P. Kindleberger (North-Holland, Amsterdam) 69–90.

Bhagwati, J.N. (1982), "Directly-unproductive profit-seeking (DUP) activities: A welfare-theoretic synthesis and generalization", Journal of Political Economy, 90:988–1002.

Bhagwati, J.N. and R.A. Brecher (1980), "National welfare in an open economy in the presence of foreign-owned factors of production", Journal of International Economics, 10:103–115.

Bhagwati, J.N.and B. Hansen (1973), "A theoretical analysis of smuggling", Quarterly Journal of Economics, 87:172–187.

Bhagwati, J.N. and V.K. Ramaswami (1963), "Domestic distortions, tariffs and the theory of optimum subsidy", Journal of Political Economy, 71:44–50.

Bhagwati, J.N. and T.N. Srinivasan (1969), "Optimal intervention to achieve non-economic objectives", Review of Economic Studies, 36:27–38.

Bhagwati, J.N. and T.N. Srinivasan (1979), "On inferring resource-allocational implications from DRC calculations in trade-distorted small open economies", Indian Economic Review, 14:1–16.

Bickerdike, C.F. (1906), "The theory of incipient taxes", Economic Journal, 16:529–535.

Boadway, R. (1978), "A note on the treatment of foreign exchange in project evaluation", Economica, 45:391–399.

Boadway, R., S. Maital and M. Prachowny (1973), "Optimal tariffs, optimal taxes and public goods", Journal of Public Economics, 2:391–403.

Brecher, R.A. (1974), "Optimal commercial policy for a minimum-wage economy", Journal of International Economics, 4:139–149.

Bruno, M. (1972a), "Market distortions and gradual reform", Review of Economic Studies, 39:373–383.

Bruno, M. (1972b), "Domestic resource costs and effective protection: Clarification and synthesis", Journal of Political Economy, 80:16–33.

Caves, R.E. (1960), Trade and economic structure (Harvard University Press, Cambridge, Mass.).

Caves, R.E. (1974), "The economics of reciprocity: Theory and evidence on bilateral trading arrangements", in: W. Sellekaerts, ed., International trade and finance: Essays in honour of Jan Tinbergen (International Arts and Sciences Press, White Plains, New York) 17–54.

Caves, R.E. (1976), "Economic models of political choice: Canada's tariff structure", Canadian Journal of Economics, 9:278–300.

Collier, P. (1979), "The welfare effects of customs unions: An anatomy", Economic Journal, 89:84–95.

Cooper, C.A. and B.F. Massell (1965a), "A new look at customs union theory", Economic Journal, 75:742–747.

Cooper, C.A. and B.F. Massell (1965b), "Toward a general theory of customs unions for developing countries", Journal of Political Economy, 73:461–476.

Corden, W.M. (1957a), "Tariffs, subsidies and the terms of trade", Economica, 24:235–242.

Corden, W.M. (1957b), "The calculation of the cost of protection", Economic Record, 33:29–51.

Corden, W.M. (1967), "Protection and foreign investment", Economic Record, 43:209–32.

Corden, W.M. (1970), "The efficiency effects of trade and protection", in: I.A. McDougall and R.H. Snape, eds., Studies in international economics: Monash Conference papers (North-Holland, Amsterdam) 1–10.

Corden, W.M. (1971), The theory of protection (Clarendon Press, Oxford).

Corden, W.M. (1972), "Economies of scale and customs unions theory", Journal of Political Economy, 80:465–475.

Corden, W.M. (1974), Trade policy and economic welfare (Clarendon Press, Oxford).

Corden, W.M. (1975), "The costs and consequences of protection: A survey of empirical work", in: P.B. Kenen, ed., International trade and finance: Frontiers for research (Cambridge University Press, London) 51–91.

Corden, W.M. (1976), "Customs union theory and nonuniformity of tariffs", Journal of International Economics, 6:99–106.

Corden, W.M. and R. Findlay (1975), "Urban unemployment, intersectoral capital mobility and development policy", Economica, 42:59–78.

Dasgupta, P., S. Marglin and A.K. Sen (for UNIDO) (1972), Guidelines for project evaluation (United Nations, New York).

Dasgupta, P.S. and J.E. Stiglitz (1974), "Benefit–cost analysis and trade policies", Journal of Political Economy, 82:1–33.

Deardorff, A.V. (1973), "The gains from trade in and out of steady-state growth", Oxford Economic Papers, 25:173–191.

Dixit, A.K. (1970), "On the optimal structure of commodity taxes", American Economic Review, 60:107–116.

Dixit, A. and V. Norman (1980), Theory of international trade (Cambridge University Press, Cambridge).

Eaton, J. and A. Panagariya (1979), "Gains from trade under variable returns to scale, commodity taxation, tariffs and factor market distortions", Journal of International Economics, 9:481–501.

El-Agraa, A.M. and A.J. Jones (1981), Theory of customs unions (St. Martins Press, New York).

Falvey, R.E. (1975), "A note on the distinction between tariffs and quotas", Economica, 42:319–26.

Findlay, R. (1973), International trade and development theory (Columbia University Press, New York).

Findlay, R. and S. Wellisz (1976), "Project evaluation, shadow prices, and trade policy", Journal of Political Economy, 84:543–552.

Findlay, R. and S. Wellisz (1982), "Endogenous tariffs, the political economy of trade restrictions and welfare", in: J.N. Bhagwati, ed., Import competition and response, National Bureau of Economic Research Conference Report (University of Chicago Press, Chicago and London) 223–243.

Foster, E. and H. Sonnenschein (1970), "Price distortion and economic welfare", Econometrica, 38:281–297.

Gehrels, F. (1971), "Optimal restrictions on foreign trade and investment", American Economic Review, 59:147–159.

Graaff, J. de V. (1949), "On optimum tariff structures", Review of Economic Studies, 17:47–59.

Grubel, H.G. (1982), "Towards a theory of free economic zones", Weltwirtschaftliches Archiv, 118:39–60.

Haberler, G. (1936), The theory of international trade (William Hodge and Co., London).

Haberler, G. (1950), "Some problems in the pure theory of international trade", Economic Journal, 60:223–240.

Hagen, E. (1958), "An economic justification of protectionism", Quarterly Journal of Economics, 72:496–514.

Hamada, K. (1974), "An economic analysis of the duty-free zone", Journal of International Economics, 4:225–241.

Hamilton, C. and L.E.O. Svensson (1982), "On the welfare effects of a 'duty-free zone'", Journal of International Economics, 13:45–64.

Harris, J.R. and M.P. Todaro (1970), "Migration, unemployment and development: A two-sector analysis", American Economic Review, 60, 126–142.

Hatta, T. (1977), "A theory of piecemeal policy recommendations", Review of Economic Studies, 44:1–21.

Hatta, T. and T. Fukushima (1979), "The welfare effect of tariff rate reductions in a many country world", Journal of International Economics, 9:503–511.

Hazari, B.R. (1978), The pure theory of international trade and distortions (Croom Helm, London).

Helpman, E. and A. Razin (1978), A theory of international trade under uncertainty (Academic Press, New York).

Hicks, J.R. (1941), "The rehabilitation of consumers' surplus", Review of Economic Studies, 9:108–116; reprinted in: K.J. Arrow and T. Scitovsky, eds., Readings in welfare economics, American Economic Association Series of Republished Articles 12 (George Allen & Unwin, London, 1969) 325–335.

Johnson, H.G. (1951), "Optimum welfare and maximum revenue tariffs", Review of Economic Studies, 19:28–35.

Johnson, H.G. (1954), "Optimum tariffs and retaliation", Review of Economic Studies, 21:142–153.

Johnson, H.G. (1960), "The cost of protection and the scientific tariff", Journal of Political Economy, 68:327–345.

Johnson, H.G. (1962), "The economic theory of customs union", Chapter 3 in: Money, trade and economic growth (George Allen & Unwin, London) 46–74.

Johnson, H.G. (1965a), "Optimal trade intervention in the presence of domestic distortions", in: R.E. Baldwin et al., Trade, growth, and the balance of payments: Essays in honor of Gottfried Haberler (Rand McNally, Chicago, and North-Holland, Amsterdam) 3–34.

Johnson, H.G. (1965b), "An economic theory of protectionism, tariff bargaining, and the formation of customs unions", Journal of Political Economy, 73:256–283.

Johnson, H.G. (1967), "The possibility of income losses from increased efficiency or factor accumulation in the presence of tariffs", Economic Journal, 77:151–154.

Johnson, H.G. (1970), "A new view of the infant industry argument", in: I.A. McDougall and R.H. Snape, eds., Studies in international economics: Monash Conference papers (North-Holland, Amsterdam) 59–76.

Jones, R.W. (1967), "International capital movements and the theory of tariffs and trade", Quarterly Journal of Economics, 81:1–38.

Joshi, V. (1972), "The rationale and relevance of the Little–Mirrlees criterion", Bulletin, Oxford University Institute of Economics and Statistics, 34:3–32.

Kahn, R.F. (1947), "Tariffs and the terms of trade", Review of Economic Studies, 15:14–19.

Kaldor, N. (1940), "A note on tariffs and the terms of trade", Economica, 7:377–380.

Katrak, H. (1977), "Multi-national monopolies and commercial policy", Oxford Economic Papers, 29:283–291.

Kemp, M.C. (1962a), "The gain from international trade", Economic Journal, 72:803–819.

Kemp, M.C. (1962b), "The benefits and costs of private investment from abroad: Comment", Economic Record, 38:108–110.

Kemp, M.C. (1964), The pure theory of international trade (Prentice-Hall, Englewood Cliffs, N.J.).

Kemp, M.C. (1966), "The gains from international trade and investment: A neo-Heckscher–Ohlin approach", American Economic Review, 65:788–809.

Kemp, M.C. (1968), "Some issues in the analysis of trade gains", Oxford Economic Papers, 20:149–161.

Kemp, M.C. (1969a), The pure theory of international trade and investment (Prentice-Hall, Englewood Cliffs, N.J.).

Kemp, M.C. (1969b), A contribution to the general equilibrium theory of preferential trading (North-Holland, Amsterdam).

Kemp, M.C. and T. Negishi (1969), "Domestic distortions, tariffs, and the theory of optimum subsidy", Journal of Political Economy, 77:1011–1013.

Kemp, M.C. and T. Negishi (1970), "Variable returns to scale, commodity taxes, factor market distortions and their implications for trade gains", Swedish Journal of Economics, 72:1–11.

Kemp, M.C. and H.Y. Wan, Jr. (1972), "The gains from free trade", International Economic Review, 13:509–522; reprinted in: M.C. Kemp, Three topics in the theory of international trade: Distribution, welfare and uncertainty (North-Holland, Amsterdam, 1976) 143–159.

Krauss, M.B. (1972), "Recent developments in customs union theory: An interpretive survey", Journal of Economic Literature, 10:413–436.

Krueger, A.O. (1966), "Some economic costs of exchange control: the Turkish case", Journal of Political Economy, 74:466–480.

Krueger, A.O. (1972), "Evaluating restrictionist trade regimes: Theory and measurement", Journal of Political Economy, 80:48–62.

Krueger, A.O. (1974), "The political economy of the rent-seeking society", American Economic Review, 64:291–303.

Krueger, A.O. and H. Sonnenschein (1967), "The terms of trade, the gains from trade, and price divergence", International Economic Review, 8:121–127.

Krugman, P.R. (1979), "Increasing returns, monopolistic competition, and international trade", Journal of International Economics, 9:469–479.

Krugman, P.R. (1981), "Intraindustry specialization and the gains from trade", Journal of Political Economy, 89:959–973.

Lal, D. (1974), Methods of project analysis: A review (World Bank, Washington).

Layard, P.R.G. and A.A. Walters (1978), Microeconomic theory (McGraw-Hill, New York).

Lerner, A.P. (1934), "The diagrammatical representation of demand conditions in international trade", Economica, 1:319–334.

Lerner, A.P. (1936), "The symmetry between import and export taxes", Economica, 3:306–313.

Lerner, A.P. (1944), The economics of control (Macmillan, New York).

Lewis, W.A. (1954), "Economic development with unlimited supplies of labour", Manchester School of Economic and Social Studies, 22:139–91.

Lipsey, R.G. (1957), "The theory of customs unions: Trade diversion and welfare", Economica, 24:40–46.

Lipsey, R.G. (1960), "The theory of customs unions: A general survey", Economic Journal, 70:498–513.

Lipsey, R.G. (1970), The theory of customs unions: A general equilibrium analysis (Weidenfeld and Nicolson, London).

Lipsey, R.G. and K. Lancaster (1956), "The general theory of second-best", Review of Economic Studies, 24:11–32.

Little, I.M.D. and J.A. Mirrlees (1969), Manual of industrial project analysis for developing countries, Vol. II: Social cost–benefit analysis (OECD Development Centre, Paris).

Little, I.M.D. and J.A. Mirrlees (1974), Project appraisal and planning for developing countries (Heinemann Educational Books, London).

Lloyd, P.J. (1974), "A more general theory of price distortions in open economies", Journal of International Economics, 4:365–386.

Lloyd, P.J. (1982), "3×3 theory of customs unions", Journal of International Economics, 12:41–63.

McCool, T. (1982), "Wage subsidies and distortionary taxes in a mobile capital Harris–Todaro model", Economica, 49:69–79.

McCulloch, R. (1973), "When are a tariff and a quota equivalent", Canadian Journal of Economics, 6:503–511.

McKinnon, R.I. (1966), "Intermediate products and differential tariffs: A generalization of Lerner's symmetry theorem", Quarterly Journal of Economics, 80:584–615.

McMillan, J. and E. McCann (1981), "Welfare effects in customs unions", Economic Journal, 91:697–703.

Magee, S.P. (1972), The welfare effects of restrictions on U.S. trade, Brookings Papers on Economic Activity, No. 3, pp. 645–701.

Magee, S.P. (1973), "Factor market distortions, production and trade: A survey", Oxford Economic Papers, 25:1–43.

Markusen, J.R. (1981), "Trade and the gains from trade with imperfect competition", Journal of International Economics, 11:531–551.

Markusen, J.R. and J.R. Melvin (1981), "Trade, factor prices, and the gains from trade with increasing returns to scale", Canadian Journal of Economics, 14:450–469.

Markusen, J.R. and J.R. Melvin (1982), The gains from trade theorem with increasing returns to scale (forthcoming).

Martin, J.P. (1978), "X-inefficiency, managerial effort and protection", Economica, 45:273–286.

Mayer, W. (1981), "Theoretical considerations on negotiated tariff adjustments", Oxford Economic Papers, 33:135–153.

Meade, J.E. (1955a), Trade and welfare (Oxford University Press, London).

Meade, J.E. (1955b), The theory of customs unions (North-Holland, Amsterdam).

Melvin, J.R. (1969), "Increasing returns to scale as a determinant of trade", Canadian Journal of Economics and Political Science, 2:389–402.

Melvin, J.R. and R.D. Warne (1973), "Monopoly and the theory of international trade", Journal of International Economics, 3:117–134.

Metzler, L.A. (1949), "Tariffs, the terms of trade, and the distribution of income", Journal of Political Economy, 57:1–29.

Michaely, M. (1965), "On customs unions and the gains from trade", Economic Journal, 75:577–583.

Michaely, M. (1976), "The assumptions of Jacob Viner's theory of customs unions", Journal of International Economics, 6:75–93.

Michaely, M. (1977), Theory of commercial policy (Philip Allan, Oxford).

Mirrlees, J.A. (1976), "Optimal tax theory: A synthesis", Journal of Public Economics, 6:327–358.

Mirrlees, J.A. (1982), "The theory of optimal taxation", in: K.J. Arrow and M.D. Intriligator, eds., Handbook of Mathematical Economics, vol. III, part 4: Mathematical Approaches to Welfare Economics (North-Holland, Amsterdam).

Mundell, R.A. (1964), "Tariff preferences and the terms of trade", Manchester School of Economic and Social Studies, 32:1–13.

Mussa, M. (1976), "Tariffs and the balance of payments: A monetary approach", in: J.A. Frenkel and H.G. Johnson, eds., The monetary approach to the balance of payments (George Allen & Unwin, London) 187–221.

Negishi, T. (1972), General equilibrium theory and international trade (North-Holland, Amsterdam).

Ohlin, B. (1931), "Protection and non-competing groups", Weltwirtschaftliches Archiv, 33:30–45.

Ohyama, M. (1972), "Trade and welfare in general equilibrium", Keio Economic Studies, 9:37–73.

Panagariya, A. (1981), "Quantitative restrictions in international trade under monopoly", Journal of International Economics, 11:15–31.

Pigou, A.C. (1947), A study in public finance, 3rd edn. (Macmillan, London).

Pearson, S.R. and W.D. Ingram (1980), "Economies of scale, domestic divergences, and potential gains from economic integration in Ghana and the Ivory Coast", Journal of Political Economy, 88:994–1008.

Ramsey, F.P. (1927), "A contribution to the theory of taxation", Economic Journal, 37:47–61.

Riezman, R. (1979), "A 3×3 model of customs unions", Journal of International Economics, 9:341–354.

Samuelson, P.A. (1939), "The gains from international trade", Canadian Journal of Economics and Political Science 5, 195–205; reprinted in: H.S. Ellis and L.A. Metzler, eds., Readings in the theory of international trade (Blakiston, Philadelphia, 1949) 239–252.

Samuelson, P.A. (1962), "The gains from international trade once again", Economic Journal, 72:820–829.

Sandmo, A. (1975), "Optimal taxation in the presence of externalities", Swedish Journal of Economics, 77:86–98.

Sandmo, A. (1976), "Optimal taxation: An introduction to the literature", Journal of Public Economics, 6:37–54.

Scitovsky, T. (1942), "A reconsideration of the theory of tariffs", Review of Economic Studies, 9:89–110; reprinted in: H.S. Ellis and L.A. Metzler, eds., Readings in the theory of international trade (Blakiston, Philadelphia, 1949) 358–389.

Scott, M.F.G. (1974), "How to use and estimate shadow exchange rates", Oxford Economic Papers, 26:169–184.

Sen, A.K. (1972), "Control areas and accounting prices: An approach to economic evaluation", Economic Journal, 82:486–501.

Sheikh, M.A. (1974), "Smuggling, production and welfare", Journal of International Economics, 4:355–364.

Shibata, H. (1968), "A note on the equivalence of tariffs and quotas", American Economic Review, 58:137–142.

Smith, M.A.M. (1979), "Intertemporal gains from trade", Journal of International Economics, 9:239–248.

Srinivasan, T.N. and J.N. Bhagwati (1978), "Shadow prices for project selection in the presence of distortions: Effective rates of protection and domestic resource costs", Journal of Political Economy, 86:97–116.

Svedberg, P. (1979), "Optimal tariff policy on imports from multinationals", Economic Record, 55:64–67.

Sweeney, R.J., E. Tower and T.D. Willett (1977), "The ranking of alternative tariff and quota policies in the presence of domestic monopoly", Journal of International Economics, 7:349–362.

Takayama, A. (1972), International trade: An approach to the theory (Holt, Rinehart and Winston, New York).

Tironi, E. (1982), "Customs union theory in the presence of foreign firms", Oxford Economic Papers, 34:150–171.

Vanek, J. (1964), "Unilateral trade liberalization and global world income", Quarterly Journal of Economics, 78:139–147.

Vanek, J. (1965), General equilibrium of international discrimination: The case of customs unions (Harvard University Press, Cambridge, Mass.).

Viner, J. (1950), The customs union issue (Carnegie Endowment for International Peace, New York).

Viner, J. (1955), Studies in the theory of international trade (George Allen & Unwin, London).

Warr, P.G. (1977a), "Shadow pricing with policy constraints", Economic Record, 53:149–166.

Warr, P.G. (1977b), "On the shadow pricing of traded commodities", Journal of Political Economy, 85:865–872.

Warr, P.G. (1979), "Shadow prices, market prices and project losses", Economics Letters, 2:363–367.

Warr, P.G. (1982), "Shadow pricing rules for non-traded commodities", Oxford Economic Papers, 34:305–325.

Wonnacott, P. and R. Wonnacott (1981), "Is unilateral tariff reduction preferable to a customs union? The curious case of the missing foreign tariffs", American Economic Review, 71:704–714.

Chapter 3

HIGHER DIMENSIONAL ISSUES IN TRADE THEORY

WILFRED J. ETHIER*

University of Pennsylvania

Contents

1.	Basic concepts	133
2.	The law of comparative advantage	135
3.	The basic propositions of the modern theory	140
4.	Many goods	141
	4.1. Factor-price equalization	142
	4.2. Stolper–Samuelson	144
	4.3. Rybczynski	145
	4.4. The Heckscher–Ohlin theorem	145
5.	Many factors	147
	5.1. The basic propositions	147
	5.2. The specific-factors model	148
6.	Strong results in even technologies	149
	6.1. Global univalence	150
	6.2. Stolper–Samuelson and Rybczynski	152
	6.3. The Heckscher–Ohlin theorems	160
7.	General results	161
	7.1. Factor-price equalization	162
	7.2. Stolper–Samuelson	163
	7.3. Rybczynski	167
	7.4. General results	169
	7.5. The Heckscher–Ohlin theorems	173
8.	Odd or even: Does it matter?	178
9.	Concluding remarks	181
	References	181

*The research for this paper was supported by the National Science Foundation. The paper itself was written during an enjoyable stay at the Institute for International Economic Studies in Stockholm. Helpful comments and suggestions were contributed by W.W. Chang, A. Dixit, E. Helpman, R.W. Jones, M.C. Kemp, A. Krueger, J.P. Neary, L. Svensson, and an April 1982 conference at Princeton University.

Handbook of International Economics, vol. I, Edited by R.W. Jones and P.B. Kenen
© *Elsevier Science Publishers B.V., 1984*

The title of this chapter could be read as an invitation to cover the entire content of this volume at a high level of generality. Acceptance of such a rash invitation would both preclude discussion of anything in depth and impinge on the turf of others. I accordingly limit myself by the ruthless application of two principles. First, I address only problems in which dimensionality is itself central. This rules out topics such as the gains from trade [e.g. Samuelson (1939, 1962), Kemp (1962), Krueger and Sonnenschein (1967), and Dixit and Norman (1980)] which are often discussed in a higher dimensional context even though, or perhaps because, dimensionality does not influence the basic argument. (This chapter will assume without elaboration that free trade confers gains relative to autarky.) Second, the issues posed by dimensionality must be important in their own right: I attempt to scale no mountains of generality simply because they are there.

An excellent example of what I want to include is the "law of comparative advantage". This principle is of the very heart and soul of our field. Yet standard textbook discussions emphasize properties which do not generalize to more than two commodities. Furthermore, the difficulties that additional goods create and the properties that do generalize both well illustrate common consequences of high dimensionality.

My two criteria guarantee that a predominant share of this chapter will concern the fate of the modern, or Heckscher–Ohlin, theory of international trade in higher dimensions. This theory, in its standard two-commodity, two-factor version (see Chapter 1) has dominated international trade theory for over thirty years. But this dominance has long been made uneasy by a widespread suspicion that world commerce does not accord well with the theoretical structure. There are two particular areas of concern. The first stems from the fact that the largest part of world trade involves the exchange of roughly similar products between similar economies, whereas the factor endowment theory – and comparative cost theory generally – teaches us to look to international dissimilarities for the causes of trade. A large part of this actual trade is classified as intraindustry even with significant disaggregation. Thus probing its causes requires a high degree of disaggregation, that is, the explicit consideration of a large number of goods. Scale economies and imperfect competition are also central, so the subject will be reserved for Chapter 7.

The second area of concern stems from the Leontief Paradox [Leontief (1953, 1956)]. Among the huge volume of resulting empirical work (see Chapter 10) the hypotheses that have by and large proved most useful (e.g. human capital, natural resources, skill groups) are not inconsistent with the view that trade has a factor endowments basis, but do demand an increase in dimensionality. Few would now dispute the conclusion of Baldwin (1971, p. 141), "that a straight-forward application of the two-factor (capital and labor) factor-proportions model along Heckscher–Ohlin lines is inadequate for understanding the pattern of U.S. trade."

The sensitivity to higher dimensions of the basic propositions of the modern theory of international trade is the key issue for the practical relevance of the logical structure that has dominated trade theory in the past thirty years.

1. Basic concepts

Before getting down to issues I introduce some notation and concepts that will prove useful. The *national product function* $y(p,V)$ records the maximal income that a country can achieve if facing the vector p of commodity prices and if endowed with the vector V of primary factors. This function therefore depends upon technology and subsumes an optimization process. Just as there is an accounting identity between the total value of national output and the total payment to primary factors, $y(p,V)$ can be given a dual interpretation: the minimal amount paid the factors V, given that factor rewards must be such as to leave the respective costs of production of all commodities no less than the elements of p. Thus

$$y(p,V) = pX = wV, \tag{1.1}$$

where X is the vector of commodity outputs and w the vector of factor rewards. X is chosen to maximize pX subject to the constraint that X be producible from V, and w is chosen to minimize wV subject to the constraint that costs be no less than p.

Differentiating y with respect to any commodity price P_i and using the first definition reflected in (1.1):

$$\frac{\partial y}{\partial P_i} = X_i + \sum_j P_j \frac{\partial X_j}{\partial P_i} = X_i, \tag{1.2}$$

where the totality of terms under the summation sign vanishes as a condition of maximization. Differentiating y with respect to any factor endowment V_j and using the second definition reflected in (1.1):

$$\frac{\partial y}{\partial V_j} = w_j + \sum_i V_i \frac{\partial w_i}{\partial V_j} = w_j, \tag{1.3}$$

where the summation vanishes as a condition of minimization. Finally, differentiating (1.2) with respect to V_j, (1.3) with respect to P_i, and noting that $\partial^2 y / \partial P_i \partial V_j$

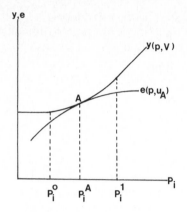

Figure 1.1. Autarkic equilibrium.

$= \partial^2 y / \partial V_j \, \partial P_i$, gives a set of what are called "reciprocity conditions":

$$\frac{\partial X_i}{\partial V_j} = \frac{\partial w_j}{\partial P_i}.$$ (1.4)

Discussion this far has been confined to the supply side of an economy. To facilitate summary of the demand side, assume a single collective utility function over national consumption (abandonment of this assumption will not be an objective of this chapter). The *national expenditure function* $e(p, u)$ records the minimum that must be spent at commodity prices p to purchase a consumption bundle yielding utility no less than u. Write

$$e(p, u) = pD,$$ (1.5)

where D denotes the chosen bundle. Then differentiation of (1.5) with respect to any commodity price P_i gives:

$$\frac{\partial e}{\partial P_i} = D_i + \sum_j P_j \frac{\partial D_j}{\partial P_i} = D_i,$$ (1.6)

where the summation vanishes as an optimization condition.[1]

Figure 1.1 depicts autarkic equilibrium. P_i is measured along the horizontal axis, and all other commodity prices are presumed set equal to their equilibrium values. The slopes of the income and expenditure functions are respectively X_i

---

[1]For surveys of duality theory see Diewert (1974, 1978). Summaries and applications to international trade are contained in Dixit and Norman (1980) and Woodland (1982). See also Samuelson's classic (1953) and Appendix One to Ethier (1983).

and D_i, from (1.2) and (1.6) so that point A reflects the autarkic equilibrium condition $X_i = D_i$, and P_i^A is the equilibrium price.

The illustrated curvatures of the income and expenditure functions follow from the respective subsumed optimizations. The position of $y(p, V)$ depends of course on the endowment vector V, and autarkic utility u_A must be such as to position $e(p, u_A)$ tangent to the income function as shown. P_i^0 denotes the price at which the economy ceases to produce good i – given the values of all other commodity prices – and P_i^1 the price at which the economy specializes completely in X_i.

2. The law of comparative advantage

In two dimensions the law of comparative advantage – that a comparison of home and foreign relative autarkic prices predicts the pattern of trade and gives bounds for the terms of trade – is rather robust across models, even though it is widely appreciated that the proposition can be vitiated by certain phenomena, such as multiple autarkic equilibria or scale economies. Ignore such possibilities so as to focus clearly on the effects of dimensionality.

Figure 2.1 shows a movement from autarky to mutual free trade for a pair of countries, when there are only two goods. This movement can be depicted as an upward shift of the expenditure function since free trade gives higher utility than autarky. Points T and T^* denote the respective trade equilibria (throughout this essay I use an asterisk to refer to the rest of the world), with common price P_i^T between the respective autarkic prices. At T, y is flatter than e so that $D_i > X_i$

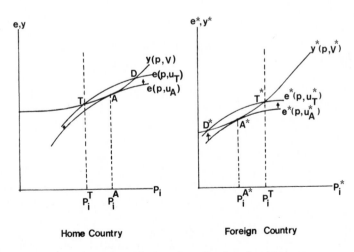

Figure 2.1. The law of comparative advantage.

from (1.2) and (1.6) and similarly $X_i^* > D_i^*$ at T^*. Thus the home country imports good i, as predicted by a comparison of autarkic prices.[2]

Is Figure 2.1 an adequate description of the movement to free trade? With only two goods it is, because then the figure's implicit assumption that all other commodity prices are fixed amounts only to a choice of numeraire: P_i^T denotes the terms of trade, and the home country exports the other good in exchange for good i. The figure is also an adequate analysis in higher dimensions if the movement to free trade involves what can be called a *two-dimensional* price change: the prices of a group of goods all move equiproportionally relative to the prices of all other goods. For then the analysis can be based upon two composite commodities. I mention this because the extent to which attempted generalizations of two dimensional results in fact apply to more interesting situations will sometimes be an issue in what follows.

When the movement to free trade does involve a change in more than one relative price – that is, when one goes beyond two goods in a substantive way – Figure 2.1 becomes inadequate. For changes in relative prices, other than that of good i in terms of the numeraire, will produce shifts of the income and expenditure functions. A little experimenting with pencil and paper convinces one that practically anything can apparently be made to happen as regards both the trade pattern and the magnitude of P_i^T.

Thus higher dimensional generalization requires restrictions of some sort. A natural point of departure is to ask when the 2×2 results remain fully valid in some respect, say as regards the pattern of trade. That is, when does it remain true, in a multidimensional context, that 2×2 comparisons determine the pattern of trade? When will the pairwise comparison,

$$\frac{P_i^A}{P_j^A} > \frac{P_i^{A^*}}{P_j^{A^*}}, \tag{2.1}$$

necessarily imply, by itself, that in free trade the home country will export good j to the rest of the world in exchange for good i? A little reflection answers, "never". The problem comes from "intervening" goods, which necessarily present themselves whenever there are more than two commodities. To grasp the point immediately, note that (2.1) is equivalent to

$$\frac{P_i^A}{P_i^{A^*}} > \frac{P_j^A}{P_j^{A^*}}.$$

---

[2] The free trade equilibrium cannot be shown by points D and T^* because this would require both countries to export good i. Likewise the pair D^* and T would require both countries to import the good. Finally, the pair D, D^* is ruled out because it would imply $P_i^T > P_i^A > P_i^{A^*} > P_i^T$.

Suppose there are three distinct goods and index them so that

$$\frac{P_i^A}{P_i^{A*}} > \frac{P_k^A}{P_k^{A*}} > \frac{P_j^A}{P_j^{A*}} \, .$$

A pairwise comparison of goods i and k indicates that the home country exports k (and imports i) whereas a pairwise comparison of k and j yields the contrary conclusion that the home country imports k (and exports j). The important point about this example is that it necessarily results as a consequence solely of an increase in dimensionality beyond two goods: *no* restrictions on technology or preferences can set matters aright (unless they undo the increase in dimensionality by implying that all price changes are two dimensional).

Given this insuperable difficulty, one asks if some modified version of the 2×2 proposition might generalize. A natural candidate would be a *chain* version: number the n goods so that

$$\frac{P_1^A}{P_1^{A*}} > \frac{P_2^A}{P_2^{A*}} > \cdots > \frac{P_n^A}{P_n^{A*}} \, . \tag{2.2}$$

Might it not be true that the free trade equilibrium would break the chain somewhere, with all goods with price ratios strictly to the left of the break imported by the home country and all those strictly to the right exported? Such a proposition subtly alters the conclusions that would be drawn from a pairwise comparison such as (2.1). Instead of saying "the home country will import good i and export good j", we now make the *conditional* prediction that "the home country will import good i if it imports good j and will export good j if it exports good i".

Such an approach is supported by the fact that chains like (2.2) do confer such predictions in certain cases. For example, in a Ricardian model, where an arbitrary number of goods are allowed but there is only one primary factor, the terms in (2.2) coincide with relative labor requirements so that, when the ratio of the domestic free trade wage to the foreign is known, the home country must import all those goods corresponding to terms in (2.2) strictly greater than this ratio and export all those goods strictly less.[3] But such a result is not generally available.

[3] See Haberler (1936). The case allows arbitrary dimensionality concerning goods, but restricts the factors to one and the countries to two. This essay will not have much to say about the consequences of additional countries, because the problems they raise are usually straightforward and sometimes tedious. But occasional exceptions will be noted. This is one. The case of two goods, one factor, and many countries yields a chain analysis analogous to the above. But allowing both many goods and

This is because in the general environment a chain of price comparisons does not translate directly into a chain of output comparisons or of demand comparisons, a fact well appreciated by students of microeconomics.[4] Suppose that the price vectors p^A and p^{A^*} in (2.1) and (2.2) refer not to two countries, but to two distinct equilibria (autarky and free trade, for example) for a single country with a given endowment vector. With only two commodities, one can expand only by drawing resources from the other; (2.1) does indeed imply:

$$\frac{X_i}{X_j} \geq \frac{X_i^*}{X_j^*},$$

if i and j are the only goods. But (2.2) does not imply:

$$\frac{X_1}{X_1^*} \geq \frac{X_2}{X_2^*} \geq \frac{X_3}{X_3^*} \geq \cdots \geq \frac{X_n}{X_n^*}.$$

Suppose that X_1 and X_3 make relatively intensive use of two disjoint groups of factors and that X_2 relies heavily on both groups. Then an expansion of X_1 that draws resources from X_2 would also free factors allowing X_3 to expand: X_3 might well rise relative to X_2 even though P_3 falls relative to P_2. Note that the existence of at least three goods is essential to this example.

On the demand side, price variations will produce changes in real incomes and these will affect demands in ways unrelated to the price change. But such possibilities arise even in two dimensions: the Giffen Paradox has graced undergraduate texts for years. What additional goods allow is complementarity between goods on the demand side, analogous to the above illustration, in response to compensated price changes.

But even though detailed predictions are dangerous, it is not true that *anything* can happen. If a rise in P_1 causes an increase in X_1 the necessary resources must come from somewhere; although X_3 may be complementary to X_1, the rest of the economy, in some average sense, cannot be. This idea can be made precise as follows. Let X^0 and X^1 be the output vectors produced with prices p^0 and p^1 by an economy with endowment V. Then $p^0 X^0 = y(p^0, V) \geq p^0 X^1$ since X^0 maximizes income at p^0 even though X^1 is feasible. Similarly $p^1 X^1 \geq p^1 X^0$. The two

---

many countries introduces problems of its own. The assignment of goods to countries to produce them that will permit the world to obtain an efficient output vector obviously depends upon the production techniques of all goods in all countries and so cannot be exposed by any sort of chain of bilateral comparisons. See McKenzie (1954, 1956), Jones (1961), and also Wilson (1980).

[4]For a discussion in the context of international trade, see Drabicki and Takayama (1979) and Dixit and Norman (1980, p. 94–96). Both provide counterexamples to the straightforward application of 2×2 results to higher dimensions.

inequalities together yield:

$$(p^0 - p^1)(X^0 - X^1) \geq 0. \tag{2.3}$$

That is, output changes must be *positively correlated* with price changes, so that the latter predict the former in an average sense.

In like fashion, if D^0 and D^1 are demanded at prices p^0 and p^1 when utility is held constant:

$$(p^0 - p^1)(D^0 - D^1) \leq 0. \tag{2.4}$$

Demand changes are negatively correlated with compensated price changes.

Note two points. First, when there are only two goods (2.3) and (2.4) imply the usual unambiguous responses. Second, (2.3) and (2.4) are quite general, especially as regards dimension, and followed directly from the optimization subsumed in the product and expenditure functions. A number of standard 2×2 results generalize along these lines.

One would certainly expect this to be true of the law of comparative advantage, since it attempts to link trade to price divergences and since trade is but the difference between production and consumption. To proceed,[5] note that, if p^A denotes the autarkic price vector:

$$p^A D^T \geq e(p^A, u_A) = y(p^A, V) \geq p^A X^T,$$

since the free trade consumption vector D^T yields at least u_A of utility, and the free trade production vector X^T can be produced from V. Then $p^A M \geq 0$ where $M = D^T - X^T$ denotes net imports. Balanced trade requires $p^T M = 0$ so that

$$(p^A - p^T) M \geq 0. \tag{2.5}$$

Imports are positively correlated with the excesses of autarkic prices over free trade prices. A similar argument yields $(p^{A^*} - p^T) M^* \geq 0$ for the foreign country, and $M = - M^*$. Thus

$$(p^A - p^{A^*}) M \geq 0. \tag{2.6}$$

Thus autarkic price differences do indeed predict trade patterns in the average sense of a positive correlation between the two. Finally, apply (2.3) to a comparison of free trade and autarkic equilibria:

$$(p^A - p^T)(X^A - X^T) \geq 0. \tag{2.7}$$

---

[5] See Deardorff (1980) and Dixit and Norman (1980, pp. 94–96), and also Appendix One of Ethier (1983).

On average, trade causes countries to redirect resources away from those sectors with lower prices than in autarky.

3. The basic propositions of the modern theory

The 2×2 Heckscher–Ohlin–Samuelson model yields four central results: the factor-price equalization, Stolper–Samuelson, Rybczynski, and Heckscher–Ohlin theorems. To establish a frame of reference I state eight propositions reflecting the principal variants of these theorems. See Chapter 1 for a fuller treatment.

Proposition 1 (Stolper – Samuelson)

A small change in relative prices will increase, in terms of both goods, the reward of the factor used intensively in the production of that good whose price has risen and will reduce, in terms of both goods, the reward of the other factor, provided that both goods are produced.

Note that there are two aspects to this proposition. First, one factor reward rises in real terms and one falls, independently of how recipients of those rewards spend them, so that commodity price changes generate conflict. Second, the identities of the favored and punished factors can be determined by relative factor intensities.

Proposition 2 (global Stolper – Samuelson)

Proposition 1 applies to large price changes as well, provided that endowments are held fixed or that the technology does not exhibit factor intensity reversals.

Proposition 3 (factor-price equalization)

For each relative commodity price there exists a cone of endowments such that all countries in the cone, and with the given technology, will have identical factor prices when freely trading at those world prices. The cone is non-trivial as long as it does not coincide with a factor-intensity reversal.

Proposition 4 (global univalence)

If there are no factor-intensity reversals, any two countries with the same technology must have equal prices if freely trading at a common world price and if both countries diversify.

Note that Proposition 3 in effect says that factor-price equalization results if the two countries have "sufficiently similar" factor endowments: widely divergent endowments preclude equalization regardless of the global nature of the technology. Proposition 4 imposes a global property to make equalization equivalent to diversification in production.

Proposition 5 (Rybczynski)

At constant relative commodity prices, a small change in factor endowments will increase, relative to both factors, the output of the good making intensive use of the factor which has become relatively more abundant and will reduce the output of the other good relative to both factors, if the economy is diversified.

Note that this proposition has two distinct aspects as did Proposition 1, and that the two propositions are in a sense dual.

Proposition 6 (global Rybczynski)

Proposition 5 applies as well to any large changes which do not disturb diversification, if the technology has no factor-intensity reversals.

Proposition 7 (quantity version of the Heckscher–Ohlin theorem)

Suppose two countries have identical technologies with no factor intensity reversals and identical homothetic demands. Then in free trade each country will export the good making relatively intensive use of the country's relatively abundant factor.

Proposition 8 (price version of the Heckscher–Ohlin theorem)

Suppose two countries have identical technologies with no factor-intensity reversals. Then each country has a lower (compared to the other country) relative autarkic price of the good making relatively intensive use of the factor which would be relatively cheap in that country in autarky. Also that good would be exported in free trade if autarkic equilibrium is unique in each country.

4. Many goods

As Jones and Scheinkman (1977) have pointed out, the 2×2 model is special in two ways: the dimensionality is low and the number of goods exactly equals the number of factors. To disentangle the individual implications, I first examine cases where the number of goods alone, and then the number of factors alone, is allowed to exceed two.

Suppose then the conventional Heckscher–Ohlin framework with the sole exception that the number of goods is arbitrary but greater than two. Equilibrium requires that (4.1), (4.2) and (4.3) hold for each country:

$$p \leq wA(w), \tag{4.1}$$

$$[p - wA(w)]X = 0, \tag{4.2}$$

$$A(w)X = V. \tag{4.3}$$

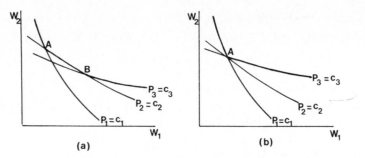

Figure 4.1. Equilibria with three goods and two factors.

In these expressions, p denotes the vector of n commodity prices, w the (two-dimensional) vector of factor rewards, X the n-vector of commodity outputs and V the vector of (two) factor endowments. The matrix $A(w)$ is the array of least-cost techniques at factor rewards w, so that $wA(w)$ is the vector of unit cost functions, $c(w)$.

4.1. Factor-price equalization

A considerable literature has concerned the question of whether additional goods render factor-price equalization more or less likely than in a 2×2 environment.[6] The sensitivity of any measure of "likelihood" to its frame of reference renders the question too sterile to be of much inherent interest. Nevertheless it has exposed the essential features of the $n \times 2$ context.

Suppose first that some country, engaged in free trade, produces positive amounts of at least two goods, say X_1 and X_2. Then the first two inequalities of (4.1) must in fact be strict equalities, and this subsystem can be analyzed in the normal 2×2 way. In particular Proposition 4 (global univalence) holds with regard to any trading partner also producing X_1 and X_2. Thus if any pair of goods is free of factor-intensity reversals, factor-price equalization must characterize free trade between any two countries both producing those two goods; if the technology has no pair-wise factor-intensity reversals at all, any countries producing at least two goods in common must have equal factor prices if freely trading. Looked at in this light, increasing the number of goods appears to broaden the opportunity for factor-price equalization.

But different viewpoints yield different interpretations. Figure 4.1 shows isocost curves for goods 1 and 2. Each curve depicts the collection of factor prices w_1 and

---

[6]References include Samuelson (1953), Tinbergen (1949), Meade (1950), Land (1959), Johnson (1967, 1970), Melvin (1968), Bertrand (1970), Chang (1979), and Dixit and Norman (1980).

w_2 that cause the minimum unit cost of the respective good to equal a specified price; the isocost curve of good i is the graph of solutions to

$$P_i = c_i(w_1, w_2) = w_1 a_{1i}(w_1, w_2) + w_2 a_{2i}(w_1, w_2), \qquad (4.4)$$

for given P_i, where a_{ij} denote elements of A. (See Chapter 1 for a fuller description.) Any $w_1 - w_2$ combination lying outside an isocost curve implies a cost for the respective good greater than its price, so the good cannot continue to be produced in equilibrium. Likewise, points below the curve imply a minimum cost less than the price of the product and are therefore inconsistent with long-run equilibrium. Thus the latter requires that factor prices be indicated somewhere along the outer envelope – called the "factor price frontier" – of all isocost curves corresponding to the actual commodity prices. (Values of the national product function $y(p, V)$ can be thought of as determined by the process of minimizing wV over all w not below the factor-price frontier determined by p.)

Suppose that in equilibrium goods 1 and 2 are produced in positive amounts. Then, with the given prices of these two goods, factor prices must be as indicated by the intersection point A in Figure 4.1(a). This equilibrium will allow good 3 to be produced also only if P_3 happens to have just the right value for its isocost curve to pass through A, that is, if the cost of producing X_3 implied by the factor prices indicated by A equals P_3, as in Figure 4.1(b). If there are n goods, complete diversification requires a common intersection for all n isocost curves.

Suppose that the three commodity prices are not just such as to yield a common intersection, as in Figure 4.1(a). Suppose that all goods are produced somewhere in the world (since we are, after all, concerned with such a case) and let there be two countries – the home economy and the rest of the world. Suppose X_1 is produced at home. Then home factor prices must be indicated by some point on the factor-price frontier in Figure 4.1(a) at or above point A. Since X_3 is necessarily produced in the rest of the world, its factor price must be reflected by a point at or below B. Neither country can be on the segment AB, exclusive of the endpoints. Thus the two countries cannot possibly have identical factor prices, and those at home must differ from those abroad by at least the distance AB. Only if the prices of the three goods happen to be such as to yield Figure 4.1(b) is factor price equalization possible, when it must occur at A if both countries completely diversify.

This argument seems to reduce factor-price equalization to a fluke. And so it would if commodity prices were drawn from an urn. But they are not: they are determined so as to clear world commodity markets.

To see what this implies note first that, from (4.4):

$$dP_i = [(dw_1)a_{1i} + (dw_2)a_{2i}] + [w_1(da_{1i}) + w_2(da_{2i})]. \qquad (4.5)$$

Now the second term in brackets on the right hand side must equal zero, as a necessary condition for cost minimization, and so the first bracketed term must likewise vanish for a movement along an isocost curve, where $\mathrm{d}P_i = 0$. Thus $(\mathrm{d}w_2/\mathrm{d}w_1) = -(a_{1i}/a_{2i})$: the slope of an isocost curve at any point equals (minus) the relative factor proportions employed in the respective industry at the relevant factor price.

A country's relative factor endowment is necessarily a weighted average of the factor proportions it employs in its operating sectors. Thus if the home economy has factor prices at A or above on the factor price frontier of Figure 4.1(a), the home relative endowment V_1/V_2 necessarily exceeds the slope of the P_3 curve at A. Likewise, for the foreign economy to be at B or below requires that the foreign relative factor endowment be less than the slope of P_3 at point B. If these conditions are not met – for example if relative endowments in the two countries are more nearly equal than the slopes of the P_3 curve at A and B – the commodity prices which give the isocost curves the position indicated by Figure 4.1(a) could not possibly clear world commodity markets.

For both countries to be at point A in Figure 4.1(b) both relative factor endowments must lie between the slopes of the P_1 and P_3 isocost curves at A. If this is not the case – for example because endowments are too dissimilar – factor prices cannot be equalized.

Then when account is taken of commodity market equilibrium the picture that emerges is qualitatively similar to that in the 2×2 case: trade between countries with "sufficiently similar" relative factor endowments will produce factor price equalization and "sufficiently dissimilar" endowments preclude such equalization.

4.2.   Stolper–Samuelson

From (4.5) we obtain, for any good actually produced,

$$\hat{P}_i = \theta_{1i}\hat{w}_1 + \theta_{2i}\hat{w}_2, \tag{4.6}$$

where a circumflex denotes proportional change (so that $\hat{P}_i = (\mathrm{d}P_i)/P_i$, etc.), and $\theta_{1i} = w_1 a_{1i}/P_i$, factor 1's distributive share in sector i (so that $\theta_{1i} + \theta_{2i} = 1$). Thus the proportional change in the price of any produced commodity is a weighted average of the proportional changes in the two factor rewards. The presence of additional produced goods does not disturb the 2×2 Stolper–Samuelson logic (see Chapter 1). Any change in the relative prices of produced goods necessarily raises one factor reward in terms of all (still) produced goods and lowers the other factor reward in terms of all (still) produced goods, and the identification of the respective factor can be deduced from the relative factor intensities of *any* pair of produced goods whose relative price changes.

But we have seen that, unless relative factor endowments are sufficiently similar across countries, some countries will not produce all goods. If more goods than factors are initially produced, a fall in any single commodity price will in fact cause some good to cease being produced.[7] If the prices of all non-produced goods fall, say, relative to produced goods, and if the latter prices do not change relative to each other, all factor rewards rise in terms of non-produced goods and remain unchanged in terms of produced goods. This is obviously analogous to the case of specialization in a 2×2 context. But different consequences arise when: (a) some non-produced goods rise in price relative to produced goods and some fall, and/or (b) the prices of produced goods change relative to each other and relative to some non-produced goods' prices. In such cases the rewards of some factors could rise relative to some goods and fall relative to other goods, a possibility that is absent when there are only two commodities. Nevertheless it is fair to conclude that the Stolper–Samuelson theorem is not fundamentally altered by an increase in the number of goods.

4.3. Rybczynski

Suppose that the home country is producing more than two goods, that is, that for a given V and an equilibrium w, eq. (4.3) possesses a solution X with at least three positive components. Then there must be many such solutions, because (4.3) is a system of two linear equations in n unknowns and will accordingly be satisfied by an $n - 2$ dimensional hyperplane of X vectors. Thus without further information national outputs are indeterminate whenever world prices and the national factor endowment permit positive production of more than two goods.[8]

Consider a change in factor endowments at unchanged commodity prices. The discussion of factor-price equalization justifies supposing that factor prices also remain unaltered. But with X indeterminate both before and after the change in V, so are the resulting changes in outputs. Thus increasing the number of goods above two profoundly affects the Rybczynski theorem.

4.4. The Heckscher–Ohlin theorem[9]

Suppose that the home and foreign economies each produce at least two goods in common. Then their factor prices must be equal so that they share a common

---

[7]Expression (4.6) and its accompanying logic can be retained even for goods which cease to be produced (or which initially become produced) if the left-hand side is reinterpreted as the change in supply price rather than market price. This is analogus to the interpretation made in Section 5 below for the Rybczynski theorem when factors outnumber goods. (I owe this observation to Avinash Dixit.)

[8]This indeterminacy of output when goods outnumber factors has often been emphasized in the literature. See Samuelson (1953), Travis (1964, 1972), Melvin (1968), Kemp (1969), Pearce (1970), Vanek and Bertrand (1971), Chang (1979), and Dixit and Norman (1980).

[9]Useful references include Jones (1956, 1974), Bhagwati (1972), Krueger (1977), Deardorff (1979), and Dornbusch, Fischer and Samuelson (1980).

technology matrix $A(w)$. (I ignore the possibility of factor-intensity reversals, since they can vitiate the Heckscher–Ohlin theorem even in a 2×2 world.) This means that the domestic hyperplane of possible outputs, defined by (4.3), is parallel to the analogous foreign hyperplane. Then the equilibrium vector of world outputs $X + X^*$ can be attained by many combinations of X and X^* consistent with (4.3) and its foreign analog. Commodity trade flows are indeterminate and cannot be predicted by any theory. Indeed the *pattern* of commodity trade need not be determinate.

If factor prices are not equalized the situation becomes more clearcut. Number the n goods in order of their relative factor intensities, good 1 making the most intensive use of factor 1. (Continue to assume away factor-intensity reversals so that this ranking is determinate.) Then the factor price frontier corresponding to the equilibrium commodity prices must consist of segments of the isocost curves for goods 1, 2, 3, etc. respectively, going downwards and to the right, as in Figure 4.2 for the case $n = 5$. (Some of the segments could be single points, if three or more isocost curves have a common intersection as at point B in Figure 4.2.) The successive segments become flatter because of the convexity of the individual isocost curves. If the home country is relatively most abundant in factor one, that is, has the highest V_1 / V_2 ratio, its factor prices must be on the steeper part of the factor-price frontier: the home economy must export those goods "higher up" in the chain of commodities and import the others. In Figure 4.2, good 1 is exported, goods 3, 4, and 5 are imported, and good 2 is in an ambiguous intermediate position, if the home economy is at A. Note that Figure 4.2, as drawn, requires at least three countries for all five goods to be produced.

If there are many countries they can also be ordered on the basis of their V_1 / V_2 ratios, and to each country there will correspond a segment of the commodity chain having the property that the country will export the goods in the segment and import the other goods. Again, "borderline" goods, producible in more than one country and of indeterminate trade status, may exist.

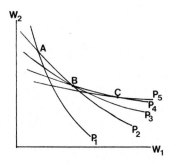

Figure 4.2. Many goods.

In the two country case, if two goods are producible in both countries factor prices are equalized and so all goods are producible in both countries: the chain proposition says nothing. With many countries, factor-price equalization between some subset of countries does not imply that all goods are producible by the members of that subset. The chain proposition still holds if the countries in the subset are treated as a single joint unit. Suppose for example that one country has an equilibrium at A in Figure 4.2, another is at B, and two others are at C. The factor prices of the latter two countries are equalized, with X_4 and X_5 producible in both of them. The two countries together import X_1, X_2, and X_3 and export X_5; X_4 is an ambiguous "borderline" good. This trade pattern need not hold for each of the two subgroup countries individually: one of them may export X_5 to the other, for example.

Factor intensity reversals prevent the construction of a unique commodity chain. However, in the two country case it is easy to see that the chain proposition still holds in a descriptive sense, when the chain is constructed on the basis of the *actual* factor intensity of each good in the country of export. (In the many country case statement of the proposition becomes cumbersome because a commodity might be exported by more than one country.)

5.   Many factors

5.1.   The basic propositions

The presence of many commodities influences but by no means disembowels the basic theory. The factor-price equalization and Stolper–Samuelson properties are basically intact, the Rybczynski and Heckscher–Ohlin theorems more significantly affected. Analytically the basic modification is that, for given factor prices and endowments, the set of equations (4.3) leaves commodity outputs X indeterminate.

Suppose now that the number of goods returns to two but that there are $m > 2$ factors of production.[10] If both goods are produced, with given commodity prices, the system (4.1) becomes a set of 2 equations in n unknowns: factor prices are not in general determined solely by commodity prices but also depend upon other information, notably factor endowments. Consider a free-trade equilibrium in which foreign endowments differ only very slightly from home endowments, by the vector dV. Then if foreign factor prices are to equal those at home, w, it follows from (4.3) that the difference dX between home and foreign outputs must

---

[10] The implications of more factors than goods are studied in Samuelson (1953), Jones (1979, ch. 8), Diewert and Woodland (1972), Batra and Casas (1976), Jones and Easton (1983), and Egawa (1978).

satisfy:

$$A(w)(dX) = dV. \tag{5.1}$$

Now the two-dimensional vector dX will in general be determined by the first two equations of (5.1) so that, except for a fluke, the remaining $m-2$ equations cannot be satisfied: factor prices will have to differ between countries.

When the same logic that has just been used for a comparison between two countries is instead applied to a comparative static change in a single country, one concludes that a change in endowments, at constant commodity prices, will produce a change in factor prices and a consequent shift in production techniques. The basis for the logic of the Rybczynski theorem is then destroyed. The proposition can be resuscitated if sticky factor rewards are maintained as an *assumption* and if factor markets are no longer required to clear, and dV in (5.1) is interpreted as the vector of factor demands. Then (5.1) gives a set of equations of the form:

$$\lambda_{j1}\hat{X}_1 + \lambda_{j2}\hat{X}_2 = \hat{V}_j, \qquad j = 1, \ldots, m, \tag{5.2}$$

where $\lambda_{ji} = a_{ji}X_i/V_j$ denotes the fraction of aggregate demand for factor j contributed by sector i. Thus every $\hat{V}_j$ is a weighted average of $\hat{X}_1$ and $\hat{X}_2$, so that any change in relative factor demands must be accompanied by an increase in the output of one good relative to all factor demands and a reduction in the other commodity output relative to all factor demands. The Rybczynski result is preserved when the number of factors rises in the same way that the Stolper–Samuelson result is preserved when the number of goods rises. But preservation of the former requires a drastic alteration in the circumstances under which it applies.

Finally, note that, with both goods produced, (4.1) leads to

$$\hat{P}_i = \theta_{1i}\hat{w}_1 + \cdots + \theta_{mi}\hat{w}_m; \qquad i = 1, 2. \tag{5.3}$$

Each $\hat{P}_i$ is a weighted average of all $\hat{w}_j$. A moment's reflection reveals that this is quite consistent with some of the $\hat{w}_j$ being weighted averages of $\hat{P}_1$ and $\hat{P}_2$: a change in relative commodity prices might well cause some factor rewards to increase in terms of one good while falling in terms of the other.

5.2. The specific-factors model

The complications introduced by more than two factors are well illustrated by the specific-factors model, sufficiently prominent in recent years to deserve mention in its own right.[11] This structure differs from the standard 2×2 one in that one of the factors is immobile between industries, so that its two sectoral allocations are distinct specific factors. Thus the model is 2×3 though each good is still produced by only two factors. Consider an increase in the endowment of one of the specific factors, with commodity prices constant. Constant factor prices would require unchanged techniques in both industries, but the sector with more of the specific factor can maintain its original factor proportions only by attracting some of the mobile factor from the other industry, thereby changing factor proportions there: the failure of factor-price equalization is transparent here.[12] An increased endowment of the mobile factor also must change techniques, with that factor allocated to the two sectors so as to preserve equality between the values of its marginal products. This produces the anti-Rybczynski result that both outputs rise but proportionally less than the endowment of the mobile factor. Finally, changes in relative commodity prices always raise the reward of the mobile factor in terms of one good and lower it in terms of the other. That factor will move towards the sector with the increased price; this lowers the value of the mobile factor's marginal product in terms of that good, while the exit of that factor from the other sector raises the value of its marginal product in terms of that other good.

6. Strong results in even technologies

Standard 2×2 conclusions are affected by increases in either the number of goods alone or the number of factors alone, with the latter the more devastating. I turn now to "even" increases in dimensionality: $n = m > 2$. The general $n \times m$ case can be thought of as a composite of the odd conclusions just derived and the even ones to come. But I shall leave to the reader the actual task of composition, except when there is reason to discuss it explicitly.[13]

Investigations of the $n \times m$ case have followed two distinct approaches. The first, to be discussed in this section, has formulated general propositions thought to retain as much as possible of familiar 2×2 properties and then derived necessary conditions for general validity. Examination of these conditions then

---

[11] For details of this model see Samuelson (1971), Jones (1971), Mayer (1974), Mussa (1974), and Neary (1978).

[12] Samuelson (1971) discusses the tendency of free trade to partially equalize factor prices between countries.

[13] This chapter does not make as intensive use of matrix algebra as has become customary in its field. For details of the mathematical structure of the general production model see, in addition to Samuelson (1953) of course, several recent valuable contributions with clear expositions and extensions: Diewert and Woodland (1977), Jones and Scheinkman (1977), Chang (1979), and Takayama (1981).

sheds light on the practical relevance of the "strong" properties of the 2×2 world.

An alternative strategy, taken up in the next section, is to ask what results remain valid in an $n \times m$ context in the absence of any assumptions stronger than those commonly imposed in a 2×2 context.

6.1. Global univalence

Perhaps most attention has been lavished on the circumstances that allow us to deduce factor price equalization from diversification in production.[14] Evidently an $n \times n$ analog to Proposition 4 would require internationally identical technology and would interpret diversification as the positive production of all n goods. Then the implied problem, in which interest was generated by Samuelson (1953), is to find technological restrictions such that the relation

$$p = wA(w) \tag{6.1}$$

yields a one-to-one mapping between w and p. In two dimensions this follows if there are no factor-intensity reversals, that is, if $A(w)$ is non-singular for all possible w. In higher dimensions the obvious analog to an absence of factor-intensity reversals is the non-singularity of $A(w)$. This condition guarantees the *local* univalence of (6.1): if $A(w)$ is non-singular for $w = w_0$, there exists some neighborhood of w_0 over which (6.1) is one-to-one. But when $n > 2$, *global* univalence of (6.1) is not guaranteed even if local univalence holds for *all* possible w, in sharp contrast to the $n = 2$ case described in Proposition 4. The distinction is described schematically in Figure 6.1. The set D is mapped into D'. Imagine the mapping as physically "bending" D so as to place point w^2 over w^0.

There is local univalence between a neighborhood of w^0 in D and a corresponding neighborhood of p^0 in D', and also a local univalence between a neighborhood of w^2 in D and one of p^0 in D'. But global univalence fails because both w^0 and w^2 are mapped into p^0.

Though complete local univalence does not imply global univalence in general one might ask whether it could do so once explicit account is taken of mathematical properties additional to (6.1) motivated by economic concerns. For example, $A(w)$ results from the choice of least-cost techniques over a technology of conventional properties, and only non-negative prices are commonly considered of interest. However, a counterexample presented by McKenzie (1967) took the wind out of the sails of such an approach.

[14]Besides the works referred to below, mention should be made of Samuelson (1949, 1967), McKenzie (1955), Harrod (1958), Pearce and James (1951), Pearce (1959, 1967, 1970), and Kuga (1972).

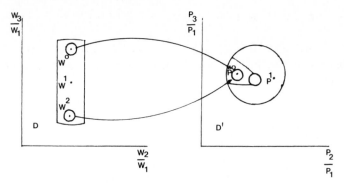

Figure 6.1.   A failure of global univalence.

The basic result is that of Gale and Nikaido (1965): the system (6.1) is globally univalent if $A(w)$ always has all positive principal minors (in which case A is sometimes called a "P-matrix"). When $n = 2$ this condition reduces (with the appropriate numbering of goods and factors) to the absence of a factor-intensity reversal. Uekawa (1971) has furnished the following interpretation for the general case.

Goods and factors can be numbered so that, no matter how the index set $\{1,\ldots,n\}$ is divided into two proper subsets J and $\bar{J}$, it is always possible to find some positive output vector X for which the goods in J together use more of *each* factor in J and less of *each* factor in $\bar{J}$ than do the goods in $\bar{J}$ together. Thus Uekawa has established a sense in which it can be said that A is a P matrix if and only if the technology resembles that of a 2×2 model.

But the Gale–Nikaido condition is only a sufficient one for global univalence which does not make use of economically reasonable restrictions. Thus the hunt is still on for weaker conditions. Mas-Colell (1979a, 1979b) has shown that positivity of the principal minors of $A(w)$ – other than the determinant of $A(w)$ itself – can be dispensed with whenever w is strictly positive. Following an earlier lead of Samuelson (1966) and Nikaido (1972), Mas-Colell (1979b) has also shown that the cost function (4.1) between *strictly* positive w and *strictly* positive p will be globally univalent if the determinant of factor shares $\theta(w) = (w_i a_{ij}(w)/p_j)$ is uniformly bounded away from zero. Both results impose restrictions notably more stringent than in the $n = 2$ context largely when some factor prices are at or near zero. Whether this should be a source of comfort is a matter of opinion. Nevertheless, the fact that the higher dimensional case does impose additional restrictions, together with both the pronounced lack of economic intuition in those conditions and also the arcane quality of the analysis used to establish them, has generated a view of global univalence as a quite fragile property.

6.2. Stolper–Samuelson and Rybczynski

To study the comparative statics of equilibria with all n goods produced, differentiate (6.1) noting the cost minimization condition $w(dA(w)) = 0$:

$$dp = (dw)A(w).$$

This can also be written as:

$$\hat{p} = \hat{w}\theta(w),\tag{6.2}$$

where $\hat{p} = (\hat{P}_1, \ldots, \hat{P}_n)$ and $\hat{w} = (\hat{w}_1, \ldots, \hat{w}_n)$. The matrix θ is column stochastic: non-negative with the elements in each column summing to unity. Each column shows the distributive shares of the various factors in the respective industry. If θ is non-singular, (6.2) can be inverted to show the proportional response of nominal factor rewards to proportional price changes:

$$\hat{w} = \hat{p}\theta^{-1}(w).\tag{6.3}$$

Since θ is column stochastic, $u\theta = u$, where u is the vector of ones. But this implies $u = u\theta^{-1}$, i.e. θ^{-1} has unit column sums.

In like manner, the condition for factor market equilibrium, $A(w)X = V$, may be differentiated to obtain, at constant prices and techniques,

$$A(w)(dX) = dV.\tag{6.4}$$

This in turn can be written as:

$$\lambda(w)\hat{X} = \hat{V},$$

where $\hat{X} = (\hat{X}_1, \ldots, \hat{X}_n)$ and $\hat{V} = (\hat{V}_1, \ldots, \hat{V}_n)$. The matrix $\lambda = (\lambda_{ji})$ is row stochastic, with each row showing the fraction of aggregate demand for the respective factor contributed by the various sectors. If λ is nonsingular, (6.4) can be inverted to show the proportional effects on commodity outputs of proportional changes in factor endowments:

$$\hat{X} = \lambda^{-1}(w)\hat{V}.\tag{6.5}$$

The row stochastic nature of λ implies that λ^{-1} has unit row sums.

For any vector d, let $I(d)$ denote the square matrix with the elements of d along its diagonal and zeroes elsewhere. Then

$$\theta \equiv I(w)A(w)I(1/p),$$

where $1/p = (1/P_1, \ldots, 1/P_n)$. Similarly $\lambda = I(1/V)A(w)I(X)$. With w, p, X and V all strictly positive, the matrices A, θ and λ are all singular or non-singular together. Also, in the latter case, $\theta^{-1} = I(p)A^{-1}I(1/w)$ and $\lambda^{-1} = I(1/X)A^{-1}I(V)$ so that A^{-1}, θ^{-1} and λ^{-1} all have the same sign pattern. These conclusions furnish the basis for a possible duality between $n \times n$ generalizations of the Stolper–Samuelson and Rybczynski theorems.

Now consider how the Stolper–Samuelson theorem might be reformulated for the $n \times n$ environment. When $n = 2$ any change in relative commodity prices will increase one factor reward in terms of both goods and reduce the other factor reward in terms of both goods. To extend fully this result to the higher dimensional context we would wish any change in relative commodity prices to cause each factor price to either rise or fall in terms of all goods. That is, we want θ^{-1} to have the property that, for *every* vector $\hat{p}$ not proportional to u, *no* component of $\hat{w}$ in (6.3) is a weighted average of the components of $\hat{p}$. When $n = 2$ it is also true that each real factor reward changes in the same direction as a particular relative commodity price – that of the good which makes relatively intensive use of the factor. To preserve this aspect one might require a one-to-one correspondence of goods and factors such that the ranking of the components of $\hat{p}$ always coincides with the ranking of the corresponding components of $\hat{w}$.

This is the full-strength higher dimensional version of the 2×2 Stolper–Samuelson property. Obviously a full-strength Rybczynski analog may be stated as well. Once these natural versions have been formulated, one obtains a striking result: they cannot in fact hold. That is, for any technology with more than two goods, there is always *some* change in relative commodity prices which will increase the reward of *some* factor in terms of one good while lowering it in terms of another good. To see this, write out the first equation of (6.3):

$$\hat{w}_1 = \theta^{11}\hat{P}_1 + \cdots + \theta^{n1}\hat{P}_n, \qquad (6.6)$$

where θ^{ij} denote elements of θ^{-1}. Suppose $\theta^{11} \neq 0$. Then set $\hat{P}_1 = (1 - a\theta^{21})/a\theta^{11}$, $\hat{P}_2 = 1$, $\hat{P}_3 = \cdots = \hat{P}_n = 0$, where a is any number exceeding unity. Then from (6.6):

$$\hat{w}_1 = \theta^{11}\hat{P}_1 + \theta^{21} = \left[(1 - a\theta^{21})/a\right] + \theta^{21} = 1/a.$$

Thus $\hat{P}_2 > \hat{w}_1 > \hat{P}_3 = \cdots = \hat{P}_n$, i.e. w_1 has fallen in terms of good 2 and risen in terms of good 3. Note that the argument depends crucially upon the existence of at least three goods.

The Stolper–Samuelson result in its strongest form is inherently a 2×2 property and offers no hope for generalization. Thus even "strong" generalizations must sacrifice something relative to the two dimensional environment in order to be guaranteed by sufficient conditions that are not vacuous. Following the seminal work of Chipman (1964, 1969) a number of alternative strong generalizations have been investigated in detail. The one that has received the most attention reduces mathematically to the stipulation that, for some numbering of goods and factors, the matrix θ^{-1} possess positive diagonal elements and negative off-diagonal elements, that is, be what is called a Minkowski matrix.

If θ^{-1} is Minkowski, then the positive diagonal elements will in fact exceed unity, by virtue of the unit column sums. Thus an increase in any commodity price, with all other commodity prices constant, will raise the reward of the corresponding factor in terms of all goods and will lower the reward of every other factor in terms of all goods. This is why the Minkowski property has interested Chipman and his followers. Our earlier discussion establishes that equally clear-cut conclusions do not apply to arbitrary changes in relative commodity prices. Exact economic characterizations have, quite surprisingly, not been featured in the literature, so it is necessary to provide some detail. Start with the following exact characterization.

Proposition 9

The matrix θ^{-1} is Minkowski if and only if, for *any* division of the n goods into two groups, a uniform proportional increase in the prices of all goods in one group relative to all goods in the second group causes the rewards of all factors corresponding to the first group to increase in terms of all goods and the rewards of all factors in the second group to fall in terms of all goods.

To prove this, suppose first that θ^{-1} is in fact Minkowski and let J denote an arbitrary non-empty proper subset of $\{1,\ldots,n\}$. Two dimensional price changes can be represented in full generality by vectors $\hat{p}$ such that $\hat{P}_i = a$ if $i \in J$ and $\hat{P}_i = 0$ if $i \notin J$ for positive a. From (6.3) we have $\hat{w}_j = \sum_{i=1}^n \hat{P}_i \theta^{ij} = a\sum_{i \in J} \theta^{ij}$. Since θ^{-1} is Minkowski, and has unit column sums, $\sum_{i \in J} \theta^{ij} > 1$ if $j \in J$ and $\sum_{i \in J} \theta^{ij} < 0$ if $j \notin J$. Thus $\hat{w}_j$ either exceeds each component of $\hat{p}$ or falls short of each component, according as j is in J or not.

Suppose next that the stipulated property regarding price changes holds. Then it must hold in particular for $\hat{p}$ such that $\hat{P}_i = 1$ for some i and $\hat{P}_j = 0$ otherwise. Thus $\theta^{ii} > 1$ and $\theta^{ji} < 0$ for $j \neq i$. Repeating the argument for each i establishes that θ^{-1} must be Minkowski.

A dual Rybczynski characterization follows in analogous fashion.

Proposition 10

The matrix λ^{-1} is Minkowski if and only if, for *any* division of the two factors into two groups, a uniform proportional increase in the endowments of all factors in one group relative to all factors in the second group causes the outputs of all goods corresponding to the first group to rise relative to all factor endowments and the outputs of the other goods to fall relative to all endowments.

Proposition 9 reveals that formulating the generalized Stolper–Samuelson theorem as the specification of conditions for which θ^{-1} is a Minkowski matrix is essentially a hunt for the circumstances under which the strong conclusions about factor rewards apply to the class of two-dimensional relative commodity price changes. The analogous Rybczynski problem likewise looks at the consequences of two-dimensional endowment changes. To approach the problem in this way is in a sense to admit defeat from the start, since a basic purpose in moving to higher dimensions in the first place is to pose questions which do not arise in two dimensions.

Nevertheless this formation does have several advantages. First, nontrivial circumstances do exist when the strong results on factor rewards apply to the class of two dimensional price changes, and we have already seen that they cannot apply to the class of all relative commodity price changes. There has as yet been no attempt to find conditions under which the strong results on factor rewards apply to a class of price changes less than universal but more extensive than the two dimensional one.

Secondly, this formulation is mathematically convenient because it amounts only to looking for a particular sign pattern for θ^{-1}. Furthermore that sign pattern has applications to other problems in economics.

Third, the present formulation possesses a strong duality. The matrices θ^{-1}, A^{-1}, and λ^{-1} all share the same sign pattern and furthermore the latter has unit row sums. Thus, if λ^{-1} has all positive diagonal elements and negative off diagonal elements, the former in fact exceed unity. The strong results on factor rewards necessarily follow from all two-dimensional relative commodity price changes if and only if analogous strong results on commodity outputs necessarily follow from all two-dimensional changes in factor endowments. Furthermore, the same association of factors and goods applies in both cases.

Finally, the present formulation can be given an alternative exact economic characterization. It is impossible to preserve in higher dimensions the full-strength results on factor rewards with respect to all relative commodity price changes, so I posed a problem that requires the former with respect to only a subset of the latter. An alternative strategy would be a formulation that accepted weakened conclusions about factor rewards in exchange for an applicability to all relative commodity price changes. Duality helps show that such an alternative formulation can also be expressed mathematically as the requirement that θ^{-1} be Minkowski, and is therefore completely equivalent to the first formulation.

Proposition 11

The matrix θ^{-1} is Minkowski if and only if, for *any* change in relative commodity prices, whenever the goods are divided into two groups with all those in the first group strictly increasing in price relative to all those in the second group, the total absolute income of the factors associated with the first group is more than sufficient to purchase whatever assortment of goods it was originally used to purchase, and the total absolute income of the factors associated with the second group can no longer buy what it initially did.

Then the first group of factor rewards *on average* increase in real terms and the second group on average fall, but nothing is claimed about individual factor rewards.

To prove the proposition, note that $dP = dwA$ or $dw = dPA^{-1}$ from which

$$(dw)I(V) = (dP)I(X)I(1/X)A^{-1}I(V) = (dP)I(X)\lambda^{-1}.$$

Then for any non-empty proper subset J of $\{1,\ldots,n\}$,

$$\sum_{j \in J} (dw_j)V_j = \sum_{j \in J} \sum_{i=1}^{n} (dP_i)X_i\lambda^{ij} = \sum_{i \in J} (dP_i)X_i\left(\sum_{j \in J} \lambda^{ij}\right)$$

$$+ \sum_{k \notin J} (dP_k)X_k\left(\sum_{j \in J} \lambda^{kj}\right) \tag{6.7}$$

and

$$\sum_{j \notin J} (dw_j)V_j = \sum_{i \in J} (dP_i)X_i\left(\sum_{j \notin J} \lambda^{ij}\right) + \sum_{k \notin J} (dP_k)X_k\left(\sum_{j \notin J} \lambda^{kj}\right). \tag{6.8}$$

Now suppose that θ^{-1} is Minkowski, and let dp be any change in relative commodity prices and J any non-empty proper subset of goods such that $dP_j/P_j > dP_i/P_i$ if $j \in J$ and $i \notin J$. We can normalize prices so that $dP_j > 0$ when $j \in J$ and $dP_j < 0$ otherwise. Now λ^{-1} has unit row sums and possesses the Minkowski sign pattern since θ^{-1} does. Thus $\sum_{j \in J}\lambda^{ij}$ exceeds unity if $i \in J$ and is negative if $i \notin J$, and the reverse is true of $\sum_{j \notin J}\lambda^{ij}$. Then from (6.7):

$$\sum_{j \in J} (dw_j)V_j > \sum_{i \in J} (dP_i)X_i > 0,$$

and from (6.8):

$$\sum_{j \notin J} (dw_j)V_j < \sum_{k \notin J} (dP_k)X_k < 0.$$

Next suppose that the stated property holds and, for arbitrary i, consider the price change $dP_i > 0$ and $dP_j = 0$ for $j \neq i$. Then from (6.7) $dw_iV_i = dP_iX_i\lambda^{ii}$ which requires $\lambda^{ii} > 1$ for the property to hold irrespective of initial conditions. Repeating the argument for each i establishes that all diagonal elements of λ^{-1}

exceed unity. Next, again for arbitrary i, consider the price change $dP_i = 0$ and $dP_k < 0$ for $k \neq i$. Then from (6.7) $dw_i V_i = \sum_{k \neq i} (dP_k) X_k \lambda^{ki}$. If any λ^{ki} were positive, $dw_i V_i$ would be made negative by appropriate choice of the dP_k, so that the assumed property would not hold for all initial conditions. Repeating the argument for each i establishes that the off-diagonal elements of λ^{-1} are non-positive. Then λ^{-1} has the Minkowski sign pattern and so θ^{-1} does as well.

In analogous fashion a dual Rybczynski result may be obtained. That is, from $dV = A \, dX$ it follows that:

$$I(P) \, dX = I(P) A^{-1} I(1/w) I(w) \, dV = \theta^{-1} I(w) \, dV,$$

from which, for any subset J of $\{1, \ldots, n\}$,

$$\sum_{i \in J} P_i \, dX_i = \sum_{j \in J} \left(\sum_{i \in J} \theta^{ij} \right) w_j (dV_j) + \sum_{k \notin J} \left(\sum_{i \in J} \theta^{ik} \right) w_k (dV_k) \qquad (6.9)$$

and

$$\sum_{i \notin J} P_i \, dX_i = \sum_{j \in J} \left(\sum_{i \notin J} \theta^{ij} \right) w_j (dV_j) + \sum_{k \notin J} \left(\sum_{i \notin J} \theta^{ik} \right) w_k (dV_k). \qquad (6.10)$$

These expressions yield the following proposition.[15]

Proposition 12

The matrix λ^{-1} is Minkowski if and only if, for any change in factor endowments where the endowments in one group of factors all increase and the remaining endowments do not increase, at constant prices, the total value of the output of all those goods associated with the first group of factors increases by a larger absolute amount than does national income, and the total value of the remaining goods rises less than does national income.

Thus if all goods are normal, the total excess demand for the first set of goods falls and that of the second rises.

Much work has been devoted to the investigation of technological properties associated with θ^{-1} having the desired sign pattern. One result is immediate from the first economic characterization. Let J be an arbitrary proper subset of $\{1, \ldots, n\}$ and let $\hat{p}$ be such that $\hat{P}_j = \varepsilon$ for $j \in J$ and $\hat{P}_j = -\varepsilon$ for $j \notin J$, where $\varepsilon > 0$. Since $\hat{p}$ constitutes a two-dimensional price change, the desired sign pattern for θ^{-1} implies that $\hat{w}_j > \varepsilon$ for $j \in J$ and $\hat{w}_j < -\varepsilon$ for $j \notin J$, where $\hat{w} = \hat{p} \theta^{-1}$. Thus

---

[15]For convenience the proposition is stated with respect to changes where some endowments increase and some fall, but it can be reformulated to apply to more general cases.

$\hat{p} = \hat{w}\theta$ gives:

$$\sum_{j \in J} w_j \theta^{ji} > \sum_{j \notin J} (-\hat{w}_j)\theta^{ji}, \qquad \text{if } i \in J,$$

$$\sum_{j \notin J} (-\hat{w}_j)\theta^{ji} > \sum_{j \in J} \hat{w}_j \theta^{ji}, \qquad \text{if } i \notin J.$$

That is, θ necessarily satisfies Uekawa's characterization of a P matrix, discussed in Section 6.1. Thus if θ^{-1} is Minkowski, θ has all positive principal minors (and therefore A and λ do as well). If this holds for all factor prices the technology must be globally univalent, by the Gale–Nikaido theorem. That the strong conclusions about factor rewards always apply to all two-dimensional price changes is then a stronger property than global univalence.

An exact characterization is found in Uekawa, Kemp and Wegge (1973). The matrix A will have an inverse with positive diagonal elements and negative off-diagonal elements if and only if for *any* non-empty proper subset J of $\{1,\dots,n\}$ and for any positive numbers $\bar{x}_j$, where $j \in J$, there exist positive numbers x_j, where $j \notin J$, such that:

$$\sum_{j \in J} a_{ij}\bar{x}_j > \sum_{j \notin J} a_{ij}x_j, \qquad \text{if } i \in J,$$

$$\sum_{j \in J} a_{ij}\bar{x}_j < \sum_{j \notin J} a_{ij}x_j, \qquad \text{if } i \notin J.$$

That this condition is strictly stronger than the characterization of a P matrix is evident in that the former must hold for all choices of positive $\bar{x}_j$ whereas the latter only requires some values that work.

The attempt to extend to higher dimensions the strong Stolper–Samuelson property that commodity price changes produce unambiguous changes in all factor rewards thus runs into serious limitations. First, either the class of applicable relative commodity price changes was restricted to the two-dimensional one or the conclusions about factor rewards were obtained only on average; secondly, the presence of the strong property for this restricted class was shown to be equivalent to the imposition on the technology of a strong factor intensity condition that can be interpreted as requiring the technology to be in some sense essentially two dimensional. The most significant accomplishment of this branch of international trade theory must surely be the basic elucidation of the notion that the strong Stolper–Samuelson property is in its very essence largely a two dimensional one.

This accomplishment is basically a destructive one: the central motivation advanced in this chapter for moving to higher dimensions is the widespread view that the salient facts of actual trade cannot be forced into the 2×2 model, so that the 2×2 questions are not really the relevant ones. Still one is sometimes interested in what basically are 2×2 questions. To this extent it is natural to buy more generality by restricting the range of relevant questions even more than in Propositions 9–12. Thus one can obtain definite results without strong conditions on technology if one is prepared *both* to admit only two dimensional price changes (or two-dimensional endowment changes) and *also* to look at conclusions about factor rewards only on average (or only at the output changes in a pair of Hicksian composites).[16] Alternative, basically "strong", extensions of the Stolper–Samuelson result have also been considered.[17] One natural possibility is to reverse the pattern of signs: require θ^{-1} to possess negative diagonal elements with all off-diagonal elements greater than unity. This is equivalent to requiring some association of goods and factors such that any two-dimensional relative price change reduces, in terms of all goods, the rewards of each factor associated with a good whose price has risen and increases, in terms of all goods, the reward of each factor associated with a good whose relative price has declined. The alternative equivalent formulation is in like manner reversed. When $n = 2$ this property is essentially the same as the earlier, differing only in the numbering of goods and factors. But when $n > 2$ the two properties are distinct, and indeed mutually exclusive, because the number of off-diagonal elements exceeds the number of diagonal elements.

Despite the obvious symmetry, this alternative is in some ways less attractive than the earlier formulation. For one thing, the fact that θ^{-1} is column-stochastic does not allow one to infer from its sign pattern that the positive off-diagonal elements in fact exceed unity. This must be imposed as a separate requirement. Thus this alternative formulation does not also reduce mathematically to simply requiring that θ^{-1} have a certain sign pattern. Secondly, the similarity of sign patterns between θ^{-1} and λ^{-1} does not imply that if the positive elements of the former exceed unity those of the latter do as well. Thus the strong duality of the earlier formulation is not retained, and Propositions 11 and 12, which exploited this duality, must be suitably rephrased. As it has happened, however, the literature has in fact strangely been concerned only with the mathematically more convenient problem of assuring that θ^{-1} have negative diagonal and positive off-diagonal elements. That the latter also exceed unity, central to the economic motivation, has not thus far even been investigated.

Further formulations apply to even more restrictive classes of price changes than the two dimensional one. One alternative is to require that θ^{-1} have no elements between zero and unity: any change in the price of a *single* commodity relative to all others should cause each factor reward to alter unambiguously in real terms. Still another alternative requires only that all diagonal elements exceed

---

[16]Details may be found in Neary (1979), which has pioneered this interesting approach.
[17]See Chipman (1969), Uekawa (1971, 1979), Inada (1971), Ethier (1974), and Egawa (1978).

unity (or yet again that they each exceed both unity and every off-diagonal element in the same row). That is, any change in the price of a single good relative to all others should increase in terms of all goods the reward of the associated factor (and increase every other factor reward a smaller amount).

6.3. The Heckscher–Ohlin theorems

In two dimensions the Heckscher–Ohlin theorems impose more restrictive assumptions than do the other fundamental propositions, so it should come as no surprise, in view of the difficulties already seen, that very little has been attempted in the way of strong generalizations of the former to higher dimensions. But what can be gleaned from the comparative statics results that have been obtained?

Suppose that the technology is indeed such that θ^{-1} always exists and has the Minkowski sign pattern for some numbering of goods and factors. Consider first the price version of the Heckscher–Ohlin theorem. In two dimensions this proposition can be thought of as consisting of two parts: the contention that differences between countries in autarkic relative factor prices correspond to differences in autarkic relative commodity prices, and the assertion that the latter predict trade patterns. The second part – a portion of what is often called the Law of Comparative Advantage – is applicable to more general circumstances than factor-endowment models. Its higher-dimensional fate was discussed earlier in this chapter. Focus now on the first part: the link between autarkic commodity price differences between countries and relative factor abundance as measured by autarkic factor prices. When the former are of the appropriate two-dimensional sort (and small) we can call on Proposition 9.

Proposition 13

Suppose that autarkic commodity prices differ in a two-dimensional fashion between two countries with an identical technology for which θ^{-1} exists and is Minkowski for some numbering of goods and factors. Then in each country the autarkic reward of each factor associated with each of the goods more costly in that country is greater, in terms of each good, than the reward of each other factor.

Next, the quantity version. Since global univalence is implied if λ^{-1} is required to have the Minkowski sign pattern, two countries will have equal factor prices if they both produce all n goods in free trade. Also they will consume the goods in identical proportions if they share identical homothetic preferences. Then Proposition 10 gives a quantity version.

Proposition 14

Suppose that two countries with identical homothetic preferences share a common technology for which λ^{-1} exists and is always Minkowski for some numbering of goods and factors. Suppose that both countries produce all goods in free trade, and that their respective factor endowments differ from each other in a two-dimensional fashion. Then each country exports each good associated with each of that country's relatively abundant factors.

These two results are patently unsatisfactory because they apply only when countries differ in very special ways, and the basic reason for moving to higher dimensions is to study the consequences of more complex differences. Propositions 11 and 12 allow us to examine more general cases, but only at the sacrifice of all attempts to specify the pattern of trade on a commodity-by-commodity basis. For example if several countries engage in free trade with factor price equalization, and the countries have identical homothetic demands, then the bundle of goods consumed by any country will have required for its manufacture a fraction of the world endowment of each factor just equal to that fraction of world income contributed by the country in question. Thus if, for some country, we let $dV_j = V_j - \gamma V_j^*$ in (6.9) and (6.10), where γ denotes the fraction of world (free trade) income contributed by the country, and V_j and V_j^* denote respectively the national and world endowments of factor j, then the dX_i will equal net exports. Let J denote the country's relatively abundant factors, i.e. those for which dV_j as thus defined are positive. Then Proposition 11 gives the following quantity version.[18]

Proposition 15

Suppose that there is free trade between all countries, factor prices are equalized, and λ^{-1} exists and has the Minkowski sign pattern. Then each country is on balance an aggregate net exporter, at world prices, of the set of goods corresponding to those factors which are relatively abundant in that country.

7. General results

The most significant message to come from the previous section is that of a basic failure to break the chains of "twoness" when it is demanded that fairly strong properties survive. This failure was manifest in both the economic meaning of the mathematical properties under consideration and also in the technological restrictions implying those properties. Such a message has seemed devastating to modern trade theory, cast in a 2×2 mold widely regarded as incapable of adequately describing reality. Thus a change in strategy is certainly of potential interest. Instead of attempting to impose results that retain as much of the strength of two dimensions as possible, enquire into what results can be obtained generally under restrictions no more severe than those conventionally adopted in the two dimensional environment.

[18] See McKenzie (1966, pp. 100, 101) and Kemp (1976, pp. 45–77).

7.1. Factor-price equalization

A natural place to start is with factor-price equalization, in contrast to the previous section's discussion of global univalence. That is, consider the higher dimensional generalization of Proposition 3 rather than, as before, of Proposition 4.

Suppose for a moment that several countries, under conditions of free trade, are alike in every way, including factor endowments, so that at existing commodity prices all goods can be produced in all countries, and in each:

$$p = wA(w). \tag{7.1}$$

Factor prices are obviously equalized now; under what circumstances will they remain equalized if endowments are allowed to vary across countries? Let K_w be the cone of factor endowments spanned by the columns of $A(w)$ in (7.1); that is, K_w consists of all vectors V satisfying $V = A(w)X$ for some non-negative X. Suppose now that we vary the endowment vectors of the countries, but that we do this so as to keep all endowments in K_w, so as to hold constant each country's national income, wV, evaluated at the original factor prices, and so as to leave world factor supplies fixed. Such variations generate potential equilibria across which world output, national demands and factor prices do not vary, so that factor price equalization holds. But need these potential equilibria actually obtain? When $n = 2$, any country with an endowment in K_w, and freely trading at the specified commodity prices, necessarily has factor prices equal to w; this is the essential constituent of the factor-price equalization theorem. The property carries over to higher dimensions. To see this, suppose that for some $V \in K_w$ another factor price vector, w', is also consistent with equilibrium, that is, $p = w'A(w')$ and for some non-negative X', $V = A(w')X'$. Since $A(w')$ is the (unique) least-cost set of techniques at factor prices w',

$$w'A(w) \geq p = wA(w), \tag{7.2}$$

with at least one strict inequality if $w' \neq w$. Similarly the fact that $A(w)$ is the least-cost set of techniques at factor prices w yields:

$$wA(w') \geq p = w'A(w'), \tag{7.3}$$

with at least one inequality if $w' \neq w$. Multiplying both sides of (7.2) by X gives $w'V \geq wV$ with strict inequality if $w' \neq w$, and multiplying both sides of (7.2) by X' gives $wV \geq w'V$ with strict inequality if $w \neq w'$. Thus $w = w'$.

For any p, all countries with endowments in an associated K_w [that is, one for which $p = wA(w)$] will have equal factor prices in free trade. This is a substantive result when K_w has full dimension, m. This is so when $A(w)$ has at least m linearly independent columns: the same condition as in the two-dimensional case. [Note that consistently with Section 5, factor-price equalization becomes a fluke when factors outnumber goods, as $A(w)$ necessarily has fewer than m columns.] Proposition 3 carries over to higher dimensions without difficulty as long as there are at least as many goods as factors.[19]

7.2. Stolper – Samuelson

7.2.1. The role of factor intensities

The conventional Stolper–Samuelson result can be decomposed into two parts: a prediction, based on factor intensities, of the direction of response of relative factor price changes to relative commodity price changes, and the assertion that factor prices move in different directions in real terms. The strong attempts at generalization tended to link these two aspects together: several forms of the relative factor-intensity hypothesis were shown to imply (or be equivalent to) certain strong relations between commodity prices and real factor rewards. In taking a more general approach it proves convenient to keep the two aspects separate. I first ask to what extent is it true that relative factor intensities allow one to infer something about the *direction* of changes in factor rewards from the direction of commodity price changes.[20]

Consider two equilibria characterized by (initial and terminal) goods price vectors p^0 and p^1, and corresponding factor price vectors w^0 and w^1. I impose no restrictions on the relative number of goods and factors, but I do look only at those goods actually produced in both the initial and terminal equilibria (though not necessarily in "intermediate" ones). Thus $p^0 = w^0 A(w^0)$ and $p^1 = w^1 A(w^1)$. Application of the mean value theorem to the function $b(w) = wA(w)(p^1 - p^0)$ yields the conclusion that, for some factor price vector $\bar{w}$,

$$b(w^1) = b(w^0) + (w^1 - w^0)[A(\bar{w}) + \bar{w}dA(\bar{w})](p^1 - p^0).$$

Now cost-minimization implies that $\bar{w}dA(\bar{w}) = 0$ so that

$$b(w^1) - b(w^0) = (w^1 - w^0)A(\bar{w})(p^1 - p^0).$$

Noting $b(w^1) - b(w^0) = (p^1 - p^0)(p^1 - p^0) > 0$ produces the conclusion:

$$(w^1 - w^0)A(\bar{w})(p^1 - p^0) > 0. \tag{7.4}$$

---

[19]See McKenzie (1955), Samuelson (1953), Uzawa (1959), Ethier (1974), and Dixit and Norman (1980).
[20]See Ethier (1982).

That is, there is a positive *correlation* between the elements of the vector $(w^1 - w^0)$ and those of $A(\bar{w})(p^1 - p^0)$ – or, equivalently, between $(w^1 - w^0)A(\bar{w})$ and $(p^1 - p^0)$. On average, high values of $w_i^1 - w_i^0$ are associated with high values of both a_{ij} and $P_j^1 - P_j^0$ or with low values of both: there is a tendency for changes in relative commodity prices to be accompanied by increases in the rewards of factors employed most intensively by those goods whose prices have relatively risen the most and employed least intensively by those goods whose relative prices have fallen the most.

Note several aspects of this result. The first is its extreme generality: the correlation is a direct result of cost minimization and requires no special restrictions on either technology or dimensionality. Furthermore the correlation, which becomes a certainty when $n = 2$, is a clear generalization of the 2×2 result. Also, for small enough changes $\bar{w} = w^0$ will work in (7.4): the pattern of factor price changes can on average be predicted from the initial factor intensities. But for large changes this is not so, and it may be necessary to choose a $\bar{w}$ near neither w^1 nor w^0 so that the pattern of intensities might not be observable for some applications. For example, consider the two dimensional case with a factor intensity reversal illustrated in Figure 7.1. A movement from A to B involves the opposite pattern of factor reward changes as one from C to D. In the former case $\bar{w}_1 / \bar{w}_2$ must be given by a point such as F whereas in the latter case it would look like E. Finally, note that $p^1 - p^0$ measures the price changes only of those goods actually produced in both states (though not necessarily in intermediate states, such as when $w = \bar{w}$). Thus the relation of real or nominal factor rewards to changes in the prices of other goods, if any, are not described.

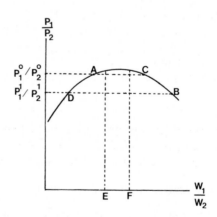

Figure 7.1. The proper choice of w.

7.2.2. Real rewards[21]

Consider an increase in the price of some good that is actually produced initially, all other commodity prices remaining unchanged. As the good was produced, price must have initially equalled its cost of production. Cost may now rise above price,[22] causing production to cease, but competition will prevent price rising above cost in any case. Thus the proportional rise in the price of this good, which I number the first, must be no greater than the proportional rise in its cost:

$$\hat{P}_1 \leq \theta_{11}\hat{w}_1 + \cdots + \theta_{m1}\hat{w}_m. \tag{7.5}$$

The θ_{ji} in this relation are non-negative and sum to unity. Thus (7.5) implies that there exists *some* factor – call it the first – such that $\hat{w}_1 \geq \hat{P}_1 > 0 = \hat{P}_2 = \cdots = \hat{P}_n$. Thus it is generally true that a rise in the price of any good initially produced must raise the reward of some factor in terms of every other good and lower it in terms of no good.

To proceed further requires that in the new equilibrium factor 1 be used in the production of some other good, say the second. As this good is produced, its price equals its cost. It may not have been produced initially, so its initial cost could have exceeded its price, but in any case competition prevented its cost from being strictly less than its price. Thus the proportional rise in the latter (zero) must have been at least as great as that in the former:

$$0 = \hat{P}_2 \geq \theta_{12}\hat{w}_1 + \cdots + \theta_{m2}\hat{w}_m. \tag{7.6}$$

We know that $\hat{w}_1 > 0$ and our assumption is that $\theta_{12} > 0$. Since the θ_{j2} are non-negative and sum to unity, (7.6) implies that some factor reward, call it the second, strictly falls: $\hat{w}_2 < 0 = \hat{P}_2 = \cdots = \hat{P}_n < \hat{P}_1$. Thus every good is "friend" to some factor and an "enemy" to some other factor, to use the terminology of Jones and Scheinkman (1977), so that any price rise is conflict-generating.

Proposition 16

A rise in any single commodity price will cause the reward of *some* factor to rise in terms of all other goods and to fall in terms of none, and it will cause the reward of *some* other factor to fall in terms of all goods – provided only that the

---

[21]References include Ethier (1974), Kemp (1976, chs. 4, 7), Jones and Scheinkman (1977), Diewert and Woodland (1977), Chang (1979), and Jones (1979, chs. 8, 18). For a consideration of joint production, see Jones and Scheinkman (1977), Woodland (1977), and Chang, Ethier and Kemp (1980).

[22]Even this possibility is easily ruled out.

good is initially produced and that every factor which it employs is subsequently also employed elsewhere in the economy.

The distinctive feature of this proposition is its extreme generality: no special condition need be imposed on the technology, and the number of commodities may fall short of, equal, or exceed the number of factors. The proposition is easily extended to encompass all two dimensional price changes as discussed in Section 6. If the prices of some subset J of goods all rise proportionally relative to those of all goods not in J, we clearly require only that some good in J be produced initially and that all factors used to produce this good also be subsequently used to produce some good not in J.

Proposition 16 does leave open the possibility that the favored factor's reward might remain constant in terms of the more expensive good, and, therefore, might not increase in real terms if spent entirely on that good. This remote possibility can be eliminated in either of two ways. One might depart from the Stolper–Samuelson tradition with the mild restriction on demand that all agents always spend increases in incomes on at least two goods. Then a factor reward which falls in terms of no good and which fails to rise in terms of at most one good necessarily increases in real terms. Alternatively one can employ a weak assumption of a purely technological nature: no good employs a *specific assortment* of factors, that is, the factors used in positive amounts by any good are precisely the factors used in positive amounts by some other good. With this assumption we can let good 2 use the same collection of factors as does good one in the above derivation of Proposition 16. Then good one uses factor two, since good two does. Thus in (7.5), $\theta_{21} > 0$ and $\hat{w}_2 < 0$. Then (7.5) in fact requires that for some factor, say the first, $\hat{w}_1 > \hat{P}_1$. It is interesting to note that both methods of resolving the problem involve imposing "twoness" at a *minimum*: income must be spent on *at least two* goods, or an assortment of factors must be common to *at least two* industries.

There remains the crucial problem of determining what can be said about the consequences of relative price changes in general, as opposed to the two-dimensional changes thus far considered. For an arbitrary relative price change, the role of good one in the above discussion can clearly be played by a commodity whose price rises at least as much, proportionally, as any other commodity price, provided that there is such a good initially produced. Similarly the role of good two can be played by any good whose price rises relative to no other, provided that there is such a commodity produced after the price change. Thus our conclusions apply to arbitrary relative price changes as long as the latter are what might be called "non-specializing": some initially-produced good falls in price relative to no other and some terminally-produced good rises in price relative to no other. These various conclusions are summarized in the following.

Proposition 17

Any non-specializing relative price change necessarily raises some factor reward in terms of all goods and lowers some other factor reward in terms of all goods, provided only that no good employs a specific assortment of factors.

Note that the conditions imposed by this proposition are trivially satisfied if all goods use all factors and if all goods are produced (the purpose of the conditions is simply to accommodate "zeros"), as in the usual two dimensional analysis. Thus the propositions meet the goal of employing restrictions no more severe than those used when $n = 2$.

Still more conclusions can be obtained by exploiting the duality embodied in the reciprocity relations derived in Section 1. But before doing this I must turn to the Rybczynski analogs of the present results.

7.3. Rybczynski

The remainder of this section is basically a collection of repetitions and applications of the logic thus far. But the process requires some care because of an asymmetry between the Stolper–Samuelson and Rybczynski problems in one respect. This involves dimensionality. Suppose that the economy is initially in equilibrium at factor prices w. As we have seen, any change in V that leaves the economy in K_w at unchanged commodity prices will also leave factor prices – and thus techniques of production – unchanged as well. Now if K_w has dimension m and if V is initially in its interior, any sufficiently small dV will leave it there. But when there are fewer produced goods than factors a change in V will, except for a fluke, involve a departure from K_w and therefore require a change in w to maintain factor market equilibrium (the previous Stolper–Samuelson discussion was not sensitive to the relative numbers of goods and factors). This is illustrated by a consideration of the role played by factor intensities in predicting the direction of output changes resulting, at constant commodity prices, from endowment changes.

7.3.1. The direction of output changes

Suppose that $V^0 = A(w)X^0$ and $V^1 = A(w)X^1$ in the initial and terminal states. Here V^0 and V^1 are assumed to both lie in K_w so that factor prices are not altered by the change. Then $V^1 - V^0 = A(w)(X^1 - X^0)$ so that multiplication of both sides by $V^1 - V^0$ gives:

$$(V^1 - V^0)A(w)(X^1 - X^0) > 0. \tag{7.7}$$

Thus we obtain a Rybczynski correlation analogous to the earlier Stolper–Samuelson one: endowment changes tend on average to increase the most those goods making relatively intensive use of those factors which have increased the most in supply, etc. But factor price equalization played a key role in this analysis which is therefore of practical significance only when $n \geq m$.

7.3.2. The magnitude of output changes

Consider an increase in the endowment of some factor, call it the first, that is fully employed after the endowment change. It may or may not have been fully employed before, but demand for the factor can have increased proportionally no less than its supply. Thus, if factor prices are unchanged,

$$\hat{V}_1 \leq \lambda_{11} \hat{X}_1 + \cdots + \lambda_{1n} \hat{X}_n. \tag{7.8}$$

The λ_{1i} are non-negative numbers summing to unity; then (7.8) requires that for some good, call it the first, $\hat{X}_1 \geq \hat{V}_1 > 0 = \hat{V}_2 = \cdots = \hat{V}_m$. So it is generally true that an increase in the endowment of a subsequently fully employed factor must increase the output of some good relatively to every other factor and lower it in terms of no factor, provided that factor prices do not change. If good one also uses an additional factor, say the second, fully employed initially,

$$0 = \hat{V}_2 \geq \lambda_{21} \hat{X}_1 + \cdots + \lambda_{2n} \hat{X}_n. \tag{7.9}$$

Since $\hat{X}_1 > 0$ and by assumption $\lambda_{21} > 0$, (7.9) requires that for some good, say the second, $\hat{X}_2 < 0$.

Proposition 18

At constant factor prices, an increase in any factor endowment will cause the output of *some* good to rise relative to all other factors and to fall relative to none, and will cause the output of *some* other good to fall absolutely – provided only that the factor is subsequently fully employed and that every industry which uses it also uses another factor that is initially fully employed.

This proposition is also extremely general, although its requirement of constant factor prices potentially gives a role to one aspect of dimensionality – the relative number of goods and factors – that did not figure at all in Proposition 16. The argument can be extended in obvious fashion to encompass arbitrary two-dimensional endowment changes.

That the output of the favored commodity actually rise relative to *all* factors, including the expanding one(s), can be guaranteed by an additional assumption: each factor is *non-specific* in the sense that it is used in positive amounts by exactly the same sectors which use some other factor. For if factor two plays this role in the above demonstration, $\lambda_{22} > 0$ implies $\lambda_{12} > 0$ so that $\hat{X}_2 < 0$ requires $\hat{X}_1 > \hat{V}_1$. Finally, the present analysis can encompass arbitrary relative endowment changes in a way analogous to the earlier inclusion of arbitrary relative price changes: the former must be "employment-maintaining" in the sense that some factor fully employed after the change increases proportionally at least as much as every other factor, and some factor initially fully employed increases proportionally no more than any other.

Proposition 19

At constant factor prices, any employment-maintaining change in relative factor endowments necessarily causes some output to expand relative to all endowments and some output to fall relative to all endowments, provided only that all factors are non-specific.

7.4. General results

7.4.1. Even technologies

Further results depend upon the number of factors and produced goods. Start with the case $n = m$. Factor prices will not change in response to (small) endowment changes if commodity prices are held constant, so Propositions 18 and 19 are now applicable to the latter case. These "Rybczynski" results can be used to obtain additional "Stolper–Samuelson" results, and vice versa, by exploiting the reciprocity relations derived in Section 1:

$$\frac{\partial X_i}{\partial V_j} = \frac{\partial w_j}{\partial P_i} \tag{7.10}$$

(with a common value of a^{ji}). Suppose that all factors are nonspecific. Then for any factor j there exists some commodity i such that $\partial X_i / \partial V_j < 0$, by Proposition 18. Then (7.10) implies that $\partial w_j / \partial P_i < 0$: for any factor there is some commodity an increase in whose price will lower the real reward of that factor. Each factor has an "enemy", in the terminology of Jones and Scheinkman.[23] Thus it is possible to control the real income of any factor by varying a single commodity price in the opposite direction.

Proposition 18 also establishes that for any factor j there is a good i such that $\partial X_i / \partial V_j > X_i / V_j > 0$. From this (7.10) implies that $\partial w_j / \partial P_i > X_i / V_j > 0$, but this does not assure that w_j rises relative to P_i. Accordingly we do not have

[23] This result also follows directly from $\theta \theta^{-1} = I$ without recourse to the reciprocity relations.

another unambiguous statement about real factor rewards, but a quite strong conclusion still follows. For, from (7.10)

$$\frac{\partial w_j}{\partial P_i} V_j - X_i = \left(\frac{\partial X_i}{\partial V_j} \frac{V_j}{X_i} - 1 \right) X_i,$$

so that $\partial X_i / \partial V_j > X_i / V_j$ implies that $V_j \partial w_j / \partial P_i > X_i$. Now the national product function $y(p, V)$ has the property $X_i = \partial y / \partial P_i = \sum_{k=1}^{n} V_k \partial w_k / \partial P_i$. Thus $\sum_{k \neq j} V_k \partial w_k / \partial P_i < 0$: the increase in P_i must cause w_j to rise by so much that the aggregate income of all other factors falls. Thus these incomes no longer suffice to purchase the bundle of goods they purchased before, so that, if after the rise in P_i the entire country can still afford its original consumption bundle, the real reward of factor j must have risen. But in general the strong positive relation between P_i and w_j does not suffice to rule out the possibility that, if the rise in P_i is associated with a fall in national income and if w_j fails to rise proportionally more than P_i, the expenditure of income accruing to factor i might be sufficiently concentrated upon good j to prevent a rise in the factor's real reward.

The phalanx of Stolper–Samuelson conclusions requires both Propositions 16 and 17's demand that no good employs a specific assortment of factors and Propositions 18 and 19's demand that all factors are non-specific. Thus the total requirement is that $A(w)$ be what can be called *fully-latticed*: a non-zero matrix in which no row or no column has a unique sign pattern.

A similar approach exploits duality to use the Stolper–Samuelson results to extend the Rybczynski results. In the end the following emerges.

Proposition 20

Suppose $n = m$ and that $A(w)$ is fully latticed. Then

(i) to each good there corresponds some factor such that an increase in the good's price raises the factor reward to a greater degree, and an increase in the factor endowment at constant commodity prices raises the output of the good by enough so that the total value of all other outputs falls;

(ii) to each good there corresponds some factor such that an increase in the good's price lowers the factor's reward, and an increase in the factor's endowment at constant commodity prices lowers the output of the good;

(iii) to each factor there corresponds some good such that an increase in the good's price lowers the factor's reward, and an increase in the factor's endowment at constant commodity prices lowers the output of the good;

(iv) to each factor there corresponds some good such that an increase in the good's price raises the factor's reward so much that the aggregate income of all other factors falls, and an increase in the factor's endowment raises the output of the good in greater proportion.

With a fully latticed, and even, technology, each good has a friend and an enemy among the factors in a Stolper–Samuelson sense, and each factor has some enemy and a "qualified" friend. In a Rybczynski sense each factor has a friend and an enemy, and each good has some enemy and a "qualified" friend.

7.4.2. Odd technologies: More goods than factors

Propositions 16 and 17, insensitive to dimensionality, remain valid, if the number of produced goods exceeds the number of factors. At constant commodity prices, endowment changes leave factor prices unaltered; thus Propositions 18 and 19 continue to describe the output effects of changes in factor supplies when the prices of goods are constant. It is true that, as indicated in Section 4, outputs – and therefore output changes as well – are now indeterminate. But this does not affect the validity of the propositions, which assert that *some* outputs must respond in certain fashions, but which do not claim that their identifies can be determined.

It is the body of results linked to duality that now require more care: for example, the left-hand terms in expressions such as (7.10) are now undefined. Proceed as follows.[24] Choose any subset, containing m goods which remain produced, out of the total of n goods. For this subset, of course,

$$(\mathrm{d}p) = (\mathrm{d}w)A(w), \tag{7.11}$$

where $A(w)$ is $m \times m$. Each good, not included in the subset, which also remains produced furnishes another relation between the respective $\mathrm{d}P_i$ and $\mathrm{d}w$, but this is additional information which does not influence (7.11) and which one can choose to ignore. Next consider the exercise of varying factor endowments subject to constant commodity prices (and thus factor prices). For each of the goods that was ignored in writing (7.11) set $\mathrm{d}X_i = 0$. If $\mathrm{d}X$ denotes the m-vector of changes in the other goods,

$$\mathrm{d}V = A(w)\,\mathrm{d}X, \tag{7.12}$$

where $A(w)$ is the same as in (7.11). The $n - m$ excluded goods use an unchanging bundle of factors in their production. Ignoring this bundle gives a standard $m \times m$ submodel for which the reciprocity relations can be derived in the usual way. (Geometrically, the basic $n \times m$ production model is being invested with the requisite strict quasi-convexity by projection into an appropriate subspace; this can obviously also be done by setting the $n - m$ "extra" $\mathrm{d}X_i$ equal to specified values other than zero.) The earlier derivation of results from duality can now be repeated and thereby extended to the $n > m$ case. The extra goods require one change in interpretation: the fact that for each good i there exists, from Proposi-

---

[24]See also Chang (1979, pp. 718–723).

tion 17, some factor j such that $\partial w_j / \partial P_i < 0$ now implies, from (7.11), that for each good i there is some factor j an increase in whose endowment *allows* a reduction in X_i. The indeterminancy of production patterns precludes a stronger statement.

Proposition 21

Proposition 20 remains fully valid when $n > m$, with the sole modification that, in parts (i) and (ii), an endowment increase at constant commodity prices *allows* the indicated response in outputs, but does not require them.

7.4.3. Odd technologies: More factors than goods

The basic even results can accommodate additional produced goods with only the slightest discomfort. The same is not true of additional factors. Suppose that $m > n$. This, again, has no effect on Propositions 16 and 17. Propositions 18 and 19 also remain valid, but they cease to apply to endowment changes with constant commodity prices, because factor prices must now change under such circumstances to maintain factor market equilibria. As Kemp and Wan point out [in Kemp (1976, p. 56)], it is necessary to choose between two mutually exclusive approaches, each faithful to 2×2 practice in one respect and unfaithful in another. One possibility is to arbitrarily hold factor prices fixed when endowments change at constant commodity prices. This requires consideration of factor market disequilibrium; in effect one moves to a "Keynesian" environment from the usual "Walrasian" one.

In this case Propositions 18 and 19 remain relevant. They should be viewed as comparisons of "Keynesian" equilibria with different factor demands – the appropriate interpretation for endowments in this context. What this approach must sacrifice are the results due to duality: the $\partial X_i / \partial V_j$ terms in the reciprocity relations (7.10) are derived on the assumption of constant commodity prices and continuous factor market equilibrium (and therefore changing factor prices if $m > n$). Thus those parts of the Stolper–Samuelson and Rybczynski results that followed from the application of (7.10) to Propositions 16 and 18 do not survive.

The alternative approach is to compare situations involving factor-market equilibria, and therefore altered factor prices. Propositions 18 and 19 now cease to apply, so that portion of the Rybczynski results is lost. But now the reciprocity relations can be applied, so that the portion of the Rybczynski results obtained by duality from Propositions 16 and 17 once again hold.

In sum, when there are more factors than goods about half the comparative statics results survive. On the Stolper–Samuelson side, it remains true that each good is a friend to some factor and an enemy to another, but each factor need no longer have some enemy and some "qualified" friend. On the Rybczynski side, if factor markets are required to clear, each good has an enemy and a "qualified" friend, but every factor need no longer be a friend to some good and an enemy to another; when factor prices are instead held fixed, just the reverse is true.

7.4.4. The multi-commodity specific-factors model

The multi-commodity extension of the specific-factors model discussed in Section 5.2 is instructive. Suppose that a positive endowment is available of each of n factors specific to each existing good, and that the technology is such that at all positive commodity price vectors positive amounts of all goods are produced. This structure is simple enough that one readily understands that the properties discussed in Section 5.2 are essentially unchanged.[25]

This model violates both of the conditions of Proposition 20: $n < m$ ($= n + 1$) and $A(w)$ is not fully latticed. But the former violation is the crucial one. Each good is a Stolper–Samuelson friend to its own specific factor and an enemy to all other specific factors; the mobile factor has neither friend nor enemy. In a Rybczynski sense, with factor markets required to clear, each good has as a qualified friend its own specific factor and every other specific factor as an enemy, while the mobile factor is neither friend nor enemy to any good. These possibilities arise because $m > n$, with the simple structure of the model assuring that the possibilities materialize in a transparent way.

The requirement that $A(w)$ be fully latticed places weak bounds on the degree of specificity: no good may use a unique collection of factors, but the collection may be shared with as few as one other sector, and so forth.[26] The specific-factors model is a limiting case with specificity so pervasive as to violate even this weak requirement. The interesting thing is how little difference it seems to make. The only purpose of requiring $A(w)$ to be fully latticed, you will recall, was to prevent "ties" between proportional increases in commodity prices (factor endowments) and factor rewards (outputs). In the specific factors model these ties nevertheless do not arise, except for the Rybczynski experiments where factor prices are kept fixed and the market for the mobile factor allowed not to clear. Then a change in any specific factor would tend to induce an equiproportional change in the output of the corresponding good and no changes in other outputs.

7.5. The Heckscher–Ohlin theorems

The Heckscher–Ohlin theorems explain the pattern of comparative advantage on the basis of factor endowments. In higher dimensions comparative advantage generalizes as a correlation between price differences and trade flows. It is

[25] For details of this model see Samuelson (1971) or Jones (1975).
[26] For a discussion of comparative statics and specificity see Fishburn and Kemp (1977).

therefore natural to enquire how endowment differences are related, in an average sense, to trade.

7.5.1. The price version

Start with an examination of factor abundance as revealed by autarkic factor prices. Recall (7.4) from the earlier Stolper–Samuelson discussion:

$$(w^1 - w^0)A(\bar{w})(p^1 - p^0) > 0. \tag{7.4}$$

Interpreting w^1 and w^0 as autarkic factor prices in the home and foreign countries, expression (7.4) establishes that countries tend to have a comparative advantage in goods intensive in their use of relatively abundant factors. Thus the price version generalizes to this degree without difficulty.

Comparative advantage is in turn correlated with the pattern of trade. To link directly factor abundance to trade flows use logic like that preceding (7.4) to obtain:

$$(p^1 - p^0)M = (w^1 - w^0)A(\bar{w})M,$$

where w^1 and w^0 denote home and foreign autarky factor prices and $M = D - X$, the vector of home imports. The discussion of comparative advantage in Section 2 established that $(p^1 - p^0)M \geq 0$ [recall expression (2.5)]. Then

$$(w^1 - w^0)A(\bar{w})M \geq 0. \tag{7.13}$$

Thus countries on average tend to import goods that make relatively intensive use of relatively scarce factors. Recall the earlier discussion of (7.4): to avoid problems arising from the presence of higher-dimensional analogs of factor intensity reversals, $\bar{w}$ must be chosen properly.

Expression (7.13) asserts that, for some "intermediate" factor price vector the price version of the Heckscher–Ohlin theorem holds. But no procedure is given for finding $\bar{w}$, that is, for measuring the relevant pattern of factor intensities. An alternative, constructive, path to generalization proceeds as follows.[27] Construct the technology matrix $\bar{A}$ on the basis of the country of origin of traded goods: the ith column of $\bar{A}$ equals the foreign technique of production if good i is imported and the domestic technique otherwise. Thus $\bar{A}$ equals the actual A matrix in each country if trade has equalized factor prices but will be a composite of the two A matrices otherwise. Define the factor content of trade as: $M_V = \bar{A} M$.

Since the two countries share a common technology, it must be feasible to produce D from the factors $V + M_V$, simply by ceasing to produce exports and

---

[27]The basic reference here is Deardorff (1981). See also Appendix One of Ethier (1983).

producing imports in the same way they are produced abroad. Of course such a process will not generally be profitable at home autarkic prices, w^A, p^A:

$$w^A(V + M_V) \geq p^A D.$$

Now $p^A D \geq p^A D^A$, where D^A denotes the vector of goods consumed in autarky, by the usual gains-from-trade argument. Thus $w^A M_V \geq p^A D^A - w^A V = 0$. The same logic applied to the rest of the world yields $w^{A\bullet} M_V^* \geq 0$. Since $M_V = - M_V^*$,

$$\left(w^A - w^{A\bullet}\right) M_V \geq 0. \tag{7.14}$$

This is a second price version, dealing with the factor content of trade: countries tend to export (indirectly via commodities) their relatively abundant (in a price sense) factors. Substitute for M_V in the correlation (7.14) to examine the pattern of commodity trade:

$$\left(w^A - w^{A\bullet}\right) \bar{A} M \geq 0. \tag{7.15}$$

This third price version says that, on average, countries tend to export goods which make relatively intensive use of relatively abundant factors.

Note that (7.14) and (7.15), like (7.13), are extremely general as they require no special assumptions on technology nor any relation between m and n. Also, like the 2×2 price version, nothing need be said about demand. But it is important that factor content be measured according to the *country of origin* of goods. This is done to avoid the problems introduced by higher-dimensional analogs of factor-intensity reversals, which must be assumed away in the 2×2 case. Consider, in the latter context, a separating factor intensity reversal between the two countries. Then (7.14) says that each country exports its relatively abundant factor: impossible for both countries if each calculates the factor content of trade according to its own techniques in use, or if the techniques of one of the countries are used by both. But the prediction is true when, as in (7.14) and (7.15), the technique of the exporting country is used for each good.

7.5.2. The quantity version

Even in the 2×2 environment the quantity version normally is based on an assumption of identical homothetic demands across countries, so do the same now. That is, tastes in both countries can be represented by a common set of radially symmetric indifference surfaces.[28]

---

[28]See Dixit and Norman (1980, pp. 96–100) and Woodland (1982, ch. 7) for treatments of the quantity version.

Recall that the national product function $y(p,V)$ measures the minimum that must be paid to factors V over all factor rewards that leave costs no lower than p. Thus $w^{A^*}V \geq y(p^{A^*},V)$ where p^{A^*} denotes foreign autarkic commodity prices. Next, if u_0 solves $y(p^{A^*},V) = e(p^{A^*},u_0)$ it follows that home autarkic utility $u_A \leq u_0$ since the opportunity to transact at prices other than p^A cannot lower utility, by the standard gains-from-trade argument. Thus,

$$w^{A^*}V \geq y(p^{A^*},V) = e(p^{A^*},u_0) = \lambda e(p^A,u_0) \geq \lambda e(p^A,u_A) = \lambda w^A V,$$

$$(7.16)$$

where $\lambda = e(p^{A^*},u_0)/e(p^A,u_0)$.

Reversing the roles of the two countries in the above argument yields:

$$w^A V^* \geq \mu w^{A^*} V^*,$$ $$(7.17)$$

where $\mu = e(p^A,u_1)/e(p^{A^*},u_1)$ and u_1 solves $e(p^{A^*},u_1) = y(k^A,V)$. Identical homothetic demands imply that $\lambda = 1/\mu$. Then combining (7.16) and (7.17) yields:

$$(w^{A^*} - \lambda w^A)(V - V^*) \geq 0.$$ $$(7.18)$$

Since λ can be viewed as a measure of the foreign autarkic price level relative to the domestic, correlation (7.18) says that countries tend to have relatively low autarkic prices for those factors with relatively large endowments: the price and quantity definitions are positively correlated. When $m = 2$ the correlation becomes an identity. The assumption of identical homothetic demands is normally the key to establishing this identity, just as that assumption is now the key to establishing a correlation for the general case.

Further progress requires increasingly severe restrictions. Suppose $n \geq m$. Since commodity prices uniquely relate to factor prices once endowments v are given, write $w = f(p,v)$. Define $h(p,v) = f(p,v)(V - V^*)$, and use logic like that preceding (7.4) to obtain, for some $\bar{w} = f(\bar{p},\bar{v})$:

$$h(p^A,V) - h(p^{A^*},V^*) = (p^A - p^{A^*})f_p(\bar{p},\bar{v})(V - V^*)$$
$$+ (V - V^*)f_v(\bar{p},\bar{v})(V - V^*),$$

where f_p and f_v denote the appropriate matrices of partial derivatives. Now $f_v(\bar{p},\bar{v}) = 0$ by the factor-price equalization theorem and $f_p(\bar{p},\bar{v}) = A^{-1}(\bar{w})$ with $A(\bar{w})$ made square, if necessary, by the arbitrary deletion of extra goods, as in subsection (7.4). Then use (7.18), with prices normalized so that $\lambda = 1$, to obtain:

$$(p^{A^*} - p^A)A(\bar{w})^{-1}(V - V^*) \geq 0.$$ $$(7.19)$$

Thus countries tend to have a comparative advantage in goods that make intensive use of factors that are relatively abundant in a physical sense. Such conclusions in a 2×2 world usually follow an assumption of no factor intensity reversals. In the more general context the proper choice of $\bar{w}$ plays the same role: recall the earlier discussion following the derivation of (7.4). The present argument can be successively applied to subsets of goods when $n > m$, but breaks down if $m > n$. Note also the interesting point that in the price version the relevant concept of factor intensity had to do with the relative magnitudes of the elements of A, whereas the quantity version uses A^{-1}. These concepts become distinct when dimensionality exceeds two.

More detailed conclusions follow when, in addition to $n \geq m$, endowments are sufficiently similar so that free trade produces factor price equalization.[29] Let V^w denote the vector of world factor endowments and g the ratio of domestic income to world income in the free trade equilibrium. Identical homothetic tastes imply that countries consume goods in identical proportions, and factor price equalization implies that each good is produced by a single technique regardless of place of production. Thus the vector of goods consumed at home must require the factors gV^w for its production so that the factor content of the home country's trade is $M_V = gV^w - V$. A country imports its relatively scarce factors, with the degree of importation proportional to the degree of scarcity. Note that, because of factor price equalization, this result also holds in value terms, with factors valued at their free trade prices.

Thus the factor content of trade can be specified precisely. What about its commodity composition? From (7.7):

$$(V^* - V)A(w)(X^* - X) > 0,$$

where w denotes the common vector of factor prices and X^* and X denote foreign and domestic production in free trade. If the foreign economy is scaled by any scalar g and the home economy by $(1 - g)$, the same method yields $[gV^* - (1 - g)V]A(w)[gX^* - (1 - g)X]$. Now if g is set equal to the ratio of home income to world income, in free trade, and if the countries share identical homothetic tastes, home imports $M = gX^* - (1 - g)X = g(X^* + X) - X$. Thus,

$$\left[(g(V + V^*) - V\right]AM \geq 0. \tag{7.20}$$

Thus a country tends on average to import those goods which make relatively intensive use of its relatively scarce factors in a quantity sense, where a factor is scarce or abundant according to whether the home country accounts for a smaller

[29]See Travis (1964), Vanek (1968), Bertrand (1972), Williams (1977), Harkness (1978), Leamer (1980), and Ethier (1982).

or greater supply of that factor than of factors in general (evaluated at the common factor prices).

8. Odd or even: Does it matter?

Higher dimensional generalization of the 2×2 theory involves consideration both of larger numbers of goods and factors and also of unequal numbers of the two. The latter has turned out to be significant. Many results, especially among those of a "strong" sort discussed in Section 6, require an even technology: the number of goods must exactly equal the number of factors.

This would seem most unfortunate. The existence of goods and factors is a fact of technology and of nature and generally taken as exogenous by economists. It is too much to ask of the world that it accommodate itself to our theories by providing factors and goods in precisely equal numbers. Furthermore the application of theory to reality is in this case sufficiently murky to destroy most people's intuition about which body of theory is the relevant one, when odd and even technologies yield distinct conclusions. The sensitivity of our results to such an arbitrary facet of technology appears fatal.

That such a pessimistic view may not be warranted is suggested by two considerations. The general impression conveyed by the "strong" literature discussed in Section 6 was of the difficulty in breaking the bounds of "twoness", whereas the alternative approach of Section 7 established the general validity of a significant core of 2×2 results. This suggests that the important question is whether the weak results depend upon the technology being odd or even. Now recall that the weak results that were valid when $n = m$ had to be altered in only trivial ways when the number of goods exceeded the number of factors, but that the opposite circumstance of relatively more factors required substantial alteration. Thus the crucial issue would seem to be not whether the technology is even or odd, but rather whether the number of goods is at least as large as the number of factors or not.

This would appear to considerably improve our odds. Also a number of writers have argued [Travis (1972), Rader (1979)] that the case of more goods than factors is in fact the practically relevant one. But this still leaves the significance of our theory subject to an arbitrary facet of technology and nature. This is where the second consideration comes in. Two distinctions between good and factor figure prominently in the theory:

(i) factors are primary inputs and goods are outputs – the definitional distinction; and

(ii) goods are internationally traded and factors are not.

Now the relative numbers of primary inputs and outputs is indeed an arbitrary matter of technology and nature, but the relative number of international and national markets is to a significant degree determined by endogenous social and economic organization and by equilibrium prices. Should the latter aspect prove to be the decisive one, the fact that basic propositions depend upon the relative numbers of goods and factors would turn out to be no embarrassment at all: properties sensitive to the number of markets in existence are the very bread and butter of economics.

Furthermore, there is in fact every reason to believe that the crucial aspect is indeed the relative number of international markets and not the technological distinction between good and factor. A basic theme of the factor endowment theory has always been the substitutability of international commodity trade for international factor trade. And from the point of view of analytical hurdles, the introduction of international capital markets into models with $m > n$ would appear on balance a simplification rather than a complication.

This question has surprisingly been ignored in the literature, despite its evident importance and the apparent ease of approaching it.[30] A full scale assault will not be attempted now, but the most strategic points can be carried forthwith.

Consider first the factor-price equalization property, which is especially susceptible to an excess of factors over goods. Let m_T of the m factors be freely traded, and let m_N be internationally immobile. Consider an equilibrium:

$$p = (w_T, w_N) A(w_T, w_N), \tag{8.1}$$

$$(V_T, V_N) = A(w_T, w_N) X, \tag{8.2}$$

where w_T and w_N denote the rentals of the respective sets of factors, V_N the endowment of immobile factors, and V_T the use of tradable factors. In (8.1), p and w_T are determined on international markets and w_N internally. If w_N satisfies (8.1) for given p and w_T, define $K_{w_N}(p, w_T)$ to be the set of all V_N satisfying (8.2) for non-negative X and V_T. An argument similar to that of Section 7 establishes that $K_{w_N}(p, w_T) \cap K_{w_N^1}(p, w_T) \neq \emptyset$ implies that $w_N = w_N^1$. Thus all countries with endowments of nontraded factors in $K_{w_N}(p, w_T)$ have factor prices (w_N, w_T) if freely trading goods and traded factors at prices p and w_T. For this to be a significant factor-price equalization result, $K_{w_N}(p, w_T)$ must be of dimensionality m_N, that is, $A(w_T, w_N)$ must have at least m_N columns (linearly independent in their use of *non-traded* factors), so the dimensionality constraint is $n \geq m_N$, or

$$n + m_T \geq m. \tag{8.3}$$

The number of international markets must be at least as great as the number of factors.

---

[30] The relevant literature includes Inada (1971), Rodriguez (1975), Neary (1980), and Svensson (1982). These papers also discuss the symmetrical possibility of nontraded goods, ignored below.

The argument of Section 7 regarding real rewards goes through as before, relating commodity price changes to the rewards of *non-traded* factors. In addition one can now note how changes in the rewards of traded *factors* influence the rewards of non-traded factors. This line of inquiry reveals some interesting contrasts to the usual one, but it will not be followed now. When condition (8.3) is imposed, the earlier Rybczynski discussion when $n \geq m$ also goes through without difficulty, regarding the effects of changes in the endowments of *non-traded* factors on commodity outputs. It now becomes possible to ask how changes in the endowments of non-traded factors influence the use of traded factors, but this will not be done. In general, when (8.3) holds the earlier Stolper–Samuelson and Rybczynski results for $n \geq m$ continue to hold; the technology need be fully latticed with respect only to non-traded factors.

Thus it would appear that the crucial consideration for the higher dimensional generalization of 2×2 results is not the exogenous happenstance of the relative numbers of goods and factors, but the economic condition of the number of international markets. But note that this is not completely true, as it would be, for example, if the crucial condition had turned out to be that the number of international markets be at least as great as the number of national. Rather we have as many international markets as there are *factor* markets: the larger the number of factors relative to goods, the larger the fraction of total markets that must be international.

Return one last time to the specific-factors model for illustration. With n goods and $n + 1$ factors, one factor market must be international for the model to satisfy condition (8.3). Suppose first that the intersectorally mobile factor is also internationally mobile. With internationally identical technology, the home country can compete in any commodity market on equal terms with the foreign country only if the respective specific factor receives the same reward in both countries, since the mobile factor fetches a single world price. Thus all factor prices are equalized: factor-price equalization is even more pervasive now than in the standard $n \times n$ world.

If instead one of the specific factors is internationally mobile, that sector can be operated in both countries only if the mobile factor receives the same reward in both countries and therefore, by the above argument, only if all factor prices are equalized. Thus factor-price equalization again follows as long as the single internationally mobile specific factor does not in equilibrium locate entirely in one country. This will not happen if endowments of the other n factors are sufficiently similar across the countries. Thus factor-price equalization becomes qualitatively about as inherent as in the $n \times n$ model.

Comparative statistics results are influenced by the fact that $A(w)$ is not fully latticed, a consideration that becomes more prominent once oddness is disposed of. The Stolper–Samuelson conclusions now emerge in full force in nearly every case, with the price of the mobile factor treated like a commodity price in the experiments. But the Rybczynski conclusions are pervaded by "ties": an increase in the endowment of any specific factor, holding constant all commodity prices and the reward of the internationally mobile factor, must cause the corresponding sector to expand in the same proportion as the factor (accompanied by an inflow of the mobile factor if that is internationally mobile, or an outflow of some specific factor if instead it is internationally mobile), with no change in all (or all but one) other outputs. An increase in the endowment of the internally mobile factor, with one of the specific factors mobile internationally, produces a more than proportional rise in the output corresponding to the latter, but no change at all in other outputs.

9. Concluding remarks

The elaborate and extensive structure of modern trade theory has been built on a foundation of several extreme assumptions, including that of low and even dimensionality. A large volume of theoretical work in recent decades has exposed the sensitivity of the structure to these assumptions, and at the same time extensive empirical work has claimed to demonstrate that low dimensionality, at least, is fundamentally inadequate. This has threatened to make a shambles of our theory. But, at least as regards dimensionality, the general implication of recent work, as surveyed in this chapter, seems to be more hopeful than that. Dimensionality has, to be sure, been seen to matter. But the interesting conclusion, to me, is the large extent to which the basic messages of elementary theory still come through.

They do so in two ways. First some results (the law of comparative advantage, Heckscher–Ohlin theorems, and the directional comparative-statistics predictions based on factor intensity) survive as correlations, or in an average sense. This happens to propositions that rely heavily on revealed preference logic and its analogues. Other results (Stolper–Samuelson and Rybczynski) survive in undiluted strength but only in a nonexclusive sense: they apply to some factors or goods but not necessarily to all. In all cases though the 2×2 theory has turned out to have pointed the way with a good deal of accuracy.

References

Baldwin, R.E. (1971), "Determinants of the commodity structure of U.S. trade", American Economic Review, 61:126–146.
Batra, R.N. and F.R. Casas (1976), "A synthesis of the Heckscher–Ohlin and the neoclassical models of international trade", Journal of International Economics, 6:21–38.
Bertrand, T.J. (1970), "On factor price equalization when commodities outnumber factors: A note", Economica 37:86–88.
Bertrand, T.J. (1972), "An extension of the *N*-factor case of factor proportions theory", Kyklos 32:592–596.

Bhagwati, J.N. (1972), "The Heckscher–Ohlin theorem in the multi-commodity case", Journal of Political Economy 80:1052–1055.

Chang, W.W. (1979), "Some theorems of trade and general equilibrium with many goods and factors", Econometrica 47:709–726.

Chang, W.W., W.J. Ethier and M.C. Kemp (1980), "The theorems of international trade with joint production", Journal of International Economics, 10:377–394.

Chipman, J. (1964), "Factor price equalization and the Stolper–Samuelson theorem (abstract)", Econometrica 32:682–683.

Chipman, J. (1969), "Factor price equalization and the Stolper–Samuelson theorem", International Economic Review 10:399–406.

Deardorff, A.V. (1979), "Weak links in the chain of comparative advantage", Journal of International Economics 9:197–209.

Deardorff, A.V. (1980), "The general validity of the law of comparative advantage", Journal of Political Economy 88:941–957.

Deardorff, A.V. (1982), "The general validity of the Heckscher–Ohlin theorem", American Economic Review, 72:683–694.

Diewert, W.E. (1974), "Applications of duality theory", in: M.D. Intriligator and D.A. Kendrick, eds., Frontiers of quantitative economics (North-Holland, Amsterdam).

Diewert, W.E. (1978), "Duality approaches to microeconomic theory", in: K.J. Arrow and M.D. Intriligator, eds., Handbook of mathematical economics (North-Holland, Amsterdam),

Diewert, W.E. and A.O. Woodland (1977), "Frank Knight's theorem in linear programming revisited", Econometrica 45:375–398.

Dixit, A.K. and V. Norman (1980), Theory of international trade (James Nisbet and Cambridge University Press, Digswell Place).

Dornbusch, R., S. Fischer and P.A. Samuelson (1980), "Heckscher–Ohlin trade with a continuum of goods", Quarterly Journal of Economics 95:203–224.

Drabicki, J.Z. and A. Takayama (1979), "An antimony in the theory of comparative advantage", Journal of International Economics 9:211–223.

Egawa, I. (1978), "Some remarks on the Stolper–Samuelson and Rybczynski theorems", Journal of International Economics 8:525–536.

Ethier, W. (1974), "Some of the theorems of international trade with many goods and factors", Journal of International Economics 4:199–206.

Ethier, W.J. (1982), "The general role of factor intensity in the theorems of international trade", Economics Letters, 10:337–342.

Ethier, W.J. (1983), Modern international economics (W.W. Norton, New York).

Fishburn, G. and M.C. Kemp (1977), "An analysis of price:rental and endowment:output relationships in terms of specific-factor and specific-product blocks, The Economic Record 142:219–226.

Gale, D. and H. Nikaido (1965), "The Jacobian matrix and the global univalence of mappings", Mathematische Annalen 159:81–93.

Haberler, G. (1936), The theory of international trade (Hodge, London).

Harkness, J. (1978), "Factor abundance and comparative advantage", American Economic Review 68:784–800.

Harrod, R.F. (1958), "Factor price relations under free trade", Economic Journal 68:245–255.

Heckscher, E. (1919), "The effect of foreign trade on the distribution of income", Ekonomisk Tidskrift 21:497–512.

Inada, K.-I. (1971), "The production coefficient matrix and the Stolper–Samuelson condition", Econometrica 39:219–240.

Johnson, H.G. (1967), "The possibility of factor price equalization when commodities outnumber factors", Economica 34:282–288.

Johnson, H.G. (1970), "On factor price equalization when commodities outnumber factors: A comment", Economica 37:89–90.

Jones, R.W. (1956), "Factor proportions and the Heckscher–Ohlin theorem", Review of Economic Studies 24:1–10.

Jones, R.W. (1961), "Comparative advantage and the theory of tariffs: A multi-country, multi-commodity model", Review of Economic Studies 28:161–175.

Jones, R.W. (1971), "A three-factor model in theory, trade and history", in: J.N. Bhagwati et al., eds.,

Trade, balance of payments and growth: Essays in honor of C.P. Kindleberger (North-Holland, Amsterdam).

Jones, R.W. (1974), "The small country in a many-commodity world", Australian Economic Papers 13:225–236.

Jones, R.W. (1975), "Income distribution and effective protection in a multicommodity trade model", Journal of Economic Theory 11:1–15.

Jones, R.W. (1979), International trade: Essays in theory (North-Holland, Amsterdam).

Jones, R.W. and S. Easton (1983), "Factor intensities and factor substitution in general equilibrium", Journal of International Economics, forthcoming.

Jones, R.W. and J. Scheinkman (1977), "The relevance of the two-sector production model in trade theory", Journal of Political Economy 85:909–935.

Kemp, M.C. (1962), "The gain from international trade", Economic Journal 82:808–819.

Kemp, M.C. (1969), The pure theory of international trade and investment (Prentice-Hall, Englewood Cliffs).

Kemp, M.C. (1976), Three topics in the theory of international trade (North-Holland, Amsterdam).

Krueger, A. (1977), "Growth, distortions and patterns of trade among many countries", Princeton Studies in International Finance, no. 40.

Krueger, A. and H. Sonnenschein (1967), "The terms of trade, the gains from trade, and price divergence", International Economic Review 8:121–127.

Kuga, K. (1972), "The factor-price equalization theorem", Econometrica 40:723–736.

Land, A.H. (1959), "Factor endowments and factor prices", Economica 26:137–142.

Leamer, E. (1980), "The Leontief paradox, reconsidered", Journal of Political Economy 88:495–503.

Leontief, W. (1953), "Domestic production and foreign trade: The American capital position re-examined", Proceedings of the American Philosophical Society 97:332–349.

Leontief, W. (1956), "Factor proportions and the structure of American trade: Further theoretical and empirical analysis", Review of Economics and Statistics 38:386–407.

Mas-Colell, A. (1979a), "Homeomorphism of compact, convex sets and the Jacobian matrix", SIAM Journal of Mathematical Analysis, 10:1105–1109.

Mas-Colell, A. (1979b), Two propositions on the global univalence of systems of cost function, in: J.R. Green and J.A. Scheinkman, eds., General equilibrium, growth and trade (Academic Press, New York).

Mayer, W. (1974), "Short-run equilibrium for a small open economy", Journal of Political Economy 82:955–968.

McKenzie, L.W. (1954), "Specialization and efficiency in world production", Review of Economic Studies 21:165–180.

McKenzie, L.W. (1955), "Equality of factor prices in world trade", Econometrica 23:239–257.

McKenzie, L.W. (1956), "Specialization in production and the production possibility locus", Review of Economic Studies 23:56–64.

McKenzie, L.W. (1966), "International trade: Mathematical theory", in: Encyclopedia of the Social Sciences (University of Chicago, Chicago).

McKenzie, L.W. (1967), "The inversion of cost functions: A counter-example", International Economic Review 8:271–278.

Meade, J.E. (1950), "The equalization of factor prices: The two-country, three-product case", Metroeconomica 2:129–133.

Melvin, J.R. (1968), "Production and trade with two factors and three goods", American Economic Review 58:1248–1268.

Mussa, M. (1974), "Tariffs and the distribution of income: The importance of factor specificity, substitutability, and intensity in the short and long run", Journal of Political Economy 82:1191–1204.

Neary, J.P. (1978), "Short-run capital specificity and the pure theory of international trade", Economic Journal 88:488–510.

Neary, J.P. (1979), "Two-by-two international trade theory with many goods and factors", Econometrica, forthcoming.

Neary, J.P. (1980), "International factor mobility, minimum wage rates and factor-price equalization", Seminar Paper no. 158, Institute for International Economic Studies, University of Stockholm.

Nikaido, H. (1972), "Relative shares and factor price equalization", Journal of International Economics 2:257–264.

Ohlin, B. (1933), Interregional and international trade (Harvard, Cambridge).

Pearce, I.F. (1959), "A further note on factor-commodity price relationships", Economic Journal 79:725-732.

Pearce, I.F. (1967), "More about factor price equalization", International Economic Review 8:255-270.

Pearce, I.F. (1970), International trade (W.W. Norton, New York).

Pearce, I.F. and S.F. James (1951), "The factor price equalization myth", Review of Economic Studies 19:111-119.

Rader, T. (1979), "Factor price equalization with more industries than factors", in: J.R. Green and J.A. Scheinkman, eds., General equilibrium, growth, and trade (Academic Press, New York).

Rodriguez, C.A. (1975), "International factor mobility, non-traded goods, and the international equalization of prices of goods and factors", Econometrica 43:115-124.

Rybczynski, T.M. (1955), "Factor endowment and relative commodity prices", Economica 22:336-341.

Samuelson, P.A. (1939), "The gains from international trade", Canadian Journal of Economics and Political Science 5:195-205.

Samuelson, P.A. (1949), "International factor-price equalization once again", Economic Journal 69:181-197.

Samuelson, P.A. (1953), "Prices of factors and goods in general equilibrium", Review of Economic Studies 21:1-20.

Samuelson, P.A. (1962), "The gains from international trade once again", Economic Journal 82:820-829.

Samuelson, P.A. (1966), "1965 postscript", in: J. Stiglitz, ed., The collected scientific papers of Paul A. Samuelson, Vol. II (M.I.T., Cambridge).

Samuelson, P.A. (1967), "Summary on factor-price equalization", International Economic Review 8:286-295.

Samuelson, P.A. (1971), "Ohlin was right", The Swedish Journal of Economics 73:365-384.

Stolper, W.F. and P.A. Samuelson (1941), "Protection and real wages", Review of Economic Studies 19:58-73.

Svensson, L.E.O. (1982), "Factor trade and goods trade", Seminar Paper no. 200, Institute for International Economic Studies, University of Stockholm.

Takayama, A. (1972), International trade (Holt, Rinehart and Winston, New York).

Takayama, A. (1981), "On theorems of general competitive equilibrium of production and trade: A survey of some recent developments in the theory of international trade", Keio Economic Studies, 19:1-37.

Tinbergen, J. (1949), "The equalization of factor prices between free trade areas", Metroeconomica 1:40-47.

Travis, W.P. (1964), The theory of trade and protection (Harvard, Cambridge).

Travis, W.P. (1972), "Production, trade and protection when there are many commodities and two factors", American Economic Review 62:87-106.

Uekawa, Y. (1971), "Generalization of the Stolper–Samuelson theorem, Econometrica 39:197-213.

Uekawa, Y. (1979), "On the concepts of factor intensities and the relation between commodity prices and factor rewards", in J.R. Green and J.A. Scheinkman, eds., General equilibrium, growth, and trade (Academic Press, New York).

Uekawa, Y., M.C. Kemp and L.L. Wegge (1973), "P and PN matrices, Minkowski and Metzler matrices, and generalizations of the Stolper–Samuelson and Samuelson–Rybczynski theorems", Journal of International Economics 3:53-76.

Uzawa, H. (1959), "Prices of the factors of production in international trade", Econometrica 27:448-468.

Vanek, J. (1968), "The factor proportions theory: The N-factor case", Kyklos 28:749-755.

Vanek, J. and T. Bertrand (1971), "Trade and factor prices in a multi-commodity world", in: J.N. Bhagwati, R.W. Jones, R.A. Mundell and J. Vanek, eds., Trade, balance of payments and growth (North-Holland, Amsterdam).

Williams, J.R. (1977), "The factor proportions theorem: The case of m commodities and n factors", Canadian Journal of Economics 10:282-288.

Wilson, C. (1980), "On the general structure of Ricardian models with a continuum of goods: Applications to growth, tariff theory, and technical change", Econometrica 48:1675-1710.

Woodland, A.D. (1977), "Joint outputs, intermediate inputs and international trade theory", International Economic Review 18:517-533.

Woodland, A.D. (1983), International trade and resource allocation (North-Holland, Amsterdam).

Chapter 4

GROWTH AND DEVELOPMENT IN TRADE MODELS

RONALD FINDLAY*

Columbia University

Contents

1. **Ricardian theory**   187
   1.1.   A dynamic Ricardian model   187
   1.2.   Lewis on the terms of trade   191
   1.3.   Unequal exchange   192
2. **Neoclassical theory**   194
   2.1.   Comparative statics of growth and trade   194
   2.2.   "Immiserizing" growth and foreign investment   198
   2.3.   Steady state growth in the open economy   203
3. **Development and asymmetrical interdependence**   212
   3.1.   Wage differentials and infant industry protection   212
   3.2.   Two-gap models and export-led growth   215
   3.3.   The open dual economy   218
   3.4.   North–South models   221

References   232

*I would like to thank J. Bhagwati, R. Brecher, A. Burgstaller, R. Feenstra, R.W. Jones, J. Ruggie and A. Smith for comments, suggestions, and encouragement.

Handbook of International Economics, vol. I, Edited by R.W. Jones and P.B. Kenen
© *Elsevier Science Publishers B.V., 1984*

Dostoevsky apparently once remarked that all of Russian literature emerged from under Gogol's *Overcoat*. It is at least as true that all of the pure theory of international trade has emerged from chapter 7 of Ricardo's *Principles*. The incredibly simple example of the exchange of cloth and wine between England and Portugal went right to the core of the concept of comparative advantage and the subsequent development of the subject has remained within the bounds set by Ricardo in a manner symbolized by the offer curves of Mill, Marshall and Edgeworth intersecting between the domestic cost ratios of England and Portugal as established by the master.

The determination of the terms of trade by reciprocal demand, the introduction of many goods, countries and factors, the analysis of tariffs, occupied the attention of subsequent writers down to the treatises of Viner (1937) and Haberler (1937). One topic, however, that was almost entirely absent from the formal literature was any consideration of the connection between economic growth and development and international trade, despite the famous quotation from Marshall that "the causes which determine the economic progress of nations belong to the study of international trade". It has only been in the last two or three decades that the "dynamization" of trade theory has gotten underway and that any systematic formal analysis of capital accumulation and technological change has been undertaken in the context of open economies. All this of course runs parallel to the development of economics as a whole, with the emergence of dynamic trade models following closely in the wake of neoclassical growth theory as developed by Solow, Swan, Uzawa, Phelps and others.

It is a strange irony, however, that Ricardo himself had constructed an implicit dynamic model of growth and trade, linked by the distribution of income, in his *Essay on the Influence of a Low Price of Corn Upon the Profits of Stock*.[1] His interest in the repeal of the Corn Laws was motivated not so much by a static "gains from trade" argument but from a "gains for growth" consideration underlying the effect of the repeal in raising the rate of profit and reducing the rent of land, capitalists being thrifty and landlords profligate in his stylized representation. The Ricardo of pure trade theory is a pale shadow of the real one. The very neatness and elegant simplicity of the chapter 7 analysis seems to have diverted attention from the more complex, but also in my opinion very rich and deep ideas contained in the *Essay*, and also, for that matter, in the rest of chapter 7. The formalization of these ideas was undertaken only rather recently by Pasinetti (1960) and Samuelson (1959). I shall describe an explicit Ricardian model of trade and growth later in this chapter drawing upon the work of these modern commentators on his closed system and on the extension to open economies in Findlay (1974).

[1] The *Essay*, originally published in 1815, is available in Volume IV, pp. 1–42, of Ricardo (1951), the Sraffa edition of the collected works and correspondence.

"Growth" and "development" are sometimes used interchangeably but I am sure that the editors intended a distinction that is usually drawn between these terms. "Growth" has the connotation of simply more of everything while "development" is taken to refer to some qualitative transformation or structural shift. In practice the "development" aspect of trade theory arises from the attempt to address problems regarded as of major significance for the less developed countries of the world economy. These have ranged from the "infant industry" problem of Hamilton and List to the "terms of trade" problem of Prebisch (1950) and Singer (1950). The insights and concerns of these critics of orthodox doctrine have led to a number of attempts, sympathetic and otherwise, to handle these issues analytically.

Ever since the creation of a unified world economy as a consequence of European voyages of discovery of the fifteenth and sixteenth centuries and the Industrial Revolution of the eighteenth century there has been a split between an advanced "center", which generates the momentum of accumulation and innovation for the system as a whole, and a backward "periphery" which responds more or less passively to or at least within the parameters set by the center. The pattern of interdependence, which orthodox theory tends to view as one between quantitatively different but qualitatively similar national economies, is viewed by "dependency" theorists and other radical schools as fundamentally *asymmetric* in character, with a center and periphery, or a "North" and a "South", linked together as "unequal partners" by the ties of trade and foreign investment. The last few years have seen some theoretical work on models of asymmetric interdependence or "North–South" models as I shall call them in this chapter.

This chapter will be divided into three sections. The first, on Ricardian theory, begins by considering some neglected aspects of Ricardo's ideas on trade and growth, based on his analysis of the distributive shares. Subsequent sections take up Arthur Lewis' three-good Ricardian model of the terms of trade and Emmanuel's concept of "unequal exchange". The second section, on neoclassical theory, contains the discussion of the major "mainstream" literature on growth and trade, with sections on comparative statics, dynamics and the concept of "immiserizing" growth and foreign investment. The final section is on various theoretical aspects of "trade and development" issues, including analyses of infant industry protection, two-gap models, the open dual economy and lastly an extensive discussion of recent work on "North–South" models.

1. Ricardian theory

1.1. A dynamic Ricardian model

In the model of Ricardo's *Essay* the size of the labor force at any moment is determined by the wage-fund, a stock of corn, and the "natural" wage-rate, also fixed in terms of corn. There are two outputs produced, corn and manufactures, and the time elapsing between input of labor and the availability of final output is fixed and equal in both sectors. Wages are paid at the beginning of each production period. The output of manufactures is simply proportional to the. input of labor into that sector but in corn there is diminishing returns to labor because of the fixed supply of land. Given the wage-fund and the natural wage-rate, the fixed supply of land and the two constant returns to scale production functions a production-possibilities frontier that is concave to the origin is obtained. At any given price-ratio perfect competition equates the rate of profit between the sectors and thus the supply of each commodity is determined.

Writing r for the rate of profit, C and M for the two outputs, p for the relative price of manufactures in terms of corn, L_c and L_m for the inputs of labor in corn and manufactures, $\bar{w}$ for the natural wage and α for the productivity of labor in manufactures we have

$$r = \frac{\left[C - \left(\frac{\partial C}{\partial T} \right) \bar{T} - \bar{w} L_c \right]}{\bar{w} L_c} = \frac{p \alpha L_m - \bar{w} L_m}{\bar{w} L_m}, \tag{1.1.1}$$

from which it follows that

$$p = \frac{1}{\alpha} \frac{\partial C}{\partial L_c} (\bar{T}, L_c), \tag{1.1.2}$$

which gives the supply of corn as the level of output corresponding to the value of L_c that solves (1.1.2) and the supply of manufactures as α times the residual labor force L_m obtained by subtracting L_c from the wage-fund divided by $\bar{w}$. Increasing p must result in falling L_c and hence C so that M and C both respond positively to an increase in their relative prices. The demand assumption is that a constant proportion of rent is spent on manufactures, regardless of relative prices. Thus as p rises L_c and hence total rents fall in terms of corn which means that the quantity of manufactures demanded by landlords declines. With all wages spent on corn this implies that the demand curve for manufactures is downward sloping. Figure 1.1 depicts the momentary equilibrium of the system as determined by the intersection of the supply and demand for manufactures. The equilibrium value of p clearly determines L_c, L_m, C, and r, which from (1.1.1) is equal to the difference between $\partial C / \partial L_c$ and $\bar{w}$, divided by $\bar{w}$.

If all profits are re-invested, as Ricardo typically assumes, the wage-fund for the next period will be $(1 + r)$ times larger than initially and the analysis can be repeated and the sequence of momentary equilibria traced out. We first determine the effect of accumulation on the relative price p of manufactures. To do this observe that from (1.1.2) it follows that at constant p we have the same value of L_c and hence of C. Thus the expansion of the labor force due to accumulation

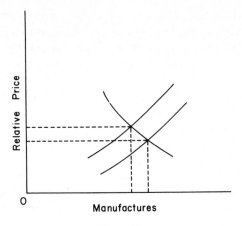

Figure 1.1

does not shift the supply curve of corn at all. The increase in the total labor force must therefore all be absorbed in the production of manufactures, the supply curve of which therefore shifts to the right. The demand curve for manufactures depends only upon the rent that is earned in the corn sector and since this is the same at each value of p the demand curve for manufactures does not shift at all. Thus the price of manufactures must decline as accumulation continues and so employment in the corn sector rises to satisfy (1.1.2). The fall in the marginal productivity of labor in the corn sector reduces the rate of profit since

$$r = \frac{\dfrac{\partial C}{\partial L_c}(p) - \overline{w}}{\overline{w}}, \quad \text{with } \frac{\mathrm{d}r}{\mathrm{d}p} > 0. \tag{1.1.3}$$

Accumulation thus drives down the relative price of manufactures until the marginal product of labor in the corn sector becomes equal to the natural wage-rate, at which point the rate of profit as expressed in (1.1.3) becomes equal to zero and the "stationary state" is reached.

International trade can readily be introduced. First consider the "small open economy" case in which the Ricardian economy has the opportunity to trade with the rest of the world at some fixed price-ratio p^* higher than the value at which the marginal product of labor in the corn sector equals the natural wage. Trade will then permanently raise the rate of profit to $r^* = r(p^*)$ and the growth rate of the wage-fund and the labor force to r^* as well. The "stationary state" can thus be averted if the expanding labor force is fed by extension of the frontier of cultivation to empty lands overseas. The fall in the relative price of the land-intensive good corn hurts landowners since the marginal product of land and hence rent per acre falls while the marginal product of labor rises. Workers of course do not gain since they cannot earn more than the natural wage but the benefit accrues to the capitalists in the form of a higher rate of profit which their thrift, "Moses and the prophets", converts into a higher rate of growth. England's agriculture is stationary but Manchester and Birmingham make her the "workshop of the world" which pays in food and primary products for the expanding output of the "workshop". It was *this* possibility, and not so much the static gains from trade, that made free trade attractive to Ricardo.

The stationary state would however once again rear its ugly head once the global frontier ran out and the "regions of recent settlement", as the League of Nations quaintly referred to the Americas and Australia, filled up. This would require a two-country model that can readily be obtained from the previous analysis by simply laterally summing the supply and demand curves of the two countries and clearing the unified world markets. The countries might of course differ in any one of several respects – technology, demand, the level of the wage-rate, the supply of land or the size of the wage-fund. Eventually however the common relative price of manufactures would have to fall to a point at which accumulation ceased in both countries with the marginal productivities of labor in corn equal to the natural wage-rates and the profit-rates equal to zero.

In view of the subsequent development of the Heckscher–Ohlin factor proportions theory of comparative advantage it is interesting to see how our Ricardian model yields the same predictions once the corresponding assumptions are made. If we suppose that technology and demand are identical in both countries, and also the natural wage-rates, it follows from the results established that the country with a higher ratio of the wage-fund to the supply of land would have to be able to produce manufactures more cheaply in isolation and hence have a comparative advantage in that commodity. Also the equalization of commodity prices would imply the same marginal productivities of land and labor and hence equalization of the rents per acre and the rates of profit. Our earlier "small open economy" analysis can already be seen to have established the Stolper–Samuelson proposition that trade benefits the "scarce" factor and also the Rybczynski theorem for the special case of land being used in only one sector, so that an expansion of labor leads to an increase in the output of the labor-intensive commodity but not to a decline in the output of the land-intensive one.

It can therefore be seen that the model of Ricardo's *Essay* leads very naturally and directly to both the Heckscher–Ohlin and the "specific factors" models so popular today and extensively discussed by Jones and Neary in Chapter 1 of this volume. It would appear that there is good reason for Samuelson (1971) to have labelled his second reconstruction of Ohlin the Viner–Ricardo model.[2] Introduc-

[2] The reference to Viner is to the celebrated 1931 article on "Cost Curves and Supply Curves". See in particular pp. 58–64 of the reprinted article in Viner (1958) and the Supplementary Note, pp. 79–84.

ing land and capital into a model of trade as Ricardo did in his *Essay* thus enables us to treat not only growth but its cessation due to the constraint of the "original and indestructible powers of the soil".

It is also of interest that the secular tendency of the terms of trade in this model is for it to turn in favor of the exporter of primary products and against manufactures, *contra* Prebisch–Singer. British economists from Jevons to Keynes, Beveridge, Robertson, and E.A.G. Robinson have been concerned with this problem.[3]

The model also indicates, however, that trade reduces the rate of growth (in comparison with autarky) in the country that exports corn, since the rise in rents is absorbed in luxury consumption while the fall in the rate of profit reduces accumulation. Thus critics of free trade orthodoxy, from List to the "dependency" theorists of today, may not necessarily have been totally off the mark in their belief that the free trade mechanism somehow benefited the already advanced center at the expense of the less developed periphery.

1.2. Lewis on the terms of trade

A Ricardian model also forms the basis of an intriguing analysis of the terms of trade between advanced and developing countries that Arthur Lewis (1954) first put forward in the second part of the celebrated paper on "unlimited supplies" of labor and then more extensively in his Wicksell Lectures for 1969. Consider two economies, in each of which labor is the only scarce factor of production. One region, call it the North, produces Food and Steel while the other region, the South, produces Food and Coffee. Outputs are simply proportional to labor inputs for all three goods, with productivity in Food being higher in the North. Since both transformation curves are linear and all goods are tradeable it is clear that the relative price of Steel and Coffee is determined strictly on the cost or supply side, independently of demand, the price of each being fixed in terms of Food by the relative labor productivities. The North exports Steel, the South Coffee, and Food is exported by whichever region has the deficit in the exchange of Steel and Coffee.

The consequences of productivity changes in all four sectors are easy to see. The "stylized facts" that Lewis introduces are that productivity growth is greater in Food than in Steel in the North, while it is greater in Coffee than in Food in the South. Thus a unit of Food is worth increasingly less Steel in the North while it is worth increasingly more Coffee in the South. It therefore follows that a unit of Coffee exported by the South is worth less and less Steel over time, i.e., there is a secular tendency for the terms of trade of the South to deteriorate.

[3]See Rostow (1958, chs. 8 and 9) for a valuable examination of this literature.

Productivity change in either Coffee or Steel, with Food productivities constant, clearly reduces the relative price of Coffee or Steel in the same proportion so that the full benefit of the improvement is passed on to the importing country. The exporter is benefited only to the extent that Coffee or Steel is consumed at home. Thus, for commodities such as Malayan rubber or Ghana's cocoa, where domestic consumption is negligible, no significant benefit is received by technical progress in the export sector since the purchasing power in terms of importables does not change. For the South modernization of the backward technology of Food production would be doubly blessed since it would not only raise real incomes directly but also raise the relative price of Coffee in terms of Steel.

A more detailed analysis and critique of the Lewis Ricardian model is given in Findlay (1981, p. 430–434).

1.3. Unequal exchange

The Ricardian model also provides a convenient framework within which to discuss the concept of "unequal exchange" advanced by Emmanuel (1972). Two fundamental assumptions made by Emmanuel are that international capital mobility equalizes the rates of profit and that real wage-rates are exogenous in each country. The simplest model to contain these ideas, based on Bacha (1978), is one in which the North is specialized in Steel and the South in Coffee, with q^N the output of Steel per unit of labor in the North, q^S the output of Coffee per unit of labor in the South, w^N and w^S the real wages in North and South respectively, both fixed in terms of Steel, p the relative price of Coffee in terms of Steel, and r the common rate of profit. Production of each good takes one period with wages paid at the beginning of each period. It therefore follows that:

$$r = \frac{(q^N - w^N)}{w^N} = \frac{(pq^S - w^S)}{w^S}, \tag{1.3.1}$$

which implies:

$$p = \frac{w^S}{w^N} \cdot \frac{q^N}{q^S}. \tag{1.3.2}$$

In this equation p represents the commodity or "net barter" terms of trade of the South. By "equal exchange" Emmanuel appears to mean a situation in which the "double factoral" terms of trade, i.e. the amount of foreign labor embodied in imports per unit of domestic labor embodied in exports, is equal to unity. The double factoral terms of trade, denoted f, are related to p by:

$$f = \frac{pq^{\mathrm{S}}}{q^{\mathrm{N}}} = \frac{w^{\mathrm{S}}}{w^{\mathrm{N}}}. \tag{1.3.3}$$

Thus f is equal to unity if and only if $w^{\mathrm{S}} = w^{\mathrm{N}}$. Emmanuel says that there is "unequal exchange", biased against the South, because $w^{\mathrm{S}} < w^{\mathrm{N}}$, i.e. the South gets commodities worth less than a day's labor in the North in exchange for commodities worth a day's labor in the South.

While there is no point in arguing about definitions it should be noted that the pejorative connotation of the term "unequal exchange" can be very misleading, as the following example illustrates. Suppose to begin with that $w^{\mathrm{S}} = w^{\mathrm{N}}$ and that consequently there is no "unequal exchange". Let q^{N} and w^{N} both increase in the same proportion, with no change in q^{S} and w^{S}. The rate of profit and the commodity terms of trade will remain unchanged but the double factoral terms of trade will deteriorate below their initial value of unity. Exchange has thus become unequal even though there is no change in the welfare of the South which still gets the same amount of Steel per unit of Coffee exported. In fact it is clear that the commodity terms of trade will improve for the South if w^{N} does not increase as much as q^{N} does, whereas the double factoral terms of trade must deteriorate due to w^{S} being constant and w^{N} rising. Thus the South's gain from trade could be increasing as a result of becoming a "victim" of unequal exchange!

In our example the only way to prevent unequal exchange as a result of the productivity increase in the North is for w^{N} to be held constant, i.e. none of the benefit passed on to Northern workers, or for w^{S} to increase pari passu with w^{N}, i.e. any benefit that Northern workers get be shared equally with Southern workers.

One way of interpreting unequal exchange is to say that international distributive justice requires a policy of open borders with regard to the migration of labor. Simply raising wages in the South to improve the terms of trade will not do since it could have very adverse consequences on employment if the North's demand for the South's exports is at all price-elastic. Free migration of labor is the only economically viable, though of course politically and socially very difficult, solution. I have explored the consequences of free migration for Marxian, Rawlsian, Libertarian and Utilitarian concepts of international distributive justice in Findlay (1982). Other explorations of this topic are by Little (1978) and Sen (1981). Section 3.4 below notes some consequences of international labor mobility in a "North–South" model of capital accumulation.

2. Neoclassical theory

2.1. *Comparative statics of growth and trade*

The major impetus to the incorporation of growth into trade theory came in the fifties with the consideration of the long-run dollar problem and related issues addressed in the famous Inaugural Lecture on that topic by Hicks (1953). The differential growth of productivity, both between sectors and national economies, was the focus of attention in that extremely stimulating paper. Hicks' lead was quickly and energetically followed by Harry Johnson (1955), whose work in turn inspired a number of other contributions, drawn together into a taxonomic synthesis in Johnson (1959).

Johnson's initial work considered trade between two completely specialized economies, Mancunia and Agraria. Letting Y_1, M_1 and Y_2, M_2 denote output levels and imports of Mancunia and Agraria respectively and p the terms of trade of Agraria the requirement of balanced trade results in:

$$pM_1(p, Y_1) - M_2\left(\frac{1}{p}, Y_2\right) = 0. \tag{2.1.1}$$

Differentiating totally and substituting we obtain:

$$\hat{p} = \frac{\varepsilon_1 \hat{Y}_1 - \varepsilon_2 \hat{Y}_2}{(\eta_1 + \eta_2 - 1)}, \tag{2.1.2}$$

in which the "hats" denote proportional changes, ε_1 and ε_2 are the income-elasticities of demand for imports and η_1 and η_2 the price-elasitcities. The denominator is required to be positive by the familiar Marshall–Lerner stability condition. Thus the terms of trade will turn against whichever country has the higher proportional growth weighted by the income-elasticities of import demand. This analysis would seem to indicate that the more "dynamic" country would experience terms of trade, or balance of payments, difficulties as a consequence of its success. This did not square well with the observation, explicitly made by Hicks, that it was the greater dynamism (at that time of course) of the US economy that created a "dollar shortage" for the then more sluggish rest of the world. Hicks saw that the greater dynamism was accompanied by a bias towards the import-competing sector in productivity growth that apparently reversed the outcome on the deficit or terms of trade. Thus most of the subsequent literature concentrated on two-sector models that permitted different degrees of export or import bias in the exogenous source of expansion.

Consider now the usual $2\times2\times2$ model in which 1 and 2 refer to countries, X and Y to goods, K and L to factors, α to a shift parameter. Equilibrium in the world market requires:

$$E_x(p,\alpha) = E_x^1(p,\alpha) + E_x^2(p) = 0, \tag{2.1.3}$$

where E_x is world excess supply of X, E_x^1 and E_x^2 the corresponding national levels and p is the relative price of X. The effect of an exogenous change in Country 1 on p can be obtained as:

$$\frac{dp}{d\alpha} = \frac{-(\partial E_x^1/\partial\alpha)}{\partial E_x/\partial p}. \tag{2.1.4}$$

The denominator is nothing but $(\eta_1 + \eta_2 - 1) > 0$ so the sign of the effect on p depends solely upon the sign of the numerator. Thus suppose Country 1 is the exporter of X and that:

$$\frac{\partial E_x^1}{\partial\alpha} < 0. \tag{2.1.5}$$

At constant prices this means that world excess supply of X is negative so that p must increase to clear the world market if it is stable. Thus Country 1 can have its terms of trade improve if the exogenous source of expansion reflected in the shift parameter causes an excess demand for its exportable product at constant relative prices.

What sort of change could produce this effect? Let X be the labor-intensive good and Y the capital-intensive good in the sense that $k_x[\omega(p)] < k_y[\omega(p)]$ for all values of the wage–rental ratio ω. Define α as an increase in the fixed amount of capital k with which Country 1 is endowed. We then have:

$$\lambda k_x[\omega(p)] + (1-\lambda)k_y[\omega(p)] = k, \tag{2.1.6}$$

in which k is the ratio of capital to labor and λ is the fraction of labor in the X industry. Differentiating with respect to k and holding p, and hence ω, k_x and k_y constant, we obtain:

$$\frac{d\lambda}{dk} = \frac{1}{(k_x - k_y)}. \tag{2.1.7}$$

Thus if $k_x < k_y$ it must follow that less labor (and consequently capital) must be allocated to X, the output of which contracts absolutely, while the output of Y must increase absolutely. This is the famous Rybczynski (1955) theorem.

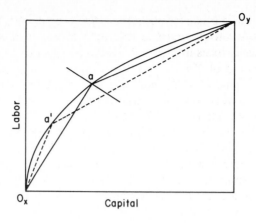

Figure 2.1

The expansion therefore contracts the supply of the exportable good when the factor that increases is used relatively more intensively in the import-competing good. The higher national income at constant prices will increase the home demand for the exportable good if inferiority in consumption is ruled out. The excess supply of the exportable must therefore become negative at constant prices and the terms of trade of the expanding country must improve. The same argument demonstrates that the terms of trade must deteriorate if the factor that increases is used relatively intensively in the exportable sector.

The other kind of expansion to consider is technical progress in either sector, which can be neutral in the well-known sense of Hicks or biased towards some factor. The effects of technical progress of various kinds on the terms of trade have been investigated in Findlay and Grubert (1959). For simplicity I shall only consider the case of Hicks-neutral technical change in detail here.

Figure 2.1 is the Edgeworth–Bowley production box for Country 1. Point a on the efficiency-locus is the initial equilibrium with wage–rental ratio ω corresponding to the equilibrium product price ratio $\bar{p}$. Let Country 1 now experience Hicks-neutral technical progress in the import-competing sector Y. Note that the efficiency locus will not shift since each point on it will continue to have X and Y isoquants tangential to each other on it at slopes equal to their original values. At point a the slope of the common tangent will continue to be equal to ω, Y output being larger and X output unchanged.

The Lerner diagram of Figure 2.2 shows the effect of the technical progress in Y on the wage–rental ratio when relative product prices remain unchanged at $\bar{p}$, which can be put equal to unity without loss of generality. The Hicks-neutral progress in Y implies that the unit isoquant for that commodity is shifted proportionally downward along each ray from the origin. The common tangent to the unit isoquants must therefore be steeper than before so that the wage–rental ratio falls and labor-intensity increases in both sectors, which implies that the point on the efficiency-locus in Figure 2.1 corresponding to $\bar{p}$ must be to the left of point a. The output of X must therefore decline at constant relative product prices and excess supply of X becomes negative if inferiority in consumption is ruled out. The same reasoning shows that the terms of trade must deteriorate if the neutral innovation occurred in the exportable sector.

The consideration of factor bias in innovations introduces the interesting possibility that the terms of trade may improve even if the innovation takes place in the export sector and, symmetrically, that they may deteriorate even if it occurs in the import-competing sector. The intuition is that a capital-saving innovation, for example, can be thought of as a combination of a neutral innovation and an increase in the endowment of capital. If such an innovation were to occur in the labor-intensive export sector X the terms of trade would deteriorate on account of the "neutral" technological effect but the notional increase in the capital stock that is implied by the capital-saving character of the innovation would result in an expansion of the output of Y and a contraction in the output of X at constant relative product prices as a consequence of the Rybczynski theorem. This effect would work in the opposite direction to improve the terms of trade. Thus an innovation in the export sector that is strongly capital-saving but only weakly cost-reducing could result in an improvement in the terms of trade. Similar reasoning would indicate that a labor-saving innovation in the import competing sector could cause a deterioration in the terms of trade.

The other country remains static in all the results reported so far in this section but it is clear that any combination of changes in factor supplies and technical

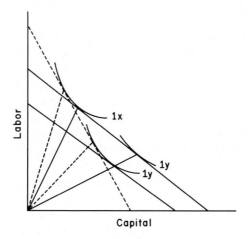

Figure 2.2

progress can be applied to both countries simultaneously and the consequences for the terms of trade deduced. Johnson (1959) provides an exhaustive diagrammatic analysis while Jones (1965) carefully works out the relevant algebra.

2.2. "Immiserizing" growth and foreign investment

The most striking result to emerge from the work of the fifties on the comparative statics of growth and trade was the demonstration by Bhagwati (1958) that growth in an open economy could be "immiserizing", i.e. that national welfare could actually decline as a result of the expansion causing a sufficiently strong deterioration of the terms of trade that exceeds the favorable effect on welfare of the expansion at constant relative product prices. This possibility had been anticipated by Edgeworth (1894) who referred to it as "damnifying" but Bhagwati's demonstration is in a much more general setting.

Edgeworth's case is simply one in which a country produces a single good that it does not consume domestically but exports in exchange for another good that it does consume. Think of Malaya or Ghana exporting rubber or cocoa in exchange for food. An expansion of production and hence of exports (equal to all of domestic production in this example) would result in a smaller volume of food imports if the price-elasticity of foreign demand is less than unity. The expansion has thus reduced national welfare. It is clear that a necessary condition for this result is that both production and trade are conducted by atomistic perfectly competitive agents, i.e. there is no private monopoly or state intervention through tariffs, export taxes or other measures that would restrict output optimally. This example has the virtue of being possibly the simplest illustration of the proposition that it does not *always* pay to rely solely on *laissez faire* or the "magic of the market".

Bhagwati considers "immiserization" in the context of the standard $2 \times 2 \times 2$ model. A key role in the analysis is played by the "zero gain" decline in the terms of trade i.e. the amount that exactly off-sets the effect of the expansion at constant relative prices. Compute the world excess supply for the importable at the "zero gain" level of the terms of trade. If it is negative then it is clear that stability would require the terms of trade to deteriorate beyond the "zero gain" level, i.e. the country is immiserized.

The condition for equilibrium in the market for the importable, prior to the change is

$$S(p, \alpha) + M(p) - C(p) = 0, \qquad (2.2.1)$$

in which S is domestic supply, M is imports, C is domestic consumption and p is the relative price of the importable and α a shift parameter.

Differentiating this expression, putting $\hat{p}$ equal to the zero gain change in the terms of trade, yields the following expression for the possibility of immiserization

$$C\left[\frac{S}{C}\sigma + \frac{M}{C}\tau + \eta\right]\hat{p} + \frac{\partial S}{\partial \alpha}\,d\alpha < 0, \tag{2.2.2}$$

in which σ is the price-elasticity of the domestic supply of the importable, τ is the price-elasticity of foreign supply of imports, η is the compensated price-elasticity of domestic demand for the importable and $(\partial S/\partial \alpha)\,d\alpha$ is the shift in the domestic supply of the importable at constant relative prices. Since σ, η and $\hat{p}$ are all positive it follows that immiserization can only occur if either τ or $\partial S/\partial \alpha$ is negative. A negative value of τ means that the foreign supply of the importable responds negatively to the rise in its price i.e. foreign demand for home exports is inelastic. A negative value of $\partial S/\partial \alpha$ means that the expansion is strongly biased against the importable at constant relative prices, i.e. a negative Rybczynski effect such as an increase in capital occurring in an economy with labor-intensive imports or a negative Findlay–Grubert effect such as a Hicks-neutral innovation in the exportable sector.

Suppose that $\partial S/\partial \alpha$ is negative and τ is positive, i.e. the foreign response to a rise in the price of their exports is "normal". Thus at constant relative prices the domestic expansion leads to a reduction in the world supply of the importable while world demand will be unchanged if real income (utility) in the expanding country is held constant. The relative price of the importable must therefore rise if the world market is to be cleared. The rise in price increases domestic supply, reduces domestic demand at unchanged real income and increases foreign supply of the importable so all the effects are working to close the gap. If σ, τ and η are all small and the absolute value of the negative $\partial S/\partial \alpha$ is large, however, it is clear that these responses may not be sufficient to close the gap when the price rise is confined to the "zero gain" value. Consequently the rise in p would have to exceed this value if equilibrium is to be restored so that immiserization results.

The sufficient condition for immiserizing growth to occur is therefore that the sum of all four terms in (2.2.2) be negative. Since σ and η are always positive a necessary condition is that either τ or $\partial S/\partial \alpha$ or both must be negative.

As in the Edgeworth case immiserization could of course never occur in the presence of rational state intervention. Growth accompanied by optimal trade intervention to satisfy all the relevant Pareto conditions must lead to an increase in national welfare.

An entirely different type of "immiserizing" growth was analyzed by Johnson (1967). Here the terms of trade are fixed for a two-sector, two-factor open economy but there is a tariff or similar distortionary trade restriction in place that results in the output of the import-competing good being too large and of the exportable good being too small. Suppose an expansion occurs that contracts the output of the exportable and increases that of the importable at constant relative domestic (tariff-inclusive) prices. Johnson shows that under some conditions it is possible for national welfare to be reduced as a result.

The necessary and sufficient condition for immiserization of the Johnson type is easily obtained. Observe that since domestic relative product prices are fixed by world prices and the tariff the domestic wage–rental ratio and hence all technical coefficients are uniquely determined also. The coefficients in the equations below can therefore all be treated "as if" they were constants. The conditions for full utilization of both factors give:

$$K = a_{11}X + a_{12}Y, \tag{2.2.3}$$

$$L = a_{21}X + a_{22}Y. \tag{2.2.4}$$

Suppose now that K increases with L constant and that X, the exportable, is labor-intensive. The effects on the output levels are given by:

$$\frac{dX}{dK} = \frac{a_{22}}{\Delta} < 0, \tag{2.2.5}$$

$$\frac{dY}{dK} = -\frac{a_{21}}{\Delta} > 0, \tag{2.2.6}$$

where

$$\Delta = (a_{11}a_{22} - a_{21}a_{12}) < 0, \tag{2.2.7}$$

by the assumption that X is labor-intensive.

The effect on welfare, however, depends upon what happens to the value of domestic production at world prices, since this determines the purchasing power of the economy in the world market and thus of the level of utility the domestic consumers in the aggregate can attain with world prices given as p_x^* and p_y^*. The change in domestic income evaluated at world prices is therefore $p_x^* dX + p_y^* dY$. Immiserization therefore implies that:

$$p_x^* \frac{dX}{dK} + p_y^* \frac{dY}{dK} < 0, \tag{2.2.8}$$

which, after substitution, becomes:

$$-p_x^* \frac{a_{22}}{\Delta} > -p_y^* \frac{a_{21}}{\Delta}. \tag{2.2.9}$$

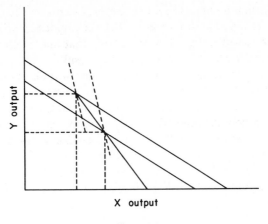

Figure 2.3

This states that immiserization will occur if and only if the value at world prices of the reduction in the output of the exportable exceeds the value at those prices of the increase in the output of the importable.

The situation is illustrated diagrammatically in Figure 2.3. Expansion of K with L constant moves the production point along the fixed labor constraint or Rybczynski line in the direction of more Y output and less X output. The value of the production bundle at world prices declines if the world price-ratio is steeper than the slope of the Rybczynski line, which is equivalent to the condition stated above.

Intuitively Johnson's immiserization occurs in this example because factor endowments change in such a way as to expand the inefficient protected sector at the expense of the efficient export sector. Any other type of expansion that has this property could be a potential source of immiserization. Note, however, that reduction in the output of the exportable is only necessary, and not sufficient, for this outcome to occur. The diagram clearly shows that if the world price-ratio is flatter than the Rybczynski line the value of domestic production at world prices must rise.

The concept of shadow prices for factors of production in distorted open economies provides a valuable tool in the analysis of immiserization.[4] If V^* denotes the value of domestic production at world prices the shadow prices of

[4]See Findlay and Wellisz (1976) and Srinivasan and Bhagwati (1978) on the determination and interpretation of shadow prices in distorted open economies and for references to the associated literature of cost–benefit analysis in developing economies.

capital and labor can be defined as:

$$r^* \equiv \frac{dV^*}{dK} = p^* \frac{dX}{dK} + \frac{dY}{dK}, \qquad (2.2.10)$$

$$w^* \equiv \frac{dV^*}{dL} = p^* \frac{dX}{dL} + \frac{dY}{dL}, \qquad (2.2.11)$$

where p^* is the ratio of the world price of the exportable to the world price of the importable. The derivatives of outputs with respect to factors are evaluated from the same tariff-distorted set of a's as before, reflecting the inherently second-best nature of the situation. The market prices of the factors, r and w, can be defined in exactly the same way except that p^* is replaced by the domestic price-ratio $\bar{p}$ which is:

$$\bar{p} = \frac{1}{(1+t)} p^* < p^*, \qquad (2.2.12)$$

where t is the rate of tariff.

Since X is the labor-intensive good we have from the Rybczynski Theorem that:

$$\frac{dX}{dK} < 0, \qquad \frac{dY}{dK} > 0, \qquad (2.2.13)$$

$$\frac{dX}{dL} > 0, \qquad \frac{dY}{dL} < 0. \qquad (2.2.14)$$

From the definitions and these inequalities it follows immediately that:

$$r^* < r, \qquad w^* > w. \qquad (2.2.15)$$

Immiserization in Johnson's sense can be seen to be equivalent to r^* being negative, i.e. the distortion caused by the tariff is so pernicious as to make capital have a negative marginal social product. Brecher and Diaz Alejandro (1977) have shown that if the additional capital is owned by foreigners, who obtain the market price as the reward, national welfare must go down. This result is immediate in view of the properties of shadow prices established above since the change in national welfare is:

$$\frac{dV^*}{dK} - r = (r^* - r) < 0. \qquad (2.2.16)$$

Thus additional capital that is domestically owned is only immiserizing if r^* is negative while additional capital is always immiserizing in the present context whenever it is foreign owned.

The impact of foreign investment on national welfare in the presence of a tariff is also shown to be negative in the context of the Viner–Ricardo or "specific factors" model by Brecher and Findlay (1983). In this paper the nationally owned stock of capital in a tariff-distorted small open economy is fixed but it is also available from abroad at a fixed (or rising) price. It is shown that an endogenously determined unrestricted inflow of foreign capital lowers national welfare in comparison with what it would be in the complete absence of international capital mobility. An optimal second-best tax, given the tariff distortion, is derived and is equal to the proportionate difference between the market and shadow prices of capital. This tax is necessarily at a higher rate than the rate of tariff, since the market price of capital is shown to exceed the shadow price by more than the level of the tariff.

Brecher and Choudhri (1982) consider the impact of foreign investment on national welfare when the country has monopoly power in international trade. They show that national welfare will rise or fall simply as a consequence of the effect of the foreign investment on the terms of trade since nationally owned factors are fixed and their welfare thus dependent only on the terms of trade.

There is thus an interesting correspondence between Brecher–Diaz and Johnson, on the one hand, and Brecher–Choudhri and Bhagwati on the other. In each case the *possibility* of immiserization is converted into a *necessity* if the source of the growth is foreign-owned.

As pointed out by Bhagwati (1971) both types of "immiserization" arise due to the failure of the necessary Paretian condition of equality between foreign and domestic rates of transformation to hold, as a result of the tariff in the small open economy Johnson case and as a result of the *absence* of an optimal tariff in the monopoly power case of the original demonstration.

2.3. *Steady state growth in the open economy*

The fifties saw the emergence of growth theory in both the neoclassical and Cambridge varieties. The former had a considerable fallout in trade theory which is not surprising in view of the fact that the 2×2 model was the common property of both these fields. Call one of the goods a capital good, introduce a savings function to provide the demand conditions, let the labor force grow exogenously and the old trade war horse is off to the races.

The core of neoclassical growth theory is the one-sector model of Solow (1956) and Swan (1956), which is easily adapted to the case of a small open economy. As a matter of fact this setting makes the heroic aggregation of that model more palatable since as we shall indicate trade makes it possible to specialize in production while permitting as much diversification and variety in consumption as one wishes.

Thus suppose that there are any number of commodities that an economy can produce with two factors of production, capital and labor, according to constant returns to scale production functions with the usual properties. The economy is embedded in a world market that determines the relative prices of all these goods independently of what goes on in the economy. With constant returns to scale and fixed relative prices it is possible to define a composite or surrogate production function that will also have constant returns to scale and the usual properties by taking the inner envelope of a set of isoquants for the goods that have the same value at world prices. I have called this the "foreign exchange" production function in Findlay (1973, p. 105). Figure 2.4 is an illustration. Some goods will never be efficient for the economy to produce at the given technology and relative prices. Goods that are on the envelope for some segment would be efficient to produce if the economy's factor proportions are within the relevant range.

Given the initial capital and labor endowment of the economy, the growth rate of the labor force and the savings function, the composite production function is all that is needed to obtain the extension of the Solow–Swan model to an open economy. The same formal apparatus applies and it is unnecessary to repeat any derivations. If a continuum of goods can be produced the "foreign exchange" production function would look just like the one-good function of the original model except that a different good would be produced at each capital–labor ratio. If there are N goods produced then there will be $(N-1)$ linear segments in the "foreign exchange" isoquant. Capital–labor ratios corresponding to each segment

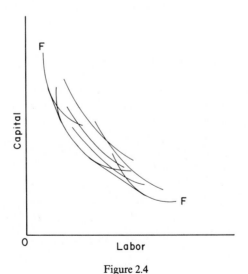

Figure 2.4

make it efficient to produce a combination of the two goods whose individual isoquants define the extremities of the segment.

Figure 2.5 depicts the solution in terms of the familiar diagram. The long-run equilibrium capital–labor ratio k^* is where the nk line indicating the "widening" capital requirement cuts the savings function $sy = sf(k)$ in which $y = f(k)$ is the foreign exchange production function in per capita form. Thus given any k_0 the economy will converge to k^* if the stability condition $sf'(k) < n$ is satisfied. The long-run equilibrium capital–labor ratio depends positively on the propensity to save and negatively on the growth rate of the "effective" labor force.

The model can illustrate the evolution of comparative advantage in response to changes in factor proportions. Goods produced initially still correspond to what is efficient at k_0. As k increases over time the original goods will cease to be produced, new ones will enter to be given up in turn until the economy settles down to a pattern of production corresponding to its "permanent" or "long run" comparative advantage corresponding to k^* given by the value of k that satisfies the equation

$$sf(k) = nk. \tag{2.3.1}$$

"Momentary" comparative advantage is therefore determined à la Heckscher–Ohlin by the $k(t)$ prevailing at time t but "long run" comparative

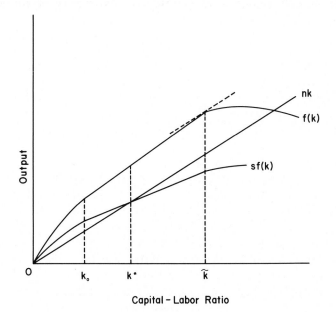

Figure 2.5

advantage is defined by the "dynamic" determinants s and n, given the technology and the structure of relative prices in the world market. For further aspects of "dynamic" comparative advantage see Findlay (1973, ch. 7). Demand conditions (other than saving) are irrelevant since they only serve to determine how the income that is efficiently produced at any moment is spent.

Figure 2.5 also can depict the "Golden Rule" capital–labor ratio $\tilde{k}$ as determined by the condition $f'(k) = n$ that maximizes sustainable per capita consumption $c = f(k) - nk$. Note that in general the Golden Rule capital–labor ratio will require the economy to specialize on only one good, unless the slope of the linear segment of $f(k)$ happens to be exactly equal to n.

The two-sector growth model, with one investment and one consumption good and the relative price given in world markets has been very popular in the literature on growth and trade. Analytically it is of course just a special case of the more general aggregation that has been described here by means of the concept of a surrogate "foreign exchange" production function. There is still however a great deal of insight that can be obtained from many of the papers in this tradition such as Johnson (1971), Vanek (1971), Deardorff (1973) and Bertrand (1975). A compact synthesis of much of this literature is provided in Smith (1977).

An intuitively satisfying result of Bertrand is that the locus of sustainable per capita consumption possibilities in a small open economy with free trade dominates that of the same economy when it is closed. This is easy to see. For the closed economy a value of k defines a production possibility frontier and hence a value of c after nk is allowed for. This function is concave and possesses a unique interior maximum. The possibility of trade at fixed prices obviously raises c for any given value of k and hence dominates the consumption-possibilities frontier for the closed economy. Varying the relative price p as a parameter generates a family of free trade consumption-possibilities loci that have the closed economy locus as their inner envelope. This is the appropriate generalization of the standard gains from trade theorem for a "small" open economy to a setting of steady growth.

Some other neat results along these lines can also be established easily. Vanek proved that an increase in the relative price of the consumption good, assumed to be the more capital-intensive of the two, will raise the steady state capital–labor ratio of a small open economy. In terms of our composite production function it is easy to see from the Lerner diagram that a rise in the relative price of the capital-intensive good must reduce the real wage and raise the return to capital $f'(k)$, measured in terms of the capital good, when the economy produces both goods. The $f(k)$ function in Figure 2.5 is shifted upwards, with a steeper slope of the linear segment associated with incomplete specialization. The steady state condition $sf(k) = nk$ can therefore only be satisfied at a higher value of k^* than before.

Deardorff pointed out that a closed economy with savings rate at the Golden Rule value would always have its steady state per capita consumption raised by entering international trade. To see this observe that there is a unique product price ratio p^* that makes $r(p) = n$ in the closed economy, the necessary condition for the Golden Rule. The per capita output of capital goods is determined by p and k, which we may express as $q = q(p, k)$ with q depending negatively on k because of the Rybczynski theorem. With p^* already given by $r(p) = n$ the Golden Rule value k^* is obtained as that which solves $q(p^*, k) = nk$. Equilibrium in the closed economy under the Golden Rule can therefore be represented by the tangency of p^* with a per capita production possibility frontier corresponding to k^*. Now let trade be possible at any price-ratio other than p^*. Per capita consumption must increase with investment maintained at nk^*. Thus the economy can increase per capita consumption even if it keeps k^* unchanged. Changing k^* to optimize under the trade opportunity can therefore only lead to a further rise in per capita consumption.

We now leave the small open economy for the analysis of the two-country equilibrium, in which the terms of trade have to be determined endogenously. The fundamental contribution in this area is Oniki and Uzawa (1965), though much of the analysis was also done independently by Bardhan (1965). Both papers are of course extensions to a two-country world economy of the Uzawa (1961) two-sector growth model of a closed economy, as is Stiglitz (1970), another important contribution. It is convenient to begin with a simple diagrammatic exposition of the essential properties of the Uzawa model that makes the extension to the two-country world relatively plain sailing. The consumption good is assumed to be always more capital-intensive than the investment good, as in all the papers cited. The investment good serves as the numeraire so that we have

$$y(p, k) = pc(p, k) + q(p, k),\qquad(2.3.2)$$

in which y is per capita income and c and q are per capita consumption and investment. We also write

$$c = \lambda f_c(k_c), \qquad q = (1 - \lambda)f_I(k_I),\qquad(2.3.3)$$

$$k = \lambda k_c + (1 - \lambda)k_I,\qquad(2.3.4)$$

in which λ is the share of labor in the consumption goods sector and the capital-intensities k_c and k_I are increasing functions of the wage–rental ratio ω, which in turn is a negative function of p. Factor allocations and output levels are thus all determined completely by p and k.

Given k the equilibrium value of p is determined by the condition that saving equals investment. The savings function makes savings proportional to income so that we have

$$sy(p,k) = q(p,k),$$ (2.3.5)

which can be solved for the unique value of p that satisfies this equation for any given value of k, which changes over time according to the accumulation equation

$$\dot{k} = q(p,k) - nk,$$ (2.3.6)

which has to equal zero in the steady state.

In Figure 2.6 we plot k on the horizontal axis and the relative price of the investment good, which is the reciprocal of p, on the vertical axis. The curve QQ indicates combinations of k and $1/p$ for which (2.3.6) holds with $\dot{k} = 0$. It is positively sloped because q depends negatively on k by the Rybczynski theorem and positively on the relative price of the investment good $1/p$. The curve SS indicates combinations of k and $1/p$ that make savings equal to the steady state level of accumulation nk. This curve is negatively sloped since

$$\frac{d(1/p)}{dk} = \frac{\left(n - s\frac{\partial y}{\partial k}\right)}{s\frac{\partial y}{\partial (1/p)}},$$ (2.3.7)

in which the denominator is negative and the numerator positive if the usual

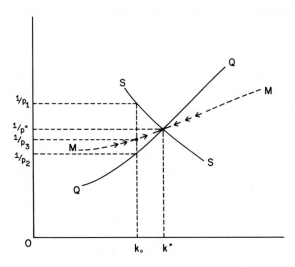

Figure 2.6

stability condition $s(\partial y/\partial k) < n$ is satisfied. The intersection of QQ and SS determine the steady state values p^* and k^* of the system.

How does the economy behave out of the steady state and does it converge to the balanced growth path defined by p^* and k^*? To answer these questions consider the dashed curve MM that passes through the rest point (p^*, k^*), cutting QQ from above. This curve shows the value of p that satisfies the saving equal investment condition (2.3.5) for any given value of k. It thus depicts the "momentary" equilibrium value of p, and hence of ω, k_c and k_I, corresponding to any given value of k. Increasing k reduces the output of investment goods and increases saving so that the reciprocal of p must increase for (2.3.5) to continue to be satisfied. This shows why MM is positively sloped.

Why must MM cut QQ from above? Consider any value of k less than k^*, say k_0. Denote the prices corresponding to k_0 on SS and QQ by $1/p_1$ and $1/p_2$ respectively. A little reflection will show that:

$$sy(p_1, k_0) = nk_0 < q(p_1, k_0),\qquad(2.3.8)$$

$$sy(p_2, k_0) > nk_0 = q(p_2, k_0),\qquad(2.3.9)$$

which means that investment exceeds savings at point (p_1, k_0) while savings exceeds investment at point (p_2, k_0). Consequently savings can only equal investment at some point (p_3, k_0) where p_3 is in between p_1 and p_2. This proves that MM must lie above QQ at k_0 or any point to the left of k^*.

Since the relative price of the investment good is higher on MM than on QQ at k_0 it follows that $\dot{k}$ must be positive. The economy must thus move along MM towards the long run equilibrium point (p^*, k^*) with k and $1/p$ both rising, so that the wage–rental ratio and the capital-intensities in both sectors rise as well. Similar reasoning would show that the model is stable in the other direction with $k_0 > k^*$ as well, though here of course the direction of change in relative prices will be reversed.

International trade in a two-country world can now be introduced very easily. Let countries A and B have identical technology and growth rates of the effective labor force. The population sizes may be different but for simplicity can be put equal to each other (it is trivial to allow for size differences). The only respect in which the economies differ is then in the savings propensities with $s_a > s_b$.

In Figure 2.7 the QQ curve remains unchanged since it depends only on the identical technology. The SS and MM curves will be different since they depend on the savings propensities. It is easy to see that the SS curve for A will be to the right of the SS curve for B while the MM curve for A will be above the MM curve for B at equal values of k. Thus, in autarky, the high-saving country A will have a higher equilibrium capital–labor ratio than the less thrifty B. The relative price of the labor-intensive good, the investment good, will be higher in A than in B under autarky.

Trade in an integrated world market without borrowing and lending implies that while saving must continue to equal investment in each economy separately the same is not true for the output of investment goods. The equilibrium condition (2.3.5) for the closed economy is replaced by

$$s_a y_a(p, k_a) + s_b y_b(p, k_b) = q_a(p, k_a) + q_b(p, k_b).$$ (2.3.10)

The equilibrium value $1/p^*$ for the world economy is determined at the point where SS^w, the SS curve for the world economy which is the simple average of SS^a and SS^b, cuts the QQ curve. This determines k_a^* and k_b^* from SS^a and SS^b for $p = p^*$. The capital–labor ratio for the world k_w^* is the average of k_a^* and k_b^*. The MM^w curve, the momentary equilibrium curve for the world economy showing the combinations of p and $(k^a + k^b)/2$ that satisfy (2.3.10) passes through the long run equilibrium point (p^*, k^*), cutting QQ from above. The world economy thus behaves like a single closed economy, moving along its momentary equilibrium curve and converging to the steady state.

International trade thus equalizes relative product prices and, assuming that both countries are not specialized in production, factor prices must be equalized also. The thrifty and hence capital-abundant country A exports the capital-intensive consumption good while the labor-abundant B exports the labor-intensive investment good. Note that trade increases the capital-labor ratio of A *above* its autarky level, while reducing that of B *below* its autarky level. The pre-trade

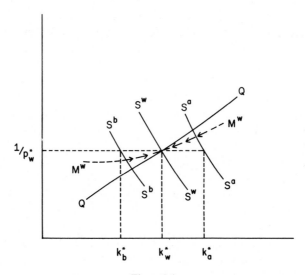

Figure 2.7

differences in factor proportions, that give rise to trade, are themselves accentuated as a result of trade.

It is interesting to note that the same effects of trade on capital stocks and per capita consumption levels as in this neoclassical growth model can also be obtained in stationary models with alternative technologies but in which factor proportions are also endogenously determined instead of simply taken as fixed as in the usual models of comparative advantage. An example is the "Austrian" model of Findlay (1978). In this model the country that has the lower rate of time discount at any given stationary level of consumption has its per capita consumption and capital stock increase as a result of trade while those of its more "impatient" partner fall.

Further investigations of the dynamic two-sector neoclassical model are provided in Hanson (1971), Fischer and Frenkel (1972, 1974) and many other papers. Fischer and Frenkel introduce trade in debt (financial instruments) into the model and link it in interesting ways to the "states of the balance of payments" an idea going back at least to J.E. Cairnes and expounded by Kindleberger (1968). A technical innovation that they introduce is an "adjustment costs" investment function to break the indeterminacy that would otherwise occur in a small open economy's portfolio choice between physical capital and financial assets. Some other papers in this area that should be mentioned are Borts (1964), Hamada (1966), Onitsuka (1974) and Hori and Stein (1977). A very simple and analytically appealing model that considers many of these issues in a neat and concise fashion has recently been presented by Ruffin (1979), who considers capital mobility between two Solow economies that each produce the same good but with different technologies and saving rates. Ruffin's model is extended to economies that produce different goods, with interesting consequences for the relationship between capital mobility, the terms of trade and welfare in the steady state by Saavedra–Rivano (1982, ch. 1).

The relationship between money and growth, analyzed in the closed economy by Tobin (1955) and others, has also given rise to some literature on the open economy. Examples are Allen (1972), Frenkel (1971), Findlay (1975) and Rodriguez (1982). The last two papers consider two-sector growing open economies in steady-state equilibrium, with given rates of monetary expansion in each country. Rodriguez proves that under flexible exchange rates an increase in the rate of monetary expansion by one country will raise its own capital–labor ratio and lower that of its partner, the net effect on the world capital–labor ratio being positive. The monetary and "real" sectors are therefore linked and money is therefore not a mere "veil" as in the usual static formulations, for reasons pointed out clearly by Marty (1961). This result is shown to hold not only for ad hoc savings functions but also with intertemporal utility maximization by consumers, under some restrictions on the demand functions for real balances.

3. Development and asymmetrical interdependence

In contrast to the tidy and systematic character of the "growth and trade" literature that has been our concern up to now the "trade and development" area presents a rather chaotic appearance, rich in historical anecdotes and intuitive insights but lacking any unified framework. Political preconceptions abound and passions run high, with most mainstream economists favoring "outward looking" strategies and policies of development and most radicals stressing the dangers of *dependencia* and consequently advocating "inward looking" policies and strategies to promote "self-reliance". The analytical task of assessing the relative costs and benefits of import substitution and export promotion as development strategies is in Anne Krueger's domain (Chapter 11) and I am happy to leave it in her expert hands. My own task here I conceive to be the examination of the more formal and theoretical aspects of the trade and development literature, relating it wherever possible to the main body of trade theory, whether as "exception" or "rule".[5]

The restriction to those aspects of the field that have undergone some formal development unfortunately excludes from discussion here many issues of great importance and interest. One example is the literature that has been inspired by the historical development of export economies, which Myint (1958) has related to the "vent for surplus" view of foreign trade advanced by Adam Smith. Caves (1965) discusses these ideas in relation to the "staples thesis" of Canadian economic historians such as H.A. Innis. Also relevant in this connection are two papers by Baldwin (1956, 1963) related to the development of mining economies in Southern Africa. The work of all these authors is rich in insights and suggestions that as yet await further analytical development. The technological characteristics of the major export products, the role of foreign capital, labor and entrepreneurship, the links between the modern export sector and the traditional agrarian economy are all in principle capable of being modelled analytically on the basis of the work already done by Baldwin, Caves and Myint.

3.1. Wage differentials and infant industry protection

The oldest controversial proposition in the field is of course the famous "infant industry" argument of Hamilton and List, taken up by Mill and Bastable, that manufacturing in "young" countries should be protected until it could compete on an equal footing with the pioneers. During the inter-war years the Rumanian Manoilesco (1931) put forward the thesis that protection to industry was justified

---

[5]See Nurkse (1961) and Kravis (1970) for moderate and balanced statements of the "pessimistic" and "optimistic" positions respectively on the empirical aspects of the trade-development nexus and the associated policy implications.

in less developed regions because the substantial urban–rural wage differential in those countries was a handicap that required off-setting by a tariff. His book was reviewed by no less eminent authorities than Viner and Ohlin, the latter giving, in a few sentences, the complete modern answer to the problem which is that the appropriate intervention to off-set the distortion was a wage subsidy to manufacturing and not a tariff. The Manoilesco argument was taken up again after World War II by Lewis (1954), whose dual economy model gave the wage differential argument an analytical underpinning by making the urban wage and hence marginal product of labor, equal to the average product of labor in rural family farms and hence greater than the marginal product of labor in agriculture. The argument was taken up in a more formal way by Haberler (1950) and Hagen (1958), finally leading to the emergence of a full-fledged theory of optimal intervention in the presence of domestic or foreign "distortions" in the work of the Delhi Trio of Jagdish Bhagwati, V.K. Ramaswami and T.N. Srinivasan, as well as by Harry Johnson and Max Corden, whose chapter in this volume will cover this topic fully. Here all I wish to do is to point out that a "development" problem has given rise to a major extension of normative trade theory. Formal trade theorists, who tend to scorn the development field for its messy and unrigorous character, should take note.

Another important but rather neglected formal extension of trade theory inspired by the infant industry problem is the work of Bardhan (1970, ch. 7) on "learning by doing" in a small open economy, inspired by the famous model of Arrow (1962). Consider an economy endowed with fixed quantities of capital and labor, producing two goods, agriculture A and manufactures M, the relative price of which is fixed from abroad. The agricultural production function is simply constant returns to scale in capital and labor but the manufacturing production function is of the form:

$$M = Q^n F_m(K_m, L_m),$$

(3.1.1)

in which Q is the cumulative volume of output of M so that

$$\dot{Q} = M.$$

(3.1.2)

The parameter n is a positive fraction so that the elasticity of output with respect to "experience" Q is less than unity. The economy's transformation curve shifts over time, purely due to the effect of "experience" in raising productivity in manufacturing, growth of the labor force and capital accumulation being assumed away for simplicity.

An optimal control problem is posed, the objective function being the integral of the discounted flow of utility from consumption of the two goods, assumed to be homothetic, subject to balanced trade with the rest of the world at a fixed relative price π, and a "dynamic" equation:

$$\dot{Q} = M - \delta Q, \tag{3.1.3}$$

in which δ is the fixed rate at which experience depreciates or "forgetting" occurs. The discount rate δ is also assumed to be fixed. The necessary conditions for a maximum are easily seen to require that the marginal rate of substitution between capital and labor be equalized between industries i.e. for given Q the economy should produce on its transformation curve and that the marginal rate of substitution in consumption of A and M be equated to π, the terms of trade. The marginal rate of transformation in production, however, should *not* be equated to the terms of trade since production of M, in addition to directly contributing to utility by making more consumption possible, also adds to experience and hence provides a social benefit in enhancing future productivity. This positive externality cannot be captured by any single firm in competitive industry and so we have the result that the manufacturing sector would be too small under laissez faire. What has to be added to the marginal product of both capital and labor in manufacturing is therefore the shadow price of the additional experience that is produced. Denoting the marginal utility of M and C by μ and λ, and the shadow price of experience in terms of utility by γ, the marginal productivity of capital in terms of utility in each sector is equated when

$$\frac{\mu + \gamma}{\lambda} = \frac{\partial A}{\partial K_a} \Big/ Q^n \frac{\partial M}{\partial K_m} = \text{MRT}, \tag{3.1.4}$$

whereas

$$\frac{\mu}{\lambda} = \frac{\partial U}{\partial C_m} \Big/ \frac{\partial U}{\partial C_a} = \text{MRS} = \pi. \tag{3.1.5}$$

The socially optimal MRT therefore differs from the socially optimal MRS by γ/λ, which yields the optimum subsidy τ on manufacturing output so that MRT equals $(1 + \tau)\pi$ instead of π as it would under laissez faire. The Lagrangians μ and λ are constants by virtue of the assumption that the utility function is homothetic but γ, the shadow price of "experience", changes over time with the level of the stock, so that τ also changes over time. Bardhan shows that the optimal solution follows a saddle path converging to a stationary solution characterized by Q and γ being at values Q^* and γ^* that satisfy:

$$Q^n F_m = \delta Q, \tag{3.1.6}$$

$$\gamma = \frac{(\mu + \gamma)r^*}{(\rho + \delta)} = \frac{\mu r^*}{(\rho + \delta - r^*)}, \tag{3.1.7}$$

where

$$r^* = nQ^{n-1}Fm = n\delta. \tag{3.1.8}$$

is the marginal productivity of experience in manufacturing evaluated at Q^*. The stock of experiences is constant when the current output of manufactures is equal to the rate at which experience depreciates. The shadow price of experience γ^* determined by (3.1.7) is equal to the current "flow" $(\mu + \gamma)r^*$ "capitalized" by the sum of the discount rate and the rate of depreciation. The optimal subsidy τ^* in the stationary solution is given by:

$$\tau^* = \frac{\gamma^*}{\mu} = \frac{n\delta}{\rho + (1-n)\delta}, \tag{3.1.9}$$

which varies inversely with ρ and directly with n and δ as one would expect. When $Q < Q^*$ it will follow that $\gamma > \gamma^*$ and the shadow price of experience and hence τ will fall over time towards τ^*.

Notice that the analysis is quite independent of whether manufactures are imported or exported. It is in fact consistent with manufactures being initially imported and later exported so that the infant can indeed grow up. The point is that it is manufacturing *output* that should always be subsidized, since it is this that contributes to experience and provides the externality, rather than imports or exports of manufactures. Bardhan also modifies his analysis to account for cumulative output ceasing to influence productivity after a certain level is reached, so that the output subsidy need not be permanent in this case.

Related work in this area has been by Clemhout and Wan (1970) and Teubal (1973).

3.2. Two-gap models and export-led growth

The early literature on development tended to emphasize domestic saving as the major constraint on the growth rate that an LDC could achieve. This view arose out of the wide-spread application of the Harrod–Domar model to problems of development planning. The experience of many LDC's in the sixties, however, indicated that the balance of payments situation tended to be a critical constraint on the rate at which capital accumulation and development could take place. Hollis Chenery, who occupied influential advisory positions at the official US foreign aid agency and later at the World Bank, put forward a simple framework in which, depending upon the values of a few parameters, a particular LDC would be identified as having its growth rate constrained by either a "domestic savings" or a "foreign exchange" gap. "Two-gap" models, as they came to be

called, were very much in vogue in the sixties and early seventies though interest
in them appears to have dwindled in recent years. Chenery and Bruno (1962), and
Chenery and Strout (1966), are perhaps the most representative papers by the
originator of this approach, McKinnon (1964) provides a detailed formalization
and Findlay (1973, ch. 10) an exposition and critique of the logical basis.

The essential idea of the two-gap approach can be brought out with the aid of
Figure 3.1. Suppose that domestic output depends only on the capital stock,
initially given. The distance OY measures domestic output, which can be exchanged at a fixed rate for imports of capital equipment. Total consumption is
simply a fraction of domestic output and is equal to OC. Domestic investment
requires imported capital equipment and the domestic good in fixed proportions.
Levels of investment are indicated by a family of L-shaped isoquants with C as
the origin. The given propensity to save, CY/OY, determines VX as the amount
of imported equipment, XY the export of the domestic good required to pay for it
and CX the domestic component of investment. The growth rate of output will be
equal to the ratio of investment, the level corresponding to the isoquant at V,
divided by the capital stock, assuming that the marginal and average capital-
output ratios are equal. This is just a modification of Harrod–Domar to an open
economy, in which growth is constrained by the savings rate.

Assume now that the maximum level of imports obtainable is UZ, regardless of
the level of exports. This reduces the attainable level of investment to the isoquant
at U. Exports of TY will be sufficient to pay for the imports of capital equipment

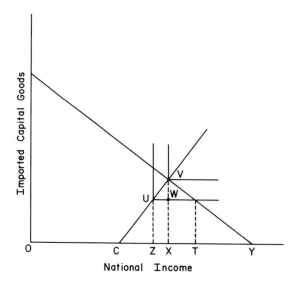

Figure 3.1

and so *ZT* of domestic output will be "redundant" in the sense that it cannot be used for investment, either directly or through exports. The "foreign exchange" gap will be measured by *VW*, the difference between *VX* and *UZ*, while the surplus of potential domestic saving is *ZT*.

Foreign aid is more growth-promoting when it is given to an LDC whose growth is constrained by the shortage of foreign exchange rather than by domestic savings. In Figure 3.2 let the amount of foreign aid be measured by *YY'*. If growth is constrained by savings investment will increase from *V* to *V'*. Notice that all of the foreign aid will not be used to import capital equipment since *XX'* of domestic output will be shifted from exports to the domestic component of investment, to provide the complementary input for the additional capital equipment that is imported. When growth is constrained by the shortage of foreign exchange, however, all of the foreign aid can be used to increase imports of capital equipment, since domestic output for investment is available in the form of the otherwise redundant supply of domestic saving.

The foreign exchange gap can also be introduced into a simple mathematical model. Let *Y* be domestic output, *X* exports, *m* the propensity to import consumer goods and α the incremental output capital ratio. Assume that export earnings increase over time at a constant rate *g*. We can therefore write:

$$\frac{dY}{dt} = \alpha \left[X_0 e^{gt} - mY \right], \tag{3.2.1}$$

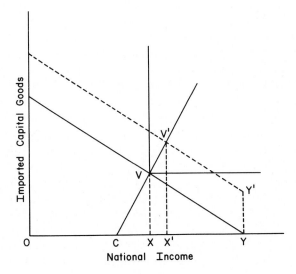

Figure 3.2

which is a simple differential equation that can be integrated to yield:

$$Y(t) = \frac{\alpha}{(g + am)} X_0 e^{gt} + \left\{ Y_0 - \frac{\alpha}{(g + am)} X_0 \right\} e^{-amt}, \qquad (3.2.2)$$

which shows that the growth rate of output will approach the growth rate of exports in the limit. This is one meaning that can be attached to the rather loosely used term "export-led growth" in the development literature.

These simple examples that we have given illustrate a crucial limitation of the two-gap approach, which is its almost complete neglect of relative prices and also its tendency to assume that the constraint on the ability of LDCs to earn the foreign exchange that they undoubtedly need for economic development is external demand and not domestic supply. The external environment is similar to what would be faced by an economic system that is undergoing a siege or a blockade. The experience of the expanding world markets of the sixties and seventies completely contradicted this ultra-pessimistic assumption about the export possibilities of the LDCs.

3.3. The open dual economy

The issues connected with "export-led" growth have also been pursued within the context of the celebrated 1954 Lewis model of economic development with unlimited supplies of labor. Though Lewis himself has not "opened up" his own analysis of capital accumulation in an economy characterized by a fixed real wage, preferring to use instead the three-good Ricardian model described earlier in this paper for his analysis of the terms of trade, other writers have introduced trade explicitly into this model in various ways. Examples include Fei and Ranis (1964), Hornby (1968), Dixit (1969), Bardhan (1970), Lefeber (1971), Paauw and Fei (1973) and Findlay (1973).

One set of problems that have been posed in the context of an open dual economy is connected with long-run development strategy when the "modern" sector is controlled by a planning authority while the "traditional" sector consists of small independent peasant producers. This situation is a relevant one for many contemporary economies in S.E. Asia and Africa and is also similar to the Soviet Union in the twenties, except for the fact that foreign trade was not of any significance. The issues of "primitive socialist accumulation" debated at that time by Bukharin, Preobrazhenski, Feldman and others and vividly discussed by Erlich (1960) continue to be relevant to contemporary developing economies and have been analyzed, with more sophisticated tools, by Hornby, Bardhan, Dixit and Findlay in the contributions listed at the end of the last paragraph. All of this work has also been influenced by the literature on development strategy and planning by Maurice Dobb, A.K. Sen, P.C. Mahalanobis and Evsey Domar.

Among some of the specific issues examined in the open dual economy context are the problem of the optimal "internal" terms of trade, or rate at which the peasant sector should be taxed to finance capital accumulation in the modern sector, the optimal allocation of resources between capital goods and consumer goods in the modern sector itself and the optimal role of foreign trade in the development of the open dual economy over time. Findlay (1973, ch. 9) analyzes this last problem in terms of the "turnpike" theorem that Dorfman, Samuelson and Solow derived from the model of Von Neumann. This application predates the simpler application of the Von Neumann model to an open economy by Steedman (1979, ch. 13).

The composite production function for tradeable goods, used to extend the Solow–Swan model to an open economy in the previous section, is again the simplest way in which to perform the analogous operation for the Lewis model, which can be thought of as a one-sector Von Neumann model. In Figure 3.3 the right hand panel is the factor-price frontier corresponding to the composite "foreign exchange" production function, which yields the rate of profit corresponding to the fixed real wage $\bar{w}$. The left-hand panel indicates the linear relationship between the profit rate ρ and the growth rate g determined by the "Anglo-Italian" equation $g = \sigma\rho$ where σ is the propensity to save out of profit, the entire wage being spent on consumption. The growth rate of a small open dual economy therefore varies inversely with the real wage, directly with the propensity to save out of profit and with the production efficiency of the economy

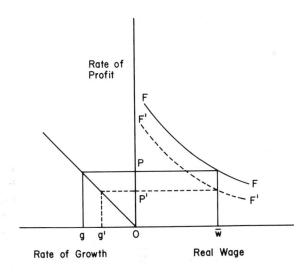

Figure 3.3

as indicated by the height of the factor-price frontier corresponding to any given real wage.

With comparatively low real wages the economy would specialize on labor-intensive exports such as textiles or footwear, or labor-intensive stages of integrated production processes, importing capital equipment, spare parts, raw materials and final consumer goods of a more capital-intensive nature. Access to modern technology, through multinational corporations for example, would keep the factor-price frontier favorably high. In conjunction with the relatively low real wage this would mean a high rate of profit and thus a high rate of growth.

A combination of circumstances such as these might help to account for the spectacular growth of manufactured exports by the newly industrializing Far Eastern economies, the so-called "gang of four" of Korea, Taiwan, Hong Kong and Singapore during the sixties, in which annual growth rates of export volume of thirty per cent per annum were achieved. The source of the additional employment in the "modern" manufacturing sector could have been domestic agriculture and the urban unemployed, as in Korea and Taiwan, or immigration from the mainland, as in Hong Kong. Eventually of course the real wage would start to rise, as it in fact has in these economies, but not as sharply as a Solow model with a perfectly inelastic supply would predict. These are simple stylized polar models of the labor market, requiring the touch of common sense for their application to particular historical and contemporary instances.

Notice the sharp contrast between this model and the "foreign exchange gap" approach. Here the lesson is to find your comparative advantage in some appropriately labor-intensive directions, which, with modern technology and at least initially low real wages will give you a high rate of profit, which you can plough back into capital accumulation and thus expand at a rapid pace. The classical forces of "productivity" and "thrift" come once again to the fore.

A strategy of import substitution behind a wall of protection, in this model, is tantamount to technological regress, since in terms of "foreign exchange" the factor price frontier of Figure 3.3 is shifted downwards to the dashed line as a result of the inefficiency in resource allocation induced by protection. Since the real wage is fixed the effect is to reduce the rate of profit and hence the rate of growth. Import substitution strategies, apparently designed to eliminate a foreign exchange "gap", may thus be the cause rather than the cure for the problem to which they are apparently addressed. Another way of putting this point is that the rate of growth of export earnings, which the two-gap approach tends to take as simply given, is an endogenous variable that depends, among other things, on trade policy itself. For a single "small" open economy there is simply no better way than finding its most profitable niche in world markets and exploiting it to the fullest extent possible. This is not to condemn the country to perpetually hewing wood and drawing water for the lords and masters of the world economy. The ploughing back into capital accumulation of profits made in primary products or labor-intensive manufactures can eventually lead the way to rising real wages, higher capital-intensities and more sophisticated technology. Economic history abounds in examples, from the raw silk and lumber of the early days of Japan and Sweden, to the East Asian newly industrializing countries of today that have gone from toys and wigs to ship-building and heavy machinery in a couple of decades.

None of this is to deny, however, that external factors do exercise an enormous influence over the possibilities that are open to the LDCs as a group. The trade-development nexus needs to be explored simultaneously at different levels – one pole being the single small country in a big world, with all relative prices given, at least within narrow limits, the other the interaction between the advanced countries as a whole, the "North" for short, with the LDCs as a whole, or the "South". Particular problems may require other groupings, that cut across these categories, such as oil exporting and oil importing countries for example.

3.4. North – South models

A common thread underlying many of the critiques of "outward looking" policies, or "development through trade" is that the "center" and the "periphery" of the world economic system are characterized by fundamental asymmetries in the structures and performance of their economies. At one level it is sometimes argued that the motivation of economic agents is different, with those in the advanced countries being more dedicated to the pursuit of self-interest and those in the less developed countries more altruistic, other-worldly or whatever. This was the sense in which the term "dualism" was first used by the influential Dutch writer Boeke, for example, in his work on colonial Indonesia. This alleged difference in motivation could be used to obtain opposite responses to price or wage increases on the part of agents in the two regions. This type of dualism or asymmetry in economic behavior, though stressed by some anthropologists, historians and others of the Karl Polanyi school, has however not been widespread among economists. The evidence of "rational" behavior by peasants in less developed countries, both in the past and in the present, is simply too overwhelming.

Another type of dualism that has been proposed is in the nature and operation of product and factor markets. Raul Prebisch has argued, for example, that large corporations and labor unions in the center combined with competitive production and trade in the periphery have introduced an asymmetry of market structure that operates to result in secular deterioration of the terms of trade of the periphery. Arthur Lewis has stressed the market for labor, with flexible wages and market clearing in the center, and exogenously given wages in the "modern" sector of the periphery. The level of the fixed wage is determined somehow by conditions in the "peasant hinterland," thus making employment depend on the demand for labor at this fixed wage. Despite wide-spread arguments to the contrary the consistency of "surplus labor" with peasant rationality is, in my opinion, convincingly demonstrated by Lewis (1973) himself and by Sen (1966).

The next two sections take up a line of work that I and some of my students have followed in the last few years that examines the characteristics of a two-region model of growth and trade, in which the labor markets of the two regions are marked by this basic asymmetry. I use the term "North–South" model to refer to any model in which there is some basic asymmetry related to the stage of development between the two regions. The model I am about to describe is an example, but by no means the only North–South model, as we shall see later on when I examine recent work by several others.

To avoid unnecessary misunderstanding I should point out that North–South models are not intended, at least not by me, to be rivals or substitutes for the conventional symmetric "Countries A and B" approach to international trade, in which the countries differ only in the quantitative magnitude of some parameter, related to technology, tastes or factor proportions or even, as in some of the recent work described in Helpman's chapter in this volume, by identical countries with trade based purely on the possibility of exploiting economies of scale. My own motivation has been that these standard models can fruitfully be supplemented by some asymmetric types, both because of the intrinsic intellectual interest and also to answer the frequently heard complaint that trade theory, as a branch of neoclassical economics, is irrelevant or pernicious in its application to developmental problems because it assumes away the problem of underemployment of the labor force, among other "structural" features of such economies. As I hope to demonstrate one *can* pay attention to such problems while at the same time respecting the canons of rigorous enquiry that trade theorists expect in their field. To argue the contrary, that trade theory should maintain its purity by avoiding contamination from such sources, seems to me to be nothing other than dogmatism and foreign to the spirit and the example of David Ricardo. In taking this view I leave entirely open the possibility that reality may conform more closely to the conventional model than to any such hybrids that I am going to discuss under the rubric of North–South models. The question of realism and relevance of models is also not one that is invariant with respect to time. The hope of all concerned with the "development" of the Third World is that eventually its structural peculiarities will disappear as it approaches more closely to the levels of productivity and income of the presently more advanced countries. "Dualism", of whatever variety, is usually considered to be a transitional phenomenon, though possibly a very protracted one. Thus the models that pay attention to this feature will one day, and perhaps even now, be of more historical than contemporary interest. This observation should not cause concern to those to whom to be parochial in time is no less a human deficiency than to be parochial in space.

Finally, it should be apparent that it would be an instance of the fallacy of composition to apply results of North–South models to any single country of either region. Thus expanding exports of labor-intensive manufactures by 25 percent a year will have very different consequences if it is one or a few individual countries that is involved or the South as a whole. It clearly would not be very intelligent for an LDC to rule out an export oriented development strategy on the grounds that the terms of trade would sharply deteriorate if the entire South followed the same strategy simultaneously. That would be like refusing to escape from a burning building on the ground that everyone could not do so at the same time due to the narrowness of the exit. It is necessary to view the trade-development connection both from a "small country" perspective and in terms of the "South" as a whole.

3.4.1.   The terms of trade and equilibrium growth

Consider two economies, North and South, each of which is completely specialized on the production of a single composite good, which can be thought of as "manufactures" for the North and "primary products" for the South, though there is no reason why the South composite good may not include labor-intensive manufactured consumer goods as well. In the North,

$$Y_N = q(k)L_N \tag{3.4.1}$$

is the constant returns to scale production function, with the usual properties, for its output with the labor force being:

$$L_N(t) = L_0 e^{nt}, \tag{3.4.2}$$

and k_N the capital–labor ratio, which changes over time according to:

$$\dot{k}_N = sq(k_N) - nk_N, \tag{3.4.3}$$

where s is the constant proportion of income that is saved. The demand for imports I_N from the South is a function of θ, the terms of trade of the South, and consumption in the North is given by:

$$I_N = m[\theta, (1-s)q(k_N)]L_N. \tag{3.4.4}$$

The North's output is thus split between investment $sq(k_N)L_N$, exports θI_N and the residual which is domestic consumption of manufactures by the North.

The North conforms exactly to the Solow growth model, except for the fact that it consumes an importable in addition to its own product.

The per capita production function for the South, also with constant returns to scale is

$$\pi = \pi(k_S). \tag{3.4.5}$$

Producers maximize profit subject to a fixed wage $\bar{w}$ so that we have

$$\pi - \pi'(k_S)k_S = \bar{w}, \tag{3.4.6}$$

which determines the capital–labor ratio k_S^* as the unique value of k_S that satisfies this equation. The rate of profit in the South is

$$\rho = \theta\pi'(k_S^*), \tag{3.4.7}$$

which determines the common growth rate of capital, output and employment in the South as $g = \sigma\rho$, where σ is the propensity to save out of profits.

The import demand function for the South is

$$I_S = \left[\theta\sigma\pi'(k_S^*)k_S^* + \mu\left(\frac{1}{\theta}, \bar{w} + (1-\sigma)\right)\pi'(k_S^*)k_S^*\right]L_S, \tag{3.4.8}$$

where μ is per capita demand for consumption of manufactures, while $\theta\sigma\pi'(k_x^*)k_S^*$ is the per capita demand for investment. The employment level L_S is determined as $K_S(t)$, which is a state variable, divided by k_S^*, the equilibrium capital–labor ratio. Given $k_N(t)$, $L_N(t)$ and $K_S(t)$ the momentary equilibrium of the model is determined by the balanced trade condition

$$\theta(t)I_N(t) = I_S(t). \tag{3.4.9}$$

Long-run steady-state equilibrium will occur when the growth rates of the two regions are equal, which occurs when the growth rate of the South $\sigma\rho(t)$ is equal to n. From (3.4.7) this condition is satisfied only when

$$\theta^* = \frac{n}{\sigma\pi'(k_S^*)}. \tag{3.4.10}$$

The long-run equilibrium for the North requires

$$k_N^* = \frac{sq(k_N^*)}{n}. \tag{3.4.11}$$

For the South define $\lambda(t)$ as the ratio $L_S(t)$ to $L_N(t)$. In the long-run equilibrium

$$\lambda^* = \frac{\theta^* m^* \left(\theta^*, k_N^* \right)}{n k_S^* + \mu^* \left(\dfrac{1}{\theta^*} \right)}. \tag{3.4.12}$$

The dynamics of the transition to the steady state values (k_N^*, λ^*) is spelled out in Findlay (1980) and is depicted in the phase diagram of Figure 3.4.

The terms of trade therefore play a key role in this model as the regulator that makes the growth rate of the South conform to the exogenously given long run growth rate of the North. Trade is the "engine of growth" for the South, but the pace of the engine is set by the growth rate of the North.

At the steady state values θ^* and k_N^* the per capita import demand $m(\theta, K_N)$ is also determined as $m^* = m(\theta^*, k_N^*)$. The export earnings of the South per each worker in the North, is therefore $\theta^* m^*$. Equation (3.4.12) above determines λ^*, the number of workers that can be employed in the South relative to one worker in the North. In the long run, employment in the South is governed by its capacity to import capital goods from the North, which in turn is governed by θ^* and k_N^*. The "iron law of the terms of trade", expressed in (3.4.10), has strong implications. It shows that increases in σ and $\pi'(k_S^*)$, i.e. greater "productivity and thrift" in the South, would reduce θ^* in the same proportion and leave the

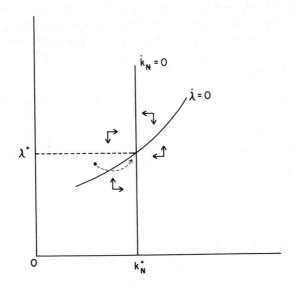

Figure 3.4

growth rate of the South unchanged, though they would serve to increase λ^* the employment ratio.

The model can be extended in various ways while preserving its essential features. Saavedra-Rivano (1982, ch. 2) introduces the relevant possibility that the South's exportable is an essential intermediate input into the North's production function, a modification that enhances the interdependence of the two regions and makes the North's steady-state capital–labor ratio a function of conditions in the South as well. Kiguel and Wooton (1982) study the incidence of tariffs by each region, both in the short and in the long run. They show that the optimum tariff is positive for the North only in the short run, since in the long run the supply of exports by the South is perfectly elastic at θ^*. The South, on the other hand, has a positive optimal tariff even in the long run, since it can benefit in increased employment from deteriorations in its international terms of trade, consistent with the domestic price-ratio being equal to θ^*, as required by the steady-state condition.

3.4.2.   International factor mobility

Burgstaller and Saavedra-Rivano (1981) have introduced international capital mobility into this model and obtained some rather remarkable results. The analysis gets rather complex and so I shall only try to provide an intuitive understanding of some of the highlights of their work.

Capital is free to move in either direction but it is natural to suppose that the incentive is for it to flow from North to South. Manufactures continue to be produced in the North but there is a foreign enclave in the South where Northern capital employs Southern labor to produce primary goods which are also produced by domestic Southern capitalists using the same production function and paying the same fixed wage. A little reflection shows that for a steady state Southern capital must grow at the same rate n as the effective labor force of the North, which continues to be sole determinant of the expansion of the system as a whole. Thus the terms of trade must continue to be equal to θ^* as in eq. (3.4.10), and the rate of profit obtainable in the South is consequently $\rho^* = \theta^* \pi'(k_\pi^*)$ where k_π^* is the capital–labor ratio that maximizes profit in the primary goods sector when the real wage is equal to $\bar{w}$. Capital mobility therefore does not affect ρ^*, which is the same as in its absence.

The North will therefore invest in manufactures only up to the point at which $q'(k_M^*) = \rho^*$ where k_M^* is the capital–labor ratio in manufacturing that makes the marginal product of capital equal to ρ^*. The quantity of capital that citizens of the North would wish to hold, however, is given by k_N^* which is the value of k_N for which $sf(k_N) = nk_N$, which leaves $(k_N^* - k_M^*)$ as the amount of capital in the steady state that will be invested by the North in the South to produce primary goods. The relation between k_N^* and k_M^* is depicted in Figure 3.5 which is the familiar diagram showing per capita income as a function of the capital–labor ratio. Foreign investment at ρ^* makes this function have a constant positive slope equal to ρ^* to the right of k_M^*. Notice that for the model to be stable we must have $s\rho^* < n$ since otherwise capital accumulation by the North would be unbounded so long as the wage was equal to $\bar{w}$ in the South. Stability could only be restored after the surplus labor pool of the South was exhausted, driving up the wage and reducing the rate of profit. To preserve dualism in the "steady state" we assume $s\rho^* < n$.

The per capita income of the North in the steady state is

$$y_N^* = q(k_M^*) + \rho^*(k_N^* - k_M^*), \qquad (3.4.13)$$

where the first term is domestic output of manufactures and the second is income from foreign investment in primary production. From θ^* and y_N^* it is immediately possible to determine that per capita demands for imports m^* and domestic consumption of manufactures c^* in the North. The balance of payments is given by:

$$x^* + \rho(k_N^* - k_M^*) = \theta^* m^* + n(k_N^* - k_M^*), \qquad (3.4.14)$$

where x^* is per capita exports of the North. The left-hand side is exports plus income from foreign investment, which together finance imports and the capital requirements of the expanding enclave in the South. It must also be true that:

$$x^* = q(k_M^*) - c^* - nk_M^*, \qquad (3.4.15)$$

since exports must equal output of manufactures less domestic consumption and investment.

We now turn to the Northern enclave in the South. For every worker in the North employment in the enclave is equal to $[(k_N^* - k_M^*)/k_\pi^*]$ which we denote λ_e^*. Investment demand to maintain the capital–labor ratio constant will be n times this amount. Demand for consumption of manufactures by workers in the enclave is $\alpha\theta^*\bar{w}$ time λ_e^*, where α is the propensity to consume manufactures by Southern workers. Employment, per worker in the North, in the domestic capitalist sector of the South is therefore:

$$\lambda_d^* = \frac{q(k_M^*) - nk_M^* - c^* - (\alpha\theta^*\bar{w} + nk_\pi^*)\lambda_e^*}{nk_\pi^* + \alpha(\theta^*\bar{w} + (1-\sigma)\rho^* k_\pi^*)}, \qquad (3.4.16)$$

where the denominator is equal to per capita import demand for both investment and consumption in the South.

The numerator of this expression clearly has to be positive for λ_d^* to be so and it is instructive to consider what this condition means. It can be seen that it is simply that there be positive excess supply of manufactures by the North after its domestic demands and that of its enclave in the South have been satisfied. Native Southern capitalists thus have to compete with the enclave in the market for primary products in the North. As we shall see immediately this fact has very significant consequences for the situation of the South.

Consider an increase in s. It is apparent from Figure 3.5 that k_M^* is unchanged while k_N^* and hence y_N^* increases as does per capita consumption since we are always to the left of the Golden Rule if $\rho^* > n$. This means that in the numerator of (3.4.16) we have $q(k_M^*)$, nk_M^* and the coefficient of λ_e^* are all constant while c^* and λ_e^* increase while the denominator remains unchanged. Thus λ_d must decline in response to an increase in s. Burgstaller and Saavedra-Rivano demonstrate, after some manipulation, that the sum of λ_d and λ_e, i.e. employment in the South relative to one worker in the North, must also decrease, the rise in λ_e being less than the fall in λ_d.

Northern capital thus "crowds out" Southern capital by entering primary production, since its opportunities in manufacturing production are exceeded by the fixed rate ρ^* obtainable abroad. Shades of Hobson and Lenin!

Essentially the same intuition explains another very striking result that perfect capital mobility reduces employment and relative real income in the South

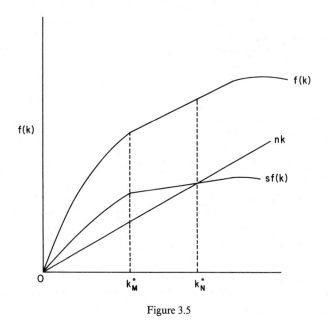

Figure 3.5

(inclusive of wage income in the enclave). The reason is again that capital mobility reduces the output of manufactures and increases the domestic consumption demand for them, thus restricting the market in the North for Southern capital.

Labor mobility, however, has entirely benign consequences in this model. Wooton (1982) has introduced labor mobility from South to North into the model in the form of a "guest worker" immigration quota set at some fraction of the Northern labor force. He shows that in the long run an increase in this fraction benefits citizens of the North, since it raises the steady-state capital–labor ratio and their real per capita income, though it reduces the real wage, and also the relative real income of the South. It does the latter in two ways – those who become *gastarbeiter* obviously have the opportunity to earn a higher wage in the North but the rise in the real income of the North itself also increases the market for the South's exports and hence permits the relative employment ratio λ^* to rise.

3.4.3. Some other North–South models

Several other interesting North–South models have recently been published. Bacha (1978), already mentioned in connection with Emmanuel in Section 1.3 of this chapter presents a simple neo-Ricardian model with exogenous wages in *both* regions, and profit rates equated by capital mobility. Though his model is not a dynamic one his comparative static exercises involving technical progress and so on capture some of the flavor of a dynamic model. I have some problems with the division of the world "wage fund" between North and South in his model and I am also not quite confident that all the stated results strictly follow from the assumptions as stated but there is no doubt that his paper made a very original and valuable contribution by presenting a simple framework in which some fresh ideas could be considered.

Krugman (1982) gives an ingenious analysis of "uneven development" by introducing external economies into the production of manufactures, varying positively with the level of the capital stock. With identical tastes and technology the region that initially has the higher capital stock, assuming equal sizes of the labor force, will have the lower unit cost in manufactures and a higher rate of profit. With classical savings behavior the higher rate of profit is tantamount to a higher rate of growth and so the advantage becomes cumulative over time in a manner described by Myrdal (1956). The lagging country finds its manufacturing becoming less competitive in a correspondingly cumulative way. Regions that start with only a slight difference in capital endowment can end up as one very rich manufacturing region and one very poor agricultural region as a result of interaction under these conditions, à la the famous case of the destruction of the once flourishing Indian textile industry by competition from Lancashire, though here of course the technology itself was very different. Krugman extends the model to permit international investment, and is able to obtain very "Leninist" conclusions, such as a phase of exports of manufactured goods being followed by one of exports of capital. The motto for the Krugman model that I find most appropriate, however, is the Biblical "to them that hath shall be given, and from them that hath not shall be taken away, even that which they hath".

Dixit (1982) considers asymmetry in the market structure for export products. His North produces and exports differentiated goods under monopolistic competition, while his South exports an essential raw material under perfect competition. He finds that greater variety can compensate the South for worsened terms of trade in response to increased exports, and a high price-elasticity of demand by the North is also a help in this regard, from the standpoint of the effect on the South's welfare.

Chichilnisky (1981) presents a North–South model that apparently obtains some startling results. In particular it is claimed that a shift in the composition of the North's demand in favor of the South's exports can worsen the terms of trade of the latter. This result is stated in Proposition 1 (p. 178 and footnote 11) which is actually self-contradictory since it implies that positive excess demand for a commodity can reduce its price even though the market is said to be stable in the Walrasian sense. Thus either the result, or Walrasian stability, has to be given up. Examination of the structure of the model shows that it possesses a unique equilibrium that is Walras stable, so it is the result that is false. A shift in the demand of the North towards the South's exports in her model actually can only produce the completely standard result that it would improve the terms of trade of the latter.

The structure of the model is easily spelt out. Two goods, called "basic" or B and "investment" or I, are each produced in the North and the South. Each good is produced with fixed coefficients of capital and labor that may differ across the regions but the I-good is the more capital-intensive in each region. Supplies of labor and capital in each region are positive functions of the real wage and rental respectively in each region. For each price-ratio P_I/P_B a wage and rental, hence labor and capital supplied and hence output levels of both goods are uniquely determined. Raising P_I/P_B raises the rental and reduces the wage by the Stolper–Samuelson theorem, and thus produces a double Rybczynski effect on each good, unambiguously raising the output of I and reducing the output of B. The supply functions of both goods are therefore positively sloped in response to a rise in their respective price. The demand for the I good in each country is assumed to be perfectly inelastic with respect to price. It is therefore convenient to examine the equilibrium in the market for the I good, leaving the B market to be determined by Walras' Law.

Each country in autarky would clearly have a stable Walrasian equilibrium at the unique value of P_I/P_B at which the positively sloped supply curve for I intersects the vertical demand curve. Let this autarky price-ratio be lower in the

North. Free trade in an integrated world market would determine a new equilibrium price-ratio, obtained as the point where the lateral sum of the two supply curves crosses the lateral sum of the two inelastic demand curves as in Figure 3.6. At this world equilibrium price the North exports the I good and the South the B good.

The comparative statics experiment is an increase in I_D^N, the fixed demand of the North. It is immediate from Figure 3.6 that P_I/P_B must rise, i.e. the terms of trade improves for the North and worsens for the South. The South imports less I goods than before, at a higher relative price in terms of B goods. The volume of the South's exports may therefore rise or fall, depending upon whether the elasticity of import demand is less than or greater than unity.

All this of course is completely elementary and would not require any comment if it were not claimed that the increase in I_D^N implied an *increase* in the North's demand for the South's exports and hence the apparent paradox. This unfortunate confusion seems to have arisen because of the gratuitous labelling of the North's exportable as an "investment" good. There is no "investment" in any sense of the word going on in the model as the supply of capital is purely a function of the rental. An increase in I_D^N is thus not an increase in investment and hence in income via a multiplier as in a Keynesian model or an increase in the

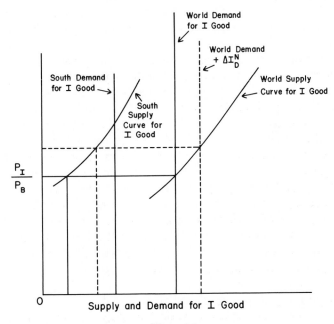

Figure 3.6

stock of capital as in a growth model. It is simply a switch in the composition of demand in favor of the North's own exportable and thus a fall in its demand for the South's exportable which, not surprisingly, leads to a worsening of the South's terms of trade.

An intensive mathematical critique by Saavedra-Rivano (1981) dissects this and associated errors in the paper. What is left is an entirely well-behaved and perhaps even useful model, but not one that produces any startling results. The differences in technology that are assumed to hold between the regions only produce differences in the magnitude of effects which are qualitatively conventional. There is no genuine asymmetry betwen North and South in either the assumptions or the correct results of the model.

Another very important distinction between North and South is with respect to the generation of technical progress. It is the North that is the source of the vast bulk of innovation in both products and processes while the South is in the position of a borrower. This of course is not without its advantages as Thorstein Veblen long ago, and Alexander Gerschenkron more recently, have stressed. The borrower or "late comer" can increase productivity much faster, given appropriate conditions, when there is a backlog of innovations available. I have combined this "relative backwardness" hypothesis with the idea of direct foreign investment as a vehicle of technological diffusion in Findlay (1978b). Other contributions of a related nature are Koizumi and Kopecky (1977), Magee (1977) and Carlos Rodriguez (1981). I shall refrain from further discussion of these and other dynamic models of technology transfer since Jones and Neary have some observations on them in Chapter 1 and also because the reader can be referred to an excellent recent survey by Pugel (1981).

Finally, I would like to end this chapter with a general observation on the relation between growth and development and the theory of international trade. As I have tried to show in the opening section on Ricardian theory the phenomena of "growth" and "development" are *not* a recent alien and messy intrusion into the tidy formal garden of trade theory. They were "present at the creation" in the mind of the founder and in his work. The present state of the world economy and its probable future indicate that there will be no lack of problems to which the traditional tools of trade theory can fruitfully be applied and also no lack of new ones that will call for extensions and modifications of that theory. General equilibrium, not of the sterile "everything depends on everything else" type but in the sense of strategic simplifications for interesting special cases, will live on.

References

Allen, P.R. (1972), "Money and growth in open economies", Review of Economic Studies, 39:213–220.
Arrow, K.J. (1962), "Economic implications of learning by doing", Review of Economic Studies, 29:155–173.

Bacha, E. (1978), "An interpretation of unequal exchange from Prebisch–Singer to Emmanuel", Journal of Development Economics, 5:319–330.

Baldwin, R.E. (1956), "Patterns of development in newly settled regions", Manchester School, 23:161–179.

Baldwin, R.E. (1963), "Export technology and development from a subsistence level", Economic Journal, 73:80–92.

Bardhan, P.K. (1965), "Equilibrium growth in the international economy", Quarterly Journal of Economics, 79:455–464.

Bardhan, P.K. (1970), Economic growth, development and foreign trade (Wiley, New York).

Bertrand, T.J. (1975), "The gains from trade: an analysis of steady state solutions in an open economy", Quarterly Journal of Economics, 89:556–568.

Bhagwati, J. (1958), "Immiserizing growth; a geometrical note", Review of Economic Studies, 25:201–205.

Bhagwati, J. (1971), "The generalized theory of distortions and welfare", in: J. Bhagwati et al., eds., Trade, balance of payments and growth (North-Holland, Amsterdam).

Borts, G. (1964), "A theory of long-run international capital movements", Journal of Political Economy, 72:341–359.

Brecher, R.A. and E.U. Choudhri (1982), "Immiserizing investment from abroad: The Singer–Prebisch thesis reconsidered", Quarterly Journal of Economics, 97:181–190.

Brecher, R.A. and C.F. Diaz Alejandro (1977), "Tariffs, foreign capital and immiserizing growth", Journal of International Economics, 7:317–322.

Brecher, R.A. and R. Findlay (1983), "Tariffs, foreign capital and national welfare", mimeographed, Columbia University Economics Department Discussion Paper No. 114; Journal of International Economics, 14:277–288.

Burgstaller, A. and N. Saavedra-Rivano (1981), "Capital mobility and growth in a North–South model", Columbia University Economics Department Discussion Paper No. 111.

Caves, R.E. (1985), "Vent for surplus models of trade and growth", in: R.E. Baldwin et al., eds., Trade, growth and the balance of payments (Rand McNally, Chicago).

Chenery, H.B. and M. Bruno (1962), "Development alternatives in an open economy: The case of Israel", Economic Journal, 72:79–103.

Chenery, H.B. and A. Strout (1966), "Foreign assistance and economic development", American Economic Review, 56:679–733.

Chichilnisky, G. (1981), "Terms of Trade and domestic distribution: Export-led growth with abundant labor", Journal of Development Economics, 8:163–192.

Clemhout, S. and H.Y. Wan (1970), "Learning-by-doing and infant industry protection", Review of Economic Studies, 37:33–56.

Deardorff, A.V. (1973), "The gains from trade in and out of steady-state growth", Oxford Economic Papers, 25:173–191.

Dixit, A.K. (1969), "Marketable surplus and dual development", Journal of Economic Theory, 1:203–219.

Dixit, A.K. (1982), "Growth and terms of trade under imperfect competition", mimeographed, Princeton University Economics Department.

Edgeworth, F.Y. (1894), "The theory of international values I", Economic Journal, 4:35–50.

Emmanuel, A. (1972), Unequal exchange (Monthly Review Press, New York).

Erlich, A. (1960), The Soviet industrialization debate (Harvard University Press, Cambridge, Mass).

Fei, J.C.H. and G. Ranis (1964), Development of the labor surplus economy (Yale University Press, New Haven).

Findlay, R. (1973), International trade and development theory (Columbia University Press, New York).

Findlay, R. (1974), "Relative prices, growth and trade in a simple Ricardian system", Economica, 41:1–13.

Findlay, R. (1975), "Dinero, commercio y crecimiento", Revista Espanola de Economia, 5:9–24.

Findlay, R. (1978a), "An 'Austrian' model of international trade and interest rate equalization", Journal of Political Economy, 56:989–1007.

Findlay, R. (1978b), "Relative backwardness, direct foreign investment and the transfer of technology: A simple dynamic model", Quarterly Journal of Economics, 92:1–16.

Findlay, R. (1980), "The terms of trade and equilibrium growth in the world economy", American

Economic Review, 70:291–299.

Findlay, R. (1981), "Fundamental determinants of the terms of trade", in Grassman, S. and E. Lundberg, eds., The world economic order: past and prospects (Macmillan, London), 425–457.

Findlay, R. (1982), "International distributive justice", Columbia University Economics Department Paper No. 104, Journal of International Economics, 13:1–14.

Findlay, R. and H. Grubert (1959), "Factor intensities, technological progress and the terms of trade", Oxford Economic Papers, 11:111–121.

Findlay, R. and S. Wellisz (1976), "Project evaluation, shadow prices and trade policy", Journal of Political Economy, 84:543–552.

Fischer, S. and J.A. Frenkel (1972), "Investment, and two-sector model, and trade in debt and capital goods", Journal of International Economics, 2:211–233.

Fischer, S. and J.A. Frenkel (1974), "Interest rate equalization, patterns of production, trade and consumption in a two-country growth model", Economic Record, 50:555–580.

Frenkel, J.A. (1971), "A theory of money, trade and the balance of payments in a model of accumulation", Journal of International Economics, 1:159–187.

Haberler, G. (1937), The theory of international trade (Hodge, London).

Haberler, G. (1950), "Some problems in the pure theory of international trade", Economic Journal, 60:223–240.

Hagen, E.E. (1958), "An economic justification of protectionism", Quarterly Journal of Economics, 72:496–514.

Hamada, K. (1966), "Economic growth and long-run capital movements", Yale Economic Essays, 6:49–96.

Hanson, J.A. (1971), Growth in open economies (Springer Verlag, Berlin).

Hicks, J.R. (1953), "An inaugural lecture", Oxford Economic Papers, 5:117–135.

Hori, H. and J.L. Stein (1977), "International growth with free trade in equities and goods", International Economic Review, 18:83–100.

Hornby, J.M. (1968), "Investment and trade policy in the dual economy", Economic Journal, 78:96–107.

Johnson, H.G. (1955), "Economic expansion and international trade", Manchester School, 23:95–112.

Johnson, H.G. (1959), "Economic development and international trade", Nationalokonomisk Tidsskrift, 5–6:253–272.

Johnson, H.G. (1967), "The possibility of income losses from increased efficiency or factor accumulation in the presence of tariffs", Economic Journal, 77:151–154.

Johnson, H.G. (1971), "Trade and growth; a geometric exposition", Journal of International Economics, 1:83–102.

Jones, R.W. (1965), "The structure of simple general equilibrium models", Journal of Political Economy, 73:557–572.

Kiguel, M.A. and J.F. Wooton (1982), "Tariff policy and equilibrium growth in the world economy", mimeographed, Columbia University Economics Department.

Kindleberger, C.P. (1968), International economics (Irwin, Homewood, Illinois).

Koizumi, T. and K.J. Kopecky (1977), "Economic growth, capital movements and the international transfer of technical knowledge", Journal of International Economics, 7:45–66.

Kravis, I.B. (1970), "Trade as a handmaiden of growth: Similarities between the nineteenth and twentieth centuries", Economic Journal, 80:850–872.

Krugman, P. (1982), "Trade, accumulation and uneven development", Journal of Development Economics, 8:149–161.

Lefeber, L. (1971), "Trade and minimum wage rates", in: J. Bhagwati et al., eds., Trade, balance of payments and growth (North-Holland, Amsterdam).

Lewis, W.A. (1954), "Economic development with unlimited supplies of labour", Manchester School, 21:139–191.

Lewis, W.A. (1969), Aspects of tropical trade 1883–1965 (Almqvist and Wiksell, Stockholm).

Lewis, W.A. (1973), "Reflections on unlimited labor", in: V. di Marco, ed. International Economics and Development (Wiley, New York).

Little, I.M.D. (1978), "Distributive justice and the new international order", in: Oppenheimer, P., ed. Issues in International Economics (Oriel Press, London), 37–53.

Magee, S. (1977), "Application of the dynamic limit pricing model to the price of technology and international technology transfer", in: K. Brunner and A. H. Meltzer, eds., Optimal policies, control theory and technology exports (North Holland, New York).

Manoilesco, M. (1931), The theory of protection and international trade (P.S. King, London).

Marty, A.L. (1961), "Gurley and Shaw on money in a theory of finance", Journal of Political Economy, 69:56–62.

McKinnon, R.I. (1964), "Foreign exchange constraints in economic development and efficient aid allocation", Economic Journal, 74:388–409.

Myint, H. (1958), "The classical theory of international trade and the underdeveloped countries", Economic Journal, 68:317–337.

Myrdal, G. (1956), An international economy (Harper and Row, New York).

Nurkse, R. (1961), Equilibrium and growth in the world economy (Harvard University Press, Cambridge, Massachusetts).

Oniki, H. and H. Uzawa (1965), "Patterns of trade and investment in a dynamic model of international trade", Review of Economic Studies, 32:15–38.

Onitsuka, Y. (1974), "International capital movements and the patterns of economic growth", American Economic Review, 64, 24–36.

Paauw, D.S. and J.C.H. Fei (1973), The transition in open dualistic economies (Yale University Press, New Haven).

Pasinetti, L. (1960), "A mathematical formulation of the Ricardian system", Review of Economic Studies, 27:78–98.

Prebisch, R. (1950), The economic development of Latin America and its principal problems (United Nations, New York).

Pugel, T. (1981), "Technology transfer and the neoclassical theory of international trade", Research in International Business and Finance, 2:11–37.

Ricardo, D. (1951), The works and correspondence of David Ricardo, P. Sfaffa, ed., (Cambridge University Press, Cambridge).

Rodriguez, A. (1982), "Long-run effects of monetary policy within a two-country model", Journal of International Economics, 12:243–256.

Rodriguez, C. (1981), "The technology transfer issue", in: S. Grassman and E. Lundberg, eds., The world economic order: Past and prospects (Macmillan, London), 167–193.

Rostow, W.W. (1952), The process of economic growth (Norton, New York).

Ruffin, R.J. (1979), "Growth and the long-run theory of international capital movements", American Economic Review, 69:832–842.

Rybczynski, T.M. (1955), "Factor endowment and relative commodity prices", Economica, 22:336–341.

Saavedra-Rivano, N. (1981), "Terms of trade and domestic distribution: A comment", Columbia University Economics Department Discussion Paper No. 109.

Saavedra-Rivano, N. (1982), North–South models and capital mobility, Ph.D. Dissertation, (Columbia University, Economics Department).

Samuelson, P.A. (1959), "A modern treatment of the Ricardian economy, I and II", Quarterly Journal of Economics, 73:1–35 and 217–231.

Samuelson, P.A. (1971), "Ohlin was right", Swedish Journal of Economics, 73:365–384.

Sen, A.K. (1966), "Peasants and dualism with or without surplus labor", Journal of Political Economy, 74:425–450.

Sen, A.K. (1981), "Ethical issues in income distribution: National and international", in: S. Grassman and E. Lundberg, eds., The world economic order: Past and prospects (Macmillan, London), 464–493.

Singer, H.W. (1950), "The distribution of gains between borrowing and investing countries", American Economic Review, 40:473–485.

Smith, M.A.M. (1977), "Capital accumulation in the open two-sector economy", Economic Journal, 87:273–282.

Solow, R.M. (1956), "A contribution to the theory of economic growth", Quarterly Journal of Economics, 70:65–94.

Srinivasan, T.N. and J.N. Bhagwati (1978), "Shadow prices for project selection in the presence of distortions", Journal of Political Economy, 86:97–116.

Steedman, I. (1979), Fundamental issues in trade theory (St. Martins Press, New York).

Stiglitz, J.E. (1970), "Factor price equalization in a dynamic economy", Journal of Political Economy, 78:456–488.

Swan, T.W. (1956), "Economic growth and capital accumulation", Economic Record, 32:334–361.

Teubal, M. (1973), "Comparative advantage and technological change: The learning-by-doing case", Journal of International Economics, 3:161–177.

Tobin, J. (1955), "A dynamic aggregative model", Journal of Political Economy, 63:103–115.

Uzawa, H. (1961), "On a two-sector model of economic growth", Review of Economic Studies, 29:40–47.

Vanek, J. (1971), "Economic growth and international trade in pure theory", Quarterly Journal of Economics, 65:377–390.

Viner, J. (1937), Studies in the theory of international trade (Harper and Row, New York).

Viner, J. (1958), The long view and the short (The Free Press, Glencoe, Illinois).

Wooton, J.F. (1982), "Labor mobility in a North–South model", mimeographed, Columbia University Economics Department.

Chapter 5

INTERNATIONAL FACTOR MOVEMENTS

ROY J. RUFFIN*

University of Houston

Contents

1.	Some statistics on labor and capital movements	238
	1.1. Labor	238
	1.2. Capital movements	240
	1.3. Direct investment	245
2.	The concept of international capital movements	246
	2.1. The transfer problem	246
	2.2. Cross-hauling and direct foreign investment	247
3.	Factor mobility and the national advantage	249
	3.1. Private versus social interests	249
	3.2. The gains from factor mobility	255
	3.3. Optimal restrictions on capital versus optimal restrictions on labor	258
4.	International factor movements and income distribution	259
	4.1. The MacDougall–Kemp model	259
	4.2. The general case of a small open economy	261
5.	Trade and capital movements	265
	5.1. The Heckscher–Ohlin model	266
	5.2. The Kemp–Jones model	269
	References	286

*I wish to thank Ronald Jones, Richard Caves, Peter Kenen, Peter Neary, Joel Sailors, Peter Zadrozny, and Oded Palmon for helpful discussions.

Handbook of International Economics, vol. I, Edited by R.W. Jones and P.B. Kenen
© *Elsevier Science Publishers B.V., 1984*

The international migration of labor and capital has substantially increased in the last twenty years. The level of immigration into the United States in the late 1970s and early 1980s rivals the massive waves that entered the country prior to World War I. During the 1970s the export of capital from the U.S. increased at an annual rate of 13 percent, nearly double the rate of growth during the 1960s. The import of capital into the U.S. grew at an annual rate of nearly 16 percent during the 1970s, which was also about double the growth rate of the 1960s.

Less developed countries are alarmed by the "brain drain" of professional, skilled, and technical workers. The U.S. is alarmed by the "brawn drain" of illegal aliens streaming across its lengthy borders. The inflow of capital into the U.S. has created fears of "America for sale" that parallels the criticisms of foreign investment in Europe and Canada. It is obvious that democratic governments will make the international migration of productive factors one of the most important policy issues of the last decades of the twentieth century.

Policy issues cannot be fully understood without a theory of the effects of international factor movements on national welfare, the distribution of income, and trade. This chapter presents a self-contained account of the real theory of international factor movements.

We begin with a general description of international factor movements in today's world. Next, we examine the appropriate conception of capital movements. We then turn to the simplest model of factor movements – the one good model with two factors. Next, we turn to income distribution and factor movements in a general setting of r factors and n goods. The basic theory of international capital movements in a world of trade, tariffs, and taxes on capital movements is then presented.

1. Some statistics on labor and capital movements

1.1. Labor

Figure 1.1 shows the amount of legal immigration into the U.S. per 1000 of the population since 1820. By historical standards the immigration rate in 1980 is small – around 2 per 1000. When supplemented by a consensus estimate of the amount of illegal immigration into the U.S. (about 500,000 per year) the immigration rate doubles to about 4 per 1000.[1] Thus, the immigration rate now is larger than at any time since immigration quotas were imposed in the 1920s. In terms

---

[1] This estimate is based on Hewlett (1981).

Immigration into the United States, 1829-1977

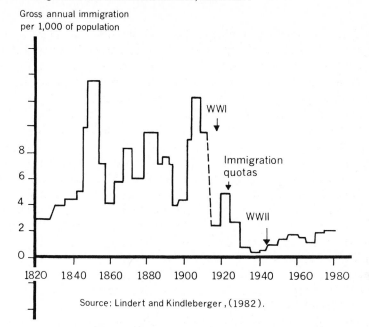

Gross annual immigration
per 1,000 of population

Figure 1.1

of sheer numbers, about one million immigrants enter the United States yearly – including both legal and estimated illegal. This compares to the level of immigration into the United States from 1905 to 1914 when over one million persons immigrated yearly (on the average).

The European guest labor program (from the late 1950s to the middle 1970s) brought about 30 million temporary workers into France, Germany, Sweden, and Switzerland from Ireland, Italy, Portugal, Spain, Finland, Greece, Turkey, Yugoslavia, Algeria, the Sudan, and Morocco. Most have now returned home, but about 5 million guest workers and 7 million dependents remain. The impact on Switzerland was the greatest. In 1970 about one-third of Switzerland's workforce was of foreign origin; in 1977 it was down to 18 percent, reflecting the abrupt halt to the guest labor program in the middle 1970s. Recruiting foreign workers came to a halt and most European countries encouraged migrants to return home (France, for example, paid their airfare plus a departure grant). A Swiss author, Max Frisch, explained it this way, "We asked for workers, but human beings came".[2]

---

[2] This paragraph draws from information provided in Hewlett (1981).

1.2. Capital movements

Labor migrations are difficult to measure, but so are capital movements. The U.S. balance of payments contain statistical discrepancies that rival the net capital outflow. In 1980, the net capital outflow was $27.7 billion. But the statistical discrepancy was a credit item of about $30 billion. Most observers treat the statistical discrepancy as an unrecorded capital inflow; if this is the case, then the United States was a net capital importer in 1980. Thus, whether the U.S. is currently a net capital importer or exporter is not even known with certainty. An incredible fact!

It is probably better to work with stocks than flows, since errors will affect the former less than the latter. In 1980, U.S. investments abroad were valued at $604 billion, while foreign investments in the U.S. were $481 billion. Thus the net international credit position of the United States was $123 billion. Table 1.1 shows the international investment position of the United States in detail for the years 1976 to 1980 and its geographical distribution in 1979 and 1980. The U.S. is a net recipient of capital from Western Europe and a net creditor to Canada and Latin America.

The basic structure of U.S. assets abroad and foreign assets in the United States is shown in somewhat more analytical fashion in Table 1.2 (1980). Portfolio investments make up about half of all U.S. assets abroad and half of all foreign assets in the U.S. Partly because of the socialized nature of OPEC (The Organization of Petroleum Exporting Countries), government-held assets are more important in foreign investments in the U.S. than for U.S. investments abroad. Finally, a much larger fraction of U.S. assets abroad are in the form of direct investments than are foreign assets in the U.S. (35 percent versus 13 percent).

A snapshot does not tell the full story. Figure 1.2 shows some basic trends in the structure of capital movements into and out of the United States. The upper curve shows the ratio of total U.S. assets abroad to total private U.S. assets abroad (portfolio plus direct). It reflects that for the 20 years following World War II the movement of international capital was dominated by the foreign economic policies of the U.S. Government, with the Marshall Plan being the best example.

The middle curve shows the proportion of U.S. private assets abroad in direct investment. U.S. direct investment exists when one U.S. person has direct or indirect ownership of 10 percent or more in a foreign business enterprise (foreign affiliate). The U.S. direct investment position is the sum of equity in and net outstanding loans to foreign affiliates of U.S. direct investors. In 1980, about 40 percent of all private assets abroad were in direct investment; from 1950 to 1972 direct investment was about two-thirds of total private assets abroad. Thus there has been a significant decline in the importance of direct foreign investment by U.S. firms. One reason would be the rise of the organized international capital

Table 1.1
International investment position of the United States at yearend (millions of dollars)

Line	Type of investment	Total					Western Europe		Canada		Japan		Latin American Republics and other Western Hemisphere		Other foreign countries		International organizations and unallocated	
		1976	1977	1978	1979	1980	1979	1980	1979	1980	1979	1980	1979	1980	1979	1980	1979	1980
1	**Net international investment position of the United States**	**83,798**	**71,320**	**77,477**	**95,043**	**122,697**	**−67,228**	**−55,243**	**60,435**	**61,369**	**118**	**843**	**65,498**	**89,418**	**16,430**	**4,754**	**19,790**	**21,556**
2	**U.S. assets abroad**	**347,173**	**379,124**	**447,852**	**508,915**	**603,614**	**157,663**	**185,813**	**86,765**	**96,185**	**28,013**	**35,378**	**128,889**	**161,843**	**80,673**	**96,484**	**26,912**	**27,911**
3	U.S. official reserve assets	18,747	19,312	18,650	18,956	26,756	2,329	7,992	(*)	(*)	1,478	2,142					15,149	16,622
4	Gold	11,598	11,719	11,671	11,172	11,160											11,172	11,160
5	Special drawing rights	2,395	2,629	1,558	2,724	2,610											2,724	2,610
6	Reserve position in the International Monetary Fund	4,434	4,946	1,047	1,253	2,852											1,253	2,852
7	Foreign currencies	320	18	4,374	3,807	10,134	2,329	7,992	(*)	(*)	1,478	2,142						
8	U.S. Government assets, other than official reserve assets	46,008	49,565	54,205	58,447	63,548	10,079	10,759	252	343	605	555	11,312	11,813	31,833	35,203	4,366	4,875
9	U.S. loans and other long-term assets[2]	44,138	47,770	52,273	56,528	61,887	9,894	10,491	248	344	603	554	11,280	11,780	30,141	33,847	4,362	4,871
10	Repayable in dollars	41,320	45,179	49,835	54,237	59,798	9,370	10,051	248	344	603	554	10,752	11,297	28,902	32,681	4,362	4,871
11	Other[3]	2,818	2,591	2,438	2,291	2,089	524	440					528	483	1,239	1,166		
12	U.S. foreign currency holdings and U.S. short-term assets	1,870	1,795	1,932	1,919	1,661	185	268	4	−1	2	1	32	33	1,692	1,356	4	4
13	U.S. private assets	282,418	310,247	374,997	431,512	513,310	145,255	167,062	86,513	95,842	25,930	32,681	117,577	150,030	48,840	61,281	7,397	6,414
14	Direct investments abroad	136,809	145,990	162,727	186,760	213,468	82,622	95,686	40,243	44,640	6,208	6,274	35,056	38,275	19,064	24,892	[4]3,567	[4]3,701
15	Foreign securities	44,157	49,439	53,384	56,626	62,118	11,909	13,418	32,458	36,158	225	1,028	2,874	3,322	5,383	5,519	3,777	2,673
16	Bonds	34,704	39,329	42,148	41,823	43,212	6,956	7,776	22,949	24,370	225	76	2,646	2,982	5,270	5,335	3,777	2,673
17	Corporate stocks	9,453	10,110	11,236	14,803	18,906	4,953	5,642	9,509	11,788	[5](*)	[5]952	228	340	113	184		
18	U.S. claims on unaffiliated foreigners reported by U.S. nonbanking concerns	20,317	22,256	28,070	31,097	33,749	10,804	11,281	5,657	5,815	1,317	1,147	9,075	11,164	4,244	4,342		
19	Long-term	5,936	6,035 }	[6]28,070 }	[6]31,097 }	[6]33,749 }	10,804	11,281	5,657	5,815	1,317	1,147	9,075	11,164	4,244	4,342		
20	Short-term	14,381	16,221 }															
21	U.S. claims reported by U.S. banks, not included elsewhere	81,135	92,562	130,816	157,029	203,975	39,920	46,677	8,155	9,229	18,180	24,232	70,572	97,269	20,149	26,528	53	40

Table 1.1 continued

Line	Type of investment	Total					Western Europe		Canada		Japan		Latin American Republics and other Western Hemisphere		Other foreign countries		International organizations and unallocated	
		1976	1977	1978	1979	1980	1979	1980	1979	1980	1979	1980	1979	1980	1979	1980	1979	1980
22	Long-term	11,898	12,649	[e]130,816	[e]157,029	[e]203,975	39,920	46,677	8,155	9,229	18,180	24,232	70,572	97,269	20,149	26,528	53	40
23	Short-term	69,237	79,913															
24	**Foreign assets in the United States**	**263,375**	**307,804**	**370,375**	**413,872**	**480,917**	**224,891**	**241,056**	**26,330**	**34,816**	**27,895**	**34,535**	**63,391**	**72,425**	**64,243**	**91,730**	**7,122**	**6,355**
25	Foreign official assets in the United States	104,238	140,793	172,852	159,514	175,717	87,373	83,130	2,044	1,747			6,368	5,740				
26	U.S. Government securities	72,572	105,386	128,511	106,640	118,164												
27	U.S. Treasury securities	70,555	101,092	123,991	101,748	111,311	(7)	(7)	(7)	(7)	(8)	(8)	(7)	(7)	(8)	(8)	(7)	(7)
28	Other	2,017	4,294	4,520	4,892	6,853												
29	Other U.S. Government liabilities	8,786	10,186	12,544	12,411	13,047	2,921	2,891	162	200	1,995	2,220	188	169	7,145	7,567		
30	U.S. liabilities reported by U.S. banks not included elsewhere	17,231	18,004	23,327	30,540	30,381	(7)	(7)	(7)	(7)	(8)	(8)	(7)	(7)	(8)	(8)	(7)	(7)
31	Other foreign official assets	5,649	7,217	8,470	9,923	14,125												
32	Other foreign assets in the United States	159,137	167,011	197,523	254,358	305,200	137,518	157,926	24,286	33,069			57,023	66,685			7,122	6,355
33	Direct investments in the United States	30,770	34,595	42,471	54,462	65,483	37,403	43,467	7,154	9,810	3,493	4,219	5,431	6,702	981	1,285		
34	U.S. securities other than U.S. Treasury securities	54,913	51,235	53,554	58,566	74,006	40,827	51,612	9,741	12,506	1,328	1,280	3,719	4,824	2,248	3,016	703	768
35	Corporate and other bonds	11,964	11,456	11,457	10,269	9,532	7,532	6,906	1,205	1,100	471	392	245	370	518	514	298	250
36	Corporate stocks	42,949	39,779	42,097	48,297	64,474	33,295	44,706	8,536	11,406	857	888	3,474	4,454	1,730	2,502	405	518
37	U.S. liabilities to unaffiliated foreigners reported by U.S. non-banking concerns																	
38	Long-term	12,961	13,435	14,869	[e]16,934	28,632	8,171	10,433	1,307	1,540	1,211	1,288	2,806	4,312	3,439	11,059		
39	Short-term	5,837	5,317[b]	8,118	[e]16,934	[b]28,632	8,171	10,433	1,307	1,540	1,211	1,288	2,806	4,312	3,439	11,059		

Table 1.1 continued

40	U.S. long-term liabilities reported by U.S. banks	1,112	1,485	(10)	(10)	(10)
41	U.S. Treasury securities and other short-term liabilities reported by					
	U.S. banks	59,381	66,261	86,629	124,396	137,097
42	U.S. Treasury securities	7,028	7,562	[11]8,910	[11]14,070	[11]16,010
43	U.S. short-term liabilities reported by U.S. banks, not included elsewhere	52,353	58,699	[10]77,719	[10]110,326	[10]121,069

(7) (7) (7) (8) (8) (7) (7) (7) (8) (8) (7) (7) (7)

‡Includes U.S. gold stock. *Less than $500,000(+).
[1] Data for 1976–79 are revised; data for 1980 are preliminary.
[2] Also includes paid-in capital subscription to international financial institutions and outstanding amounts of miscellaneous claims that have been settled through international agreements to be payable to the U.S. Government over periods in excess of 1 year. Excludes World War I debts that are not being serviced.
[3] Includes indebtedness that the borrower may contractually, or at its option, repay with its currency, or by delivery of materials or transfer of services.
[4] For the most part, represents the estimated investment in shipping companies registered primarily in Honduras, Panama, and Liberia, and in U.S. affiliated multinational trading companies, finance and insurance companies, not designated by country.
[5] U.S. holdings of Japanese shares may be underestimated. This is due in part to the recording of security transactions by the country of transactor rather than the country of issuer.
[6] Maturity breakdown is not available.
[7] Details not shown separately are included in totals in lines 25 and 32.
[8] Details not shown separately are included in line 24.
[9] Primarily includes U.S. Government liabilities associated with military sales contracts and other transactions arranged with or through foreign official agencies.
[10] Maturity breakdown is not available: see line 43.
[11] Includes U.S. Treasury notes denominated in foreign currencies sold through foreign central banks to domestic residents in country of issue; these notes are subject to restricted transferability.

Source: Survey of Current Business, August 1981.

Table 1.2
International investment position of the
United States (analytical breakdown), 1980 (billions)

	U.S. assets abroad	Foreign assets in U.S.
Government-held assets	$91	$176
Private portfolio investments	300	240
Private direct investments	213	65
Total	$604	$481

Source: Table 1.1.

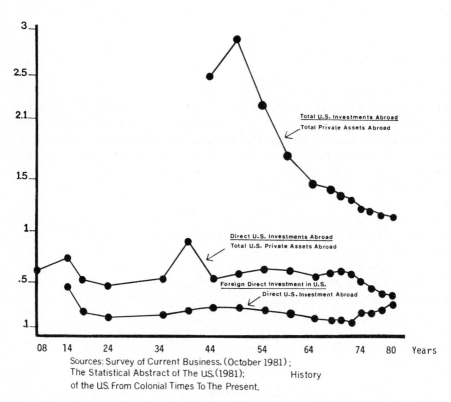

Sources: Survey of Current Business. (October 1981);
The Statistical Abstract of The US. (1981);   History
of the US. From Colonial Times To The Present.

Figure 1.2

Table 1.3
Specialization ratios

	U.S. parent specialization ratio	Affiliate specialization ratio
Mining	67.3	92.7
Petroleum	86.7	87.9
Manufacturing	87.9	94.9
Trade	90.7	96.1
Finance, insurance, and real estate	89.9	99.4

Source: Barber (1981).

market (which consists of Eurocredits, Eurobonds, and foreign bond markets), which encourages impersonal investment.[3]

The bottom curve shows the ratio of foreign direct investments in the U.S. to U.S. direct investments abroad. In 1980, this ratio was about one-third and is up significantly since the late 60's and early 70's when it was about one-sixth.

1.3. Direct investment

A simple definition of a multinational company (MNC) is simply a company that has direct investment abroad.[4] In 1977 there were 3425 U.S. MNCs. There were 187 MNCs with affiliates in more than one country. The consolidated assets of all U.S. MNCs were an astounding $1.8 trillion, with 42 percent in manufacturing, 23 percent in finance (except banking), real estate, and insurance, and 16 percent in petroleum. The overwhelming majority (83 percent) of affiliates were majority-owned, and 71 percent were wholly-owned. The assets of the affiliates themselves were $490 billion: $118 billion was in integrated refining and extraction of petroleum and coal products; $54 billion in transportation equipment; $47 billion in chemicals; $44 billion in finance, insurance, and real estate; $30 billion in metals; $24 billion in office and computing machines; and $17 billion in food and kindred products (mostly grain mill and bakery products).

Affiliates are in the same industry as their parents – only more so. If parents and affiliates are classified in the one industry in which they had the largest sales, the specialization ratio (defined as the ratio of industry sales to total sales) of affiliates is higher than the ratio for their U.S. parents. The higher specialization ratios for affiliates (Table 1.3) partly reflects the higher level of consolidation for the parent.

---

[3] The story of the rise of the organized international capital markets is told in Mendelsohn (1980).
[4] The information in this and the following paragraphs is based on Barker (1981).

Where were the U.S. MNCs foreign operations located? The following countries held 77 percent of the $490 billion in affiliate assets.

Canada	$87.2	Brazil	$17.3
United Kingdom	54.7	Bermuda	17.2
Japan	41.8	Switzerland	14.2
Germany	37.8	OPEC	12.4
France	24.3	Italy	12.2
Netherlands	18.5	Spain	11.9
Australia	18.3	Mexico	9.5

It should be pointed out that in Japan, Spain, and Mexico the U.S. ownership interest in those assets is far smaller than in the other countries due to government restrictions in those countries.

2. The concept of international capital movements

2.1. The transfer problem

Physical capital is transferred abroad through a trade surplus and corresponds to the accumulation of ownership claims against capital located in a foreign country. Hence, the appropriate concept of international capital movements simply involves a change in the location but not the ownership of physical capital. In growth models, such as in Fischer and Frenkel (1974) and Ruffin (1979), the trade surplus corresponding to the transfer of capital must be taken into account. In static models, such as in MacDougall (1960), Kemp (1966), and Jones (1967), there is a one-time stock adjustment in which a portion of a fixed stock of physical capital simply moves abroad (and is itself the trade surplus).

John Maynard Keynes (1929) and Bertil Ohlin (1929) debated the effects of a transfer of funds on the paying and receiving countries. The essence of the matter was summed up by Keynes when he observed: "If £1 is taken from you and given to me and I choose to increase my consumption of precisely the same goods as those of which you are compelled to diminish yours, there is no Transfer Problem." It is part of doctrinal history that Keynes himself took a different point of view than that expressed in the above quote and that modern analysis has followed the path pioneered by Ohlin.

According to the classics [Meade (1951), Ohlin (1929, 1967), Samuelson (1952)] the transfer problem applies to loans, gifts, and reparation payments. The main conclusion of this literature is that the paying country will suffer a secondary burden (in addition to the transfer itself) if the sum of the marginal propensities to import is less than unity. The idea behind this criterion is simplicity itself. Let m be the paying country's marginal propensity to import and let m^* be the receiving country's marginal propensity to import. If there are two goods, exportables and importables, a dollar transfer from the paying country to the receiving country will, at constant prices, reduce the paying country's demand for its exportables by $1 - m$ and increase the receiving country's demand for the paying country's exportable by m^*. The paying country's terms of trade will decline if m^* is less than $1 - m$ or, equivalently,

$$m + m^* < 1.$$

Viewed from the standpoint of rational expectations – where the agents in the models must be assumed to have some knowledge about the structure of the model itself – the classical view seems incorrect when applied to capital transfers. If country A transfers \$100 to country B in period 1 and country B transfers \$110 to country A in period 2, it seems somewhat ridiculous to treat international capital movements as simply a "reverse transfer". The difficulty with the orthodox treatment is that it requires changes in the terms of trade to occur when the sum of the marginal propensities to import differ from unity. If this is the case, it would seem that speculators could then make a profit by anticipating the change in relative prices between periods 1 and 2.

The economics of a loan and its repayment appears to be substantially different from the economics of a forced reparations payment. In the case of a forced reparations payment, the welfare of the paying country falls while that of the recipient rises. In the case of a capital movement, under standard assumptions to be reviewed shortly, both countries gain from the exchange. The key issue in the classical transfer problem is whether the paying country must suffer a secondary burden of the transfer in the form of reduced terms of trade. There are no "burdens" in a capital transfer; it is a sharing of gains rather than a wealth redistribution. The repeated empirical puzzle of scholars failing to find painful adjustments [Yeager (1976, p. 73n)] in the case of capital transfers may be explained by this simple observation: the application of the wrong model. The classical transfer problem's domain, therefore, should not include the theory of capital transfers. Work remains in integrating the rational expectations hypothesis into the theory of capital transfers.

2.2. Cross-hauling and direct foreign investment

The real world consists of simultaneous capital exports and imports. What is the explanation? Two main explanations have been offered. First, there is the elementary point that in a world of uncertainty rational investors will not choose to put all of their eggs in one basket. The optimal portfolio of a rational investor is likely to carry both home and foreign securities [Grubel (1966)]. This undoubtedly explains much of portfolio investment. Another view is represented by the specific factors model [Caves (1971)]. According to Caves, foreign investment involves a bundle of capital, technology, and market skills. The appropriate model is, therefore, a specific factors model. Each sector has its own specific type of capital (+ technology + market skills). Thus a country may export sector 1 capital and import sector 2 capital. Such a model has been developed in considerable detail by Jones, Neary and Ruane (1981).

Most scholars now emphasize that the key ingredient of foreign direct investment is *not* foreign investment (the transfer of capital). Hymer (1960) and Kindleberger (1969) refer to MNCs as existing in order to overcome some market imperfection. Buckley and Casson (1976), McManus (1972), Hood and Young (1979), and Caves (1982) treat MNCs as devices for internalizing the returns to ownership-specific assets (secret technology, marketing skills, etc.) in a world of significant transaction costs. Without transaction costs, foreign firms would simply be licensed or would simply rent management consulting teams. The basic hypothesis is that the MNC must have some non-marketable advantage over foreign firms that is sufficient to overcome the natural obstacles of operating in some distant foreign market. This latter view of the MNC appears broad enough to encompass the Hymer–Kindleberger view, but without the objectionable feature of identifying transaction costs with market "imperfections".

The specific factors model appears closely allied with the modern view; however, there is an essential difference. The specific factors model assumes that the capital invested in foreign affiliates comes from the home country. If a significant fraction of the capital invested in foreign affiliates came from home countries, the specific factors model would be a particularly simple way to capture the phenomenon of direct foreign investment. But most of the financing of foreign affiliates comes from foreign sources [Hood and Young (1979, p. 39)]. Even newly established affiliates in 1980 acquired two-thirds of their investment funds from foreign sources [Belli (1981)].

Little work has gone into testing the new view [Hood and Young (1979, p. 75)]. But casual evidence does suggest that direct foreign investment involves the internalization of ownership-specific assets. The list of U.S. firms acquired or established by foreign MNCs in 1980 is a manifesto of foreign comparative advantages: A tobacco firm by the British; an auto firm by the French; a textile plant by the British; a cement plant by the Germans; a beverage firm by the French; a beverage firm by the Japanese; grain milling by the Canadians; meat packing by the British; construction and mining machinery manufacturing by the Canadians; industrial chemicals by the Germans; electric motors by the British; and a U.S. petroleum company by the Canadians [Belli (1981)]. Likewise, a list of U.S. acquisitions abroad would reveal a roster reflecting U.S. comparative advantages.

In what follows I will treat foreign investment as a change in the location but not the ownership of physical capital. The above discussion indicates that it is probably best not to interpret this as foreign direct investment.

3.   Factor mobility and the national advantage

The relationship between the national advantage and international factor movements is a perennial issue. Two central questions can be raised: What is the
division of the gains between factor importing and factor exporting countries?
And, to what extent is the interest of the factor-owner the same as the national
interests? Most of the literature has been devoted to the second question. The first
question has been largely untouched in the standard literature. We shall here
discuss both questions.

3.1.   Private versus social interests

3.1.1.   The MacDougall – Kemp model

Hobson (1914), Jassay (1960), MacDougall (1960), and Kemp (1964) set down the
simplest possible model for analyzing the consequences of international capital
mobility: two factors, one good, full employment, perfect competition, and
constant returns to scale. While these writers used the model for analyzing
international capital mobility, subsequent writers, beginning with Johnson (1967),
applied the same model to international labor migration [see Grubel and Scott,
(1966), and Berry and Soligo, (1969)]. We shall call this model the MacDougall–
Kemp model.

Let K be the amount of capital the home country owns and L its native
population (assumed for simplicity to be the same as the labor force). The home
country invests Z units of its capital stock in the foreign country and receives M
migrants from the foreign country. Of course, if $Z < 0$ and $M < 0$ the reverse is
true: the home country imports capital and exports labor. But we shall assume
that the home country exports capital. Starred variables refer to the foreign
country. It is convenient to define everything in per capita terms. Thus define the
variables:

$$z = Z/L,$$

$$m = M/L,$$

$$b = L/L^*,$$

$$k = K/L,$$

$$k^* = K^*/L^*,$$

$$c = (K - Z)/(L + M) = (k - z)/(1 + m),$$

$$c^* = (K^* + Z)/(L^* - M) = (k^* + bz)/(1 - bm).$$

The variables $k(k^*)$ and $c(c^*)$ are the capital–labor ratios in the home (foreign) country before and after the movement of factors. The production functions in intensive form are $f(c)$ and $g(c^*)$ in the home and foreign countries, respectively. I invoke the neoclassical assumptions, i.e.

$$f' > 0, \quad f'' < 0, \quad f(0) = 0. \tag{3.1}$$

Conditions (3.1) hold for $g(c^*)$ as well.

Let $w(w^*)$ and $r(r^*)$ denote the wage and rental rates in the home (foreign) country. With competitively determined employment of labor and capital, wages and rents are equal to their relevant marginal products. Thus:

$$w = f(c) - cf'(c), \qquad r = f'(c), \tag{3.2}$$
$$w^* = g(c^*) - c^*g'(c^*), \qquad r^* = g'(c^*). \tag{3.3}$$

Capital is supposed to be perfectly mobile, with the exception of taxes imposed by each country. We shall generalize the MacDougall–Kemp model by supposing that labor is mobile, but subject to strict quantitative restrictions (QRs). As far as the capital market is concerned

$$r = (1-t)r^0 \tag{3.4}$$

and

$$r^*(1-t^*) = r^0, \tag{3.5}$$

where t and t^* are the tax rates the home and foreign countries impose on internationally mobile capital. The interest rate r^0 may be considered the "world" interest rate. When taxes are non-negative, it is clear that $r \leq r^0 \leq r^*$. The quantity of home capital located abroad, z, is determined by the equation

$$r = (1-t)(1-t^*)r^*. \tag{3.6}$$

We follow the convention of attributing all income to the *native* populations. Thus, Mexican or Taiwanese workers in the United States contribute to Mexican or Taiwanese income. Migrants earn the wage of their country of residence. Hence, if $m > 0$ (the home country receives labor from the foreign country), migrants earn w per person; if $m < 0$, migrants earn w^* per person.

Letting Y and Y^* be the total incomes of the native populations of the two countries, when the home country imports foreign labor $(m > 0)$ we have:

$$Y = (L + M)f(c) + r^0 Z - wM, \tag{3.7}$$
$$Y^* = (L^* - M)g(c^*) - r^0 Z + wM. \tag{3.8}$$

In per capita terms, these can be rewritten as:

$$y = (1+m)f(c)+r^0z - wm,$$ (3.9)

$$y^* = (1-bm)g(c^*)-r^0bz + wbm.$$ (3.10)

When the home country sends labor to the foreign country ($m < 0$) the per capita incomes of the native populations are:

$$y = (1+m)f(c)+r^0z - w^*m,$$ (3.11)

$$y^* = (1-bm)g(c^*)-r^0bz + w^*bm.$$ (3.12)

Let us first consider the case where the home country imposes a restriction on capital exports (i.e. raises t). This will, of course, lower the quantity of capital exports, z. Since t^* is constant and $r^0 = r^*(1-t^*)$, reducing z will raise both r^* and r^0. Thus $\partial r^0/\partial z < 0$ when the home country manipulates z through lowering or raising t. The impact of a change in z on the home country that imports labor is found by differentiating (3.9) with respect to z, i.e. (note $\partial c/\partial z = -1/(1+m)$)

$$\partial y/\partial z = r^0 - r + z\,\partial r^0/\partial z - m\,\partial w/\partial z.$$ (3.13)

When there is an incipient restriction beginning with $r^0 = r$ we have:

$$\partial y/\partial z = z\,\partial r^0/\partial z - m\,\partial w/\partial z.$$ (3.13')

Since an additional amount of z lowers domestic wages, w, $\partial w/\partial z < 0$. The sign of (3.13') is ambiguous as long as $m > 0$. We reach an important conclusion: a capital exporting country with a foreign workforce (fixed in number) may not gain from restricting its capital exports. On the other hand, if $m = 0$ we obtain the traditional MacDougall–Kemp result. If $m = 0$, $\partial y/\partial z < 0$ and home income can be raised by lowering (i.e. restricting capital exports) z.

The results are the same if the capital exporting country happens to be a labor exporting country as well. Differentiating (3.11) with respect to z yields:

$$\partial y/\partial z = r^0 - r + z\,\partial r^0/\partial z - m\,\partial w^*/\partial z.$$ (3.14)

When there is an incipient restriction beginning with $r^0 = r$ we have:

$$\partial y/\partial z = z\,\partial r^0/\partial z - m\,\partial w^*/\partial z.$$ (3.14')

The first term is again negative, but $m\,\partial w^*/\partial z$ is also negative since $m < 0$ and $\partial w^*/\partial z > 0$. It follows that a small restriction on the export of capital has an ambiguous effect on home welfare (unless m is very small).

When $m \neq 0$ the ambiguity arises from a very simple observation. Restricting capital exports raises r^0, and, hence, benefits the inframarginal units of capital that are already invested in the foreign country. This is a clear social bonus. If there is a foreign workforce ($m > 0$), restriction raises home wages and, hence, increases the cost of imported labor. If some home labor is located abroad ($m < 0$), restriction of capital exports lowers their wage, w^*, and, hence, the national gains from sending labor abroad. In either case, there is ambiguity. To eliminate the ambiguity we must have $m = 0$.

Summarizing:

Theorem 1 (MacDougall–Kemp).

If $m = 0$, it pays the capital-exporting country that is large enough to influence the world interest rate to restrict incipiently its capital exports if the rest of the world does not retaliate.

Theorem 2

If $m \neq 0$, it may not pay the large capital exporting country to restrict incipiently its capital exports even if the rest of the world does not retaliate.

We therefore see (Theorem 2) that the MacDougall–Kemp theorem (Theorem 1) needs modification in the general case.

What about the capital importing country? To analyze the capital importing country we must differentiate equations (3.10) and (3.12) with respect to z. Here we note that now $\partial r^0 / \partial z$ is positive rather than negative because the restriction of capital imports by the capital importing country lowers the world rate of return (lower z, lower r^0). Noting that $\partial c^* / \partial z = b/(1 - bm)$, eqs. (3.15) and (3.16) show $\partial y^* / \partial z$ for (3.10) and (3.12), respectively:

$$\partial y^* / \partial z = b\left(r^* - r^0 - z \partial r^0 / \partial z + m \partial w / \partial z\right), \qquad m > 0, \tag{3.15}$$

$$\partial y^* / \partial z = b\left(r^* - r^0 - z \partial r^0 / \partial z + m \partial w^* / \partial z\right), \qquad m < 0. \tag{3.16}$$

In the incipient case where $r^* = r^0$ we have:

$$\partial y^* / \partial z = b\left(- z \partial r^0 / \partial z + m \partial w / \partial z\right), \qquad m > 0, \tag{3.15'}$$

$$\partial y^* / \partial z = b\left(- z \partial r^0 / \partial z + m \partial w^* / \partial z\right), \qquad m < 0. \tag{3.16'}$$

Since $\partial w / \partial z < 0$ and $\partial w^* / \partial z > 0$, we find that in both (3.15') and (3.16') $\partial y^* / \partial z < 0$. We therefore conclude that in all cases it pays the capital-importing country to incipiently restrict its capital imports by raising taxes on the income paid to foreign-sourced capital. No ambiguity arises.

The reason for there to be no ambiguity is straightforward. Restricting its capital imports lowers the foreign country's cost of borrowed capital, r^0, on the inframarginal units, z. If some of the foreign country's workforce is located abroad, these migrants are benefited by the higher wage paid abroad. If the foreign country imports labor ($m < 0$), the restriction lowers the wage paid to its imported workforce.

Theorem 3

It pays the capital-importing country that is large enough to influence the world interest rate to restrict incipiently its capital imports by taxation if the rest of the world does not retaliate.

The above analysis is consistent with the restriction in the case of a capital exporting country being in the form of a quantitative restriction, since capital located in the foreign country is paid the foreign rate of return. But a capital importing country must use a tax since otherwise the imported capital will take out the domestic rate of return. This is like a voluntary export quota. For example, with a quantitative restriction instead of a tax eq. (3.10) would be:

$$y^* = (1 - bm) g(c^*) - r^* bz + wbm. \qquad (3.10')$$

The derivative now would be $\partial y^* / \partial z = b(-z \partial r^* / \partial z + m \partial w / \partial z)$, which can be positive or negative as $\partial r^* / \partial z < 0$, $m > 0$, and $\partial w / \partial z < 0$.

We now calculate the optimum tax rates in the case where $m = 0$. We employ the naive assumption that when one country restricts the rest of the world does not retaliate. This is the standard MacDougall–Kemp story. In the case of the capital exporting country we set $\partial y / \partial z = 0$ in (3.13). The foreign country's elasticity of demand for imported capital is $-(\partial z / \partial r^0)(r^0 / z) = n^*$. Accordingly, we have [using (3.4)]:

$$t = 1/n^*. \qquad (3.17)$$

In the case of the capital importing country we set $\partial y^* / \partial z = 0$ in (3.15). With $m = 0$ and defining the elasticity of supply of exported capital as $\xi = (\partial z / \partial r^0)(r^0 / z)$ we have [using (3.5)]:

$$t^* / (1 - t^*) = 1/\xi. \qquad (3.18)$$

Table 3.1 shows some sample calculations of the optimal tax for a capital exporting country. We assume that both countries are identical and that the production function is $f(c) = c^{0.25}$ with the home country's capital stock being twice the foreign. The optimal tax rate varies from 19.8 percent for $b = 2$ to 3.25 percent for $b = 0.05$. Since most countries are a small fraction of the world

Table 3.1
Optimum tax on income from capital exports[a]

L/L^*	t^{opt} (in percent)
2	19.76
1	17.63
0.5	14.42
0.25	10.51
0.1	5.74
0.05	3.25

[a] Each country's production function is $f(c)$ = $c^{0.25}$, and $k = 100$, and $k^* = 50$.

population, we are safe in assuming that optimal taxes on capital movements must be of an order of magnitude not far different from 3 percent.

Ruffin (1980) shows that when capital accumulation is taken into account the long-run optimum export tax exceeds the short-run optimum tax while the long-run optimum import tax falls short of the optimum. The reasoning is that capital import and export taxes hurt the foreign country and thus reduce the foreign country's capital stock in the long run. This creates secondary benefits for a capital exporting country and a secondary burden for the capital importing country that must be taken into account in the long-run.

3.1.2. Keynes's argument

J.M. Keynes (1924) argued that the private benefits of foreign investment exceeded the social benefits, but for substantially different reasons than the MacDougall–Kemp case. Keynes felt that uncertainty made a difference. Imagine two investments, one at home and the other abroad, that are identical in the distribution of possible returns. The private investor will be indifferent. But should the nation? To quote Keynes: "If the Grand Truck Railway of Canada fails its shareholders by reason of legal restriction of the rates chargeable or for any other cause, we have nothing. If the Underground System of London fails its shareholders, Londoners still have their Underground System." We now know that uncertainty does not lead to market failure unless there are missing markets (Arrow, 1970) that can be filled by government action (Coase, 1960). Without an explicit statement of the costs and benefits of various market arrangements no conclusion is possible. If the Canadian railway fails, its default value to Canada will accrue to British stock-holders just as the default value of the London Underground would accrue to British stockholders. Moreover, physical capital can be moved. In Honduras during the 1930s, the United Fruit Company took up

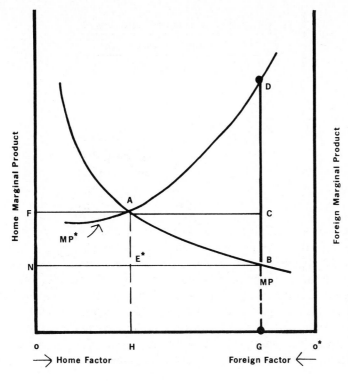

Figure 3.1

its railroad tracks from its failed banana operations (due to the Panama fungus) near Port Castilla.[5]

3.2. The gains from factor mobility

That it always pays to export or import capital in the MacDougall–Kemp model can be seen by setting $z = m = 0$ in (3.13) and (3.15). We then see that:

$$\partial y / \partial z = r^0 - r, \tag{3.19}$$

$$\partial y^* / \partial z = r^* - r^0. \tag{3.20}$$

When there is no trade in capital services $r^* > r$. For any world interest rate r^0

---

[5]I am indebted to Mr. Aguillar Pompeyo for this story.

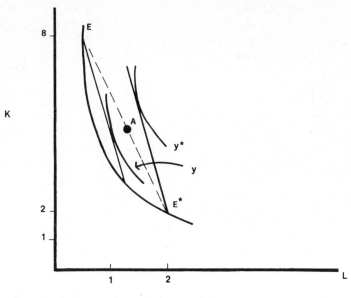

Figure 3.2

between these extremes it clearly pays the home country to shift capital from where its return is r to the higher return r^0 capital can earn abroad. It also pays the foreign country to borrow cheap capital from abroad.

The gains from free trade in capital services are illustrated in Figure 3.1. The home country's marginal product of capital curve is labeled MP. The foreign country's is labeled MP^*, and is measured from the origin O^*. The home country's capital stock is OG. The foreign country's capital stock is O^*G. With free and perfect capital mobility, HG units of capital are located in the foreign country. When the rates of return are equalized, where $r = r^*$ at point A, the home country gains ACB and the foreign country gains ACD. The reason the capital exporting home country gains ABC is that its output falls by the area under the curve MP from A to B but the benefit is HG times the interest rate. The foreign country gains the output equal to the area under MP^* from A to D and loses the cost of the borrowed capital HG times the interest rate. We have depicted a situation in which the home country's gains fall short of the foreign country's gains – the capital importing country gains more from the free exchange of capital services. In this particular case, we have in fact started from an initial situation where both countries have the same output (with no trade).[6]

---

[6]Figure 3.1 is based on the marginal product of capital curves: $r = 0.414(K - Z)^{-2/3}$ and $r^* = 0.653(K^* + Z)^{-2/3}$.

If the world interest rate is the country's interest rate it gains nothing from trade of its capital services. As always, large countries gain little from trade. The interesting question is: If two countries are the same size, which country gains the most? Do capital-importing countries or capital-exporting countries tend to gain the most from free trade in capital services?

Consider Figure 3.2. This shows a Cobb–Douglas isoquant where the production function is of the form $Q = AL^{1-\alpha}K^{\alpha}$ and $\alpha = 1/3$. The endowment for the home country is E; the endowment for the foreign country is E^*. With free and complete capital mobility, capital will be imported into the foreign country until the installed capital–labor ratio in each country is given by the slope of the ray OA, where A bisects the arc EE^*. Who gains most from this trade depends on the slope of the isoquant through point A. If the slope of the isoquant exceeds the slope of the arc EE^* (in absolute value), the capital-importing country gains most from trade. Figure 3.2 illustrates the case where with free trade the capital-importing foreign country has the income Y^* greater than the capital-exporting home country with the income Y. Indeed, we can show:[7]

Theorem 4

If both countries have the same autarkic output, the production functions are Cobb–Douglas and identical in the MacDougall–Kemp model, free and perfect

---

[7]*Proof*

In Figure 4.1, the absolute slope of the arc between E and E^* is:

$$S = (bk - k^*)/(1 - b).$$

The slope of the marginal rate of substitution is:

$$w/r = ((1-\alpha)/\alpha)(bk + k^*)/(1+b).$$

When both countries are the same size $b = (k/k^*)$. Under these circumstances the wage–rent ratio with free trade will exceed S if, and only if:

$$(kk^*)^{\alpha}(k - k^*)(1 - 2\alpha) + k^{2\alpha}k^* - (k^*)^{2\alpha}k > 0.$$

Define $x = k/k^*$. The above expression will be positive if and only if:

$$H(\alpha) \equiv (x-1)(1-2\alpha) + x^{\alpha} - x^{1-\alpha} > 0,$$

where $x > 1$. It is clear that:

$$H(0) = H(0.5) = 0.$$

We can also see that

$$H''(\alpha) = (\ln x)^2(x^{\alpha} - x^{1-\alpha}) < 0,$$

for $x > 1$ and $\alpha < 1/2$. This means that $H(\alpha)$ is positive for $0 < \alpha < 1/2$.

factor mobility leads to greater (or less) gains for the capital-importing country than the capital-exporting country as the capital-share coefficient is less than (greater than) 0.5.

The intuitive reason that the capital-importing country gains more than the capital-exporting country when both countries are the same size and the share of capital is less than 0.5 with Cobb–Douglas technology is simple: the world has a taste for labor. If there is free trade in factor services and both countries start from the same total output, the labor-rich country will gain the most from the trade.

3.3. Optimal restrictions on capital versus optimal restrictions on labor

Suppose the home and foreign countries have identical production functions and $k > k^*$. The home country will export capital, import labor, or both. Using optimal restrictions, is it better for the home country to optimally restrict labor imports with prohibitions on capital export or optimally restrict capital exports with a prohibition on labor imports? In an elegant note, Ramaswami (1968) shows that it is better to restrict labor imports and keep capital at home.

The proof of this theorem is as follows. If labor does not move, capital will move from the home country to the foreign country. Suppose the home country restricts the flow of capital (optimally or not) so that r remains less than r^* (and w more than w^*). Thus, in the restricted situation c exceeds c^*. Suppose now that the exported capital, Z, is brought back along with the $M = Z/c^*$ units of foreign labor working with that capital. This bundle of capital if used as an enclave in the home country will produce the same goods as it did in the foreign country. No loss to the home country is entailed if such a separate enclave is used. But since c exceeds the c^* of the enclave it is better to integrate the enclave with the rest of the home economy; ordinarily, this would raise the wages of immigrant labor. But tax this and give the proceeds to the native population of the home country. Thus we have shown that for any level of restricted capital exports there exists a tax on labor immigration combined with prohibited capital exports that makes the home country better off.

A differential tax on immigrant labor, imposed by the country of immigration, is not only odious it is probably unconstitutional in many countries. But this is not a fatal objection, because the theorem applies with equal force should the country imposing the restrictions be a natural capital importer and a natural labor exporter – or the foreign country in the above scenario.

The significance of the Ramaswami theorem is somewhat limited by the assumption that both countries share the same technology. It turns out that productivity differences can either magnify or reverse the Ramaswami result. For example, if foreign labor is only slightly less productive in the home environment than in the foreign country, then the theorem breaks down. Straightforward calculation shows that if the home country's production function is $Q = 0.99L^{0.75}K^{0.25}$ while the foreign country's is $Q^* = L^{0.75}K^{0.25}$, then the Ramaswami result will be reversed, i.e. it pays the home country to substitute optimal restrictions on exports of capital for optimal restrictions on imports of labor. On the other hand, productivity differences in favor of the home country intensify the Ramaswami result.

4. International factor movements and income distribution

International factor movements alter the relative domestic supplies of productive factors and, hence, should change the internal distribution of income. Who gains? Who loses? What are the sizes of the redistribution? This section gives some illustrative calculations using the MacDougall–Kemp model and then turns to a more general framework with r factors and n goods.

4.1. The MacDougall – Kemp model

The MacDougall–Kemp model is useful for making illustrative calculations of the impact of, say, immigration on income distribution. The model is limited by the fact that it uses only two productive factors, though it would be easy to extend the model to more than two factors at the cost of losing its sharp predictive powers. Suppose that the production function is Cobb–Douglas, the intensive form of which is $f(c) = c^\alpha$. We know that the wage rate $w = f - cf'$. Substituting we find that $w = (1 - \alpha)c^\alpha$. If the initial capital stock is k, the autrakic wage rate is $w_A = (1 - \alpha)k^\alpha$. Since $c = k/(1 + m)$, the impact of immigration on the domestic wage rate is simply:

$$w/w_A = (1/(1 + m))^\alpha.$$

The effect of immigration on the per capita income of the native population is also simple to calculate. Since $y = (1 + m)f(c) - wm$, substitution shows that:

$$y/y_A = (1/(1 + m))^\alpha (1 + m),$$

where $y_A = k^\alpha$.

Table 4.1 shows some calculations for m running from 1 percent to 50 percent of the native population for two cases: a capital share coefficient of 0.25 and one of 0.333. If the foreign population is 20 percent of the native population ($= 16$

percent of the total workforce), national income rises by 0.3 to 0.4 percent while wages fall by 4.5 to 6 percent. If $m = 0.5$ (33 percent of the workforce), income rises by 1.6 to 2 percent while wages fall by 10 to 13 percent. As we pointed out earlier, such migration figures are not unrealistic (e.g. in 1970 one-third of the Swiss workforce was foreign).

Let us now consider the effects of emigration on the income of non-emigrants. Writers on the brain drain [Bhagwati (1976)] have placed special emphasis on this issue. We have earlier seen that emigration increases the income of the native population. In Figure 3.1, which we earlier interpreted in terms of the movement of capital, we could have just as easily described the impact of labor movements. There are OG units of labor in the home country and $O*G$ in the foreign country; the wage in the former is initially GB and in the latter GD (much higher). HG units of labor emigrate to the foreign country. The non-emigrants, OH lose the area ABE; for the income to capital (which does not move) falls by $FABEN$ and non-emigrant labor OH gains only $FAEN$.

Harry Johnson (1967) pointed out that the fate of non-emigrants depends on the amount of capital the emigrants take with them. In Figure 4.1, based on Johnson, before migration the equilibrium wage-rent ratio is shown by the slope of the tangent at point E. The endowment of non-emigrants is shown to be point E_N, so emigrants own the endowment K_M and M. Before emigration, non-emigrant income is Y_1. After emigration the non-emigrants receive Y_0. The loss clearly depends on the capital–labor ratio of the emigrants: the closer E_N is to the ray OE, the smaller the loss to non-emigrants. We can also see the source of the loss: the trade of factor services between emigrants and non-emigrants. In Figure 4.1, non-emigrants are more richly endowed with capital than the emigrants. The loss they suffer is due to the trade gains they enjoyed renting their capital to the emigrants before the latter decided to leave with their relatively abundant capital.

Table 4.1

The impact of immigration on domestic wages and national income: $f(c) = c^\alpha$

$m = M/L$	$\alpha = 0.25$		$\alpha = 0.333$	
	w/w_A	y/y_A	w/w_A	y/y_A
0.01	0.9975	1.000009	0.9967	1.000011
0.05	0.9879	1.000225	0.9839	1.000266
0.10	0.9765	1.000865	0.9687	1.00102
0.15	0.9657	1.001875	0.9545	1.002205
0.2	0.9554	1.003215	0.941	1.003772
0.25	0.9457	1.00485	0.9283	1.005678
0.30	0.9365	1.00675	0.9163	1.007886
0.4	0.9193	1.011255	0.8939	1.013091
0.5	0.9036	1.016552	0.8736	1.019177

   This argument has been criticized by McCulloch and Yellen (1974). If capital is internationally mobile the capital that emigrants take with them will be replaced by compensating inflows.

4.2.   The general case of a small open economy

MacDougall–Kemp is limited by the fact that it cannot deal with questions involving, say, immigration of unskilled workers when there are skilled workers and capital present in the economy. With three factors and one good, virtually anything can happen. The general two-by-two (two factors and two goods) Heckscher–Ohlin trade model is also of limited use because of the factor price equalization property. Basically, factor price equalization implies that factor prices are independent of factor supplies for certain ranges and makes analysis of the effects of factor movements a trivial question: nothing happens or else the model reduces to the MacDougall–Kemp model if specialization is forced.
   The way out of this puzzle is to use a model with more factors than goods. A good example of such a model is the specific factors model analyzed by Samuelson (1971) and Jones (1971). Suppose capital is specific to the manufacturing sector and land is specific to the agricultural sector, with labor being used in both sectors. If the economy is a small open economy, so the relative prices of

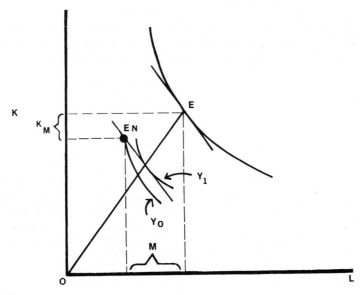

Figure 4.1

manufactured and agricultural goods are fixed, changes in the supply of capital, land, and labor have predictable effects on income distribution. Additional capital will draw labor out of agricultural activities and, hence, reduce agricultural rents and raise wage rates. Additional labor will spill over into both sectors and raise the rents on both agricultural land and manufacturing capital. In this specific factors model, the specific factors are "natural enemies" and the mobile factor is everybody's "friend".

What can be said in the general case? Ruffin (1981) shows that with three factors and two goods a result similar to the specific factors model holds.

4.2.1. Enemies and friends

It is useful to begin with the r-factor, n-good model ($r > n$). This model has been studied by Jones and Scheinkman (1977) and Diewert and Woodland (1977). They prove the theorem that if the supply of a factor increases, its return diminishes when commodity prices are given in a small open economy.

Assume constant returns to scale, diminishing returns, fixed factor supplies, and flexible factor prices (permitting full employment). Let $w = (w_1, \ldots, w_r)$ be the vector of r-factor prices; let $p = (p_1, \ldots, p_n)$ be the vector of fixed world prices of the n goods; and let $V = (V_1, \ldots, V_r)$ be the vector of r-factor supplies. The amount of input i used in a unit of good j depends on w, i.e.

$$a_{ij} = a_{ij}(w), \qquad i = 1, \ldots, r, \quad j = 1, \ldots, n. \tag{4.1}$$

The minimum cost of producing good j is:

$$c_j(w) = \sum w_i a_{ij}(w). \tag{4.2}$$

Letting $X_i (i = 1, \ldots, n)$ denote the output of good i, the set of outputs $X = (X_1, \ldots, X_n)$ and factor prices w are determined by:

$$\sum_i w_i a_{ij}(w) = p_j, \qquad j = 1, \ldots, n, \tag{4.3}$$

$$\sum_j a_{ij}(w) X_j = V_i, \qquad i = 1, \ldots, r. \tag{4.4}$$

The endogenous variables X_j and w_i obviously depend on the V_i's and p_j's. National income, Y, can be defined as:

$$Y = \sum w_i V_i \tag{4.5}$$

or

$$Y = \sum p_j X_j. \tag{4.6}$$

The following results are useful [Samuelson (1953), Jones and Scheinkman (1977)]:

$$\sum_i V_i \, \partial w_i / \partial V_h = 0. \tag{4.7}$$

A corollary of (4.7) is that an additional unit of V_h raises national income by its factor price, w_h:

$$\partial Y / \partial V_h = w_h. \tag{4.8}$$

Since the order of differentiation does not matter, the relationship between factors h and k is entirely reciprocal:

$$\partial w_h / \partial V_k = \partial w_k / \partial V_h. \tag{4.9}$$

Let us now prove the following interesting result. Define friendship between factors i and j as $\partial w_i / \partial V_j > 0$. Factors i and j are enemies if $\partial w_i / \partial V_j < 0$. Conditions (4.9) imply that friendship is reciprocal. The interesting result follows almost directly from (4.7). Since $\partial w_h / \partial v_h < 0$ under normal conditions, it follows that there must be some factor g such that $\partial w_g / \partial V_h > 0$. This implies, by reciprocity, that $\partial w_h / \partial V_g > 0$. Hence, *every factor has a friend when the number of factors n exceeds the number of goods r.*

4.2.2. The three-factor, two-good model

When there are three factors and two goods, it appears there are two possible friendship patterns (ignoring the case where $\partial w_i / \partial V_j = 0$). The sign pattern A of the matrix $(\partial w_i / \partial V_j)$ corresponds to the case where all factors are friends; and sign pattern B to the case where factors 1 and 3 are enemies. There are no other patterns, since every factor has a friend. Of course, renaming the enemies could change the sign pattern of B.

$$A = \begin{bmatrix} - & + & + \\ + & - & + \\ + & + & - \end{bmatrix}, \qquad B = \begin{bmatrix} - & + & - \\ + & - & + \\ - & + & - \end{bmatrix}.$$

We now show that with a suitable re-numbering of factors only sign pattern B is possible; sign pattern A is impossible when there are three genuinely different factors producing two genuinely different goods.

For any given set of factor endowments V_i ($i = 1, 2, 3$) and commodity prices p_j ($j = 1, 2$), eqs. (4.1), (4.3), and (4.4) determine the input-output coefficients, a_{ij}. Form the three ratios a_{i1} / a_{i2} ($i = 1, 2, 3$) indicating relative factor usage across industries. Clearly, factors can always be re-numbered so that:

$$a_{11}/a_{12} \geqq a_{21}/a_{22} \geqq a_{31}/a_{32}. \tag{4.10}$$

If no two factors are used the same way across industries we have the stronger condition:

$$a_{11}/a_{12} > a_{21}/a_{22} > a_{31}/a_{32}. \tag{4.11}$$

When (4.11) prevails we shall call factors 1 and 3 the "extreme" factors and factor 2 the "middle" factor. I shall call (4.11) the *factor extremity condition*. Notice that for any given set of factor endowments and commodity prices two of the factors must normally be extreme factors and the third factor must be a middle factor. Naturally, with changes in the exogenous variables there may be factor extremity reversals.

We shall now prove that with the factor extremity condition (4.11) sign pattern *B* is the only one possible. We need only show that factors 1 and 3 are enemies; for that implies, since every factor has a friend, that factor 2 is everybody's friend (except, of course, other members of the same class).

For a given set of commodity prices and factor endowments, Figure 4.2 illustrates the solution to (4.4) for the factor endowments V_1, V_2, and V_3. Point *A* satisfies (4.4); and the implicit a_{ij}'s satisfies (4.3). Now suppose V_1 increases to V_1' and V_3 decreases to V_3', so that the new equilibrium is at point *C* *at the old set of factor prices*. Now let the supply of factor 3 rise again to the original level V_3. By the theorem in the previous section, the price of factor 3 must fall, since factor demand curves are downward sloping. Hence, we have proven that factor 1, which increased in supply to V_1', must bring about a reduction in w_3 if the supply of factors 2 and 3 are constant. Hence, we have shown that the two *extreme* factors 1 and 3 must be enemies while factor 2, the middle factor, is everybody's friend.

This argument suggests that whether factors are substitutes or complements does not matter when seeking to determine the impact of a change in one factor supply on another factor reward. The reason: to know the impact of a change in the supply of a factor on the price of another factor we need only know the state of excess demand created for the other factor at the original set of factor prices when two of the factors have zero excess demands. At a single set of factor prices, the forces of factor substitution are not set in motion to determine whether a particular factor price will rise or fall.

Summarizing our result:

Theorem

If there are three factors and two goods produced in a competitive, small open economy operating under constant returns to scale, an increase in the supply of

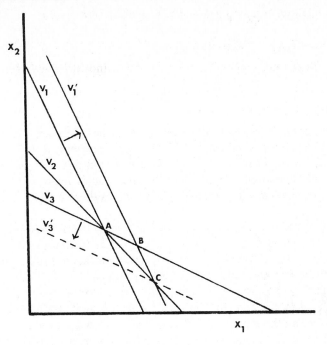

Figure 4.2

the middle factor will benefit the extreme factors and a small increase in the supply of an extreme factor will benefit the middle factor and hurt the other extreme factor. The condition for this result is simply that a change in the supply of any factor affects factor prices.

5. Trade and capital movements

We have so far neglected the interaction between trade, tariffs, and factor movements. The most complete analysis of this subject is Jones' (1967) classic, which was based on a pioneering investigation by Kemp (1966). The Kemp–Jones model consisted of the basic Heckscher–Ohlin production structure, capital mobility, and technology differences between the two trading countries. Earlier work [Mundell (1957)] had assumed that both trading countries shared the same technology. Since the original contributions by Mundell, Kemp, and Jones, there has been additional work by Brecher and Diaz-Alejandro (1977), Markusen and Melvin (1979), and Bhagwati and Brecher (1980). The pattern of trade and specialization has been examined by Jones and Ruffin (1975), Doug Purvis (1972), and Chipman (1971).

5.1.   The Heckscher – Ohlin model

Ohlin (1967), Heckscher (1919), Meade (1951), Lerner (1952), Samuelson (1949), and many others have suggested that trade is a substitute for factor movements. The basis for this suggestion is the factor endowment theory of international trade pioneered by Ohlin and Heckscher: countries export goods that are intensive in their relatively abundant factors. Abundant factors are indirectly exported through the goods they produce; scarce factors are indirectly imported through the importation of goods using those factors. If factors are shipped from where they are relatively abundant to where they are relatively scarce, the basis for trade is narrowed: thus, trade substitutes for factor movements. When factor price equalization holds [Lerner (1952), Samuelson (1949)], trade is a perfect substitute for factor movements.

Figure 5.1 illustrates (and proves) the factor price equalization theorem. Imagine two countries have access to the same constant-returns-to-scale technology, two goods (G_1 and G_2), and two factors [capital (K) and labor (L)]. Assume G_2 is always capital-intensive, i.e. uses a higher capital–labor ratio than G_1's capital intensity for any common wage–rent (w/r) ratio. Let p denote the price of G_2 in terms of G_1. Then the isoquant $X_2 = 1/p$ is the unit value isoquant for G_2 and the

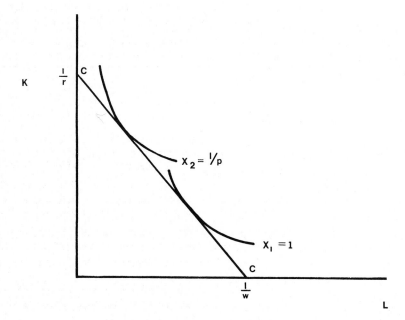

Figure 5.1

isoquant $X_1 = 1$ is the unit value isoquant for G_1. Competitive production of both goods requires that the unit value quantity of each be produced at the same minimum cost of unity. Hence, both unit value isoquants must be tangent to the unit isocost line, which intersects the capital and labor axes at $1/r$ and $1/w$ respectively. Notice that there is only one factor price pair (w, r) associated with any given p that is compatible with producing both goods. It follows that if both countries face the same p and produce both goods, both countries must have the same factor prices.

The relationship between commodity prices and factor prices reflects the technology of a country when both goods are produced – factor endowment is irrelevant. Inspection of Figure 5.1 shows that a higher p will raise r and lower w. Indeed, it will be true (the Stolper–Samuelson theorem) that raising the relative price of the capital-intensive good, p, will raise the reurn to capital by an even greater proportion. The intuition behind this result is that since w falls, r must rise by an even larger percentage in order for the cost of good 2 to rise to the new higher price for good 2. Figure 5.2 illustrates the technological link between p and r imbedded in Figure 5.1 and reflects the magnification effect of p on r.

Let us now look at the relationship between commodity prices and factor prices in the light of a country's factor endowment. For a given factor endowment of capital and labor there are only certain commodity prices that are compatible

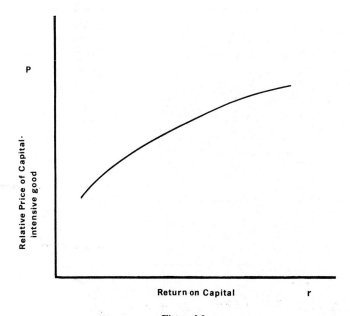

Figure 5.2

with diversified production of both goods. If p is too low, G_2 will not be produced; if p is too high, G_1 will not be produced. Let p and $\bar{p}$ indicate the limits on the relative price of G_2 consistent with positive production of both goods; these are shown in Figure 5.3. Notice that when $p < p$, the rental on capital does not change. The reason is that only G_1 is now produced; since G_1 is the numeraire the rental on capital, r, is simply the marginal product of capital in the G_1 industry and changes in p below p have no effects. When $p > \bar{p}$, only G_2 is produced. The rental on capital is simply the product of p and the marginal product of capital in G_2 production, which is now fixed when all resources are allocated to G_2. Hence, p and r are now proportional. The heavy line $ABCD$ in Figure 5.3 shows the link between p and r when factor endowment is taken into account. Along the segment BC both goods are produced.

The remaining properties of the Heckscher–Ohlin model are common to all models of competitive, non-joint, constant-returns-to-scale production:

$$\partial X_1/\partial p + p\,\partial X_2/\partial p = 0, \tag{5.1}$$

$$\partial X_1/\partial C + p\,\partial X_2/\partial C = r, \tag{5.2}$$

$$\partial X_2/\partial C = \partial r/\partial p; \quad \partial X_1/\partial C = \partial(r/p)/\partial(1/p) = r - p\,\partial r/\partial p. \tag{5.3}$$

Eq. (5.1) is that the slope of the production-possibility curve is equated to the price ratio; eq. (5.2) is that an extra unit of capital raises national income by the rental on capital. Eqs. (5.3) are the Samuelson duality relations.

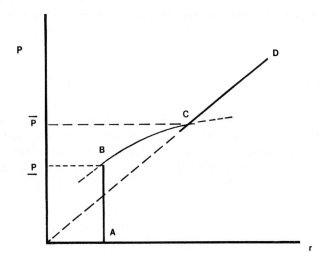

Figure 5.3

5.2. The Kemp–Jones model

When technology differences and perfect capital mobility are introduced into the Heckscher–Ohlin model a number of important properties obtain. (i) Trade patterns are "Ricardian" since they reflect technology differences rather than factor endowments and at least one country must be specialized. (ii) There may be comparative cost advantage reversals along the world production possibility curve. (iii) International capital movements may complement trade in goods rather than substitute for trade in goods. (iv) The direction of capital flow must always be reversed as the commodity price ratio goes from high to low values. (v) A rise in a commodity's relative price may attract capital towards the country with a comparative disadvantage in producing that commodity. (vi) With tariffs in place capital inflows or outflows may prove to be immiserizing. Finally, (vii) perfect capital mobility may alter the optimal tariff strategy of a country.

Let us begin with a very simple exercise. The $p-r$ relationship in Figure 5.2 plays a central role in the Kemp–Jones model, since it shows the relative cost of production in a country for a particular rate of return on capital. Since we will be studying two countries with different technologies it is useful to ask: how does technology change affect the $p-r$ curve?

When both goods are produced we know that competitive pricing requires:

$$a_{L1}w + a_{K1}r = 1,$$

$$a_{L2}w + a_{K2}r = p. \tag{5.4}$$

Eqs. (5.4) correspond to the common tangency in Figure 5.1. Let θ_{ij} denote the cost shares, e.g. $\theta_{L1} = a_{L1}w$. We know further that minimum cost production requires:

$$\theta_{Li}\hat{a}_{Li} + \theta_{Ki}\hat{a}_{Ki} = 0, \tag{5.5}$$

where $\hat{x} = dx/x$ is the proportionate change in a variable. Eq. (5.5) holds for all small changes in the w/r ratio when the technology is constant. Define now π_i as the percentage reduction in the cost of producing G_i due to reductions in the a_{ji} coefficients at constant factor prices. By totally differentiating (5.4) and collecting the technological change parameters in the π_i coefficients, we obtain [compare Jones (1970)]:

$$\theta_{L1}\hat{w} + \theta_{K1}\hat{r} = \pi_1,$$

$$\theta_{L2}\hat{w} + \theta_{K2}\hat{r} = \pi_2 + \hat{p}. \tag{5.6}$$

Solving (5.6) for $\hat{r}$ yields:

$$\hat{r} = \frac{\theta_{L1}(\pi_2 + \hat{p}) - \pi_1\theta_{L2}}{\theta}, \qquad \theta = \theta_{K2} - \theta_{K1} = \theta_{L1} - \theta_{L2} > 0. \qquad (5.7)$$

When $\pi_i = 0$, (5.7) reduces to:

$$\hat{r} = \theta_{L1}\hat{p}/\theta,$$

which shows that $\hat{r}/\hat{p} > 1$ (the magnification effect or Stolper–Samuelson theorem). We are interested in the case when $\hat{p} = 0$. Eq. (5.7) then gives us the horizontal shift in the $p-r$ relationship due to an improvement in technology. In particular, the $p-r$ curve will shift to the right if

$$\theta_{L1}\pi_2 - \theta_{L2}\pi_1 > 0. \qquad (5.8)$$

Indeed, if we assume Hicksian-uniform technical progress:

$$\hat{r} = \pi_1 = \pi_2. \qquad (5.9)$$

It is clear that if there is a Cobb–Douglas technology, where the θ_{ji}'s are constant, the $p-r$ curve will shift wholly to the left or wholly to the right. But, in general, it would be possible for the new $p-r$ curve to intersect the old $p-r$ curve if the expression in (5.8) changed signs.

5.2.1. The Ricardian nature of the Kemp–Jones model

Jones and Ruffin (1975) and Ferguson (1978) have noted the Ricardian flavor of the current model. Figure 5.4 summarizes the Heckscher–Ohlin model with capital mobility and differences in technology. Assume that the home country is more advanced than the foreign country in both sectors and that condition (5.8) holds. This means that the home $p-r$ curve is below and to the right of the foreign $p-r$ curve. Figure 5.4 would prevail if, for example, the home country were uniformly more advanced ($\pi_1 = \pi_2$) than the foreign country or simply more advanced in the capital-intensive (G_2) industry (i.e. $\pi_2 > 0$ and $\pi_1 = 0$). The opposite would hold if the home country were substantially more advanced in the labor-intensive industry than in the capital-intensive industry.

Suppose that OR in Figure 5.4 is the common rate of return on capital when the world economy is in equilibrium. It is easy to see that the world p must be in between RA and RB. For if $p > RB$, both countries would specialize in G_2; and if $p < RA$, both countries would specialize in G_1. Thus for the world economy to produce both goods, p must be in between the limits set by RA and RB. Just

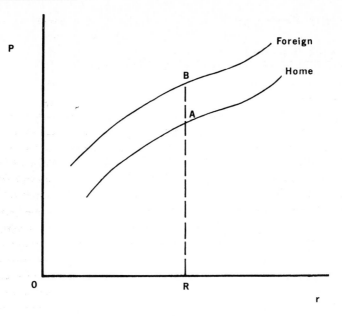

Figure 5.4

where p will be will depend on world demand and the sizes of the two countries (as in the Ricardian model). If p is strictly in between RA and RB, both will specialize in the good in which they have a comparative cost advantage; if p equals the relative cost of one of the countries, that country may diversify or, at least, be incipiently specialized. But, whatever the case, the home country exports G_2. Clearly, when technological differences confer unique comparative cost advantages on each country, the pattern of trade depends only on technology differences.

The model shares much with the Ricardian model. But when one examines the technology differences more closely, the analogy breaks down in certain instances. Let us solve for the comparative cost difference at a common rate or return. When $\hat{r} = 0$, eq. (5.6) implies:

$$\hat{p} = \frac{(\theta_{L2}\pi_1 - \theta_{L1}\pi_2)}{\theta_{L1}}. \tag{5.10}$$

The home country has a comparative cost advantage in G_1 or G_2 as $\hat{p}$ is positive or negative. The Ricardian analogy does *not* break down if the home country is more advanced in only one industry; for eq. (5.10) shows that the home country would export that good, just as in the Ricardian model. But even here we shall later see that there are important differences. The analogy clearly breaks down if the home country is equally more advanced in both industries, since the present model implies the home country will export the capital-intensive good whereas the Ricardian model implies no trade. This crucial result [noted in Jones (1970)] makes good intuitive sense. The fact that the home country is equally more advanced than the foreign country does not confer any advantages one way or the other; but since the home country must have a higher wage–rent ratio than the foreign country with mobile capital, the labor-intensive good is penalized.

5.2.2. Comparative cost reversals

It is clear that the advanced country will tend to export the capital-intensive good unless it is relative more efficient in the labor-intensive good. A necessary, but not sufficient, condition for exporting the labor-intensive good is that $\pi_1 > \pi_2$. When this is true it is possible for the home $p-r$ curve to lie above the foreign curve everywhere or for the two curves to intersect, i.e. a cost reversal. Figure 5.5 shows a possible cost reversal situation.

When Figure 5.5 obtains, the more advanced home country will have a comparative advantage in the labor-intensive good if the relative price of the

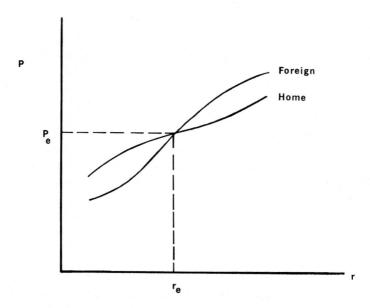

Figure 5.5

capital-intensive good G_2 is below p_e and a comparative advantage in the capital-intensive good when p exceeds p_e. In short, the advanced country has a comparative advantage in the good for which world demand is relatively "high."

From (5.10) it is clear that:

$$\hat{p} \gtrless 0, \quad \text{as} \quad \frac{\pi_1}{\pi_2} \gtrless \frac{\theta_{L1}}{\theta_{L2}}. \tag{5.11}$$

Hence, Figure 5.5 can obtain if θ_{L1}/θ_{L2} is an increasing function of p ($\hat{p}$ initially positive and then becoming negative).

I investigate the behavior of θ_{L1}/θ_{L2} on the assumption that technology is constant. Indeed, it is only necessary to examine the ratio of labor shares in a single economy. From (5.6) it is clear that when $\pi_i = 0$,

$$\hat{w} = - \hat{p}\theta_{K1}/\theta \quad \text{and} \quad \hat{p} = -\theta(\hat{w} - \hat{r}). \tag{5.12}$$

By definition $\hat{\theta}_{L1} = \hat{w} + \hat{a}_{L1}$ and $\hat{\theta}_{L2} = \hat{w} + \hat{a}_{L2} - \hat{p}$. From the cost-minimizing condition and the definition of the elasticity of substitution, it may be shown that:

$$\hat{a}_{Li} = -\theta_{Ki}\sigma_i(\hat{w} - \hat{r}), \tag{5.13}$$

where σ_i is the elasticity of substitution in industry i. From (5.12), (5.13), and the definitions of $\hat{\theta}_{Li}$ it may be seen that:

$$\hat{\theta}_{L1} - \hat{\theta}_{L2} = (\hat{p}/\theta)(\theta_{K1}(\sigma_1 - 1) - \theta_{K2}(\sigma_2 - 1)). \tag{5.14}$$

To simplify, let both elasticities equal the same number, σ. In that case we get:

$$\hat{\theta}_{L1} - \hat{\theta}_{L2} = \hat{p}(1 - \sigma). \tag{5.15}$$

If the elasticities of substitution are less than unity, cost reversals will tend to be of the type depicted in Figure 5.5.

The major consequences of a comparative cost reversal are: technology differences no longer confer a unique position of comparative advantage; if the (p_e, r_e) intersection point in Figure 5.5 prevails, both countries can be diversified even though one country is more advanced in both sectors; and, as Chipman (1973) has pointed out and as will be discussed below, world production will be indeterminate over a finite range of outputs.

5.2.3. Trade and capital movements

In the Heckscher–Ohlin model trade and capital movements are substitutes. This no longer holds in the Kemp–Jones model. Let us take the case where the technology difference confers a unique comparative advantage, as in Figure 5.4. The more advanced home country will tend to have a comparative advantage in the capital-intensive good, since with capital mobility both countries have the same rent and the advanced country will have a higher wage–rent ratio. This means that trade and capital movements will tend to be complements since trade will increase with capital flows.

To see the dramatic contrast between a world with technology differences and one with identical technologies, suppose that the home country is equally more advanced in both industries than the foreign country. Assume identical and homothetic tastes. With the same factor endowment (and no capital movements) there would be no trade; the home country would simply have uniformly higher wages and rents. Now open up capital mobility. Since the home r > the foreign r^*, capital will flow to the home country. This necessarily drives the specialization patterns apart à la Rybcyznski – the home country's output of the capital-intensive good rises and the foreign country's output of the capital-intensive good falls. But one does not have to go this far. The tendency for the volume of trade to expand will be enormous. Without capital mobility the home country will have a higher rate of return on capital if both countries are diversified. As long as the home country exports the capital-intensive good without capital mobility, the movement of capital will encourage more trade.

These tendencies will be counteracted only if before capital mobility is introduced the home country exports the labor-intensive good. This will hold, for instance, when the home country is uniformly more advanced and has a higher ratio of labor to capital than the foreign country. In this case, capital will still be attracted to the home country but this time the volume of trade is likely to diminish.

The complimentarity between trade and capital movements in the Kemp–Jones model helps explain the enormous expansion of both international trade and capital movements in the decade of the 1970s. Such a combination is difficult to explain with a simple Heckscher–Ohlin view of the world.

5.2.4.   *Capital flows and the terms of trade*

We now summarize the properties of the world production possibility curve when there is capital mobility. Jones and Ruffin (1975), and Chipman (1971) provide more detailed arguments. However, the essential arguments are quite simple.

I first derive the world production possibility curve with perfect capital mobility when the home country has a unique comparative advantage in the capital-intensive good, G_2. The method is to start with the world specialized in (say) G_1 and raise p until the world specializes in G_2, observing along the way the various patterns of specialization and capital flows.

In Figure 5.6 the vertical heights of points p_1 and p_2 denote the world specialization prices in G_1 and G_2, respectively. The way they are determined is simple. Suppose both countries are specialized in G_1 and capital is allocated to equalize r and r^*. Point p_1 represents the relative cost of producing G_2 in the low-cost country – the home country. Any p less than or equal to p_1 causes specialization in G_1. Point p_2 is determined in a similar way, but it reflects relative costs in the foreign country, which is the low-cost country for G_1. It is easy to see that lowering p below p_1 or raising p above p_2 has no impact on the optimal allocation of the world capital stock. The hard part is considering what happens in between.

Figure 5.6 makes it clear that for p to move from p_1 to p_2 it must travel along the home curve for a finite distance, jump the gap, and then travel along the foreign curve to p_2. The principles governing the movement of capital in response to a change in p are simple: (i) if one country is diversified so that magnification effects operate, an increase (decrease) in p attracts capital to the diversified (specialized) country; and (ii) if both countries specialize an increase (decrease) in p attracts capital to the country with a comparative advantage in the capital-intensive (labor-intensive) good. Accordingly, from p_1 to p_0 capital is moving to the home country, from p_0 to p_{00} capital is moving to the home country, and from p_{00} to p_2 capital is moving to the foreign country. As p rises, the world output of G_2 rises and that of G_1 falls – in case (i) because of magnification and price effects

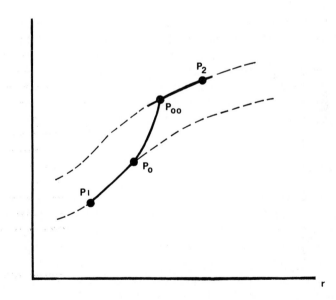

Figure 5.6

and in case (ii) because capital is productive. Figures 5.7 and 5.8 summarize the argument.

Return now to the cost reversal of Figure 5.5. If the world r is less than r_e, the foreign country has a comparative cost advantage in G_2; if the world r is greater than r_e, the home country has a comparative cost advantage in G_2. Again, p_1 and p_2 denote the world specialization prices in G_1 and G_2.

What determines whether the cost reversal point is effective? The question is whether both countries can be diversified at the common $r-p$ combination (r_e, p_e). Consider a single country. A country can be diversified at a particular (r, p) if its supply of capital is higher than the amount of capital it would use if specialized in the labor-intensive good and lower than the demand for capital if specialized in the capital-intensive good. The same is true for the world economy (merely replace *world* demand and supply for capital in the above condition). If this "Chipman condition" is not satisfied, the specialization prices would lie on one side of p_e and the previous analysis would hold.

An effective cost-reversal point implies that the world production possibility curve is flat over a certain range, as first noted by Chipman. Moreover, in the case where $\partial r^*/\partial p < \partial r/\partial p$ (Figure 5.5), along the "Chipman flat" capital moves from the foreign country to the home country as more of the capital-intensive good, G_2, is produced.

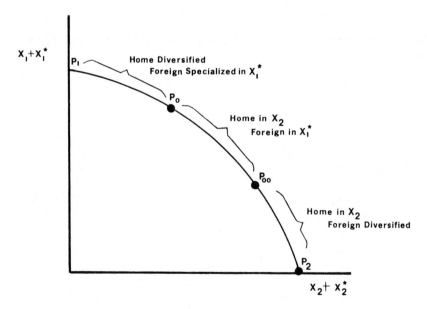

Figure 5.7

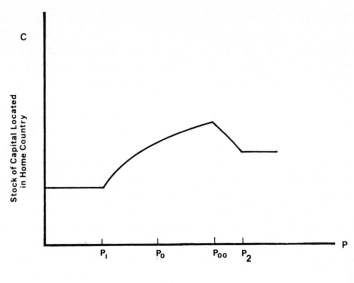

Figure 5.8

To establish these points note that from Samuelson's duality relation, (5.3):

$$\partial r^*/\partial p = \partial X_2^*/\partial C^* < \partial X_2/\partial C = \partial r/\partial p. \tag{5.16}$$

But from (5.2) we have $\partial X_1/\partial C + p_e \partial X_2/\partial C = \partial X_1^*/\partial C^* + p_e \partial X_2^*/\partial C^* = r_e$. Thus, (5.16) implies:

$$\partial X_1^*/\partial C^* > \partial X_1/\partial C. \tag{5.17}$$

It is also clear that the $(\partial X_i/\partial C)$'s are constants at the cost reversal point. From (5.16) and (5.17) it is clear that a movement of capital from the foreign to the home country will raise the output of G_2 and lower the world output of G_1. Since the net changes in world outputs are constants, the world production possibility curve is flat.

One paradoxical implication of the world economy being on the Chipman flat is that the link between capital exports and wages is reversed from what one would expect. Normally, we expect capital exports will lower domestic wages. Suppose, however, that a small tax is imposed on capital exports from the foreign to the home country in the vicinity of the Chipman flat. As capital backtracks from the home country to the foreign country the world output of G_2 will fall. This lowers p and, therefore, raises the wage rate in both countries. The home country finds that its domestic supply of capital is falling while its wage rate is rising! This curiosity was overlooked by both Jones and Ruffin (1975) and Chipman (1971). Paradox must prevail because in the Chipman flat wages and rents are linked to prices rather than factor movements. If a factor movement stimulated by a tax on capital exports or imports occurs it will cause a sympathetic change in wages in the two countries in response to the policy-induced capital flow.

5.2.5. Tariffs and capital movements

The interaction of tariffs, trade, and capital movements has been the subject of much recent investigation [e.g. Brecher and Diaz–Alejandro (1977), Markusen and Melvin (1979), and Bhagwati and Brecher (1980)]. Most of this work is related to the difficult and lengthy paper by Jones (1967) which was based on Kemp (1966). I shall attempt here to explain, in simplified form, the theory of restrictions on trade and capital movements in the Kemp–Jones model.

We begin with the assumptions that (1) the home country has a comparative cost advantage in the capital-intensive good, G_2 – as in Figure 5.4 – and (2) the foreign country maintains a posture of non-interference with trade and capital movements.

The basic balance of payments constraint is simply that the net import balance plus foreign investment income equals zero. Letting $E_i = D_i - X_i$ denote the excess demand for G_i, and Z the home country's foreign investment, the constraint is:

$$E_1 + p^*E_2 = r^*Z.$$

Through the income from foreign investments the home country can finance an excess demand for goods. Recalling that

$$E_i + E_i^* = 0 \tag{5.16}$$

in equilibrium, we write the budget constraint as:

$$E_1^* + p^*E_2^* + r^*Z = 0 \tag{5.17}$$

or

$$D_1^* + p^*D_2^* = X_1^* + p^*X_2^* - r^*Z. \tag{5.17'}$$

These expressions simply state that the foreign country must have an export surplus (if $Z > 0$) with expenditure equal income minus the repatrition of dividends or interest on home-owned foreign capital. The important thing about (5.17) is that it holds regardless of the interferences imposed by the home country.

Since $C = K - Z$ and $C^* = K^* + Z$, we can rewrite (5.2) and (5.3) as:

$$\partial X_2 / \partial Z = -\partial r / \partial p \quad \text{and} \quad \partial X_2^* / \partial Z = \partial r^* / \partial p^*, \tag{5.18}$$

$$\partial X_1 / \partial Z + p \partial X_2 / \partial Z = -r \quad \text{and} \quad \partial X_1^* / \partial Z + p^* \partial X_2^* / \partial Z = r^*. \tag{5.19}$$

These expressions may be used to simplify the impact of restrictions on home and foreign welfare.

Imagine now that the world economy is in equilibrium so that (5.16) holds. The only assumption we need now about capital mobility is that internationally mobile capital earns the foreign rate of return, r^*; this can be justified if capital is perfectly mobile and the home country imposes any taxes on such capital or if capital is imperfectly mobile and the home country invests in the foreign country. Suppose now that the world settles on a certain p^*, Z, and r^*. Now assume that the home country introduces a policy change. The change in foreign welfare is defined to be: $\mathrm{d}y^* = \mathrm{d}D_1^* + p^* \mathrm{d}D_2^*$. Totally differentiating (5.17) and using (5.1) and (5.19) we obtain:

$$\mathrm{d}y^* = -\left(E_2^* \mathrm{d}p^* + Z \mathrm{d}r^*\right). \tag{5.20}$$

If we think of the foreign country as importing G_2 ($E_2^* > 0$) and capital ($Z > 0$), foreign welfare falls by the increase in the cost of imports of goods and capital. The intuition behind (5.20) is clear; indeed, Keynes (1930, p. 345) wrote down a similar equation in his *Treatise on Money*.

The change in home welfare is slightly more complicated since the home country has taxes or restrictions on trade. But it also makes good intuitive sense:

$$\mathrm{d}y = \left(E_2^* \mathrm{d}p^* + Z \mathrm{d}r^*\right) + \left(p^* - p\right) \mathrm{d}E_2^* + \left(r^* - r\right) \mathrm{d}Z. \tag{5.21}$$

To understand this equation, imagine the home country exports G_2 and capital. Then the increase in home welfare is the increase in the terms of trade for goods and the increase in the return on capital plus the national profit from the increase in the exports of goods and capital that arises from the difference between home and foreign prices or rentals caused by the taxation of goods and foreign income. Eq. (5.21) can be derived by noting that $\mathrm{d}y = \mathrm{d}D_1 + p \mathrm{d}D_2$, totally differentiating (5.17) again, and using the equilibrium condition (5.16) as well as (5.1) and (5.19) again.

Equations (5.20) and (5.21) apply to the case where internationally mobile capital earns r^* (the foreign rate of return) in the balance of payments [eq. (5.17)]. This need not be the case if the home country imports capital ($Z < 0$) in a regime of quantitative restrictions; in that case, the appropriate interest rate is r rather than r^*. With quantitative restrictions and $Z < 0$ we have instead of (5.17), (5.20), and (5.21) (define $Z^* = -Z$):

$$E_1^* + p^*E_2^* = rZ^*, \tag{5.22}$$

$$dy^* = -E_2^* dp^* + Z^* dr, \tag{5.23}$$

$$dy = E_2^* dp^* - Z^* dr + (p^* - p) dE_2^*. \tag{5.24}$$

In (5.24) [compared to (5.21)] the term $(r^* - r)dZ$ falls off because foreign capital is paid the same as domestic capital. In Kemp–Jones, eqs. (5.17), (5.20), and (5.21) are used. But some literature, noted later, implicitly uses (5.22), (5.23), and (5.24).

Since we have precise expressions for the change in real income it is useful to use the compensated demand functions $D_i(p, y)$ or $D_i^*(p^*, y^*)$. The excess demand functions we use are then:

$$E_i(p, y, Z) = D_i(p, y) - X_i(p, Z), \tag{5.25}$$
$$E_i^*(p^*, y^*, Z) = D_i^*(p^*, y^*) - X_i^*(p^*, Z).$$

Similarly, we have:

$$r = r(p, Z) \quad \text{and} \quad r^* = r^*(p^*, Z). \tag{5.26}$$

Now let us turn to the arbitrage relationships. If the home country exports G_2 the link between p and p^* is shown by:

$$p^* = p(1 + \tau), \tag{5.27}$$

where τ is the export duty or import duty [Lerner (1936)]. If the home country imports G_2 the link is:

$$p = p^*(1 + \tau'). \tag{5.27'}$$

If the home country exports capital:

$$r = r^*(1 - t); \tag{5.28}$$

and if the home country imports capital:

$$r^* = r(1 - t'), \tag{5.28'}$$

where t or t' are the appropriate tax rates. Unless otherwise specified, we shall assume (5.27) and (5.28) hold, so the home country exports G_2 and capital.

The equilibrium values for p, p^*, and Z are determined by the following equations:

$$E_2(p, y, Z) + E_2^*(p^*, y^*, Z) = 0 \tag{5.29}$$

$$r(p, Z) = (1 - t)r^*(p^*, Z), \tag{5.30}$$

$$p = p^*(1 + \tau). \tag{5.31}$$

Real income, of course, is a function of p, p^*, and Z as well so the above three equations suffice to determine the solution.

The following definitions [based on Jones (1967)] will be useful in the subsequent remarks.

D.1   The elasticity of rentals on capital to price:

$$\gamma^* = (\partial r^*/\partial p^*)(p^*/r^*), \qquad \gamma = (\partial r/\partial p)(p/r).$$

D.2   The elasticity of rentals to foreign investment:

$$\delta^* = (\partial r^*/\partial Z)(Z/r^*), \qquad \delta = -(\partial r/\partial Z)(Z/r).$$

D.3   The ratio of foreign investment income to home exports:

$$\mu^* = r^* Z / p^* E_2^*.$$

D.4   The uncompensated foreign price elasticity of demand for E_2^*:

$$\eta_2^* = (dE_2^*/dp^*)(p^*/E_2^*),$$

where $dE_2^*/dp^* = \partial E_2^*/\partial p^* + (\partial E_2^*/\partial y^*)(dy^*/dp^*)$.

D.5   The compensated price elasticities:

$$\bar{\eta}_2 = (\partial E_2/\partial p)(p/E_2^*) \quad \text{and} \quad \bar{\eta}_2^* = (\partial E_2^*/\partial p^*)(p^*/E_2^*).$$

D.6   The marginal propensities to consume:

$$m_2 = p(\partial E_2/\partial y) \quad \text{and} \quad m_1 + m_2 = 1$$

(similar expressions for foreign country).

Assume the home country always produces G_2 and the foreign country always produces G_1. Thus $X_1 \neq 0$ or $X_2^* \neq 0$ imply the home or foreign countries are diversified. It follows that:

$$\gamma = \begin{cases} 1, & \text{if } X_1 = 0, \\ >1, & \text{if } X_1 \neq 0 \text{ and } G_2 \text{ is capital-intensive,} \\ <0, & \text{if } X_1 \neq 0 \text{ and } G_2 \text{ is labor-intensive;} \end{cases} \tag{5.32}$$

$$\gamma^* = \begin{cases} 0, & \text{if } X_2^* = 0, \\ >1, & \text{if } X_2^* \neq 0 \text{ } G_2 \text{ is capital-intensive,} \\ <0, & \text{if } X_2^* \neq 0 \text{ } G_2 \text{ is labor-intensive;} \end{cases} \tag{5.33}$$

$$\delta = \begin{cases} =0, & \text{if } X_1 \neq 0, \\ <0, & \text{if } X_1 = 0 \quad \text{and} \quad Z > 0, \\ >0, & \text{if } X_1 = 0 \quad \text{and} \quad Z < 0; \end{cases} \tag{5.34}$$

$$\delta^* = \begin{cases} =0, & \text{if } X_2^* \neq 0, \\ <0, & \text{if } X_2^* = 0 \quad \text{and} \quad Z > 0, \\ >0, & \text{if } X_2^* = 0 \quad \text{and} \quad Z < 0. \end{cases} \tag{5.35}$$

The above derive from the basic properties of the Heckscher–Ohlin model – summarized in Figure 5.3. The factor price equalization property implies δ is zero when both goods produced; specialization implies γ is unity or zero; and diversification implies γ reflects the Stolper–Samuelson result.

5.2.6. The small country

We begin our analysis with the case of the home country being small: thus, $dp^* = dr^* = 0$ from the standpoint of policy. We shall also assume that capital movements are subject to quantitative restrictions, so that the policy variable is the quantity of mobile capital. If the home country is a capital exporter, we have from (5.21) and $dp^* = dr^* = 0$:

$$dy = (p^* - p)dE_2^* + (r^* - r)dZ. \tag{5.36}$$

If the home country is a capital importer, we have from (5.24) and $dp^* = 0$:

$$dy = -Z^* dr + (p^* - p)dE_2^* = -Z^* dr + (p - p^*)dE_2, \tag{5.37}$$

where $Z^* = -Z$ and we have used $dE_2^* = -dE_2$.

Let us first, briefly, consider the case in which the home country is a capital exporter – so that (5.36) applies. If the Heckscher–Ohlin trade pattern prevails, the capital-intensive good is exported (G_2). With tariffs in place $p^* > p$ and, initially, $r^* > r$. Clearly, an increase in Z will have an ambiguous impact on home welfare. The increase in Z will contract trade and, hence, lower tariff revenues but will increase the rents to the capital exporters ($r^* > r$). The first term in (5.36) is negative, the second is positive.

The case that has attracted most of the attention in the literature is the small capital importing country – so (5.37) applies. This case has been studied by Brecher and Diaz–Alejandro (1977) and commented upon by Bhagwati (1979). If the Heckscher–Ohlin trade pattern prevails, the capital-intensive good, G_2, is imported. With tariffs in place $p > p^*$. When $p = p^*(1 + \tau)$ the rental, r, is always fixed so that $dr = 0$. Thus, when capital is imported in the incipient stages only the second term ($p - p^*$)dE_2 matters. Since the Rybczynski theorem implies $dE_2 < 0$ when capital is imported, home welfare falls. Capital imports into a tariff-distorted small country that also imports capital-intensive goods are immiserizing. The source of immiserization is the loss of tariff revenue. When imports of G_2 are eliminated by successive capital imports, we will then have $p^* \le p \le p^*$ ($1 + \tau$). Further capital imports lower p and since G_2 is capital-intensive, r falls. The second term in (5.37) is now zero and the first term is positive! When capital inflows push p down to equal p^*, we reach the free trade level where trade and capital movements are perfect substitutes [Mundell (1957)] and $dy = 0$.

When the Heckscher–Ohlin trade pattern does not hold so that the capital-importing country imports the labor-intensive good, capital imports increase imports and so add to the tariff revenue. Welfare in this case will initially increase.

5.2.7. The large country case

We now return to the large country case of Kemp–Jones and eqs. (5.29) through (5.31). The change in real incomes are again defined by (5.20) and (5.21).

Let us begin by considering the optimum tariff and tax strategy of the home country. We may assume that tariffs improve a country's terms of trade, though in this case Jones (1967) has shown this need not hold in a narrow range. The benefits from tariffs can then be measured by $\partial y / \partial p^*$ and the benefits of restricting capital flows can be measured by $\partial y / \partial Z$. From (5.21) it is clear that when $dZ = 0$ we can immediately write:

$$\partial y / \partial p^* = E_2^* + Z \partial r^* / \partial p^* + (p^* - p) E_2^* \eta_2^* / p^*.$$

We have used D.4 in the above expression. Substituting D.1 and D.3 into the above expression we can write

$$\partial y/\partial p^* = E_2^*\left(1 + \mu^*\gamma^* + (p^* - p)\eta_2^*/p^*\right). \tag{5.38}$$

Calculating $\partial y/\partial Z$ is somewhat more difficult. When $dp^* = 0$ we have $dr^* = (\partial r^*/\partial Z)dZ$ and $dE_2^* = dD_2^* - dX_2^* = (m_2^*/p^*)dy^* - (\partial X_2^*/\partial Z)dZ$. Using (5.20) and (5.3) we can write:

$$dE_2^* = \left(-(m_2^*/p^*)Z\partial r^*/\partial Z - \partial r^*/\partial p^*\right)dZ.$$

Substituting into (5.21) and using D.1, D.2, and D.6 we have:

$$\partial y/\partial Z = \left(1 + (m_1^* + pm_2^*/p^*)\delta^* - (p^* - p)\gamma^*/p^*\right)r^* - r. \tag{5.39}$$

Beginning with the case of unimpeded flows of goods and capital so that $p = p^*$ and $r = r^*$, we have:

$$\left(\partial y/\partial p^*\right)_{p = p^*} = E_2^*\left(1 + \mu^*\gamma^*\right), \tag{5.40}$$

$$\left(\partial y/\partial Z\right)_{\substack{r = r \\ p = p^*}} = \delta^*. \tag{5.41}$$

Think of the home country as exporting G_2 and capital. If the foreign country is specialized, $\gamma^* = 0$; hence, $\partial y/\partial p^* = E_2^* > 0$ and $\partial y/\partial Z = \delta^* < 0$. It pays to raise p^* and lower Z; thus, it pays the country to impose a tariff on trade and a tax on foreign investment income. Incipient restriction of both trade and capital movements pays. If the home country were a capital importer, $\partial y/\partial Z = \delta^* > 0$. It pays to increase Z. But since Z is now negative, foreign capital placed in the home country should be reduced. Thus we reach the general conclusion that if the foreign country is specialized the usual conclusion that restricting trade and capital movements follows. By setting $\partial y/\partial p^* = \partial y/\partial K = 0$ in (5.38) and (5.39) we can derive the following formulae for the optimal tariff and tax policy:

$$\tau^{opt} = -1/\left(1 + \eta_2^*\right), \tag{5.42}$$

$$t^{opt} = -\left(m_1^* + pm_2^*/p^*\right)\delta^*, \tag{5.43}$$

where we have used the arbitrage relations (5.27) and (5.28).

When the foreign country is diversified r^* no longer depends on Z; instead, r^* depends on p^*. What now is the optimal policy of the home country? We shall make the assumptions that the home country exports G_2 and that G_2 is capital-intensive. Under our new assumptions $\gamma^* > 1$ and $\delta^* = 0$. From (5.38) and (5.39) we can calculate:

$$(\partial y/\partial p^*)_{p=p^*} = E_2^*(1+\mu^*\gamma^*), \tag{5.44}$$

$$(\partial y/\partial Z)_{r=r^*} = (p-p^*)\gamma^*/p^*. \tag{5.45}$$

If the home country exports capital, $\mu^* > 0$ (from D.3). It follows that $\partial y/\partial p^* > 0$. The home country should restrict trade. If it restricts trade $p < p^*$; hence, $\partial y/\partial Z < 0$, and capital exports should also be restricted. We thus reach the conclusion: if the foreign country is diversified and the Heckscher–Ohlin trade pattern holds, it pays the home country to impose sufficiently small tariffs and taxes on trade and capital movements.

When the Heckscher–Ohlin trade pattern holds, an export duty (or import duty) raises the price of the country's exportable abroad. If the country exports capital, the return to capital abroad is increased by restricting trade. A positive tariff sets up no conflict between the terms of trade on the commodity account and the terms of trade on the capital account.

Now suppose that the Heckscher–Ohlin trade pattern does not hold. In the present case, this means that capital is imported. A tariff now still raises p^* and r^* abroad. Since there free capital mobility this means that the cost of borrowed capital rises to the home country. There is now a conflict between the commodity terms of trade and the capital terms of trade. Jones (1967) argued that it is now possible for the optimal tariff or tax (but not both) to be negative.

Let us now show that if the optimal tax is negative, the optimal tariff must be positive. By assumption it pays to encourage capital inflows by a subsidy. This means that $\partial y/\partial Z < 0$ because Z is now negative. But by (5.45) this implies $p^* > p$. Since G_2 is exported, a positive tariff is implied.

If the optimal tariff is negative, the optimum tax will be positive when $Z < 0$. With a negative optimum tariff $p > p^*$. This implies that $\partial y/\partial Z > 0$ from (5.45). Thus, capital imports should be restricted.

When the Heckscher–Ohlin trade pattern does not prevail it may still, nevertheless, pay the country to have positive optimal tariffs and taxes. We have shown that in the optimal strategy both cannot be negative [Jones (1967)].

5.2.8. *Capital exports and the terms of trade*

We close out our discussion of the basic Kemp–Jones model with some remarks on the link between capital exports and the terms of trade. The classic view of the significance of foreign investments has been that capital exports improve a country's terms of trade [Mill (1971, p. 490), Iversen (1935, p. 230)]. The emigration of English capital was supposed to keep up a supply of cheap food and raw materials to British workmen and factories. Capital imports in Denmark made butter and bacon cheap to the creditor countries of Western Europe.

Consider the case in which the home country has free trade in goods and restrictions on capital exports. Since $p = p^*$:

$$\mathrm{d}y = -\mathrm{d}y^* + (r^* - r)\,\mathrm{d}Z.$$

When there is a change in Z, due either to taxes or changes in quantitative restrictions, we know that $\mathrm{d}E_2 + \mathrm{d}E_2^* = 0$. What are the conditions in which additional capital exports improve the home country's term of trade, i.e. $\mathrm{d}p^*/\mathrm{d}Z > 0$? If we make the simplifying assumption that $m_2 = m_2^*$ it turns out that:

$$\left(\partial E_2/\partial p + \partial E_2^*/\partial p^*\right)\mathrm{d}p^*$$
$$+ \left((r^* - r)m_2/p + (\partial r/\partial p - \partial r^*/\partial p^*)\right)\mathrm{d}Z = 0. \qquad (5.46)$$

Since $r^* > r$ for the case of a capital exporter, it follows that as long as $\partial r/\partial p \geq \partial r^*/\partial p^*$, $\mathrm{d}p^*/\mathrm{d}Z > 0$. This occurs if the home country exports the capital-intensive good and the foreign country is specialized ($\partial r^*/\partial p^* = 0$). Ambiguity arises when the Heckscher–Ohlin trade pattern does not hold. Suppose, for example, that G_2 is labor-intensive. If the foreign country is specialized $\partial r/\partial p < \partial r^*/\partial p^* = 0$. When capital exports occur the country's production of importables is reduced; and this must be pitted against the increase in the output of the importable abroad.

References

Arrow, K.J. (1970), Essays in the theory of risk bearing (North-Holland, Amsterdam) ch. 4.

Barker, B.L. (1981), "A profile of U.S. multinational companies in 1977", Survey of Current Business, 61 (10):38–57.

Belli, R.D. (1981), "U.S. business enterprises acquired or established by foreign direct investors in 1980", Survey of Current Business, 61 (8):58–71.

Berry, R. and R. Soligo (1969), "Some welfare aspects of international migration", Journal of Political Economy, 77:778–794.

Bhagwati, J. and R. Brecher (1980), "National welfare in an open economy in the presence of foreign-owned factors of production", Journal of International Economics, 10, p. 103.

Bhagwati, J. and K. Hamada (1974), "The brain drain, international integration of markets for professionals and unemployment", Journal of Development Economics, 1:19–42.

Bhagwati, J. and C. Rodriguez (1975), "Welfare-theoretical analyses of the brain drain", Journal of Development Economics, 2.

Bhagwati J., ed. (1976), The brain drain and taxation, Vol. II (North-Holland, Amsterdam).

Bhagwati, J. (1979), "International factor movements and the national advantage", V.K. Ramaswami Memorial Lecture, mimeo.

Brecher, R.A. and C.F. Diaz-Alejandro (1977), "Tariffs, foreign capital and immerserizing growth", Journal of International Economics, 7:317–322.

Buckley, P.J. and M. Casson (1976), The future of the multinational enterprise (MacMillan, London).

Cairncross, A.K. (1953), Home and foreign investment, 1870–1913 (Cambridge University Press).

Caves, R.E. (1971), "International corporations: The industrial economics of foreign investment", Economica, 38:1–27.

Caves, R.E. (1982), Multinational enterprises and economic analysis (Cambridge University Press, Cambridge).

Chipman, J.S. (1971), "International trade with capital mobility: A substitution theorem", in: Bhagwati, Jones, Mundell, and Vanek, eds., Trade, balance of payments and growth (North-Holland, Amsterdam) 201–237.

Coase, R.H. (1960), "The problem of social cost", Journal of Law and Economics, 3:1–44.

Diewert, W.E., and A.D. Woodland (1977), "Frank Knight's theorem in linear programming", Econometrica, 45:375–398.

Ethier, W.J. (1981), "International trade and labor migration", Department of Economics (University of Pennsylvania), mimeo.

Ferguson, D.G., (1978), "International capital mobility and comparative advantage: The two country, two factor case", Journal of International Economics, 8:373–396.

Grubel, H.G. and A.D. Scott (1966), "The international flow of human capital", American Economic Review, 56:268–274.

Hamada, K. (1974), "An economic analysis of the duty free zone", Journal of International Economics, 4:225–241.

Heckscher, E.F. (1919), "The effect of foreign trade on the distribution of national income", Ekonomisk Tidskrift, 21; reprinted in Ellis and Metzler, Readings in the theory of international trade (Philadelphia, 1949).

Hewlett, S.A. (1981/82), "Coping with illegal immigrants", Foreign Affairs, 60:358–378.

Hobson, C.K. (1914), The export of capital (London, Constable).

Hood, N. and S. Young (1979), The economics of multinational enterprise (Longman, London).

Hymer, S. (1960), "The international operations of national firms: A study of direct investment", doctoral dissertation (Massachusetts Institute of Technology).

Iversen, C. (1936) Aspects of the theory of international capital movements (London, Oxford University Press).

Jasay, A.E. (1960), "The social choice between home and overseas investments", Economic Journal, 70:105–113.

Johnson, H.G. (1967), "Some economic aspects of the brain drain", Pakistani Development Review, 7:379–411.

Jones, R.W. (1965), "The structure of simple general equilibrium models", Journal of Political Economy, 73:557–572.

Jones, R.W. (1967), "International capital movements and the theory of tariffs and trade", Quarterly Journal of Economics, 81:1–38.

Jones, R.W. (1970), "The role of technology in the theory of international trade", in: Raymond Vernon, ed., The technology factor in international trade (National Bureau of Economic Research) 73–92.

Jones, R.W. (1971), "A three-factor model in theory, trade, and history", in Bhagwati, Jones, Mundell, and Vanek, eds., Trade, balance of payments and growth (North-Holland, Amsterdam) 3–21.

Jones, R.W. (1980), "Comparative and absolute advantage", Schweizerisch Zeitschrift fur Volkswirtschaft und Statistik, 3:235–260.

Jones, R.W. and R.J. Ruffin (1975), "Trade patterns with capital mobility", in M. Parkin and A.R. Nobay, eds., Current economic problems, (Cambridge) 307–332; reprinted as "Production patterns with capital mobility", Chapter 13 in: R.W. Jones, International trade: Essays in theory (North-Holland, Amsterdam, 1979).

Jones, R.W., J.P. Neary, and F.P. Ruane (1981), "Two-way capital flows: Cross-hauling in models of foreign investment", mimeo.

Jones, R.W. and J. Scheinkman (1977), "The relevance of the two-sector production model in trade theory", Journal of Political Economy, 85:909–935.

Kemp, M.C. (1964), The pure theory of international trade (Englewood Cliffs, Prentice-Hall).

Kemp, M.C. (1966), "The gain from international trade and investment: A Neo–Heckscher–Ohlin approach", American Economic Review, 56:788–809.

Kemp, M.C. (1969), The pure theory of international trade and investment (Englewood Cliffs, Prentice-Hall) ch. 9.

Keynes, J.M. (1924), "Foreign investment and the national advantage", The Nation and Athenaeum, 35:584–587.

Keynes, J.M. (1929), "The German transfer problem", Economic Journal, 39:1–7.

Keynes, J.M. (1930), The treatise on money, Vol. 1 (London, MacMillan).

Kindleberger, C.P. (1967), Europe's postwar growth: The role of labor supply (Harvard University Press, Cambridge).

Kindleberger, C.P. (1969), American business abroad: Six letters on direct investment (Yale, New Haven).

Lerner, A.P. (1936), "The symmetry between import and export taxes", Economica, 3:306–313.

Lerner, A.P. (1952), "Factor prices and international trade", Economica, 19:1–16.

Lindert, P.H. and C.P. Kindleberger (1982), International economics, 7th edn. (Richard Irwin, Homewood).

MacDougall, G.D.A. (1960), "The benefits and costs of private investment from abroad: A theoretical approach", Economic Record, 36:13–35.

Markusen, J.R. and J.R. Melvin (1979), "Tariffs, capital mobility, and foreign ownership", Journal of International Economics, 9:395–409.

McCulloch, R. and J.L. Yellen (1974), "Factor mobility and the steady state distribution of income", Discussion Paper No. 369 (Harvard).

McMannus, J.P. (1972), "The theory of the multinational firm", in: G. Pacquet, ed., The multinational firm and the nation state (Collier-MacMillan, Ontario).

Meade, J.E. (1951), The balance of payments (Oxford University Press, London).

Meade, J.E. (1955), Trade and welfare (Oxford University Press, London).

Mendelsohn, M.S. (1980), Money on the move (McGraw-Hill, New York).

Mill, J.S. (1971), Principles of political economy, 7th edn., (London).

Mundell, R.A. (1957), "International trade and factor mobility", American Economic Review, 47:321–337.

Ohlin, B. (1929), "The German transfer problem: A discussion", Economic Journal, 39:172–173.

Piore, M.H. (1979), Birds of passage: Migrant labor and industrial societies (Cambridge University Press, London).

Purvis, D.D. (1972), "Technology, trade and factor mobility", Economic Journal, 82:991–999.

Ramaswami, V.K. (1968), "International factor movements and the national advantage", Economica, 35:309–310.

Ruffin, R.J. (1979), "Growth and the long-run theory of international capital movements", American Economic Review, 69:832–842.

Ruffin, R.J. (1980), "Taxing international capital movements in a growing world", Seminar Paper No. 165 (Institute for International Economic Studies, Stockholm).

Ruffin, R.J. (1981), "Trade and factor movements with three factors and two goods", Economics Letters, 7:177–182.

Rybczynski, T.N. (1955), "Factor endowment and relative commodity prices", Economica, 22:336–341.

Samuelson, P.A. (1949), "International factor price equalization once again", Economic Journal, 59:181–197.

Samuelson, P.A. (1952), "The transfer problem & transfer costs", Economic Journal, 62:278–304.

Samuelson, P.A. (1953), "The prices of factors and goods in general equilibrium", Review of Economic Studies, 21:1–20.

Samuelson, P.A. (1971), "Ohlin was right", Swedish Journal of Economics, 73:365–384.

Scholl, R.B. (1981), "The international investment position of the United States: Developments in 1980", Survey of Current Business, 61 (8):52–57.

Thomas, B. (1954), Migration and economic growth: A study of Great Britain and the Atlantic economy (Cambridge University Press, Cambridge).

Whichard, O.G. (1981), "U.S. direct investment abroad in 1980", Survey of Current Business, 61 (8):20–39.

Yeager, L.B. (1976), International monetary relations: Theory, history, and policy, 2nd edn. (Harper & Row, New York).

Chapter 6

CAPITAL THEORY AND TRADE THEORY

ALASDAIR SMITH*

University of Sussex

Contents

1. Introduction   290
2. A general intertemporal model of production and trade   290
    2.1. Comparative statics and comparative dynamics   290
    2.2. The intertemporal welfare economics of trade   293
3. Capital and growth in non-steady-state models   297
    3.1. The Heckscher–Ohlin–Samuelson model   297
    3.2. Trade in capital assets   307
    3.3. Two-period models   309
    3.4. A footnote   310
4. Steady-state models with many capital goods   311
    4.1. Comparative dynamics of prices   311
    4.2. Comparative dynamics of quantities   316
    4.3. An alternative theory of trade?   318
5. Conclusion   320
References   321

*I am grateful for comments on earlier drafts from Stan Metcalfe and Ian Steedman, and from Ronald Findlay, John Pomery, Avinash Dixit, and other participants in the Princeton Conference.

Handbook of International Economics, vol. I, Edited by R.W. Jones and P.B. Kenen
© *Elsevier Science Publishers B.V., 1984*

1. Introduction

Twenty years ago, Bhagwati (1964) in a major survey of the theory of international trade reported that "dynamic trade theory still calls for further, systematic analysis and synthesis", and noted "the negligible dent made so far by intermediate and capital goods in the theoretical models employed by analysts of international trade". The purpose of this chapter is to survey the progress that has now been made in incorporating capital goods into trade theory, and such a survey inevitably leads us to look at part of the literature on dynamic models of trade and growth, though a fuller survey of that area is found in Chapter 4.

We start with a very general treatment of capital in Section 2. Within this model it is possible to develop a treatment of welfare economics which broadly follows the well-known static theory of the gains from trade, although with some important features peculiar to intertemporal theory. Few positive-economic results are obtainable within such a general model and Sections 3 and 4 of the chapter pursue two alternative ways of simplifying the general model so as to obtain useful results: reducing the number of goods, factors and time-periods in the model, or considering only steady states.

As we look at various special models we see the importance of such details as the number of primary inputs, the number of capital goods, and whether some goods are non-traded. Economic theorists should be unsurprised by the observation that results depend on assumptions, or by the idea that whether a particular theory is interesting generally depends on the problem in hand. We should therefore be wary of jumping excitedly to the conclusion that the introduction of capital destroys the main body of orthodox trade theory, just because one or two particular models have come up with unorthodox results. Equally, results in particular cases which turn out to be similar to the standard results in models without capital may not be sufficient to show that capital makes no difference. Finally, let us be wary of steady-state analysis: when a comparative dynamic result in steady state is formally very similar to a comparative static result in a timeless model it is tempting to give the former result the same title as the latter, but such terminology may sometimes be misleading.

2. A general intertemporal model of production and trade

2.1. Comparative statics and comparative dynamics

Let us start with a very general intertemporal linear production model with perfect competition and constant returns to scale.

There are m linear activities, n produced goods and p non-produced primary inputs. The jth activity takes the vector a_j of goods and the vector c_j of primary inputs at time $t-1$ and produces at time t the vector b_j of goods. The $n \times m$ matrix whose columns are a_j is denoted A, B is the $n \times m$ matrix with columns b_j, and C is the $p \times m$ matrix whose columns are c_j, where in each case $j = 1, \ldots, m$. The matrices A, B and C are non-negative. The vector of activity levels of processes operating from $t-1$ to t is x_t, the vector of goods available for consumption or trade at time t is y_t, and z_t is the vector of primary inputs available for use from $t-1$ to t. Thus:

$$Bx_t \geq Ax_{t+1} + y_t, \tag{2.1}$$

$$z_t \geq Cx_t. \tag{2.2}$$

Let p_t be the vector of goods prices and w_t the vector of primary input prices, each at time t, and each relative to a numeraire at time 0. This choice of numeraire means that all prices are measured as present values with respect to time 0. [There is an extended discussion of present-value prices in Bliss (1975, ch. 3).] Suppose primary inputs are paid at the end of the production period. Competitive pricing with perfect foresight requires that no production process make a positive profit, so

$$p_t B \leq p_{t-1} A + w_t C. \tag{2.3}$$

It is also required in competitive equilibrium that goods or inputs in excess supply have zero prices, while production processes which make losses are not operated: this complementary slackness of (2.1) with p_t, (2.2) with w_t and (2.3) with x_t implies that

$$p_t B x_t = p_t A x_{t+1} + p_t y_t, \tag{2.4}$$

$$w_t z_t = w_t C x_t, \tag{2.5}$$

$$p_t B x_t = p_{t-1} A x_t + w_t C x_t, \tag{2.6}$$

so that

$$p_t y_t = (p_{t-1} A x_t - p_t A x_{t+1}) + w_t z_t. \tag{2.7}$$

The capital stock used from $t-1$ to t is Ax_t. The goods available at t for consumption in a closed economy are y_t, so $p_t y_t$ is the value of consumption. In an open economy in which some goods can be traded at the prices p_t, the goods consumed need not be y_t; but, if there is no international borrowing or lending, trade must balance each period and the value of consumption must still be equal to $p_t y_t$. In either case, (2.7) simply expresses the fact that consumption is income less gross investment.

Most models of production involving capital are special cases of this general model, although some technical amendments are required if there is smooth substitutability of techniques in production, for that implies the existence of an infinity of potential techniques.

For example, the version of the standard two-by-two Heckscher–Ohlin–Samuelson model which is discussed in detail below (Section 3.1) has labour as the only primary input, one perfectly durable capital good, and one pure consumption good, and the techniques *in use* at any one time are described by the matrices:

$$A = \begin{pmatrix} a_{KI} & a_{KC} \\ 0 & 0 \end{pmatrix}, \qquad B = \begin{pmatrix} 1 + a_{KI} & a_{KC} \\ 0 & 1 \end{pmatrix}, \qquad C = (a_{LI} \quad a_{LC}).$$

Formally, the general model is a competitive production system involving nT goods and pT primary inputs, where T is the number of time periods under consideration and could be countably infinite. In such a model there are essentially only two general comparative static results: an increase in one p_{it} with all other p_{jt} and all z_t constant will raise y_{it}; and an increase in one z_{kt} with all p_t and all other z_{jt} constant will reduce w_{kt}. The ceteris paribus qualifications make these results uninteresting in the present context. In addition, there are the various reciprocity results: the effect on y_{jt} of a ceteris paribus increase in $p_{i\tau}$ is the same as the effect on $y_{i\tau}$ of a ceteris paribus increase in p_{jt}, the effect on w_{kt} of an increase in $p_{i\tau}$ is the same as the effect on $y_{i\tau}$ of an increase in z_{kt}, and so on; but these results too are of no great interest.

To obtain interesting results we depart from generality in two respects. First, we can make special assumptions about the size and structure of the A, B and C matrices, and about the number of time periods in the model. The literature on higher-dimensional trade theory (see Chapter 3) should make one cautious of expecting too much out of this approach, since it seems to imply that only the very simplest models give definite results, but we shall see below that there are some intertemporal models which are both simple and useful.

The second possibility is to consider only an economy that is on a steady-state growth path; and seek comparative dynamic rather than comparative static results. On a steady growth path, all quantities grow at the constant rate g: $x_t = x(1 + g)^t$, $y_t = y(1 + g)^t$, $z_t = z(1 + g)^t$. Note what a strong assumption this is if there is more than one primary input. Future goods prices are related to current prices by a single interest rate applicable to all goods and all time periods: $p_{t-1} = (1 + r)p_t$. Although the latter assumption may superficially seem more acceptable than the former, it really is no less restrictive for it is hard to see how prices could have the constant interest rate property unless all quantities have a common growth rate. With these assumptions, eqs. (2.1)–(2.7) become:

$$Bx \geq (1+g)Ax + y, \tag{2.8}$$

$$z \geq Cx, \tag{2.9}$$

$$pB \leq (1+r)pA + wC, \tag{2.10}$$

$$pBx = (1+g)pAx + py, \tag{2.11}$$

$$wz = wCx, \tag{2.12}$$

$$pBx = (1+r)pAx + wCx, \tag{2.13}$$

$$py = (r-g)pAx + wz. \tag{2.14}$$

The analysis of chapter 4 of Bliss (1975) should make one pessimistic about the prospects of obtaining even steady-state results in a fully general production structure: the only result which holds in general is the "golden rule" result, that a path on which $r = g$ provides more consumption than any other path. (In a many-consumption good model, the consumption vector y_1 gives "more consumption" than the vector y_2 if $p_1 y_1 \geq p_1 y_2$, where the price vector p_1 is the set of prices associated with the consumption vector y_1.) Thus it should be no surprise to find that much of the literature on capital and trade departs from generality in restricting the production structure as well as confining attention to steady states.

2.2. The intertemporal welfare economics of trade

Even a fairly casual comparison of writings on positive trade theory with those on the welfare economics of trade, for example Chapters 1 and 2 of this volume, will reveal that in discussions of welfare theory the detailed specifications of models are of much less concern than in positive theory. Thus we can study the welfare economics of trade involving capital in the very general model introduced in the previous section, without having to make the sort of restrictive assumptions discussed at the end of that section. In particular, note that the economy is not assumed to be in steady state.

Suppose that an economy described by (2.1)–(2.7) is following an autarkic path up until time 0, but then switches to a path on which there is free trade. Let a variable on the autarky path be superscripted a, while a variable on the free trade path is not superscripted. The matrices A, B and C are common to both paths, since they describe the technology. We compare the welfare attainable on the free trade path with that which would have been attained on the autarky path.

The activities x_0^a of the time period ending at time 0 produce the vector of goods Bx_0^a. In the next period there is free trade, the activity levels are x_1, and the vector Ax_1 is required as inputs. The free trade prices p_0 are the competitive prices at time 0 so the value of consumption is:

$$p_0 y_0 = p_0 B x_0^a - p_0 A x_1. \tag{2.15}$$

In subsequent periods (2.7) holds, so the value of total consumption from 0 to T is:

$$C_T = \sum_{t=0}^{T} p_t y_t = p_0 B x_0^a - p_T A x_{T+1} + \sum_{t=1}^{T} w_t z_t. \tag{2.16}$$

Now consider the value of consumption that would have been obtained had the economy remained on the autarky path, with the same primary inputs being supplied. *The free-trade prices are used in making this valuation.* Noting that complementary slackness of (2.1)–(2.3) with p_t, w_t and x_t does not hold when the prices refer to one path and the quantities to the other, we obtain:

$$p_0 y_0^a \leq p_0 B x_0^a - p_0 A x_1^a, \tag{2.17}$$

and, for $t = 1, \ldots T$:

$$p_t y_t^a \leq p_{t-1} A x_t^a - p_t A x_{t+1}^a + w_t z_t, \tag{2.18}$$

so that the value at free-trade prices of consumption on the autarky path from 0 to T is:

$$C_T^a = \sum_{t=0}^{T} p_t y_t^a \leq p_0 B x_0^a - p_T A x_{T+1}^a + \sum_{t=1}^{T} w_t z_t. \tag{2.19}$$

From (2.16) and (2.19) it follows that:

$$C_T - C_T^a \geq - p_T A (x_{T+1} - x_{T+1}^a). \tag{2.20}$$

Since in this argument (2.3) is not used at time 0, it is immaterial whether or not the switch from autarky to free trade was foreseen in the preceding time period.

Two results now follow from (2.20).

(1) If both the free trade path and the autarky path converge to a steady state in which all quantities grow at the rate g, and if the trade steady state prices have constant interest rate r, with $r > g$, then as $T \to \infty$, $x_{T+1} - x_{T+1}^a$ tends towards steady growth at the rate g while p_T tends towards steady decline at the rate r, and the right-hand side of (2.20) tends to zero, so that in the obvious notation:

$$C_\infty - C_\infty^a \geq 0. \tag{2.21}$$

2) If at some time T, free trade is abandoned and the economy rejoins the autarky path with which free trade is being compared, then $Ax_{T+1} = Ax^a_{T+1}$ and (2.20) implies that:

$$C_T - C^a_T \geqq 0. \tag{2.22}$$

These two results are very closely related to two results proved by Bliss (1975, ch. 10). It will be clear to a careful reader of Bliss's discussion why the first result cannot be extended to the case of a steady state with $r = g$. In the context of a gains from trade discussion the second result is a powerful one; for to establish the inefficiency of autarky it is sufficient to show that a temporary shift to free trade is welfare increasing.

The technical source of the inequalities in (2.20)–(2.22) is the fact that the value of net production in one competitive equilibrium is higher than the value of net production at another equilibrium if the prices of the first equilibrium are used in the valuation. The application of the inequalities to the valuation of consumption then follows from the first equilibrium being one of free trade so that the value of consumption is equal to the value of net production, while at the second, autarkic, equilibrium the consumption and net production vectors are the same.

All of this is strictly analogous to the development of the gains from trade argument in the simplest static model. The rest of the argument proceeds along standard lines too. If the economy is treated as if there were one consumer, then on revealed preference grounds the inequalities (2.21) or (2.22) establish the welfare superiority of free trade to autarky. If there are different individuals with distinct endowments and preferences, we have to assume the existence of sufficiently powerful redistributive tools, which need not include lump-sum taxation, to establish the Pareto superiority of free trade to autarky. It is obvious that the inequalities above imply that autarky cannot be Pareto superior to free trade. The details of the type of arguments required are in Dixit and Norman (1980, ch. 3). We conclude that with lump-sum redistribution, or with a complete set of commodity and factor taxes, (1) a path that permanently shifts to free trade and converges to steady state with $r > g$ can be made Pareto superior to an autarky path with the same starting point; and (2) a path that temporarily shifts to free trade but later reverts to autarky can be made Pareto superior to an autarky path that has the same starting point and that coincides with it after the reversion to autarky.

The discussion above is a modification of the discussion in Smith (1979) and an elaboration of the argument of Samuelson (1975, sections 4, 5). Clearly it could be developed further, to encompass comparisons involving trade restricted by taxes and tariffs in strict analogy to the static cases discussed in Ohyama (1972), Dixit and Norman (1980, ch. 3) and Smith (1982), for example, but it seems unlikely that new theoretical insights or difficulties would emerge in such an extension.

Allowing international capital flows makes for some extra complications. Consider a path on which there is free trade in goods and on which international capital flows start at time 0. Prices and quantities on this path are superscripted b, and the present value at time 0 of the net foreign assets held by the country at time t is S_t. The value of consumption at time t is now not $p_t^b y_t^b$ but $p_t^b c_t^b = p_t^b y_t^b + S_t - S_{t+1}$, where c_t^b denotes the vector of goods consumed at time t. Analogously to (2.16) we have:

$$C_T^b = \sum_{t=0}^T p_t^b c_t^b$$

$$= p_0^b B x_0 - p_T^b A x_{T+1}^b - S_{T+1} + \sum_{t=1}^T w_t^b z_t. \tag{2.23}$$

The value at the prices p_t^b of the consumption vectors c_t on the path with free trade in goods but portfolio autarky is:

$$C_T^c = \sum_{t=0}^T p_t^b c_t$$

$$\leqq p_0^b B x_0 - p_T^b A x_{T+1} + \sum_{t=1}^T w_t^b z_t + \sum_{t=0}^T p_t^b (c_t - y_t), \tag{2.24}$$

so that, using the fact that with portfolio autarky $p_t c_t = p_t y_t$:

$$C_T^b - C_T^c \geqq - p_T^b A \left(x_{T+1}^b - x_{T+1} \right) - S_{T+1}$$

$$+ \sum_{t=0}^T \left(p_t - p_t^b \right) (c_t - y_t). \tag{2.25}$$

If, at some time T, the economy reverts to portfolio autarky, then $x_{T+1}^b = x_{T+1}$ and $S_{T+1} = 0$ and the first two terms on the right-hand side of (2.25) are zero. Alternatively, if we consider a path which converges to a steady state with $r > g$, these first two terms tend to zero as $T \to \infty$, for S_T is the present value of cumulative future trade deficits. But to establish the welfare superiority of international capital mobility to portfolio autarky it is necessary to assume in each case that the final term is non-negative: that is, that the terms of trade in goods have not deteriorated as the scope of trade has been widened to encompass capital assets. A move to free trade is a special kind of terms-of-trade improvement; the opening up of new forms of trade when some trade already exists is, in the absence of optimal trade (and investment) taxes, an unambiguous terms-of-trade improvement only if the terms of the existing trade do not deteriorate. [I owe this observation, and the consequent correction of the argument in Smith (1979) to Avinash Dixit.]

The fact that the technological specification of the model discussed here is very general should direct attention to the fact that it is the behavioural assumptions of perfect competition and perfect foresight which are critical to our results. If one wished to make an argument for the non-optimality of trade in an intertemporal model, surely agents' uncertainty and incorrect expectations about the future are the obvious lines to pursue, extending the sort of arguments discussed in Chapter 9 into an intertemporal context. That writers on trade theory and capital theory have not generally taken this path seems to be a consequence of over-concentration, indeed, in a welfare context, quite unnecessary concentration, on steady states, for it is only in steady state that perfect foresight and absence of uncertainty become plausible. In steady state discussions of intertemporal economics [Mainwaring (1979) and Steedman (1979a, pp. 8–9) for example] there is a tendency to emphasise technological assumptions at the expense of behavioural assumptions.

It is also worth directing attention to the assumptions about redistributive taxation that are needed when we take account of differences between individuals. Formally there is no difficulty: if the achievement of Pareto superiority requires a lump sum transfer between groups of individuals who are members of different generations, then the transfer will require the temporary creation of public debt or the temporary public acquisition of assets. Nonetheless, the intertemporal aspect of the problem gives good grounds for scepticism about whether the required redistributions would actually be effected. This is a point worth some further attention in specific models, and we shall return to it below.

3. Capital and growth in non-steady-state models

3.1. The Heckscher–Ohlin–Samuelson model

The standard two-sector Heckscher–Ohlin–Samuelson (HOS) model is a natural starting point for an exploration of specific models of capital and trade, if only because of the frequency with which it is asserted in the literature that this model provides an inadequate or inappropriate treatment of capital.

In the relevant version of the HOS model there are two factors, homogeneous labour and homogeneous capital. Each factor is perfectly mobile intersectorally. This model has come under fire on the one hand on the grounds that perfect intersectoral mobility of capital is an indefensible assumption, at least in the short-run, and this criticism has led to more attention being given to models with sector-specific factors. If, however, we are to think of the HOS model as being a model of the medium to long run, and maintain the usual assumption that factor supplies are exogenous, we run into the difficulty that, as Neary (1978, p. 507) puts it,

> medium-run resource reallocation does not for the most part take the form of a diversion of physical capital equipment from one use to another, with the total stock of homogeneous, infinitely long-lived machines remaining constant throughout. Rather it appears frequently to take the form of a slowing down in the rate of replacement of depreciating capital goods in the declining sector, coinciding with a rechannelling of new investment towards the expanding sector. Once it is recognised that investment requires abstinence from consumption, it is clear that except under very strong assumptions, this process will lead to a change in the total capital stock between the old and the new long-run equilibria.

Essentially the same point is made by Steedman (1979a, pp. 4–5; 1979b, pp. 4–5) who argues that the essential feature of capital is "that it consists of, or at the very least is embodied in, *produced* means of production" and doubts that this is well-represented by the "capital" found in many HOS analyses which is "simply given in quantity, even in long-run equilibrium...an apparently homogeneous, malleable productive input".

One response to these criticisms of the HOS model (though it is not Steedman's response, as we shall see) is simply to introduce into the model an account of saving and investment so that the capital stock becomes an endogenous variable.

Consider then an open economy with a two-output two-input constant-returns production structure in which one output is a pure investment good and the other is a pure consumption good. Output levels of the goods are respectively X_I and X_C while domestic absorption levels are I and C. Let the goods prices be respectively p_I and p_C. With free trade, p_C/p_I is both the domestic and the world relative price. The rental rate on capital is rp_I, where r is the rate of interest. Supplies of capital and labor are K and L respectively. For simplicity, assume there is no depreciation. The relation between this model and the general model of the previous section is brought out by explicit indication of time in the statement of the equilibrium relations of the model.

Competitive pricing requires that

$$p_I(t) \leqq r(t)p_I(t)a_{KI}(t) + w(t)a_{LI}(t), \tag{3.1}$$

$$p_C(t) \leqq r(t)p_I(t)a_{KC}(t) + w(t)a_{LC}(t), \tag{3.2}$$

with equality in (3.1) and (3.2) respectively if $X_I(t) > 0$ or $X_C(t) > 0$, and where $a_{MN}(t)$ is the amount of input M used in the production of one unit of X_N in time period t. These inequalities correspond to the inequalities (2.3) of the general model. It should be observed that, since there is only one capital good, no loss of generality is involved in the use of the single own interest rate $r(t)$, for it can be regarded as being defined by $r(t)p_I(t) = p_I(t-1) - p_I(t)$. If we divide both inequalities by $p_I(t)$ to obtain two inequalities in $r_t(=r(t))$, $w_t(=w(t)/p_I(t))$ and $p_t(=p_C(t)/p_I(t))$, we have a system which gives a fully general account of the relationships between all relevant relative prices. If, for the sake of clarity, we drop the time variable from (3.1) and (3.2), and assume both goods are produced, then with all prices being relative to p_I, we obtain the equations:

$$1 = ra_{KI} + wa_{LI} \tag{3.1a}$$

$$p = ra_{KC} + wa_{LC}. \tag{3.2a}$$

The version of the Stolper–Samuelson theorem thus derivable has two slightly different interpretations: it can be used to describe the relationship at any point in time between a hypothetical change in p_t and the consequent changes in w_t and r_t; or it can be used to describe how w_t and r_t change over time, if the time path of p_t is known. It should be noted that the actual derivation of the theorem is identical to the derivation in the standard static model in which inputs and outputs are separate goods. For a detailed derivation see Caves and Jones (1981, pp. 512–514) and for further discussion see Chapter 1, Section 2.3 of this volume.

Full employment of inputs means that:

$$K(t) = a_{KI}(t)X_I(t) + a_{KC}(t)X_C(t), \tag{3.3}$$

$$L(t) = a_{LI}(t)X_I(t) + a_{LC}(t)X_C(t) \tag{3.4}$$

(if we ignore the possibility of an input being a free good in excess supply). These equations correspond to the inequalities (2.1) and (2.2) of the general model. The rest of the analysis of the model follows precisely the familiar lines: the Rybczynski theorem can be derived from (3.3) and (3.4) for comparisons involving a fixed wage rental ratio w_t/r_t; and for two countries satisfying the standard assumptions about "tastes" and technology, one can establish the Heckscher–Ohlin and factor price equalisation theorems.

All of this is a perfectly natural extension of the standard model, in which the characteristics of the trading equilibrium *at each point in time* are determined by the factor endowments of the respective economies. The only new twist to the story arose in the pricing equations where the price of the investment good appeared on both sides of the equations, but this complication was easily dealt with by judicious choice of numeraire.

The next step is to give a systematic account of how the economy (or economies) evolve over time, and for this we need an hypothesis about saving, to explain the evolution of the capital stock. (We need, too, an hypothesis about labour supply, but steady growth at an exogenously fixed rate seems to be the standard assumption). Most of the writers on the theory of trade and growth, starting with Oniki and Uzawa (1965) and including, for example, Johnson (1971) and Deardorff (1973), have adopted the hypothesis that saving is a fixed fraction of income. The "classical" hypothesis that saving is a fixed fraction of profits is technically easier to work with, and is adopted, for example, by Stiglitz (1970). ("Profits" being, of course, the income rK accruing to capital owners. With competitive pricing and constant returns there are no disequilibrium profits.) A closely-related and interesting alternative investigated by Stiglitz (1970) and Srinivasan and Bhagwati (1980) is to suppose that saving is determined by the optimisation of an intertemporal social welfare function. A further possibility [see Fried (1980) and the references in the next subsection] is that saving behaviour is determined by individual optimisation in a Samuelson–Diamond overlapping-generations model.

Consider the simplest case: a small open economy in which saving and, therefore, investment is a fixed fraction s of profit income. The evolution of the capital stock is described by:

$$dK/dt = srK, \tag{3.5}$$

so that the capital–labour ratio $k = K/L$ satisfies:

$$dk/dt = (sr - n)k, \tag{3.6}$$

where n is the steady growth rate of the labor force L. In steady state $sr = n$. Suppose that the consumption good is capital-intensive, so that, with incomplete specialisation, p is a decreasing function of ω, the wage–rental ratio, as shown in Figure 3.1. [The assumption that the consumption good is capital-intensive is convenient because it ensures that in autarky the economy has a unique momentary equilibrium – see, for example, Burmeister and Dobell (1970, ch. 4).] Let the economy start in an autarkic steady state with $r_0 = n/s$. The world relative price is fixed at p_1, independently of this country's behaviour and of time. If $p_1 > p_0$, where p_0 is the autarkic steady state price, then when trade opens up, the country has a comparative advantage in the capital-intensive consumption good, and instantly factors will be moved from the investment to the consumption goods sector. The price differential shown in Figure 3.1 is insufficient to induce complete specialisation. However, the rise in the profit rate, say to r_1, raises per-worker profits to $r_1 k_0 > r_0 k_0$. Since the autarky equilibrium was a steady state in which savings per worker $s r_0 k_0$ equalled the investment $n k_0$ necessary to keep the capital–labour ratio constant, we now have $s r_1 k_0 > n k_0$ and the capital–labour ratio rises. As k rises above k_0 the economy eventually becomes completely specialised in consumption goods, and r then begins to fall, but k continues to grow until r falls to r_0. Let $a_{KC}(1)$, $a_{LC}(1)$, and w_1 be the input coefficients and wage rate corresponding to the specialised equilibrium when $r = r_0$; while $a_{KC}(0)$, $a_{LC}(0)$ and w_0 correspond to the initial autarky equilibrium. Since $r_0 a_{KC}(0) + w_0 a_{LC}(0) = p_0 < p_1 = r_0 a_{KC}(1) + w_1 a_{LC}(1)$, it follows that $w_1 > w_0$. Hence the restoration of the profit rate to r_0 does not restore the original wage–rental ratio. The wage–rental ratio will in fact be greater than ω_0 and is shown as ω_2 in Figure 3.1.

The path of the economy over time is indicated by the arrowed line in the top half of Figure 3.1: the economy starts at the autarky steady state A, jumps to B on the opening up of trade, accumulates capital and becomes completely specialised at C, and finally attains the trade steady state at D.

If the initial comparative advantage were in the opposite direction the time path of the economy would be as shown in Figure 3.2. Essentially the process described above is reversed: capital accumulation is less than labour force growth so the capital–labor ratio falls and there is specialisation, eventually complete specialisation, in the labour-intensive investment good. In this case, however, the wage–rental ratio returns exactly to ω_0 when r falls to r_0, since in the final steady state the fact that the equation $1 = r_0 a_{KI} + w a_{LI}$ is satisfied implies that $w = w_0$.

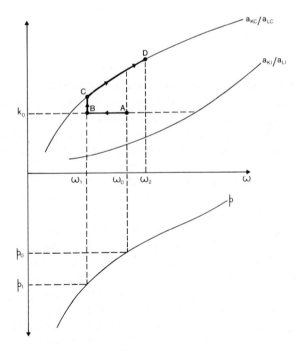

Figure 3.1

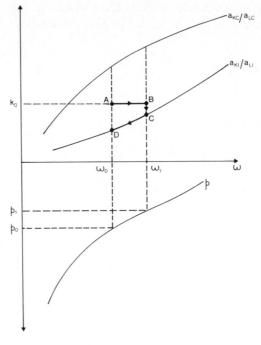

Figure 3.2

If we now add to our model the additional assumption that the rest of the world has the same technology and the same rate of growth of the labour force, then to the standard Heckscher–Ohlin and factor price equalisation theorems which are short-run results we can add a new long-run result: the country accumulates capital and specialises in the capital-intensive good if it has a higher saving propensity than the rest of the world, while it decumulates capital and specialises in the labour-intensive good if its saving propensity is lower than the rest of the world. This is a long-run analogue to the Heckscher–Ohlin theorem. [One could drop the equal growth rates assumption, allow this country to have a lower growth rate than the rest of the world and focus on the steady-state profit rate differential as the determinant of long-run specialisation. See Dixit (1981b, p. 283), however, on why unequal growth rates must be handled with care.]

We have now analysed how the capital stock and factor prices evolve over time as the economy moves from the autarkic steady state to the trade steady state. It is interesting also to look in some detail at what happens to consumption. For this purpose it is helpful to develop an equation which describes the comparative dynamics of consumption across steady states. Let I be the level of investment and C the level of consumption. In an open economy facing world relative price

p, with no trade in capital assets (that is, in the ownership titles to capital goods; capital goods themselves are traded) balance of trade at each moment of time requires that:

$$I + pC = X_I + pX_C \tag{3.7}$$

$$= rK + wL, \tag{3.8}$$

where (3.8) follows from (3.1)–(3.4). Taking differentials gives:

$$p\,dC = r\,dK + w\,dL + K\,dr + L\,dw - dI - C\,dp. \tag{3.9}$$

Applying the envelope theorem of cost minimisation [see Caves and Jones (1981, p. 508)] to (3.1a) and (3.2a) we obtain:

$$0 = a_{KI}\,dr + a_{LI}\,dw, \tag{3.10}$$

$$dp = a_{KC}\,dr + a_{LC}\,dw, \tag{3.11}$$

and together with (3.3) and (3.4), these imply:

$$K\,dr + L\,dw = X_C\,dp, \tag{3.12}$$

so that

$$p\,dC = r\,dK - dI + w\,dL + (X_C - C)\,dp. \tag{3.13}$$

At all times $I = srK$ so $dI = sK\,dr + sr\,dK$ and

$$p\,dC = (1 - s)r\,dK + w\,dL - sK\,dr + (X_C - C)\,dp. \tag{3.14}$$

In steady state, $sr = n$ so in comparing steady states we can use the equation:

$$p\,dC = (r - n)\,dK + w\,dL + (X_C - C)\,dp. \tag{3.15}$$

Now consider what happens, first in the case where $p_1 > p_0$ so the country has comparative advantage in the consumption good. When trade opens up, with given K and L, the rise in p is associated with the country becoming an exporter of the consumption good and with a rise in r. Only the last two terms in (3.14) are non-zero but they are of opposite sign so the impact effect of trade on consumption is ambiguous. To compare the steady states we use (3.15). Since $s \leq 1$, $r > n$, and in a hypothetical shift from the autarky to the free trade steady state at the same point in time we have $(r - n)\,dK \geq 0$, $dL = 0$, and $(X_C - C)\,dp > 0$ so that $dC > 0$. Thus the path of consumption per worker over time is as shown in Figure

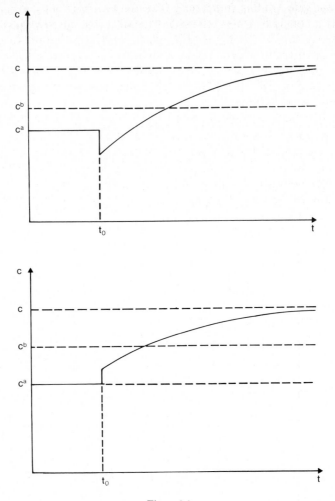

Figure 3.3

3.3(a) or (b), where in each case c^a is the autarky steady state level, c the free trade steady state level, and t_0 the time trade opens up.

The case where $p_1 < p_0$ so the country has comparative advantage in the investment good can be similarly analysed. Now the impact effect is unambiguous, but the steady state effect is ambiguous, because capital decumulation takes place. The outcome is as in Figure 3.4(a) or (b).

The outcome shown in Figure 3.4(a) is the most striking of the four: steady state consumption is lower with free trade than in autarky. The implication for actual consumption on the free trade path is that there exists a time $t_2 > t_0$ such that consumption is lower at all times beyond t_2 than it would have been in autarky. The case shown in Figure 3.3(a) has consumption on the free trade path lower than in autarky for all times up to some t_1. The two cases have in common the feature that consumption is not raised by trade at every point in time. By contrast, in the cases shown in Figures 3.3(b) and 3.4(b), consumption is raised by trade at every point in time.

The steady-state consumption level labelled c^b in Figures 3.3 and 3.4 is attainable instantaneously on the opening up of trade if the economy were to follow the alternative saving policy of keeping the capital stock per worker constant at its autarky steady-state level. That $c^b \geq c^a$ follows at once from (3.14), the difference between c^b and c^a being given by the term $(X_C - C)dp$ and corresponding to the usual static gains from trade. Given that the actual paths

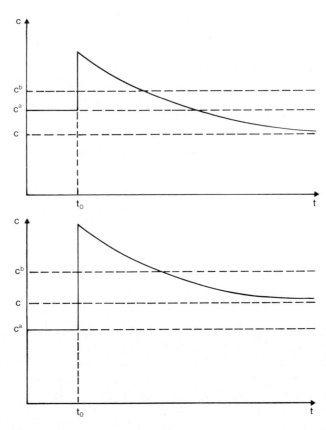

Figure 3.4

shown in Figures 3.3 and 3.4 give consumption levels below c^b for part of the time, it is evident that the cases shown in Figures 3.3(a) and 3.4(a) can arise if $c^b - c^a$ is sufficiently small.

The fact that trade can bring about such striking intertemporal reallocation of consumption is, of course, quite compatible with the general results discussed in Section 2.2. We know that when there are consumption losses at some times on the trade path, the present value of such losses is outweighed by the present values of the gains which exist at other times. Note, in this context, that the case where there were short-run losses and long-run gains [Figure 3.3(a)] was one where the country specialised in the capital-intensive good and thus must have a relatively low interest rate; while the converse case [Figure 3.4(a)] arose when the interest rate was relatively high. An "impatient" country tends to take the gains from trade in the present rather than the future and may even use the opportunity presented by free trade to reallocate consumption from the future to the present; a "patient" country makes the reverse choice.

Thus quite dramatic consumption reallocations consequent on the opening up of trade are entirely compatible with intertemporal accumulation and distribution decisions being optimal. Equally valid, however, is the observation that in the presence of suboptimal intertemporal decision-making such reallocations might be welfare-decreasing so that trade could be welfare-inferior to autarky. This is simply a variant, albeit a particularly interesting variant, of a well-known general second-best principle.

So far in this subsection we have worked with the hypothesis that there is a fixed ratio of savings to profits. The effects of trade in a two-sector model with a fixed ratio of savings to income are most simply analysed by observing [following Stiglitz (1970) and Deardorff (1974)] that the small open two-sector economy is isomorphic to a closed one-sector Solow model in which the per-worker production function has a flat segment. The principal difference between this and the "classical savings" case is that there is no necessity for the steady state to display complete specialisation. As in the "classical savings" case, the standard HOS results can be applied to the analysis of the economy as it moves along a transition path; while in the steady state it is easy to prove the comparative dynamic result that for a given world price ratio p, the higher the saving rate, the higher will be the capital–labour ratio, so the closer will be the economy to specialisation in the capital-intensive good. See Findlay (1970; 1973, ch. 7) for a similar result in a slightly different model. This "long-run Rybczynski theorem" may be generalised to the case of different saving propensities out of wages and profits – see Dixit (1978).

The effects of trade on consumption in both the short and the long run can be analysed too. In the classical savings case we were constrained by the saving propensity being not greater than 1 to consider only cases where $r \geq n$. With savings proportional to income the restriction $r \geq n$ need no longer hold, and when we analyse the effect of capital accumulation on consumption there is, apparently, a richer menu of possibilities. Since, however, a steady state with $r < n$ is dynamically inefficient and since the saving assumption is essentially arbitrary it is unclear that these cases are interesting. See Smith (1977) for details of how these cases can be simply analysed using the techniques employed above.

Further exploration along the lines so far investigated is clearly possible. Fried (1980) analyses the development of a small open economy with life-cycle savings, and this is a class of models whose possibilities have been by no means exhausted; in particular, the question of how compensation could be paid to those generations which lose from trade is one which is best tackled in an overlapping-generations model.

Another possibility would be to graft the short-run analysis of the specific-factors model on to the models analysed above to give a new model with the appealing property of capital being inter-sectorally shiftable only through net investment. Findlay (1973, Chapter 8) discusses a model with this characteristic. Vintage capital models [see Smith (1976) for discussion and references] are another class in which the issue of adjustment costs arises. But our concern here is not to give a comprehensive treatment of the theory of trade and growth, rather to show how simple models of capital accumulation, firmly in the "neoclassical" tradition, can be naturally and unproblematically integrated into the traditional static trade theoretic framework. Thus we have a benchmark against which to judge the contribution of those theories which have adopted alternative approaches.

3.2. Trade in capital assets

Before we consider alternatives to the "neoclassical" model, however, let us consider one development of that model, in which there is trade in titles to the ownership of capital goods. This is a natural development, for once the capital endowment of an economy ceases to be an exogenously fixed quantity it becomes difficult to justify the assumption that ownership of the capital stock may not be internationally transferable. Simply to allow trade in securities in the two-sector model of the previous section runs, however, into the difficulty described by Fischer and Frenkel (1972, p. 213): "if a country can both import securities and import investment goods, then it is a matter of indifference what its capital stock is. Its income will be the same at all times – so long as it is not specialised – whether it acquires income streams from abroad by buying securities or whether it owns physical capital".

However, to study trade in assets we no longer need two goods: a one-sector model is adequate to illustrate some interesting issues. But it is desirable to give a clearer motivation for saving and capital accumulation than is provided by the arbitrarily fixed saving ratio assumptions of the previous subsection. The overlapping generations model of life-cycle saving due to Samuelson (1958) and Diamond (1965) is a more suitable framework in which to look at the issues raised.

Models of this type have been analysed by Gale (1971) [on which see also Green (1972)], Gale (1974), Kareken and Wallace (1977) and Buiter (1981). The detailed specification differs significantly from author to author: the exposition here follows Buiter's model.

Suppose the world consists of two countries, identical in every respect except taste. Each generation lives for two time periods, supplying a fixed amount of work in the first period but not working in the second. The capital stock for the working generation is provided by the savings of the previous generation. The technology is described by the standard competitive one-sector model. A typical member of generation t chooses consumption c_t^1 while young and c_t^2 while old to maximise utility:

$$u = v\left(c_t^1\right) + \left(1+\rho\right)^{-1} v\left(c_t^2\right), \tag{3.16}$$

subject to the budget constraint:

$$w_t - c_t^1 = c_t^2 \left(1 + r_{t+1}\right)^{-1}, \tag{3.17}$$

where the wage rate w_t is determined by the existing capital stock available as this generation works, while this generation's own consumption choices determine the next period's capital stock and the rate of return r_{t+1} on that capital. The autarkic comparative statics results derived by Buiter are: (i) if two economies are identical in all respects except the pure rate of time preference, and both begin from a common initial capital–labour ratio at time $t = t_0$, then the capital–labour ratio of the high-time-preference country will be below that of the low-time-preference country for all $t > t_0$ if second-period consumption is a normal good and if a higher interest rate does not reduce saving; (ii) locally, the country with the higher rate of time preference will have the lower steady-state capital–labour ratio if the model is locally stable, if consumption in both periods is a normal good and if an increased interest rate lowers first-period consumption.

Now let there be international trade in the good and in the capital asset. The interest rate will be equalised internationally, and in consequence the wage rate and the capital stock per worker are equalised also. (Interest rates can be equalised between countries with differing time-preference rates because the first-order condition derived from maximising (3.16) subject to (3.17) is $v'(c_t^1)(1+\rho) = v'(c_t^2)(1 + r_{t+1})$.] The steady state equilibrium of the trading world has the following properties: (i) the country with the higher pure rate of time preference will in steady state have the higher value of first-period consumption and will run a current account deficit; (ii) locally, the common steady-state open-economy capital–labour ratio lies between the two autarky capital–labour ratios if the model is stable under autarky, if consumption in both periods is a normal good and if an increase in the interest rate lowers first period consumption. Property (ii) implies that the steady-state real wage of the capital exporting country is below its autarky real wage and conversely for the capital-importing country. [See Gale (1974) for discussion of why there is nothing necessarily paradoxical about an economy having a permanent imbalance of trade.]

When we look at how the pattern of consumption evolves over time we find remarkable similarities with the conclusions of the previous subsection. There we confined attention to cases where the rate of interest exceeded the growth rate of the economy, and we do the same here. When the existing capital stock cannot be relocated, the high-time-preference country finds the welfare of the younger generation alive in the period when trade opens lowered by the opening of trade, the older generation being unaffected by the change, but the steady state utility level is higher in the trade equilibrium. This is exactly analogous to the pattern shown in Figure 3.3(a). (There is here no ambiguity about the impact effect, so a case analogous to Figure 3.3(b) cannot arise, because there are no static efficiency gains from trade). In the low-time-preference country, the younger generation alive when trade opens up finds its welfare raised, and the effect of trade on steady state utility is ambiguous – two possibilities exactly analogous to those shown in Figure 3.4(a) and (b).

That the impact of trade on the intertemporal allocation of consumption and distribution of welfare is rather similar in the models of this and the previous subsection is a natural consequence of the fact that, in the sense described above by Fischer and Frenkel, trade in goods and trade in securities may be alternative ways of integrating separate economies.

3.3. Two-period models

Models with only two time periods are commonly used for simple expositions of intertemporal economics, and it is perhaps a little surprising that their use in models of international trade is so recent. Consider the very simplest such model: each of two countries has an endowment of a single good in each of two time periods, and that good may not be stored. In autarky, the endowments are consumed. With trade, differences in marginal rates of intertemporal substitution (that is, in time preference rates) will give rise to mutually gainful trading possibilities in the form of international borrowing and lending. In each country, consumption in one of the periods is reduced by trade; and in each period one of the countries has a balance of trade deficit. Consideration of such a simple model may help to clarify the discussion of consumption reallocation through trade in Sections 3.1 and 3.2 above.

The model of Razin (1980) is more complex, though still fairly simple: there is production in each period of both traded and non-traded goods and capital investment can take place, and the impact of various government policies on the intertemporal allocation of resources and the pattern of international payments can be analysed.

Then we have a series of two-period models focused on aspects of contemporary problems arising out of oil price changes; starting with the model of Dixit (1981a) which considers a world with two non-reproducible factors, labour and oil, as well as capital. In the first period in each country there are endowments of labour, capital and oil; while in the second there is a labour endowment, the previous period's capital stock is carried over, augmented by any real investment that has taken place, and the stock of oil is carried over, depleted by first-period use. Various comparative static results are derived, including the possibility that producing countries' income effects may cause a price-inelastic long-run demand for oil despite large elasticities of substitution.

The effects of terms of trade changes in general, or oil price changes in particular, on the balance of trade are analysed in two-period models of various specifications by Sachs (1981), Svensson and Razin (1983), Svensson (1981), Marion and Svensson (1981, 1982). A notable feature of some of this work is the use of the techniques of duality theory.

In short, the desire to analyse various issues arising from the dramatic changes in the real price of oil in the 1970s motivated the development of models a little more complicated in technology than the two-sector workhorse. The maintenance of analytical tractability required a sacrifice of generality elsewhere, whence the restriction to two time periods.

3.4. A footnote

The models considered in this section should give a fair impression of what is possible when we try to dynamise the standard static models of trade theory; but what has been offered is a selection of the most important models rather than an exhaustive inventory. One significant omission is the set of models of Findlay (1973, Parts 1 and 2), where capital accumulation and allocation in open dual economies are considered under the policy objective of maximising growth. Closer in spirit the static HOS model is another omission: the model of Samuelson (1965) and Findlay (1970; 1973, ch. 7) with two traded consumer goods and a non-traded but reproducible capital good. (This model, indeed, has as much claim as the model of Section 3.1 to be called a dynamic HOS model.) However, as we see in the next section, once we try to go much beyond the type of model presented here, we are forced into the confines of steady-state analysis.

4. Steady-state models with many capital goods

4.1. Comparative dynamics of prices

Useful as the models of capital accumulation discussed above are, it cannot be denied that they are rather special and that one can legitimately be sceptical of what they tell us of the real world. Steedman (1979a, p. 6) certainly believes that: "one cannot feel confident that such analyses give much insight into the long-run equilibrium properties of the multi-capital good models which must be developed to deal adequately with real-world problems of trade and accumulation".

However, once more than one capital good is introduced into the model, the derivation of definite results requires us to confine attention to the comparative dynamics of steady state paths. This emerges clearly if we contrast the model of Samuelson (1965) with later models. In Samuelson's model there are two traded consumption goods (indexed 1 and 2) and one non-traded investment good (indexed 0). The motivation for this structure is that it is the simplest in which one can sensibly ask the question Samuelson wishes to answer: whether international equalisation of the rental of a non-traded capital good implies also equalisation of the rate of interest. The capital stock in sector i decays at the rate m_i, so the competitive pricing equations are

$$p_i = (r + m_i) p_0 a_{0i} + w c_{Li}, \qquad i = 0, 1, 2. \tag{4.1}$$

Some fairly simple modifications of the standard argument show that all the p_i depend on w and on the rental $R = r p_0$ in such a way that p_1/p_2, p_0 and r are all monotonic functions of w/R on the standard factor-intensity assumption, giving an affirmative answer to the question.

The equations (4.1) incorporate no restrictive assumptions beyond those required by perfect competition with constant returns to scale and intersectorally mobile capital. In particular, the use of a single rate of interest implies no loss of generality in the intertemporal price system, for the same reason as in equations (3.1) and (3.2). Contrast the models of Acheson (1970), Metcalfe and Steedman (1972; 1973), Steedman and Metcalfe (1977), and Kemp (1973; 1976, ch. 5) in which there are two capital goods. The precise specification differs between authors but all the models differ in one significant respect from the models whose pricing equations are (3.1)–(3.2) or (4.1). Take Kemp's first specification, for example, in which the two capital goods are perfectly durable and serve also as consumption goods and in which there are also two primary inputs. The pricing equations are:

$$p_i = r(p_1 a_{1i} + p_2 a_{2i}) + w_1 c_{1i} + w_2 c_{2i}, \qquad i = 1, 2. \tag{4.2}$$

(in the notation of Section 2, not the original notation). These equations embody the restrictive steady state assumption that the same own rate of interest applies to both goods prices; and this is a genuine restriction because there are two capital goods.

The derivation of a "long-run Stolper–Samuelson theorem" in this model requires one further restriction: that r is constant when other prices change. Now write (4.2) in matrix notation as:

$$p = rpA + wC, \tag{4.3}$$

and take differentials with r constant, using "envelope" equations to eliminate the effects of input coefficient changes, to give:

$$dp = rd pA + dwC. \tag{4.4}$$

Now (4.3) can be rewritten:

$$p = wC(I - rA)^{-1}, \tag{4.5}$$

and if p is to be non-negative, we require the Hawkins–Simon condition that $(I - rA)^{-1}$ be a non-negative matrix. Eq. (4.4) can be rewritten:

$$dp = dwC(I - rA)^{-1}. \tag{4.6}$$

In the standard static model (4.5) and (4.6) hold with I replacing $(I - rA)^{-1}$ and the Stolper–Samuelson theorem is derived by showing that p_1/p_2 is increasing or decreasing with w_1/w_2 according as the determinant of C is positive or negative, and the determinant of C has the sign of $(c_{11}/c_{21}) - (c_{12}/c_{22})$. In the present case, therefore, p_1/p_2 increases or decreases with w_1/w_2 (in the standard "magnified" way) according as the determinant of $C(I - rA)^{-1}$ is positive or negative. But since $(I - rA)^{-1}$ is a positive matrix, its determinant is necessarily positive so the determinant of $C(I - rA)^{-1}$ has the same sign as the determinant of C and the "long-run" Stolper–Samuelson theorem depends on *exactly* the same conditions as the standard static Stolper–Samuelson theorem.

If we drop one of the primary factors we can drop the assumption that r is constant. Eq. (4.2) becomes:

$$p_i = r(p_1 a_{1i} + p_2 a_{2i}) + w c_i, \tag{4.7}$$

or, in matrix notation:

$$p = rpA + wc. \tag{4.8}$$

Taking differentials and using envelope equations gives:

$$dp = rd\,pA + dr\,pA + dw\,c, \tag{4.9}$$

which can be written as:

$$dp(I - rA) = d\omega C, \tag{4.10}$$

where $d\omega$ is the vector $(dr\ dw)$ and C is now a matrix of "input coefficients" which has pA in its first row and c in its second row. Since $(I - rA)^{-1}$ must be a positive matrix for (4.8) to give positive prices, we can derive a second "long-run Stolper–Samuelson theorem" where the direction of the relationship between p_1/p_2 and w/r depends on the sign of the determinant of C, that is, on the relative factor intensity of the two activities. This, however, is not quite as satisfactory as a result as the static theorem or the previous long-run result, for the factor intensities are not derived solely from physical input coefficients (which in general are functions of factor prices) but also depend on the commodity price vector p which enters into the evaluation of capital intensity. [See the exchange between Metcalfe and Steedman (1981), and Ethier (1979, 1981) on this issue.]

Alternative assumptions about capital deterioration make no real difference to the analysis. Generalisation to greater numbers of goods and of primary inputs raises all the difficulties of generalising the static theorem, and some more too. [See Uekawa et al. (1973).] Indeed the close correspondence between the static and the long-run comparative dynamic analyses makes it clear that significant generalisation beyond the types of models already considered is unlikely to be productive of further simple results.

Thus it is no surprise to find a non-monotonic relationship between the relative price of the two final goods and the ratio of the wage to the interest rate in the model of Metcalfe and Steedman (1973) for that model has two (non-traded) capital goods. Bliss (1973), in commenting on Metcalfe and Steedman (1973), points out that it is Wicksell effects – the effect of interest rate changes on the prices of capital goods – which are the source of the non-monotonicity of the relationship between the relative price of the two traded consumption goods and the ratio of the wage to the interest rate.

Commentators on the "neo-Ricardian" models of Steedman and his associates have persistently raised the question of the extent to which their results are due to the existence of many *capital* goods in their model or are simply standard many-goods problems. It is as well, therefore, to make it clear that the non-monotonicity in Metcalfe and Steedman (1973) does arise because the intermediate goods are capital goods attracting interest payments. For consider a static model involving non-traded intermediate goods, with pricing equations:

$$p = \pi A_1 + w C_1, \tag{4.11}$$
$$\pi = \pi A_2 + w C_2, \tag{4.12}$$

where p, π and w are the prices of final goods, intermediate goods, and primary factors respectively. If A_2 is square and $I - A_2$ is non-singular, we can write:

$$p = w \left[C_2 (I - A_2)^{-1} A_1 + C_1 \right]. \tag{4.13}$$

Price changes satisfy (4.11) and (4.12) with dp, $d\pi$ and dw replacing p, π and w respectively, so:

$$dp = dw \left[C_2 (I - A_2)^{-1} A_1 + C_1 \right], \tag{4.14}$$

and the price relationship therefore depends on the *total* input coefficient matrix $C_1 (I - A_2)^{-1} A_1 + C_1$, which, as Bliss observes, may display different factor intensity relations to the direct input coefficient matrix C_1. Metcalfe and Steedman's fig. 4.2, however, makes it clear that in their model the price relationship is non-monotonic even though *total* factor intensities display no reversal. Consider, therefore, a model like the previous one except that the intermediate goods are capital goods. The steady-state price equations are:

$$p = (1 + r) \pi A_1 + w C_1, \tag{4.15}$$
$$\pi = (1 + r) \pi A_2 + w C_2, \tag{4.16}$$

so

$$p = w \left[(1 + r) C_2 (I - (1 + r) A_2)^{-1} A_1 + C_1 \right], \tag{4.17}$$

while the price change equations are:

$$dp = dr \pi A_1 + (1 + r) d\pi A_1 + dw C_1, \tag{4.18}$$
$$d\pi = dr \pi A_2 + (1 + r) d\pi A_2 + dw C_2, \tag{4.19}$$

so that:

$$dp = dw \left[(1 + r) C_2 (I - (1 + r) A_2)^{-1} A_1 + C_1 \right]$$
$$+ dr w C_2 (I - (1 + r) A_2)^{-2} A_1, \tag{4.20}$$

and there is no simple relationship between (4.20) and (4.17) like that between (4.14) and (4.13) or even between (4.10) and (4.8). Thus even if there is only one primary factor and if relative factor intensity is unambiguously defined, the Stolper–Samuelson theorem need not hold. [See Sanyal (1980) for an alternative analysis of this issue in a rather less general model.]

The other major theorem concerning the relationship between commodity prices and factor prices is the factor price equalisation theorem. In the static two-by-two model, it is natural to approach the factor price equalisation problem via the Stolper–Samuelson theorem. In a more general setting, however, the univalence of the price mapping which is required for factor price equalisation is a weaker requirement than some versions of the Stolper–Samuelson theorem [see Chipman (1969), Uekawa (1971), and Chapter 3 of this volume] and it is natural to tackle the factor price equalisation problem directly. Relevant literature is Bliss (1973), Steedman and Metcalfe (1973), Samuelson (1975, 1978a), Mainwaring (1976, 1978), Burmeister (1978), Ethier (1979) and Dixit (1981b). Some of the discussion is quite technical. One would do well to start with Dixit (1981b), where we are given a clear account of the central problems, an indication of the issues which still have to be settled, and a caution about whether this is an area where further research is worthwhile.

Finally, there are some models which have departed significantly from the HOS paradigm, but which are not really classifiable simply as multi-capital good models either. Their structure, though specific, is sufficiently complex to require steady state analysis, and their most interesting results concern price relations, so this is the appropriate point to take note of them.

Kenen (1965, 1968) retains the notion of capital as a single good, but does not have that capital good enter directly into the production function like any other factor. Rather, capital is applied to the primitive factors of labour and land in order to make them productive, and then improved labour and land enter the conventional production function. The most striking result derived from this model is the fact that free international trade does not imply interest rate equalisation even when the prices of the improved factors are equalised. Kenen's model seems not to have been productive of further work, perhaps because of its algebraic complexity, though it does find an echo in more recent work on "multi-level trade" discussed in Chapter 1.

Still further from the beaten track we find the "Austrian" models of Brecher and Parker (1977) and Findlay (1978). Here the idea of capital as a good or class of goods is virtually abandoned. Thus in Findlay's model, there is one sector in which labour produces "wood" in a point-input point-output Austrian process. The quantity of "wood" produced per unit of labour increases at a decreasing rate as a function of the time elapsed from the input point. In the other sector, labour and "wood" can be instantaneously combined to produce a consumer good. Both "wood" and the consumer good are traded. In autarky, a more patient country produces in a more time-intensive fashion and has a higher level of consumption. Trade between countries with different time preferences leads the more patient country to move towards specialisation in the more time-intensive production of wood, but, in the familiar way, free trade leads to equalisation of the wage and the interest rate so long as neither country is completely specialised and so long as there are no "time intensity reversals". It is not literally true that there are no capital goods in the model: "immature wood" is an intermediate good and there is a continuum of processes requiring no labour whereby immature wood becomes slightly more mature wood. But this way of looking at the model does it a disservice, by obscuring its essential simplicity and its Austrian "vision".

4.2. Comparative dynamics of quantities

In a static setting the Rybczynski and Stolper–Samuelson theorems are dual. In steady state the price equations with constant r are dual to the quantity equations with constant g. Since we saw above that a long-run Stolper–Samuelson theorem holds under various circumstances, it is no surprise to find that essentially the same argument establishes a steady-state Rybczynski theorem; and then since the static "quantity version" of the Heckscher–Ohlin theorem can be derived directly from the Rybczynski theorem, a steady-state version of that theorem follows too. The details are so easily worked out from the quantity equations of the model of eqs. (4.3)–(4.6) and the final result of so little interest that the derivation is omitted. One can also look at the one-primary-factor model of eqs. (4.8)–(4.10), define the capital endowment of the economy as pAx, and derive the corresponding Rybczynski and Heckscher–Ohlin theorems along the lines of Ethier (1979). These results are less interesting than the corresponding timeless results for the same reason as the price results derived in the same model: they do not relate endogenous variables to exogenous conditions; but they are not wholly devoid of content. See the interchange between Metcalfe and Steedman (1981) and Ethier (1981).

Now we arrive at an interesting contrast between the timeless and the steady state models. The price version of the Heckscher–Ohlin theorem is a very robust result in a static setting, because it is derived from the very general property of a competitive model that supply of a good is an increasing function of its own price. Contrast the rest of the standard results which are sensitive to the dimensionality of the model. But whereas these results have been shown above to have comparative dynamic analogues, the steady-state price-output relation may easily be perverse, as Metcalfe and Steedman (1972) point out. [Kemp and Khang (1974) give some conditions which are sufficient to rule out perversity.]

The fact that the analysis of the steady-state price-output relation when $r > g$ is isomorphic to the analysis of the static price-output relation in the presence of distorting taxes [as is pointed out, for example, in many places in Steedman (1979a) and, in a particularly illuminating way, by Samuelson (1975)] should not mislead us into thinking that an interest rate in excess of the growth rate *is* a distortion or that there is a theoretical presumption that the steady-state price-output response should not be "perverse". The basic point is rather easily seen. Consider the general steady state model described by eqs. (2.8)–(2.14). That model is formally identical to a static model with intermediate goods input matrix $(1 + g)A$ except that the intermediate goods price vector on the right-hand side of (2.10) is $(1 + r)p/(1 + g)$; so it is as if there were taxes on intermediate inputs at the rate $(1 + r)/(1 + g) - 1$. If $r = g$, the system is identical to a perfectly competitive production system and all static results have exact comparative dynamic analogues: in particular, net output of any good is an increasing function of the price of that good. With $r \neq g$, that is no longer so.

When we reduce the number of primary factors to one but allow the interest rate to be variable, then some positive, though rather weak, results appear. Ethier (1979) shows that the price-output response is positive on a transformation curve defined by holding the quantity of labour and the "real value of capital" (in a sense defined by Ethier) constant. The problem with this is that there is simply no reason to suppose that the endowment of "real capital" should be constant across the steady states being considered.

Smith (1976) proves another result: in the general model of eqs. (2.8)–(2.14) but with labour being the only primary factor, two countries with identical technology but different factor prices specialise so that the capital intensity of all the processes in use in the low-interest high-wage country is higher than that of all the processes in use in the other country. [See also Ethier (1979), proposition 7. Sanyal (1980) strengthens the result by showing that factor intensity can be defined independently of prices, but only in a very special model with two goods and fixed coefficients.] This result is subject to the, by now familiar, criticism that, except when the interest rate differential is determined by time preference differences, the result simply associates one endogenous phenomenon with another. Nonetheless, it does serve to make the point that the capital-valuation issues discussed by Metcalfe and Steedman (1973) could not, as they imply, be an explanation of the Leontief paradox. Certainly one could not look at autarkic capital–labour ratios in a world with many capital goods and predict from them the pattern of trade, but that is not what is done in the Leontief type of calculations where all the data necessarily relate to the observed, trading, situation. (Another way to put this point is to say that when the world price vector can be used to value heterogeneous capital goods, one has less cause to worry about the issues raised in the "capital controversy" of the late 1960s.)

4.3. *An alternative theory of trade?*

The models discussed in this section have been presented as a natural extension of the models of Section 3: the limitation to steady states being the price of having many capital goods. However, much of the work in this area has been done, or inspired, by the "neo-Ricardian" theorists whose principal papers are collected in Steedman (1979a), and the neo-Ricardians' objective seems to have been to make a radical revision of, rather than an extension to, the theory of international trade. The introductory essay of Steedman (1979a) regrets the limitations of steady state analysis, but sees virtue in focusing on "the long-period equilibria which give meaning to the concept of comparative advantage". Steedman regards the dynamic HOS models discussed in Section 3 not as providing a complementary approach which may in some applications be the more fruitful, but as providing a quite inadequate treatment of important aspects of production, trade and growth. He is remarkably modest in his claims for what the neo-Ricardians have actually achieved: "a cautious, preliminary attempt...too soon to assess the degree of success" (p. 7), "the alternative approach...is [n]either complete [n]or free from problems" (p. 10); but such modesty should not deter one from posing the question of whether a fundamental revision of trade theory is achieved or promised by this approach.

A further question to be addressed is the relationship between the neo-Ricardian approach and the various Marxist and neo-Marxist theories of trade and imperialism. An excellent, sympathetic but critical, survey of Marxist theories of imperialism is provided by Brewer (1980) who makes it clear (p. 208, for example) that the main body of Marxist theory focuses on issues which are outwith the concerns of this chapter: the development and effects of monopoly, and the expansion of capitalism at the expense of pre-capitalist modes of production. The writings of Arghiri Emmanuel and Samir Amin, however, seem to stand apart from the Marxist mainstream and to express the view that international trade may be inefficient in a capitalistic economy with a positive rate of profit.

Now the precise nature of the propositions being advanced by Emmanuel is unclear, and even sympathetic critics such as Evans (1979) and Brewer (1980) raise serious questions about the coherence and completeness of his theoretical structure, but there can be little ambiguity about the meaning of conclusions such as: "[the] international division of labor based on comparative costs [may] lead, not to a gain, but to a loss for the world as a whole" [Emmanuel (1972, p. 248)]; or "[we] refute the premise that a general and absolute advantage accrues automatically to the world as a whole from free trade and the international division of labor" [Emmanuel (1972, p. 267)]. Emmanuel's analysis has been criticised by Samuelson (1973, 1976), on which see also Emmanuel (1977, 1978) and Samuelson (1978b).

This proposition of Emmanuel's seems to be essentially the same as the proposition advanced by the neo-Ricardians that the level of consumption per head in a free-trade steady state with the profit rate in excess of the growth rate may be less than the level in an autarkic steady state. There is discussion of this proposition in Steedman (1979b, p. 11, and ch. 5) and in Steedman (1979a, chs. 4, 9, 11 and 12) [respectively, Metcalfe and Steedman (1974), Mainwaring (1974), Steedman and Metcalfe (1979) and Mainwaring (1979)].

In Metcalfe and Steedman (1974), the analogy, which we have already discussed in Section 4.1, between a profit rate different from the growth rate in a steady state competitive price system and a tax-induced distortion in a static competitive price system is used in the presentation of the result.

There is, however, no distinctive neo-Marxian or neo-Ricardian contribution in this result, for we have seen it already in the discussion of the two-sector model in Sections 3.1 and 3.2. Nor, as we have seen, can comparative dynamics results of this type have welfare significance in themselves. The analogy of profit rates with distortionary taxes is an analogy only, not to be taken literally.

The neo-Ricardians have generally been appropriately cautious about attaching welfare significance to steady-state comparisons. However, Mainwaring (1979) argues that the gains from trade results presented in Section 1 can be overturned if capital goods are non-malleable. But the analysis of Section 1 makes no special assumptions about malleability or sector-specificity of capital, and comparison of that analysis with Mainwaring's results makes it clear that it is Mainwaring's behavioural assumption of a fixed wage that is the source of his result that trade may not be beneficial. Similarly, Evans (1979, 1980) in defending Emmanuel against Samuelson's criticisms focuses on the consequences of the wage being exogenously fixed. The proposition that trade may fail to be gainful in the presence of a factor price rigidity is, however, a well-known second-best proposition in the standard static gains-from-trade theory (see Chapter 2, Section 3.3), and it is not clear that our understanding of its significance is enhanced by its being restated in an intertemporal setting.

It would not be appropriate here to make a judgement about the contribution of Emmanuel (or of Amin). Emmanuel himself (1977, p. 88, footnote 3) remarks that his efficiency theorem is "far from being the most important one in the theory...a side issue". His main concern is the effect of international wage differentials on the terms of trade and the international distribution of income. Explorations of this issue and of the general idea of "unequal exchange" have been undertaken by Bacha (1978), Findlay (1980), Taylor (1981) and Brewer (1982), but such analysis is outside the scope of this chapter, and is discussed in Chapter 4, Sections 1.3 and 3.4.

What then of the neo-Ricardian contribution? There is no doubt that it is substantial and useful, and that at least some of the "neoclassical" theoretical developments surveyed above would have been different and poorer without the stimulus provided by the neo-Ricardians. On the grand question of whether we really are given an alternative "vision" of international trade, only a personal view can be expressed and my answer is negative, particularly with respect to the welfare economics issues discussed above, where one could argue that dispute over whether the "neoclassical" theory is valid in an intertemporal context and the suggestion that its validity is somehow sensitive to the technological specification of the model have rather obscured the incredibility of the assumptions about behaviour, foresight and intergenerational redistribution which are required to establish the results discussed in Section 1. Incredible though they may be, these assumptions provide a natural benchmark and no comparable benchmark is provided by the neo-Ricardian approach. It seems more sensible to treat models in which an exogeneously fixed profit rate has no relationship to individuals' time preference rates as providing examples of the consequences of nonoptimal intertemporal decision-making rather than as providing a class of models of very general application. Similarly on the positive-economic side, all the neo-Ricardian analysis can be interpreted from a "mainstream" viewpoint as variants of or extensions to the "mainstream" theory, but the converse statement cannot be made; and I agree with Dixit (1981b) that the types of models surveyed in Section 2 are more fruitful in many respects than those of Section 3. A corollary of the importance of behavioural as opposed to technological assumptions to the neoclassical theory is that a successful radical critique of that theory and its application to policy is more likely to be mounted along traditional Marxist lines than from a neo-Ricardian standpoint.

5. Conclusion

Much progress has been made in the twenty years since Bhagwati's (1964) survey, and some of that progress has been genuinely exciting. At this point, however, many of the other areas surveyed in chapters in this Handbook seem to have more promise of future excitements than does the area surveyed in this chapter. The topics which do seem to have scope for interesting development seem generally to lie within the areas covered in Section 3: in particular, the overlapping-generations model invites further exploitation by trade theorists, both for positive results and to explore the issue of intergenerational redistribution that is not explicitly treated in the general model of Section 2. The steady-state models discussed in Section 4 have aroused considerable and justifiable interest, but I am sceptical about whether interesting future developments can be expected there; and certainly the key, if it exists, to understanding the benefits or evils of "capitalism" is not labelled "capital theory".

References

Acheson, Keith (1970), "The aggregation of heterogeneous capital goods and various trade theorems", Journal of Political Economy, 78:565–571.

Bacha, Edmar L. (1978), "An interpretation of unequal exchange from Prebisch–Singer to Emmanuel", Journal of Development Economics, 5:319–330.

Bhagwati, Jagdish (1964), "The pure theory of international trade: A survey", Economic Journal, 74:1–84.

Bhagwati, Jagdish (1981), International trade: Selected readings (M.I.T. Press, Cambridge, Mass.).

Bliss, Christopher J. (1973), "Heterogeneous capital and the Heckscher–Ohlin–Samuelson theory of trade: discussion", in: J.M. Parkin, ed., Essays in modern economics (Longman, London) 61–64.

Bliss, Christopher J. (1975), Capital theory and the distribution of income (North-Holland, Amsterdam).

Brecher, Richard A. and Ian C. Parker (1977), "Time structure of production and the theory of international trade", Journal of International Economics, 7:385–402.

Brewer, Anthony (1980), Marxist theories of imperialism: A critical survey (Routledge and Kegan Paul, London).

Brewer, Anthony (1982), "Trade with fixed real wages and mobile capital", typescript, University of Bristol.

Buiter, Willem H. (1981), "Time preference and international lending and borrowing in an overlapping-generations model", Journal of Political Economy, 89:769–797.

Burmeister, Edwin (1978), "An interest rate and factor price equalization theorem with non-traded commodities", Journal of International Economics, 8:1–9.

Burmeister, Edwin and A. Rodney Dobell (1970), Mathematical theories of economic growth (Macmillan, New York).

Caves, Richard E. and Ronald W. Jones (1981), World trade and payments, 3rd edn. (Little, Brown, Boston).

Chipman, John S. (1969), "Factor price equalization and the Stolper-Samuelson theorem", International Economic Review, 10:399–406.

Deardorff, Alan V. (1973), "The gains from trade in and out of steady state growth", Oxford Economic Papers (N.S.), 25:173–191.

Deardorff, Alan V. (1974), "A geometry of growth and trade", Canadian Journal of Economics, 7:295–306.

Diamond, Peter A. (1965), "National debt in a neo-classical growth model", American Economic Review, 55:1126–1150.

Dixit, Avinash (1978), "On Rybczynski's theorem in a setting of growth", Journal of International Economics, 8:127–129.

Dixit Avinash (1981a), "A model of trade in oil and capital", Discussion paper in Economics, No. 16 (Woodrow Wilson School, Princeton University).

Dixit, Avinash (1981b), "The export of capital theory", Journal of International Economics, 11:279–294.

Dixit, Avinash and Victor Norman (1980), Theory of international trade: A dual, general equilibrium approach (James Nisbet, Welwyn, and Cambridge University Press, Cambridge).

Emmanuel, Arghiri (1972), Unequal exchange: A study of the imperialism of trade (Monthly Review Press, New York).

Emmanuel, Arghiri (1977), "Gains and losses from the international division of labor", Review, 1:87–108.

Emmanuel, Arghiri (1978), "A note on 'trade pattern reversals'", Journal of International Economics, 8:143–145.

Ethier, Wilfred (1979), "The theorems of international trade in time-phased economies", Journal of International Economics, 9:225–238.

Ethier, Wilfred (1981), "A reply to Professors Metcalfe and Steedman", Journal of International Economics, 11:273–277.

Evans, David (1979), "Unequal exchange and economic policies: Some implications of the neo-Ricardian critique of the theory of comparative advantage", in: Ian Livingstone, ed., Development economics and policy: Readings (Allen and Unwin, London) 117–128.

Evans, David (1980), "Emmanuel's theory of unequal exchange: Critique, counter critique and theoretical contribution", Discussion paper 149, Institute of Development Studies, Sussex, March 1980.

Findlay, Ronald (1970), "Factor proportions and comparative advantage in the long run", Journal of Political Economy, 78:27–34, and Chapter 5 of Bhagwati (1981).

Findlay, Ronald (1973), International trade and development theory (Columbia University Press, New York).

Findlay, Ronald (1978), "An 'Austrian' model of international trade and interest rate equalization", Journal of Political Economy, 86:989–1007.

Findlay, Ronald (1980), "The terms of trade and equilibrium growth in the world economy", American Economic Review, 70:291–299.

Fischer, Stanley and Jacob A. Frenkel (1972), "Investment, the two-sector model and trade in debt and capital goods", Journal of International Economics, 2:211–233, and Chapter 28 of Bhagwati (1981).

Fried, Joel (1980), "The intergenerational distribution of the gains from technical change and from international trade", Canadian Journal of Economics, 13:65–81.

Gale, David (1971), "General equilibrium with imbalance of trade", Journal of International Economics, 1:141–158.

Gale, David (1974), "The trade imbalance story", Journal of International Economics, 4:119–137.

Green, Jerry (1972), "The question of collective rationality in Professor Gale's model of trade imbalance", Journal of International Economics, 2:38–56.

Johnson, Harry G. (1971), "Trade and growth: A geometrical exposition", Journal of International Economics, 1:83–101.

Kareken, John and Neil Wallace (1977), "Portfolio autarky: A welfare analysis", Journal of International Economics, 7:19–43.

Kemp, Murray C. (1973), "Heterogeneous capital goods and long-run Stolper–Samuelson theorems", Australian Economic Papers, 12:253–260, and Chapter 5 of Kemp (1976).

Kemp, Murray C. (1976), Three topics in the theory of international trade: Distribution, welfare and uncertainty (North-Holland, Amsterdam).

Kemp, Murray C. and Chulsoon Khang (1974), "A note on steady-state price: output relationships", Journal of International Economics, 4:187–197.

Kenen, Peter B. (1965), "Nature, capital and trade", Journal of Political Economy, 73:437–460.

Kenen, Peter B. (1968), "Toward a more general theory of capital and trade", in: Peter B. Kenen and Roger Lawrence, eds., The open economy: Essays on international trade and finance (Columbia University Press, New York).

Mainwaring, L. (1974), "A neo-Ricardian analysis of international trade", Kyklos, 27:537–553, and Chapter 9 of Steedman (1979a).

Mainwaring, L. (1976), "Relative prices and 'factor price' equalisation in a heterogeneous capital goods model", Australian Economic Papers, 15:109–118, and Chapter 6 of Steedman (1979a).

Mainwaring, L. (1978), "The interest rate equalisation theorem with non-traded goods", Journal of International Economics, 8:11–19, and Chapter 7 of Steedman (1979a).

Mainwaring, L. (1979), "On the transition from autarky to trade", Chapter 12 of Steedman (1979a).

Marion, Nancy P., and Lars E.O. Svensson (1981), World equilibrium with oil price increases: An intertemporal analysis, Seminar paper no. 191, Institute for International Economic Studies, Stockholm, December, 1981.

Marion, Nancy P. and Lars E.O. Svensson (1982), "Structural differences and macroeconomic adjustment to oil price increases in a three-country model", Working paper no. 839, National Bureau of Economic Research, Cambridge, Mass., January, 1982.

Metcalfe, J.S. and Ian Steedman (1972), "Reswitching and primary input use", Economic Journal, 82:140–157, and Chapter 2 of Steedman (1979a).

Metcalfe, J.S. and Ian Steedman (1973), "Heterogeneous capital and the Heckscher–Ohlin–Samuelson theory of trade", in: J.M. Parkin, ed., Essays in modern economics (Longman, London) 50–60, and Chapter 5 of Steedman (1979a).

Metcalfe, J.S. and Ian Steedman (1974), "A note on the gain from trade", Economic Record, 50:581–595, and Chapter 4 of Steedman (1979a).

Metcalfe, J.S. and Ian Steedman (1981), "On the transformation of theorems", Journal of International Economics, 11:267–271.

Neary, J. Peter (1978), "Short-run capital specificity and the pure theory of international trade", Economic Journal, 88:488–510.

Ohyama, Michihiro (1972), "Trade and welfare in general equilibrium", Keio Economic Studies, 9:37–73.

Onika, H. and H. Uzawa (1965), "Patterns of trade and investment in a dynamic model of international trade", Review of Economic Studies, 32:15–38.

Razin, Assaf (1980), "Capital movements, intersectoral resource shifts and the trade balance", Seminar paper no. 159, Institute for International Economic Studies, Stockholm, October.

Sachs, Jeffery (1981), "The current account and macroeconomic adjustment in the 1970s", Brookings Papers on Economic Activity, 201–268.

Samuelson, Paul A. (1958), "An exact consumption-loan model of interest with or without the social contrivance of money", Journal of Political Economy, 66:467–482.

Samuelson, Paul A. (1965), "Equalization by trade of the interest rate along with the real wage", in: R.E. Baldwin, R.E. Caves, H.G. Johnson and P.B. Kenen, eds., Trade, growth and the balance of payments: Essays in honor of Gottfried Haberler (Rand-McNally, Chicago) 35–52.

Samuelson, Paul A. (1973), "Deadweight loss in international trade from the profit motive?", in: C. Fred Bergsten and William G. Tyler, eds., Leading issues in international economic policy: Essays in honor of George N. Halm (Lexington Books, Lexington, Mass.) 149–154.

Samuelson, Paul A. (1975), "Trade pattern reversals in time-phased Ricardian systems and intertemporal efficiency", Journal of International Economics, 5:309–363.

Samuelson, Paul A (1976), "Illogic of neo-Marxian doctrine of unequal exchange", in: David A. Belsey, Edward J. Kane, Paul A. Samuelson and Robert M. Solow, eds., Inflation, trade and taxes: Essays in honor of Alice Bourneuf (Ohio State University Press, Columbus, Ohio) 96–107.

Samuelson, Paul A. (1978a), "Interest rate equalization and non-equalization by trade in Leontief–Sraffa models", Journal of International Economics, 8:21–27.

Samuelson, Paul A. (1978b), "Free trade's intertemporal Pareto-optimality", Journal of International Economics, 8:147–149.

Sanyal, Kalyan K. (1980), "Commodity prices, factor rewards and the pattern of trade in a time-phased model", chapter of Ph.D. thesis, University of Rochester.

Smith, M. Alasdair M. (1976), "Trade, growth and consumption in alternative models of capital accumulation", Journal of International Economics, 6:371–384.

Smith, M. Alasdair M. (1977), "Capital accumulation in the open two-sector economy", Economic Journal, 87:273–282, and Chapter 25 of Bhagwati (1981).

Smith, M. Alasdair M. (1979), "Intertemporal gains from trade", Journal of International Economics, 9:239–248.

Smith, Alasdair (1982), "Some simple results on the gains from trade, from growth and from public production", Journal of International Economics, 13:215–230.

Srinivasan, T.N., and Jagdish N. Bhagwati (1980), "Trade and welfare in a steady state", in: John S. Chipman and Charles P. Kindleberger, eds., Flexible exchange rates and the balance of payments: Essays in memory of Egon Sohmen (North-Holland, Amsterdam) 341–353.

Steedman, Ian, ed. (1979a), Fundamental issues in trade theory (Macmillan, London).

Steedman, Ian (1979b), Trade amongst growing economies (Cambridge University Press, Cambridge).

Steedman, Ian and J.S. Metcalfe (1973), "The non-substitution theorem and international trade theory", Australian Economic Papers, 12:267–269, and Chapter 10 of Steedman (1979a).

Steedman, Ian and J.S. Metcalfe (1977), "Reswitching, primary inputs and the Heckscher–Ohlin–Samuelson theory of trade", Journal of International Economics, 7:201–208, and Chapter 3 of Steedman (1979a).

Steedman, Ian and J.S. Metcalfe (1979), "The golden rule and the gain from trade", Chapter 11 of Steedman (1979a).

Stiglitz, Joseph E. (1970), "Factor price equalization in a dynamic economy", Journal of Political Economy, 78:456–488.

Svensson, Lars E.O. (1981), "Oil prices and a small oil-importing economy's welfare and trade balance: An intertemporal approach", Seminar paper no. 184, Institute for International Economic Studies, Stockholm, October, 1981.

Svensson, Lars E.O. and Assaf Razin (1983), "The terms of trade and the current account: The Harberger–Laursen–Metzler effect", Journal of Political Economy, 91:97–125.

Taylor, Lance (1981), "South–North trade and Southern growth: Bleak prospects from the structuralist point of view", Journal of International Economics, 11:589–602.

Uekawa, Yasuo (1971), "Generalization of the Stolper–Samuelson theorem", Econometrica, 39:197–218.

Uekawa, Yasuo, Murray C. Kemp and Leon L. Wegge (1973), "P and PN matrices, Minkowski and Metzler matrices, and generalizations of the Stolper–Samuelson and Samuelson–Rybczynski theorems", Journal of International Economics, 3:53–76, and Chapter 3 of Kemp (1976).

Chapter 7

INCREASING RETURNS, IMPERFECT MARKETS, AND TRADE THEORY

ELHANAN HELPMAN*

Tel Aviv University

Contents

1. Introduction   326
2. Types of economies of scale   327
3. Types of competition   330
4. Homogeneous products   332
5. International returns to scale   337
6. National returns to scale   341
7. Limited entry and market segmentation   348
8. Differentiated products   355
References   363

*This chapter is a revised version of Working Paper no. 18-82, The Foerder Institute of Economic Research, Tel Aviv University. As with much of my previous work, the present one has also benefited from discussions at the Tel Aviv Workshop on International Economics. I would like to thank especially Eitan Berglas for his many wise comments on a written draft and in oral discussions. This version also benefited from the comments of Alan Deardorff, Wilfred Ethier, James Markusen, James Melvin, Arvind Panagariya and Lars Svensson, as well as from discussions at the conference of the *Handbook*'s authors at Princeton University. Finally, I would like to thank the Foerder Institute for Economic Research for financial support.

Handbook of International Economics, vol. I, Edited by R.W. Jones and P.B. Kenen
© *Elsevier Science Publishers B.V., 1984*

1. Introduction

The effects of increasing returns to scale and noncompetitive behavior on international trade have been discussed for many years. They have a bearing on a host of trade problems such as explanations of trade patterns, gains from trade, commercial policy, transnational corporations and direct foreign investment. This survey concentrates on two major issues: explanations of trade patterns and gains from trade.[1]

Early writers on this subject whose approach was grounded in the classical tradition were mainly concerned with gains from trade and other welfare effects. Thus Marshall (1879, p. 13) discussed terms of trade effects, arguing that with increasing returns to scale (economies of scale) a country may improve its terms of trade by expanding demand for its imports, while Graham (1923) argued that economies of scale may cause a country to lose from trade, concluding that in this case a tariff is beneficial. Later, with the development of the neoclassical trade theory, the pattern of trade became of major concern. Thus Ohlin (1933) pointed out that economies of scale serve as one explanation of foreign trade patterns, while other post 1933 writers emphasized the role of monopolistic competition in differentiated products. In the preface to the English edition of his famous book, Haberler (1936) wrote:

> it seems to me that the theory of international trade, as outlined in the following pages, requires further development, in two main directions. The theory of imperfect competition and the theory of short-run oscillations (business cycle theory) must be applied to the problems of international trade. It will soon be possible to do this in a systematic way, since much progress has been made in both fields in recent years. With regard to the first of these questions, there is the literature which centers around the two outstanding books, *Monopolistic Competition* by Professor E. Chamberlin and *Imperfect Competition* by Mrs. Joan Robinson. In the second field where further development is required, it is not easy to refer to a body of accepted theory."

The hope that was expressed by Haberler was probably shared in the thirties by other trade experts as well. Indeed, there exist early attempts to extend trade theory on the basis of Chamberlin's work [see, for example, Beach (1936) and Lovasy (1941)]. However, only recently has this goal been achieved.

In what follows I survey the theory of international trade in the presence of economies of scale and monopolistic (not monopsonistic) competition, with an

---

[1] Some issues which are not dealt with in this survey are surveyed in Caves (1974).

emphasis on predictions of trade patterns and gains from trade. I will take a unified approach to the subject trying to bring out the common logic in much of the seemingly unrelated parts of the literature. The main ingredient of this logic is that the allocation of productive resources is guided in every country by the reward level of every sector's employed combination of factors of production.

In order to obtain an idea what these sectoral rewards are, consider two examples. First, suppose there is pure competition, no joint production, and constant returns to scale. Then the commodity price, which is equated to marginal costs of production, is the reward to a combination of factors of production that produce a single unit at minimum costs. Without impediments to trade, the reward levels – which equal prices – are the same in every country, and trade patterns are predicted by the standard theories. Secondly, suppose there is monopolistic competition and constant returns to scale. Suppose also that there exists one producer of each good in every country. Since a monopolist equates marginal costs to marginal revenue, marginal revenue is the sectoral reward to the cost minimizing combination of factors of production that produce a single unit at minimum costs. If in a trading equilibrium marginal revenues are the same in every country, identical reward levels guide the allocation of productive resources in every country and we can again predict trade patterns by means of standard theories. If they are not, other avenues have to be explored. Whether marginal revenues are the same depends on the nature of the monopolistic competition.

After discussing types of economies of scale in Section 2 and types of competition in Section 3, I present in Section 4 a general model of trade in homogeneous products when there are variable returns to scale and free entry into industries. This model covers many of the cases discussed in the literature. International returns to scale are explored in Section 5 while national returns to scale are explored in Section 6. In Section 7 the assumption of variable returns to scale is abandoned and cases of monopolistic competition with limited entry and market segmentation are considered. In the final section, Section 8, I discuss differentiated products.

2. Types of economies of scale

The role of economies of scale (increasing returns to scale) in international trade cannot be dealt with unless their nature is specified, because the behavioral assumptions which are appropriate for firms depend on them. Consequently, the resulting market structure and equilibrium allocations depend on the underlying economies of scale. The importance of this point emerged in discussions of international trade with increasing returns to scale, starting with the debate between Knight and Graham [see Graham (1923), Knight (1924), Graham (1925) and Knight (1925)]. Knight's view was that Graham's analysis of the possible losses from trade is valid if the economies of scale are external to the firm and internal to the industry, but that it is wrong if the economies of scale are internal to the firm.[2] We will come back to the Graham–Knight debate in Section 4. It has been brought up at this point only in order to argue the relevance of alternative specifications.

Variable returns to scale which are internal to the firm are defined as follows. Let $f(v)$ be the firm's quasi-concave production function, where v is a vector of inputs. Then $f(\cdot)$ exhibits economies of scale (increasing returns to scale) at v if for $\lambda > 1$, but sufficiently close to one, $f(\lambda v) > \lambda f(v)$. Namely, a small proportional increase in all factor inputs increases output more than proportionately. Similarly, there are diseconomies of scale (decreasing returns to scale) if $f(\lambda v) < \lambda f(v)$. The *local* degree of returns to scale can be measured by the elasticity of $f(\lambda v)$ with respect to λ, evaluated at $\lambda = 1$. If this elasticity is larger than one there are economies of scale, if it equals one there are constant returns to scale, and if it falls short of one there are diseconomies of scale.

An alternative way of measuring the degree of economies of scale is by means of the cost function $C(w, x)$ which is associated with the production function $f(v)$, where w is the vector of factor prices and x is the output level $[x = f(v)]$. Using the cost function, the local measure of returns to scale is defined as the inverse of the elasticity of costs with respect to output, which equals average costs divided by marginal costs:

$$\theta(w, x) = \frac{C(w, x)/x}{\partial C(w, x)/\partial x}. \tag{2.1}$$

It can be shown [see Hanoch (1975)] that there are increasing returns to scale according to the original definition – which rests on properties of the production function – if and only if $\theta(w, x) > 1$. I will use the measure $\theta(\cdot)$ in the following analysis. Clearly, $\theta(\cdot) < 1$ means that marginal costs exceed average costs or that average costs are increasing with output. Explanations of economies of scale which are internal to the firm are based on economies of internal organization and specialization [see Marshall (1920, Book IV, ch. IX) and Stigler (1951)], on indivisibilities [see Ohlin (1933, p. 52)] and on the existence of fixed costs.

Economies or diseconomies of scale which are external to the firm but internal to the industry are usually represented by a production function of the form $x = \tilde{f}(v, X)$, where x is the output level of the single firm, v is its vector of inputs and X is the industry's level of output [see Jones (1968)]. The function $\tilde{f}(\cdot)$ is assumed to be quasi-concave and positively linear homogeneous in v. This means that from the point of view of a single firm which considers the industry's output

---

[2] This view was supported by Haberler (1936, pp. 204–208). See Caves (1960, pp. 169–176) for a clear description of the debate. The concepts of internal and external economies of scale are extensively discussed in Marshall (1920, Book IV, chs. IX–XI).

level as invariant to its decisions, the production process exhibits constant returns to scale. Assuming that all firms in the industry have identical production functions, the industry's output level is $X = \sum_{k=1}^{n} x^k = \sum_{k=1}^{n} \tilde{f}(v^k, X)$ where n is the number of firms in the industry and k is an index of firms. Since $\tilde{f}(\cdot)$ is positively linear homogeneous in v, then assuming that all firms pay the same factor prices and that factor inputs are cost minimizing, we get $X = \tilde{f}(\sum_{k=1}^{n} v^k, X)$ or $X = \tilde{f}(V, X)$, where V is the vector of inputs employed by the industry. Hence, if all firms are identical and factor markets are competitive, the implicit relationship between the industry's input vector and output level is given by:[3]

$$X = \tilde{f}(V, X). \tag{2.2}$$

Assume that (2.2) can be inverted to yield a solution:

$$X = F(V), \tag{2.3}$$

where $F(\cdot)$ is a function, then with competitive factor markets the industry operates as if $F(\cdot)$ is its implicit production function.

It is now straightforward to show that the industry's implicit production function exhibits decreasing returns to scale when the elasticity of $\tilde{f}(\cdot)$ with respect to X is negative, that it exhibits constant returns to scale when this elasticity is zero, and increasing returns to scale when this elasticity is positive but smaller than one. It is assumed that the elasticity of the firm's production function with respect to the industry's output is smaller than one in order to avoid land of Cockaigne phenomena.[4]

Explanations of external economies – economies of scale which are external to the firm but internal to the industry (I will not discuss diseconomies of scale of this type) – rest on the argument that a larger industry takes better advantage of within-industry specialization (the division of labor is limited by the extent of the market, and so is probably the division of other factors of production), as well as better advantage of conglomeration, indivisibilities, and public intermediate inputs such as roads [see Marshall (1920, Book IV, chs. X–XI), Ohlin (1933, p. 53) and Stigler (1951)]. The process by means of which higher output levels lead to more intra-industry specialization is not spelled out explicitly. Early writers on the subject were aware of the difficulties inherent in the concept of external economies of scale [see Chipman (1965) for a summary of the views on this matter and Chipman (1970) for a general equilibrium analysis of external economies of scale].

---

[3] These assumptions are really stronger than required, but they facilitate the exposition.

[4] Using eq. (2.2), the elasticity of $F(\lambda v)$ with respect to λ evaluated at $\lambda = 1$ is calculated to be $[1 - \varepsilon(V, X)]^{-1}$, where $\varepsilon(\cdot)$ is the elasticity of $\tilde{f}(\cdot)$ with respect to X. The conclusion discussed in the text follows from here.

It has, nevertheless, remained a concept of major use in the theory of international trade.

It is clear from our discussion that the specification of what constitutes an industry for the definition of external economies is of major importance. Most of the literature has used a national basis for this purpose. Namely, it assumed that a firm operating in a particular country derives cost savings from the expansion of output of that country's industry. This view was criticized by Ethier (1979) who suggested that in a world economy which is integrated via international trade, the international basis is more appropriate for the definition of external economies. According to this view, a firm derives cost savings from the expansion of world output of its product [see also Viner (1937, p. 480)] due to within-industry specialization which is diffused throughout the world via intra-industry trade in intermediate inputs and stages of production. However, economies of scale which arise from conglomeration or public intermediate inputs (such as roads) seem to be country specific, and due to transportation costs within-industry specialization in some stages of production may also be country specific. It seems, therefore, that the size of a domestic industry plays a role in the determination of external economies of scale. But it is also clear that some sources of these scale economies affect more than a single industry, which implies cross-industry spillovers of external economies of scale. Cross industry spillovers are not discussed in detail in this chapter [see, however, Anderson (1936), Haberler (1936, p. 208), Manning and Macmillan (1979), Chang (1981), and Herberg, Kemp and Tawada (1982)].

In what follows I confine attention to the type of economies of scale that have been discussed in the formal part of this section. The reader should, however, be aware of the fact that these concepts are rather limited. Firstly, the suggested formulation is restricted to output generating economies of scale. From the verbal discussion it is clear that this need not be the case. In each case the precise specification should be derived from more basic microeconomic structures. Secondly, a firm may be able to save costs when other sectors expand. I have mentioned earlier some of the reasons for such effects. Thirdly, pecuniary external effects which are derived from other industries when output expands as well as from domestic factor markets might play a role [see Viner (1937, p. 481)]. These spillover effects can conceptually also be derived from more basic microeconomic structures. However, we will proceed with what is available.

3. Types of competition

The literature on international trade under increasing returns to scale employs a variety of assumptions concerning firms' behavior. These assumptions play an important role in the determination of trade patterns and welfare effects. In addition it is necessary to specify whether there is free entry, because the ease with which firms can enter significantly affects the degree of competition in an industry.

Broadly speaking, there are three types of assumptions about firms' behavior that have been employed. When possible, it has been assumed that firms behave purely competitively. Namely, that firms take prices of inputs and outputs as given, and that they choose the input–output combination that maximizes profits. The consequence is, of course, marginal cost pricing. This pricing procedure is viable if the resulting profits are non-negative, which means that perceived marginal costs exceed perceived average costs, or – using eq. (2.1) – that at the resulting input–output combination there do not exist economies of scale. If the process of production is characterized by global economies of scale, the competitive assumption is inappropriate. Indeed, this assumption has been employed exclusively in cases in which the economies (or diseconomies) of scale are external to the firm but internal to the industry, in which case the single firm operates under perceived constant returns to scale.

The second behavioral assumption that has been employed is that of price competition, which is associated with the name of Bertrand [see Modigliani (1958)]. Under this assumption a firm takes as given the prices that are charged by its competitors and it chooses a price for its product so as to maximize profits. Clearly, this assumption is appropriate when the firm faces a downward sloping demand curve for its product, but it can also be employed on other occasions.[5]

The third assumption in the broad classification is that of quantity competition, which is associated with the name of Cournot [see Modigliani (1958)]. In the international trade literature it has been used mainly for industries which produce a homogeneous product. Under this assumption a firm observes the quantities of the product offered for sale by its competitors. It assumes that variations in its own sales will not affect the sales of its competitors. Then it calculates the response of the price to changes in its sales and it chooses a profit maximizing level of sales.

Existing models can be classified along several lines, generating a multi-dimensional matrix. However, not all of the entries in this matrix have been investigated; some of them may even be meaningless. The three categories of behavioral assumptions that have been described above represent a single axis of the matrix. Other axes which are relevant to the literature include the following:

(a) Entry: It can be assumed that there are barriers to entry so that the number of firms in an industry is predetermined, or, alternatively, that there is free entry. The second assumption leads to long-run equilibria with "normal" profit levels (usually assumed to be zero).

---

[5]I will come back to this point at a later stage.

(b) Product type: An industry's product may be a homogeneous good or it may be a differentiated product with many possible varieties. In the second case an additional dimension of competition is added; competition in product type.

(c) Market type: Markets of different countries for the same product may be integrated or segregated. In particular, it makes a significant difference whether a firm recognizes this interdependence or it ignores it.

This classification is in the domain of competition types. If we add the possible types of economies of scale (internal or external), the number of cases is doubled. There is, of course, no intention to go over all these cases in this survey. I will survey the major combinations that have been discussed in the literature and I will present the main conclusions that have been reached in other cases.

4. Homogeneous products

International trade in homogeneous products has received most of the attention in the theoretical literature. In this section I describe a model of trade in homogeneous products which is general enough to cover the cases of national and international returns to scale, and I prove a gains from trade theorem for the model.

Many of the important issues that have a bearing on the problems discussed in this section were discussed in connection with the Graham–Knight debate. Graham (1923) constructed a numerical example (or so he believed) which shows that when a country has a sector with increasing returns to scale and a sector with decreasing returns to scale it may lose from trade. Graham's argument can be restated as follows. Suppose there is a single factor of production, say labor, and equal prices of both goods. Also suppose that as a result of foreign trade a country shifts labor from the increasing returns to scale industry to the decreasing returns to scale industry. Then output per man falls in both industries, thereby reducing gross domestic product at constant commodity prices. This leads to a welfare loss.

Knight (1924) accused Graham of not distinguishing between internal and external economies. If the economies of scale are internal to the firm there can be no competition and one has to deal explicitly with monopoly. Graham (1925) denied the need to distinguish between internal and external economies of scale. Haberler (1936, p. 204) and Viner (1937, p. 473) agreed with Knight's position on this matter. Viner also pointed out that Graham confused average and marginal costs in his pricing rules and that external economies may depend on world output rather than national output, in which case Graham's argument is significantly weakened.

First consider the case of external economies, and recall that the firm's production function is assumed to be of the form $x = \tilde{f}(v, X)$, where X is the relevant industry's (national or international) output level. The literature under survey deals mainly with the following multiplicatively separable form of $\tilde{f}(\cdot)$:

$$\tilde{f}(v, X) = g(X)f(v), \tag{4.1}$$

where $f(\cdot)$ is increasing, strictly quasi-concave, and positively linear homogeneous. The function $g(X)$ has an elasticity $\varepsilon(X)$ smaller than one. If $g(\cdot)$ is an increasing function of X, there are economies of scale, and if it is a decreasing function there are diseconomies of scale.

The specification of the production function in (4.1) has a convenient interpretation. The function $f(\cdot)$, which has the standard properties, can be considered as representing factoral value added. This value added is augmented by the productivity of the scale effect, which is represented by $g(\cdot)$, to yield total output. It is clear from this specification that if $c(w)$ represents unit costs of factoral value added [the unit cost function associated with $f(v)$] then competitive firms in the industry engage in *marginal* cost pricing according to $p = c(w)/g(X)$, where p is the product price [$c(w)/g(X)$ is the firm's marginal cost function]. Put differently:

$$pg(X) = c(w), \tag{4.2}$$

where $pg(X)$ is the reward per unit factoral value added. It is now straightforward to show that $c(w)X/g(X)$ is the industry's cost function so that $c(w)/g(X)$ represents its average costs.[6] Hence, the industry prices its output according to average costs.

Let $g(\cdot)$ be increasing in X, then the industry's implicit production function $F(V)$ exhibits increasing returns to scale. Now change the assumption and assume that $F(v)$ is a firm's production function, so that the scale economies are internal to the firm. But assume also that there is free access to this technology, free entry (and exit) into the industry, and price competition á la Bertrand. If an entering firm conjectures that by charging the market price it can get any market share it desires, that by charging a higher price it will get a zero market share, and by charging a lower price it will get the entire market, then in the resulting equilibrium there will be a single firm in the industry and it will charge a price equal to average costs [see Kemp (1969, p. 155) and Grossman (1981)]. In this case the pricing equation (4.2) is also applicable. Despite there being a single firm in the industry, *entry* competition forces the monopolist to engage in average cost

---

[6]From (4.1) the industry's implicit production function is $F(V) \equiv \tilde{g}^{-1}[f(V)]$, where $\tilde{g}^{-1}(\cdot)$ is the inverse of $\tilde{g}(\cdot)$, defined by $\tilde{g}(X) \equiv X/g(X)$. Hence, if $C_f(w, Z)$ is the cost function associated with $f(v)$ and $C_F(w, X)$ is the cost function associated with $F(V)$, the two are related by $C_F(w, X) \equiv C_f[w, \tilde{g}(X)]$. Since $f(\cdot)$ is positively linear homogeneous, $C_f[w, \tilde{g}(x)] \equiv c(w)\tilde{g}(x)$, implying $C_F(w, X) \equiv c(w)X/g(X)$.

pricing.[7] It seems, therefore, that Graham (1925) had a point when he argued that he does not care whether the economies of scale are internal or external. It is also clear that in our cases average cost pricing is the proper specification, and I will adopt it in the following presentation.

In order to represent the equilibrium conditions consider a many sector economy, with $f_i(V^i)$, $i = 1, 2, \ldots, m$, being the factoral value added function in sector i. Given the aggregate endowment of factors of production one can define the economy's transformation surface between factoral value added levels.[8] This surface has the usual properties of a transformation surface derived from constant returns to scale technologies. Equilibrium factoral value added levels will be on this surface due to cost minimization. In addition, due to the average cost pricing rule (4.2) the economy's factoral value added levels will be chosen at a point of tangency between this surface and a hyperplane with weights $[p_1 g_1(X_1), p_2 g_2(X_2), \ldots, p_m g_m(X_m)]$. The economy's GDP can, therefore, be represented by the function $\text{GDP}[p_1 g_1(X_1), p_2 g_2(X_2), \ldots, p_m g_m(X_m); V]$, where $\text{GDP}(\cdot)$ has the usual properties of a restricted profit function which is derived from constant returns to scale technologies.[9] It is positively linear homogeneous in the first m arguments, it is positively linear homogeneous in V, its partial derivative with respect to $p_i g_i(X_i)$ equals the factoral value added in sector i,[10] and its derivative with respect to V_l equals the competitive reward to factor l. In addition, it is convex in the first m arguments and concave in V [see Varian (1978, ch. 1)]. Since $\text{GDP}(\cdot)$ is positively linear homogeneous in V and the competitive reward of factor l equals $\partial \text{GDP}/\partial V_l$, factor payments exhaust the entire GDP, and there are no pure profits. In what follows I will use the notation

---

[7]This discussion was confined to the case of increasing returns to scale. If there are decreasing returns to scale, free entry and free access to the technology lead to infinitely many firms which operate at an infinitesimal level and the industry's implicit production function exhibits constant returns to scale.

[8]Let $Z = (Z_1, Z_2, \ldots, Z_m)$ be a vector of factoral value added levels. Then, given an endowment vector V, this transformation surface is defined as follows:

$$T(V) = \left\{ Z \mid V^i \geq 0, i = 1, 2, \ldots, m, \text{ such that } \sum_{i=1}^{m} V^i \leq V, \text{ and} \right.$$

$$Z_i = f_i(V^i), \text{ and } \hat{V}^i \geq 0, i = 1, 2, \ldots, m \text{ such that } \sum_{i=1}^{m} \hat{V}^i \leq V$$

$$\left. \text{and } f_i(\hat{V}^i) \geq Z_i, i = 1, 2, \ldots, m, \text{ with strict inequality holding for some } i \right\}.$$

See also Herberg and Kemp (1969) and Inoue (1981).

[9]By definition, $\text{GDP}(q, V) \equiv \max q \cdot Z$, s.t. $Z \in T(V)$. In our case $q_i = p_i g_i(X_i)$.

[10]For economies in which the number of goods is larger than the number of factors of production, such as in the Ricardian case, the GDP function may not be differentiable with respect to the first m arguments. In this case its gradient with respect to these arguments should be interpreted as a set.

GDP$[pg(X), V]$, where $pg(X)$ is interpreted as the vector $[p_1 g_1(X_1),$ $p_2 g_2(X_2), \ldots, p_m g_m(X_m)]$. Observe that the employed specification admits also sectors with constant returns to scale. Such sectors are represented by constant $g(\cdot)$ functions. In particular, one may choose $g_i(X_i) \equiv 1$ for a constant returns to scale sector.

In the remaining part of this section I specify the equilibrium conditions of a trading world in which the economies of scale are national in some sectors, international in others or have a more general form, and I prove a gains from trade theorem. For some purposes we will also need autarky equilibrium conditions. However, these will not be formalized in order to save space; their nature will become clear from the trading equilibrium conditions.

Let superscript j denote functions and variables of country j. For example, GDP$^j(\cdot)$ is country j's GDP function, which depends on its technologies of production of factoral value added. Let $D^j(p, I)$ be country j's *vector* of demand functions. Then the following are equilibrium conditions:

$$\sum_j D^j\{p, \text{GDP}^j[pg^j(\bar{X}^j), V^j]\} = \sum_j X^j, \tag{4.3}$$

$$X^j = \text{GDP}_p^j[pg^j(\bar{X}^j), V^j], \quad \text{for all } j, \tag{4.4}$$

$$w^j = \text{GDP}_V^j[pg^j(\bar{X}^j), V^j], \quad \text{for all } j. \tag{4.5}$$

Condition (4.3) is the equilibrium condition in commodity markets, where X^j is the output vector in country j. All goods are traded and there are no impediments to trade. Hence, p is the vector of commodity prices in every country. Countries are allowed to differ in demand patterns, technologies [including the $g(\cdot)$ functions] and factor endowments.

Condition (4.4) says that a country's output vector equals its supply. The supply equals the gradient (GDP$_p$) of the GDP function with respect to p.[11] Condition (4.5) represents equilibrium factor prices. These equal marginal product values or the gradient (GDP$_V$) of the GDP function with respect to the factor endowment vector.

It remains to explain the $\bar{X}^j$ that appears in $g(\cdot)$. This vector represents the relevant type of returns to scale. If in sector i the returns to scale are national and sector specific, then $\bar{X}_i^j = X_i^j$, i.e. only the national output level of sector i affects productivity in sector i. If, on the other hand, the returns to scale in sector i are international and sector specific, then $\bar{X}_i^j = \sum_k X_i^k$, i.e. world output of sector i affects productivity in sector i. By an appropriate specification of the $\bar{X}_i^j$'s one obtains every desired mixture of national and international returns to scale.

---

[11] From the properties of the GDP function, we have: $\partial \text{GDP}/\partial p_i = g_i[\partial \text{GDP}/\partial(p_i g_i)] = g_i f_i = X_i$. If the GDP function is not differentiable, the gradient is a set and (4.4) should be interpreted as $X^j \in \text{GDP}_p^j(\cdot)$.

Moreover, for present purposes $\bar{X}_i^j$ may be a vector which represents intersectoral spillover effects of economies of scale [in this case $g_i^j(\cdot)$ is a function of a vector], or irreversible economies of scale as discussed in Marshall (1920, appendix H) and Negishi (1972, ch. 5). Some sectors may also exhibit constant returns to scale. This specification together with (4.3)–(4.5) provide a complete description of equilibrium conditions.

It remains to formulate the gains from trade theorem. Let $X^{\Lambda j}$ be the autarky output vector in country j. In the absence of trade only national output levels affect productivity in sectors with variable returns to scale, so that in autarky $g_i^j(\cdot)$ depends on $X^{\Lambda j}$ [here I allow $g_i^j(\cdot)$ to be a function of the entire output vector].

Gains from trade theorem 1

The following is a sufficient condition for gains from trade:

$$\sum_{i=1}^{m} p_i \left[g_i^j(\bar{X}_i^j) - g_i^j(X^{\Lambda j}) \right] f_i^{\Lambda j} \geq 0,$$

where $f_i^{\Lambda j}$ is autarky factoral value added in country j's sector i.[12]

This condition is necessarily satisfied if $\bar{X}_i^j$ is a scalar which represents the post trade output level of sector i in country j or the world's post trade output level of

---

[12] The proof of this theorem is as follows. Let $e^j(p, u)$ be country j's minimum expenditure function (associated with its utility function from which the vector of demands $D^j(p, I)$ has been derived). Then:

$$e^j(p, u^{\Lambda j}) \leq \sum_{i=1}^{m} p_i X_i^{\Lambda j} = \sum_{i=1}^{m} p_i g_i^j(X^{\Lambda j}) f_i^{\Lambda j},$$

where $u^{\Lambda j}$ is the autarky utility level, p is the post-trade commodity price vector and $f_i^{\Lambda j}$ is the autarky factoral value added in country j's sector i. However, according to the condition of the theorem,

$$\sum_{i=1}^{m} p_i g_i^j(X^{\Lambda j}) f_i^{\Lambda j} \leq \sum_{i=1}^{m} p_i g_i^j(\bar{X}_i^j) f_i^{\Lambda j}.$$

Hence:

$$e^j(p, u^{\Lambda j}) \leq \sum_{i=1}^{m} p_i g_i(\bar{X}_i^j) f_j^{\Lambda j}.$$

Now, the right-hand side of the last inequality is smaller or equal to $\text{GDP}^j[pg(\bar{X}^j), V^j]$ which equals $e^j(p, u^j)$, where u^j is the post-trade utility level, yielding $e^j(p, u^{\Lambda j}) \leq e^j(p, u^j)$. The last inequality implies $u^j \geq u^{\Lambda j}$. As usual, strict gains from trade are obtained whenever a strict inequality holds in at least one place in the chain of inequalities.

industry *i* and:
- (a) for $g_i^j(\cdot)$ strictly increasing (economies of scale) $\overline{X}_i^j \geq X_i^{Aj}$;
- (b) for $g_i^j(\cdot)$ strictly decreasing (diseconomies of scale) $\overline{X}_i^j \leq X_i^{Aj}$.

The interpretation of conditions (a) and (b) is that a country gains from trade if (i) as a result of trade it expands output of industries with national economies of scale and it contracts output of industries with national diseconomies of scale, and if (ii) the post trade world output of industries with international economies of scale is larger than the country's output of these industries in autarky and the post trade world output of industries with international diseconomies of scale is smaller than the country's output of these industries in autarky. No restrictions are imposed on industries with constant returns to scale. This is a generalization of the gains from trade theorem proved by Kemp and Negishi (1970), who dealt only with the case of national economies of scale.[13] Negishi (1972, ch. 5) proved that irreversible national economies of scale assure gains from trade, where irreversibility means that a contraction of output does not reduce productivity [if X_i^0 initially, then $g_i(X_i) = g_i(X_i^0)$ for all $X_i \leq X_i^0$]. His case is covered by my sufficient condition as is the case of irreversible international economies of scale and cases of intersectoral interdependencies.

I have provided a sufficient condition for gains from trade. This condition makes clear the point that international economies of scale are more conducive to gains from trade than national economies of scale. Moreover, the smaller the country compared to the rest of the world, the more it stands to gain from trade due to international economies of scale (because the more likely it is that *world* output of these industries will exceed significantly its pre-trade output levels). By the same token international diseconomies of scale are more harmful to gains from trade than national diseconomies of scale. If economies of scale are irreversible, then a country always gains from trade. The sufficient condition described in the theorem states simply that trade does not reduce the economy's average productivity (as measured at the autarky factor allocation).

5. International returns to scale

The relevance of international economies of scale for trade problems was pointed out by Viner (1937, p. 480) in his evaluation of the Graham–Knight debate. However, only in Ethier (1979) has this concept been seriously explored. Ethier expressed the view that international economies of scale are more important than national economies of scale. He developed a two sector model; one operating under constant returns to scale and the other (manufacturing) operating under

---

[13] Eaton and Panagariya (1979) provide a stronger version of the Kemp–Negishi theorem. However, their global analysis, which should have relied on line integrals, is incomplete.

internationally sector specific increasing returns to scale. Then he showed that for fixed budget share demand patterns and an exponential $g(\cdot)$ function in manufacturing, there exists a unique equilibrium in which trading takes place according to standard theories of comparative advantage.[14] Although he did not state explicitly a gains from trade theorem, his discussions give the impression that countries do gain from trade.

First consider the pattern of trade. Suppose that every country has the same $g_i(\cdot)$ function in sector i. If all returns to scale are international and sector specific (we admit both economies and diseconomies of scale), as assumed by Ethier (1979), then $\bar{X}_i^j = \sum_k X_i^k$ and the reward to factoral value added in sector i, $p_i g_i(\sum_k X_i^k)$, is the same in every country. However, for predictions of trade patterns what is required is to have the same $\bar{X}_i^j$ in every country. This means that we can allow $\bar{X}_i^j$ to be a vector which represents also intersectoral effects, with $\sum_k X_i^k$ being its ith coordinate. In this case it can be easily shown that when factoral value added is produced by means of Ricardian technologies with a single factor of production (labor) the pattern of specialization is predicted according to comparative costs, just as in the classical model of trade [see eqs. (4.3) and (4.4)].[15] If instead of the Ricardian technology factoral value added is produced by means of Heckscher–Ohlin type technologies which are identical across countries and preferences are homothetic and identical across countries, then due to the fact that the reward to factoral value added is the same in every country (in each sector) relative output levels are determined by relative factor endowments while relative consumption levels are the same in every country. Hence, the pattern of trade is predicted by the Heckscher–Ohlin theory [see eqs. (4.3) and (4.4)]. In addition, due to (4.5), factor price equalization obtains if V^j belongs to the cone of diversification (see Chapter 3).

It is clear from this discussion that the key to our ability to predict trade patterns for economies with internationally variable returns to scale lies in the fact that in a trading equilibrium the real reward to factoral value added is the same in every country sector by sector. This is not the case with national returns to scale. It is also clear that due precisely to the same key feature and the assumed homotheticity of preferences, under international returns to scale the pattern of trade does not depend on country size. On the other hand, since autarky scale productivity levels $(g_1, g_2, \ldots, g_m)$ depend on autarky output levels, pre-trade

---

[14]Ethier (1979) has developed in that paper a new analytical construct, the allocation curve, in order to analyze the problems at hand.

[15]In this case $T^j(V^j)$ is the non-negative part of a hyperplane and

$$\text{GDP}^j[\,pg(\bar{X}), V^j\,] \equiv \max \sum_{i=1}^{m} p_i g_i(\bar{X}_i^j) Z_i, \quad \text{s.t.} \ Z \in T^j(V^j),$$

implies corner values of Z_i's except for special combinations of $p_i g_i$, $i = 1, 2, \ldots, m$.

relative commodity prices or factor rewards serve as biased predictors of trade patterns. Take, for example, the case of two countries which produce two goods by means of two factors of production with identical technologies. One sector is a constant returns to scale sector while the other is subject to sector specific internationally increasing returns to scale. Suppose also that the countries have identical homothetic preferences and the same relative factor endowments. Then according to our prediction these countries will not trade with each other. However, if one country is larger than the other, the larger country will have in autarky a lower relative price of the good that is produced with increasing returns to scale. Under these circumstances pre-trade commodity prices and factor rewards do not serve as reliable predictors of the pattern of trade.

The idea that there are international externalities when trade is allowed to take place but it does not take place and no such externalities exist in autarky, sounds like a bizarre one. However, the above discussion should be interpreted as dealing with predictions of *intersectoral* trade patterns. If one interprets the international economies of scale as being obtained via intra-industry trade (despite the absence of an explicit modeling of its existence), the paradox is resolved.

Now consider the uniqueness problem. It has been known for a long time that with nationally increasing returns to scale there exist multiple equilibria [see Chipman (1965)]. In the case analyzed by Ethier (1979) this difficulty does not exist, but it remains a problem in other cases, just as it is a problem in a closed economy. To see this point as well as some welfare implications, take the following example. There are two goods and a single factor of production, say, labor. One sector produces with sector specific internationally increasing returns to scale while the other produces with constant returns to scale. In particular:

$$f_i(L_i) = L_i, \qquad i = 1, 2, \qquad L_1 + L_2 = L,$$
$$g_1(\bar{X}_1) \equiv \bar{X}_1^\varepsilon, \qquad 0 < \varepsilon < 1, \qquad g_2(\bar{X}_2) \equiv 1.$$

Preferences are of the CES form with equal weights on both goods and an elasticity of substitution $\sigma > \varepsilon^{-1} > 1$. If p stands for the relative price of the first good, this implies that its budget share is $[1 + p^{\sigma-1}]^{-1}$, and the budget share declines in p. Let good two serve as numeraire. Then in autarky the wage rate equals one and according to (4.2):

$$p = X_1^{-\varepsilon}. \tag{5.1}$$

In addition, autarky versions of (4.3)–(4.4) imply that the budget share of good one should equal $pX_1/L = X_1^{1-\varepsilon}/L$, where the equality is obtained by means of (5.1). Hence,

$$[1 + p^{\sigma-1}]^{-1} = X_1^{1-\varepsilon}/L, \tag{5.2}$$

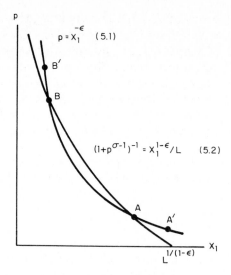

Figure 5.1.   An example of multiple equilibria and losses from trade in the presence of international economies of scale.

where the left-hand side represents the first commodity's budget share. The curves described by (5.1) and (5.2) are drawn in Figure 5.1. For sufficiently large values of L the two curves have several points in common [observe that condition (5.1) does not depend on L], these represent autarky equilibria. Two equilibrium points of interest are points A and B. Assuming that L is large enough, the existence of these points can be seen as follows. Point A exists because the curve described by (5.1) is asymptotic to the horizontal axis while the curve described by (5.2) cuts this axis at $X_1 = L^{1/(1-\varepsilon)}$. Given the existence of A, the existence of B can be verified by observing that for X_1 sufficiently small the curve described by (5.1) lies above the curve described by (5.2).[16] Hence, we have identified two autarky equilibrium points. These can also be interpreted as equilibrium points of a trading world which consists of two identical countries, each one of size $L/2$, with X_1 being world output of the first commodity.

Apart from demonstrating the possibility of multiple equilibria, this example also brings out another important feature of models with internationally increasing returns to scale; under these circumstances an economy may lose from free trade. To see this, consider two identical economies, each one in an equilibrium at point B in Figure 5.1 prior to trade. Now suppose that these economies engage in trade. Trading equilibria can be described by moving out the curve that intersects

---

[16] This relationship holds if and only if $\varepsilon\sigma > 1$. In Ethier (1979) $\sigma = 1$, implying $\varepsilon\sigma < 1$. Hence, in Ethier's case point B does not exist.

the horizontal axis. The new equilibrium corresponding to point B will be to the left of B on the curve described by (5.1), say B'. If this is the resulting equilibrium point, both countries lose from trade, because their income has not changed and they pay higher prices for the first commodity. As a result of trade world output of good one is lower than each country's autarky output level (which means that the sufficient condition of our gains from trade theorem is not satisfied). There will be gains from trade if the new equilibrium is at A', which corresponds to A.

I have demonstrated the possibility of losses from trade. There remain, however, open questions which have to be answered before the relevance of this possibility can be evaluated. These have to do with dynamic adjustment processes which should help determine both autarky and trading equilibria.

6. National returns to scale

The case of national returns to scale has been investigated more than others. It was discussed by Marshall (1879) in relation to terms of trade effects,[17] by Graham (1923) in relation to gains from trade, by Ohlin (1933) in relation to trade patterns, and by Lerner (1932) in relation to efficient world production. Later writers have expanded on some of these issues.

As far as the trade pattern is concerned, it has been argued by Ohlin (1933, p. 54) that economies of scale per se cause international trade. This should be interpreted to mean that in the absence of other causes of trade – such as differences in preferences, relative productivity levels, and relative factor endowments – there will be foreign trade due to the existence of economies of scale. This was indeed shown to be true by Matthews (1949–50) and later by Melvin (1969).[18] (I will come back to this point when discussing a specific example.) Apart from causing international trade, nationally increasing returns to scale are capable of assigning trade patterns on the basis of relative country size. This is a new feature. Remember that in the presence of internationally variable returns to scale there could be no intersectoral trade between identical economies and relative country size played no role in the determination of the trade pattern.

---

[17]"…an increase in Germany's demand for English cloth may to an extent develop the facilities which England has for producing cloth as to cause a great and permanent fall in the value of cloth in England. …an increase in Germany's demand for English cloth may cause her to obtain an import of English cloth increased in a *greater ratio* than is her export of linen to England" [Marshall (1879, p. 13)]. Italics in original.

[18]Melvin (1969) concentrates his analysis on complete specialization and misleads the reader to believe that severe restrictions on preferences are required to assure the existence of an equilibrium. When incomplete specialization is not excluded by assumption (as it should not be), his restrictions are not required (see his discussion on pp. 392–393 and especially footnote 8).

With nationally sector specific variable returns to scale the reward to factoral value added in sector i, $p_i g_i(X_i^j)$, depends on the country's output level in this sector. As a result, countries which have different factor endowments have different factor prices [see (4.5)] even if relative factor endowments are the same, thereby inducing factor movements.[19] But if factors do not move, the differences in factor rewards will affect the trading countries' cross-industry ordering of relative costs, and therefore also the pattern of specialization.

For concreteness, consider a world which consists of two economies. There are two goods; good one is produced with nationally increasing returns to scale and good two is produced with constant returns to scale. The production functions are the same in both countries, $g_1(X_1) = X_1^\varepsilon$, $0 < \varepsilon < 1$, and $V^2 = \lambda V^1$, $\lambda > 1$ [the assumption of a constant elasticity $g_1(\cdot)$ function is not trivial]. The last assumption means that the second country is larger than the first, but that it has the same composition of factors of production. Assume also that both countries have the same homothetic preferences. In this case there exists an equilibrium in which the larger country (country 2) exports the commodity produced with increasing returns to scale [see Markusen and Melvin (1981)].

The proof proceeds as follows. For a fixed output ratio X_2/X_1, the MRT $(= -\partial X_2/\partial X_1)$ of the larger country is smaller than the MRT of the smaller country, because the scale effect makes marginal resource requirements for the production of good one lower in the larger country. Since under the current specification output is determined by $p = \text{MRT}/(1 - \varepsilon)$, where $p = p_1/p_2$ [see Herberg and Kemp (1969)], this means that when the autarky equilibrium is unique, the homotheticity of preferences assures that in autarky the relative price p is smaller in the larger country.[20] The last point is demonstrated in Figure 6.1. Point A represents the autarky equilibrium point of the smaller country. At this

---

[19] Melvin's (1969) discussion of factor mobility is inaccurate, because he lets *relative* factor rewards determine factor movements. However, with economies of scale, a higher relative return is not necessarily associated with a higher absolute return.

[20] The most technical step in the proof consists of showing that for the same X_2/X_1 ratio MRT is smaller in the larger country. Since $p = \text{MRT}/(1 - \varepsilon)$, this can be proved by showing that (4.4) implies a lower p when V expands proportionately and $\delta \equiv X_2/X_1$ is kept constant. In the current two sector economy, with $g_1(X_1) = X_1^\varepsilon$ and $g_2(X_2) \equiv 1$, (4.4) can be written as:

$$X_1^{1-\varepsilon} = G_1(q,1;\lambda V); \qquad \delta X_1 = G_2(q,1;\lambda V),$$

where $q = pX_1^\varepsilon$.

If there exists a single factor of production, $G_i(\cdot)$ does not exist, but then q does not change with λ, implying that X_1 increases and p declines when λ rises. If there exist at least two factors of production and the transformation curve of factoral value added is strictly concave, $G_1(\cdot)$ increases in q and $G_2(\cdot)$ decreases in q. Since $G_1(\cdot)$ and $G_2(\cdot)$ are positively linear homogeneous in V, it is straightforward to calculate from the first two equations that in this case an increase in λ raises X_1 and reduces q. This implies by means of the last equation that p declines, proving the required result. Markusen and Melvin (1981) provide a complicated proof for the two factor case.

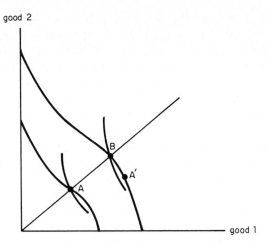

Figure 6.1. A comparison between autarky equilibria of two countries which differ only in size.

point the slope of the indifference curve is $(1-\varepsilon)^{-1}$ times larger than the slope of the transformation curve, i.e. $MRS = MRT/(1-\varepsilon)$.[21] If we draw a ray through the origin and point A, we obtain point B on the larger country's transformation curve. At B the slope of the indifference curve is the same as at A, but the slope of the transformation curve is smaller, i.e., at B we have $MRS > MRT/(1-\varepsilon)$. However, unless there is a corner equilibrium in the larger country there is a point of tangency between an indifference curve and the transformation curve ($MRS = MRT$) to the right of B, implying by continuity that between that point and B there is a point, say A', at which $MRS = MRT/(1-\varepsilon)$. Point A' is the larger country's equilibrium point. Since at A' the consumption of good 1 is relatively higher than at A, MRS is smaller at A' than at A. If we have a corner solution, MRS in the larger country is also higher than at A. This proves that when the equilibrium is unique the autarky relative price of good one is lower in the larger country.

Taking advantage of the fact that in autarky the relative price of good one is lower in the larger country, draw each country's offer curve to find out that there exists at least one intersection point of the offer curves at which the larger country exports the commodity that is produced under increasing returns to scale. One of

[21] There are two opposing forces which shape the transformation curve. The factoral value added transformation curve makes the commodity transformation curve concave to the origin while the scale effect in the first industry makes it convex to the origin. With the employed $g(\cdot)$ function, the first factor dominates near the axis of the increasing returns to scale good while the second factor dominates near the other axis [see Herberg and Kemp (1969)]. Starting with Tinbergen (1945), it became a common mistake to draw this curve with reversed concavity–convexity properties.

these equilibrium points is also stable according to the Kemp (1969, ch. 8) adjustment process, in which producers bear the burden of adjustment. Consumers are always on their demand curves, but producers may be off their supply curves. Whenever production takes place off a supply curve, output is adjusted to approach the supply curve [see Markusen and Melvin (1981)]. For the case of a single factor of production the stability property of the above mentioned equilibrium point was also confirmed for the adjustment mechanism under which output is expanded whenever the demand price exceeds the supply price and output is contracted whenever the supply price exceeds the demand price [see Ethier (1982a)]. Although the implications of adjustment mechanisms have been explored for economies with nationally increasing returns to scale more than for economies with internationally increasing returns to scale, it seems that we have not yet reached a satisfactory state of knowledge in this area. Competing mechanisms (such as Kemp's and Ethier's) cannot claim too much in terms of well based operating assumptions, but if we do not rely on them, we have no way of comparing the many possible equilibria in order to make a judgment about which are the more likely to occur. More work in this area is certainly required.

We have seen that there exist equilibria in which the larger country exports the commodity that is being produced with increasing returns to scale. However, even if both countries are of the same size, trade will exist. To see this possibility as well as some welfare effects, further specialize the example and assume that there is a single factor of production, say labor L, with $f_i(L_i) \equiv L_i$. Also assume that each country spends the same fixed budget share α on good one. Suppose $L^1 = L^2 = L$. Then for $\alpha < 1/2$ the following is an equilibrium:

$$L_1^1 = 2\alpha L, \qquad\qquad L_1^2 = 0,$$

$$L_2^1 = (1 - 2\alpha)L, \qquad L_2^2 = L,$$

$$X_1^1 = (2\alpha L)^{1/(1-\varepsilon)}, \qquad X_1^2 = 0,$$

$$X_2^1 = (1 - 2\alpha)L, \qquad X_2^2 = L,$$

$$w^1 = 1, \qquad\qquad w^2 = 1,$$

$$p = (2\alpha L)^{-\varepsilon/(1-\varepsilon)}.$$

Here country 2 specializes in good 2 while country 1 is incompletely specialized. Clearly, the roles of each country can be reversed, which demonstrates that there are multiple equilibria, a possibility that was pointed out by Ohlin (1933, p. 55). Due to the fact that $\alpha < 1/2$, the demand for good 1 is low enough to enable a single unspecialized country to supply the market for that good.[22]

---

[22] If the second industry was to produce under decreasing returns to scale with $g_2(X_2) = X_2^\eta$, $\eta < 0$, then, as shown in Panagariya (1981), each country would have produced at least some of good 2.

In autarky $L_1^{Aj} = \alpha L$, $L_2^{Aj} = (1-\alpha)L$, $X_1^{Aj} = (\alpha L)^{1/(1-\varepsilon)}$, $X_2^{Aj} = (1-\alpha)L$, $w^{Aj} = 1$ and $p^{Aj} = (\alpha L)^{-\varepsilon/(1-\varepsilon)}$. This is also a trading equilibrium without active trade, but it is unstable for some adjustment mechanisms [see Ethier (1982a)]. Since $p^{Aj} > p$ and the wage rate equals one in autarky and under free trade, each country gains from trade in the above described equilibrium. In addition, in the active trading equilibrium output is on the world's transformation curve. Observe, however, that despite there being gains from trade the conditions of the gains from trade theorem due to Kemp and Negishi (1970) are not satisfied. Recall that according to that theorem a sufficient condition for a country with the example's data to gain from trade is that as a result of trade it expands production of the good produced with nationally increasing returns to scale. In our example both countries gain, but one of them reduces to zero its output of the good produced with nationally increasing returns to scale. This implies that their sufficient conditions for gains from trade are quite restrictive.[23] In fact, the general sufficient condition for gains from trade presented in Section 4 in the gains from trade theorem is also not satisfied for the country that specializes in the second commodity, which means that that condition is also quite restrictive.

Now take the case $\alpha > 1/2$. In this case the demand for good one is too large for a single unspecialized country to supply the demanded quantities. In the following asymmetrical equilibrium one country specializes in good one while the other specializes in good two:

$$L_1^1 = L, \qquad\qquad L_1^2 = 0,$$

$$L_2^1 = 0, \qquad\qquad L_2^2 = L,$$

$$X_1^1 = L^{1/(1-\varepsilon)}, \qquad X_1^2 = 0,$$

$$X_2^1 = 0, \qquad\qquad X_2^2 = L,$$

$$w^1 = \alpha/(1-\alpha), \qquad w^2 = 1,$$

$$p = \frac{\alpha}{1-\alpha} L^{-\varepsilon/(1-\varepsilon)}.$$

In this equilibrium the first country's real wage rate is higher than in autarky in terms of every good $[w^1 = \alpha/(1-\alpha) > w^{A1} = 1$ for $\alpha > 1/2$ and $w^1/p = L^{\varepsilon/(1-\varepsilon)} > w^{A1}/p^{A1} = (\alpha L)^{\varepsilon/(1-\varepsilon)}]$, while the second country's real wage rate is as high as in autarky in terms of good two but may be higher or lower than in autarky in terms of good one $[w^2 = 1 = w^{A2}$ and $w^2/p = \alpha^{-1}(1-\alpha)L^{\varepsilon/(1-\varepsilon)}$, $w^{A2}/p^{A2} =$

---

[23] Eaton and Panagariya (1979) provide weaker conditions. They require expansion of output in industries with a degree of economies of scale which exceeds some reference degree and contraction of output in industries with a lower degree of economies of scale. However, their sufficient conditions are also not satisfied in our example.

$\alpha^{\varepsilon/(1-\varepsilon)}L^{\varepsilon/(1-\varepsilon)}$]. For α sufficiently close to one the country that specializes in good two has a wage rate which is lower in terms of good one than in autarky and it loses from trade.

This example shows that identical countries may engage in trade, it shows that both countries may gain from trade or one of them may lose, and it shows that gains from trade depend on the strength of demand for the good that is produced under nationally increasing returns to scale. It confirms Graham's argument that a country may lose from trade [see Graham (1923)]. Viner (1937) attributes a similar argument to Nicholson (1897).[24] It also shows that there need not be factor price equalization even when the trading partners are identical. In the example there is factor price equalization in autarky while trade brings about unequal factor prices [Ohlin (1933, p. 106) points out the unequalizing effect of trade on factor prices in the presence of economics of scale]. This shows again that with economies of scale neither commodity prices nor factor rewards serve as reliable predictors of the pattern of trade. When the countries are of unequal size there is an equilibrium in which the larger country exports the good produced with economies of scale.

Apart from the issues discussed so far, comparative statics responses of the production structure of economies with nationally increasing returns to scale have been investigated. In this context factoral value added is assumed to be produced by means of Heckscher–Ohlin-type technologies resulting in the following equilibrium conditions in production (the country specific superscript j is dropped at this stage):

$$p_i = c_i(w)/g_i(X_i), \quad \text{for all } i, \tag{6.1}$$

$$\sum_{i=1}^{m} \left[a_{li}(w)/g_i(X_i) \right] X_i = V_l, \quad \text{for all } l, \tag{6.2}$$

where it is assumed that the returns to scale are sector specific.[25] Eq. (6.1) is just a reproduction of the pricing equation (4.2). Eq. (6.2) represents equilibrium in factor markets. The coefficient $a_{li}(w)$ is the demand for factor l per-unit factoral value added in sector i $[= \partial c_i(w)/\partial w_l]$. Divided by $g_i(X_i)$ this coefficient represents demand for factor l per-unit output in sector i. Seen in this form, it is clear that changes in output levels affect both productivity and costs. Therefore we should not expect the standard results – such as the Stolper–Samuelson and the Rybczynski theorems – to remain intact in the present framework.

---

[24] For an analysis of gains from trade with decreasing returns to scale in one industry, which was Graham's original assumption, see Panagariya (1981) and Ethier (1982a).

[25] See Jones (1968), Kemp (1969), Panagariya (1980), and Inoue (1981). Jones (1968) does not assume homotheticity. Chang (1981) and Herberg, Kemp and Tawada (1982) discuss also intersectoral spillovers.

Take, for example, the Stolper–Samuelson theorem in the two-commodity two-factor case. It states that in an incompletely specialized economy an increase in the relative price of a good increases the real reward of the factor that is being used relatively intensively in the production of this good. The standard proof relies on the fact that the relationship between commodity prices and factor rewards is independent of output levels [this is indeed the case when $g_i(X_i) \equiv 1$; see (6.1)]. However, in the present context changes in output levels affect both absolute and relative costs [see (6.1)], which means that the effect of a relative price increase on real factor rewards depends on the feedback of output changes (that are caused by the relative price change) on sectoral cost structures. By logarithmic differentiation of (6.1) and (6.2) given $i = 1, 2$, $l = 1, 2$, calling the first factor of production labor (with $w_1 \equiv w$), and the second factor of production capital (with $w_2 \equiv r$), we obtain:

$$\begin{pmatrix} \theta_{L1} & \theta_{K1} \\ \theta_{L2} & \theta_{K2} \end{pmatrix} \begin{pmatrix} \hat{w} \\ \hat{r} \end{pmatrix} = \begin{pmatrix} \hat{p}_1 \\ \hat{p}_2 \end{pmatrix} + \begin{pmatrix} \varepsilon_1 \hat{X}_1 \\ \varepsilon_2 \hat{X}_2 \end{pmatrix}, \tag{6.3}$$

$$\begin{bmatrix} (1-\varepsilon_1)\lambda_{L1} & (1-\varepsilon_2)\lambda_{L2} \\ (1-\varepsilon_1)\lambda_{K1} & (1-\varepsilon_2)\lambda_{K2} \end{bmatrix} \begin{pmatrix} \hat{X}_1 \\ \hat{X}_2 \end{pmatrix} = \begin{pmatrix} \hat{L} \\ \hat{K} \end{pmatrix} + (\hat{w}-\hat{r}) \begin{pmatrix} \delta_L \\ -\delta_K \end{pmatrix}, \tag{6.4}$$

where θ_{ji} is the cost share of factor j in industry i, λ_{ji} is the allocative share of factor j in industry i, $\delta_L = \lambda_{L1}\theta_{K1}\sigma_1 + \lambda_{L2}\theta_{K2}\sigma_2$, $\delta_K = \lambda_{K1}\theta_{L1}\sigma_1 + \lambda_{K2}\theta_{L2}\sigma_2$, $\sigma_i =$ elasticity of substitution between labor and capital in sector i, ε_i is the elasticity of $g_i(X_i)$, and hats indicate proportional rates of change. Assuming that sector 1 is relatively labor intensive, the determinant of the matrix on the left-hand side of (6.3), θ, is positive, i.e. $|\theta| > 0$, and so is the determinant of the matrix on the left-hand side of (6.4), which equals $(1-\varepsilon_1)(1-\varepsilon_2)|\lambda|$, where $|\lambda| = \lambda_{L1}\lambda_{K2} - \lambda_{K1}\lambda_{L2}$.

Using (6.3) and (6.4), we can calculate the link between commodity prices and factor rewards which takes into account both the direct and indirect (through output changes) effects. This calculation yields:

$$\theta' \begin{pmatrix} \hat{w} \\ \hat{r} \end{pmatrix} = \begin{pmatrix} \hat{p}_1 \\ \hat{p}_2 \end{pmatrix}, \tag{6.5}$$

where

$$\theta' = \begin{pmatrix} \theta_{L1} - \xi_1 & \theta_{K1} + \xi_1 \\ \theta_{L2} + \xi_2 & \theta_{K2} - \xi_2 \end{pmatrix},$$

$$\xi_i = \frac{\varepsilon_i (\lambda_{Kj}\delta_L + \lambda_{Lj}\delta_K)}{|\lambda|(1-\varepsilon_i)}, \qquad i = 1, 2; \quad j = 1, 2; \quad j \neq i.$$

A typical element of the matrix θ' represents the effect of a factor price increase on *average* costs of production, given constant factor endowments [see Jones (1968)]. It takes into account the direct cost increase (represented by θ_{ij}) and the indirect cost effect that stems from changes in output levels (represented by ξ_j). If all the elements of θ' are positive, which means that average costs increase with a rise in every factor price, then the Stolper–Samuelson theorem remains valid if the determinant of θ', $|\theta'|$, is positive, i.e. if the sign of $|\theta'|$ is the same as the sign of $|\theta|$ [see Jones (1968)]. However, if θ' is a positive matrix but $|\theta'| < 0$, then the converse of the Stolper–Samuelson theorem holds. Indeed, for $\varepsilon_i > 0$ the sign of $|\theta'|$ becomes negative for sufficiently small values of X_i [see Panagariya (1980)]. Hence, with economies of scale in at least one sector, there always exist combinations of commodity prices and a corresponding resource allocation for which an increase in the relative price of a good will reduce the real reward of the factor used relatively intensively in its production and it will increase the real reward of the other factor of production. This means, for example, that one cannot use tariff policies to protect a factor of production by knowing only sectoral relative factor intensities; one needs much more information for this purpose. It should also be pointed out that the converse of the Stolper–Samuelson theorem does not rely on non-concavity of the production transformation curve; the validity of the Stolper–Samuelson theorem is neither necessary nor sufficient for the local concavity of the production possibility curve [see proposition 3 in Panagariya (1980)].

It is also possible to discuss the Rybczynski theorem and show similar implications in terms of the richness of outcomes. For example, in the presence of sector specific national variable returns to scale an increase in any input may cause all outputs to expand (at constant commodity prices). Chang (1981) and Herberg, Kemp and Tawada (1982) have also analyzed similar issues in a model with cross industry externalities, but I will not describe more comparative statics results. It should, however, be pointed out that all these are local results, both in the usual sense and also in the sense that for given commodity prices and factor endowments the initial allocation of resources around which the comparative statics is performed should be specified as *one* of the possible equilibrium allocations. The point is that commodity prices and factor endowments do not imply a unique equilibrium allocation of factors of production; multiple equilibria are possible.

7. Limited entry and market segmentation

So far we have dealt with trade in homogeneous products when there exists price competition à la Bertrand with free access to the technology and free entry into the industry, or pure competition with external economies. In either case commodities are priced according to average costs. Another line of investigation, which has received relatively little attention, considers market structures with limited entry. An extreme form of this case arises when the market for a commodity is supplied by a single monopolist. This assumption raises the natural question: what prevents other firms from entering, and in particular when the monopolist makes positive profits and there is "room" in terms of profitability for more firms? There is no obvious answer to this question. One possible answer is the existence of public licensing. Why have then the authorities issued a single licence? For our purposes nothing significant changes if instead of a single firm there exists a small given number of firms in the industry.

The role of monopoly power can be dealt with in the presence or in the absence of economies of scale in production. In order to isolate the role of monopoly power, it is instructive to assume that goods are produced with constant returns to scale [see, however, Markusen (1981) for a discussion of monopoly with economies of scale]. A firm with monopoly power, which faces a downward sloping demand curve, maximizes profits by equating marginal costs to marginal revenue. Under constant returns to scale marginal costs equal average costs and they depend only on factor prices. The structure of the marginal revenue function depends on the nature of demand. Marginal revenue for good i equals $p_i(1 - E_i^{-1})$, where E_i is the relevant elasticity of demand. Each monopolist takes as given all commodity prices except for his own. If preferences are homothetic, the elasticity of demand E_i depends only on relative prices. In this case marginal revenues depend also only on commodity prices, and each firm's profit maximizing condition becomes:

$$\text{MR}_i(p) = c_i(w), \qquad i = 1, 2, \ldots, m, \tag{7.1}$$

where p is the vector of commodity prices, $\text{MR}_i(p)$ is the marginal revenue function and $c_i(w)$ is the unit cost function. For a purely competitive industry $\text{MR}_i(p) \equiv p_i$. Factor market equilibrium conditions are the standard ones:

$$\sum_{i=1}^{m} a_{li}(w) X_i = V_l, \quad \text{for all } l, \tag{7.2}$$

where $a_{li}(w) = \partial c_i(w)/\partial w_l$ is the input of factor l per unit output of good i. In addition, there are the commodity market clearing conditions. It is clear from this representation that factor rewards are related to commodity prices by:

$$w = Y_V[\text{MR}_1(p), \text{MR}_2(p), \ldots, \text{MR}_m(p); V], \tag{7.3}$$

where $Y(\cdot)$ is defined as maximum $\sum_{i=1}^{m} \text{MR}_i(p) X_i$ s.t. $(X_1, X_2, \ldots, X_m)$ belongs to the production transformation surface and $Y_V(\cdot)$ is the gradient of $Y(\cdot)$ with respect to V. The function $Y(\cdot)$ represents factor income and it has the properties of the GDP$(\cdot)$ function previously discussed. In particular,

$$X = Y_{\text{MR}}[\text{MR}_1(p), \text{MR}_2(p), \ldots, \text{MR}_m(p); V] \tag{7.4}$$

whenever these derivatives exist. But $Y(\cdot)$ does not represent gross domestic product. The relationship between Y and GDP is as follows:

$$GDP = \sum_{i=1}^{m} p_i X_i = Y + \sum_{i=1}^{m} (p_i - MR_i) X_i$$

$$= Y + \sum_{i=1}^{m} (p_i - c_i) X_i$$

$$= Y + \Pi,$$

where Π represents monopoly profits.

An equilibrium described by (7.1)–(7.4) and appropriate commodity market clearing conditions does not always exist. Melvin and Warne (1973) have shown, however, that for a two sector economy with a CES utility function in which the elasticity of substitution is larger than one there exists a unique autarky equilibrium.[26] The key feature behind their uniqueness result is that with the CES utility function $MR_i(p)$ is increasing in p_i/p_j, $j \neq i$ [$MR_i(\cdot)$ is homogeneous of degree zero]. Using (7.4), this implies that the relative supply X_1/X_2 increases with p_1/p_2 and it ranges from zero (when $p_1/p_2 = 0$) to infinity (when $p_1/p_2 \rightarrow \infty$). Since the relative demand D_1/D_2 declines with p_1/p_2 and it is independent of the income level, there exists exactly one intersection point of the relative demand and relative supply functions. More generally, the uniqueness result applies to all preferences which yield the above described monotonicity property of the marginal revenue function. Although a two sector analysis of our economy with a monopolized sector in which the monopolist does not exercise monopsony power may seem superficial, it can be interpreted as a simulation of results which are appropriate for a multisector economy. Surely, with many sectors in existence, as in my formulation, this objection loses its force. In any case, it is instructive to isolate the effects of monopoly power from those of monopsony power.

Now suppose that there exist two countries with the same technologies and the same homothetic preferences. Assume also that when trade takes place there remains a single producer in each sector, i.e. every commodity is produced by a single profit maximizing producer who allocates production between the countries so as to minimize costs. Cost minimization implies equal marginal costs in every country (or no production in countries with higher marginal costs), while profit maximization implies that these marginal costs equal the marginal revenue of aggregate world demand. The result is that the same $MR_i(\cdot)$'s are applicable in every country's factor income function $Y(\cdot)$. Hence, under the usual conditions of no specialization and no factor intensity reversal, we obtain factor price equalization. Eq. (7.4) implies that each country produces relatively more of the goods

---

[26] Using my representation, their proof can probably be generalized to the m commodity case.

which are intensive in the factors with which the country is relatively well endowed. Since relative consumption levels are the same in every country, the pattern of trade is predicted by the Heckscher–Ohlin theory, provided each country's spending (income) equals its GDP. This is achieved when monopoly profits are distributed across countries in proportion to their consumption levels. Observe that for this result we do not have to require demand patterns which generate a unique trading equilibrium; all that is required is that an equilibrium exists.[27] Observe also that in the case of Ricardian technologies the pattern of trade is predicted by the classical theory. More generally, in the present setup production and trade patterns which are based on supply considerations remain valid. The driving force behind this outcome is the applicability of the *same* marginal revenue functions in every country. This has been achieved by means of the assumption that there exists a single firm in every sector. Clearly, nothing changes if some of the sectors are competitive [in a competitive sector $MR_i(p) \equiv p_i$].

A similar result is obtained if the market structure is such that in every country there exists a single firm in each noncompetitive sector and each firm believes that its share of the world's market is constant [see Melvin and Warne (1973)]. The point is that as long as the firm considers its market share to be constant, it faces the market demand elasticity independently of its market share (in the previous formulation this share was assumed to be one). Clearly, consistency requires the actual market share to equal the firm's perceived market share. But this means that every equilibrium with a single world monopolist in each industry is also an equilibrium of the two monopolists per-industry economy who consider their market shares as fixed, when the perceived market shares in the latter case equal the actually produced market shares in the former case. In the perceived fixed market share interpretation of the model, each country's income equals necessarily its GDP and the pattern of trade is predicted without further restrictions.

In the present framework the structure of the model is related to the model with internationally variable returns to scale, and it also implies that differences in country size do not affect the pattern of trade. As shown by Markusen (1981), this changes when in every country there exists a single firm in a noncompetitive sector and instead of considering its market share as constant the firms play a Cournot game. Namely, each firm takes as given the output (equals sales) level of its competitors and chooses its output level so as to maximize profits. In this case marginal revenue equals $p_i(1 - s_i E_i^{-1})$, where s_i is the firm's market share and E_i is the world's elasticity of demand for the product. If the countries have the same endowments of factors of production, there is a symmetric equilibrium in which MR_i is the same in every country and all countries have the same share of each market. In this case there is no trade. If, however, countries differ, say in size,

[27] This is a generalization of the Melvin and Warne (1973) result.

then marginal revenues will not be necessarily the same in every country, because they will have different market shares. The last point can be seen as follows. Suppose there are two countries with the same composition of factors of production but with $V^2 = \lambda V^1$, $\lambda > 1$,-i.e. with country two being larger than country one. Suppose also that these countries have the same homothetic preferences. In a trading equilibrium they cannot have the same market shares, because if they did they would have had the same MR_i's and therefore also – due to (7.3) – the same factor prices. But with the same factor prices they cannot produce the same quantities of goods when factors of production are fully employed [see (7.2)]. Factor price equalization is, therefore, out of the question in this case.

What can we say about the pattern of trade? Take the case considered by Markusen (1981) in which there are two sectors; the first is monopolized while the second is purely competitive. The utility function is homothetic (Markusen assumes a CES type utility function with an elasticity of substitution larger than one, but this is not required for the following argument as long as existence is assured). Then in a trading equilibrium the larger country gets a larger share of the market for good one (see footnote 28 below), which means that it faces a lower marginal revenue in this market [remember that $MR_1 = p_1(1 - s_1 E_1^{-1})$]. Reintroducing superscript j for countries, we have $MR_1^1 > MR_1^2$ and $MR_2^1 = MR_2^2 = p_2$ (the last equality stems from the fact that the second sector is competitive). Due to (7.4), the difference in marginal revenues in sector one implies that the larger country produces relatively more of the second commodity, i.e. $X_1^1/X_2^1 > X_1^2/X_2^2$. Since both countries consume the same relative quantities of every good, this means that the larger country exports the commodity that is being produced in the competitive sector and it imports the commodity that is being produced in the monopolistic sector; the smaller country has a revealed comparative advantage in the monopolistically marketed good while the larger country has a revealed comparative advantage in the competitively marketed good.[28] Observe also that in autarky the small country has the same factor prices as the large country, but that in the presence of trade they have different factor prices (because the marginal revenues become different as a result of trade). In particular, if there are two factors of production, the relative reward of the factor used relatively intensively in the monopolistic sector is lower in the larger country. Hence, in this example trade unequalizes factor rewards.

The presence of monopoly power substantially complicates the analysis of gains from trade. Clearly, if a country has a monopolized sector and trade eliminates this monopoly power, there are gains from trade from two sources; the elimination of monopoly power and the usual gains from trade. But when there is

---

[28] It is clear from the argument in the text that the larger country cannot have the smaller market share of good one. For suppose it does. Then $MR_1^2 > MR_1^1$ and $X_1^2/X_2^2 > X_1^1/X_2^1$. Since country 2 is larger than country 1, the last inequality implies $X_1^2 > X_1^1$, which contradicts the initial assumption that country 2 has a smaller market share of good one.

monopoly power in autarky as well as in the presence of trade, gains from trade cannot be assured. However, we can state the following gains from trade theorem:

Gains from Trade Theorem 2

In the absence of economies of scale in production, the following is a sufficient condition for gains from trade in country j:[29]

$$\sum_{i=1}^{m} \left(p_i - \mathrm{MR}_i^j \right)\left(X_i^j - X_i^{Aj} \right) \geq 0,$$

where p is the post-trade price vector, MR_i^j is the post-trade marginal revenue in country j, X_i^{Aj} is autarky output and X_i^j is post-trade output.

Since marginal revenue equals marginal costs [see (7.1)], $p_i - \mathrm{MR}_i^j$ equals marginal monopolistic profits in sector i, and my sufficient condition states that aggregate monopolistic profits in the trading equilibrium exceed the monopolistic profits that would have been obtained with these profit margins if the autarky output levels were produced [in the Melvin–Warne case MR_i^j equals $p_i(1 - E_i^{-1})$ and it equals $p_i(1 - s_i^j E_i^{-1})$ in the Markusen case]. When all sectors are competitive $\mathrm{MR}_i^j = p_i$ and this condition necessarily holds. We have, therefore, a proper generalization of the standard gains from trade theorem. But when some of the sectors are monopolized, the condition of the theorem holds if trade leads to an expansion of output in all the monopolized industries (since $p_i > \mathrm{MR}_i^j$ in a monopolized sector). If as a result of trade some monopolized industries expand while others contract, then our condition is still satisfied if the expanding industries have large monopolistic marginal profits while the contracting industries have small marginal monopolistic profits and they contract little relative to the expansion of the high profit industries. In the two sector case, in which one sector is monopolized while the other is competitive, the condition of the theorem is satisfied if the first industry expands output; i.e. if $X_1^j > X_1^{Aj}$. Markusen (1981)

---

[29]*Proof*

Let $e(p, u)$ be the minimum expenditure function of country j. Then, if p represents the price vector when trade takes place, u^A its autarky utility level and u its post-trade utility level, then:

$$e\left(p, u^A\right) \leq \sum_i p_i X_i^{Aj} = \sum_i \mathrm{MR}_i^j X_i^{Aj} + \sum_i \left(p_i - \mathrm{MR}_i^j \right) X_j^{Aj} \leq Y^j\left(\mathrm{MR}_1^j, \mathrm{MR}_2^j, \ldots, \mathrm{MR}_m^j; V^j\right)$$

$$+ \sum_i \left(p_i - \mathrm{MR}_i^j \right) X_i^{Aj} = \sum_i p_i X_i^j - \sum_i \left(p_i - \mathrm{MR}_i^j \right)\left(X_i^j - X_i^{Aj} \right) \leq \sum_i p_i X_i^j = e(p, u).$$

The last inequality stems from the condition of the theorem. However, $e(p, u^A) \leq e(p, u)$ implies $u^A \leq u$.

has indeed shown that this leads to gains from trade. Moreover, considering two countries which are identical except for size and which have the same CES utility functions he has shown that $X_i^j > X_i^{A,j}$ is always the case for the smaller country but may or may not happen in the larger country. This means that the small country gains from trade, but it does not resolve the large country's welfare change. If the countries are of equal size both gain from trade despite there being no active trade. Here the gains result from the reduction of the degree of monopoly power which comes with the doubling (from one to two) of the number of firms in each sector.

Melvin and Warne (1973) argue that in their case the country with a comparative advantage in the low elasticity good gains from trade. The other country may gain or lose. I have not been able to relate this result to my gains from trade theorem.

In all the models that have been discussed so far international commodity markets were assumed to be integrated. Namely, a commodity was assumed to be sold for one price everywhere and monopolists considered the aggregate demand for the good as the basic factor that determines the demand curve faced by them. Brander (1981) has deviated from this tradition by assuming market segmentation. According to Brander a typical monopolistic firm faces distinct country-specific downward sloping demand curves. It chooses profit maximizing sales in every country under the assumption that the quantity sold by its competitors in *each* market is invariant to its decisions. Firms do not recognize the fact that markets are interrelated; they operate under the assumption of segregated markets. Assuming that in the monopolized sector there exists a single firm in every country, it is obvious that in this case there might be two-way trade in the same good. For suppose marginal costs of production are the same in every country and one market is served by a single firm. For the servicing firm marginal revenue equals marginal costs, i.e. $p_i(1 - E_i^{-1}) = c_i$, and its market share equals one. For the other firm marginal revenue equals $p_i(1 - s_i E_i^{-1}) = p_i$ because its market share s_i is zero. Hence, for the other firm marginal revenue exceeds marginal costs, making it worthwhile to penetrate the market.

Market segregation leads to two-way trade in the same good (intra-industry trade). This property is preserved when the number of firms is larger than one as long as it is finite. If there are internal economies of scale, free entry will lead to a finite number of firms with zero profits and intra-industry trade in identical commodities. The existence of transport costs does not eliminate this possibility too, but it does introduce the possibility of two-way dumping – a situation in which in every country the f.o.b. export price is less than the domestic price of the same commodity [see Brander and Krugman (1980)]. In addition, the existence of transport costs makes two-way trade wasteful in terms of real resources. Hence, even if trade is desirable because it increases competition, the wasteful transport costs may dominate the welfare effect, causing overall losses from trade.

8. Differentiated products

The need for an extension of trade theories in order to deal with differentiated products was recognized many years ago [see the preface to the English edition of Haberler (1937)]. The publication of Chamberlin's and Robinson's works on monopolistic competition [Chamberlin (1933) and Robinson (1933)] raised hopes that it will be possible to accomplish the desired extension. There were, at the time, several attempts to evaluate the implications of Chamberlin's work for international trade theory [see, for example, Anderson (1936), Beach (1936), and Lovasy (1941)] but these were not very successful [see Caves (1960)].

The new interest in trade in differentiated products has arisen primarily from empirical observations, in particular due to Balassa (1967), Kravis (1971) and Grubel and Lloyd (1975), one of the major observations being a tremendous increase in the post World War II period of the share of intra-industry trade [see Barker (1977)]. These were followed by attempts to provide a theoretical underpinning to these observations both by the observers themselves and by others [see, for example, Grubel (1970), Gray (1973), and Barker (1977)].[30]

A new wave of theoretical developments began with the work of Krugman (1979) and Lancaster (1979, ch. 9), who presented one sector models in which all international trade is intra-industry trade. This was followed by an integration of traditional trade theories with the theory of intra-industry trade [see Lancaster (1980), Dixit and Norman (1980, ch. 9), and Helpman (1981)].

The major innovation of the new theory lies in its accommodation of two assumptions: (a) that there exist sectors with product differentiation and there exists in every country a demand for a wide spectrum of varieties; and (b) that each variety of a differentiated product is produced with internal economies of scale. The second assumption has lead to the adoption of a monopolistic market structure in the differentiated product industries, and to equilibria in which a finite number of varieties is produced, with every firm producing a different variety. If in an equilibrium there exist differentiated products which are produced in more than one country, then – since each variety is produced in only one country – the first assumption assures intra-industry trade. This is the central innovation of this theory. As simple as it might seem, once embedded in a general equilibrium trade model it enriches significantly the model's implications.

There are two approaches that have been used for the modeling of the demand for varieties. One approach, which is based on Dixit and Stiglitz (1977), assumes that a representative consumer likes to consume a large number of varieties. Suppose the utility function is weakly separable so that $u = U[u_1(\cdot), u_2(\cdot), \ldots, u_m(\cdot)]$, where $u_i(\cdot)$ is the sub-utility derived from consuming sector i's goods, and $U(\cdot)$ is homothetic. In the case of differentiated products it is assumed

---

[30] I will discuss the empirical observations in relation to the theory at a later stage.

that:

$$u_i(y_{i1}, y_{i2}, \ldots) \equiv \left(\sum_{k=1}^{\infty} y_{ik}^{\beta_i} \right)^{1/\beta_i}, \qquad 0 < \beta_i < 1, \tag{8.1}$$

where y_k is consumption of variety k of product i. Since only a finite number of varieties is available, $u_i(\cdot)$ is bounded in equilibrium. The taste for varieties represented by this utility function can be seen by observing that with equal commodity prices for available varieties the maximal $u_i(\cdot)$ attained for a given expenditure level increases with the number of varieties. According to this representation the elasticity of substitution is the same between every pair of varieties. Hence, there do not exist good and bad substitutes; all can be equally well substituted for each other. In addition, if a large number of varieties is available, the elasticity of demand for a single variety is approximately equal to $1/(1-\beta_i)$, i.e. all elasticities of demand are equal and constant.[31] This greatly facilitates the analysis.

The alternative approach is due to Lancaster (1979). It is based on the assumption that products are differentiated by the combination of some basic characteristics. Every consumer has an ideal product, i.e. his most desired combination of characteristics. Representing a variety by a point on a line or the circumference of a circle,[32] a consumer who is forced to consume a variety which is not his ideal product prefers the one which is closest to his ideal product. Hence, there is a measure of "closeness" of varieties such that the closer two varieties are the better substitutes they are for each other. Here the subutility of a differentiated product i is:

$$u_i(y_i, d_i) \equiv y_i / h_i(d_i), \tag{8.2}$$

where y_i is the quantity consumed, d_i is the distance between the consumed variety and the ideal product, and $h_i(\cdot)$ is a compensation function which is increasing, convex, with $h_i(0) = 1$ and $h_i'(0) = 0$.

The need for an aggregate demand for a wide spectrum of varieties is satisfied by assuming that the distribution of tastes is uniform, which is the analogue of

---

[31] In the case of a continuum of varieties with a finite number N:

$$u_i = \left[\int_0^N [y_i(k)]^{\beta_i} dk \right]^{1/\beta_i},$$

and $1/(1-\beta_i)$ is the exact elasticity of demand. Krugman (1979) used a more general utility function.
[32] Other representations are also possible.

the assumption of identical consumers in the previous case (this assumption should be relaxed in future work). All consumers are also assumed to have the same utility functions $U[u_i(\cdot),\ldots,u_m(\cdot)]$ and $u_i(\cdot)$, $i=1,2,\ldots,m$, with $U(\cdot)$ being homothetic. This means in particular that irrespective of the most desired variety, they have the same compensation functions. These assumptions enable one to derive the demand for a single variety of a given product. Here the elasticity of demand is not constant; it depends on the number of available varieties and on the price of the variety under consideration as well as on prices of its closest substitutes [see Lancaster (1979)].

We have seen that the alternative specifications of preferences have different implication for the demand elasticity. They also have different implications for welfare evaluations and for the competition in product choice. Under the Dixit–Stiglitz formulation a firm need not worry about the product type that it chooses to produce, as long as it does not choose an already available variety. Under the Lancaster specification the variety choice is significant. In both cases it is assumed that firms engage in price competition [except Dixit and Norman (1980, ch. 9)], taking advantage of their limited monopoly power (the monopoly power is limited by the available substitutes in the form of other varieties). In the second case they also compete on variety choice.

Suppose that preferences are identical across countries. Assuming that all varieties of the same product are equally priced (which will follow from the assumptions to be specified at a later stage), the elasticity of world demand for a particular variety will generally depend on the vector of commodity prices $p = (p_1, p_2,\ldots, p_m)$ and the numbers of each product's available varieties, $N = (N_1, N_2,\ldots, N_m)$. If a particular product i is not differentiated, then N_i has no effect on its elasticity of demand. This means also that the degree of monopoly power, defined as the ratio of average to marginal revenue, $R_i \equiv p_i/\mathrm{MR}_i = (1 - E_1^{-1})^{-1}$, depends on p and N, i.e. $R_i = R_i(p, N)$. In the Dixit–Stiglitz case $R_i(\cdot)$ is constant, and it equals β_i^{-1}. In the Lancaster case it is generally a complicated function, but it depends only on N_i if the consumer spends fixed budget shares on each product [see Lancaster (1979)].

Now assume that there are internal economies of scale in the production of each variety and that the same production functions apply to all varieties of the same product. Production functions are the same in every country. This strong symmetry assumption together with the symmetry assumed about consumers, makes symmetrical equilibria of prime interest. Every producer who maximizes profits by taking as given the prices charged by his competitors and the varieties that they produce chooses a distinct variety (one that is not produced by his competitors) and charges a price which equates his marginal costs to his marginal revenue. In equilibrium all varieties of a given product are equally priced and in Lancaster's case available varieties are equally spaced in product space. Assuming free entry, prices equal average costs, so that when varieties of product i are produced in country j:

$$p_i x_i = C_i(w^j, x_i), \qquad i = 1, 2, \ldots, m, \tag{8.3}$$

where x_i is output of a single variety of product i and $C_i(\cdot)$ is the cost function. The quantity x_i is the same in every country that produces this product because given our symmetry assumptions the same quantity of every variety is demanded by consumers. Due to the economies of scale the elasticity of costs with respect to output, $1/\theta_i(w^j, x_i)$ [see eq. (2.1)], is smaller than one.

Now combine the condition that marginal costs equal marginal revenue with (8.3) to obtain:

$$R_i(p, N) = \theta_i(w^j, x_i), \qquad i = 1, 2, \ldots, m. \tag{8.4}$$

Namely, the degree of economies of scale equals the degree of monopoly power. If there is no product differentiation by consumers, or if there are sufficiently many varieties for products to be custom made, then $R_i(\cdot) = 1$. If there are constant returns to scale, then $\theta_i(\cdot) = 1$. Hence, (8.4) is also satisfied for products of the standard type used in trade theory.

Now, it is clear from (8.3) that with more goods than factors of production and no factor intensity reversal at x_i, the vector of factor rewards w^j is the same in every country. In fact, there are conditions under which (8.3) and (8.4) imply factor price equalization and equalization of output per firm [see Helpman (1981a)]. Observe also that this is obtained with increasing returns to scale and even without requiring homotheticity in production.[33]

In what follows assume factor price equalization. Denoting by n_i^j the number of firms in industry i of country j, factor market clearing conditions can be represented by:

$$\sum_{i=1}^{m} A_{li}(w, x_i) n_i^j = V_l^j, \quad \text{for all } l, \tag{8.5}$$

where $A_{li} = \partial C_i / \partial w_l$ is the employment of factor l by a representative firm in sector i. If sector i produces a homogeneous product with constant returns to scale, then $A_{li}(w, x_i) n_i^j = a_{li}(w) n_i^j x_i = a_{li}(w) X_i^j$, where $X_i^j = n_i^j x_i$, as in the standard model. In this case the number of firms in the industry is undetermined, but the industry's output level X_i^j is determined.

It is clear from (8.5) that a country which is relatively well endowed with certain factors of production will have a relatively large output X_i^j in industries which use these factors intensively. If an industry produces a homogeneous

---

[33] See Helpman and Razin (1980) and Lawrence and Spiller (1983) for explicit examples.

product, this is reflected in its aggregate output X_i^j. If an industry produces a differentiated product this is reflected in X_i^j through the number of firms n_i^j (and therefore also varieties) that exist in the industry, because output per-firm x_i is the same in every country. Hence, if a country is well endowed with factors of production which are used intensively in a differentiated product industry i, then this country produces relatively many varieties n_i^j of this product.

Due to our assumptions about preferences, every country has the same composition of consumption, i.e. every country consumes a fixed proportion of every variety produced in the world economy and the same proportion of every homogeneous product, with this proportion being equal to its share in world income. Since different varieties of a product are produced in different countries, this means that there is intra-industry trade in differentiated products. Also, since relative production levels are determined by relative endowments of factors of production, this means that intersectoral trade is as predicted by the Heckscher–Ohlin theory [see Helpman (1981)].[34, 35] However, as in other cases with economies of scale pre-trade commodity prices and factor rewards do not serve as reliable predictors of the pattern of trade [see Lancaster (1980) and Helpman (1981a)]. In special cases factor rewards and scale-adjusted commodity prices can be used to predict the pattern of trade [see Helpman (1981)].

It is clear from this that the Chamberlin–Heckscher–Ohlin model explains intra-industry trade as well as inter-industry trade. It shoud, however, be pointed out that its explanation of two-way trade in similar commodities is not based on the assumption of market segmentation [as in Brander (1981)]; we have assumed integrated markets. Here intra-industry trade arises from the fact that due to internal economies of scale every country specializes in different varieties. Chamberlin is used to explain intra-industry trade while Heckscher–Ohlin are used to explain inter-sectoral trade.[36] Although we have confined attention to final products only, the theory can be modified in order to deal with trade in middle products, without altering its main explanatory power. This is shown in Ethier (1982b) and Helpman (1983). Ethier (1982b) assumes a homogeneous final output which can be produced with infinitely many varieties of middle products.

---

[34] In the special case in which all production functions are homothetic, $C_i(w, x_i) = c_i(w)\tilde{g}_i(x_i)$, where $c_i(\cdot)$ represents unit costs to produce factoral value added. Now condition (8.3) can be written as $p_i g_i(x_i) = c_i(w)$, where $g_i(x_i) \equiv x_i/\tilde{g}_i(x_i)$, just as in (4.2). In this case (8.5) reads $\sum_{i=1}^m [a_{li}(w)/g_i(x_i)] n_i^j x_i = V_l^j$. This means that gross domestic product can be written as a function $\mathrm{GDP}[p_1 g_1(x_1), p_2 g_2(x_2), \ldots, p_m g_m(x_m); V^j]$, with $\partial \mathrm{GDP}/\partial p_i = n_i^j x_i$ and $w_l = \partial \mathrm{GDP}/\partial V_l$. This makes clear the link between the present result and those discussed in Sections 4–6. Also using the technique employed in Helpman and Razin (1983, Section 3), one can define a $\mathrm{GDP}(\cdot)$ function $\mathrm{GDP}(p_1, p_2, \ldots, p_m; V; x_1, x_2, \ldots, x_m)$ which has the usual properties with respect to (p, V) (with $\partial \mathrm{GDP}/\partial p_i = n_i x_i$) and in which the x_i's operate like technical progress coefficients, without requiring homotheticity.

[35] Horn (1983) presents a comparative statics analysis of this model for the case of a constant degree of monopoly power, with an emphasis on non-homotheticity in production.

The production function of the final good has the CES form as in (8.1), so that with equal input prices costs of a given output decline with the available number of varieties of the middle product. Each variety is produced with internal economies of scale, which limits their available number. This way one obtains economies of scale in the production of the final output and they have the form of international economies of scale, because the larger world output the more varieties of the middle product become available. Helpman (1983) assumes that the final product and the middle product are differentiated, with preferences being of the Lancaster type. Each variety of the final product has an ideal variety of the middle product which is most suited for its production. If one has to employ a variety of the middle product which is not the ideal one, it is necessary to employ more labor and capital, with the required quantities of the primary inputs being larger the less suitable is the employed variety of the middle product. Each variety of the middle product is produced with internal economies of scale. In both cases there is monopolistic competition in the industry producing middle products and there is intra-industry trade in middle products.

In what follows, I discuss the case in which there do not exist middle products [see, however, Helpman (1983) for analogies in results]. If all goods are differentiated products, then the volume of trade between a pair of countries conforms to the gravity equation. Namely, the volume of trade is proportional to the product of their GDPs. This can be seen as follows.[37] If y_i^j is consumption of a single variety of product i in country j, then $y_i^j = \mu^j x_i$, where μ^j is the share of country j in world GDP. Exports of country l to country k equal

$$EX^{lk} = \sum_{i=1}^{m} p_i n_i^l y_i^k = \mu^k \sum_{i=1}^{m} p_i n_i^l x_i = \mu^k \text{GDP}^l = \text{GDP}^k \text{GDP}^l \bigg/ \sum_j \text{GDP}^j,$$

which also equals exports of country k to country l, EX^{kl}. Hence,

$$E^{lk} = EX^{kl} = \text{GDP}^k \text{GDP}^l \bigg/ \sum_j \text{GDP}^j,$$

and the bilateral value of trade is proportional to the product of GDP levels, with the factor of proportionality being the inverse of world income. Can this explain

---

[36] In the presence of transport costs domestic market size differences generate a predictable pattern of trade. If two countries of equal size trade with each other in two classes of differentiated products and they differ only in the composition of demand, then each country is a net exporter of the product for which it has a relatively larger demand. The relatively larger demand translates into a relatively larger domestic market (both in terms of consumption and production) so that each country exports the good for which it has a relatively larger domestic market [see Krugman (1980a)].

[37] Krugman (1980) derives this equation for a special case.

the fact that the volume of trade has grown faster than income? According to Krugman (1980) it cannot, because in his model (which uses Dixit–Stiglitz-type preferences) a proportionally equal increase in all countries' factors of production increases every country's income by the same factor of proportionality, implying via (8.6) an increase in the volume of trade at the common rate of GDP growth.[38]

More can be said about the volume of trade if we assume a two sector economy with one differentiated product and one homogeneous product, and two factors of production – labor and capital. In a world composed of two countries which differ only in size, i.e. $V^2 = \lambda V^1$, $\lambda \geq 1$, a redistribution of factors of production which leaves each country with the same composition increases the volume of trade if and only if it reduces the difference in relative country size. The volume of trade is maximized when the countries are of equal size [see Proposition 6 in Helpman (1981)]. On the other hand, if countries differ in the endowed capital–labor ratio, a redistribution of labor and capital which does not change GDP levels increases the volume of trade if and only if it increases the difference in factor proportions [see Proposition 5 in Helpman (1981)]. These two results imply that similarity in incomes per capita need not breed large volumes of trade as argued by the Linder hypothesis [see Burestam Linder (1961)]. On the other hand, a redistribution of factors of production reduces the *share* of intra-industry trade independently of its effect on relative country size if and only if it increases the difference in the endowed capital–labor ratios [see Proposition 4 in Helpman (1981) and the example in Krugman (1981)]. This means that similarities in income per capita are associated with a larger share of intra-industry trade [Loertscher and Wolter (1980) provide empirical support for this result].

Although there does not exist a general gains from trade theorem for economies with differentiated products, gains from trade can be shown for specific models. A new source of gains from trade which is specific to economies with differentiated products is an increase in available varieties that comes with trade. In the Dixit–Stiglitz case this has a direct positive welfare effect because individuals have a taste for many varieties, while in the Lancaster case trade enables more individuals to consume varieties which are closer to their ideal product so that on average welfare increases.[39] In addition, trade may lead to higher output levels of each variety, thereby reducing average resource use as well as prices. The result is

---

[38] With the Dixit–Stiglitz-type CES preferences $R_i = \beta_i^{-1}$, implying a constant x_i. Hence, if production functions are homothetic, real production, consumption, and trade, rise at the rate of factor growth through an increase in n_i^j. Hence, Krugman (1980) could not obtain a rate of growth of the volume of trade which exceeds the rate of GDP growth, even if he was to admit the existence of homogeneous goods which are produced with constant returns to scale.

[39] This means that if in the Lancaster case varieties are drawn from a uniform distribution both in autarky and when trade takes place, then the expected utility is higher when trade takes place.

an increase in welfare.[40, 41] The larger the trading partners, the more a country stands to gain from trade.[42]

Suppose we consider gainful trade among several economies. Does every factor of production gain from trade? In the Heckscher–Ohlin world some factors of production necessarily lose as implied by the Stolper–Samuelson theorem [see Jones and Scheinkman (1977) for the many factors many goods case as well as Chapter 3 in this volume]. However, in the Chamberlin–Heckscher–Ohlin world it is possible for all factors of production to gain. Take the case of trade among economies which spend fixed budget shares on every product which they produce with homothetic production functions, and which have the same composition of factors of production. Such economies gain from trade if the degree of monopoly power decreases in the number of varieties and the degree of economies of scale decreases in output. In addition, in this case relative factor rewards do not change with trade.[43] Hence, every factor of production gains. This means that for sufficiently small differences in the composition of factors of production the variety effect dominates the Stolper–Samuelson effect and every factor of production gains from trade. But for sufficiently dissimilar compositions of factors of production some factors of production may lose from trade [see Krugman (1981) for an example]. Since similarity in the composition of factors of production breeds intra-industry trade while dissimilarity breeds intersectoral trade, observed larger shares of intra-industry trade make it more likely that many (and perhaps all) factors of production gain from trade. Can this explain the fact noted by Balassa (1967) that the formation of the EEC was not followed by severe structural reallocations of resources and little resistance by interest groups, as argued by Krugman (1981)? It might, although the current analysis deals with gains from trade while the formation of the EEC involved reductions of impediments to trade. So far, tariff policies have not been investigated in this framework.

[40] Take the homothetic case with fixed budget shares discussed in Helpman (1981, section 6). If countries with the same factor proportions engage in trade, it is clear from that analysis that as a result of trade x_i increases and p_i falls in the differentiated product industry. Since income does not change, every country gains from trade.

[41] Similar effects appear in the welfare analysis of international factor movements in Helpman and Razin (1983). Due to the effects that factor movements have on the number of varieties available to consumers and output levels per firm, market rewards do not represent the social marginal product value of a factor of production.

[42] This is obvious from the analysis suggested in footnote 40. For another example see Proposition 10 in Lawrence and Spiller (1983).

[43] See footnote 40.

References

Anderson, K.L. (1936), "Tariff protection and increasing returns", in: Explorations in economies: Notes and essays contributed in honor of F.W. Taussing (McGraw-Hill, New York).

Balassa, B. (1967), Trade liberalization among industrial countries (McGraw-Hill, New York).

Barker, T. (1977), "International trade and economic growth: An alternative to the neoclassical approach", Cambridge Journal of Economics, 1:153–172.

Beach, W.E. (1936), "Some aspects of international trade under monopolistic competition", in: Explorations in economies: Notes and essays contributed in honor of F.W. Taussing (McGraw-Hill, New York).

Brander, J.A. (1981), "Intra-industry trade in identical commodities", Journal of International Economics, 11:1–14.

Brander, J.A. and P.R. Krugman (1980), "A 'reciprocal dumping' model of international trade", mimeo.

Burestam Linder, S. (1961), An essay on trade and transformation (Almqvist A. Wicksell, Uppsala).

Caves, R.E. (1960), Trade and economic structure (Harvard University Press, Cambridge).

Caves, R.E. (1974), "International trade, international investment, and imperfect markets", Special Papers in International Economics no. 10 International Finance Section, Princeton University.

Chamberlin, E.H. (1933), The theory of monopolistic competition (Harvard University Press, Cambridge).

Chang, W.W. (1981), "Production externalities, variable returns to scale and theory of trade", International Economic Review, 22:511–525.

Chipman, J.S. (1965), "A survey of the theory of international trade: Part 2, the neoclassical theory", Econometrica, 33:685–760.

Chipman, J.S. (1970), "External economics of scale and competitive equilibrium", Quarterly Journal of Economics, 84:347–385.

Dixit, A.K. and V.D. Norman (1980), Theory of international trade (Cambridge University Press, Cambridge).

Dixit, A.D. and J.E. Stiglitz, (1977), "Monopolistic competition and optimum product diversity", American Economic Review, 67:297–308.

Eaton, J. and A. Panagariya (1979), "Gains from trade under variable returns to scale, commodity taxation, tariffs and factor market distortions", Journal of International Economics, 9:481–501.

Ethier, W.J. (1979), "Internationally decreasing costs and world trade", Journal of International Economics, 9:1–24.

Ethier, W.J. (1982a), "Decreasing costs in international trade and Frank Graham's argument for protection", Econometrica, 50:1243–1268.

Ethier, W.J. (1982b), "National and international returns to scale in the modern theory of international trade", American Economic Review, 72:389–405.

Graham, F.D. (1923), "Some aspects of protection further considered", Quarterly Journal of Economics, 37:199–227.

Graham, F.D. (1925), "Some fallacies in the interpretation of social costs: A reply", Quarterly Journal of Economics, 39:324–330.

Gray, H.P. (1973), "Two-way international trade in manufactures: A theoretical underpinning", Weltwirtscaftliche Archiv, 19–38.

Grossman, S.J. (1981), "Nash equilibrium and the industrial organization of markets with large fixed costs", Econometrica, 49:1149–1172.

Grubel, H.G. (1970), "The theory of intra-industry trade", in: I.A. McDougall, ed, Studies in international economics (North-Holland, Amsterdam).

Grubel, H.G. and P.J. Lloyd (1975), Intra-industry trade: The theory and measurement of international trade in differentiated products (Macmillan, London).

Haberler, G. (1936), The theory of international trade with its applications to commercial policy (William Hodges, London).

Hanoch, G. (1975), "The elasticity of scale and the shape of average costs", American Economic Review, 65:492–497.

Helpman, E. (1981), "International trade in the presence of product differentiation, economies of scale and monopolistic competition: A Chamberlin–Heckscher–Ohlin approach", Journal of International Economics, 11:305–340.

Helpman, E. (1983), "International trade in differentiated middle products", in: D. Hague and K.G. Jungenfelt, eds., Structural adjustment in developed open economies (Macmillan, London).

Helpman, E. and A. Razin (1980), "Monopolistic competition and factor movements", Seminar Paper no. 155 Institute for International Economic Studies, University of Stockholm.

Helpman, E. and A. Razin (1983), "Increasing returns, monopolistic competition and factor movements: A welfare analysis", Journal of International Economics, 14.

Herberg, H. and M.C. Kemp (1969), "Some implications of variable returns to scale", Canadian Journal of Economics, 11:403–415.

Herberg, H., M.C. Kemp and M. Tawada (1983), "Further implications of variable returns to scale", Journal of International Economics, 13: 65–84.

Horn, H. (1981), "Some implications of non-homotheticity in production in a two-sector general equilibrium model with monopolistic competition", Journal of International Economics, 13: 85–101.

Inoue, I. (1981), "A generalization of the Samuelson reciprocity relation, the Stolper–Samuelson theorem and the Rybczynski theorem under variable returns to scale", Journal of International Economics, 11:79–98.

Jones, R.W. (1968), "Variable returns to scale in general equilibrium theory", International Economic Review, 9:261–272.

Jones, R.W. and J.A. Scheinkman (1977), "The relevance of the two-sector production model in trade theory", Journal of Political Economy, 85:909–935.

Kemp, M.C. (1969), The pure theory of international trade and investment (Prentice-Hall, Englewood Cliffs).

Kemp, M.C. and T. Negishi (1970), "Variable returns to scale, commodity taxes, factor market distortions and their implications for trade gains", Swedish Journal of Economics, 72:1–11.

Knight, F.H. (1924), "Some fallacies in the interpretation of social costs", Quarterly Journal of Economics, 38:582–606.

Knight, F.H. (1925), "On decreasing costs and comparative costs: A rejoinder", Quarterly Journal of Economics, 39:331–333.

Kravis, I.B. (1971), "The current case for import limitations", in: United States economic policy in an interdependent world (Commission on International Trade and Investment Policy, Washington).

Krugman, P.R. (1979), "Increasing returns, monopolistic competition, and international trade", Journal of International Economics, 9:469–479.

Krugman, P.R. (1980a), "Scale economies, product differentiation, and the pattern of trade", American Economic Review, 70:950–959.

Krugman, P.R. (1980b), "Differentiated products and multilateral trade", (mimeo).

Krugman, P.R. (1981), "Intraindustry specialization and the gains from trade", Journal of Political Economy, 89:959–973.

Lancaster, K. (1979), Variety, equity, and efficiency (Columbia University Press, New York).

Lancaster, K. (1980), "Intra-industry trade under perfect monopolistic competition", Journal of International Economics, 10:151–175.

Lawrence, C. and P.T. Spiller (1983), "Product diversity, economies of scale and international trade", Quarterly Journal of Economics, XCVII: 63–83.

Lerner, A.P. (1932), "The diagrammatic representation of cost conditions in international trade", Economica, 34:346–356.

Loertscher, R. and F. Wolter (1980), "Determinants of intra-industry trade: Among countries and across industries", Weltwirtschafliches Archiv, 8:280–293.

Lovasy, G. (1941), "International trade under imperfect competition", Quarterly Journal of Economics, LV:567–583.

Manning, R. and J. Macmillan (1979), "Public intermediate goods, production possibilities, and international trade", Canadian Journal of Economics, XII:243–257.

Markusen, J.R. (1981), Trade and gains from trade with imperfect competition, Journal of International Economics, 11:531–551.

Markusen, J.R. and J.R. Melvin (1981), "Trade, factor prices, and gains from trade with increasing returns to scale", Canadian Journal of Economics, XIV:450–469.

Marshall, A. (1879), The pure theory of foreign trade (reprinted by the London School of Economics in 1930).

Marshall, A. (1920), Principles of economics, 8th edn. (Macmillan, London).

Matthews, R.C.O. (1949–1950), "Reciprocal demand and increasing returns", Review of Economic Studies, 37:149–158.

Melvin, J.R. (1969), "Increasing returns to scale as a determinant of trade", Canadian Journal of Economics, 11:389–402.

Melvin, J.R. and R.D. Warne (1973), "Monopoly and the theory of international trade", Journal of International Economics, 3:117–134.

Modigliani, F. (1958), "New developments on the oligopoly front", Journal of Political Economy, 66:215–232.

Negishi, T. (1972), General equilibrium theory and international trade (North-Holland, Amsterdam).

Nicholson, J.S. (1897), Principles of political economy.

Ohlin, B. (1933), Interregional and international trade (Harvard University Press, Cambridge).

Panagariya, A. (1980), "Variable returns to scale in general equilibrium theory once again", Journal of International Economics, 10:499–526.

Panagariya, A. (1981), "Variable returns to scale and patterns of specialization", American Economic Review, 71:221–230.

Robinson, J. (1933), The economics of imperfect competition (Macmillan, London).

Stigler, G.J. (1951), "The division of labor is limited by the extent of the market", Journal of Political Economy, 59:185–193.

Tinbergen, J. (1945), International economic cooperation (Elsevier, Amsterdam).

Varian, H.R. (1978), Microeconomic analysis (Norton, New York).

Viner, J. (1937), Studies in the theory of international trade (Harper & Brothers, New York).

Chapter 8

THE ROLE OF NATURAL RESOURCES IN TRADE MODELS

MURRAY C. KEMP

University of New South Wales

and

NGO VAN LONG

Australian National University

Contents

1.	The need for new theories	368
2.	Anti-Heckscher–Ohlin theory	370
3.	Generalized Heckscher–Ohlin theory	377
4.	Generalized anti-Heckscher–Ohlin theory	388
5.	Hybrid theory	388
6.	Resource-renewal and resource-replacement	395
	6.1. Resource-renewal	395
	6.2. Resource-replacement	397
7.	Cartels – introduction	405
8.	Cartels – the case of binding contracts	406
9.	Cartels – no binding contracts	411
10.	The formation of cartels	412
11.	Bibliographical notes	413
	References	415

*We are very grateful to Tracy Lewis and Alistair Ulph for guiding us in our search of the literature, to Makoto Tawada for picking up several mistakes in an early draft, and to Roy Ruffin and Alasdair Smith for useful suggestions concerning the organisation of the chapter.

Handbook of International Economics, vol. I, Edited by R.W. Jones and P.B. Kenen
© *Elsevier Science Publishers B.V., 1984*

1. The need for new theories

Much of the modern long-run theory of international trade derives from what has come to be called the 2×2 or Heckscher–Ohlin model of production; and the rest of the theory derives from straightforward extensions of that model achieved by the accommodation of additional factors and products and by the addition of more-or-less durable produced intermediate goods. In all versions of the model, final goods are produced, directly or indirectly, by two primary or non-produced factors of production, a unit of any factor yielding its services in a given and steady flow for ever and ever (one thinks of Ricardo's indestructible powers of the soil).

On the other hand, raw materials extracted from exhaustible deposits now contribute a considerable part of the annual value of international trade. (According to the *Annual Report of International Trade*, published by GATT in 1980, minerals and fuels alone accounted for 29 percent of the value of world commodity exports. If the accounting had been in terms of value added, the share undoubtedly would have been even higher.) And the distinctive feature of such deposits is that they yield their services in a controlled and variable flow for only as long as the stock survives (one thinks now of coal deposits and oil reserves, that is, of Hotelling's destructible powers of the soil).

Thus we appear to rely on a theory of trade patterns which denies the existence of a major component of trade.

In defense of conventional theory it might be argued that formally there is little difference between man-made deposits of equipment, which can be run down (depreciated) by using them and deposits of exhaustible resources which can be artificially renewed by means of scrap recycling, plant nurseries and fish hatcheries. However there is a very important difference betwen natural resources and man-made equipment. Each component of a stock of equipment is used continuously; hence the entire stock depreciates, and changes in its economic characteristics, at a rate which depends on the intensity of its use. On the other hand, only the marginal scrapings of a resource stock are utilized at any moment, and they are entirely used up; hence the economic characteristics of the surviving stock are independent of the rate at which the stock is exploited. In short, depreciation of a homogeneous resource-stock involves simple contraction whereas depreciation of a homogeneous stock of equipment involves the transformation of one homogeneous stock into another. In fact those who have constructed models of growth and trade invariably ignore the heterogeneity of equipment and, if they bother at all about depreciation, assume that it is some very simple function of time, quite independent of the intensity with which the equipment is used. Evidently exhaustible natural resources cannot be treated in that way, even if they happen to be renewable. They force one to fashion new habits of thought and new modelling clichés.

There is need of a theory of international trade which accommodates both exhaustible natural resources and the traditional Ricardian primary factors and of which the standard Heckscher–Ohlin theory appears as a special case. The new theory can be expected to differ in important respects from the old, for in a context of exhaustible resources there are no nontrivial steady states, only transitions. In particular, it is not to be expected that one will be able to transplant unchanged the familiar comparative steady-state propositions: the Rybczynski, Stolper–Samuelson, Heckscher–Ohlin and Factor Price Equalization theorems.

However it is possible that in some cases comparative-dynamical counterparts of those propositions can be established. At any rate it has seemed to us that before all else we should examine that possibility. That is the purpose of Sections 2–5. In those sections we follow a step-by-step strategy. Thus we begin (in Section 2) by constructing a theory in which the traditional pair of non-wasting primary factors is replaced by a pair of Hotelling's exhaustible resources and which therefore is polar to the conventional theory. We then proceed (in Sections 3 and 4) to generalize the two polar theories by providing them with non-homogeneous factor bases. Finally (in Section 5) we examine hybrid theories, resting on a base of one Ricardian and one Hotelling factor and therefore neither more general than the Heckscher–Ohlin theory nor more general than the Hotelling theory. Models of this type indeed were among the first constructed.

Throughout Sections 2–5 we abstract from the costliness of extraction. The assumption that resources can be extracted without cost simplifies the calculations and enables us to concentrate on the implications of exhaustibility as such. Moreover, in the canonical case in which the available processes of extraction display constant returns to scale and are independent of the amount already extracted, costs of extraction make no difference to our qualitative conclusions. This is obviously so in an anti-Heckscher–Ohlin world for, there, costs of extraction simply reduce the "effective" initial resource stocks; but it is true also in the context of Sections 3–5.

Section 6 forms an addendum to earlier sections. In that section we allow for the possibility that there exist costly flow substitutes for exhaustible resources, that is, substitutes produced by means of Ricardian factors. Such substitutes make possible time-patterns of production and trade which are otherwise impossible; for example, they make possible the re-switching of competitive trade patterns. They may also give rise to abrupt or "jump" changes in production and trade. In that section we allow also for the possibility that some resources, like forests and fisheries, are self-renewing.

In Sections 7–10 we recognize the historical fact that the extraction and processing of some exhaustible resources have sometimes been under the control (possibly incomplete, possibly indirect) of cartels. In those sections we abandon the assumption of competition and allow for the possibility that the extraction of an exhaustible resource is under the partial control of a cartel.

The survey ends with a brief bibliographical section. That section is not intended to be merely ornamental. It directs the reader to the sources upon which our text is based and guides his reading to topics which, in spite of their importance, have been played down for lack of anything systematic to report or because of overlap with other chapters. [One thinks of uncertainty, commonality of property, "resource-skewness" (the uneven distribution of resources across the face of the earth), and the conditions of a country's survival.]

2. Anti-Heckscher–Ohlin theory

Sticking as close as possible to the form of the Heckscher–Ohlin model of production, let us suppose that two final or consumption goods are produced non-jointly under conditions of constant returns to scale by two raw materials, each derived from an exhaustible and non-renewable stock. Let $R_i(t)$ be the amount of the ith resource outstanding at time t, so that $R_i(0)$ is the size of the initial stock; let $E_i(t)$ be the rate at which the ith stock is depleted at time t; let $E_i^j(t)$ be the rate at which the ith resource is used by the jth industry at time t; and let $X_j(t)$ be the rate of output of the jth final good at time t. Then we may write the production functions:

$$X_j(t) = F^j\big(E_1^j(t), E_2^j(t)\big), \qquad j = 1, 2, \tag{2.1}$$

where F^j is assumed to be homogeneous of degree one, strictly quasi-concave and such that each input is essential.

Given E_1 and E_2, the two rates of extraction, one can construct the usual set of production possibilities. If (as is assumed) the two industries differ in their relative factor intensities, the set has a strictly concave upper boundary. Given in addition $P = P_2/P_1$, the price of the second commodity in terms of the first, one can read off that unique combination of industrial outputs which maximizes total output in terms of the numeraire. Thus we may write:

$$X_j(t) = X^j\big(P(t), E_1(t), E_2(t)\big), \qquad j = 1, 2, \tag{2.2}$$

and

$$
\begin{aligned}
Y_1(t) &= Y^1\big(P(t), E_1(t), E_2(t)\big) \\
&\equiv X^1\big(P(t), E_1(t), E_2(t)\big) + P(t)X^2\big(P(t), E_1(t), E_2(t)\big).
\end{aligned}
\tag{2.3}
$$

Since production of each commodity is subject to constant returns, so is total output:

$$Y^1(P, E_1, E_2) = E_1 Y^1(P, 1, E_2/E_1)$$

$$\equiv E_1 y^1(P, E_2/E_1) \equiv E_1 y^1(P, \mathscr{E}). \tag{2.4}$$

The properties of the function Y^1 are displayed in Figure 2.1. Both parts of the figure are drawn on the assumption that P is fixed at the particular value $\bar{P}$. In Figure 2.1(a) is displayed the curve of average total product for the first input. Between the input ratios $\underline{\mathscr{E}}$ and $\bar{\mathscr{E}}$ production is incompletely specialized, so there the curve is linear. Figure 2.1(b), on the other hand, contains a pair of iso-value loci, with linear segments between the rays $O\underline{\mathscr{E}}$ and $O\bar{\mathscr{E}}$.

Turning to the demand side of the model, it is assumed that the community is composed of identical individuals and that their preferences are time separable. Thus the objective of each individual and of the community is to maximize an

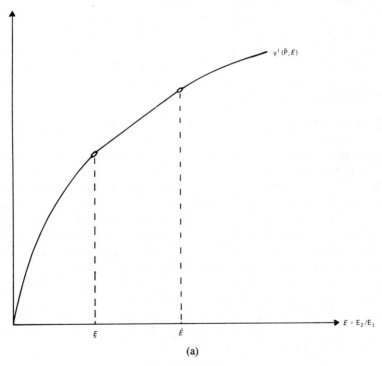

(a)

Figure 2.1

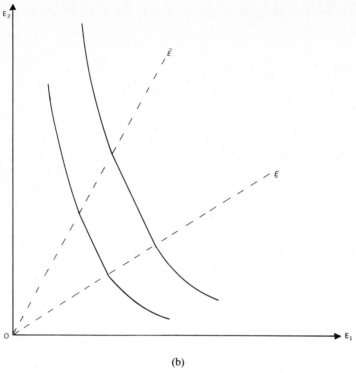

(b)

Figure 2.1. *continued.*

integral of instantaneous utilities, with each utility a function of the two rates of consumption and discounted in the light of a constant and positive rate of time preference.

The social maximization is to be carried out in the light of several constraints defined by the production functions and initial resource-stocks. For much of this and the next two sections we also impose the small-country assumption of given and constant terms of trade. Finally, throughout the present section we rule out the possibility of international borrowing and lending. For if a small country had access to a perfectly competitive international capital market our problem would be trivial: it would be optimal to use up both resource deposits at once, sell the product at the given terms of trade, and invest the proceeds at the given world market rate of interest. The need to impose such a strong assumption suggests that a model with only exhaustible resources as inputs is likely to be no more useful than the Heckscher–Ohlin model itself. However it does nicely prepare us for the hybrid and more general models of Sections 3 and 4.

In full detail the planning (or competitive-market) problem facing a small country is to find:

(P2.1)

$$\max_{\{E_1, E_2\}} \int_0^\infty \exp(-\rho t) W\left[Y^1(\bar{P}, E_1(t), E_2(t)), \bar{P}\right] dt$$

$$\text{s.t.} \quad \left.\begin{array}{l} \dot{R}_i(t) = -E_i(t) \\ R_i(t) \geq 0 \\ R_i(0) \text{ given and positive} \\ E_i(t) \geq 0 \end{array}\right\}, \quad i = 1, 2,$$

where ρ is the positive rate of time preference and W is an indirect utility function, assumed to be increasing and strictly concave in Y_1. [If ρ were zero, (P2.1) would have no solution and it would be necessary to resort to some form of the "overtaking" criterion.]

Recalling that each factor is indispensable in each industry we have, as necessary conditions for (P2.1):

$$\left(\frac{\partial W}{\partial Y_1}\right)\left(\frac{\partial Y^1}{\partial E_i}\right) = \psi_i \exp(\rho t), \tag{2.5a}$$

where ψ_i is a positive constant; that is, the present value of the marginal social product of each factor is constant. (The analogy with the simplest cake-eating problem will be apparent.) Whenever extraction takes place, therefore,

$$\frac{\partial Y^1}{\partial E_2} \bigg/ \frac{\partial Y^1}{\partial E_1} = \psi \equiv \psi_2/\psi_1 = \text{pos. const.} \tag{2.5b}$$

It follows from (2.5b) and the shape of $y^1(\bar{P}, \mathscr{E})$ that if $\mathscr{R}(0) \equiv R_2(0)/R_1(0) \leq \underline{\mathscr{E}}(\bar{P})$ or if $\mathscr{R}(0) \geq \bar{\mathscr{E}}(\bar{P})$ then, while production lasts, $\mathscr{E}(t)$ must be constant and equal to $\mathscr{R}(0)$. It also follows, from (2.5a) and from the concavity of W in Y_1, that national income Y_1 declines through time. Whether the rates of extraction and output go to zero in finite time depends on the behavior of marginal utility as consumption goes to zero. If, on the other hand, $\underline{\mathscr{E}}(\bar{P}) < \mathscr{R}(0) < \bar{\mathscr{E}}(\bar{P})$ then the day-by-day factor ratio $\mathscr{E}(t)$ is, within the bounds $\underline{\mathscr{E}}$ and $\bar{\mathscr{E}}$, undetermined; hence the day-by-day output ratio $X_2(t)/X_1(t)$ also is undetermined. From (2.5a),

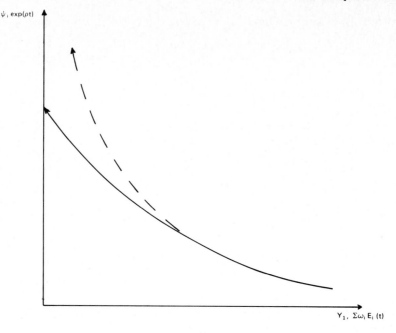

Figure 2.2

however, total output (in terms of either commodity) is fully determined whatever the value of $\mathscr{R}(0)$ and it declines through time.

Figure 2.2 is the phase diagram in the space of $Y_1(t)$ and $\psi_i \exp(\rho t)$, or in the space of total resource input $\omega_1 E_1(t) + \omega_2 E_2(t)$ and $\psi_i \exp(\rho t)$, where $\omega_i \equiv \partial Y^1 / \partial E_i$.

We proceed to demonstrate that the standard Heckscher–Ohlin trade theorems survive, in recognizable form, their transference to an anti-Heckscher–Ohlin world. We begin by recording two lemmas, the first of which is implicit in the foregoing discussion.

Lemma 2.1

If there is a solution to (P2.1) with each good produced during some common non-degenerate interval of time then there is a solution with the two goods produced in the same constant proportion whenever production takes place.

Henceforth, when we say that both goods are produced we must be understood to mean that the goods are produced in constant proportion for as long as production lasts.

Lemma 2.2

In a small country of the type considered, extraction declines at the rate $-\rho/\eta$, where $\eta(Y_1, P)$ is the partial elasticity of marginal utility $\partial W/\partial Y_1$ with respect to Y_1.

Proof

From (2.5a), along an optimal trajectory $(\partial W/\partial Y_1)(\partial Y^1/\partial E_i)$ grows exponentially at rate ρ; and, from Lemma 2.1 and the properties of Y^1, $\partial Y^1/\partial E_i$ is constant. Hence $\partial W/\partial Y_1$ grows exponentially at rate ρ, implying in turn that:

$$(\partial^2 W/\partial Y_1^2)\sum(\partial Y^1/\partial E_i)\dot{E}_i = \rho(\partial W/\partial Y_1). \tag{2.6}$$

Recalling that Y^1 is homogeneous of degree one in E_1 and E_2 and that $\dot{E}_1/E_1 = \dot{E}_2/E_2$, (2.6) reduces to

$$\dot{E}_i/E_i = \rho/\eta, \qquad i=1,2. \quad \text{Q.E.D.}$$

Theorem 2.1 (Rybczynski)

Let both goods be produced along an optimal trajectory, and let the same be true after a small increase in $R_i(0)$. As a result of the increase in $R_i(0)$ there is, at each point of time at which production takes place, an increase in the relative and absolute output of the commodity which is relatively intensive in its use of the ith resource.

Proof

Without loss, let the jth industry be relatively intensive in its use of the jth resource. Then an increase in $R_i(0)$ entails an increase in $E_i(t)/E_j(t)$ and, by standard reasoning, in $X_i(t)/X_j(t)$ for all t such that $X_i(t)$ and $X_j(t)$ are positive.

Moreover an increase in $R_i(0)$ entails an increase in the total resource stock $\omega_1 R_1(0) + \omega_2 R_2(0)$. In terms of Figure 2.2, therefore, the new optimal trajectory begins farther to the right but otherwise coincides with the old trajectory. Hence for each t $Y_1(t)$ is greater along the new trajectory.

Putting together the conclusions of the above paragraphs, the proposition follows. Q.E.D.

Remark

It has been assumed that $\mathcal{R}(t)$ is constant. However it is possible to reformulate the theorem in terms of undiscounted cumulative outputs without making use of that assumption. Thus, under the assumptions of Theorem 2.1 it is always true that an increase in $R_i(0)$ gives rise to an increase in the relative and absolute cumulative output of the commodity which is relatively intensive in its use of the ith resource.

Theorem 2.2 (Stolper–Samuelson)

Let both goods be produced along an optimal trajectory and let the same be true after a small increase in $\bar{P}_j$, the given price of the jth good. As a result of the increase in $\bar{P}_j$ there is, for each point of time at which production takes place, an increase in the marginal product (in each industry) of the resource used relatively intensively in the jth industry and a reduction in the marginal product (in each industry) of the other resource.

Proof

Before and after the price change, $\mathscr{E}(t) = \mathscr{R}(0)$. Thus the ratio of total factor inputs is independent of commodity prices. The conclusion of the theorem then follows by standard Stolper–Samuelson reasoning.   Q.E.D.

Remark

The assumption that $\mathscr{E}(t) = \mathscr{R}(0)$ for all t is inessential.

Theorem 2.3 (Heckscher–Ohlin)

(i) If preferences are strictly convex, homothetic and the same in each of two free-trading countries, and if there is a trading equilibrium with constant terms of trade, then, for as long as production continues, the country which initially is relatively well endowed with the ith Hotelling factor will export the commodity which is relatively intensive in its use of that factor. (ii) If in addition the rate of time preference is everywhere the same and marginal utility is of constant elasticity then there is a trading equilibrium with constant terms of trade.

Proof

(i) If the terms of trade are constant then for each country there is an optimal program with $\mathscr{R}(t)$ constant. The proof then follows standard static lines. (ii) Consider any constant world price ratio. From the homotheticity of like preferences, at each point of time the two commodities are everywhere demanded in the same proportion. On the other hand, from Lemma 2.1, in each country the two commodities are always produced in the same proportion, a different proportion in each country; and, from Lemma 2.2 and the assumed constancy of the elasticity of marginal utility, all inputs and outputs everywhere decline at the same rate ρ/η. It follows that if at the given constant price ratio world markets clear at any point of time then at that price ratio they always clear.

That there does exist a market-clearing world price ratio follows from the twin facts that the world output ratio $\sum X_2 / \sum X_1$ is a monotone non-decreasing function of P, ranging from zero to infinity for positive values of P, and that the corresponding world demand ratio is a monotone non-increasing function of P.

Moreover, if both goods are demanded at all positive price ratios then the world equilibrium is unique.

That establishes the existence and (under an additional assumption) uniqueness of a market-clearing constant price ratio. It remains to notice that, as an implication of the international uniformity of demand ratios and the international disparity of output ratios, each country must export that commodity which is relatively intensive in its use of that country's relatively abundant Hotelling factor.   Q.E.D.

Remark

If the elasticity of marginal utility is not at each point of time the same in both countries then the relative sizes of the two countries must change through time, and in general this is inconsistent with constant terms of trade.

The standard static Factor Price Equalization Theorem remains valid. However in an anti-Heckscher–Ohlin world both the extraction vector and the cone of diversification may shift through time. Hence the conditions of the theorem may be satisfied at some points of time and not satisfied at others. Moreover the extraction vector is not given by Nature, as is the endowment vector of Heckscher–Ohlin theory, but is to be determined by the theory itself. Thus the standard theorem begs even more questions in an anti-Heckscher–Ohlin world than in a Heckscher–Ohlin world. An interesting theorem must state conditions which ensure the international equalization of factor prices at all points of time.

Theorem 2.4 (Factor Price Equalization)

(i) If and only if the extraction vectors of some two free-trading countries lie in a common cone of diversification defined by the equilibrium terms of trade then the marginal product of each resource is the same in both countries. (ii) If preferences are everywhere the same and homothetic, and if in addition marginal utility is of constant elasticity, then there exists an equilibrium terms of trade and an associated cone of diversification which is the same for all points of time at which production takes place and, moreover, in each country the extraction ratio is constant, equal to the initial endowment ratio.

Proof

(i) is the standard theorem. (ii) follows from Theorem 2.3(b).   Q.E.D.

3.   Generalized Heckscher–Ohlin theory

At the opposite pole from the anti-Heckscher–Ohlin theory of Section 2 we find models with one or more exhaustible resources added to the two traditional primary factors. Suppose that a single exhaustible resource is added. It will be shown that, for a particular class of production functions, recognizable versions of the four standard theorems are available.

In each country two final goods can be produced with the aid of three internationally-immobile factors of production, two conventional or Ricardian primary factors and an exhaustible resource. Let V_i be the endowment of the ith primary factor, V_i^j the amount of that factor allocated to the jth industry, $R(0)$ the initial stock of the resource, E the rate of extraction and E^j the rate at which the resource is used in the jth industry. The two production functions are assumed to be positively homogeneous of degree one in all inputs and, to eliminate the possibility that in some industry the exhaustible resource is used relatively more intensively than either Ricardian factor, of the special separable form:

$$X_j = (E^j)^\alpha F^j (V_1^j, V_2^j),$$ (3.1)

where F^j is homogeneous of degree $1 - \alpha$ ($0 < \alpha < 1$). Alternatively, defining

$$Q_j \equiv \phi^j (V_1^j, V_2^j) \equiv [F^j (V_1^j, V_2^j)]^{1/(1-\alpha)},$$ (3.2)

we may rewrite (3.1) as:

$$X_j = (E^j)^\alpha (Q_j)^{1-\alpha},$$ (3.3)

with Q_j interpreted as an intermediate input. Each industry is relatively intensive in its use of one of the two Ricardian factors. That is,

$$\text{if } \frac{\partial F^1}{\partial V_1^1} \Big/ \frac{\partial F^1}{\partial V_2^1} = \frac{\partial F^2}{\partial V_1^2} \Big/ \frac{\partial F^2}{\partial V_2^2}, \quad \text{then } \frac{V_1^1}{V_2^1} \neq \frac{V_1^2}{V_2^2}.$$ (3.4a)

or, equivalently,

$$\text{if } \frac{\partial \phi^1}{\partial V_1^1} \Big/ \frac{\partial \phi^1}{\partial V_2^1} = \frac{\partial \phi^2}{\partial V_1^2} \Big/ \frac{\partial \phi^2}{\partial V_2^2}, \quad \text{then } \frac{V_1^1}{V_2^1} \neq \frac{V_1^2}{V_2^2}.$$ (3.4b)

At each moment the factor allocations must satisfy the constraints:

$$\sum E^j \leq E,$$ (3.5a)

$$\sum_j V_i^j \leq V_i.$$ (3.5b)

For given commodity prices $\bar{P}_1$ and $\bar{P}_2$, a competitive economy maximizes the value of output $\Sigma \bar{P}_j X_j$ subject to constraints (3.2), (3.3) and (3.4). The first-order conditions are:

$$\bar{P}_1(E^1)^\alpha (1-\alpha)(\phi^1)^{-\alpha}\phi_i^1 = \bar{P}_2(E^2)^\alpha (1-\alpha)(\phi^2)^{-\alpha}\phi_i^2, \qquad i=1,2, \qquad (3.6a)$$

$$\alpha \bar{P}_1(E^1)^{\alpha-1}(\phi^1)^{1-\alpha} = \alpha \bar{P}_2(E^2)^{\alpha-1}(\phi^2)^{1-\alpha}, \qquad (3.6b)$$

where $\phi_i^j \equiv \partial \phi^j / \partial V_i^j$. From (3.6a):

$$\frac{(\phi^2)^{-\alpha}\phi_i^2}{(\phi^1)^{-\alpha}\phi_i^1} = \frac{\bar{P}_1(E^1)^\alpha}{\bar{P}_2(E^2)^\alpha}, \qquad i=1,2; \qquad (3.7a)$$

and, from (3.6b):

$$\frac{E^1}{E^2} = \left(\frac{\bar{P}_1}{\bar{P}_2}\right)^{1/(1-\alpha)} \left(\frac{\phi^1}{\phi^2}\right). \qquad (3.7b)$$

Substituting from (3.7b) into (3.7a),

$$\frac{\phi_i^2}{\phi_i^1} = \left(\frac{\bar{P}_1}{\bar{P}_2}\right)^{1/(1-\alpha)} \equiv \pi, \qquad i=1,2, \qquad (3.8)$$

where π can be interpreted as the relative price of the first intermediate input in terms of the second. Given π, V_1 and V_2, the equilibrium allocations of the two Ricardian factors are completely determined by (3.5b) and (3.8). Thus we have:

Lemma 3.1

The competitive allocation of Ricardian factors is independent of the rate of resource extraction.

And once the allocations of the Ricardian factors are known so are the values of Q_1 and Q_2. Eqs. (3.5b) and (3.8) enable us to write:

$$Q_i = Q^i(\pi, V_1, V_2), \qquad (3.9a)$$

where

$$\partial Q^1/\partial \pi > 0, \quad \partial Q^2/\partial \pi < 0 \qquad \text{if } Q_1, Q_2 > 0. \qquad (3.9b)$$

The familiar Figure 3.1 provides a partial illustration.

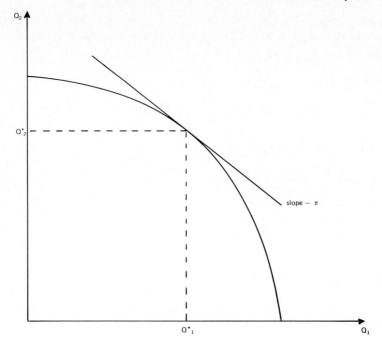

Figure 3.1

We turn our attention next to the total output function. From (3.7b), (3.8) and (3.9):

$$\frac{E^1}{E^2} = \pi \frac{Q^1(\pi, V_1, V_2)}{Q^2(\pi, V_1, V_2)} \equiv k(\pi, V_1, V_2), \tag{3.10a}$$

where

$$\frac{\partial k}{\partial \pi} = \frac{-\pi Q_1[\partial Q^2/\partial \pi] + Q_2[\pi(\partial Q^1/\partial \pi) + Q_1]}{(Q_2)^2} > 0. \tag{3.10b}$$

Recalling (3.5a), with strict equality, it follows from (3.10a) that:

$$E^1 = \frac{k}{1+k} E = \frac{\pi Q_1}{Q_2 + \pi Q_1} E, \tag{3.11a}$$

$$E^2 = \frac{1}{1+k} E = \frac{Q_2}{Q_2 + \pi Q_1} E. \tag{3.11b}$$

Substituting from (3.11) into (3.3):

$$X_1 = \left[\pi Q_1 / (Q_2 + \pi Q_1) \right]^\alpha E^\alpha Q_1^{1-\alpha}, \tag{3.12a}$$

$$X_2 = \left[Q_2 / (Q_2 + \pi Q_1) \right]^\alpha E^\alpha Q_2^{1-\alpha}. \tag{3.12b}$$

Hence total output $Y_1 = X_1 + PX_2$ can be written in the separable form:

$$
\begin{aligned}
Y_1 &= Y^1(P, E, V_1, V_2) \\
&\equiv E^\alpha \left[\left(\frac{\pi Q_1}{Q_2 + \pi Q_1} \right)^\alpha Q_1^{1-\alpha} + P \left(\frac{Q_2}{Q_2 + \pi Q_1} \right)^\alpha Q_2^{1-\alpha} \right] \\
&\equiv E^\alpha \hat{Y}^1(\pi, V_1, V_2) \\
&\equiv E^\alpha \tilde{Y}^1(P, V_1, V_2).
\end{aligned}
\tag{3.13}
$$

Consider now a small competitive economy facing given and constant terms of trade $\bar{P}$ and able to borrow from and lend to other countries at the given but not necessarily constant rate of interest $r(t)$. Such a country seeks

(P3.1)

$$\max_{\{E\}} \int_0^\infty \exp\left(- \int_0^t r(s)\,ds \right) Y^1(\bar{P}, E, V_1, V_2)\,dt$$

s.t. $\dot{R} = -E$

$R \geq 0$

$R(0)$ positive and given.

Lemma 3.2

In a small country of the type just described, the rate of extraction declines at the relative rate $r(t)/(1-\alpha)$.

Proof

Along a solution path of (P3.1), $\partial Y^1 / \partial E$ grows at the relative rate $r(t)$. However, from (3.13), $\partial Y^1 / \partial E = \alpha \tilde{Y}^1 / E^{1-\alpha}$. It follows that the rate of extraction declines at the relative rate $r(t)/(1-\alpha)$.   Q.E.D.

Corollary 3.1

The rate of extraction, and therefore the interval (possibly infinite) over which extraction and production takes place, is independent both of the constant terms of trade and of the Ricardian factor endowment.

Lemma 3.3

If at some point of time a small economy of the type described produces both commodities then it must produce both commodities whenever production takes place.

Proof

From Lemma 3.1, the allocation of Ricardian factors is independent of the rate of extraction, depending only on the stationary technology, the constant terms of trade and the constant Ricardian factor endowment. Q.E.D.

Theorem 3.1 (Rybczynski)

Let both goods be produced along an optimal trajectory and let the same be true after an increase in the ith Ricardian endowment V_i. As a result of the increase in V_i, at each point of time such that production takes place the output of whichever commodity is relatively intensive in its use of the ith resource increases and the output of the other commodity declines; moreover, if α is sufficiently small then the output of the commodity relatively intensive in its use of the ith resource increases in greater proportion than V_i.

Proof

Suppose that the jth good is relatively intensive in its use of the jth Ricardian factor. Then, by standard Rybczynski reasoning,

$$\hat{Q}_1 > \hat{V}_1 > \hat{V}_2 = 0 > \hat{Q}_2, \tag{3.14}$$

where the circumflexes indicate relative changes. On the other hand, from Corollary 3.1, the path of extraction is undisturbed by the change in V_1; and, from (3.10a), k must increase. It then follows from (3.11) that, for all t such that extraction is positive, $E^1(t)$ must increase, $E^2(t)$ decrease. Hence $X_1(t)$ must increase, $X_2(t)$ decrease. Indeed, from (3.3), (3.11a) and (3.14):

$$
\begin{aligned}
\hat{X}_1(t) &= \alpha \hat{E}^1(t) + (1-\alpha)\hat{Q}_1(t) \\
&= \hat{Q}_1(t) - \alpha\left[\hat{Q}_1(t) - \hat{E}^1(t)\right] \\
&= \hat{Q}_1(t) - \alpha\left[\frac{\pi \, dQ_1(t) + dQ_2(t)}{\pi Q_1(t) + Q_2(t)}\right] \\
&\geq \hat{Q}_1(t) - \alpha\left[\frac{\pi \, dQ_1(t)}{\pi Q_1(t) + Q_2(t)}\right] \\
&\geq \hat{Q}_1(t) - \alpha\hat{Q}_1 \\
&= (1-\alpha)\hat{Q}_1(t) \\
&> (1-\alpha)\hat{V}_1.
\end{aligned}
\tag{3.15}
$$

It follows that if α is sufficiently small then $\hat{X}_1(t) > \hat{V}_1$.   Q.E.D.

Theorem 3.2 (Stolper–Samuelson)

Let both goods be produced along an optimal trajectory and let the same be true after an increase in $\bar{P}_j$, the given price of the jth commodity. After the increase in $\bar{P}_j$ there is at each point of time a higher marginal product (in each industry) of whichever Ricardian factor is used relatively intensively in the jth industry and a lower marginal product of the other factor.

Proof

Let w_i be the marginal product of the ith Ricardian factor in terms of the first intermediate good, let W_i be the marginal product of the ith Ricardian factor in terms of the first final good, and suppose again that the jth good is relatively intensive in its use of the jth Ricardian factor. By standard Stolper–Samuelson reasoning:

$$\hat{w}_1 > \hat{\pi} > 0 > \hat{w}_2 . \tag{3.16}$$

On the other hand:

$$W_i = \partial X_1 / \partial V_i^1 = (E^1)^{\alpha}(1 - \alpha)(\phi^1)^{-\alpha}\phi_i^1 , \tag{3.17}$$

which, with (3.11a), implies that:

$$\begin{aligned} \hat{W}_i &= \alpha \hat{E}^1 - \alpha \hat{Q}_1 + \hat{w}_i \\ &= \alpha(\hat{Q}_1 - \hat{z}) - \alpha \hat{Q}_1 + \hat{w}_i \\ &= -\alpha \hat{z} + \hat{w}_i . \end{aligned} \tag{3.18}$$

From a well-known envelope theorem, $\partial z / \partial \pi = Q_1$, implying that $\hat{z} = (\pi Q_1 / z)\hat{\pi}$. Substituting for $\hat{z}$ in (3.18),

$$\hat{W}_i = -\alpha(\pi Q_1 / z)\hat{\pi} + \hat{w}_i \tag{3.19}$$

From (3.16) and (3.19), and the fact that both α and $\pi Q_1 / z$ are positive factors, $\hat{W}_1 > 0 > \hat{W}_2$.   Q.E.D.

Theorem 3.3 (Heckscher–Ohlin)

(i) If preferences are the same and homothetic in each of two free-trading countries then there is a world trading and borrowing-lending equilibrium with constant terms of trade; moreover, the country which initially is relatively well endowed with the ith Ricardian factor, if it exports at all, will export the commodity which is relatively intensive in its use of that factor. If both goods are demanded at all positive price ratios then the equilibrium is unique. (ii) If in addition to the assumptions introduced under (i) the elasticity of marginal utility is constant and the same rate of time preference prevails everywhere then there is a world equilibrium such that the terms of trade and rate of interest are constant, net international indebtedness is always zero, and the country which initially is relatively well endowed with the ith Ricardian factor always exports the commodity which is relatively intensive in its use of that factor.

Proof

(i) Suppose that at time t world commodity markets clear at the price ratio P. Then P is market-clearing at all points of time; for, from the homogeneity of like preferences, at each point of time the two commodities are everywhere demanded in a proportion which depends on the price ratio only, and, from Lemmas 3.1 and 3.2, given the price ratio all outputs everywhere decline at the same relative rate $\alpha r(t)/(1-\alpha)$.

That there does exist a market-clearing world price ratio follows from the twin facts that the world output ratio $\Sigma X_2/\Sigma X_1$ is a monotone nondecreasing function of P, ranging from zero to infinity for positive values of P, and that the corresponding world demand ratio is a monotone non-increasing function of P. Moreover if both goods are demanded at all positive price ratios then the world equilibrium is unique.

(ii) Suppose that the rate of interest is constant. Then each country must solve, in addition to (P3.1),

(P3.2)

$$\max_{\{c\}} \int_0^\infty \exp(-\rho t) u(c(t)) \, dt$$
$$\text{st. } \dot{S}(t) = rS(t) - c(t)$$
$$S(0) = 0,$$

where c is the rate of consumption and $-S$ is the level of indebtedness. From the first-order conditions one easily calculates that:

$$\dot{c}/c = (\rho - r)/\eta.$$

On the other hand, from (3.13) and Lemma 3.2, output changes at the rate

$$\alpha \dot{E}/E = -\alpha r/(1-\alpha).$$

The two rates are equal if and only if

$$r = \rho(1-\alpha)/[1-\alpha(1+\eta)];$$

and if the two rates are equal for all t then consumption must equal output for all t, that is, net indebtedness must be always zero.

It remains to notice that, as an implication of the international uniformity of demand ratios and the international disparity of output ratios, each country must export the good which is relatively intensive in its use of that country's relatively abundant Ricardian factor.   Q.E.D.

Theorem 3.4 (Factor Price Equalization)

(i) If and only if the Ricardian endowment vectors of some two free-trading countries, say A and B, lie in a common cone of diversification defined by the equilibrium terms of trade then the ratio of marginal products of the Ricardian factors is the same in each country. (ii) If preferences are homothetic and the same in each country then there exists an equilibrium terms of trade and an associated cone of diversification which is the same for all points of time at which production takes place. If in addition the two Hotelling endowments, say $R^A(0)$ and $R^B(0)$, stand in the relationship:

$$\frac{R^A(0)}{R^B(0)} = \frac{Q_2^A(\pi) + \pi Q_1^A(\pi)}{Q_2^B(\pi) + \pi Q_1^B(\pi)}, \tag{3.20}$$

then the marginal product of each Ricardian factor is everywhere the same.

Proof

(i) From (3.17), $W_1/W_2 = \phi_1^1/\phi_2^1$; and, from Lemma 3.1, the ratio $w_1/w_2 = \phi_1^1/\phi_2^1$ is equalized across countries if and only if the two Ricardian endowment vectors lie in the cone of diversification defined by the equilibrium terms of trade.

(ii) The first part of (ii) follows from Theorem 3.3. It remains to verify the second part. Applying (3.11a) and (3.13) to (3.17):

$$W_1 = \frac{\partial}{\partial V_1^1}\left[(E^1)^\alpha\left(\phi^1(V_1^1, V_2^1)\right)^{1-\alpha}\right]$$

$$= (1-\alpha)E^\alpha\left(\frac{k}{1+k}\right)^\alpha (Q_1)^{-\alpha}\phi_1^1$$

$$= (1-\alpha)E^\alpha\phi_1^1/[Q_1(\pi) + \pi Q_2(\pi)]. \tag{3.21}$$

Hence $W_1^A = W_1^B$ if and only if both

$$\left(\phi_1^1\right)^A = \left(\phi_1^1\right)^B \tag{3.22}$$

and

$$\frac{(E^A)^\alpha}{Q_2^A(\pi, V_1^A, V_2^A) + \pi Q_1^A(\pi, V_1^A, V_2^A)} = \frac{(E^B)^\alpha}{Q_2^B(\pi, V_1^B, V_2^B) + \pi Q_1^B(\pi, V_1^B, V_2^B)}.$$

(3.23)

But (3.22) follows from the standard argument for factor-price equalization, applied to the two intermediate goods. And (3.23) holds for all t if and only if (3.20) is satisfied. Q.E.D.

Remark

From (3.21), W_i fall over time if the terms of trade are constant.

To this point it has been assumed that there is a perfect international capital market. We now take the opposite tack and assume (as in Section 2) that international borrowing and lending are impossible. The task facing a small country is then to find:

(P3.3)

$$\max_{\{E\}} \int_0^\infty \exp(-\rho t) W\left[Y^1(\bar{P}, E(t), V_1, V_2), \bar{P}\right] dt$$

s.t. $\dot{R}(t) = -E(t)$

$R(t) \geq 0$

$R(0)$ positive and given

$E(t) \geq 0.$

where (as in Section 2) W is assumed to be increasing and strictly concave in Y_1. Lemmas 3.1 and 3.3 remain valid. Lemma 3.2 must be modified.

Lemma 3.2'

In a small country of the type now considered the rate of extraction declines at the rate $\rho/[1 - \alpha(1 + \eta)]$.

Proof

After noting that along an optimal trajectory $(\partial W/\partial Y_1)(\partial Y^1/\partial E)$ grows exponentially at rate ρ, the proof is similar to that for Lemma 3.2. Q.E.D.

Corollary 3.1'

If η is a constant, independent of Y_1 and of P, then the rate of extraction, and therefore the interval (possibly infinite) over which extraction and production take place, is independent both of the constant terms of trade and of the Ricardian factor endowment.

Remark

Lemma 3.2 can be obtained as a special case of Lemma 3.2′ by setting $\eta \equiv 0$.

Theorem 3.1′ (Rybczynski)

Let both goods be produced along an optimal trajectory and let the same be true after an increase in the ith Ricardian endowment V_i. (i) As a result of the increase in V_i, at each point of time such that production takes place the relative output of whichever commodity is relatively intensive in its use of the ith factor increases. (ii) If in addition the marginal utility function $\partial W / \partial Y_1$ is of constant elasticity with respect to income then, as a result of the increase in V_i, at each point of time at which production takes place the output of whichever commodity is relatively intensive in its use of the ith factor increases, and in greater proportion than V_i, and the output of the other commodity decreases.

Proof

(i) follows from Lemma 3.1. (ii) follows from Lemma 3.1 and Corollary 3.1′. Q.E.D.

Theorem 3.2′ (Stolper–Samuelson)

Let both goods be produced along an optimal trajectory and let the same be true after an increase in $\bar{P}_j$, the price of the jth commodity. (i) After the increase in $\bar{P}_j$, at each point of time at which production takes place the marginal product of the Ricardian factor used intensively in the jth industry rises in relation to the marginal product of the other factor. (ii) If in addition the marginal utility function $\partial W / \partial Y_1$ is of constant elasticity with respect to income then, as a result of the increase in $\bar{P}_j$, at each point of time at which production takes place there is a higher marginal product (in each industry) of whichever Ricardian factor is used intensively in the jth industry and a lower marginal product of the other factor.

Proof

(i) follows from Lemma 3.1. (ii) follows from Lemma 3.1 and Corollary 3.1′. Q.E.D.

Similarly, Theorems 3.3(i), 3.3(ii) and 3.4 remain valid.

Finally we notice that all theorems carry over with only nominal changes if, instead of (3.1), we write:

$$X_j = \left[\psi \left(E_1^j, \ldots, E_n^j \right) \right]^{\alpha} \left[\phi^j \left(V_1^j, V_2^j \right) \right]^{1-\alpha}, \quad j = 1, 2,$$

where ψ and ϕ^j are homogeneous of degree one.

4. Generalized anti-Heckscher–Ohlin theory

Just as it is possible to generalize the Heckscher–Ohlin model of production by multiplying each production function by a homogeneous function of a single Hotelling input, so it is possible to generalize the anti-Heckscher–Ohlin model by multiplying each production function by a homogeneous function of a single Ricardian input. Instead of (2.1) we then have

$$X_j(t) = (V^j)^\alpha F^j\big(E_1^j(t), E_2^j(t)\big)$$

$$\equiv (V^j)^\alpha \big[\phi^j\big(E_1^j(t), E_2^j(t)\big)\big]^{1-\alpha},$$

where V^j is the amount of the Ricardian factor employed by the jth industry, F^j is homogeneous of degree $1 - \alpha$, and ϕ^j is homogeneous of degree one.

Without dwelling on details, we simply report that the analysis of Section 3 up to eq. (3.13) remains valid if the roles of Ricardian and Hotelling factors are interchanged. Given the further analysis of Section 3 it can be accepted perhaps that for a country facing given and constant terms of trade and given rate of interest it is optimal to set $E_2(t)/E_1(t) = \mathcal{R}(0)$ and let extraction decline at the rate $r(t)/\alpha$, so that the marginal product of each factor rises at the rate of interest. It is then easy to verify that the theorems of Section 3 carry over if only the labels "Hotelling" and "Ricardian" are interchanged. Of course, in the Remark attached to Theorem 3.4 "falls" must be replaced by "rises."

Further straightforward generalizations are obtained by writing:

$$X_j = \big[\psi\big(V_1^j,\ldots,V_n^j\big)\big]^\alpha \big[\phi^j\big(E_1^j, E_2^j\big)\big]^{1-\alpha},$$

where ψ and ϕ^j are homogenecus of degree one.

5. Hybrid theory

We now turn our attention to a theory which is neither more nor less general than the Heckscher–Ohlin theory and which is not polar to that theory. In the present section we change the standard assumptions as little as possible, simply substituting an exhaustible resource for one of the two Ricardian primary factors of Heckscher–Ohlin theory.

In each country two final goods are produced by means of one (Ricardian) primary factor and one (Hotelling) exhaustible natural resource. Let V be the endowment of the Ricardian factor, $R(0)$ the initial stock of the resource and $E(t)$ the rate of extraction of the resource. For given P, V and E, the economy produces maximum total output:

$$Y_1 = Y^1(P, E, V) = X^1(P, E, V) + PX^2(P, E, V) = X_1 + PX_2.$$

For given P and V, the function Y^1 has the properties displayed in Figure 5.1.

For a small country, able to buy and sell at given and constant terms of trade and able to borrow and lend at a given and constant rate of interest, the task is to find

(P5.1)

$$\max_{\{E\}} \int_0^\infty \exp(-rt) Y^1(P, E, V) \, dt$$

s.t. $\dot{R} = -E$
$R(0)$ positive and given
$R \geq 0, \qquad E \geq 0.$

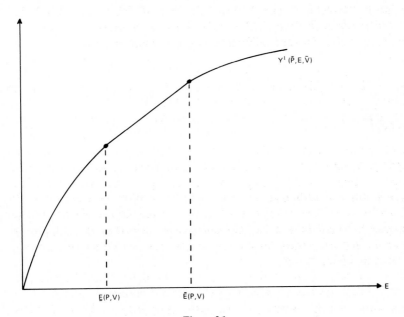

Figure 5.1

Among the necessary conditions we have:

$$\partial Y^1/\partial E \leq \bar{\psi}\exp(rt) \quad (= \text{if } E > 0),$$
$$\equiv \psi(t), \tag{5.1}$$

where $\bar{\psi}$ is a positive constant.

From (5.1) and the concavity of $Y^1(\bar{P}, E, \bar{V})$ we see that E declines monotonely to zero, reaching zero in finite time or approaching it asymptotically according to the behavior of Y^1 at the origin. We note also that, in the interval $[\underline{E}, \bar{E}]$, $\partial Y^1/\partial E$ is constant, implying that E cannot remain in that interval for more than a moment. It follows that along an optimal trajectory either $E(0)$ is greater than $\bar{E}(\bar{P}, \bar{V})$, in which case production is initially specialized to the resource-intensive industry, later switching abruptly to the opposite specialization; or the resource-intensive good is never produced. Typical trajectories, in (R, ψ)-space, are displayed in Figure 5.2. Notice that the trajectories have "kinks" at $\psi(t) = \partial Y^1(\bar{P}, E, \bar{V})/\partial E|_{\underline{E} \leq E \leq \bar{E}}$, where the switch in specialization and jump in $E(t)$ take place. Of course if $R(0) \leq R^*$ the kink is irrelevant, for then the resource-intensive good is never produced.

Theorem 5.1 (Rybczynski)

Let $R(0)$ be such that along an optimal trajectory each good is produced during some interval of time. Then any increase in $R(0)$ raises the output of the resource-intensive good for all t at which it is produced and, moreover, delays the switch to the opposite specialization.

Proof

The conclusion of the theorem follows from (5.1) and the transversality condition that $\lim_{t \to \infty} R(t) = 0$, or from Figure 5.2.   Q.E.D.

Corollary 5.1

Under the conditions of Theorem 5.1, if $R(0)$ increases then the cumulative output (discounted or undiscounted) of the resource-intensive good increases and the cumulative discounted output of the other good declines (cumulative undiscounted output is unchanged).

Since output is always specialized, it is not to be expected that there is a close analogue of the Stolper–Samuelson Theorem. However the implications of a change in the commodity price ratio are of independent interest, whether or not they can be related to that theorem.

Theorem 5.2

Suppose that along an optimal trajectory each good is produced during some interval of time. Then any increase in the price of the relatively resource-intensive

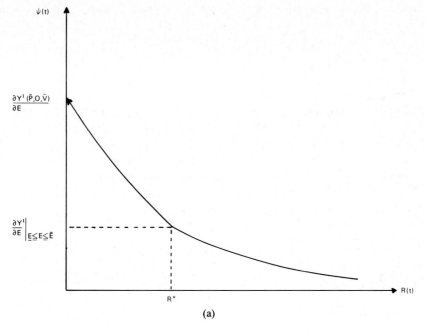

(a)

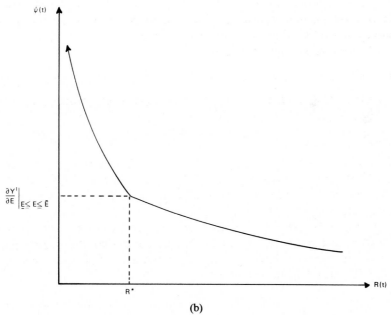

(b)

Figure 5.2

good entails (a) a reduction in both $\underline{E}$ and $\overline{E}$ and (b) an increase in the interval of time during which the relatively resource-intensive good is produced and a reduction in the interval of time during which the relatively resource-unintensive good is produced.

Proof

For concreteness, suppose that the second good is relatively resource-intensive.

(a) An increase in P shifts the Y^1-curve in the manner indicated by Figure 5.3. Evidently, for $\Delta P > 0$:

$$\Delta \underline{E}(P,V) \equiv \underline{E}(P + \Delta P, V) - \underline{E}(P,V) < 0,$$

$$\Delta \overline{E}(P,V) \equiv \overline{E}(P + \Delta P, V) - \overline{E}(P,V) < 0.$$

(b) It follows from the first of the inequalities that there is a decline in the amount of the resource used while only the resource-unintensive good is produced and therefore an increase in the amount of the resource used during the initial phase of specialization in the resource-intensive good. On the other hand, from

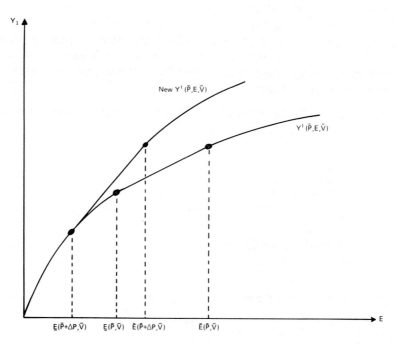

Figure 5.3

(5.1), when only the resource-intensive good is produced:

$$\dot{E}/E = \left[r(\partial Y^1/\partial E)\right]/\left[E(\partial^2 Y^1/\partial E^2)\right]$$
$$= \left[r(\partial F^2(E,V)/\partial E)\right]/\left[E(\partial^2 F^2(E,V)/\partial E^2)\right],$$

which is independent of commodity prices. Hence the interval of time during which the resource-intensive good is produced increases.   Q.E.D.

Theorem 5.3 (Heckscher–Ohlin)

If preferences are the same and homothetic in each of two free-trading countries then that country which initially is relatively well-endowed with the exhaustible resource will always export the relatively resource-intensive good.

Proof

Since returns to scale are constant and preferences are homothetic there is no loss in assuming that the two countries enjoy the same Ricardian endowment.

Suppose that at some point in time the same rate of extraction prevails in each country. The two countries must then produce each good at the same rate. Since preferences are homothetic and the same everywhere, there is no trade. Moreover $\partial Y^1/\partial E$, and therefore $\psi(t)$, are the same in both countries. It follows that $\partial Y^1/\partial E$ and E must be the same in both countries always, contradicting the assumption that the initial resource-stocks differ from country to country. It follows further that the rate of extraction is always larger in the relatively resource-rich country. That country therefore always produces more of (and exports) the resource-intensive good.   Q.E.D.

Suppose now that the possibility of international borrowing and lending is removed. A small country must find:

(P5.2)

$$\max_{\{E\}} \int_0^\infty \exp(-\rho t) W\left[Y^1(\bar{P}, E, V), P\right] dt$$

s.t. $\dot{R} = -E$
   $R(0)$ positive and given
   $R \geq 0, \qquad E \geq 0.$

Instead of (5.1) we have the necessary condition:

$$(\partial W/\partial Y_1)(\partial Y^1/\partial E) \leq \bar{\psi} \exp(\rho t) \quad (= \text{if } E > 0)$$
$$\equiv \psi(t). \tag{5.2}$$

From (5.2), and from the concavity of W in Y_1 and Y^1 in E, the rate of extraction again declines monotonely to zero. However, W is strictly concave in Y_1, and therefore in E. Hence there is no longer an abrupt switch in specialization as E reaches some critical value. Rather there is a smooth progression from complete specialization in the resource-intensive good through degrees of incomplete specialization to complete specialization in the other good. If the kink is removed, Figure 5.2 still faithfully depicts the optimal trajectory. Theorems 5.1–5.3 remain valid. Figure 5.3, the diagram accompanying Theorem 5.2, is transformed into Figure 5.4.

Theorems 5.1 and 5.2, and their no-borrowing counterparts, are based on the assumption of constant terms of trade. However that assumption is now less plausible than in earlier sections. For if all economies are hybrid and the terms of trade are constant then, after finite time, all economies must specialize in producing the commodity which is relatively intensive in its use of the Ricardian factor. Evidently such an outcome would never be observed if, for example, the resource-intensive good is essential in consumption, in the sense that the indifference contours never reach the axis of the other good. In such circum-

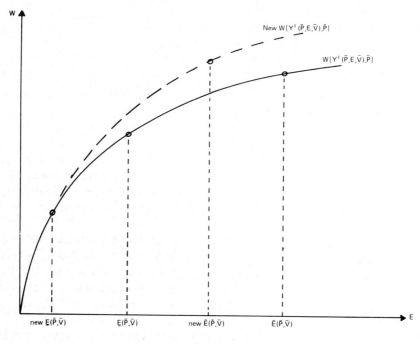

Figure 5.4

stances it might be more plausible to assume that the terms of trade move exponentially in favor of the resource-intensive good. Kemp and Long (1981a) have shown that under the alternative assumption it still is possible to establish a theorem of Rybczynski type.

6. Resource-renewal and resource-replacement

So far we have considered only those resources which are not only exhaustible but also non-renewable and non-replaceable. In fact some resources are self-renewing – one thinks of "biological" resources like forests and fisheries; some can be artificially renewed – one thinks of plant nurseries, fish hatcheries and all kinds of "recycling" processes; and some can be replaced, either by perfect substitutes (one thinks of the sun replacing fossil fuel as an immediate source of energy) or by imperfect substitutes (one thinks of resorting to methods of production which are more capital-intensive but also more parsimonious in their use of exhaustible resources). In a more complete survey we should have wanted to examine the robustness of standard theorems in the face of several types of resource-renewal and several types of resource-replacement. Since pages are in short supply we content ourselves with a brief discussion of some of the implications of self-renewal and of one type of resource-replacement and, for the rest, refer the reader to the relevant paragraph of the final bibliographical section.

6.1. Resource-renewal

That resources are self-renewing suggests the possibility of non-trivial steady states in which the several rates of extraction are exactly matched by rates of renewal. Whether the optimal trajectory does indeed approach a steady state depends on the rate of interest and on the properties of the renewal or growth functions of the resources.

Space does not allow a complete reworking of all earlier theories. We focus on that version of the hybrid theory of Section 5 in which international borrowing and lending are possible, simply appending a growth function $g(R)$ for the single resource. It is assumed, conventionally, that $g(R)$ is strictly concave, with $g'(0) > 0$ and $g(0) = 0 = g(\bar{R})$ for some positive $\bar{R}$. It then follows that $g(R)$ attains a maximum at some unique $\hat{R}$, $0 < \hat{R} < \bar{R}$.

For a small country, able to buy and sell at a given, positive and constant terms of trade and able to borrow and lend at a given, positive and constant rate of interest, the task is to find:

(P6.1)

$$\max_{\{E\}} \int_0^\infty \exp(-rt)Y^1(\bar{P}, E(t), V)\,dt$$

s.t. $\dot{R} = -E + g(R)$

$R(0)$ positive and given $\qquad\qquad$ (6.1)

$R \geq 0, \quad E \geq 0.$

Among the necessary conditions we have

$$\partial Y^1/\partial E \leq \psi(t) \quad (= \text{if } E > 0) \qquad\qquad (6.2)$$

and

$$\dot{\psi} = (r - g'(R))\psi, \qquad\qquad (6.3)$$

where $g'(R) \equiv dg/dR$.

We see at once that if $r - g'(0)$ is non-negative, so that $r - g'(R)$ is positive for all positive R, then along the optimal trajectory E declines monotonely to zero. In that case, all the qualitative conclusions of Section 5 remain intact. In particular, the resource is exhausted, perhaps only asymptotically, in spite of its capacity for self-renewal.

Suppose then that there exists some positive value of R, say R^*, such that $r = G'(R^*)$. Evidently $R^* < \hat{R}$. With the aid of (6.1)–(6.3), the phase diagram in (R, ψ)-space is easily constructed. Thus, from (6.3), the locus $\dot{\psi} = 0$ consists of the non-negative R-axis and the line defined by $R = R^*$. From (6.1) and (6.2), on the other hand, the locus $\dot{R} = 0$ has one of the shapes displayed in Figure 6.1. Thus if $g(\hat{R}) \leq \underline{E}$ then $\dot{R} = 0$ implies that $E \leq \underline{E}$, so that only the relatively labor-intensive good is produced, and the locus has the shape displayed in Figure 6.1(a); if $\underline{E} < g(\hat{R}) \leq \bar{E}$ then $\dot{R} = 0$ implies that $E \leq \bar{E}$, so that either both goods are produced or only the relatively labor-intensive good is produced, and the locus has the shape of Figure 6.1(b); and if $g(\hat{R}) > \bar{E}$ then production may be specialized to either good or neither, and the locus has the shape of Figure 6.1(c). The intersection of the two loci, $\dot{\psi} = 0$ and $\dot{R} = 0$, defines the steady state (ψ^*, R^*) where $\psi^* \equiv (\partial Y^1/\partial E)|_{E=g(R^*)}$. In the steady state it may be optimal to produce only the labor-intensive good [as in Figure 6.1(a)], only the resource-intensive good [as in Figure 6.1(c)], or both goods [as in Figure 6.1(b)]. Evidently the stationary state is a saddlepoint. As the economy passes along one or other of the stable arms of the saddle, production may switch from one pattern of specialization to another. The sequence may but need not be the one traced in

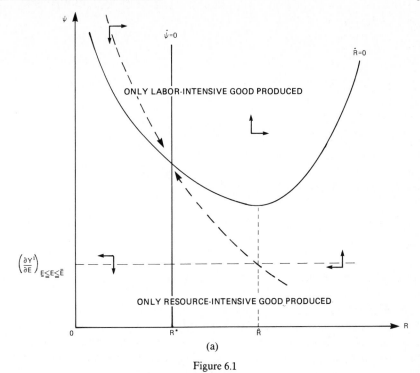

Figure 6.1

Section 5. The old sequence (specialization in producing the resource-intensive good giving way to specialization in producing the labor-intensive good) is reproduced by the right-hand arm of Figure 6.1(a); but along the left-hand arm of Figure 6.1(c) one encounters the reversed sequence; and along other trajectories there is no switching of patterns (along the left-hand arms of Figures 6.1(a) and 6.1(b) only the labor-intensive good is produced, and along the right-hand arms of Figures 6.1(b) and 6.1(c) only the resource-intensive good is produced).

Armed with eqs. (6.1)–(6.3) and with the phase diagram (6.1) it can be verified without difficulty that Theorems 6.1 to 6.3 survive the recognition of self-renewal. One need only remember that, when the switch of specialization is *away* from the labor-intensive good, an increase in the resource-endowment *advances* the switch-point.

6.2. Resource-replacement

The possibility of resource-replacement raises a set of questions which could not be posed in the context of earlier sections. Thus one may wish to compare the

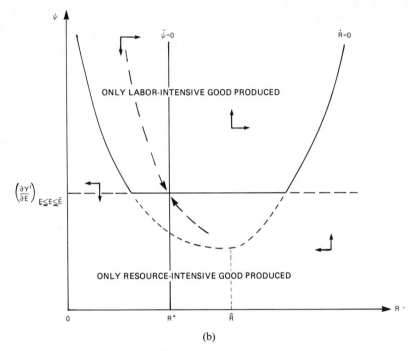

(b)

Figure 6.1.   *continued.*

patterns of output and trade in the pre- and post-replacement phases and, in particular, to trace the behaviour of output and trade at the point of time at which the substitute is brought into production. It will emerge that abrupt jumps in both are possible.

Again sticking as close to the orthodox Heckscher–Ohlin framework as possible, we suppose that two tradeable goods are produced by means of non-traded labor and "energy", with the first good relatively labor-intensive and the second relatively energy-intensive. Energy in turn may be derived either from an oil deposit of given initial extent or directly from the sun. By convention, a unit of extracted oil is equivalent to a unit of solar energy. The extraction of a unit of oil requires b_1 units of labor; the harnessing of a unit of solar energy requires b_2 units of labor; and $b_1 \gtreqless b_2$. It is possible that the utilization of solar energy requires the construction of a "solar plant" at some given cost K in terms of the first commodity. However we do not rule out the case $K = 0$. For simplicity we take K to be independent of the rate of utilization of solar energy.

A small country faces constant and given terms of trade $P \equiv P_2/P_1$ and a constant and given world rate of interest (in terms of the first commodity) r. It therefore may be taken to maximize the present value of its income flow.

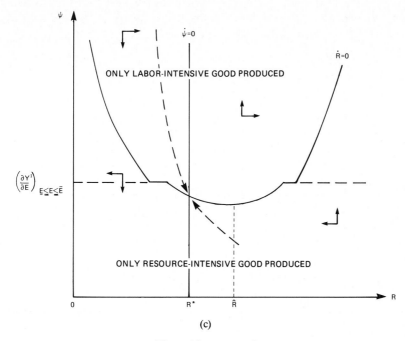

(c)

Figure 6.1. *continued.*

To avoid triviality it is assumed both that b_1 is not so much greater than b_2 that the oil is not worth extracting and that b_2 and the interest rK on the set-up cost K are not so great as to make solar energy forever unattractive. Given that assumption, we can be sure that an initial interval, during which oil is the sole source of energy, will be followed by a second interval during which the sun is the sole source. That there will be no interval during which both sources of energy are tapped can be explained intuitively. At any time t the social cost of extracted oil is composed of the direct labor cost b_1 plus an imputed scarcity rent which steadily rises as the resource-stock is depleted. Eventually the social cost of extracted oil exceeds b_2, the average variable cost of harnessing the sun, by rK. At that moment it is optimal to install the solar plant; and at that moment the stock of oil comes to an end.

It follows that we can approach the social problem in two stages. In the first stage we take as arbitrarily given the time T at which the transition from oil to sun takes place, then determine both the optimal path of oil extraction from the initial moment to T and the optimal rate of production of solar energy thereafter. Given the paths of oil extraction and production of solar energy, the net social benefit from both can be calculated as a function of T. In the second stage, T is chosen to make the benefit a maximum.

Suppose then that T has been assigned some arbitrary value. We seek the optimal path of extraction over the interval $(0, T)$. To this end we introduce the net-output function:

$$Y^{(1)}(E) \equiv Y^1(P, E, V - b_1 E) \equiv Y^1(P, E, V^{(1)}), \qquad (6.4)$$

where E is, as usual, the rate of extraction and $V^{(1)} \equiv V - b_1 E$ is the labor available for producing the two tradeable goods. The function $Y^{(1)}$ is strictly concave except for $E \in (\tilde{E}^{(1)}, \hat{E}^{(1)})$, where $\tilde{E}^{(1)}$ and $\hat{E}^{(1)}$ are the values of E at which the input-feasibility frontier $V^{(1)} = V - b_1 E$ cuts the rays α and β defining the cone of diversification. See Figures 6.2 and 6.3. The function $Y^{(1)}$ attains its maximum at say $E^{*(1)}$ which is unique if the slope of the straight segments of the constant-price isoquants of $Y^1(P, E, V^{(1)})$ differs from $-b_1$. Figure 6.2 illustrates the case in which $E^{*(1)} > \hat{E}^{(1)}$, Figure 6.3 the case in which $E^{*(1)} < \tilde{E}^{(1)}$. Given T, we seek:

(P6.1)

$$\max_{\{E\}} \int_0^T \exp(-rt) Y^{(1)}(E(t)) \, dt$$

s.t. $\quad \dot{R}(t) = -E(t)$

$\qquad R(0)$ positive and given, $\qquad R(T) = 0,$

$\qquad E(t) \geq 0.$

The Hamiltonian for (P6.1) is:

$$H = \exp(-rt) Y^{(1)}(E(t)) - \phi(t) E(t) \qquad (6.5)$$

and as necessary conditions we have:

$$\exp(-rt)(dY^{(1)}/dE) - \phi(t) \leq 0 \quad (= 0 \text{ if } E > 0), \qquad (6.6)$$

$$\dot{\phi} = -\partial H/\partial R = 0. \qquad (6.7)$$

From (6.7), $\phi(t) = \phi(0)$, a constant. From (6.6), therefore, $dY^{(1)}/dE$ must fall at the rate r, implying that diversification of production is suboptimal. Let $W^{(1)}(R(0), T)$ be the required maximum value for (P6.1).

Let us now consider the interval $[T, \infty)$. The stock of oil has been exhausted and the solar plant installed. The relevant net-output function is:

$$Y^{(2)}(E) \equiv Y^1(P, E, V - b_2 E) \equiv Y^1(P, E, V^{(2)}), \qquad (6.8)$$

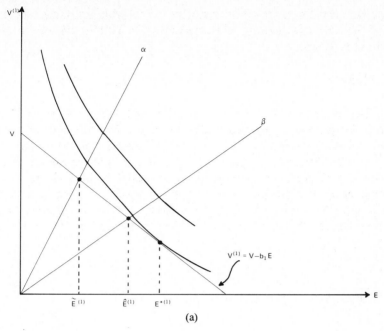

(a)

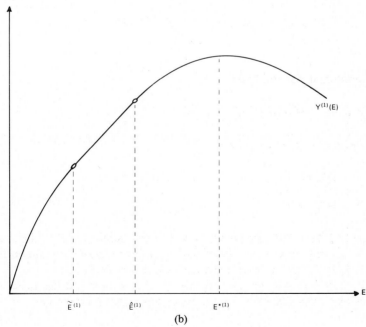

(b)

Figure 6.2. (a) $E^{*(1)} > \hat{E}^{(1)}$; (b) $E^{*(1)} > \hat{E}^{(1)}$.

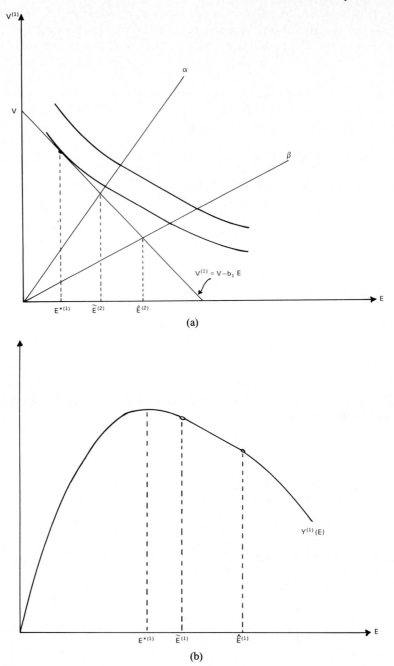

Figure 6.3.   (a) $E^{*(1)} < \tilde{E}^{(1)}$; (b) $E^{*(1)} < \tilde{E}^{(1)}$.

where E is now the rate of production of solar energy and $V^{(2)}$ is the labor available for the production of the two tradeable goods. The function $Y^{(2)}(E)$ has the same qualitative properties as $Y^{(1)}(E)$. In particular, it attains a unique maximum, at say $E^{*(2)}$, if the slope of the straight segments of the constant-price isoquants of $Y^1(P, E, V^{(2)})$ differs from $-b_2$. Depending on whether $E^{*(2)} > \hat{E}^{(2)}$ or $E^{*(2)} < \tilde{E}^{(2)}$, it is optimal to specialize in the second (relatively energy-intensive) good or in the first (relatively labor-intensive) good. In either case, the present value of the stream of outputs is:

$$\left(Y^{(2)}(E^{*(2)}) - rK \right)/r. \tag{6.9}$$

Clearly the solar plant should be built only if (6.9) is positive.

The transition time T is chosen to maximize:

$$W(R(0), T, K, r) \equiv W^{(1)}(R(0), T) + \exp(-rT)\left(Y^{(2)}(E^{*(2)}) - rK \right)/r.$$

The necessary condition for a maximum is:

$$\partial W/\partial T \equiv \partial W^{(1)}/\partial T - \exp(-rT)\left(Y^{(2)}(E^{*(2)}) - rK \right) = 0. \tag{6.10}$$

However it is a theorem in control theory that

$$\partial W^{(1)}/\partial T = H(T). \tag{6.11}$$

[See, for example, Hadley and Kemp (1971, pp. 117–120).] Moreover H is a continuous function of time. Hence (6.5), (6.6) and (6.11) can be brought into play to rewrite (6.10) as:

$$\lim_{t \to T} \left[Y^{(1)}(E(t)) - E(t)(\mathrm{d}Y^{(1)}/\mathrm{d}E) \right] = Y^{(2)}(E^{*(2)}) - rK, \tag{6.12}$$

or, defining $E^- \equiv \lim_{t \to T} E(t)$, as:

$$Y^{(1)}(E^-) - E^-(\mathrm{d}Y^{(1)}/\mathrm{d}E) = Y^{(2)}(E^{*(2)}) - rK. \tag{6.13}$$

Given $E^{*(2)}$, (6.13) determines E^-; and, given E^-, (6.6) and (6.7), together with the requirement that $R(T) = 0$, determine T.

We now seek to compare E^- and $E^{*(2)}$. Since $\mathrm{d}Y^{(2)}/\mathrm{d}E = 0$ if $E = E^{*(2)}$, (6.13) can be rewritten as:

$$Y^{(1)}(E^-) - E^-(\mathrm{d}Y^{(1)}/\mathrm{d}E)|_{E=E^-}$$

$$= Y^{(2)}(E^{*(2)}) - E^{*(2)}(\mathrm{d}Y^{(2)}/\mathrm{d}E)|_{E=E^{*(2)}} - rK, \quad (6.14)$$

or, defining

$$S^{(i)}(E) \equiv Y^{(i)}(E) - E\left(dY^{(i)}/dE\right), \qquad i = 1, 2, \tag{6.15}$$

as

$$S^{(1)}(E^-) = S^{(2)}(E^{*(2)}) - rK. \tag{6.16}$$

The functions $S^{(1)}(E)$ and $S^{(2)}(E)$ are depicted in Figure 6.4, drawn on the assumption that $b_2 > b_1$. (For the case $b_1 > b_2$, the superscripts are interchanged; and, for the case $b_1 = b_2$, the two curves coincide.) With the aid of Figure 6.4 it can be seen that the rate of energy production jumps up at T if rK is sufficiently large, down if rK is sufficiently small, and is continuous at T for a singular intermediate value of rK. (For the case $b_1 > b_2$ production necessarily jumps up; for the case $b_1 = b_2$ production jumps up if rK is positive and otherwise is continuous.) This conclusion is valid whether $E^{*(2)} > \hat{E}^{(2)}$, as in Figure 6.4, or $E^{*(2)} < \tilde{E}^{(2)}$.

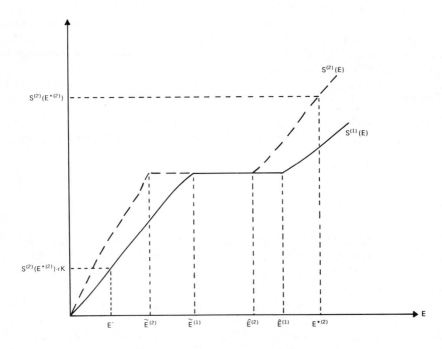

Figure 6.4

Our conclusions are summarized in

Theorem 6.1

Under the general assumptions of this section it is optimal to exhaust the oil deposit before turning to solar energy. During the oil phase, the production of energy steadily declines at the rate r. An initial subphase of specialization in the relatively resource-intensive good is succeeded by a subphase of specialization in the relatively labor-intensive good. Either (but not both) of the subphases may be degenerate. At the point of transition to solar power the production of energy jumps up if:

(a) (i) $b_1 > b_2$ *or* (ii) $b_1 = b_2$ and $rK > 0$ *or* (iii) $b_1 < b_2$ and rK is sufficiently large.

Production jumps down if:

(b) $b_1 < b_2$ and rK is sufficiently small.

Production is continuous if:

(c) (i) $b_1 = b_2$ and $rK = 0$ *or* (ii) $b_1 < b_2$ and rK takes on a particular positive value.

Corollary

It is possible that during the oil phase there is a switch in the pattern of trade, with first the relatively energy-intensive good and later the relatively labor-intensive good exported. If any of the conditions (a) (i)–(iii) is satisfied then at T there may be a *re*-switching of the pattern of trade, with the relatively energy-intensive good resuming its role of export-good.

Remark

If (a) (i) is satisfied and if (as we have assumed) oil is used during an initial phase then $rK > 0$. Thus if $rK = 0$ then (a) is violated. In fact, if $rK = 0$ then reswitching is impossible.

7. Cartels – introduction

Throughout Sections 2–6 the assumption of perfect competition was maintained intact. Historically, however, the extraction of some important exhaustible resources has been under the control, more or less complete, of large international cartels. One thinks of tin, rubber, bauxite, coffee and oil. Almost always, the cartels have been incomplete, hemmed in and disciplined by a "fringe," visible or merely potential, of smaller price-taking producers; almost always, the cartels have been temporary – forming, sticking together for a time, then breaking up, to be replaced at a later date by a new coalition.

Since price-setting is one of the objectives of cartelization the competitive analysis of earlier sections should be supplemented by an integrated theory of the formation, operation and dissolution of cartels. Unfortunately there is available only the most primitive of theories concerning the formation and collapse of cartels and it is not closely integrated with the theory of the operation of cartels. For the most part therefore we follow tradition and concentrate on the interaction of an established cartel and fringe, without asking how the cartel came into being and without admitting that it has an uncertain lifetime or that some of its operating decisions may be taken merely with an eye to maintaining or changing its identity. Only at the end of our analysis of the operation of cartels do we pull together a few ideas concerning their formation and dissolution.

The recognition of cartels calls for explicitly game-theoretical analysis. Not surprisingly, in all work so far available the formulations have been severely partial equilibrium in character. In the most interesting formulation, the extraction of a homogeneous exhaustible resource is undertaken by an industry which comprises one large or "dominant" firm D and many small or "fringe" firms, collectively F. Possibly the large "firm" is a cartel of small firms. The members of the fringe and the members of the cartel may be located in any country. In a case of special interest, all fringe firms are located in one set of countries and all members of the cartel in a second set disjoint from the first. The price path of the extracted resource is set by D and passively accepted by F. In that sense, D is a leader, F a follower. Moreover in setting the price D makes full allowance for the responses of F to changes in price. Thus the setting is of Stackelberg rather than, say, Nash–Cournot type.

Given the Stackelberg approach it is still necessary to choose a solution concept. Here we concentrate on price paths which can be announced by D at the outset, which D either will be unable to change later or will not wish to change later, which are market-clearing, and which therefore can be confidently accepted by F as a basis for planning; that is, we concentrate on perfect-foresight or rational-expectations equilibria. It will turn out that membership of the set of perfect-foresight equilibria depends on whether D is bound or not bound by the announcement. We begin by considering the subcase in which D is bound by its announcement, as it would be if there were a complete set of futures markets with binding contracts entered into at the outset and extending into the indefinite future and if there were no other markets.

8. Cartels – the case of binding contracts

Demand for the extracted resource is a stable monotone-decreasing function of price P, with a negative elasticity ε non-increasing in P. There may or may not exist a finite price $\bar{P}$ such that demand is extinguished at $\bar{P}$ but positive at $P < \bar{P}$.

For D the average cost of extraction is k_D, a non-negative constant; and for F the average cost of extraction is k_F. If $\bar{P}$ exists then $k_D, k_F < \bar{P}$.

At some initial moment ($t = 0$), D announces the entire price path $\{P(t)\}$ and thereafter sticks to it. D seeks to maximize the present value of its sales but is constrained in its choice of price by the presence of F. Let q_F be the rate of extraction by F. Then the constraint takes the following form.

Price constraint

If q_F is positive at time t^* then

$$[P(t^*) - k_F]\exp(-rt^*) \geqq [P(t) - k_F]\exp(-rt), \quad \text{for all } t, \qquad (8.1)$$

with strict inequality only if $q_F = 0$ at $t \neq t^*$.

If (8.1) is binding then the economy is said to be in a competitive phase at t^*; otherwise it is said to be in a monopolistic phase at t^*. By definition, F does not extract during a monopolistic phase; but D may extract during a competitive phase. In principle the optimal path may call for repeated switching from one phase to the other. For simplicity, however, it will be assumed that there is at most one switch.

What are the properties of an optimal price path? Consider first the behaviour of the optimal price at junction or switch points. If neither the extracted resource nor the numéraire can be stored across the junction without cost then it seems possible that a switch from monopoly to competition might be associated with an upward jump of the optimal price and that a switch from competition to monopoly might be associated with a downward jump of the price.[1] (We have been able to exclude the latter possibility when $k_F \leqq k_M$, but those are not the only circumstances in which a switch from competition to monopoly may occur.) However if each good can be stored without cost it is possible to rule out jumps of both kinds. For an upward jump would enable consumers to make a certain profit (in terms of the numéraire and in terms of utility) by holding the extracted resource across the junction point, and a downward jump would enable them to make a certain profit (in terms of the extracted resource and in terms of utility) by holding the numéraire across the junction point. To minimize complications, it will be assumed that costless storage is available.

While the optimal price must be continuous across junctions it need not be continuously differentiable. During any competitive phase the price of the extracted resource must satisfy (8.1) with strict equality for all t and t^* in that phase; that is, net price (price less the average cost of extraction for F) must rise at the rate of interest. And it is easy to see that during any monopolistic phase

---

[1] Since the period of storage is degenerate, only set-up costs of storage are relevant.

price must be such that marginal net revenue (marginal revenue less the marginal cost of extraction for D) must rise at the rate of interest. Let T be the point of transition from a monopolistic to a competitive phase, and let $\phi(t)$ be the competitive supply price during the monopolistic phase. Immediately to the left of T, (8.1) holds with strict inequality. Together with the continuity of the optimal price, this implies that:

$$\left.\frac{dP(t)}{dt}\right|_{t=T^-} > \left.\frac{d\phi(t)}{dt}\right|_{t=T^-}.$$

The implied kink in $P(t)$ at $t = T$ is displayed in Figure 8.1. Now let T be the point of transition from a competitive to a monopolistic phase. Evidently:

$$\left.\frac{dP(t)}{dt}\right|_{t=T^+} < \left.\frac{d\phi(t)}{dt}\right|_{t=T^+},$$

for, otherwise, the competitive phase would extend beyond T. The implied kink in $P(t)$ is displayed in Figure 8.2.

It is now easy to show that the optimal price rises at a rate not greater than the rate of interest. During a competitive phase, net price rises at the rate of interest, hence price rises at a not-greater rate (at a lower rate if k_F is positive). During a monopolistic phase, marginal net revenue rises at the rate of interest. Hence

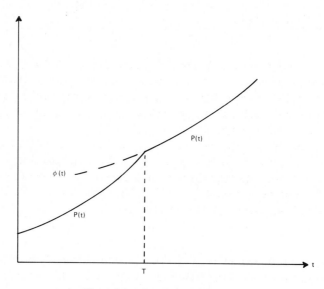

Figure 8.1.   Competitive phase last.

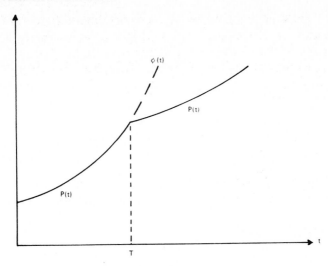

Figure 8.2. Monopolistic phase last.

marginal revenue rises at a not-greater rate (at a smaller rate if k_D is positive). But marginal revenue is equal to $P(1+(1/\varepsilon))$ and the relative change in that expression per unit of time is

$$\frac{\mathrm{d}\ln P}{\mathrm{d}t} + \frac{\mathrm{d}\ln(1+(1/\varepsilon))}{\mathrm{d}t}.$$

Moreover by assumption ε is a non-increasing function of P. Hence P must increase through time at a rate not greater than the rate at which marginal revenue is changing. Hence, finally, P must increase during the monopolistic phase at a rate not greater than the rate of interest (at a lower rate if k_D is positive or if ε is a decreasing function of P).

Finally we notice that, whatever the phasing of monopoly and competition, the terminal price must be $\bar{P}$. For if the terminal price were less than $\bar{P}$ consumers would be able to make a certain profit (in terms of the numéraire or utility) by stockpiling the extracted resource.

Pulling together the foregoing information we obtain:

Lemma 8.1

If both the extracted resource and the numéraire are storable without cost then the optimal price is a continuous function of time, increases at a rate which except at points of transition is positive but not greater than the rate of interest, and terminates at $\bar{P}$. At points of transition the rate of price increase drops discontinuously.

We have set down some of the properties of the path of optimal prices, both when a monopolistic phase precedes a competitive phase and when a competitive phase comes first. But what determines the phasing itself? In particular, how is the phasing related to the values of k_D and k_F? It can be shown by example that, whatever the relative values of k_D and k_F, the competitive phase can precede the monopolistic phase. On the other hand, the monopolistic phase can precede the competitive phase only if $k_D < k_F$. To see this, suppose that the monopolistic phase comes first, beginning at $t = 0$ and ending at $t = T$. Then, for some $t \in (T - \delta, T)$ and some $\delta > 0$,

$$P(t) = \frac{\varepsilon(t)}{1 + \varepsilon(t)} \pi(t)$$

$$= \frac{\varepsilon(t)}{1 + \varepsilon(t)} [k_D + (\pi(T^-) - k_D)\exp(-r(T^- - t))],$$

where $\pi(t)$ is marginal revenue at time t. It follows that:

$$\left. \frac{dP(t)}{dt} \right|_{t=T^-} = \left[\frac{\varepsilon(T^-)}{1 + \varepsilon(T^-)} \right] r [\pi(T^-) - k_D] + \frac{\pi(T^-)}{(1 + \varepsilon(T^-))^2} \left. \frac{d\varepsilon(t)}{dt} \right|_{t=T^-}$$

$$= rP(T^-) - \left[\frac{\varepsilon(T^-)}{1 + \varepsilon(T^-)} \right] rk_D$$

$$+ \left[\frac{(T^-)}{\varepsilon(T^-)(1 + \varepsilon(T^-))} \right] \left. \frac{d\varepsilon(t)}{dt} \right|_{t=T^-}$$

$$> \left. \frac{d\phi(t)}{dt} \right|_{t=T^-} \quad \text{[from Lemma 8.1]}$$

$$= r[P(T) - k_F] \quad \text{[from the continuity of } P(t)\text{]}.$$

Thus if $\varepsilon < -1$ the monopolistic phase comes first only if:[2]

$$k_F > \left[\frac{\varepsilon(T)}{1 + \varepsilon(T)} \right] k_D - \left[\frac{P(T)}{r\varepsilon(T)(1 + \varepsilon(T))} \right] \left. \frac{d\varepsilon(t)}{dt} \right|_{t=T} > \left[\frac{\varepsilon(T)}{1 + \varepsilon(T)} \right] k_D > k_D.$$

---

[2] If demand is inelastic, so that marginal revenue is negative, there is no monopolistic phase.

Lemma 8.2

The monopolistic phase cannot precede the competitive phase if $k_D \geq k_F$.

That concludes our discussion of the price path. Given that path, and knowing the demand function, we can deduce the path of total extraction. There remains for discussion only the division of extraction between D and F during the competitive phase; but here some surprises lie in wait.

Two questions emerge. First, is it always optimal for D to extract during the competitive phase, is it never optimal, or is it sometimes optimal? It can be shown by example that, whatever the phasing of extraction and whatever the relative values of k_D and k_F, it may be optimal for D to extract during the competitive phase. Beyond that, it can be shown that if the monopolistic phase comes first (implying that $k_D < k_F$) then D necessarily extracts during the competitive phase.

Second, if it is optimal for D to extract during the competitive phase, at what points during that phase should extraction take place? Suppose that the monopolistic phase comes first, with the transition at $t = T$. Then, from Lemma 8.2, $k_F > k_D$. From (8.1), the value of sales by D at $t > T$, discounted to $t = T$, is:

$$[P(t) - k_D]\exp(-r(t - T)) = [P(T) - k_F] + (k_F - k_D)\exp(-r(t - T)).$$

Since $k_F > k_D$, this expression reaches a maximum at $t = T$. Thus any extraction by D during the competitive phase will be concentrated in a subinterval beginning at $t = T$. Similarly, if $k_F > k_D$ but the competitive phase comes first, with the transition point T, then any extraction by D during the competitive phase will be concentrated in a subinterval beginning at $t = 0$. Finally, if $k_F < k_D$, with the competitive phase first, then any extraction by D during the competitive phase will be concentrated in a subinterval ending at $t = T$.

Now in a competitive closed economy, or in a competitive trading world with a perfect capital market, a set of deposits differing one from the other in extraction costs will be exploited in strict sequence, beginning with the lowest-cost deposit. [See Herfindahl (1967).] But this is no longer true in the context of a dominant firm; in particular, it is no longer true if the competitive phase comes first and if $k_F > k_D$. Moreover, by considering the possibility that all fringe firms are in one set of countries and all cartel firms in another we arrive at the following proposition.

Proposition

If there is a perfect world capital market then the direction of trade between low-cost and high-cost countries may change and then change again.

9. Cartels – no binding contracts

We have assumed that the price path announced by D at $t = 0$ is binding on D, and we have noted that this would be the case in the institutional setting of complete futures markets. We now show that if the announced path is not binding, as when the announcement relates to future spot prices, but D nevertheless announces a path which coincides with the binding-contract path then at points in time $t > 0$ D may have an incentive to depart from the announced path. Thus suppose that the competitive phase comes first and that $k_F < k_D$, so that any extraction by D during the competitive phase is concentrated at the end of that phase. Suppose also that along the initial binding-contract path D would extract during the competitive phase. The amount which D would extract depends on F's initial holding; to see this one need only reflect that if F's initial holding were zero then there would be no competitive phase. It follows that, as time goes by and F's holding declines with extraction, the extraction planned by D for the competitive phase will be continually revised. When F's holding is completely exhausted, D will be free to set the unrestricted monopoly price. If the competitive phase comes first but $k_F > k_D$ then, as soon as F's extraction begins, D will have an incentive to depart from the announced price path. In particular, once F's holding has been exhausted D will be free to set the unrestricted monopoly price.

It follows from the above argument that, even if F accepts the binding-contract path of prices as a reliable guide to future spot prices, realized prices will deviate from that path, implying that the path of realized prices cannot be a perfect-foresight or rational-expectations path. And being in possession of all relevant information F will know that the announced prices will not be realized and therefore will reject them at the outset. The binding-contract equilibrium price path is "dynamically inconsistent" if in fact the announcement is not binding.

This raises the question whether there exists a rational-expectations equilibrium price path in the context of spot markets. Evidently we need a price path which D has an incentive to abide by and which therefore will seem credible to F, rather than a path which is merely optimal in the sense that its announcement has a desirable effect on F's current decisions. Subject to that requirement, the path must maximize the present value of D's profits.[3] If along the binding-contract path the monopolistic phase comes first then that path is consistent with rational expectations. In other cases the required equilibrium exists but may be extremely difficult to compute, even when very simple functional forms are assumed.

10. The formation of cartels

There seems to exist very little successful analysis of the process of cartel-formation. It can be shown that, given any initial allocation of firms between fringe and

---

[3]In terms of the theory of differential games we need a closed-loop or feedback solution, with the strategies of the players conditional on the state of the game, rather than an open-loop solution, with strategies conditional on time only. See Starr and Ho (1969a, b).

cartel and given any initial binding-contract price path it is always possible to enlarge the cartel and find both a new binding-contract price path and a system of compensatory payments involving only members of the enlarged cartel such that all members of the enlarged cartel are better off. With the aid of this proposition one can understand why, in a context of complete markets, cartels form and expand. In fact the proposition is, if anything, too successful for it fails to explain why not all firms join the cartel. Presumably a more realistic analysis would allow for inertia in the face of changing circumstances, for ignorance, for difficulties in agreeing on a formula for profit sharing and, of course, for the absence of a complete set of futures markets.[4]

11. Bibliographical notes

Sections 2–5 are directly based on a series of papers by Kemp and Long (1980, Essays 10, 13 and 15; 1982a) and by Tawada (1982). Indirectly they flow from the first-generation work on trade and exhaustible resources by Vousden (1974), Long (1974, 1975b), Kemp and Suzuki (1975) and Suzuki (1976). However these early contributions not only introduced the essential element of exhaustibility but also departed from the symmetrical Heckscher–Ohlin format in several other respects, with the result that the contribution of exhaustibility as such was masked. The reader may refer also to Ono (1982).

For the material covered in the first part of Section 6 the most useful reference is Tawada (1982). (Whereas we have postulated a perfect international capital market, Tawada ruled out all international borrowing and lending.) Also relevant are Long (1975c), Kemp and Suzuki (1975), McRae (1978), Kemp and Long (1980, Essays 13 and 15), and Tawada (1981). For the topics treated in the second part of Section 6 we can find no really appropriate reference. However the analysis of that part is closely related to that of the closed-economy paper by Hung, Kemp and Long (1983).

For the topics discussed in Sections 7–10, on the other hand, there is a plentiful supply of suitable references. In a series of papers, some written jointly with Michael Folie, or David Ulph, Alistair Ulph has provided a systematic treatment of dominant-firm markets in exhaustible resources. See especially Ulph and Folie (1981), Ulph and Ulph (1981) and Ulph (1980, 1982). The possibility that the binding-contract equilibrium might be dynamically inconsistent was first noted by

---

[4]Ulph (1982) has gone to the opposite extreme, developing a completely non-cooperative theory of cartel formation. In particular he provides a careful examination of the incentives to join and leave the cartel in terms of the marginal profits of member and non-member firms as functions of the cartel size. However the analysis is based on a very special case and, as Ulph recognizes, the assumption of non-cooperativeness in cartel formation sits uncomfortably with the assumption that members of the cartel act cooperatively in setting price and outputs.

Newbery (1976), in a context of consumer cartelization. A rational-expectations equilibrium price path was computed by Newbery (1980) for a very special case. Also relevant are Maskin and Newbery (1978), Kemp and Long (1980, Essays 16 and 18) and Newbery (1981). For a proof of a proposition closely related to that of Section 10, see Kemp and Wan (1976), also Grinols (1981).

Finally we turn to the omitted topics noted at the end of Section 1. The first of these is uncertainty. A systematic analysis of the interaction of trade and uncertainty may be found in Chapter 9. However in a context of exhaustible resources uncertainty may have implications of an unusual sort. Specifically, uncertainty about the extent of a resource-stock ("endowment uncertainty") is, in general, incompatible with competitive behaviour [Kemp and Long (1980, Essay 4)], may entail that the optimal rate of extraction is increasing over non-degenerate intervals of time [Kemp (1976)] and may entail that problems of the type discussed in Sections 2–5 have no solution [Kasanen (1982)]. For particular analyses of trade under conditions of endowment uncertainty the reader may refer to Kemp and Suzuki (1976) and Kemp and Okuguchi (1979). For the implications of uncertain title to resources he may consult Long (1975a). And for the implications of uncertainty about future demand and prices he may consult Dasgupta, Eastwood and Heal (1978) and Eaton (1979), respectively.

Many resource-deposits are the common property of individuals and firms of more than one country. One thinks of fisheries and of ocean-floor mineral resources, including off-shore oil. In these circumstances intervention of national governments is inevitable and one looks for a game-theoretical treatment of their behaviour. So far, little formal analysis is available. However the reader may consult the work of Markusen (1976), Khalatbari (1977), Kemp and Long (1980, Essay 10), Bolle (1980), Levhari and Mirman (1980), Chiarella, Kemp, Long and Okuguchi (1984), Sinn (1983) and McMillan and Sinn (1984).

Some resources are very unevenly distributed across the surface of the earth. Trade theorists have responded to this fact by developing asymmetrical models of trade between countries rich in resources but without the ability to process those resources and countries without resources but with well-developed manufacturing industries. The purpose of such activity is to throw light on the long-run drift of the terms of trade between materials and finished products and of the ownership of the world's capital-stock (including its resource-stock). The literature is fragmentary. The reader might begin with Kemp and Long (1980, Essay 17), Chiarella (1980) and Hoel (1981).

Central to the historical development of the economics of exhaustible resources has been the question of survival. In the form given the question by Solow (1974), one asks for conditions on the technology which ensure that a closed economy for which some resource is an essential input can survive in the sense of being able to bound per capita consumption above zero by progressively substituting capital for the resource. [Solow's analysis was later extended by Mitra (1978), Cass and

Mitra (1981) and Kemp and Long (1982c).] It is natural that trade theorists should want to re-examine Solow's question in the context of a trading world. Typically they have sought conditions for the survival (in Solow's sense) of a small country without resources of its own but able to buy them with its own product on terms which move steadily against it. It is a common finding that if the terms of trade move exponentially against the country then it cannot survive without technical progress. The reader might consult Mitra, Majumdar and Ray (1982), Kemp and Long (1982b) and Ray (1981).

References

Aarrestad, J. (1978), "Optimal savings and exhaustible resource extraction in an open economy", Journal of Economic Theory, 19:163–179.

Bolle, F. (1980), "The efficient use of a non-renewable common-pool resource is possible but unlikely", Zeitschrift für Nationalökonomie, 40:391–397.

Cass, D. and T. Mitra (1979), "Persistence of economic growth despite exhaustion of natural resources", University of Pennsylvania.

Chiarella, C. (1980), "Trade between resource-poor and resource-rich economies as a differential game", Essay 19 in: M.C. Kemp and N.V. Long (1980).

Chiarella, C., M.C. Kemp, N.V. Long and K. Okuguchi (1984), "On the economics of international fisheries", International Economic Review, to be published.

Dasgupta, P., R. Eastwood and G. Heal (1978), "Resource management in a trading economy", Quarterly Journal of Economics, 92:297–306.

Eaton, J. (1979), "The allocation of resources in an open economy with uncertain terms of trade", International Economic Review, 20:391–403.

Grinols, E.L. (1981), "An extension of the Kemp–Wan theorem on the formation of customs unions", Journal of International Economics, 11:259–266.

Hoel, M. (1981), "Resource extraction by a monopolist with influence over the rate of return on non-resource assets", International Economic Review, 22:147–157.

Hung, N.M., M.C. Kemp and N.V. Long (1983), "The transition from an exhaustible resource-stock to an inexhaustible substitute", in: A.M. Ulph, ed., Demand, equilibrium and trade, Essays in honour of Professor Ivor F. Pearce (Macmillan, London).

Kasanen, E. (1982), "Dilemmas with infinitesimal magnitudes: The case of the resource depletion problem", Journal of Economic Dynamics and Control, 4:295–301.

Kemp, M.C. (1976), "How to eat a cake of unknown size", Essay 23 in: M.C. Kemp, Three topics in the theory of international trade (North-Holland Publishing Company, Amsterdam).

Kemp, M.C. and N.V. Long (1980), Exhaustible resources, optimality, and trade (North-Holland Publishing Company, Amsterdam).

Kemp, M.C. and N.V. Long (1982a), "Rybczynski's theorem in a context of exhaustible resources: The case of time-contingent prices", International Economic Review, 23:699–710.

Kemp, M.C. and N.V. Long (1982b), "Conditions for the survival of a small resource-importing economy", Journal of International Economics, 13:135–142.

Kemp, M.C. and N.V. Long (1982c), "A note on Solow's survival problem", Economics Letters, 10:381–384.

Kemp, M.C. and K. Okuguchi (1979), "Optimal policies for exhaustible resources in open economies", Zeitschrift für die gesamte Staatswissenschaft, 135:207–215.

Kemp, M.C. and K. Okuguchi (1980), "Exhaustible resources and optimal consumption in an open economy", Economic Studies Quarterly, 31:79–83.

Kemp, M.C. and H. Suzuki (1975), "International trade with a wasting but possibly replenishable resource", International Economic Review, 16:712–732; reprinted as Chapter 18 in: M.C. Kemp, Three topics in the theory of international trade (North-Holland Publishing Company, Amsterdam,

1976) 277–254.

Kemp, M.C. and H. Suzuki (1976), "Optimal international borrowing with a wasting resource", Chapter 24 in: M.C. Kemp, Three topics in the theory of international trade (North-Holland Publishing Company, Amsterdam) 309–316.

Kemp, M.C. and H.Y. Wan, Jr. (1976), "An elementary proposition concerning the formation of customs unions", Journal of International Economics, 6:95–97.

Khalatbari, F. (1977), "Market imperfections and the optimum rate of depletion of natural resources", Economica, 44:409–414.

Khang, C. (1971), "An isovalue locus involving intermediate goods and its applications to the pure theory of international trade", Journal of International Economics, 1:315–325.

Kydland, F.E. and E.C. Prescott (1977), "Rules rather than discretion: The inconsistency of optimal plans", Journal of Political Economy, 85:473–491.

Levhari, D. and L.J. Mirman (1980), "The great fish war: An example using a dynamic Nash–Cournot solution", Bell Journal of Economics, 11:322–334.

Long, N.V. (1974), "International borrowing for resource extraction", International Economic Review, 15:168–183.

Long, N.V. (1975a), "Resource extraction under uncertainty about possible nationalization", Journal of Economic Theory, 10:42–53.

Long, N.V. (1975b), International borrowing for resource extraction. Doctoral thesis, Australian National University.

Long, N.V. (1975c), "Optimal exploitation and replenishment of a natural resource", in: J.D. Pitchford and S.J. Turnovsky, eds., Application of control theory to economic analysis (North-Holland Publishing Company, Amsterdam), 81–106.

McMillan, J. and H.-W. Sinn (1984), "Oligopolistic extraction of a common-property resource: Dynamic equilibria", Chapter 11 in: M.C. Kemp and N.V. Long, eds., Essays in the economics of exhaustible resources (North-Holland Publishing Company, Amsterdam).

McRae, J.J. (1978), "Optimal and competitive use of replenishable natural resources by open economies", Journal of International Economics, 8:29–54.

Markusen, J.R. (1976), "Production and trade from international common property resources", Canadian Journal of Economics, 9:309–319.

Maskin, E. and D. Newbery (1978), "Rational expectations with market power–the paradox of the disadvantageous tariff in oil", University of Warwick.

Mitra, T. (1978), "On maintainable consumption levels and exhaustible resources", State University of New York at Stony Brook.

Mitra, T., M. Majumdar and D. Ray (1982), "Feasible alternatives under deteriorating terms of trade", Journal of International Economics, 13:105–134.

Newbery, D.M.G. (1976), "A paradox in tax theory: Optimal tariffs on exhaustible resources", University of Cambridge.

Newbery, D.M.G. (1981), "Oil prices, cartels, and the problem of dynamic inconsistency", Economic Journal, 91:617–646.

Newbery, D.M.G. (1980), "Credible oil supply contracts", University of Cambridge.

Ono, H. (1982), "Note on 'International trade with an exhaustible resource: A theorem of Rybczynski type'", International Economic Review, 23:165–170.

Ray, D. (1981), "Survival, growth and technical progress in an open economy facing deteriorating terms of trade", Cornell University.

Sinn, H.-W. (1983), "Resource depletion, seepage losses, and oligopoly: A Cournot model of the oil market", Economica, to be published.

Solow, R.M. (1974), "Intergenerational equity and exhaustible resources", Review of Economic Studies, Symposium, 29–45.

Starr, A.W. and Y.C. Ho (1969a), "Non-zero-sum differential games", Journal of Optimization Theory and Applications, 3:184–206.

Starr, A.W. and Y.C. Ho (1969b), "Further properties of non-zero-sum differential games", Journal of Optimization Theory and Applications, 3:207–219.

Suzuki, H. (1976a), "Models of economic development with wasting resources", Doctoral thesis, University of New South Wales.

Suzuki, H. (1976b), "On the possibility of steadily growing *per capita* consumption in an economy with a wasting and non-replenishable resource", Review of Economic Studies, 43:527–535.

Suzuki, H. and M. Ogawa (1979), "International trade with exhaustible natural resources", Zeitschrift für Nationalökonomie, 39:131–142.

Tawada, M. (1981), "International trade with a replenishable resource: The steady-state analysis", Kobe University of Commerce.

Tawada, M. (1982), "A note on international trade with a renewable resource", International Economic Review, 23:157–163.

Ulph, A.M. (1980), "Stackelberg models of partially cartelised markets for exhaustible resources", University of Southampton.

Ulph, A.M. (1982), "Modelling partially cartelized markets for exhaustible resources", Chapter 21 in: W. Eichhorn, R. Henn, K. Neumann and R.W. Shephard, eds., Economic theory of natural resources (Physica-Verlag, Würzburg).

Ulph, A.M. and M. Folie (1981), "Dominant firm models of resource depletion", in: D. Currie, D. Peel and W. Peters, eds., Microeconomic analysis (Croom Helm, London) 77–106.

Ulph, A.M. and D.T. Ulph (1981), "International monopoly-monopsony power in oil and capital: Part 1 – characterization of equilibria", University of Southampton.

Vousden, N. (1974), "International trade and exhaustible resources: A theoretical model", International Economic Review, 15:149–167.

Chapter 9

UNCERTAINTY IN TRADE MODELS

JOHN POMERY*

Purdue University

Contents

1.	Some preliminaries	420
2.	Walrasian-international models: Pure exchange	426
3.	Walrasian-international models: Production	435
4.	Welfare and government intervention	449
5.	Miscellany	457
6.	Concluding remarks	461
	References	461

*This chapter was written while the author was at Northwestern University. The original version benefitted from comments at presentations at Northwestern and Purdue Universities, at the Mid-West International Economics Meetings, and at the Princeton conference of Handbook contributors. The remarks of Bill Ethier, Elhanan Helpman, and Peter Kenen were particularly helpful. Deficiencies of this chapter, both stylistic and technical, remain the responsibility of the author and are positively correlated with failure to execute fully suggestions from those mentioned above.

Handbook of International Economics, vol. I, Edited by R.W. Jones and P.B. Kenen
© *Elsevier Science Publishers B.V., 1984*

The purpose of this chapter is to outline and to evaluate a variety of models, each involving uncertainty in the context of international trade. Uncertainty has many potential roles in microeconomic models of international trade. It can create a rationale for additional markets and hence both added dimensions for potential gains from trade and a plethora of results contingent upon the particular market structure assumed. In addition uncertainty may arise in issues concerning the existence and form of extramarket organizations and institutions.

It is beyond the scope of this chapter to examine all the possible roles for uncertainty in international trade; indeed this would invite a major reassessment of the domain of international microtheory, affecting both the "international" and the "uncertainty" aspects of models. Uncertainty has been appended to many traditional trade models, where it is natural to ask to what extent basic results are altered by, or generalizable given, the presence of uncertainty. A second question asks what results arise specifically because of the introduction of uncertainty. While much of the earlier literature addressed the first question, the second merits considerable attention – particularly where it leads beyond traditional classes of models.

This chapter will try to balance the inward-looking "basic results" and the outward-looking "new directions" approaches. In the spirit of the latter, think of the research program for uncertainty in international trade as exploring under what circumstances the index of nationality interacts nontrivially with uncertainty in a variety of forms of collective behavior.

1. Some preliminaries

Among the many forms uncertainty can take in economic models, it may be imposed, as a model-exogenous datum, on preferences, technology or endowments. It can arise as a consequence of strategic behavior of agents in the model, although formally strategic behavior need not imply uncertainty. It may appear through the failure of information-transmitting devices, such as the price mechanism, to perform flawlessly. Since pure trade theory is rooted in Walrasian general-equilibrium theory, it is natural to start with the first form of uncertainty. However it is then useful to consider a broader perspective where other forms of uncertainty might arise in an international context, recognizing that the competitive allocation mechanism does not capture the entire institutional framework within which international trade occurs, and that the existence and behavior of extramarket organizations and institutions is often linked to the latter two forms of uncertainty.

420

International economics can be said to begin with markets, and in particular with competitive (although possibly segmented) markets. For this chapter, think of a "Walrasian model" in the following terms. Economic agents are model-exogenous and classified as either households or firms. Households are linked to model-exogenous endowments and preferences (taken to include consumption sets), while firms are linked to model-exogenous technological opportunity sets. There are only two pure forms of economic activity: (i) trade, i.e. transferring ownership of a given bundle of goods, and (ii) production, i.e. transforming bundles of goods, given ownership. Actions are coordinated via the price mechanism, under the assumptions of price-taking and profit-maximization, resulting in a Pareto-efficient outcome (interpretable as minimization of aggregate rents).

"Walrasian-international models" are then Walrasian models where the index of nationality is introduced in a nontrivial fashion. Typically agents are partitioned by nationality and then some attributes – endowments, preferences and/or technology – are made nation-specific. (Markets segmented along national boundaries can be introduced by appropriate indexation.) The rationale for international trade in Walrasian-international models arises from the opportunity to coordinate activities globally, as opposed to merely nationally, via the competitive mechanism. The ultimate source of trade, and the determinant of the pattern of trade, arises out of differences across nations in endowments, preferences or technology.

Uncertainty can be introduced into Walrasian-international models by assuming state-dependence (taken here as synonymous with randomness) of endowments, preferences, technology, or prices. Random preferences have not been considered widely in the general-equilibrium literature, although this is often a convenient way to generate endogenous randomness in prices [cf. Kemp and Liviatan (1973), also Ethier (1981, 1982)]. Outside of pure exchange models and the topic of international trade involving depletable resources – the latter neglected in this chapter – randomness in endowments has received little coverage [although cf. Kemp (1976, ch. 21)]. In the current chapter, following the supply-side orientation of past Walrasian-international models, the major focus will be on technological randomness (or endowment randomness in exchange models). Direct imposition of randomness on prices, as opposed to randomness in prices induced from some more fundamental source, must be recognized as an implicitly partial-equilibrium approach; extension to a general-equilibrium framework may depend critically on the ultimate cause of the price randomness.

With supply-side randomness in Walrasian-international models comes the potential for additional markets, namely markets which permit trade across states of the world, not (just) across physical commodities within a given state. In general this "randomness rationale for trade" will not be separable unambiguously from the "commodity rationale for trade", but the extent of market structure imposed on the model has important consequences for the results obtained.

The purest extension of Walrasian-international models to incorporate supply-side randomness arises when markets are assumed to be complete, that is all physical commodities can be traded contingent upon each state of the world. In this situation all trade decisions are made ex-ante, i.e. occur prior to the realization of the state of the world [although there exist equivalent trading structures involving a mixture of ex-ante and ex-post trade, as in Arrow (1971b)]. Jointness introduced by supply-side randomness can be unpackaged for the purposes of trade. In such a world differences in beliefs, attitudes to risk, or ownership of randomness, are among potential sources of gains from trade. Free trade has standard optimality properties, and the agency problem of firms with respect to preferences of stockholders is solved by profit maximization in terms of contingent commodity prices.

Once outside the domain of complete markets a greater variety of possibilities can be found. The combination of ex-ante trade and/or production with ex-post trade can lead to situations where, with incomplete markets, free trade is Pareto-dominated by autarky [cf. Newbery and Stiglitz (1981), Cornes and Milne (1981)]. Another failure can arise in the agency problem for production – even with a single physical commodity if randomness is not multiplicative – [cf. Drèze (1974), also Stiglitz (1981, 1982)].

The problems with incomplete markets can be explained by recalling the nature of the price mechanism. Start from a collective behavior situation where individual agents each choose actions, these actions then jointly determine outcomes, the outcomes then jointly determine individual utilities, and the individual utilities are somehow weighted for a measure of collective well-being. The competitive mechanism is of this form, with the additional feature that actions are simultaneously determined with outcomes in the form of prices (and hence implicitly the distribution of income).

With complete markets and no non-pecuniary externalities, the competitive mechanism implies Pareto-efficiency for the following reason. Outcomes can be partitioned into private outcomes (i.e. incomes given prices) and public or joint outcomes (i.e. the price vector). Private actions optimize private outcomes, on individual and collective criteria, both because price-taking individuals have no incentive to attempt to use private actions to alter public outcomes and because of the absence of non-pecuniary externalities. Even though private actions do affect public outcomes, this does not matter at the collective level in terms of the Paretian criterion because of coordination induced via the price mechanism (whether we think of equalized marginal rates of substitution or more generally in terms of separation theory).

With incomplete markets, it is not guaranteed that marginal rates of substitution will be equalized across all individuals for all dimensions. Thus the impact of private actions on public outcomes can matter; pecuniary externalities are potentially important [cf. Loong and Zeckhauser (1982)]. Newbery and Stiglitz (1981) talk of ex-post commodity markets performing both their traditional role and also as an implicit insurance market; then private production decisions alter the distribution of ex-post prices and hence alter the effectiveness of ex-post markets as (second-best) insurance markets.

It should be clear that the existence of incomplete markets expands the list of potential reasons for government intervention; yet the government is just one form of extramarket organization or institution. At this stage it is useful to introduce the concept of a simple economic agent. A simple economic agent is one who has no problems of internal organization. It may be easiest to get a feel for this concept by contrasting with a complex economic agent, e.g. a firm, a nation, or other group – even an individual, as in Thaler and Shefrin (1981). Collective behavior in terms of complex economic agents is potentially ridden with a variety of well-known difficulties: aggregation of preferences of the constituent agents into a well-defined representation of collective preferences; obtaining correct revelation of constituent preferences; coordinating activity, even with no ex-post divergence of incentives; ex-post divergence of incentives (e.g. managers vs. stockholders, politicians or bureaucrats vs voters, employer vs employee, regulator vs regulatee); monitoring behavior and enforcing ex-ante agreements. A simple economic agent has none of these problems.

The notion of a complex economic agent is almost too broad, in that any form of collective behavior can be interpreted, from the global perspective, as the action of a complex agent. As is well known, the competitive mechanism can be viewed (under certain assumptions) as a particularly acceptable means of de-centralization for a global economy. Yet the concept forces attention to some simple observations. (i) Any form of collective behavior can be viewed both as a means of partial decentralization and as a form of partial coordination. (ii) Complex agents such as firms exist both as actors within the market system but also as alternatives to markets; this in the spirit of Coase (1937), Arrow (1974), Williamson (1975), Schotter (1981) among many others. (iii) Models of uncer-tainty where economic agents are treated as if simple agents and where simple agents interact in non-strategic manner with no information asymmetries will have different domains of applicability from models where the same agents are viewed as complex, with strategic behavior and/or information asymmetries among constituent agents. (iv) Models of pure trade theory have been heavily oriented to the competitive mechanism and have had a tendency to use strong aggregation assumptions; both these features tend to pull the focus away from some interesting topics involving the function of complex economic agents – mul-tinational firms, interest groups, groups of firms (whether rivalrous or collusive), supranational organizations and/or international institutions.

The notion of complex economic agent can become part of an informal classification of various difficulties in collective behavior in the presence of a price system. Thus a complex agent, when modelled as a single decision-making unit within a larger group, may be thought of as "internally dysfunctional" if the actions of that agent are not privately-optimal in terms of its own objective functions. Other difficulties such as nonpecuniary externalities, and pecuniary externalities with incomplete markets, involve an "insensitivity dysfunction" in that an agent undertakes a private action for private benefit, ignoring the additional social impact (whether this falls on only one other agent or on the entire group). Another form of dysfunction – a "manipulative dysfunction" – arises when an agent deliberately chooses private actions to alter the public outcome in its favor, either by directly manipulating a public outcome or by influencing the choices of others.

As an example, international trade between two countries each with factor market distortions would be collective behavior (at the global level) with internally dysfunctional agents. The familiar optimal tariff story would be an example of a manipulative dysfunction from the global perspective, although not from the perspective of the imposing country; in such situations, of course, it is necessary to distinguish between within-group and global optimality (as in the literature on clubs). The presence of uncertainty is consistent with all the forms of collective dysfunction of traditional trade theory, but draws attention, for example, to (i) internal dysfunctions, (ii) pecuniary externalities in the presence of incomplete markets, (iii) manipulative behavior, and (iv) externalities based on asymmetric information.

The actions, outcomes, satisfactions framework suggests another way of classifying the appearance of uncertainty. Uncertainty can occur in the form of randomness in the link from private action to private outcome (e.g. as in technological randomness), or with respect to the actions of others, to the extent that such actions affect joint outcomes. This latter category includes both conscious recognition of others (as in oligopoly) and sensitivity solely to aggregate effect (as with price randomness).

Once a private-sector agent faces uncertainty in his environment, there are a variety of possible responses. Given the existence of, say, technological randomness, the risk can be spread with different agents each taking a small share, or it can be pooled via mixing with other sources of randomness (if they are not perfectly positively correlated) – although both options are limited by the extent of markets and, frequently, by information problems. Altering behavior with respect to commodity trade, production or inventories may also mitigate the impact of randomness. Sometimes information acquisition or postponement of decisions may be appropriate, while manipulative dysfunctions might be helped by internalization within a complex agent (such as a firm). Uncertainty can generate new markets, alter the functioning of existing markets, and generate a variety of responses at both the individual and collective level.

Alternative assumptions about private sector options for response lead to a variety of models. For example, bearing in mind the "mixed-motive" notion of

Schelling (1960) and that the competitive mechanism is a pure coordination device where the element of conflict is neutralized via the price-taking assumption, there exists a modelling void to be filled by the literatures on rent-seeking, strategic tariff behavior, etc. Other types of situation may arise, such as with a regulator and a regulatee, either on a one-to-one basis as in many principal-agent problems or on a one-to-many basis. In such cases the regulator may be pursuing his own objective or simply acting as a means to allow those regulated to achieve a collective objective. In the context of regulated behavior, the options for mobility of those regulated become important [as emphasized, for example, by Cooper (1976)]. With uncertainty, mobility options such as substitution in production or consumption, lobbying or exit, are supplemented, for example, by cheating on ex-ante agreements or by altering an allocation mechanism by dissembling.

Another form of classification of models is by form of gains from collective behavior. While Walrasian price-coordination has dominated the traditional literature and is based on differences in autarkic price vectors, more recent work gives (new) examples of gains in the absence of explicit differences in autarkic price [e.g. Krugman (1979)], trade which may be inefficient and/or mutually disadvantageous [e.g. Brander (1981), Newbery and Stiglitz (1981), Cornes and Milne (1981)]. Moreover there is a branch of literature suggesting that jurisdictional issues and public goods, rather than competitive trade, should be the prime focus of international economists [e.g. Cooper (1976), Whitman (1977)].

All this suggests concern both for the sources of potential gains in any given example of collective behavior and for the relevant constraints in realizing those gains. Ultimately such gains must arise from some form of superadditivity in real incomes, but this may arise from price coordination, superadditivity in consumption or production technology (as with economies of scale, of scope, or agglomeration or in provision of pure public goods), or other sources. The gains may be realisable by the private sector without supervision, may require regulatory intervention, or may be imperfectly realisable in almost any framework. In addition it must be expected that changes in environments may be beneficial in some settings but adverse in others. For example it might be presumed that additional information is always beneficial, but the non-trade literature points out that information revealed at a certain juncture can destroy the possibility of insurance markets, or that decentralized agents reacting to common information may respond in identical (perfectly-positively correlated) fashion, thus destroying risk-pooling opportunities available if each reacts to somewhat coarser private information.

The point behind this preliminary section is that in order fully to appreciate what the recognition of uncertainty can contribute to international trade, it is necessary to adopt a very broad focus in terms of possible forms of collective behavior across national boundaries. The various rationales for tariffs under uncertainty provides a good example, as evidenced in Section 4 by the work of Helpman and Razin (1978c, 1978d, 1980b), Newbery and Stiglitz (1981) and Eaton and Grossman (1981), Bhagwati and Srinivasan (1976), and – tangentially – in Section 5 by the work of Ethier (1982).

It is tempting to include in this list of tariff models the literature on global tariff structures as the outcome of a non-cooperative game, or the work of Magee and Brock (1980). In the latter the government is viewed as a complex agent and a form of politically-endogenous collective decision-making agency, whose behavior is the outcome of strategic interaction between politicians and interest groups. Formally such inclusions would be inappropriate, since strategic behavior (in its broadest game-theoretic sense) need not imply uncertainty. Yet there are many contexts where uncertainty is suppressed in terms of formal modelling, but perhaps should be acknowledged as at least incipient. Ignoring uncertainty in, say, Walrasian models often relies implicitly on risk-pooling or related arguments: randomness in output of individual farmers need not imply randomness at the industry level if individual shocks are independent (although aggregate supply may be affected if risk-pooling opportunities are not available for individual farmers); randomness in food prices is not important for consumers if the randomness is independent of randomness in other consumer prices and food is a minor part of consumer budgets; in exchange of private goods, misrepresentation of preferences may be beneficial in bilateral exchange but decreases in value as market size is replicated (although this is not true in general for misrepresentation with respect to public goods).

When collective behavior involves small numbers, as in firm–firm, firm–government and government–government interactions in international economics, it is hard to use pooling-type arguments to assume away the uncertainty. In formal modelling this is often done by appealing to the notion of conjectural variation or by employing game-theoretic solution concepts such as Nash non-cooperative equilibrium. An alternative method is to introduce the concept of reputation in repeated situations, and think of "trust" as a public good providing imperfect social insurance in a world of incomplete and asymmetric information [cf. Kreps, Milgrom, Roberts and Wilson (1982), also more generally Schotter (1981)]. In any event the boundary lines between strategic behavior and uncertainty and information and uncertainty have been drawn very imperfectly in this chapter.

2. Walrasian-international models: Pure exchange

This section considers aspects of Walrasian-international models under uncertainty in the context of pure exchange. This implies ex-ante and/or ex-post trade is the only form of transformation, postponing discussion of the agency problem facing managers of firms with random output. However the exchange context is sufficient to discuss gains from trade, links between ex-ante and ex-post markets, some implications of incomplete markets, and some preference-side portfolio results. In some of the production literature such as the Helpman and Razin extension of Heckscher–Ohlin theory, with multiplicative technological randomness and global stock markets, there is little reason to emphasize the demand side. However when alternative forms of randomness are introduced, or markets are more segmented or less complete, then the demand side – with portfolio-type theories of preferences over assets – becomes more important.

Throughout this section attention will be focused on randomness in endowments. Start with a situation with no production, one physical commodity, two states of the world, and two countries – each of which behaves as if a single price-taking individual. This gives an Edgeworth-box framework with the two goods as the two contingent commodities. The index of nationality can be applied to expectations (i.e. the subjective probabilities of the two states), preferences, and/or endowments. Any story about gains from trade and the pattern of trade must, at this level, originate from one or a combination of these sources. Also notice the traditional high level of aggregation, particularly here with respect to the representative-individual assumption. Treating each country as a simple economic agent implicitly assumes that either intranational markets are operating perfectly or they are redundant (as in the case of a clone-economy), a point not emphasized in the literature until Helpman and Razin explicitly introduced stock markets. Further this implies a country's randomness is irreducible at the national level and any internal redistribution effects are ignored.

Throughout it will be assumed (unless otherwise stated) that objective functions can be represented in von Neumann–Morgenstern fashion as the expected utility of consumption, that solutions exist both for individual optimization problems and for market-clearing, that sufficient continuity and differentiability prevails, that first-order conditions hold with equality and that second-order conditions hold. At this stage, no special theoretical issues are raised with respect to these assumptions, but note the results of Hart (1974b) – and also Milne (1980).

Formally let $s = 1, 2$ represent the states of the world. Let $U(c(s))$ be the home country utility of consumption in state s, with $U(\cdot)$ being independent of state and with $c(s)$ the quantity of the single physical commodity consumed in state s. The endowment is given by $x(s)$ in state s. The home country's subjective probability of state s, recall it acts as a simple economic agent, is $b(s)$, where the probabilities are positive and sum to unity. Prices of the contingent commodities are given by $p(s)$, $s = 1, 2$. Variables for the foreign country will be denoted by a "*". The home country maximizes an induced objective function $V(c(1), c(2))$ with respect to its arguments, subject to its budget constraint. Thus its problem is:

Maximize, by choice of $c(s), V(c(1), c(2))$

$\overset{\text{df}}{=} b(1) \cdot U(c(1)) + b(2) \cdot U(c(2))$,

subject to $p(1) \cdot c(1) + p(2) \cdot c(2) = p(1) \cdot x(1) + p(2) \cdot x(2)$.

The foreign country solves an analogous problem, facing the same world prices. Utility functions are assumed to be monotonically increasing and strictly concave, and with Walras' Law we can focus on a single independent market with clearing condition $c(1) + c^*(1) = x(1) + x^*(1)$.

The following results are easily obtained and are, although far from exhaustive, representative and robust to increasing the number of states of the world beyond two.

(i) Gains from trade occur is any one of the following holds in isolation: (a) both countries have non-random (i.e. state-independent) endowment but have different probability vectors; (b) both countries have identical probability vectors and identical endowments which are not independent of state, and one country is unambiguously more risk-averse than the other; (c) both countries have identical probabilities and identical intrastate utility functions, and their endowment vectors do not lie on the same income-consumption path in contingent-commodity space. In case (b) the more risk averse country pays a premium (in the sense that its expected consumption is less than its expected endowment in physical terms) and trades toward its certainty ray.

(ii) If both countries have identical probability vectors and the home country's endowment is not state-dependent but the foreign country's endowment is state-dependent, then there exist gains from trade where the home country (the insurer) trades away from its certainty ray while the foreign country (the insuree) pays a premium and trades towards – but not completely to – its certainty ray.

(iii) If each country has the same probability vector and both have state-dependent endowments such that the world endowment is non-random, then there exist gains from trade with both countries moving to their certainty rays and neither paying a premium in trade.

These propositions reflect the fact that, in a two-country, two-good, competitive model of this type the pattern of trade can be deduced from relative autarkic prices; differences in expectations, or in attitudes to risk, or in endowments could each in isolation generate gains from trade, and at this level gains from trade can only arise from some combination thereof.

By one country being unambiguously more risk-averse than another is meant that the utility function of the former is a monotone-increasing, strictly concave transformation of the utility of the latter. [Cf. Pratt (1964).] This only generates a partial ordering over utility functions, but for comparable utility functions implies the more risk-averse country has larger coefficients of absolute and of relative risk aversion. (Sometimes the concept of an unambiguously more random distribution is required; here the partial ordering of Rothschild and Stiglitz [1971] is appropriate.)

Proposition (ii) illustrates the potential for one-sided insurance as the rationale for trade. Proposition (iii) gives the example of mutual insurance via perfect risk-pooling. (In general there is no reason to be in either of these extreme cases.)

Having noted that differences in expectations may, in isolation, generate trade – since even in a perfectly state-independent environment on the endowment side, different probabilities create a rationale for trade – from now on we will assume identical probabilities.

Propositions (ii) and (iii) serve as reminders that while randomness is welfare-reducing for risk averters in some circumstances, there are situations where this intuition must be qualified. The strict concavity of the utility function (plus monotonicity) is directly equivalent to the assertion that a risk averter prefers a given quantity of consumption with certainty to random consumption with the same (or lower) arithmetic mean. This leads directly to the proposition that a risk averter with non-random autarky will take no part of an actuarially fair or unfavorable bet, and also to the proposition that the introduction of mean-preserving randomness into the endowment structure of a previously non-random model is welfare reducing for risk averters – in that the Pareto-frontier (in terms of expected utility) is pulled in. However in proposition (ii) the loss from randomness coexists with gains from trade created by the presence of the randomness; the country acting as insurer is unambiguously better off as the result of its imports of randomness – because this is done at actuarially favorable terms in response to the trading opportunity in world markets. Proposition (iii) illustrates another straightforward point, that introducing a source of randomness may be welfare-increasing if it allows risk-pooling relative to previously undiversifiable randomness; this is related to the proposition that a risk averter with random autarky might well take an actuarially unfavorable bet.

There is little difficulty in extending this model to many states of the world, and the discussion of this section was worded to suggest its broader applicability. Extending to many countries, or allowing countries to consist of heterogeneous individuals who cannot be aggregated into a simple economic agent, creates no more or less problems than in any other context.

Consider now, still with a single physical commodity, a share-trading model in the spirit of Diamond (1967), but in an exchange context. Treat the home and the foreign countries as competitive, simple economic agents. Let there be S states of the world (where $S > 2$ or we are effectively back in a complete market setting) and let $x(s)$ be the home country's endowment of the physical commodity in state s, with $s = 1, \ldots, S$. Let m_1 and m_2 respectively represent the home country's share of the home and foreign endowments held after trading; these shares lie between zero and one, while by the nature of the model each country has one unit share in its own endowment and zero share in the other country's endowment before trade. Let q_1 and q_2 respectively stand for the prices of a unit share in the home and the foreign endowment. Then the home country has an induced objective function $V(m_1, m_2) \stackrel{\mathrm{df}}{=} \sum_s b(s) \cdot U(m_1 \cdot x(s) + m_2 \cdot x^*(s))$, which is maximized subject to $q_1 \cdot m_1 + q_2 \cdot m_2 = q_1 \cdot 1 + q_2 \cdot 0$. The foreign country faces a similar problem, with the unit and the zero switched on the right-hand side of the budget constraint. The single independent market-clearing condition can be stated as $m_1 + m_1^* = 1$.

The competitive solution will imply the equalization of $V_1(m)/V_2(m)$ across countries, where $V_1(m) = \sum_s b(s) \cdot U'(c(s)) \cdot x(s)$, and similarly for $V_2(m)$. Now markets are incomplete, and typically equalization of marginal rates of substitution in asset-space, i.e. (m_1, m_2)-space, will not imply (but will be implied by) equalization of marginal rates of substitution in all directions in contingent-commodity space. In the special case of one physical commodity, the incomplete, but competitive, market structure gives a "constrained Pareto optimum" [Diamond (1967)] – that is, an allocation which is Pareto-optimal given the constraint that only share-trading is permitted.

The propositions obtained in the context of the previous contingent-commodity model now are weakened to some extent. For example, if the two countries are identical with respect to endowments and attitudes to risk, i.e. if $x(s) = x^*(s)$ for $s = 1,\ldots, S$ and $U(\cdot) = U^*(\cdot)$, differences in probability vectors need not generate gains from trade. The pattern of trade in terms of assets is trivially determined in this model by the skewed nature of the asset-endowments. However since a risk averter from non-random autarky takes some part of an actuarially-favorable bet, [Arrow (1971a)], proposition (ii), that a non-random country will act as partial insurer to a random country in return for actuarially-favorable trade, goes through. Also valid is proposition (iii) concerning the actuarially-fair complete mutual insurance if world endowment is non-random but country endowments are random.

Next consider the situation with two physical commodities, still in an exchange setting. Assume first a complete set of contingent commodity markets. There is little advantage in restricting attention to two states of the world, so assume there are S states of the world, indexed by $s = 1,\ldots, S$; two physical commodities, indexed by $j = 1, 2$; two countries, home and foreign, each acting as a simple economic agent; endowments, denoted by $x_j(s)$; markets for contingent commodities, with prices $p_j(s)$; consumption denoted by $c_j(s)$. The home country induced objective function, defined over the vector of choice variables $c \stackrel{\mathrm{df}}{=} (c(1),\ldots, c(S))$ $\stackrel{\mathrm{df}}{=} (c_1(1), c_2(1),\ldots, c_1(S), c_2(S))$ is given by $V(c) \stackrel{\mathrm{df}}{=} \sum_s b(s) \cdot U(c(s))$. This is maximized subject to the budget constraint $p \cdot c = p \cdot x$, where p and x are vectors defined analogously to the vector c. The foreign country faces a similar problem, and market clearing is defined (prior to application of Walras' Law) by $c_j(s) + c_j^*(s) = x_j(s) + x_j^*(s)$, $j = 1, 2$; $s = 1,\ldots, S$. Trade can occur across physical commodities but intrastate, across states in the same physical commodity, and across states and physical commodities. Full Pareto optimality requires equalization across countries of all ratios of the form $[b(s) \cdot U_j(c(s))]/[b(t) \cdot U_k(c(t))]$ for $j, k = 1, 2$ and $s, t = 1,\ldots, S$ [where $U_j(c(s))$ is the marginal utility of physical commodity j in state s]. This will be achieved under the complete set of contingent commodity markets, or the operationally equivalent situation of Arrow–Debreu securities plus ex-post trade.

Since at this stage we maintain the assumption of completeness of markets, the simple two-good framework has been lost. Moreover additional structure is required on the utility function $U(\cdot)$ to be able to talk about attitudes to risk. It is necessary to have ordinally-identical preferences, although a stronger technique is to assume homotheticity with respect to preferences over physical commodities; then we can write $U(c) = u(f(c))$, where $f(\cdot)$ is positively homogeneous of degree one and the strict concavity of $u(\cdot)$ represents risk aversion. To get even more structure on preferences, one can assume constant coefficient of relative risk aversion and constant elasticity of substitution (with respect to the two physical commodities) which are reciprocals. Such an assumption generates additive separability of the objective function $V(c)$, an appealing property which has been employed elsewhere in the international literature [also note Krugman (1979)]. Beyond imposing values of unity on the constant and reciprocal coefficients, it is hard to envisage more structure being placed on preferences.

Rather than pursue the contingent-commodity case, consider restricted forms of trade. One restricted form of trading is share-trading with two physical commodities. To keep the two-asset structure one can assume that each country is specialized (in terms of endowment) in a single physical commodity – an assumption which may be appropriate in some contexts – or assume both countries are endowed with both physical commodities but trade occurs in "national shares" which yield proportionate claims on the national endowment of both commodities, or assume that the randomness is industry-specific but not nation-specific. The simultaneity of ex-ante trade in shares and ex-post trade in physical commodities is handled using an indirect utility function.

It is at this stage that we encounter the complication introduced by Hart (1975) and subsequently developed in an international trade context by Cornes and Milne (1981) and Newbery and Stiglitz (1981). If both ex-ante and ex-post trade occur in the presence of incomplete markets, then the pecuniary externalities generated as trading decisions alter ex-post prices will alter the role of such prices as implicit providers of insurance. Such models need not achieve the constrained Pareto-efficiency of the Diamond one-physical-commodity models with multiplicative randomness.

Among share-trading exchange models with two physical commodities, consider the Helpman-Razin type of situation (stripped of its production aspects) where both countries have an endowment of both physical commodities, with randomness commodity-specific but not nation-specific and with ex-post trade also possible. Using for expediency the assumption of identical probabilities, let $x_j(s) = x_j \cdot e_j(s)$ and $x_j^*(s) = x_j^* \cdot e_j^*(s)$ for $j = 1, 2$ and $s = 1, \ldots, S$. Assume $e_j(s) = e_j^*(s)$ for all j and s, with $\sum_s b(s) \cdot e_j(s) = 1$ for $j = 1, 2$. This says that randomness is perfectly positively correlated for endowments of the same physical commodity across countries – the industry-specificity assumption – and that units of shares can be measured in units of expected quantity of endowment.

Treat each country as a simple economic agent. Let z_1 and z_2 be the quantities of the two shares held by the home country after asset trade, then in state s the home country has "ex-post endowment" $(z_1 \cdot e_1(s), z_2 \cdot e_2(s))$ and maximizes by choice of $c_1(s)$ and $c_2(s)$ the objective function $U(c(s))$ subject to the constraint $p_1(s) \cdot c_1(s) + p_2(s) \cdot c_2(s) = p_1(s) \cdot z_1 \cdot e_1(s) + p_2(s) \cdot z_2 \cdot e_2(s)$. By assumption the agent can correctly predict the ex-post commodity prices conditional on the occurence of state s. The ex-post relative price is given by a market-clearing condition, $c_1(s) + c_1^*(s) = z_1 \cdot e_1(s) + z_1^* \cdot e_1(s)$, for $s = 1, \ldots, S$. Taking physical-commodity one as numeraire in each state, let $p(s) \overset{\mathrm{df}}{=} p_2(s)/p_1(s)$ and $y(s) \overset{\mathrm{df}}{=} z_1 \cdot e_1(s) + p(s) \cdot z_2 \cdot e_2(s)$ for $s = 1, \ldots, S$. Now let $W(p(s), y(s))$ be defined as $U(c_1(p(s), y(s)), c_2(p(s), y(s)))$; that is, $W(\ )$ is the indirect utility function in state s, with $c_j(p(s), y(s))$ the demand function for the jth physical commodity evaluated at the prevailing price ratio and ex-post endowment.

Prior to asset trade, the home-country induced objective function over quantities of shares is $V(z_1, z_2) \overset{\mathrm{df}}{=} \sum_s b(s) \cdot U(c(p(s), y(s)))$. The home country must choose (z_1, z_2) to maximize $V(z_1, z_2)$ subject to $q_1 \cdot z_1 + q_2 \cdot z_2 = q_1 \cdot x_1 + q_2 \cdot x_2$, where q_1 and q_2 are the respective prices of the shares in the two physical-commodity endowments. The foreign country faces a similar problem. The asset prices can be normalized, and the single independent asset-market clearing condition can be represented by $z_1 + z_1^* = x_1 + x_1^*$.

First-order conditions are linked to $V_1(z) = \sum_s b(s) \cdot W_y(p(s), y(s)) \cdot e_1(s)$ and $V_2(z) = \sum_s b(s) \cdot W_y(p(s), y(s)) \cdot p(s) \cdot e_2(s)$, where $W_y(p(s), y(s))$ is the marginal utility of income, using commodity one as numeraire, in state s. Under price-taking behavior, $q_1/q_2 = V_1(z)/V_2(z)$, so that the marginal rate of substitution in asset space is equalized across countries. From here, for comparative statics exercises, it is straightforward to differentiate the first-order conditions and the asset budget constraint in each country.

The special case of skewed endowments can be obtained by, say, setting $x_2 = x_1^* = 0$ in the above model. Note that the skewed endowment assumption implies that share-trading in part performs the function of trading physical commodities. It may be worth pointing to a result which can be found, for example, in Newbery and Stiglitz (1981), which is applicable to the skewed-endowment share-trading model if there is no ex-post commodity trade. Suppose the foreign endowment involving physical commodity two is random, but the home endowment involving physical commodity one is non-random. Also assume the home country has an additively separable objective function where the constant coefficient of relative risk aversion is greater than unity and hence its reciprocal, the constant elasticity of substitution with respect to the physical commodities, is less than unity. The home country is then fairly risk averse but has difficulty substituting between physical commodities; for such a country a major concern is being caught with the "wrong" proportions of consumption of the two physical commodities in states when the foreign endowment is low.

Consequently the home country will tend to export more of its own endowment when the foreign endowment is random than it would if the foreign endowment were non-random. (Note that if the constant elasticity of substitution were fixed at unity, then the home country would export the same fraction of its endowment irrespective of the extent of randomness in the foreign endowment.)

Thus randomness need not deter in some circumstances, since the risk averter is concerned about randomness in real income, not in quantities of one of two physical commodities. To avoid statements to the effect that "the risky asset is not risky", and because of earlier examples where a source of randomness may generate either gains from trade for a market participant or risk-pooling for the entire economy, this chapter uses the neutral terms "random" and "non-random" rather than "risky" and "safe".

One could envisage a case where trade is only permitted if it is not state-dependent. That is, if $z_j(s) \overset{\text{df}}{=} c_j(s) - x_j(s)$ is the net import of physical commodity j in state s, then this restriction requires $z_j(s) = z_j(t) \overset{\text{df}}{=} z_j$ for $j = 1, 2$; $s, t = 1, \ldots, S$. The induced objective function can be given as $v(z_1, z_2) \overset{\text{df}}{=} \sum_s b(s) \cdot U(x(s) + z)$, to be maximized with respect to $z \overset{\text{df}}{=} (z_1, z_2)$ subject to the budget constraint $q_1 \cdot z_1 + q_2 \cdot z_2 = 0$; here q_j is simply the market price of a unit of physical commodity j traded irrespective of state. The foreign country faces a similar problem, and the market-clearing condition for the single independent market is given by $z_1 + z_1^* = 0$. We leave the interested reader to pursue this case. This kind of ex-ante trade is a general-equilibrium relative of what can be called "commitment trade". Such models have been analyzed by Brainard and Cooper (1968) and Ruffin (1974b), also Batra and Russell (1974); on the last paper, cf. the comments of Kemp and Ohyama (1978), Helpman and Razin (1978d), also Hartman (1976), Akiba (1980), Batra and Russell (1976), plus Anderson's (1976b) comments on Batra (1975a). In commitment models a country, viewed as a simple economic agent, makes decisions to trade quantities of physical commodities before knowing the terms of trade. Thus in effect quantities of one or both commodities are thrown on the world market (typically but not necessarily these quantities are export rather than import commitments), with ex-ante random quantities of the other commodities being received in amounts determined by the initial commitments and the realized terms of trade in the world market. A fuller discussion is to be found in Pomery (1979); cf. also Ethier (1979).

Another situation, where strictly there is no uncertainty, arises when the terms of trade are random but the economy can postpone all trading decisions until after the realization of the terms of trade. This type of model can be called a "fluctuations" model. This literature dates back to Waugh (1944), Oi (1961); for more references, including Samuelson (1972), see Pomery (1979). Note that analysis of fluctuations in the exchange context is an implicit component of production models where production decisions are made ex-ante but consumption decisions ex-post, as for example in Eaton (1979).

The major topic in fluctuations models is whether the economy is better or worse off with fluctuating terms of trade compared to some benchmark level of the terms of trade with certainty. Let $p(s) \stackrel{\text{df}}{=} p_2(s)/p_1(s)$ be the relative price of physical commodity two in world markets in state s. Taking the arithmetic mean of p as the benchmark, the country is better (worse) off with fluctuating terms of trade if the indirect utility function $V(p, y) \stackrel{\text{df}}{=} U(c_1(p, y), c_2(p, y))$ is strictly convex (concave) in p; here, $y \stackrel{\text{df}}{=} x_1 + p \cdot x_2$. It can be shown:

$$\left(p^2/V_y \cdot y \right) \cdot \left(\mathrm{d}^2 V/\mathrm{d} p^2 \right)$$

$$= S_{c1} \cdot S_{c2}(ESD) - 2 \cdot \left(S_{x2} - S_{c2} \right) \cdot S_{c2} \cdot e_{2y} - \left(S_{x2} - S_{c2} \right)^2 \cdot (RRA),$$

where S_{cj} = the consumption share of commodity j in national income, S_{xj} = the endowment share of commodity j in national income, $j = 1, 2$, (ESD) = the demand-side elasticity of substitution around the indifference curve in physical-commodity space, e_{2y} = the income elasticity of demand for commodity two, and (RRA) = the coefficient of relative risk aversion.

In the neighborhood of autarky, fluctuations in relative price are beneficial. To see this, take the autarkic price as the benchmark and then let price fluctuate on either side. Provided there is non-zero elasticity of substitution in the indifference map at autarky, the standard gains from trade argument implies the country always does strictly better when trading at the fluctuating prices (which differ from the autarkic price) than at the autarkic benchmark. This is picking up the fact that minimum expenditure, to achieve a given level of satisfaction, is a strictly concave function of relative price. However, as Samuelson (1972) has emphasized, this is not a result of interest for a closed economy. If the randomness arose in a closed economy via exogenous endowment randomness, then welfare analysis would have to take into account the (dominating) adverse effect of ownership of randomness; if the closed economy artificially manufactured the randomness in an otherwise non-random environment, then it would not be feasible to generate price fluctuations with an arithmetic mean equal to the non-random level.

A second complication arises because, given fluctuating terms of trade, the choice of benchmark is numeraire-dependent if the arithmetic mean is used. As the reciprocal function is strictly convex, by Jensen's inequality $E(1/p) > 1/[Ep]$, where E is the expectation operator. That is, it is impossible simultaneously to set p and $1/p$ equal to their respective arithmetic means; in fact if we create a fair bet at the margin in one direction then the reverse bet must be actuarially favorable. As a consequence, Flemming, Turnovsky and Kemp (1977) have argued that for fluctuations in relative price the geometric mean is the appropriate benchmark, since in this case there is no numeraire dependency. The geometric mean has been adopted in subsequent literature, e.g. Eaton (1979). (Choice of benchmark is irrelevant to the dominance of fluctuating prices if autarky is the benchmark; that conclusion is not an artifact of the use of arithmetic mean.) While the geometric mean has the property of numeraire-independence it is not automatically the appropriate choice. Use of the geometric mean, or the arithmetic mean for the relative price of commodity two, or the arithmetic mean for the relative price of commodity one simply represent different conceptual experiments, and the appropriate benchmark cannot be determined without considering the underlying randomness in the economy which induces the price randomness. [Cf. Boonekamp and Donaldson (1979) on this topic.]

3. Walrasian-international models: Production

The introduction of production introduces a second form of transformation into Walrasian-international models under uncertainty. It also creates a potential agency problem in terms of transmitting preferences of either existing or potential shareholders to managers of firms. When production is introduced it is necessary to consider both the timing of production and trade decisions, and also the interrelation of market structure, form of randomness, and objective of the firm. This section will focus mainly on the case of ex-ante production decisions and ex-post trade in physical commodities, where the input-allocation decision, (even) for an industry producing a single physical product, implies a vector of joint outputs – each element of the vector corresponding to output in a particular state of the world. The ex-ante production decision generates randomness which has to be owned by some set of agents; agents may respond to this randomness in many ways, but the presence of markets in randomness may allow a larger group of agents each to take a smaller fraction of the randomness and/or the randomness from one firm to be pooled with randomness elsewhere in the economy. The demand side of models with ex-ante production and ex-post trade in physical commodities has already been discussed in Section 2.

Consider differentiation of models arising from alternative assumptions about specificity of the randomness. (Randomness is, say, nation-specific if all firms producing in any given nation have equiproportional joint-product vectors of output while, in general, this is not true for firms across national boundaries.) With respect to technology, randomness might be global, nation-specific but not industry-specific, industry-specific but not nation-specific, both nation-specific and industry-specific, or even firm-specific. The literature has given little attention to motivating the particular assumption employed in any given model.

Globally-identical randomness is of little interest if it is ubiquitous and completely undiversifiable. Randomness which is nation-specific but not industry-specific presumably reflects some countrywide shock, possibly linked to aggregate demand or political shocks. With political risk of expropriation or default the randomness could vary according to nationality (or some other index) of the holder of the asset as well as according to the nationality of source of the asset. Much of the literature has assumed that randomness is industry-specific but not nation-specific. This assumption is hard to justify convincingly: it is necessary to find some form of randomness which affects uniformly all the U.S. export industries and all the corresponding industries in the rest of the world, but has no effect on U.S. import-competing industries. Even with attention restricted to countries at similar levels of development, as is one rationalization of the identical-technology assumption of the Heckscher–Ohlin framework, it is unclear this assumption has a good interpretation. Agricultural examples do little better, for while climatic factors are an explanation of random output, it is not obvious that randomness is identical within countries, let alone across countries, for the same crop.

In a sense the industry-specific assumption is related to the very simple aggregation and indexation properties of the Heckscher–Ohlin model on the production side. With technology industry-specific but not nation-specific, and with industries in a given country treated as if single (price-taking) firms, the production structure is difficult to preserve when randomness is introduced unless randomness is industry-specific but not nation-specific – preserving indexation – and multiplicative – preserving aggregation. Firm-specific randomness is easier to understand but it is unclear how far this can be extended across firms in the same industry without requiring a reevaluation of the nature of the assumption. Firms may be subject to random output because of internal breakdowns in coordination, variability in availability and quality of inputs, including breakdowns in equipment or labor strikes. Some of these could affect entire industries relatively uniformly, but others should not; moreover it is unclear whether such effects should be uniform across national boundaries or should affect the entire export industry but not the import-competing industry in the same country.

It should be remarked (i) that one role of the firm may be to minimize the intra-production-unit randomness, in the limit leaving only external-source shocks; (ii) that the explanation of the nature of randomness should be consistent, if we are operating in a Heckscher–Ohlin context, with the view of Heckscher–Ohlin as a longer-run model; (iii) that it may be useful to model some of these possible shocks explicitly since the threat of production disruption from, say, partial labor withdrawal could in some circumstances modify a firm's choice of techniques; (iv) some forms of randomness – even if relatively uniform within an industry – may not be diversifiable via equity-trade because of information constraints involving moral hazard and/or adverse selection.

Another differentiating characteristic of models is extent of markets, with two-way classification: are markets global or segmented on national (or some other) basis? Are markets complete or incomplete, and if incomplete do they have sufficient spanning properties for the purposes of production decisions? The first question was not explicitly posed in the early literature, particularly prior to the work of Helpman and Razin (1978a, b, d). There was a tendency to assume nations behaved as simple economic agents, maximizing the expected utility of aggregate consumption, without bearing in mind that this implicitly assumed a freely-functioning internal market for trading randomness (or redundancy of such a market as individuals are sufficiently similar not to need the market at national autarky). Other assumptions used, particularly in the earlier literature, were that firms in a random industry maximize the expected utility of profits, or that firms maximize expected profits.

With complete markets, it is well known that the formal structure of an Arrow–Debreu model under uncertainty is equivalent to the structure in the absence of uncertainty. The price mechanism allows equalization of marginal rates of substitution across individuals for any given tradeoff (across states, across physical commodities within a state, or across physical commodities in different states). This allows a price-taking firm to maximize the market value of its vector of state-dependent returns, irrespective of heterogeneity of expectations or preferences of stockholders. The assumption of complete contingent-commodity markets is often felt to be too strong in the context of international trade models. Yet it is unclear what the assumption of complete markets entails at the level of aggregation prevalent in trade theory, given there is no story offered about the nature of the randomness; it may suffice to have markets which are complete relative to the randomness being modelled.

There appear to be two strongly opposed views concerning the completeness of markets. One, found for example in Loong and Zeckhauser (1982), holds that the relative paucity of markets in the face of uncertainty is self-evidently a major weakness of market economies. The other, espoused for example in Satterthwaite (1981), argues that if markets are incomplete then there exists, in general, unexploited gains from trade because of the failure to equalize (in all dimensions) marginal rates of substitution across individuals; hence there is a theoretical presumption that those missing markets will be created by market-making arbitrage. In this view, existence of complete markets is an equilibrium property of the model rather than an arbitrary assumption. At this level not much can be said, since the relevant concept of completeness is determined by the uncertainty being modelled. A related question, not addressed in the formal literature on international trade, is the extent to which national boundaries affect the relative completeness of market structures by affecting information flows and transactions costs impeding market creation.

It is a virtually universal characteristic of the formal literature to toss in assumptions about market structure, as well as specificity of randomness, without much comment. The early literature ignored the implicit role of (segmented) equity markets, while Helpman and Razin go straight to the assumption of a globally-unsegmented market. Yet an asset transaction often involves a closer relationship between the two trading partners than arises for many transactions involving physical commodities, since the former automatically raises questions of trust that are muted in situations of contemporaneous exchange. Hence the impact of national boundaries is worth exploring; for example, the possibility of lack of local knowledge may be balanced by the possible emergence of firms which perform screening services on an international basis.

With randomness in output price or in technology, profit maximization is not well defined, since profits are a random variable. Maximization of expected profits is inadequate as a criterion since in general this may not reflect the risk attitudes or expectations of the owners of the firm; similarly maximization of the expected utility of profits is in general deficient. The criterion of maximization of the market value of the firm, and the related issue of whether ex-post stock-holders, i.e. those holding shares after the completion of asset trading, will unanimously (dis)approve the decision of a firm to undertake a particular investment project is tied to the concept of spanning. Spanning occurs for a firm if the vector of returns generated by a production decision of the firm lies in the subspace spanned by the returns of all traded assets, for then it could deduce (i) the impact of a decision on its market value from prices implied by asset markets, and (ii) from the impact on its market value the unanimous reaction of stock-holders to its decisions.

Note that satisfaction of the spanning property for a firm is weaker than the assumption of complete commodity markets. For example, with multiplicative randomness and either a single physical commodity or the assumption of given ex-post prices, the firm's vector of returns across states spans its own one-dimensional subspace. However in the absence of multiplicative randomness the situation is less simple, cf. Drèze (1974) for example, while with multiplicative randomness, incomplete markets and two or more physical commodities there arises the issue of nonpecuniary externalities. Stiglitz (1981, 1982) discusses many of the issues concerning (sub)optimality of stock markets. Since arguments for free trade which are based on price coordination are effectively corollaries of optimality properties of the competitive mechanism, such issues must be acknowledged in the international literature.

Until the work of Dumas (1980a), followed by Grinols (1981), the literature considered multiplicative randomness. In terms of market structure there have been a variety of assumptions. The earliest literature did not explicitly model stock markets, although inevitably implicit assumptions were present. Helpman and Razin [e.g. (1978a)] introduced Diamond-style stock markets, extended to more than one physical commodity – an extension they credit to Hart (1974a) – complete with multiplicative randomness. Dumas has criticized this analysis as unduly restrictive and has derived a variety of propositions, relating to the Heckscher–Ohlin production structure, assuming in effect a complete market structure but relaxing the assumption of stochastic constant returns. Grinols has dropped both the multiplicative randomness and the Dumas assumption of spanning relative to the production-relevant subspace (or the coincidental irrelevance of such spanning), replacing it by a procedure suggested by Drèze (1974) whereby management polls shareholders to obtain a revelation of their preferences. It is not clear how far this line of attack will go, since deficiencies in market structure can presumably be offset with increasingly complex direct-revelation approaches. Whether this is a relatively costless decision-making procedure for, say, a multinational corporation and to what extent, if any, nationality plays a role in the efficacy of these procedures, remains to be discussed. (Note that the assumption of multiplicative uncertainty precludes any choice of risk class at the level of the firm.)

Start the discussion of particular models with a two-state, one-physical-commodity model where there are two production techniques, each drawing on two factors of production (labor and capital) which are inelastically supplied to the economy at the aggregate level. Most of the time the Heckscher–Ohlin production structure, plus multiplicative randomness, will be considered (with a brief digression into non-multiplicative randomness). The basic ideas of this section could be applied to any constant-returns production structure under competition; the focus on Heckscher–Ohlin merely imposes a specific production structure, chosen for concreteness and to follow much of the literature.

Let $x_1(s) = F(L_1, K_1) \cdot e_1(s)$ and $x_2(s) = G(L_2, K_2) \cdot e_2(s)$, where here $x_1(s)$ and $x_2(s)$ represent quantities of the same physical commodity. One can say that technique one is relatively well-adapted to state one, or state-one intensive, if $e_1(1)/e_2(1) > e_1(2)/e_2(2)$. If $p(s)$ is the price of the single physical commodity, contingent on state s, then profit maximization for the aggregate production sector requires maximization of $p(1) \cdot x(1) + p(2) \cdot x(2) - w \cdot L - r \cdot K$; here w and r are the, non-random, returns to labor and capital resulting from implicit competition among firms in the factor markets. (With additive technology and price-taking, profit-maximizing firms there is no loss of generality in treating the supply side of the economy as a single price-taking firm.) Let $x(s) \overset{\text{df}}{=} x_1(s) + x_2(s)$ for $s = 1, 2$.

Assuming identical probabilities for all individuals, let $b(1) \cdot e_j(1) + b(2) \cdot e_j(2) = 1$ for $j = 1, 2$, i.e. the expected value of the random variable is unity in each industry, implying that units of assets can be denominated in units of expected output. Expected output is given by $F(L_1, K_1) \overset{\text{df}}{=} x_1$ or $G(L_2, K_2) \overset{\text{df}}{=} x_2$ respectively. (This normalization is only well-defined under uniform probabilities and is not essential; however because of the simplicity of interpretation permitted, we will maintain the uniform-probabilities assumption.) Define $a_{L1} = L_1/F(L_1, K_1) = L_1/x_1$ and similarly for a_{ij}, $i = L, K$ and $j = 1, 2$.

Let $q_j \overset{\text{df}}{=} p(1) \cdot e_j(1) + p(2) \cdot e_j(2)$ for $j = 1, 2$. Then q_j can be interpreted as the price of a claim to one unit of expected output from industry j. If both industries produce (implying unit cost equals unit revenue under free entry and exit) and both factors are fully employed, then the input side of the model can be represented by:

$$w \cdot a_{L1} + r \cdot a_{K1} = q_1, \tag{3.1}$$

$$w \cdot a_{L2} + r \cdot a_{K2} = q_2, \tag{3.2}$$

$$a_{L1} \cdot x_1 + a_{L2} \cdot x_2 = L, \tag{3.3}$$

$$a_{K1} \cdot x_1 + a_{K2} \cdot x_2 = K. \tag{3.4}$$

The notation is taken from Jones (1965), recognizing that the structure of this model is formally equivalent to the standard Heckscher–Ohlin model without uncertainty, at least on the input side.

In addition the output side can be treated in the joint-production framework, a point explicitly noted by Chang, Ethier and Kemp (1980). Thus:

$$p(1) \cdot e_1(1) + p(2) \cdot e_1(2) = q_1, \tag{3.5}$$

$$p(1) \cdot e_2(1) + p(2) \cdot e_2(2) = q_2, \tag{3.6}$$

$$x_1 \cdot e_1(1) + x_2 \cdot e_2(1) = x(1), \tag{3.7}$$

$$x_1 \cdot e_1(2) + x_2 \cdot e_2(2) = x(2). \tag{3.8}$$

Here $x(s)$ is aggregate output from the combined industries in state s, for $s = 1, 2$. The random terms $e_j(s)$ are assumed fixed, whereas the a_{ij} terms on the input side will typically vary with the wage–rental ratio. The joint-product side exhibits "contractionary effects", as opposed to the "magnification effects" on the input side. Thus a one percent increase in the price of contingent-commodity one, ceteris paribus, will result in an increase in both q_1 and q_2, but by less than one percent and with q_1 increasing proportionately more than q_2 if industry one is state-one intensive.

Suppose in a two-country framework there is identical technology in the strong sense, meaning not only production functions $F(\cdot)$ and $G(\cdot)$ are respectively identical across the two countries but also that $e_j(s) = e_j^*(s)$ for all j and s. Then in the absence of intensity reversals (currently only relevant on the input side, given fixed coefficients on the joint-product side), if all four financial equations hold as equalities in both countries, then free trade in contingent commodities implies equalization of the implicit industry-asset prices, which in turn implies equalization of factor prices. (Note the introduction of the strong assumption of identical industry-specific randomness at the stage of generating inter-country propositions.) Similarly if we assume industry one is labor-intensive, plus identical technology in the strong sense, plus absence of intensity-reversals, plus identical constant coefficients of relative risk aversion in the two countries (ensuring identical homothetic preferences in contingent-commodity space), then the country with the relatively abundant labor supply will have the relatively cheap autarkic price of the industry-one asset and the relatively cheap autarkic price of contingent-commodity one. Hence the home country would export contingent-commodity one under free trade.

The model above could easily be extended to many states of the world. The input-side equations would be unaltered, while on the joint-product-side the two-by-two structure is lost. Thus the equations become:

$$p(1)\cdot e_j(1) + \cdots + p(S)\cdot e_j(S) = q_j, \qquad j = 1,2; \tag{3.9}$$

$$x_1 \cdot e_1(s) + x_2 \cdot e_2(s) = x(s), \qquad s = 1,\ldots, S. \tag{3.10}$$

Trade in contingent commodities implies equalization of equity prices if both industries produce in both countries, but equalization of equity prices would not guarantee equalization of contingent-commodity prices.

Now retain multiplicative randomness with one physical commodity, and introduce share-trading. In general, let $x_1(s) = F(L_1, K_1)\cdot e_1(s) \stackrel{\mathrm{df}}{=} x_1 \cdot e_1(s)$ and $x_2(s) = G(L_2, K_2)\cdot e_2(s) \stackrel{\mathrm{df}}{=} x_2 \cdot e_2(s)$ for $s = 1,\ldots, S$. Assume identical probabilities for the convenience of letting x_1 and x_2 be interpretable as units of expected output. Let q_1 be the market price of a claim to the joint-product vector generated by one unit of expected output in industry one, while q_2 is the price of a unit claim in industry two. The coefficients a_{ij} represent the amount of factor i per unit of expected output in industry j.

Under competition firms will maximize $q_j \cdot x_j - w \cdot L_j - r \cdot K_j$ for $j = 1,2$, with the constraints that there are zero economic profits and that factor markets clear. If it is assumed that both industries produce, in addition to factor-market clearing, then the production structure can be represented by eqs. (3.1)–(3.4) above. Again equity prices replace prices of physical commodities while quantities of equities, here interpreted as quantities of expected output, replace quantities of output of physical commodities. This can be done even if both industries are producing different physical commodities. (Only for the demand side does a single source of randomness and/or a single physical commodity give more results.) The logic can be applied directly to any constant-returns production structure with multiplicative randomness, given competitive firms and some price-taking market for equities.

Trivially all the standard propositions of the Heckscher–Ohlin framework go through if appropriately reinterpreted. [The qualification will not be completely innocent for the pattern of trade with two equities and two physical commodities; cf. Helpman and Razin (1978d, p. 107) and Anderson (1981).] An increase in the endowment of labor, freezing equity prices and hence freezing the wage–rental ratio, implies a more than proportionate increase in the size of the labor-intensive industry and a contraction in the capital-intensive industry. An increase in equity price for the labor-intensive industry increases the return to labor more than proportionately while the return to capital falls. If both countries have identical technology in the strong sense [i.e. if $e_j(s) = e_j^*(s)$ for all j and for all s, in addition to identical non-random components of technology], both countries produce both equities, and there are no intervening intensity-reversals, then equalization of equity prices, e.g. via free trade in equities, will result in factor-price equalization. The theorem concerning the pattern of trade is potentially more complicated precisely because this theorem requires some treatment of the demand side. With a single physical commodity, in the absence of intensity reversals and with identical technology in the strong sense, if the demand side is neutralized by identical constant coefficients of relative risk aversion across countries (implying identical homothetic preferences in asset-space) then the relatively labor-abundant country will export the labor-intensive equity, this being cheaper at autarky.

While the basic propositions of the Heckscher–Ohlin model are preserved generally under multiplicative randomness in technology and free trade in equities, more mileage can be obtained in the special case of not only a single physical commodity but also a single source of randomness. With this kind of one-physical commodity model the economy has two methods of generating output, one random and one non-random; thus it gives an example of choice of risk-reducing techniques in the face of technological randomness. Assume both industries produce, and industry two is non-random, so that q_2 is simply the price of one unit of the physical commodity with certainty. For this part of the paper set $q_2 = 1$. In an equity model, factor prices are denominated in units of numeraire equity; here that reduces to non-random factor payments, given one physical commodity and the numeraire industry non-random.

Interpret the behavior of managers in the random industry as follows. Having hired labor and capital at their respective non-random market returns, and having produced a vector of state-dependent outputs, this randomness has to be sold in an implicit competitive market. This randomness will be sold at terms actuarially favorable to the purchaser, so write $q_1 = 1 - z_1$, where z_1 is the price the manager has to pay per unit of expected output to get rid of the randomness. Think of z_1 as a "risk premium", although not in the exact sense of Pratt (1964), and q_1 as a "certainty-equivalent price".

All that remains here is to explain how z_1 is determined, since z_1 feeds back into the equity-production equations at only one point, (3.1). To explain the possibilities assume the economy is segmented into two groups, A and B. If an individual belongs to group A then he is entitled to participate in the market for randomness as a buyer, taking z_1 as given. If an individual belongs to group B, then he is excluded from the market for randomness and simply consumes the proceeds from his non-random income as owner of physical factors of production (labor and capital). Members of group A may have non-random income from physical factors in addition to their participation in the market for randomness. The introduction of multiplicative randomness in production is being implicitly met by an additional market. The supply side of the market is trivially determined from the production possibility frontier, in terms of expected outputs or equities; the marginal rate of product transformation must equal $q_1 = 1 - z_1$, allowing supply of randomness, measured in units of expected output in random industry one, to be linked to q_1 (or z_1).

On the demand side for individual h belonging to group A, he must choose the level of x_1^h (his purchases in the market for randomness) to maximize the expected utility of his consumption, given his non-random physical-factor income and given q_1. He maximizes $\sum_s b(s) \cdot U(x_1^h \cdot (e(s) - q_1) + w \cdot L^h + r \cdot K^h)$, where L^h and K^h respectively are his endowments of labor and capital and where $(e(s) - q_1)$ is the state-dependent return per unit of randomness purchased.

It is easy to consider a variety of cases in the literature. Batra (1975a, b) assumes the random industry is operated by maximization of the expected utility of profits in the random industry; also Das (1977), and for an exposition in the spirit of the current discussion, Sakai (1978). The representative-entrepreneur assumption is captured by the assumption that $L^h = K^h = 0$ for all h in group A. In other words the defining characteristic of the implicit buyers of randomness is that they are fixed in number and have zero physical endowments. [Cf. Mayer (1976) for another way of modelling entrepreneurial activity; also Baron and Forsythe (1979), and Kihlstrom and Laffont (1979).]

Another possibility, e.g. Kemp (1976), is to assume the economy acts as a simple economic agent, maximizing expected utility of aggregate consumption. This is captured by assuming fixity of the number of demand-side participants with $L^h = L$ and $K^h = K$, that is the representative buyer of randomness owns the entire national endowment of physical factors. This reflects an earlier observation that treating an economy as a simple economic agent implies assuming sufficient internal markets or sufficient homogeneity that internal markets are redundant. With a representative entrepreneur or a representative consumer buying the randomness, there are no income redistribution effects to consider. Changes in equity price q_1 will alter the wage and the rental via the competitive profit conditions, and in general this affects the demand side of the market for randomness by altering the non-random factor-remuneration of members of group A. However this effect cannot occur for a representative entrepreneur, who by definition has no non-random factor remuneration; also with a representative consumer, no internal redistribution occurs. In these two cases, the sensitivity of the economy to changes in attitudes to risk or extent of randomness involves little more than standard Arrow–Pratt portfolio theory, linked to the Heckscher–Ohlin equity-production structure through the price z_1.

Extension of the above model to many physical commodities is straightforward for the small country case with non-random world prices, since this reduces – for the purposes of portfolio theory – to the one-commodity case. With random world price the extension is more complicated, in that non-random factor prices in terms of the numeraire commodity do not imply absence of randomness in real terms if both goods are consumed.

Next introduce the possibility of non-multiplicative randomness in production, linking to the work of Dumas (1980a) without introducing his second physical commodity and using other simplifications. Start with the multiple-state, two-industry, two-factor, one-physical-commodity setting. Following Dumas, production in industry one in state s is given by $x_1(s) = F^s(L_1, K_1)$, where the state-dependent production function exhibits constant returns to scale. (That is, the constant returns property holds within any given state.) The production side is given by:

$$\sum_s q(s) \cdot x_1(s) = w \cdot L_1 + r \cdot K_1,$$
(3.11)

$$\sum_s q(s) \cdot x_2(s) = w \cdot L_2 + r \cdot K_2,$$
(3.12)

$$L_1 + L_2 = L,$$
(3.13)

$$K_1 + K_2 = K.$$
(3.14)

The first two equations above represent the zero-profit conditions under competitive freedom of entry and exit, while the last two equations represent the factor-market clearing conditions. All four equations are, in a sense, the same as eqs. (3.1)–(3.4) in the two-state model with multiplicative randomness – but there has been no attempt to state them in terms of a_{ij} coefficients, if only because there is no natural unit in which to measure the scale of production.

The treatment here of the financial side is simpler than in Dumas, who assumes Arrow–Debreu security-trade plus commodity markets, this giving the desired unanimity result with firms maximizing market value. We assume identical probabilities and one physical commodity, so that $q(s) = b(s) \cdot p(s)$ is the implicit contingent-commodity price in state s, and $p(s) = 1$ for all s (assuming no discounting over the production lag). As Dumas explains, we still have the concept of factor intensities and the factor-market clearing conditions can be expressed in familiar fashion:

$$(L_1/L) \cdot (K_1/L_1) + ((L - L_1)/L) \cdot (K_2/L_2) = (K/L);$$
(3.15)

and furthermore the factor prices can be expressed as:

$$r = \sum_s q(s) \cdot F_K^s(\cdot) = \sum_s q(s) \cdot G_K^s(\cdot),$$
(3.16)

$$w = \sum_s q(s) \cdot F_L^s(\cdot) = \sum_s q(s) \cdot G_L^s(\cdot).$$
(3.17)

Dumas, employing the factor-price frontier, obtains conditions for factor-price equalization – although with "generalized uncertainty", as opposed to "multiplicative uncertainty", the possibility of an intensity reversal is increased.

To get propositions such as Rybczynski's theorem, it is necessary to replace output as in the non-random model, or even the state-independent component of output as in the multiplicative-randomness case, by a form of average, namely the market value of output. Define $R_j = \sum_s q(s) \cdot x_j(s)$ for $j = 1, 2$. Also define $A_{Lj} = L_j / R_j$ and $A_{Kj} = K_j / R_j$. Now the factor-market clearing conditions, (3.13) and (3.14), can be rewritten:

$$A_{L1} \cdot R_1 + A_{L2} \cdot R_2 = L, \tag{3.18}$$

$$A_{K1} \cdot R_1 + A_{K2} \cdot R_2 = K. \tag{3.19}$$

Moreover the competitive profit conditions, (3.11) and (3.12), can be rewritten:

$$(R_1 / L_1) = w + r \cdot (K_1 / L_1), \tag{3.20}$$

$$(R_2 / L_2) = w + r \cdot (K_2 / L_2). \tag{3.21}$$

One way to understand what is going on with generalized uncertainty is to note that labor and capital generate expected revenue, i.e. with Dumas' assumption of Arrow–Debreu securities, the market value of the firm R_j. Thus we could draw isoquants linking L_j and K_j to R_j. However, since $R_j = \sum_s q(s) \cdot F^s(L_j, K_j)$, these iso-market-value loci shift not only with technological change in any state but also with changes in the prices $q(s)$. Were randomness multiplicative we could define a mapping from L_j and K_j to x_j, the expected level of output in industry j, and use this for the isoquant map; define $q_j = \sum_s q(s) \cdot e_j(s)$; also then $R_j = q_j \cdot x_j$ and $A_{ij} = a_{ij} / q_j$. Substitution back into the factor-market relations and the competitive profit conditions brings the framework to the original form obtained for multiplicative randomness, i.e. (3.1)–(3.4). However with generalized uncertainty there is no natural unit with which to measure physical output.

To go a step further, let $(\% X)$ denote the logarithmic derivative of variable X. Then:

$$(\% R_j) = \sum_s n_{Rj}(s) \cdot \left[(\% q(s)) + (\% x_j(s)) \right], \tag{3.22}$$

where $n_{Rj}(s) \stackrel{\mathrm{dt}}{=} R_j(s) / R_j$ is the fraction of the market value of the firm attributed to state s. Thus if $(\% q(s)) = 0$ for $s = 1, \ldots, S$ – or more generally if $\sum_s n_{Rj}(s) \cdot (\% q(s)) = 0$ – then this implies:

$$(\% R_j) = \sum_s n_{Rj}(s) \cdot (\% x_j(s)). \tag{3.23}$$

Given the technology exhibits constant returns to scale within any given state, and given the wage, for example, will be equated to the expected value of marginal product of labor, Euler's theorem implies we have:

$$\sum_{s} n_{R_j}(s) \cdot \left(\% x_j(s) \right) = S_{Lj} \cdot \left(\% L_j \right) + S_{Kj} \cdot \left(\% K_j \right), \tag{3.24}$$

where S_{ij} is the financial share of factor i in R_j. With $q(s)$ constant, all s:

$$\left(\% R_j \right) = S_{Lj} \cdot \left(\% L_j \right) + S_{Kj} \cdot \left(\% K_j \right), \tag{3.25}$$

But since $R_j = w \cdot L_j + r \cdot K_j$, differentiation of this competitive profit condition, holding $q(s)$ constant for all s, gives:

$$0 = S_{Lj} \cdot \left(\% w \right) + S_{Kj} \cdot \left(\% r \right) \quad \text{for} \quad j = 1, 2. \tag{3.26}$$

In other words, given non-singularity of the S_{ij} matrix, holding all the $q(s)$ constant implies holding the wage and rental constant, and this in turn implies holding the A_{ij} constant (because with the $q(s)$ constant and no technological progress, R_j is an invariant function of L_j and K_j and the firm is effectively cost-minimizing subject to a representative level set of this function). As a consequence of this logic, if the $q(s)$ are held constant then the A_{ij} coefficients in the factor-market clearing conditions can be treated as constants, giving:

$$T_{L1} \cdot \left(\% R_1 \right) + T_{L2} \cdot \left(\% R_2 \right) = \left(\% L \right), \tag{3.27}$$

$$T_{K1} \cdot \left(\% R_1 \right) + T_{K2} \cdot \left(\% R_2 \right) = \left(\% K \right), \tag{3.28}$$

where T_{ij} = physical share of industry j in the factor market for input i. But this is exactly the structure required for the Rybczynski and related physical-side magnification propositions. Now the theorem says that an increase in the labor endowment, for fixed quantity of capital, holding the $q(s)$ constant for all s, leads to a more than proportionate expansion of the labor-intensive industry and a contraction of the capital-intensive industry in terms of market values.

It should be clear that the name of the game is to reduce the production structure to something formally the same as that of the Heckscher–Ohlin model without uncertainty, and then to reinterpret the theorems. The less structure imposed beforehand, e.g. generalized uncertainty rather than multiplicative randomness, the stronger the market structure (or the supplements to the market structure) and the more complex the reinterpretation. As Dumas points out, there is a further complication with "generalized uncertainty" in that factor-intensity reversals can arise in a greater variety of ways.

Returning to the world of multiplicative randomness it is now easy to introduce the model of Helpman and Razin (1978a, b, d) since so much of it has been anticipated by earlier discussion. There are two physical commodities, two countries, two industries per country – each producing a single physical commodity – and two physical factors of production. Production decisions are made ex-ante but there is both ex-ante free trade in equities and ex-post free trade in physical commodities. Randomness occurs multiplicatively in Heckscher–Ohlin technology, which is identical by industry across countries in the strong sense, and technological randomness induces randomness in ex-post terms of trade in a manner which consumers are able to predict contingent on the realized state of the world.

All this leads directly to an equity-production structure which is isomorphic to the production structure without randomness, with equity prices replacing prices of physical commodities, with levels of equity-output replacing levels of output of physical commodities, and with factor returns denominated in units of numeraire equity. The production structure representation is identical to the share-trading model earlier in this section with one physical commodity and multiplicative randomness, i.e. (3.1)–(3.4), but the physical outputs of the two industries differ – affecting the preference-side determination of equity prices. However, with more than one physical commodity and more than one source of randomness, preference-side results will not be abundant. We will not repeat the earlier model, but reemphasize the roles of multiplicative randomness, the strong form of identical technology, plus a strong identical homotheticity assumption in equity-space [introduced later by Anderson (1981)].

The demand side of the Helpman–Razin model is handled using an indirect utility function approach, exactly as discussed in Section 2 for the two-physical commodity case with commodity-specific randomness and share-trading. Let m_1 and m_2 be the home countries choices of asset holdings after ex-ante trade. Then the consumer/country maximizes $V(m_1, m_2) \overset{\text{df}}{=} \sum_s b(s) \cdot U(c_1(p(s), y(s)),$ $c_2(p(s), y(s))$ subject to $q_1 \cdot m_1 + q_2 \cdot m_2 = w \cdot L + r \cdot K$. Here $p(s) \overset{\text{df}}{=} p_2(s)/p_1(s)$ is the relative price of the second physical commodity in state s, $y(s) \overset{\text{df}}{=} m_1 \cdot e_1(s)$ $+ p(s) \cdot m_2 \cdot e_2(s)$ is the income, measured in units of physical commodity one, obtained from the chosen asset bundle if state s is realized. Note also from the constant returns structure, $w \cdot L + r \cdot K = q_1 \cdot x_1 + q_2 \cdot x_2$, so the ex-ante constraint is for the entire economy $q_1 \cdot m_1 + q_2 \cdot m_2 = q_1 \cdot x_1 + q_2 \cdot x_2$.

Ex-post utility, conditional on the equity-production and the equity-trading decisions, arises from ex-post consumption choice in each state s to maximize $U(c(s))$ subject to $c_1(s) + p(s) \cdot c_2(s) = y(s)$. As with the one-physical-commodity model it is possible to draw the production possibility frontier in equity-space, i.e. (m_1, m_2)-space, and then to draw indifference maps representing combinations of m_1 and m_2 which keep $V(m)$ constant. However all the ex-post trading is buried in these indifference maps in equity-space, and any disturbance to the system may, by altering the distribution of ex-post prices, alter the indifference map in equity-space.

Helpman and Razin show the robustness of Stolper–Samuelson, Rybczynski and factor-price equalization theorems when free trade in equities makes the equity-production structure isomorphic to that in the absence of randomness. The later paper of Anderson (1981) showed that one could also extend the pattern-of-(equity)-trade result by putting sufficient structure on preferences to obtain the appropriate analogy of identical homothetic preferences. Specifically, identical homothetic preferences over physical commodities and identical constant coefficients of relative risk aversion are required. Helpman and Razin give counterexamples to, for example, the validity of the Stolper–Samuelson proposition when international equity markets do not exist. These counterexamples should come as no surprise since all the basic propositions of Heckscher–Ohlin theory are consequences of the specific production structure and, once this production structure is no longer preserved in moving to equity-production, there is no presumption that propositions should be robust. In effect if production has become production of equities rather than production of physical commodities, then trade – viewed as an alternative means of transformation relative to production – should be equity trade rather than solely trade in physical commodities. (The presence of ex-post trade of physical commodities is permissible, but its impact on equity-production feeds through equity prices.) Helpman and Razin, with multiplicative randomness, identical technology in the strong sense, and explicit internationally-unsegmented equity markets, in effect present the case for treating technological randomness as a restatement of traditional propositions in terms of equities rather than physical commodities. Dumas (1980b) is investigating the relaxation of the assumption of identical technologies in the strong sense.

What remains on the production side is models of ex-ante production choice and ex-post consumption choice, and also fluctuations models of ex-post production and consumption, when randomness occurs in exogenous terms of trade. The case of price randomness with ex-ante production decision and ex-post consumption decision has been considered by a number of authors, e.g. Ruffin (1974a), Turnovsky (1974), Anderson and Riley (1976), Eaton (1979). Note also the model with an inventory option by Feder, Just and Schmitz (1977). Some of these papers are discussed in Pomery (1979), to which the interested reader is referred. These models do not explicitly consider the role of asset markets, although by assuming the economy can be treated as if a simple economic agent they implicitly assumed intranational markets for randomness either operate perfectly or are redundant. The production decision is handled using the indirect utility function approach.

With fluctuations models, the terms of trade are random and all decisions can be made ex-post. We have already discussed in the context of an exchange model the conditions for the indirect utility function to be convex or concave in relative price (for arithmetic mean). Adding substitutability in production merely adds a positive term $+ S_{x1} \cdot S_{x2} \cdot$ (ESS), where $S_{xj} =$ the share of industry j in the national income, and (ESS) = the elasticity of substitution around the production possibility frontier. Thus the opportunity to substitute in production adds to the potential benefit of exogenous price variability.

4. Welfare and government intervention

Governments are a major form of extramarket organization in traditional trade theory. From the Walrasian perspective, extramarket organizations and institutions are symptomatic of market failure. In the literature on uncertainty in trade models there are at least four categories of interventionist analysis. (i) The traditional monopoly-power argument for an optimal tariff can be found in, for example, Helpman and Razin (1978b, d; 1980a). Recall this is an example of manipulative dysfunction from the global viewpoint, but can simultaneously be thought of as an internalization of a pecuniary externality for (subgroup) redistributive purposes. With uncertainty the situation is complicated by the presence of both ex-ante and ex-post markets. (ii) A variety of other explicitly interventionist arguments can be found. Prominent is the notion of tariffs as a (second-best) corrective for the pecuniary externalities created by an incomplete market structure. Another situation of internalization arises in the Bhagwati–Srinivasan (1976) framework of trade disruption, where tariffs impose on exporters their contribution to the aggregate national cost of (uncertain) trade restrictions levied by the importing country in response to "excessive" levels of such imports. More tangential are the implicit-contract models of Ethier, discussed in Section 5 of this chapter, where there is a potential role for intervention to offset "importing of distortions".

(iii) Nontariff intervention arises in a paper by Chiang and Masson (1981), where information asymmetries generate an externality with respect to product quality levels. [In this vein, note in passing the Magee (1977) appropriability view of multinational corporations, where extramarket organizations – the multinationals – choose to operate across national boundaries because of their limited ability to appropriate the benefits of comparative advantage in information/technology via market transactions.] (iv) There is also an abundant literature on the relative merits of tariffs and quotas under uncertainty. There is an ad hoc element about much of this literature, in that it is not obvious how the government objective is related to general-equilibrium Paretian criteria.

Section 2 of this survey started with some simple contingent-commodity models where existence and optimality of a competitive equilibrium are not major issues, and where the standard gains from trade arguments can be reinterpreted in terms of trade in randomness (with or without simultaneous trade in physical commodities). In the Diamond share-trading model with one physical commodity, we have a form of restricted optimality, i.e. the competitive allocation is Pareto-optimal given the restriction that only share-trading is possible, but still the gains from trade logic goes through.

However as more than one physical commodity is combined with incomplete markets, the issue becomes less clearcut. Hart (1975) has shown there may exist multiple equilibria under rational expectations where some equilibria are Pareto-dominated by others. Hart also gives examples where the introduction of an additional market makes all market participants worse off. Cornes and Milne (1981) have offered an explanation of the Hart result in terms of implicit distortions arising from failure to equalize marginal rates of substitution in sufficient directions under incomplete markets, and suggest analogies with the literature on externalities. The notion that trade may be mutually disadvantageous is alien to the free-trade bias of non-dysfunctional Walrasian-international models. However if one considers a broader framework of international collective behavior, encompassing a variety of forms of externalities including prisoners' dilemma type situations, then it is less surprising that voluntary collective behavior is not automatically beneficial. [Note again the Brander paper (1981) involving oligopolistic interdependence, and – in a non-trade model – Loong and Zeckhauser (1982) on the possibility of pecuniary externalities preventing the achievement of a Pareto-optimum in the presence of randomness and incomplete markets.]

Newbery and Stiglitz (1981) give an example, where with incomplete markets, free trade may be Pareto-dominated by autarky, an idea which has been adopted by Eaton and Grossman (1981) to give a second-best argument for tariffs as a form of insurance when internal markets are incomplete. Newbery and Stiglitz's example, where free trade may be Pareto-inferior to autarky and to restricted trade, appears likely to spawn a variety of applications and so may be worth spelling out in some detail. The essence is that there exists an implicit role for a risk-pooling market, but that no such explicit market (including trade in shares of producers) exists either within or across countries. Ex-post commodity markets perform (imperfectly) this role as well as satisfying the commodity rationale for trade.

Let two countries each produce two commodities, with only one commodity having random output. We will take the simplest and strongest statement of the model, assuming countries are identical except that outputs of the random commodity are perfectly negatively correlated across the two countries. At autarky the negative relation between price and quantity for the random commodity provides income insurance for producers – here assume unit price elasticities so that income insurance is complete at autarky. Note the negative correlation of outputs implies the insurance-providing prices tend to be negatively correlated across countries.

Now permit free trade in physical commodities. With the symmetry assumption, world price is uniform across states of the world, in contrast to autarkic prices. This provides stability for consumers, but destroys the insurance role of price for producers. Producers' welfare drops monotonically the greater the extent of trade, while consumers are faced by a beneficial effect of increased stability and an adverse effect of a changed supply pattern as producers tend to move out of the now (individually) riskier commodity. Near autarky the former, beneficial effect for consumers will dominate but, if consumers are not very risk averse, then at free trade the latter adverse effect may dominate (particularly if producers are strongly risk averse and adjust the supply pattern significantly). Hence this can create a situation where both producers and consumers are worse off under free trade than at autarky; as the two countries are symmetric, except that output in the random industry is negatively-correlated across countries, this implies a situation where all agents are worse off under free trade than under autarky. In general in this situation restricted trade will be the desirable regime.

Explicitly utilizing the insight stated in Newbery and Stiglitz, Eaton and Grossman (1981) consider the role of tariffs as a substitute for internal insurance markets. Starting from an economy of identical individuals, where internal insurance markets would be redundant, they add a constraint that each individual must allocate his entire endowment of one factor (call it capital) to one or other industry before realization of the terms of trade. At the aggregate level, once the capital has been allocated, the model is a small-country, Ricardo–Viner fluctuations model – since all other production and consumption decisions are made ex-post. The constraint on ex-ante specialization of capital at the individual level, in the absence of markets to trade randomness, leaves a potential for gains from trade with individuals falling into two groups according to sector-specific randomness from capital.

Eaton and Grossman distinguish between anticipated and unanticipated intervention policies, arguing that the former are probably more useful but show that even with unanticipated intervention, in the sense that at the time when capital is allocated ex-ante it is assumed that free trade will prevail, free trade is not optimal. The driving force of this conclusion is that tariff policy can redistribute income from those with relatively low marginal utility of income to those with relatively high marginal utility – thus acting as an imperfect form of insurance. Note that tariffs here are state-contingent, and may be subsidies in some cases. Eaton and Grossman consider two types of anticipated policies. First, anticipated policies may be time-consistent, in that the policy anticipated by the private sector must be optimal from the governmental perspective after the capital has been allocated. This because while the government may try to influence the allocation of capital by announcing a specific policy, at the time of executing the intervention decision the capital-allocation decision is a bygone and, in general, ex-post the government has no incentive to follow through on its stated policy. (In effect the government is a complex agent, with government-today and government-tomorrow as constituent agents.) It may be anticipated that the government will, in fact, do what is ex-post optimal despite its ex-ante statements.

Second, the government may be able to commit itself in a credible fashion, in which case its stated policy is anticipated. The issue of credibility is linked to concepts such as reputation. Holding to a commitment, even when not ex-post optimal in isolation, may be sensible if this is part of generating trust over a longer term repeated situation. The question of time-consistency hinges in part on whether the particular ex-post decision is tied in some way to other decisions. Since this cannot be known a priori, it may be necessary to consider both general precommitted and time-consistent policies as alternatives. With an optimal precommitted and anticipated policy, as with the unanticipated case, free trade is not optimal and, the analysis being conducted in a two-state framework, in the state where the terms of trade are favorable it is optimal to impose a tariff rather than a subsidy. Eaton and Grossman also consider state-independent tariffs, and production subsidies and taxes (both state-contingent and state-independent).

Now return to the welfare conclusions of Helpman and Razin (1978b, d; 1980a), which tend to end – by virtue of frequent use of the small-country assumption – where the Newbery–Stiglitz type of example begins. Helpman and Razin show that in their model for a small country, free trade in physical commodities dominates complete autarky (i.e. the absence of trade in both equities and physical commodities), and that free trade in both physical commodities and equities dominates trade in physical commodities alone. Ex-post trade alone is always beneficial for a country of any size.

Now add in free trade for equities for a country which cannot affect world prices in either equities or physical commodities. By adjusting equity-production and by trading in the equity market, the country can expand its equity-consumption possibility set. The small-country assumption avoids the potential complication, should ex-post commodity terms of trade alter in moving from zero international trade in equities to free trade in equities, that the equity-indifference map is altered and the levels of expected utility for the two situations are non-comparable. The complication leads back to the conclusion that for large countries we cannot exclude the possibility that, given ex-post commodity trade, both countries are hurt by the introduction of equity trade.

Improvements in the commodity terms of trade in any state(s) will be unambiguously welfare-improving if either there is no equity-trade or the relative price of equities remains unchanged. If equity terms of trade do not remain fixed, then the previous logic does not go through. The situation is reminiscent of models of capital mobility where there is more than one terms of trade.

Next consider Helpman and Razin's conclusions (1978c, d; 1980b) on government intervention, bearing in mind that their discussion of tariffs under uncertainty is closest to the traditional tariff literature. Suppose a country cannot affect price in the ex-post commodity markets, so that the equity-indifference map is unaltered throughout in the strong sense that not only are the indifference curves geometrically immobile but the level of expected utility for each is unchanged. Then it should, from a national perspective, impose a tariff on equity-trade if and only if it has monopoly power in equity-trade. This follows since, with constant ex-post terms of trade in each state, the equity allocation problem reduces to the standard tariff discussion. This a first-best argument for intervention, with the representative consumer assumption implying no market failure within the economy.

Helpman and Razin also provide a second-best case for intervention in equity-trade, assuming a fixed tariff wedge in ex-post commodity trade which cannot be eliminated either directly or indirectly. Then it can be shown, paralleling results in the literature on capital mobility, that in general it is optimal to intervene in equity markets (given tariff proceeds are redistributed in lump-sum fashion). For intervention in commodity markets, Helpman and Razin show by example another consequence of the incomplete market structure. In the absence of international trade in equities it is possible to have a Metzler paradox for a small country, an impossibility for the case of certainty. However, if trade in equities also occurs but the country cannot influence either equity or commodity prices in the world markets, then the Metzler paradox cannot occur (and a commodity tariff, by raising the domestic ex-post price above the corresponding exogenous world price in each state, is effectively an equity tariff). It can be shown, by restating some earlier logic, that tariffs on commodity trade are harmful for a country with no ability to influence price either in equity or commodity markets. Finally Helpman and Razin are able to show that, if tariff revenues are redistributed, then restricted commodity trade, with either zero or unrestricted trade in equities, dominates complete autarky. If the tariff revenues are undistributed, then restricted commodity trade plus unrestricted equity trade dominates restricted commodity trade with no equity trade.

Now return to some of the work of Newbery and Stiglitz (1979, 1981), which has a different emphasis than the production-side models of Section 3. Newbery and Stiglitz are concerned with the function and properties of commodity-price stabilization schemes, viewed as potential form of risk-bearing activity. Their analysis links up with the earlier preference-side sections of this survey, since there is no emphasis on Heckscher–Ohlin or other specific production structures. It overlaps with the discussion of incomplete markets, given the interpretation of price-stabilization schemes as at best imperfect vehicles for insurance, and with a literature on tariffs versus quotas under uncertainty, given commodity-price stabilization schemes as partial substitutes for government intervention via tariffs or quotas (or for private institutions such as futures markets).

A major policy conclusion of Newbery and Stiglitz is that commodity-price stabilization schemes are probably highly overrated, in that prior studies have employed inappropriate methodology leading to misestimation of both costs and benefits and a likely overall overestimation of net benefits. Some of their arguments are paraphrased here. Government-operated commodity-price stabilization schemes represent an intervention in the environment in which the private sector already operates. Thus it is necessary to ask why the private sector cannot perform the same operation, what alternative forms of intervention are open to the government, to what extent government activity acts as a substitute for existing private sector activity, and how – in the face of government activity – the private sector will respond.

To answer some of these questions it is necessary to step back and to consider the objective of commodity-price stabilization schemes. Newbery and Stiglitz argue that the purpose, ideally, is to stabilize incomes (particularly in real terms) and that price stabilization per se has little independent merit. Price stabilization is neither necessary nor sufficient for stabilization of income (in either nominal or real terms). Given the predominance of supply-side shocks then, if these are perfectly positively correlated across producers, increased output is associated with decreased price. With unit elasticity of demand, nominal income is stabilized in the face of output variability by induced price variability – while price stabilization implies induced nominal – income variability. If output shocks are not perfectly positively correlated across producers, then the impact of output variability on income variability need not be potentially damped for a given producer by price variability. Further, with non-traded goods whose prices may be sensitive to the sources of these shocks, real income may be less variable than nominal income.

Given real-income stabilization is the objective, the first-best solution would seem to be direct income insurance. However this raises obvious difficulties from information asymmetry; there is the moral hazard problem that incentive to work and to protect the crops is diminished, and the adverse selection problem that with insurance offered at actuarially fair terms the high-risk producers (unidentifiable to the insurers) have an incentive to take advantage of the (personally favorable) insurance terms while the (unidentifiable) low-risk producers are driven from the market by the same (personally unfavorable) terms. Futures markets do not exist in sufficient variety, especially with respect to longer time periods, and in any event neither provide full income stabilization (but merely approximate certainty about the realized selling price as of the time the contract is purchased) nor can be fully utilized if the quantity of the commodity to be harvested is unknown. This explains market failure in the private sector.

Suppose the government were to succeed in eliminating price variability via a stabilization scheme. Producers may have alternative opportunities to stabilize income. They may hold limited inventories privately as small-scale stabilization schemes, and these may be abandoned. They may diversify by planting more than one commodity, and stabilization of the price of one commodity may lead to

abandonment of other crops despite the socially-desirable diversification provided. Similarly they may adopt less risky techniques for production in the face of
price variability. With perfect capital markets consumption can be smoothed by
lending when income is high and borrowing when income is low. Alternative
methods of (partial) stabilization, such as futures markets and long-term contracts
may be utilized. All this suggests that government activity may not be operating
in a private-sector vacuum with respect to stabilization and diversification behavior. Moreover as the private sector responds to price stabilization by the government, it may expand production of the commodity in question and increase the
strain on the government buffer stock.

Newbery and Stiglitz also point out that complete price stabilization is impossible in many situations. Thus if buffer stock were to follow a random walk then
with probability one either the stock will be exhausted at some point or it will
expand beyond any finite storage capacity. In this case the best that could be
hoped for is partial stabilization, but the amount of storage required to provide
an x percent probability that the stock will last for at least y years increases
dramatically as x and y increase. (Presumably this is a disincentive for large-scale
private stabilization schemes.)

In summary Newbery and Stiglitz suggest that prior analysis tends to be
misleading for a number of reasons. The common assumption of linear demand
and supply curves implies that stabilizing price also stabilizes quantity in the
market, which is a special case and draws attention away from the issues in the
previous paragraphs. No distinction between stabilization of price and stabilization of real income is made. The use of surplus measures implies a form of
risk-neutrality, thus ignoring a major purpose of stabilization, i.e. meeting the
risk-averse needs of producers. However the tendency of the private sector to
substitute governmental activity for private methods of stabilization and diversification suggests this important role may be smaller than appears at first glance. In
addition the costs of stabilization, via the expensiveness of long-term, high-proba-
bility partial stabilization and via the response of the private sector increasing the
strain on the buffer stock, are probably significantly underestimated. Overall the
authors conclude that price stabilization may be significantly less attractive than
suggested by prior analysis. They suggest more attention be paid to the distinction
between purely redistributive effects (transfers) and efficiency effects; while the
latter may have been overestimated, the former are probably significant.

Another topic covered in the Newbery and Stiglitz book, and which has
generated a growing literature in the journals, is that of the relation of tariffs
(specific and ad valorem) and quotas under uncertainty. If we also include some
work on buffer stocks and related topics this literature more recently includes
Anderson (1976a), Dasgupta and Stiglitz (1977), Fishelson and Flatters (1975),
Helpman and Razin (1980b), Ohta (1978), Pelcovits (1976, 1979), Tower (1981),
Toyoda (1976), Young (1979, 1980a, b, 1982), Young and Anderson (1980, 1982),

and Young and Kemp (1982). Note also the survey by Turnovsky (1978). Much of this literature operates in terms of consumer and producer surplus concepts. The limitations of such analysis are discussed in Newbery and Stiglitz. However some recent contributions – e.g. Young (1982), Young and Anderson (1982) – have emphasized the role of risk aversion and/or drawn attention to the link to the literature on price versus quantity instruments for planners [as in Wietzman (1974)].

This literature is distinguished by alternative objectives to be achieved via trade intervention. A useful insight is obtained from the interpretation of a tariff as a set of state-dependent quotas [cf. Young and Anderson (1980)]. Consider the case of a small country facing randomness in world price of an importable commodity, and trying to maximize the expected consumer surplus subject to some additional constraint. A ceiling on expected imports implies arbitrage of the quota across states, which is done optimally by a specific tariff, given the objective of maximizing expected consumer surplus, since the rent on a unit of contingent quota licenses is identical in all states of the world. A ceiling on foreign exchange expenditure implies the arbitrage of this expenditure quota across states, which is done optimally by an ad valorem tariff since an ad valorem tariff equalizes rent across states.

Newbery and Stiglitz (1981) discuss tariffs and quotas in terms of their impact on the expected utility of producers and of consumers (thus allowing for risk spreading benefits) with explicit supply-side randomness, in the context of symmetric countries trading physical commodities internationally without the benefit of either national or international equity markets. They show that for this model, (i) starting from a symmetric free trade equilibrium, some trade restriction is Pareto-improving if producers are sufficiently risk averse, (ii) starting from autarky, some trade is Pareto-improving, (iii) near the symmetric free trade equilibrium, with sufficiently risk averse producers, quotas are preferable to tariffs, but (iv) near autarky, tariffs are preferable to quotas. The links to implicit insurance (in Newbery and Stiglitz in particular) and to implicit arbitrage markets for quotas (in Young and Anderson) are suggestive and consistent with a continuing and inevitable theme of this survey, namely that results will be dependent on the extent of existing markets relative to the first-best structure for the objectives of the model in question.

Another literature that may generate a rationale for intervention in the presence of uncertainty – if individual agents are insensitive to their contribution to aggregate behavior – involves models of trade disruption, as pioneered by Bhagwati and Srinivasan (1976). They consider the situation of a country over two periods (subsequently extended to longer time horizons in the same paper), where the private sector makes trade decisions in the first period ignoring the (aggregate) effect that too large a quantity of exports could provoke quantitative restrictions on trade in the second period by their trading partner. The endogenous probability of quantitative restrictions leads to an ex-ante diminution of expected utility, since the original country is worse off if it triggers the restrictions. (Bhagwati and Srinivasan consider both the case where adjustment to a new situation in the second period is unconstrained and the case where there is some inflexibility in input allocation after the initial decision.) Thus there is a justification for intervention by the government of the original country in order to internalize this cost of trade in terms of ex-ante welfare. In the absence of adjustment costs it is not hard to see that the appropriate policy is a trade-related intervention in the first period, leaving the marginal rate of substitution in consumption congruent with the marginal rate of product transformation – since the externality is trade-related. (Second-period activity should be undistorted in a two-period framework; with adjustment costs, intervention should be directed at both trade and production.)

Kemp and Ohta (1978) extend the Bhagwati–Srinivasan analysis, with particular emphasis on the longer time horizon and the possibility that the exportable commodity may be storable, with the threat of trade disruption a function of the cumulative total of exports. Other papers in this area include Mayer (1977, also 1981), Tolley and Wilman (1977), and Arad and Hillman (1979a, b).

A paper by Chiang and Masson (1981) offers both a departure from traditional approaches to trade and uncertainty, and an alternative rationale for some form of intervention at the collective level. The basic idea here is taken from industrial organization theory, and is intuitively straightforward. The argument is that some LDCs may have difficulty upgrading the product-quality of their exports because of information asymmetry and an externality it creates. If buyers in international markets are not aware of the quality levels of individual firms within a country, but do have a perception of overall quality for the entire country (then attributing this quality level uniformly to firms in the country), it follows that the national benefit of improved quality by a single firm is greater than the benefit to the firm itself. This because the benefit is "diluted" across all firms in the industry, a problem which is more severe and harder partially to internalize – cf. Olson (1965) on large versus small groups – in an approximately competitive industry of many producers than in an oligopolistic industry of few producers or in a nation where industrial activity is partially coordinated by government agencies. As the authors suggest, this may have some implications for the ability to upgrade quality of exports in, say, Taiwan compared to Japan.

5. Miscellany

While the Chiang and Masson paper draws from industrial organization, two papers by Ethier (1981, 1982) apply implicit contract theory to the topics of labor migration and of dumping. In Ethier's paper on dumping, his purpose is to show how differences in the underlying nature of labor markets can explain why countries sell below cost in some states of the world. [Davies and McGuinness (1982) use uncertainty facing a monopolist as one explanation for dumping, defined as sales below marginal cost.] In the Ethier model countries differ, amongst other things, according to the fraction of tenured to nontenured workers, and in the level of unemployment compensation available to the nontenured workers when laid off. The intuition is that countries with high proportions of tenured workers (and hence high proportions of fixed to variable costs) and with relatively low unemployment compensation are likely to export unemployment by dumping in low-demand states of the world. Thus we get an implication, familiar in other contexts in Cooper (1973, 1976), that linkages via the private sector – here via the international market for the good in question – generate externalities across jurisdictions tending to encourage similar institutional structures across countries. As this offers a different perspective from the production models of Section 3, an outline of the model is sketched below.

Assume two countries, one composite traded good, satisfying the law of one price. Firms are price-takers, and employ two factors, which are in fixed supply to the traded-goods sector, with constant returns technology. There are two equiprobable states of the world, with state-dependent demand; one state will be termed the high demand state. Both factors of production are paid a remuneration which is state-independent, but one factor (managers) is guaranteed employment irrespective of state while the other (laborers) may be laid off, in which case the firm pays nothing and the laborers receive unemployment compensation. Firms are risk-neutral and maximize expected profits, implying managers are paid their expected value of marginal product.

For laborers, firms are aware that hiring additional workers ex-ante tends to increase the probability for any given laborer that he will be laid off if the low-demand state occurs, and that the higher probability of layoff must be compensated for by a higher wage if the firm is to remain competitive in the labor market. Hence the firm "overemploys" labor in the low-demand state, in the sense of going beyond the level consistent with the usual value of marginal product pricing criterion, because additional labor in that state not only produces more output but lowers the wage rate required to maintain the firm's position in the labor market. The firm, which is subject in equilibrium to a zero-expected profit condition, "underemploys" labor in the high-demand state. (Equilibrium in the factor markets implies that all managers are employed and that all laborers are employed in the high-demand state.) Since the fixed number of managers have more cooperating laborers in the high-demand state than in the low-demand state, and hence under constant returns a higher marginal physical product, both managers and laborers are paid less than their value of marginal product in the high-demand state and the opposite in the low-demand state. From the homogeneity property of production, this implies the firm makes profits in the high-demand state and makes losses, i.e. sells below cost, in the low-demand state.

The model is closed by an aggregate market-clearing condition for the traded good in world markets, and randomness is introduced by characterizing each country's demand via a state-independent component (as a function of price) plus a multiplicative state-dependent term. Rather than spell out the detailed workings of the model, we state some of the conclusions. From a symmetric initial point, with demand variability correlated across countries, the country with a higher ratio of managers to laborers tends to dump, i.e. to export goods below cost, in the low-demand state. In the same context, the country with the lower level of unemployment compensation tends to dump in low-demand states, increasing the variability of employment in the other country and decreasing employment variability for itself. If the two countries are symmetric except that randomness is negatively correlated ("out-of-phase" to use Ethier's expression), then the whole discussion is moot, in the sense that the pooling of demand shocks provides for a state-independent world demand, so that there is no role for uncertainty generated by the possibility of layoffs. If demand fluctuations are negatively correlated, but more pronounced in one country, then that country tends to dump when in recession but the other country exports at above cost during its own recession.

Such a model is a partial representation of a trading situation and, as Ethier points out, it is difficult to make policy conclusions on the basis of this model alone. In part the model reflects incompleteness of markets for allocating randomness, and there may be a presumptive role for at least a small tariff even when this model is embedded in a broader framework. Although the intuitive story will not come as a surprise to international economists, it is useful to have a formalized model which ties into the theory of implicit contracts, the industrial-organization notion of high- versus low-fixed cost producers, and ideas about spillovers across national boundaries in the spirit of Cooper.

Ethier's second implicit-contract paper (1981) considers a small country completely specialized in a single commodity, which is produced using two factors of production (under constant returns to scale), with firms maximizing expected profits which are driven to zero by competition. (Note the risk-neutrality assumption may be strong for an industry which is the only one in the economy.) One factor is domestic labor, in fixed supply, paid a state-independent wage, but subject to layoff in the low-demand state; the second factor is migrant labor, an imperfect substitute for domestic labor, which can be chosen ex-post at an exogenous – and possibly state-dependent – wage. The country is a price-taker in its import market, but influences price in its export market. Since migrant labor is freely available ex-post, it is paid its value of marginal product in each state. However domestic labor is paid less than its value of marginal product in the low-demand state (and more in the high-demand state), as in the previous paper.

The model now permits the output to be sold below cost in the low-demand state and/or for migrant labor to be curtailed to the benefit of domestic workers, or even the possibility that low-cost migrant labor is substituted for domestic labor, and by allowing output to expand via lower costs, indirectly benefiting domestic employment.

Next, although strategic models do not belong under the uncertainty heading, we mention two of the settings where game-theoretic techniques have been employed in international economics. The justification for inclusion lies in the incipient uncertainty of small-group interactions, combined with the new perspective on collective interaction. One line involves the link between the choice of platform of political parties, the interests of groups in the electorate, and the interaction between interest groups and political parties, modelled as a multi-level game endogenously determining trade taxes or subsidies via the political process. This by Magee and Brock (1980), to choose one in a series including Brock and Magee (1978, 1980) and Magee (1980). The second is a small formal literature considering the determination of tariffs as a strategic equilibrium at the international level. This literature, whose roots can perhaps be traced to Johnson (1953), considers the global structure of tariffs as a Nash equilibrium where the strategy space for each country is its vector of tariffs. In other words, each country chooses its best tariff vector, given the choices of the remaining countries, and an equilibrium is a consistent set of choices. In this vein are the papers of Ichiishi and Riezman (1981), Jensen and Thursby (1980, 1982), Kuga (1973) and Otani (1980).

Any survey is, inevitably, selective and this is no exception. One omission is the literature on uncertainty in the presence of natural resources, a topic covered by Kemp and Long in Chapter 8 of this volume. Another omission is the various formulations of the international capital-asset pricing model, typically in the Sharpe–Lintner portfolio framework. This literature is useful for estimates of the opportunities available for international portfolio diversification, which in turn leads to another topic neglected here – the link of multinational corporations to portfolio diversification. It is a commonplace that multinational firms transfer across national boundaries a package of resources, possibly including management skills, firm-specific technology, access to financing and risk-bearing. Much of this is related to uncertainty, either via the information asymmetries which imply market failures and hence a need to internalize transnational activity within firms, or via strategic behavior between groups of firms or between firms and governments. However very little of this has filtered through to the mainstream formalized theory of international trade – although cf. Caves (1979) and Magee (1977) for example. Another omission is the literature, particularly on the empirical side, of the opportunities for export diversification and the impact of export instability on national welfare and growth (particularly for LDCs); the early paper by Brainard and Cooper (1968) was in this spirit, but subsequently mainstream pure trade theory has tended to diverge from literature based on development and agricultural perspectives, a situation which may be altered by the work of Newbery and Stiglitz. Another topic which it might be useful to link to this survey is the work on debt and repudiation by Eaton and Gersovitz (1981). There also is a significant literature on the behavior of the firm in the face of exchange rate uncertainty; many of these models are close relations of real models discussed in this survey, and the dividing line between real and financial models becomes somewhat arbitrary with exchange rate variations being tied to variations in prices and/or with the role of international financial markets.

6. Concluding remarks

There is little value in reiterating specific results, while the general thrust of this chapter should need no further emphasis. The role of uncertainty, and its policy implications, varies both across models of a given type – consider the advisibility of free trade with and without complete markets – and across types of models. For some purposes, results are preserved (if interpreted with care) by treating trade and production in equities rather than in the traditional physical commodities. In other areas, the presence of uncertainty increases the possible explanations of market failure – consider the role of pecuniary externalities with incomplete markets. In addition uncertainty can be linked to the existence and extent of extramarket institutions and organizations.

While uncertainty can contribute to a broader view of international trade, it does not have a monopoly in this respect. The variety of potential models, even within the context of uncertainty and international trade, suggests that we must forgo the comfort of strong conclusions, either positive or normative. Where results are most powerful, as in the Helpman–Razin production models of Section 3, the applicability is unclear because of the uncertain interpretation of (joint) assumptions such as industry-specific randomness with global equity markets. Where powerful results would be most welcome, e.g. on the desirability of free trade, there appears no justification for an unambiguous conclusion. The outcome often depends on the extent of markets and/or the extent of extramarket institutions, with their implicit patterns of potential externalities – yet perhaps the justification for the study of international economics is that national boundaries do affect the nature and extent of markets and institutions in many ways.

References

Akiba, H. (1980), "Gains from trade under uncertainty: Further comment", American Economic Review, 70:515–517.
Anderson, J.E. (1976a), "Optimal buffering policies for a small trading country", Southern Economic Journal, 43:1067–1076.

Anderson, J.E. (1976b), "Book review (of The pure theory of international trade under uncertainty, R.N. Batra)", Journal of Economic Literature, 14:1321–1322.

Anderson, J.E. (1981), "The Heckscher–Ohlin and Travis–Vanek theorems under uncertainty", Journal of International Economics, 11:239–247.

Anderson, J.E. and J.G. Riley (1976), "International trade with fluctuating prices", International Economic Review, 17:76–97.

Arad, R.W. and A.L. Hillman (1979a), "The collective good motive for immigration policy", Australian Economic Papers, 18:243–257.

Arad, R.W. and A.L. Hillman (1979b), "Embargo threat, learning and departure from comparative advantage", Journal of International Economics, 9:265–275.

Arrow, K.J. (1971a), "The theory of risk aversion", reprinted in: K.J. Arrow, Essays in the theory of risk-bearing (North-Holland, Amsterdam).

Arrow, K.J. (1971b), "The role of securities in the optimal allocation of risk-bearing", reprinted in: K.J. Arrow, Essays in the theory of risk-bearing (North-Holland, Amsterdam).

Arrow, K.J. (1974), The limits of organization (W.W. Norton & Co., New York).

Baron, D.P. and R. Forsythe (1979), "Models of the firm and international trade under uncertainty", American Economic Review, 69:565–574.

Batra, R.N. (1975a), The pure theory of international trade under uncertainty (Halsted Press, New York).

Batra, R.N. (1975b), "Production uncertainty and the Heckscher–Ohlin theorem", Review of Economic Studies, 42:259–268.

Batra, R.N. and W.R. Russell (1974), "Gains from trade under uncertainty", American Economic Review, 64:1040–1048.

Batra, R.N. and W.R. Russell (1976), "Gains from trade under uncertainty: Reply", American Economic Review, 66:928.

Bhagwati, J.N. and T.N. Srinivasan (1976), "Optimal trade policy and compensation under endogenous uncertainty: The phenomenon of market disruption", Journal of International Economics, 6:317–336.

Boonekamp, C.F.J. and D. Donaldson (1979), "Certain alternatives for price uncertainty", Canadian Journal of Economics, 12:718–728.

Brainard, W.C. and R.N. Cooper (1968), "Uncertainty and diversification in international trade", Food Research Institute Studies, 8:257–285.

Brander, J.A. (1981), "Intra-industry trade in identical commodities", Journal of International Economics, 11:1–14.

Brock, W.A. and S.P. Magee (1978), "The economics of special interest politics: The case of the tariff", American Economic Review, 68:246–250.

Brock, W.A. and S.P. Magee (1980), "Tariff formation in a democracy", in: J. Black and B. Hindley, eds., Current issues in commercial policy and diplomacy (Trade Policy Research Centre, London).

Caves, R.E. (1979), "International cartels and monopolies in international trade", in: R. Dornbusch and J.A. Frenkel, eds., International economic policy: Theory and evidence (The Johns Hopkins University Press, Baltimore).

Chang, W.W., W.J. Ethier, and M.C. Kemp (1980), "The theorems of international trade with joint production", Journal of International Economics, 10:377–394.

Chiang, S.-C. and R.T. Masson (1981), "Domestic industrial structure and export upgrading: A quality signaling approach", manuscript.

Coase, R.N. (1937), "The nature of the firm", Economica N.S., 4:386–405.

Cooper, R.N. (1973), Economic mobility and national economic policy (Almqvist and Wiksell, Stockholm).

Cooper, R.N. (1976), "Worldwide versus regional integration: Is there an optimum size of the integrated area?", in: F. Machlup, ed., Integration worldwide, regional, sectoral (MacMillan Press, London).

Cornes, R. and F. Milne (1981), "A simple analysis of mutually disadvantageous trades", Working paper No. 036 (The Australian National University, Faculty of Economics and Research School of Social Sciences).

Das, S.K. (1977), "Uncertainty and the Heckscher–Ohlin theorem: A comment", Review of Economic Studies, 44:189–190.

Dasgupta, P. and J. Stiglitz (1977), "Tariffs versus quotas as revenue raising devices", American Economic Review, 67:975–981.

Davies, S.W. and A.J. McGuinness (1982), "Dumping at less than marginal cost", Journal of International Economics, 12:169–182.

Diamond, P.A. (1967), "The role of a stock market in a general equilibrium model with technological uncertainty", American Economic Review, 57:759–776.

Drèze, J.H. (1974), "Investment under private ownership: Optimality, equilibrium and stability", in: J.H. Drèze, ed., Allocation under uncertainty: Equilibrium and optimality (John Wiley, New York).

Dumas, B. (1980a), "The theorems of international trade under generalized uncertainty", Journal of International Economics, 10:481–498.

Dumas, B. (1980b), "Trade theorems with less than perfectly correlated disturbances across countries", manuscript.

Eaton, J. (1979), "The allocation of resources in an open economy with uncertain terms of trade", International Economic Review, 20:391–403.

Eaton, J. and M. Gersovitz (1981), "Debt with potential repudiation: Theoretical and empirical analysis", Review of Economic Studies, 48:289–309.

Eaton, J. and G.M. Grossman (1981), "Tariffs as insurance: Optimal commercial policy when domestic markets are incomplete", Working paper 797, National Bureau of Economic Research.

Ethier, W. (1979), "Comment", in: R. Dornbusch and J.A. Frenkel, eds., International economic policy: Theory and evidence (The Johns Hopkins University Press, Baltimore).

Ethier, W.J. (1981), "International trade and labor migration", Department of Economics, University of Pennsylvania, mimeo.

Ethier, W.J. (1982), "Dumping", Journal of Political Economy, 90:487–506.

Feder, G., Just, R.E. and A. Schmitz (1977), "Storage with price uncertainty in international trade", International Economic Review, 18:553–568.

Fishelson, G. and F. Flatters (1975), "The (non)equivalence of optimal tariffs and quotas under uncertainty", Journal of International Economics, 5:385–393.

Flemming, J.S., Turnovsky, S.J. and M.C. Kemp (1977), "On the choice of numeraire and certainty price in general equilibrium models of price uncertainty", Review of Economic Studies, 44:573–584.

Grinols, E.L. (1981), "A model of international trade, welfare and risk sharing", manuscript.

Hart, O.D. (1974a), "A model of the stock market with many goods", Research Memorandum No. 165, Princeton University.

Hart, O.D. (1974b), "On the existence of equilibrium in a securities model", Journal of Economic Theory, 9:293–311.

Hart, O. (1975), "On the optimality of equilibrium when the market structure is incomplete", Journal of Economic Theory, 11:448–443.

Hartman, R. (1976), "Gains from trade under uncertainty: Comment", American Economic Review, 66:925–927.

Helpman, E. and A. Razin (1978a), "Uncertainty and international trade in the presence of stock markets", Review of Economic Studies, 45:239–250.

Helpman, E. and A. Razin (1978b), "Welfare aspects of international trade in goods and securities", Quarterly Journal of Economics, 92:489–508.

Helpman, E. and A. Razin (1978c), "The protective effect of a tariff under uncertainty", Journal of Political Economy, 86:1131–1141.

Helpman, E. and A. Razin (1978d), A theory of international trade under uncertainty (Academic Press, New York).

Helpman, E. and A. Razin (1980a), "Welfare aspects of international trade in goods and securities: An addendum", Quarterly Journal of Economics, 94:615–618.

Helpman, E. and A. Razin (1980b), "Efficient protection under uncertainty", American Economic Review, 70:716–731.

Ichiishi, T. and R. Riezman (1981), "Customs union formation", Working paper 81-20 (College of Business Administration, University of Iowa).

Jensen, R. and M. Thursby (1980), "Free trade: Two non-cooperative equilibrium approaches" (Working paper #58, Department of Economics, Ohio State University).

Jensen, R. and M. Thursby (1982), "A conjectural variation approach to strategic tariff equilibria" (Working paper #76, Department of Economics, Ohio State University).

Johnson, H.G. (1953), "Optimal tariffs and retaliation", Review of Economic Studies, 55:142–153.

Jones, R.W. (1965), "The structure of simple general equilibrium models", Journal of Political Economy, 73:557–572.

Kemp, M.C. (1976), Three topics in the theory of international trade: Distribution, welfare and uncertainty (North-Holland, Amsterdam).

Kemp, M.C. and N. Liviatan (1973), "Production and trade patterns under uncertainty", Economic Record, 49:215–227.

Kemp, M.C. and H. Ohta (1978), "The optimal level of exports under threat of foreign import restriction", Canadian Journal of Economics, 11:720–725.

Kemp, M.C. and M. Ohyama (1978), "The gain from free trade under conditions of uncertainty", Journal of International Economics, 8:139–141.

Kihlstrom, R.E. and J.-J. Laffont (1979), "A general equilibrium entrepreneurial theorem of firm formation based on risk aversion", Journal of Political Economy, 87:719–748.

Kreps, D.M., P. Milgrom, J. Roberts and R. Wilson (1982), "Rational cooperation in the finitely repeated prisoners' dilemma", Journal of Economic Theory, 27:245–252.

Krugman, P.R. (1979), "Increasing returns, monopolistic competition, and international trade", Journal of International Economics, 9:469–479.

Kuga, K. (1973), "Tariff retaliation and policy equilibrium", Journal of International Economics, 3:351–366.

Loong, L.H. and R. Zeckhauser (1982), "Pecuniary externalities do matter when contingent claims markets are incomplete", Quarterly Journal of Economics, 97:171–179.

Magee, S.P. (1977), "Information and the multinational corporation: An appropriability theory of foreign direct investment", in: J. Bhagwati, ed., The new international economic order: The North–South debate (M.I.T. Press, Cambridge, Mass.).

Magee, S.P. (1980), "The simple tests of the Stolper–Samuelson theorem", in: P. Oppenheimer, ed., Issues in international economics (Oriel Press, London).

Magee, S.P. and Brock, W.A. (1980), "A model of politics, tariffs and rent seeking in general equilibrium", forthcoming in: H. Hughes, ed., Conference volume of International Economic Association sixth world congress of economists.

Mayer, W. (1976), "The Rybczynski, Stolper–Samuelson, and factor-price equalization theorems under price uncertainty", American Economic Review, 66:797–808.

Mayer, W. (1977), "The national defense argument reconsidered", Journal of International Economics, 7:363–377.

Mayer, W. (1981), "Some theoretical considerations on negotiated tariff adjustments", Oxford Economic Papers, 33:135–153.

Milne, F. (1980), "Short-selling, default risk and the existence of equilibrium in a securities model", International Economic Review, 21:255–267.

Newbery, D.M.G. and J.E. Stiglitz (1979), "The theory of commodity price stabilisation rules: Welfare impacts and supply responses", Economic Journal, 89:799–817.

Newbery, D.M.G. and J.E. Stiglitz (1981), The theory of commodity price stabilization: A study in the economics of risk (Oxford University Press, Oxford).

Ohta, H. (1978), "On the ranking of price and quantity controls under uncertainty", Journal of International Economics, 8:543–550.

Oi, W.Y. (1961), "The desirability of price instability under perfect competition", Econometrica, 29:58–64.

Olson, M. (1965), The logic of collective action (Harvard University Press, Cambridge).

Otani, Y. (1980), "Strategic equilibrium of tariffs and general equilibrium", Econometrica, 48:643–662.

Pelcovits, M.D. (1976), "Quotas versus tariffs", Journal of International Economics, 6:363–370.

Pelcovits, M. (1979), "The equivalence of quotas and buffer stocks as alternative stabilization policies", Journal of International Economics, 9:303–307.

Pomery, J. (1979), "Uncertainty and international trade", in: R. Dornbusch and J.A. Frenkel, eds., International economic policy: Theory and evidence (The Johns Hopkins University Press, Baltimore).

Pratt, J.W. (1964), "Risk aversion in the small and in the large", Econometrica, 32:122–136.

Rothschild, M. and J.E. Stiglitz (1971), "Increasing risk II: Its economic consequences", Journal of

Economic Theory, 3:66–84.

Ruffin, R.J. (1974a), "Comparative advantage under uncertainty", Journal of International Economics, 4:261–273.

Ruffin, R.J. (1974b), "International trade under uncertainty", Journal of International Economics, 4:243–259.

Sakai, Y. (1978), "A simple general equilibrium model of production: Comparative statics with price uncertainty", Journal of Economic Theory, 19:287–306.

Samuelson, P.A. (1972), "The consumer does benefit from feasible price stability", Quarterly Journal of Economics, 86:476–493.

Satterthwaite, M.A. (1981), "On the scope of stockholder unanimity theorems" International Economic Review, 22:119–133.

Schelling, T.C. (1960), The theory of conflict (Harvard University Press, Cambridge).

Schotter, A. (1981), The economic theory of social institutions (Cambridge University Press, Cambridge).

Stiglitz, J.E. (1981), "Pareto optimality and competition", Journal of Finance, 36:235–251.

Stiglitz, J.E. (1982), "The inefficiency of the stock market equilibrium", Review of Economic Studies, 49:241–261.

Thaler, R.H. and H.M. Shefrin (1981), "An economic theory of self-control", Journal of Political Economy, 89:392–406.

Tolley, G.S. and J.D. Wilman (1977), "The foreign dependence question", Journal of Political Economy, 85:323–347.

Tower, E. (1981), "Buffer stocks are better stabilizers than quotas", Journal of International Economics, 11:113–115.

Toyoda, T. (1976), "Import instability and tariffs: Some welfare implications of price stabilization", Journal of Political Economy, 84:395–400.

Turnovsky, S.J. (1974), "Technological and price uncertainty in a Ricardian model of international trade", Review of Economic Studies, 41:201–217.

Turnovsky, S.J. (1978), "The distribution of welfare gains from price stabilization: A survey of some theoretical issues", in: F.G. Adams and S.A. Klein, eds., Stabilizing world commodity markets (Lexington Books, Lexington).

Waugh, F.V. (1944), "Does the consumer benefit from price instability?", Quarterly Journal of Economics, 58:602–614.

Weitzman, M.L. (1974), "Prices vs. quantities", Review of Economic Studies, 41:50–65.

Whitman, M.v.N. (1977), "Sustaining the international economic system", Essays in International Finance, No. 121, International Finance Section, Princeton University.

Williamson, O.E. (1975), Markets and hierarchies: Analysis and antitrust implications (The Free Press, New York).

Young, L. (1979), "Ranking optimal tariffs and quotas for a large country under uncertainty", Journal of International Economics, 9:249–264.

Young, L. (1980a), "Tariffs versus quotas under uncertainty: An extension", American Economic Review, 70:522–527.

Young, L. (1980b), "Optimal revenue-raising trade restrictions under uncertainty", Journal of International Economics, 10:425–439.

Young, L. (1982), "Quantity controls vs. expenditure controls in international trade under uncertainty", Journal of International Economics, 12:143–163.

Young, L. and J.E. Anderson (1980), "The optimal policies for restricting trade under uncertainty", Review of Economic Studies, 47:927–932.

Young, L. and J.E. Anderson (1982), "Risk aversion and optimal trade restrictions", Review of Economic Studies, 49:291–305.

Young, L. and M.C. Kemp (1982), "On the optimal stabilization of internal producers' prices in international trade", International Economic Review, 23:123–141.

Chapter 10

TESTING TRADE THEORIES AND PREDICTING TRADE FLOWS

ALAN V. DEARDORFF*

University of Michigan

Contents

1.	Introduction	468
2.	How do you test a trade theory?	469
3.	Tests of the Ricardian model	475
4.	Tests of the Heckscher–Ohlin model	478
	4.1. Leontief-type analysis of the factor content of trade	480
	4.2. Regression analysis of the commodity composition of trade	485
	4.3. Tests of the Heckscher–Ohlin theorem	492
5.	Tests of technology theories of trade	493
6.	Other patterns of trade and theories to explain them	499
	6.1. Empirical regularities	500
	6.2. Gravity-type models of bilateral trade flows	503
	6.3. The Linder hypothesis	504
	6.4. Homogeneous-product explanations of intra-industry trade	506
	6.5. Product differentiation	507
	6.6. Scale economies and country size	510
7.	Conclusion	511
	References	513

*I benefited greatly from comments on earlier drafts from Robert E. Baldwin, Richard A. Brecher, W. Max Corden, Robert M. Stern and many other participants in the conference at Princeton and the Research Seminar on International Economics at Michigan. I would also like to thank Jewell Ray Bowen II for his able research assistance.

Handbook of International Economics, vol. I, Edited by R.W. Jones and P.B. Kenen
© *Elsevier Science Publishers B.V., 1984*

1. Introduction

Empirical implementation and testing of the major theories of international trade began in the early 1950s with MacDougall's (1951, 1952) application of the Ricardian model of comparative labor costs and Leontief's (1954) applications of the Heckscher–Ohlin model of factor proportions. I say "application" rather than "test" of the models because both were acknowledged then and since as being either misdirected or incomplete as tests of the models. Rather, they used the models only as the basis for their empirical analyses of trade. Nonetheless, the results of both studies were striking in what they seemed to suggest about the validity of the models upon which they were based, and they stimulated a large body of research that continues today in an effort more rigorously to test these and other theories of the determinants of international trade.[1]

Throughout this period the major obstacle to the testing of trade theories has been the difficulty of constructing tests that all would agree· were theoretically sound. The intuitive content of most trade theories is quite simple and straightforward. But empirical tests of the theories are often faulted on the grounds that they test propositions that do not derive rigorously from the theories. The reason is not usually that the empirical models are sloppy. Rather, the problem seems to lie in the theories themselves, which are seldom stated in forms that are compatible with the real world complexities that empirical research cannot escape.

These problems are most severe for the model that has also received the most attention in the literature: the Heckscher–Ohlin model. In its simplest form as exposited for example by Jones (1956–57), the Heckscher–Ohlin theorem is derived from a model of only two each of goods, countries, and factors of production. It is unclear what the theorem says should be true in the real world where there are many of all three, and it is therefore difficult to form a consensus as to what would constitute a valid test. Similar problems arise when one tries to account for intermediate goods, nontraded goods, and unbalanced trade. In each case there has been at least some confusion as to what the theory implies in the presence of these complications. Empirical tests must rely on data in which these complications are facts of life. No wonder, then, that the tests have been less than uniformly successful.

These problems and others like them provide the theme of this survey of the literature on testing trade theories. Considerable progress has been made, especially in the last few years, with refinements of the theories to improve their empirical relevance. But it remains true nonetheless that no unambiguously

---

[1] Oddly enough, the consensus today seems to favor a generalized version of the Heckscher–Ohlin model over the Ricardian model, even though in these early applications the latter seemed to perform far better than the former.

correct and conclusive test of any trade theory has been formulated and applied. Instead there have been piecemeal improvements in the empirical applications of trade theories. Together these have given us a body of evidence that, though it proves little, is highly suggestive and has fostered a consensus as to what the economic factors are that contribute most to the understanding of international trade.

I will begin this survey in Section 2 with a general discussion of the problems that arise in testing trade theories independently of the theory being tested. To the extent that many of the specific explanations of trade have a common foundation in the theory of comparative advantage, they also share some of the same empirical complications and it is useful to look at these before becoming immersed in the particular problems that arise from specific theories.

In Sections 3, 4, and 5, I review the empirical tests and implementations of, respectively, the Ricardian Theory, the Heckscher–Ohlin theory, and the technology theory. Of these, Section 4 on the Heckscher–Ohlin model is by far the most extensive.

Finally, in Section 6, I review an assortment of other approaches to trade. These include both recently articulated theories that have not yet been tested, such as the monopolistic competition model, and empirical tests that have been done without benefit of theory, such as the so-called gravity models. In both cases I will try to sketch how future research might be directed so as to fill in these gaps.

2. How do you test a trade theory?

Theories of international trade have taken a variety of forms. One would therefore not expect to be able to make general statements about how they should be tested, since surely a test of a theory should be tailored specifically to the theory itself. However there is enough similarity among the most popular theories of trade that some such general discussion is in order. This similarity, as I will explain in a moment, reflects the fact that all of these theories are particular applications or elaborations of the theory of comparative advantage. Thus the theory of comparative advantage and what is known about it provide some guidance as to how more specific explanations of international trade may be tested.

There are three questions that a theory of international trade might be expected to answer and that would seem to be easy enough to check against the data on actual trade. It may be useful to list these questions at the outset, if only to highlight how limited most theories are in this respect:

(1) *What goods* do countries trade?
(2) *With whom* do countries trade?
(3) *How much* do countries trade?

As will be seen later in this survey, empirical work has been done on all three of these questions and on combinations of them. But the fundamental theories of international trade deal only with the first.

There are several reasons for this. Many trade models start with the assumption that there are only two countries, and with that assumption the question of with whom a country trades is meaningless. But even when the models are extended to multiple countries, most assume that the products of all are identical. Thus all exports of a particular good from all countries that export it compete in a single world market and there is no way of determining bilateral trade. Realistically one might suppose that transport costs might remove this indeterminacy, the bilateral pattern of trade being determined so as to minimize transport costs. But like friction in physics, transport costs are almost universally ignored in trade models in the sanguine hope that if included they would not materially affect the results. The cost of this omission, however, is to remove bilateral trade patterns from the list of things to be explained.

The omission of transport costs also accounts for the failure of most trade models to explain adequately the volume of trade, both in particular goods and overall. Melvin (1968, p. 1265) for example has suggested that indeterminacy of the pattern of trade in a more-goods-than-factors Heckscher–Ohlin model could be removed by introducing and then minimizing transport costs. And even when there is no such indeterminacy, I doubt that most of us would take literally the apparent implications of any trade models for the volume of trade when they are based on the assumption of costless transport.

Thus, most trade models are designed to answer only the first of the three questions above: What goods do countries trade, and why? And most models explain the commodity pattern of trade in terms of the Law of Comparative Advantage: Countries tend to export those goods which have the lowest relative costs – and therefore prices – in autarky. Particular models, such as the Ricardian model, the Heckscher–Ohlin model and others, focus on particular commodity and/or country characteristics that in turn determine the relative autarky prices.[2] But with the exception of a few models that I will look at in Section 6 below, all agree that it is comparative advantage, or the structure of relative autarky prices, that is the proximate determinant of the pattern of commodity trade. Thus it is useful to begin by discussing how one might test the theory of comparative advantage.

There are two reasons why tests of the theory of comparative advantage are difficult. The first and more obvious is that relative autarky prices are not observable. Almost all countries have engaged in trade throughout history, so that

---

[2] The Ricardian model is sometimes regarded as a more general model of comparative advantage, encompassing both the labor-costs and Heckscher–Ohlin models as special cases. I will follow the more common current practice of identifying the Ricardian model as that in which labor is the only factor of production.

there is no experience with autarky from which to draw data. Even if there were, unless that experience were very recent, it would be highly unlikely that the prices that prevailed then would be the same as those that would arise now if trade were to be suspended. Yet it is only the latter that are relevant for determining the current pattern of trade.

Fortunately, however, tests of trade theories do not require that we test the theory of comparative advantage directly. The theories we are discussing here explain trade by first explaining comparative advantage itself in terms of other factors that may be observable. If such an explanation can be formulated rigorously, then it can be incorporated into the theory of comparative advantage to yield a testable proposition regarding trade. Suppose, for example, that a vector of relative autarky prices, $\tilde{p}$, can be shown in some model of an economy to be linearly related to certain characteristics of the goods contained in a matrix X as follows:

$$\tilde{p} = Xa, \tag{2.1}$$

where the coefficients in the vector a may reflect characteristics of the country relative to its trading partners. Then whatever may be the relationship between trade and $\tilde{p}$ implied by the law of comparative advantage, (2.1) implies a similar or at least easily derivable relationship between trade and the characteristics contained in a and X.

The second difficulty, however, is that the relationship between trade and $\tilde{p}$ is not well understood. That is, the Law of Comparative Advantage does not, as far as is known, imply the sort of deterministic relationship between trade and $\tilde{p}$ that would lead to a simple test.[3] It would be simplest, for example, if one could show that the volume of trade by commodity must be linearly related to $\tilde{p}$:

$$T = B'\tilde{p}, \tag{2.2}$$

where T is a vector of net exports and B is a coefficient matrix, ideally diagonal and positive. This would be the case, for example, if trade could be determined on an industry-by-industry basis by partial equilibrium supplies and demands. If $\tilde{p}$ contained the difference between domestic and foreign autarky prices in a common numeraire, then the coefficients in B would be derivable from the slopes of the supply and demand curves. In that case (2.1) and (2.2) together would

---

[3] Nonetheless many find such a relationship to be so plausible that they assume it anyway as the basis for empirical work. Balassa (1965), for example, used indices of export performance as a way of "revealing" comparative advantage. See Hillman (1980) and Bowen (1982) for critiques of this procedure.

imply a simple and linear relationship between trade and its determinants that could be tested using ordinary regression analysis.

Unfortunately, the partial equilibrium model of supply and demand is too obviously inappropriate for analysis of a country's or the world's complete pattern of trade. And the general equilibrium models that we have do not, even in simple cases, imply a relationship such as (2.2). In the Ricardian model with free trade, for example, the direction of trade depends on autarky prices but its quantity does not. Once a good is determined to be exported by a country, the quantity that it exports depends either on world demand for it or on the country's capacity to produce, whichever is smaller, and neither has much to do with autarky prices. Similar problems also arise in the Heckscher–Ohlin model when the number of goods and factors are equal, and they are made even worse when there are more goods than factors and even the direction of trade may become indeterminate.

As will be seen below, this problem has often been ignored in the literature. Many investigators have run regressions of trade on its proposed determinants as though a relationship like (2.2) were valid. But without a rigorous justification the results of such regressions are difficult to interpret since it is not known what they really represent. Also this approach invites disagreement among investigators as to the appropriate forms for their regression equations. Debates, for example, as to the appropriate form of the trade variable – gross versus net, scaled versus unscaled, value versus quantity – cannot be resolved conclusively when the regression itself has no rigorous basis in theory.

Lest we give up too easily on regression analysis, however, I should point out that the studies that have used this technique have been relatively successful in spite of its dubious theoretical heritage. In later sections I will refer to what has come to be quite a large body of literature of this type. The results in this literature are strong enough, and consistent enough, that I believe it would be foolish to dismiss them as misguided and therefore meaningless. Perhaps, then, what is needed is more effort to provide a rigorous justification for a relationship like (2.2).

This is not the place for an exploration of new models, and I would have none to offer if it were, but I would like to suggest several possibilities for modeling trade as a well-defined function of autarky prices as in (2.2). The first and most obvious would again be to allow for transport costs. However it is not sufficient merely to add constant costs of transportation to a standard trade model. That would only prevent trade at all until autarky price differences reached a threshold value, and it would leave trade unrelated to autarky prices once the threshold was surpassed. Instead one would need to assume that the costs of transportation rise with the amount transported over a particular route or between particular pairs of countries. One might argue that as trade expands it is necessary for exports to penetrate deeper and deeper into the importing country and that this is increasingly costly. With this assumption it should follow that quantities traded would depend positively on autarky price differences, though in general equilibrium there would be room for many and perhaps ambiguous cross effects as well.

Other possible avenues for modeling a functional trade-autarky-price relationship involve greater departures from standard perfectly competitive models.[4] One approach would be the so-called Armington assumption: that products of the same industry produced in different countries are viewed as imperfect substitutes by demanders.[5] Another would be to allow markets to be monopolistically competitive, as in Krugman (1979). Yet a third would be to assume that government-imposed tariff and non-tariff barriers, including the threat of such barriers being imposed, increase endogenously with the level of import penetration of domestic markets.[6] Each of these assumptions if handled carefully might lead to a functional relationship between trade and autarky prices, such as (2.2), without invalidating the standard theories of autarky prices themselves as in (2.1). If so they might provide justification for the pervasive practice of regressing trade on the determinants of comparative advantage, as well as guidance for improving the specification of such regressions.

An alternative is to try to test trade theories without reliance on a relationship like (2.2). This can be done by looking at something other than trade itself, as in the Leontief-type tests to be discussed in Section 4. Or it can be done using trade but assuming only a weak relationship between trade and factor prices. The latter is the approach taken by Harkness and Kyle (1975), and by the others following their lead in testing the Heckscher–Ohlin model, but the argument could apply to other theories of trade as well.

The idea is that, as already noted, comparative advantage and its determinants explain only the direction, not the quantity, of trade. Trade should therefore be analyzed empirically using a statistical technique that is appropriate to a model in which the dependent variable is binary rather than continuous. Such a technique is probit analysis which is based on a model in which the probability of the dependent variable being of a particular sign is related to a list of explanatory variables. As will be seen below, probit analysis and a similar technique, logit analysis, have taken a place along OLS regression analysis as standard techniques for the empirical analysis of trade.

However it is hard to see that the theoretical basis for using these bivariate techniques is really any stronger than for OLS regressions. Simple models of

[4]Without perfect competition, of course, the gains from trade are no longer assured.

[5]This assumption was used by Armington (1969) as a way of accounting for the low elasticities of demand for imports and exports that have usually been estimated. See Stern et al. (1976) for a compendium of this elasticity evidence. Variants of the Armington assumption have become a standard feature of computational models of trade such as Brown and Whalley (1980) and Deardorff and Stern (1981).

[6]Travis (1964) stresses the idea that tariffs are set in response to trade and uses this to explain the Leontief paradox.

comparative advantage determine the direction of trade unambiguously, and not probabilistically as required for probit analysis. And even when the direction of trade is theoretically uncertain as in the more-goods-than-factors Heckscher–Ohlin model, the process by which the indeterminacy is resolved is simply unknown, and not subject to any well-defined stochastic process. Perhaps the trade models could be elaborated to include a stochastic structure and so provide a firmer foundation for probit and logit tests of trade theories. But such elaboration remains to be done.

A final approach to resolving this difficulty is suggested by recent work establishing the Law of Comparative Advantage in the form of various correlations between measures of trade and of relative autarky prices. In Deardorff (1980) I used a quite general model to derive several results of this sort. At the heart of these results is the following inequality relating trade and autarky prices:

$$\tilde{p}'T < 0. \tag{2.3}$$

With various appropriate specifications of the price and trade variables this implies in turn that the two are negatively correlated.

Now (2.3) is considerably weaker than (2.2), but it nonetheless may permit us to derive testable propositions relating trade and the determinants of comparative advantage. As an almost trivial example, suppose that only one variable suffices to determine relative autarky prices, so that X in (2.1) is a vector instead of a matrix and a is a scalar. Then when (2.1) is substituted into (2.3), a can be factored out to yield:

$$\text{sign } X'T = -\text{sign } a. \tag{2.4}$$

With appropriate normalization this implies that the pattern of trade will be positively correlated with whatever it is that determines comparative advantage. This result also provides a reason for analyzing trade by means of a regression of T on X, since $X'T$ has the same sign as the OLS-estimated coefficient. Thus the regression yields useful information, even though it has not been possible to derive a linear relationship between T and X as would normally be required for the classical linear regression model.

The problem is more complicated when more than one variable is needed to determine relative autarky prices. It is still possible to substitute (2.1) into (2.3), which now yields:

$$a'X'T < 0. \tag{2.5}$$

If a, X, and T can all be observed, this is itself a testable relationship. Alternatively one can again consider regressing T on X, this time getting the following vector of estimated coefficients using OLS:

$$\hat{\beta} = (X'X)^{-1}X'T. \tag{2.6}$$

Relationship (2.5) can then be rewritten as:

$$a'(X'X)\hat{\beta} < 0, \tag{2.7}$$

which, with appropriate normalization, implies a negative correlation between the estimated coefficients from the least squares regression and a transformation of the country-specific variables that indicate where its comparative advantage should lie.

In short, the correlation relationships between autarky prices and trade permit testable propositions to be derived from any trade theory that relies on the Law of Comparative Advantage, whether or not such a theory permits one to derive a deterministic relationship between trade and its determinants. Furthermore, the running of OLS regressions of trade on its hypothesized determinants may be appropriate after all, even for theories that purport to explain only the direction, and not the quantity, of trade. For the estimated coefficients from such regressions can also be incorporated into testable propositions regarding trade.

A word of warning is in order here, however. If a regression is used only as a convenient way of testing a relationship such as (2.4) or (2.7), and without functional justification such as (2.2), then the usual OLS test statistics have only limited meaning. Without a foundation in the classical linear regression model, $\hat{\beta}$ in (2.6) is not an estimate of a "true" coefficient. Nor, therefore, does the standard error on a coefficient place bounds on the "true" value or indicate its significance. Because of our experience with such statistics they may still be of interest as descriptions of how well the data have fit together. But the true significance of the results should be judged independently of such statistics.

3. Tests of the Ricardian model

The Ricardian model attributes comparative advantage entirely to differences in labor requirements of production. In terms of the framework set out in Section 2:

$$\tilde{p} = c, \tag{3.1}$$

where c is a vector of a country's relative labor costs of production. Thus the matrix X is just the vector c and a is unity. With such a simple structure one might expect tests of the Ricardian model to be straightforward. If relative labor costs of production could be observed, a simple regression of trade on these labor costs would suffice to test the theory, just as explained in Section 2. Several problems arise, however, most having to do with the observability of c.

The first problem is implicit in the simple Ricardian model itself. With free trade the model implies complete specialization in equilibrium. A good will be produced in more than one country only if labor costs in both are the same when expressed in a common numeraire. If relative labor requirements differ between countries, as they must for the model to explain trade at all, then at most one good will be produced in common by two countries. This in turn means that the differences in labor requirements cannot be observed, since imported goods will almost never be produced in the importing country. Relative labor requirements therefore ought to be just as difficult to observe as relative autarky prices.

All of this seems irrelevant, however, since such a high degree of specialization obviously does not occur in the real world. The reason for incomplete specialization may be that the Ricardian model is simply incorrect – that something more like the Heckscher–Ohlin model is more appropriate for explaining trade. But if we are to give the Ricardian explanation of trade a chance, we must modify it so as to explain incomplete specialization without giving up relative labor requirements as the determinant of comparative advantage. I already discussed in Section 2 several ways this might be done, such as assuming increasing transport costs. If trade is sufficiently restricted that all goods continue to be produced in a trade equilibrium, then it will be possible to measure relative labor requirements after all.

A second problem with observing relative labor requirements concerns the difficulty of making international comparisons when there are many countries. Ideally one would observe and compare labor requirements in all countries of the world simultaneously, but this poses prohibitive practical difficulties. Instead it is tempting to compare labor requirements in only two countries, and this is in fact what MacDougall (1951, 1952) and others who have tested the Ricardian model have done.

The obvious procedure, based on the simple two-country Ricardian model, would be to examine the bilateral trade between two countries and see whether each country's exports to the other display lower relative labor requirements than its imports. In practice however the volume of bilateral trade is small between pairs of countries compared with their trade with the rest of the world, and the direction of that bilateral trade is difficult to ascertain since goods often flow in both directions. Therefore MacDougall chose instead to focus on two countries' exports to third markets and see whether that trade could be explained in terms of the countries' relative labor requirements.

Bhagwati (1964) has objected that there is no theoretical basis for such a test – that there is nothing in the Ricardian model to predict that a country with a greater cost advantage will export more to third markets. Actually, though, the simple Ricardian model has the even more extreme implication that the country with the greater cost advantage will be the *only* one to export to third markets. If, as I have suggested, the Ricardian model were to be extended to allow, for example, for increasing transportation costs so as to be consistent with the reality of several different-cost suppliers in the same market, then the McDougall test seems reasonable after all.

In any case, whatever may be the justification for the procedure, the results turn out to be, in Bhagwati's words, "remarkably successful,"[7] While several specific tests have been performed, the most direct has been a log linear regression of the ratio of U.S. to U.K. exports on the ratio of U.S. to U.K. labor productivities. The results, estimated by both MacDougall et al. (1962) and Stern (1962) using 1950 quantity of export data, and by Balassa (1963) using 1951 value of export data, show a consistently positive and significant correlation between these two variables.[8]

Unlike Bhagwati, I interpret these results as evidence in favor of a valid relationship. I have already noted my willingness to accept an analysis of third-country trade performance as relevant for the Ricardian model, if suitably modified to be compatible with incomplete specialization. Bhagwati (1964) did not accept this procedure, but also objected even more strongly for another reason. His own analysis of the data failed to turn up a significant positive correlation between export price ratios and appropriate ratios of labor productivity or labor costs. I disagree that this undermines the Ricardian theory of trade, which should be tested as directly as possible in terms of its ability to explain trade, not prices. Depending on how the Ricardian model is modified to be compatible with incomplete specialization, I could easily imagine that trade would tend to equalize export prices without undermining the role of comparative costs in determining trade.

However before I would accept the results of MacDougall and others as supporting the Ricardian theory, I would want to be sure that their results cannot also be explained by some other model of trade. In an interchange begun by Ford (1967) and generalized by Falvey (1981b), it has been established that other trade models are likely to predict the same relationship between labor productivities and trade that is implied by the Ricardian model. I will conclude this discussion, therefore, by showing that MacDougall's results would also be expected in the Heckscher–Ohlin model.

If factor prices were equalized by trade and if production functions were everywhere homogeneous and identical, then labor productivities would not differ

---

[7]See Bhagwai (1969, p. 16). Bhagwati also provides a convenient summary of the results.
[8]The three authors also produced some evidence relating trade to unit labor costs rather than productivities. The two would be equivalent if wages were the same in all industries, as assumed in the Ricardian model. If wages are different across industries then this is a test of a somewhat different hypothesis than the Ricardian model and the support it provides for the Ricardian model is therefore weaker.

internationally and MacDougall's analysis would have been impossible. But now suppose instead that factor prices are not equalized, in a two-factor, many-commodity Heckscher–Ohlin model. Factor price differences imply labor productivity differences in a given industry as follows:

$$\hat{x} = \theta_k \sigma \hat{\omega}, \tag{3.2}$$

where $\hat{x}$ and $\hat{\omega}$ are the log-differences of labor productivities (output per unit labor) and wage–rental ratios between countries respectively, and θ_k and σ are the capital share and elasticity of substitution in the industry.[9]

Now suppose that the more capital abundant country has a comparative advantage in more capital intensive goods, as the Heckscher–Ohlin theorem predicts. Then if σ were the same for all industries (3.2) would imply that its relative labor productivity would be positively related to capital intensity and thus to comparative advantage and trade. Likewise, in the labor abundant country, where labor is relatively cheap, labor productivities would all be smaller than abroad. But they would tend to be reduced the least in labor intensive industries, so that again relative labor productivities would be highest where there is greater comparative advantage.

Thus, the MacDougall test of the Ricardian model is deficient, in my view, not because it fails to identify a valid relationship but because the relationship is also likely to hold in the Heckscher–Ohlin model.[10] Thus it fails to distinguish between the two models.

With this in mind, I should mention one other test of the Ricardian model that has appeared more recently. McGilvray and Simpson (1973) examined the trade of the Republic of Ireland with the United Kingdom and used it to test both the Ricardian and Heckscher–Ohlin models. In rank correlations between trade and comparative labor productivities, they fairly consistently found the relationship to be insignificant but of the wrong sign. Since such a relationship finds theoretical support in both models of trade, their failure to find empirical support for it is doubly surprising.

4. Tests of the Heckscher–Ohlin model

The Heckscher–Ohlin theorem says that countries will tend to export those goods which use relatively intensively their relatively abundant factors of production. In

---

[9] Equation (3.2) is obtained by differentiating the production function to get $\hat{x} = \theta_k \hat{k}$, where k is the capital–labor ratio, and combining this with the definition of the elasticity of substitution, $\hat{k} = \sigma \hat{\omega}$.

[10] That it need not necessarily be the case can be seen from (3.2) if the elasticity of substitution differs systematically across industries, being largest in the industries that are least capital intensive. However, if substitution elasticities are independent of capital intensities, or only weakly correlated, then this relationship would be expected to hold. Falvey (1981b), who derives the required relationship in more detail, also provides some empirical evidence that this is in fact the case.

the $2 \times 2 \times 2$ model, it says simply that the capital-abundant country will export the capital-intensive good. The theorem is therefore a three-way relationship – among factor abundance, factor intensity, and trade – and a proper test of it must include all three. Few if any investigators have managed this, and what we have instead is therefore a large body of evidence that is suggestive but hardly conclusive as to the empirical validity of the Heckscher–Ohlin theorem.

The theorem has actually been stated and applied in two forms. What I stated above has been called the "commodity version" of the Heckscher–Ohlin theorem. It has been somewhat difficult to prove with any generality as a theoretical proposition.[11] As a result, attention has often been directed to an alternative "factor content version" of the Heckscher–Ohlin theorem. This says that countries will tend to export the services of their abundant factors, embodied as factor content in the goods they trade. The standard proof is due to Vanek (1968), but Travis (1964) and Melvin (1968) also deserve credit, as does Leamer (1980a) for an important extension to a model with unbalanced trade.

Empirical application of the theorem has also been of two forms, corresponding roughly to the two theoretical propositions even though much of the empirical work predated the contributions to theory. Leontief's (1954) classic result may be interpreted as an application of the factor content version. His paradoxical conclusion led to numerous attempts to replicate his work in other contexts and the Leontief-type test continues today, though in a modified form, to be a standard method for the analysis of trade. I will devote the first subsection below to such tests.

Those who have wished to focus more directly on the commodity composition of trade, however, have had to take another approach. Commonly they regress some measure of trade performance on measures either of factor intensity or factor abundance, so as to assess the importance of these variables in determining trade. Those regression analyses have also been used a great deal and I will devote a second subsection below to considering them.

Before proceeding, though, I should address an issue that arises in both kinds of empirical analysis. This concerns whether the factor intensities and factor contents in the two versions of the theorem are to reflect only direct inputs or should instead be based on "direct-plus-indirect," or gross, input–output coefficients. At one level the issue seems to depend on the empirical question of whether inputs are or are not tradable. Factors required for producing a non-traded input should surely be accounted for in assessing the potential for trade in a good, since the costs of these factors will have to be passed through. For inputs that are available as imports, on the other hand, this does not seem necessary. Intuitively a country might have a comparative advantage in one stage of producing a product even though earlier stages require unduly scarce resources. If the semiprocessed

---

[11]See, however, Deardorff (1982) where a general statement of the commodity version is shown to hold as an average relationship among the variables.

input can be obtained cheaply through trade, then it might pay to import it, process it, and export the result, even though the gross factor intensity of the product seems inappropriate.

However on the basis of the framework laid out in Section 2, it is clear that gross factor intensities are the appropriate determinant of trade, since it is these that determine autarky prices. Also, I have been able in Deardorff (1982) to generalize both versions of the theorem, and the concept of factor intensity that turns out to work in these generalizations is again a gross one. In the discussions below the reader should therefore assume unless told otherwise that factor intensities are of the gross, or direct-plus-indirect, variety.[12]

4.1. Leontief-type analysis of the factor content of trade

Leontief obtained his classic "paradox" when he used an input–output table for the U.S. economy to measure the capital and labor embodied in representative bundles of U.S. exports and import substitutes. He found, to everyone's surprise, that the ratio of capital to labor embodied in U.S. exports was smaller than that embodied in import substitutes. His was not a test of the Heckscher–Ohlin theorem, since he did not measure factor endowments. Leontief himself tended to accept the theorem and therefore interpreted his results as demonstrating that the U.S. is in some sense well endowed with labor. But subsequent literature has so often referred to his result as a paradox, that this interpretation has apparently not been accepted.

Leontief's results led to a spate of objections to his methodology, but his paradoxical result has, until recently, survived what minor improvements in his technique were needed. The reader can consult the surveys by Bhagwati (1964) and Stern (1975) for more detail on these issues. Leontief's basic methodology has been reapplied for more recent years by Baldwin (1971), Mitchell (1975) and Stern and Maskus (1981) among others and the results have typically reaffirmed the paradox for the early years but found that it may have disappeared by 1970. A sample of these results will be reported below. The methodology has also been applied to a number of other countries, in some cases again with paradoxical results.

The main byproduct of Leontief's results and the debate that followed has been on the theoretical front. The Heckscher–Ohlin theorem itself has been extended to allow for additional factors beyond just capital and labor. Most of these theoretical developments need not concern us here as they are covered elsewhere in this volume.[13]

---

[12] This agrees with the conclusion of Hamilton and Svensson (1982).

[13] DeMarchi (1976) discusses several paths that the trade literature has followed, some in response to Leontief's findings, others apparently in spite of them.

An understanding of Leontief's methodology and its implications requires a brief review of the factor content version of the Heckscher–Ohlin theorem.[14] Let the matrix A, with elements a_{kj}, represent the quantities of factors k used in producing a unit of output of goods, j. Suppose that, due to factor price equalization and internationally identical homogeneous technologies, these technical coefficients are the same everywhere in the world. If T_i is a vector of country i's net commodity trade, then AT_i is a vector representing the country's net trade in embodied factor services. Letting E_i and E be vectors of factor endowments for country i and for the world as a whole and assuming that all countries allocate expenditure identically, it can be shown that:

$$AT_i = E_i - Ew_i, \tag{4.1}$$

where w_i is a scalar representing country i's share of world expenditure. If trade is balanced, so that each country's expenditure equals its factor income, then w_i is country i's share of world factor endowments. It follows directly from (4.1) that if a country is endowed with more (less) than its share of a particular factor, then it will be a net exporter (importer) of the services of that factor as embodied in its trade.

It is this relationship that Leontief's paradoxical result seems to have violated. If, as commonly supposed, the U.S. is capital abundant and labor scarce relative to the rest of the world, then according to this result it should embody more capital in its exports than in its imports, and less labor. This would imply a higher capital–labor ratio in exports than in imports, contrary to what Leontief observed.

In response to this paradox various investigators have suggested that U.S. trade could be better explained in terms of factors other than capital and labor. Natural resources have been singled out for special treatment on the grounds that certain categories of trade depend more on the availability of natural resources than on the subtleties of their capital and labor intensities.[15] And more generally, a number of studies have pointed to skilled labor, or human capital, as a factor distinct from physical capital and unskilled labor, and have indicated that this may be the primary source of U.S. comparative advantage.[16]

Allowance for more than two factors is usually done using regression analysis, and so will be considered more fully below. At this point I want to consider only whether acknowledgement of additional factors of production can in theory explain Leontief's paradoxical results regarding capital and labor. The answer, I believe, is no.

[14] This discussion follows Leamer and Bowen (1981).
[15] See Vanek (1963).
[16] Keesing (1965, 1966) found labor skills to be an important determinant of U.S. export performance, while Kenen (1965) focused on a measure of human capital.

Suppose we could agree that some factor, such as human capital, is relatively more abundant in the U.S. than are both physical capital and labor. We might then find the U.S. to be an importer of both capital and labor services, in quantities that depend on the total importance of capital and labor in the world economy, and there would be no presumption that the ratio of capital to labor in exports would be either higher or lower than in imports. The paradox seems no longer paradoxical.

But Leontief did not measure only the ratios of capital to labor in trade. Instead, for equal values of exports and import substitutes, he found more labor in exports than in imports and more capital in imports than in exports. If trade were balanced one could derive from (4.1) that the U.S. must be endowed with a higher fraction of the world's labor than its capital, and the paradox remains. Thus, no matter how much our understanding of trade has improved as a result of accounting for the role of other factors of production such as human capital, these explanations have not helped at all to alter the seemingly inappropriate implication of Leontief's results for the U.S. endowments of capital and labor.[17]

An important step toward resolving the paradox was provided recently by Leamer (1980a) who noted that the U.S. in Leontief's data was a net exporter of both capital and labor services. This could have happened either because U.S. trade was unbalanced, or because factors other than capital and labor were involved. Consider the case when trade is not balanced. Eq. (4.1) is still correct, but its interpretation differs. Letting Y_i and Y be *GNP* for country i and the world respectively, and letting B_i be country i's balance of trade, the country's share of world expenditure can be written as:

$$w_i = (Y_i - B_i)/Y. \tag{4.2}$$

Together with (4.1) it follows that a trade surplus, for example, makes it possible for a country to be a net exporter even of the services of factors with which it is relatively poorly endowed. And Leamer shows by counter example that when this happens, the ratios of factors embodied in exports and imports need bear no particular relationship to relative factor endowments. Thus a capital abundant country need not, after all, embody a higher ratio of capital to labor in its exports than its imports and Leontief's results are not paradoxical at all.

Instead Leamer shows that a valid test of the pattern of unbalanced trade must be stated in terms of the factor ratios embodied in production versus consumption, rather than exports versus imports. Taking this approach to Leontief's data he finds that the U.S. was a net exporter of both labor and capital services and

---

[17]Allowing for human capital can resolve this paradox if it is viewed not as an additional factor but as more of the same factor, capital. This would require, however, that human and physical capital be perfect substitutes, and this seems implausible. Also, the regression analyses of Stern (1976) and Branson and Monoyios (1977) demonstrate the inappropriateness of such aggregation.

that the capital–labor ratio embodied in production was indeed greater than that embodied in consumption. The presumed abundance of U.S. capital relative to labor is supported after all and the paradox disappears.

Most recently, however, Brecher and Choudhri (1982) have pointed out that a slightly different paradox still exists in Leontief's data. They show, by a simple manipulation of eq. (4.1) applied to labor, that a country can be a net exporter of labor services only if its expenditure per worker is less than in the rest of the world. Citing data that the latter is far from true for the U.S., Brecher and Choudhri therefore argue that Leamer's observation that the U.S. was a net exporter of labor services in Leontief's data itself constitutes a paradox.

A selection of the results of Leontief and others is provided in Table 4.1. Each column shows, for the particular study selected, various measures of factor content of trade, production and consumption. Leontief's initial results, and the original paradox, are in the first column. The ratio of capital labor ratios in imports and exports is shown in row (3c). The value of 1.30 for 1947 is dramatically larger than one, indicating the paradox of relatively capital intensive imports. Subsequent studies by Leontief (1956) and Baldwin (1971) are also reported in that row and reconfirm the paradox with both 1951 and 1962 trade. However, still more recent studies typified by Stern and Maskus (1981) show the disappearance of the paradox in more recent years.[18] The table also shows another result that has been found by some but not all investigators: that the ratio in row (3c) falls below one when natural resource industries are excluded.

Column (2) of the table shows Leamer's calculations, from Leontief's data, of the factor intensities of production and consumption in 1947. As shown in rows (3e) and (3f), U.S. production was slightly more capital intensive than was consumption in 1947. These calculations were also made for later years by Stern and Maskus (1981). They too failed to find a paradox with 1972 data, but, while it is not reported here, their calculation for 1958 was paradoxical in spite of using Leamer's method.

Finally, the indicator of paradox stressed by Brecher and Choudhri (1982) can be seen in row (1d), where the U.S. is shown as a net exporter of labor services in 1947. This paradox too seems to disappear by 1972, when Stern and Maskus found the sign to be reversed, although Brecher and Choudhri would argue that the *size* of U.S. net imports of labor services is still paradoxically low.

Table 4.1 also shows two sets of calculations showing the human capital intensity of trade. While different measures of human capital were used by Baldwin and by Stern and Maskus, both found, in row (5c), that imports embody less of it relative to labor than do exports. Thus whatever may be the roles of physical capital and labor in determining U.S. comparative advantage, it seems

---

[18]Baldwin's (1979) re-examination of 1969 U.S. trade data had also shown the paradox beginning to disappear.

Table 4.1

Selected estimates of the factor content (direct plus indirect) of U.S. trade

Author (date)		Leontief (1954)	Leamer (1980)	Leontief (1956)[b]		Baldwin (1971)		Stern and Maskus (1981)	
Year of trade data		1947	1947	1951		1962		1972	
Year of input data		1947	1947	1947		1958		1972	
Coverage		All industries	All industries	All industries	Excl. N.R.[a]	All industries	Excl. N.R.[a]	All industries	Excl. N.R.[a]
1. Labor:									
(a) Imports	(Man years/$million)	170		168	207	119	106	96	29
(b) Exports	(Man years/$million)	182		174	224	131	107	99	24
(c) Imports/exports	(Ratio)	0.93		0.96	0.92	0.91	0.99	0.98	1.18
(d) Net exports	(Million man years)		1.99					-0.43	
(e) Production	(Million man years)		47.27					228.52	
(f) Consumption	(Million man years)		45.28					228.95	
2. Capital:[c]									
(a) Imports	($thousand/$million)	3091		2303	2093	2132	1259	1368	497
(b) Exports	($thousand/$million)	2551		2257	2577	1876	1223	1478	455
(c) Imports/exports	(Ratio)	1.21		1.02	0.81	1.14	1.03	0.92	1.09
(d) Net exports	($billion)		23.45					-2.26	
(e) Production	($billion)		328.52					3163.35	
(f) Consumption	($billion)		305.07					3165.61	
3. Capital / Labor:									
(a) Imports	($thousand/man year)	18.1		13.7	10.1	18.0	11.9	14.2	17.3
(b) Exports	($thousand/man year)	14.0		13.0	11.5	14.2	11.5	15.0	18.7
(c) Imports/exports	(Ratio)	1.30		1.06	0.88	1.27	1.04	0.95	0.93
(d) Net exports	($thousand/man year)		11.8					5.25	
(e) Production	($thousand/man year)		6.9					13.84	
(f) Consumption	($thousand/man year)		6.7					13.83	
4. Human Capital:[d]									
(a) Imports	($thousand/$million)					1226	1187	5046	1553
(b) Exports	($thousand/$million)					1376	1305	5245	1480
(c) Imports/exports	(Ratio)					0.89	0.91	0.96	1.05
(d) Net exports	($billion)							-16.18	
(e) Production	($billion)							11,184.59	
(f) Consumption	($billion)							11,200.77	
5. Human Capital / Labor:									
(a) Imports	($thousand/man year)					10.3	11.2	52.4	54.2
(b) Exports	($thousand/man year)					10.5	12.2	53.2	60.7
(c) Imports/exports	(Ratio)					0.97	0.92	0.99	0.89
(d) Net exports	($thousand/man year)							37.62	
(e) Production	($thousand/man year)							48.94	
(f) Consumption	($thousand/man year)							48.92	

[a] Excluded natural-resource sectors differ slightly across studies. See original sources for details.

[b] Leontief (1956) used input coefficients that include capital replacement.

[c] Capital requirements reported from Baldwin (1971) are on a net basis, while those from Stern and Maskus (1981) are gross.

[d] Human capital requirements reported for Baldwin (1971) are total costs of education, while those of Stern and Maskus are discounted industry wage differentials.

clear that human capital intensity has a positive effect. There will be more evidence on this point in the next section.

What then is the current state of the evidence as far as the Leontief paradox is concerned? As an empirical phenomenon in any of several forms, it seems to have disappeared by the early 1970s. Still, its stubborn persistence in the data from the earlier decades continues to cast doubt on the overall validity and usefulness of the Heckscher–Ohlin model of trade. Leamer's (1980a) contribution showed that Leontief's original observation was not, after all, inconsistent with that model. But his result also means that the Heckscher–Ohlin *theorem* as to the determinants of trade, as it is usually understood, is not even theoretically valid when there is unbalanced trade. Furthermore, the model itself is still contradicted empirically in some years, as Brecher and Choudhri (1982) especially have shown. A full understanding of U.S. postwar trade seems therefore to require some departure from the Heckscher–Ohlin assumptions.

4.2. Regression analysis of the commodity composition of trade

Analysis of the commodity composition of trade in terms of a generalized factor proportions model is most readily done via regressions of trade on its determinants. The justification for such regressions has already been sketched in Section 2 presuming only that one can establish a relationship like (2.1) between autarky prices and factor proportions. This is not difficult, especially if we consider the problem in the context of a relatively simple model.

Suppose, then, that preferences and production functions are given by the following Cobb–Douglas functions, identical in all countries, for n goods and m factors:

$$U = \prod_{j=1}^{n} X_j^{\alpha_j}, \tag{4.3}$$

$$X_j = \prod_{i=1}^{m} \left(L_{ij} \right)^{\theta_{ij}}, \tag{4.4}$$

where U is utility, X_j is output and consumption of good j, L_{ij} is the amount of factor i employed in producing good j, and α_j, θ_{ij} are non-negative fractions. With the additional assumptions of full employment of fixed endowments of the factors, $\bar{L}_i$, plus perfect competition, autarky prices can be derived as:

$$\ln p_j = A_j - \sum_{i=1}^{m} \theta_{ij} \ln \bar{L}_i, \tag{4.5}$$

where

$$A_j = \ln \bar{Y} - \sum_{i=1}^{m} \theta_{ij} \ln \left(\theta_{ij} \Big/ \sum_{k=1}^{n} \alpha_k \theta_{ik} \right), \tag{4.6}$$

and $\bar{Y}$ is nominal GNP.[19] Using as a basis for comparison the equilibrium prices in the world as a whole assuming free trade of both goods and factors, autarky prices for country c relative to the world, w, can be written as follows:

$$\ln\left(p_j^c / p_j^w \right) = \sum_{i=1}^{m} \theta_{ij} \left[\ln(\bar{Y}^c / \bar{Y}^w) - \ln(\bar{L}_i^c / \bar{L}_i^w) \right]. \tag{4.7}$$

This is a linear form relating relative autarky prices on the left to a matrix of factor intensities, θ_{ij}, and the measure of relative factor abundance shown in square brackets. This can play the role of eq. (2.1) in Section 2 and thus motivates the analysis of trade by means of multiple regression of trade on factor intensities.
  A typical regression equation might take the following form:

$$T_j = \beta_1 \theta_{1j} + \cdots + \beta_m \theta_{mj} + u_j, \qquad j=1,\ldots,n, \tag{4.8}$$

where u_j is a stochastic disturbance term. Quite a number of studies have appeared reporting regressions of this type, and a sample of these will be reported below. These studies have not always agreed, however, on the precise form that (4.8) should take, in terms of the definitions and measurement of the variables it contains, and I will examine a few of these issues first before discussing the specific studies.

4.2.1. Measurement of factor intensity

As derived above, the factor intensity variables, θ_{ij}, are pure numbers representing factor shares, and these by definition sum over i to unity if all factors are considered. Until recently, however, most studies have used factor ratios, rather

---

[19] This is easily derived by first solving for equilibrium factor prices, w_i, from the factors' shares of GNP implied by the Cobb–Douglas functions:

$$w_i L_i = \sum_{j=1}^{n} \alpha_j \theta_{ij} \bar{Y}.$$

These can then be substituted into the Cobb–Douglas unit cost functions:

$$c_j = \prod_{i=1}^{m} \left(w_i / \theta_{ij} \right)^{\theta_{ij}},$$

and set equal to prices to yield, with some manipulation, (4.5).

than factor shares, as the independent variables in this equation. With labor in the denominators of these ratios, as it normally is, this is equivalent to dividing (4.8) throughout by the labor share and incorporating factor prices into the coefficients to be estimated. This however also alters the dependent variable and the error term, in ways that seem undesirable. It is notable that one of the most recent regression studies, by Harkness (1978), does use factor shares instead of factor ratios as independent variables.

4.2.2. Selection of the trade variable

Because of the uncertainty regarding the form of the link between comparative advantage and trade, it is not surprising that a variety of specifications of the dependent variable in this regression has appeared in the literature. The most common is net exports, but separate regressions for gross exports and for imports have also been attempted. Also I have already noted the procedure of Harkness and Kyle (1975) who essentially used only the sign of net exports as the dependent variable. My own preference would be for the simple use of net exports, on the grounds that gross exports, if they behave much differently from net exports, reflect the phenomenon of intraindustry trade about which the standard factor proportions model has little to say.

4.2.3. Scaling of the trade variable

The volume of trade in any particular good depends rather obviously on the importance of that good in world markets. No degree of comparative advantage will permit a country to export much of a good that nobody wants. This suggests, quite properly, that the trade variable in (4.8) should include some sort of scaling in order to normalize for world market size. Unfortunately, while scaling has often been done, the method used has usually been to divide by industry shipments in the exporting country.[20] It is hard to see how this could be appropriate, since it artificially reduces the apparent trade flow in precisely those industries where comparative advantage is strongest and a great deal is produced. It would be preferable to use some measure of the size of the world market for scaling purposes.

4.2.4. Heteroscedasticity

A related issue is that the variance of the error term in (4.8) is likely to be related to industry size. The appropriate correction involves scaling the entire

---

[20]An alternative has been to regress unscaled trade on the total employment of all factors, rather than on factor ratios. Relative to scaled regressions on factor ratios, this procedure is equivalent to using industry employment, instead of shipments, as a scaling variable and is open to the same objections.

equation – not just the dependent variable – by a measure of industry size. This should be less of a problem if scaling of the trade variable has already been done appropriately as described in the preceding paragraph. But if evidence of hetero-scedasticity persists, then a further scaling of the regression by industry ship-ments, or their square root, may be appropriate.

4.2.5. Cross-commodity versus cross-country regression

My discussion so far has implicitly assumed that the objective was to explain, for a given country, its pattern of trade in goods. This has indeed been the objective of the majority of studies that have appeared, and they have therefore run regressions on a cross-section of industries for particular countries. However there has also been some effort to determine, for particular goods, which countries are most likely to export or import them. Thus, for example, Leamer (1974) used Bayesian techniques to estimate equations across countries relating imports of particular goods to characteristics of the countries.

Table 4.2 reports representative results of several of the more important studies which have applied regression analysis to trade. While most of these studies fitted several alternative forms of their equations, I have reported only one for each. To facilitate comparison among them, I have not always selected the equation that was most preferred by the author(s) of each study, but rather that which is most comparable to the others in terms of trade and factor coverage. For each study, a column of Table 4.2 reports the estimated coefficients from one of its estimated equations, together with information on the specification of the equation, the estimation method, and the date and level of disaggregation of the trade data that were used. In all cases, the trade to be explained was U.S. net exports.

The first of these studies, and the one which pioneered the technique of analysis, was Baldwin's (1971) now classic article. As reported above, Baldwin began by replicating Leontief's results with more recent data, and he provided an excellent review of the literature that had attempted to explain these results. In order to evaluate some of these explanations, he then ran regressions of U.S. net exports by industry, either bilaterally vis-à-vis particular trading partners or multilaterally, on various suggested determinants of comparative advantage. Table 4.2 reports one of the multilateral regressions, in which trade was explained by capital–labor ratios and the shares of each industry's labor force in each of several skill groups. In other regressions, not reported here, Baldwin replaced these labor skill variables with others representing either the years or the costs of education. In all cases he found, as in the first row of Table 4.2, that the physical capital–labor ratio was related negatively and very significantly to U.S. net exports. Thus the Leontief paradox was confirmed using a quite different mode of analysis.

Table 4.2
Selected estimated equations to explain cross-sections of U.S. net exports

	Baldwin (1971)	Harkness and Kyle (1975)	Branson and Monoyios (1977)	Harkness (1978)	Stern and Maskus (1981)	Hilton (1981)
Dependent variable	Adjusted[a] net exports	Sign of adjusted[a] net exports	Net exports	Net exports per final output	Net exports	Sign of net exports
Year of trade data	1962	1962	1963	1958	1976	1972
Year of input data	1958	1958	1963	1958	1976	1972
Coverage	50 1958-USIO industries	45 1958-USIO non-resource industries	90 3-digit SITC industries	60 1958-USIO industries	128 3-digit SIC industries	52 1972-USIO Manuf. indus.
Estimation method	Regression	Logit	Regression	Regression	Regression, scaled	Probit
Measure of factor intensity	Total[b] factors per worker	Total[b] factors per worker	Direct factors employed	Total[b] factor share	Direct factors employed	Total[b] factor share
Estimated Coefficients:						
Physical capital	−1.37**	7.762*	−0.05*	10.208**	−0.08*	−0.63
Human capital			0.04**		0.06**	8.40**
Labor categories:						
Scientists and engineers	7011*			8.087**		
Other prof. and managers	−1473	0.785*		−6.048		
Clerical and sales	71			3.860		
Craftsmen and foremen	1578*	0.682*	−0.67**	4.672**	−2.83**	−3.95**
Operatives	−248			0.465		
Unskilled and service	−761	−0.045		−3.889**		
Farmers and farm workers	845**			−0.731*	−18.54	
Constant		3.78	18.54			
Other	Indices of Scale and Unionization			Various Land and Natural Resource Shares		
R^2 or χ^2 (degrees of freedom)	.44**	37.61(9)**	0.45**	0.948**	0.17***	15.32(2)**

[a]Adjusted net exports are industry exports per $-million of total exports minus industry imports per $-million of total imports.
[b]"Total" factors include direct plus indirect factor requirements.
*, **indicate 95 and 99 percent level of significance, respectively.

489

Baldwin also found that skill and education variables tend to perform well in explaining U.S. trade. His results here are not as clear cut as those of later studies, perhaps because he did not focus directly on a measure of human capital. But he did find a clear positive role for education and for certain skill intensities in determining U.S net exports.

At about the same time, Branson and Junz (1971) did a similar study, not reported here, using estimates of human capital per man, rather than skill variables, to explain U.S. net exports. Following Kenen (1965), they constructed estimates of human capital by capitalizing the difference between an industry wage estimate and an estimate of the economy-wide unskilled wage. Their results were similar to Baldwin's and included a clearly significant coefficient on human capital per man. The results continued to be similar when Branson (1971) repeated the exercise using a scaled dependent variable for reasons explained above. He used gross trade – exports plus imports – to scale the net export variable and found that this improved the significance of the earlier results and strengthened the conclusion that U.S. exports are intensive in human capital, rather than physical capital.

One of these conclusions appeared to be reversed by Harkness and Kyle (1975) who used logit analysis to estimate an otherwise fairly similar equation. As shown in the second column of Table 4.2, they found a positive and significant coefficient on the capital labor ratio. This result has not, however, been replicated by subsequent research, and given the ambiguous justification for the technique that I noted in Section 2, it is probably best not to take it too seriously.

Alternative specifications and estimation methods were explored extensively by Branson and Monoyios (1977). They regressed net exports on industry levels of physical capital, human capital, and labor, plus a constant term. They also experimented with the use of skilled and unskilled labor variables and with the use of a shipments variable either as an additional explanatory variable or to scale the equations to correct for heteroscedasticity. Finally, Branson and Monoyios also experimented with the use of probit analysis in the spirit of Harkness and Kyle. In their results, none of these complications change the basic message. As shown in the third column of Table 4.2, U.S. net exports are best explained by human capital intensity. The effects of both physical capital and raw labor are usually negative and often significantly so.

The same conclusions were reached and strengthened by Stern and Maskus (1981), with some refinement of the technique. They repeated the analysis for each year from 1958 through 1976. The results for 1976, shown in the fifth column of Table 4.2, are typical. Over time, the negative coefficient on labor was found to grow in both size and significance. Stern and Maskus also experimented with probit analysis and were unable by that means alone to obtain a positive coefficient on the capital–labor ratio, though the sign did become positive when natural-resource industries were excluded.

Harkness (1978) was the first to use factor shares as the measure of factor intensity. He included shares of some 16 different factors of production in his regressions, and there is room to report only a few of these in Table 4.2. While Harkness himself did not focus attention on this result, it is notable that his coefficient on physical capital was both positive and highly significant.[21] This seems likely to be a result of his inclusion of a number of natural resource intensities among his explanatory variables. Given their close association with only a few industries, this is very similar simply to excluding natural-resource-intensive industries from the regression altogether. Thus this result reflects the tendency, already noted, for the Leontief paradox to be reversed when natural-resource-intensive industries are excluded.

The final column of Table 4.2 shows one set of estimates obtained recently by Hilton (1981). It is of interest because it too uses factor shares as explanatory variables and also because it fails to confirm Harkness and Kyle's reversal of the Leontief paradox using a binary estimation technique.

However, the results in Table 4.2 are not those that Hilton himself prefers. He argues persuasively on theoretical grounds that the Heckscher–Ohlin theorem should not be applied on a multilateral basis, but rather that only bilateral trade flows should correspond to factor intensities. The argument is most easily seen in a world of two factors, many goods, and many countries. A country of intermediate capital abundance relative to the world would be expected to export goods of intermediate capital intensity and to import both more capital-intensive and less capital-intensive goods from different countries abroad.[22] Its total trade would therefore not be readily explainable in terms of capital intensity, but its trade with individual trading partners would.

While it is not obvious that this argument is relevant for the U.S., where factor abundance is presumably extreme rather than intermediate, Hilton nonetheless prefers to estimate equations explaining bilateral trade, and only reports the multilateral results of Table 4.2 for comparison with other studies. Surprisingly his estimates for U.S. bilateral trade with each of eight countries and regions all yield positive coefficients on the capital share, several of which are at least mildly significant. Since this contradicts the results of bilateral regressions run by Baldwin (1971), this is a result which deserves further attention to clarify what is going on.

Other work has been done along these lines and I can only briefly allude to some of it. Studies of this sort have been done for other countries than the U.S. For example, Stern (1976) looked at West Germany and Heller (1976) looked at Japan. Most recently, Baldwin (1979) repeated his earlier analysis on some 28

---

[21] This was true only when inventories were excluded from capital.
[22] See, for example, Krueger (1977).

countries. Finally, mention should also be made again of Leamer's (1974, 1980b) innovative analyses of patterns of trade across countries.[23]

4.3.   Tests of the Heckscher – Ohlin theorem

As I noted at the outset of this section, the Heckscher–Ohlin theorem is a relationship among *three* variables: factor abundance, factor intensity, and trade. Most of the studies reviewed so far have looked at only two of these – usually trade and factor intensities – and have therefore not even pretended to *test* the theorem.[24] This is true of both the Leontief-type measurements of factor content and of the regressions of trade on factor intensities à la Baldwin and others. In both cases a true test of the Heckscher–Ohlin theorem would require that their results be combined with data on factor endowments to see whether the two together are consistent. This is just as true of cross-country studies of trade patterns such as Leamer (1974), who did use data on factor endowments but not on factor intensities. All of this work is very useful in describing the determinants of trade, and perhaps even in predicting trade flows, but as a body of evidence actually testing the Heckscher–Ohlin theorem it is at best only suggestive.[25]

Even given data on all three components of the theorem, it is not entirely clear what an acceptable test would be. The factor content version is likely to be the easiest, since its simple theoretical derivation implies that the ranking of factors by the factor content of trade should be the same as the ranking of factor endowments. With trade impediments and unequal factor prices the theorem weakens to require only a positive correlation between these variables, and this correlation is not difficult to calculate.

Something like this correlation has been calculated by Hufbauer (1970). However because he viewed physical capital and human capital as the subjects of separate theories of international trade, rather than as interacting with each other and with other factors in a many-factor version of a single model, he did not compute quite the correct correlations for a test of that generalized model. He did find, for example, a significant positive correlation across countries between capital per man embodied in exports and the national endowments of fixed capital per man. He also found similar results for the export embodiment and

---

[23] In addition, the same framework has been used to analyze problems other than trade in goods. Baldwin (1979) extended it to direct investment, while Sapir (1982) applied cross-country regressions to trade in services.

[24] Heller (1976), in his study of Japanese trade, is an exception. He runs a Leontief test for several years from 1956 to 1968 and compares the results to changes over time in Japan's factor endowments. The dramatic increase in Japan's capital abundance over this period shows up, however, in increases in the relative capital content of both Japan's exports and imports. The factor content of net trade does not seem to show such a clear pattern.

[25] One can, however, view these studies as tests of the *joint* hypothesis that the Heckscher–Ohlin theorem is valid and that some relationship among factor endowments holds.

national endowments of labor skills.[26] However he never ran his correlations across factors of production, or across both factors and countries simultaneously, as the argument in the multifactor model would suggest. Similar results have been obtained by Bowen (1983) who also ran such correlations on trade and endowment data from several years and compared them.

So far as I know, the only other author who has claimed to do a proper test of the Heckscher–Ohlin theorem is Harkness (1978). He took greater pains than usual to provide theoretical motivation for both a Leontief-type multi-factor analysis and for a regression analysis. He then used the former as a measure of relative factor endowments and tested the Heckscher–Ohlin theorem by correlating these with the estimated coefficients from his regression. The latter procedure is analogous to that suggested by my result in Section 2, inequality (2.7). But as (2.7) suggests and as Leamer and Bowen (1981) have pointed out, the connection between factor endowments and the regression coefficients of trade on factor intensities is not so simple and direct unless $X'X$, where X is a matrix of factor shares, has very special properties.

Even more serious, it seems to me, is Harkness' reliance on a Leontief-type test as his source for data on factor endowments in a test like this. He ends up correlating two sets of numbers that were themselves calculated from the same set of data on trade and factor intensities. Were it not for the problems Leamer and Bowen, and also Anderson (1981), point out, he could hardly fail to get a positive correlation regardless of whether the underlying data conforms with the theory. Therefore while I am impressed with the bulk of the evidence that Harkness presents, and with the care he has taken at least to attempt a theoretical motivation of his procedure, I do not regard his results as telling us anything at all about the validity of the Heckscher–Ohlin theorem.[27]

5. Tests of technology theories of trade

Partly in response to the difficulties posed by the Leontief paradox, and partly out of efforts to explain trade and investment in particular industries where technological differences seemed of obvious importance, the past two decades have seen the development of several technology-oriented theories of trade. The common feature of these theories is an emphasis on technological change and the resulting pattern of trade in new products. While the details of this process differ among

---

[26]Yahr found a similar relationship for labor skills. While she did not look directly at trade, her analysis of value added and skill endowments across countries does support the view that countries poorly endowed with labor skills tend to specialize in low-skill industries.

[27]Though apparently not intended as a test of the theorem, Balassa's (1979) paper does correct this deficiency by regressing estimated factor intensity coefficients for 36 countries on separate measures of their factor endowments. The results provide encouraging support for the factor proportions theory.

theories, all are apparently designed to explain the pattern of trade of the United States, and tests of the theories using U.S. data have tended to be successful.

The first major theoretical effort to explain observed trade patterns in terms of technical progress was the technology gap model sketched by Posner (1961).[28] He observed that as new products and processes are continually being developed, the country in which these innovations occur will for a time enjoy a technological advantage over its trading partners in these particular products. This advantage will last only until the new technology is imitated in other countries, but before that happens the innovating country may export the good even though it has no obvious basis for comparative advantage in terms of factor intensities and endowments. Over time, each innovation is eventually diffused around the world and the initial advantage is lost, but as progress continues new discoveries are constantly being made and there exists a constantly changing list of new products in which the innovating country enjoys a comparative advantage.

While Posner (1961) did not lay out a formal model, his theory can readily be viewed as a generalization of the Ricardian model. Trade takes place because of differences across countries in technologies. Posner's contribution was to describe the dynamic process by which this progress is continually renewed in different products, at the same time that existing technologies are being transferred to other countries. His model was further elaborated by Hufbauer (1966) and has recently been formalized by Krugman (1982) who has put it in the context of Dornbusch, Fischer and Samuelson's (1977) Ricardian model with a continuum of goods.

A possible drawback of the technology gap model is that it fails to explain why an innovation, once discovered, is not taken advantage of in the least cost location. One can easily understand why the innovating party itself would refuse to share its knowledge with others. But in today's world of multinational firms, why does the innovating firm not itself go abroad immediately to produce where costs are lowest, rather than producing in the country where the innovation takes place as Posner suggests? Two different answers to this question have been provided, along with further structure on why and where the innovations themselves take place.

Hirsch (1967) follows Kuznets (1953) in arguing that new products go through a cycle of systematic changes in technology. New products at first require large amounts of skilled labor in their production and development. As larger quantities are demanded, however, more capital intensive production techniques become appropriate. Finally, when products mature and become standardized, the production process becomes routine, and less skilled labor can play a greater and

---

[28] There had, of course, been numerous previous attempts to introduce technological change into an otherwise Heckscher–Ohlin model. A classic example is Findlay and Grubert (1959), as well as others cited in Chacholiades (1978, ch. 12). Also, the concept of "availability," used by Kravis (1956) to explain trade patterns, is quite general and can include the availability of new products.

greater role. Hirsch then goes on to explain the location of production by essentially applying the multi-factor Heckscher–Ohlin theorem to this pattern of factor intensities among new, growing, and mature products.

Vernon (1966), alone among these authors, departs from the theory of comparative advantage in constructing his own "product cycle" hypothesis.[29] He follows Linder (1961) in arguing that the developers of new products must stay in close proximity to their markets, so as to benefit from customer feedback in modifying the product and also to provide service. In addition he argues that discovery of the innovation itself is helped by close proximity to those whose needs the innovation will satisfy. Thus both innovation and production tend to be concentrated in countries where new needs and wants are first making themselves known. Vernon explicitly rejects not only factor proportions but also comparative costs as determining the location of production – and later export – of new products. Instead he predicts that new products will be first produced in, and later exported from, the country where they are first demanded. Only later still, as the product matures and becomes standardized, does its production move to a location of lower cost.

These three attempts to explain trade in terms of technology may best be understood by seeing what they imply about U.S. trade. All three predict that the U.S. will be an exporter of new products, but their reasons for this prediction are quite different. Posner has the technology for producing new products be available only in the U.S. Hirsch has the technology available everywhere, but says that it is intensive in the use of skilled labor which is abundant in the U.S.[30] Finally, Vernon has new products produced in the U.S. in order to be close to their markets and perhaps in spite of a higher cost of producing them there than elsewhere.

Key to Vernon's hypothesis as it applies to the U.S. is also the notion that new products are needed either to satisfy the wants of high income consumers or to economize on labor costs of producers. As the U.S. has led the world in both per capita incomes and relative wages throughout most of the post-war period, it follows that innovations will have been concentrated there as well. In a more recent piece, however, Vernon (1979) has suggested that this pattern may be shifting. On the one hand, wages and incomes have caught up to the U.S. in several other countries. At the same time, raw materials have replaced labor as the focus of cost-reducing innovations.

Tests of these technology theories of trade can, to the extent that they are consistent with the theory of comparative advantage, proceed along the same lines

---

[29]Vernon's work preceded that of Hirsch, who was Vernon's student. I discuss Vernon last because his work embodies the most radical departures from traditional trade-theoretic assumptions.

[30]Hirsch also argues that this same skill intensity gives even greater comparative advantage to small developed countries such as Britain, Switzerland, Holland, Sweden, and Israel.

developed in Section II. Thus both Posner (1961) and Hirsch (1967) propose particular dynamic explanations of evolving comparative advantage. The argument of Section 3 then suggests correlating trade patterns with their proposed determinants of comparative advantage. This has been done in a number of studies, though the theoretical basis for such a test has never been explicit.

Tests of Vernon's (1966) product cycle theory need to be separately motivated, since he rejects comparative advantage as a determinant of trade. Without any formal model as a guide, tests of his theory have had to rely more on intuition and have sought evidence wherever it could be found of relationships between trade and its suggested determinants.

Aside from particular industry studies, which I will not discuss here, the first empirical test of the technology explanations of trade were by Keesing (1967) and Gruber, Mehta and Vernon (1967). Both papers sought and found positive correlations between U.S. export performance across industries and various measures of research and development (R&D). Since R&D is related to technological progress, whatever its cause or effects, this evidence lends support to all three technology theories of trade without at all distinguishing among them.

Hufbauer (1970) tried to make such a distinction, between Posner's technology gap and Vernon's product cycle. The former is viewed as emphasizing time, while the latter is viewed as emphasizing product differentiation versus standardization. Hufbauer therefore constructed measures of these two product characteristics using, for the former, the "first trade date" of a product and, for the latter, a normalized standard deviation of U.S. export unit values.[31] The embodiment of these characteristics in exports was then calculated and correlated across his sample of countries with GDP per capita which was taken to measure "industrial sophistication." Both correlations were positive and significant, indicating that advanced countries tend to export products that are both new and differentiated. Thus both the Posner and the Vernon theories receive some support.

Additional evidence relating to the technology theories and their relationship with more traditional approaches has been gathered by a number of authors who have incorporated technology-related variables into regression analyses of U.S. trade similar to those reported in Table 4.2. A sample of these results is shown in Table 5.1.

Wells (1969) sought support for another aspect of Vernon's product cycle theory be regressing export performance on income elasticity of demand. The significant coefficient that he obtained using a selection of consumer durables

---

[31] The latter measure is intended to capture the extent to which otherwise similar products differ in price. Grey and Martin (1980) criticize it for confusing strategic oligopolistic product differentiation with technological product differentiation, only the second of which is related to the product cycle. They suggest, but do not apply, a better measure based on hedonic price indices.

Table 5.1

Selected regression equations testing technological determinants of U.S. manufacturing trade

Author (date)	Wells (1969)	Morrall (1972)	Lowinger (1975)	Finger (1975)	Stern and Maskus (1981)
Dependent variable	Growth ratio of exports	Net exports/shipments	Export share of world trade	% of change of exports	Net exports
Year (s) of trade data	1952–53 to 1962–63	1965	1968–70	1958–61 to 1967–69	1970
Coverage	20 consumer durable products	20 2-digit SIC industries	16 2- and 3-digit SIC industries	97 3-digit SITC industries	74 3-digit U.S. census industries
Estimated coefficients:					
Technology-related variables:					
Research and Development	3.171**		0.058**	18.3*	24.71**
Income elasticity of ownership					
Materials + payroll/shipments		−20.47*			
Labor vs. capital efficiency growth		27.93*			
Turnover				3.17*	
Age				7.83	
Other Variables:					
Capital or capital per man				0.20	0.003
Human capital or labor skill ratio		0.2714**		1.42	0.002**
Labor					−0.76*
Scale economies				−1.53**	
Foreign tariffs			−0.010**		
Constant	0.784	13.70	0.230		−113.22
R^2	0.896	0.770	0.891	0.27	0.24

*, **indicate 95 and 99 percent level of significance, respectively.

497

supports Vernon's argument that the U.S. ought to innovate and export in areas that cater to the emerging wants of her high income consumers.[32]

Morrall (1972) tested U.S. exports against a number of variables that are suggested by the technology theories of trade. Of these the two that performed best were those whose coefficients appear in the second column of Table 5.1. The first – the cost of materials plus payroll as a fraction of industry shipments – is an inverse measure of industry profitability and thus indicates (negatively) the monopoly rents enjoyed by innovators. The second – the relative growth rates of labor efficiency versus capital efficiency – is a measure of labor saving innovation. The significance of both these coefficients again supports both the technology gap and product cycle explanations of U.S. trade.

Finally, Finger (1975a) has argued that the product characteristics that Hirsch (1967) and Vernon (1966) associated with technology are more accurately associated with product turnover even when such turnover is not a result of technical change. To test this Finger constructed a measure of turnover based upon the appearance and disappearance of 7-digit items on the U.S. export schedule between 1965 and 1971. Using this variable together with R&D and a measure of product age taken from Hufbauer's (1970) first trade dates, Finger finds support for his hypothesis. In addition, the continued significance of R&D, together with the insignificance and wrong sign for age, suggest to Finger that R&D may promote U.S. exports more by lowering costs of existing products than by introducing new ones.

Whatever its source, the importance of research and development as a determinant of U.S. exports continues to find strong support in regression analyses, such as those reported from Lowinger (1975) and Stern and Maskus (1981). Thus the significant correlations found by Keesing (1967) and by Gruber et al. (1967) easily survive the introduction of additional explanatory variables, including those that are appropriate to the factor proportions theory.

Most of the work described so far, with the exception of Hufbauer (1970), has dealt exclusively with U.S. trade.[33] This is a significant drawback in tests of these theories, since they seem to have had their origins in observation of the U.S. What is needed is a multicountry analysis to determine whether the technology theories are capable of explaining the pattern of trade across countries. Except for Hufbauer's (1970) correlations, such evidence is hard to find.

Leamer (1974) included research and development as one of several "resource variables" determining imports across countries in various industries. Although his resource variables as a group did not perform well, within the group the R&D

---

[32]Wells' results were strengthened by Adler (1970) using income elasticities of foreign demands for U.S. exports, rather than elasticities of domestic demands as done by Wells.

[33]Another exception is Finger (1975a), who included regressions for Japan. He did not, however, do a cross-country analysis.

variable did as well as any, suggesting some small support for technology theories of trade.

Hirsch (1975) also reports a cross-country regression analysis as a test of his particular version of the product cycle. As described above, however, his theory stresses factor proportions in a dynamic context, and his regressions really only test whether skilled labor plays a role in addition to physical capital in explaining trade. His results provide additional support for a three factor Heckscher–Ohlin theory, but they do not directly bear on the dynamic and technology-related issues being discussed here.

More recently Soete (1981) uses data on the shares of U.S. patents held by industries in other countries to test whether export performance is related to this indicator of "output" of new technology. The test is reasonably successful, but I suspect that causation here may run from trade to patents, rather than the reverse.[34]

Where does all this leave us? It seems clear, from the results reported for the U.S. at least, that the technology theories have identified an important set of variables that can help to explain trade. These variables all relate to the "newness" of products or processes, but they also relate to the special knowledge possessed by individuals, firms, and countries that enable them to develop and exploit technologies. Thus it is difficult to distinguish evidence supporting technology from evidence supporting human capital or skills as determinants of trade.

There is also some question as to whether the role of technology, whatever it has been in the past, may be diminishing in importance for explaining patterns of trade that are emerging today. I have already noted Vernon's (1979) reservations about carrying over his earlier explanation of U.S. trade to today's world of higher foreign incomes and materials costs. He also suggests that the growth and spread of multinational corporations has lessened the need for production of new products to start near their markets and thus has undermined part of the rationale for product cycle trade. Giddy (1978) also questions the adequacy of the product cycle model in today's world. He suggests a more general, but so far rather vague, approach based on market imperfections and the means used by firms to avoid or exploit them. It will be interesting to see whether the existing technology theories of trade will be refined and convincingly tested before they are left behind by a changing world.

6. Other patterns of trade and theories to explain them

The Ricardian and Heckscher–Ohlin theories are thought by many to provide a less than complete explanation of world trade. The reason for this dissatisfaction

---

[34]Bowen (1981) has also run a multi-country test of the product cycle model, focusing on rates at which prices decline over time as an indicator of their newness. His results do not support the model, but this may only reflect inadequacy of this indicator.

lies only partly in the somewhat ambiguous support that tests of the theories have provided. Rather, many authors have noted a number of empirical regularities in the data of international trade that seem, on the surface at least, to be unexplainable in terms of these dominant theories. As a result, a variety of other theories have been suggested in recent years to supplement, if not replace, these traditional models. The technology theories that I looked at in Section 5 fall into this category to some extent and have received enough attention to warrant a separate section of this chapter. In this section I examine several other attempts that have been made to explain trade, both empirically and theoretically.

I will begin by noting the empirical regularities in the trade data that often have motivated alternative approaches. These will be examined first to see whether they are indeed unexplainable in terms of, say, the factor proportions theory. Then in subsequent subsections I will turn to the alternative models, describe them briefly, and note the extent to which they have received empirical support.

There is a tremendous amount of literature to be covered here, and not much space to cover it. I will therefore have to be more brief than I would like. In particular, I will not present any numerical results in this section, even though several of these models rely more heavily on data than on theory for their support.

6.1. Empirical regularities

Alternative trade theories often begin by pointing out aspects of the pattern of international trade that are seemingly inconsistent with other theories and which the new theories attempt to explain. These empirical regularities, sometimes called paradoxes, need to be examined first since the interest in the alternative theories depends so heavily on their validity.

6.1.1. Trade among industrialized countries

The first paradox is that a disproportionately high amount of international trade takes place among the industrialized countries. Since these countries share similar factor endowments, this observation contradicts what one would expect from the factor proportions theory. According to it, countries' trade should be based on differences in factor endowments. One could perhaps reconcile the empirical fact with theory by introducing transportation costs and noting that the industrialized countries are often neighbors. But it is also true, as documented by Hufbauer and Chilas (1974), that the proportion of trade among industrialized countries has grown over time. Since over time these countries have also become more similar in per capita incomes, and therefore presumably also in factor endowments, it is hard to see how the factor proportions theory even including transport costs can account for this phenomenon.

6.1.2. Intra-industry trade

A good deal of trade, especially among the industrialized countries, seems to take place within industries rather than between them. That is, it is quite normal to find countries both exporting and importing goods from the same industrial classification and very often this "intra-industry trade" accounts for a substantial fraction of total trade. This was noted by Kojima (1964), Balassa (1966), and Grubel (1967) and has led to a huge literature attempting further to document and explain such trade.

Much of this literature has concerned the issue of aggregation. Lipsey (1976), for example, in reviewing Grubel and Lloyd's (1975) book on the subject, objects that the three-digit SITC industries within which they normally measure intra-industry trade are far too large. Indeed it is true that much of the apparent intra-industry trade disappears when finer levels of disaggregation are used in measuring it. Grubel and Lloyd (1975) for example report that Australian intra-industry trade declines from 43 percent at the one-digit level of aggregation to only 6 percent at the seven-digit level, with even more dramatic reductions for Australia's bilateral trade. Whether the amount of intra-industry trade that remains at low levels of aggregation is enough to be worth studying, and whether such extreme disaggregation is even appropriate, are matters of judgment on which disagreement still exists.

Whatever the level of aggregation, intra-industry trade requires special consideration only if it cannot be explained by traditional theories. But this and the aggregation question cannot be separated, since the definition of the industry must correspond to the meaning of an industry in the model used to explain trade. Finger (1975b) for example argues that intra-industry trade within three-digit SITC categories can be explained by the factor proportions theory, since, as he measures them, factor intensities vary almost as much within these groups as among them. What this means, of course, is that SITC groups do not constitute industries in the sense the term is used in the Heckscher–Ohlin model, and the term "intra-industry trade" is a misnomer. Falvey (1981a) has presented a theory of intra-industry trade that relies precisely on such variations of factor intensities among products within an "industry," and his model is therefore more properly viewed as an extension or elaboration of the Heckscher–Ohlin model than as an alternative to it.

This sort of explanation of intra-industry trade in terms of factor proportions and aggregation may suffice for explaining the fact that it occurs at all, but it is less adequate to deal with yet another empirical observation: As measured by Grubel and Lloyd (1975) and many others in other contexts, the proportion of intra-industry trade has grown significantly over time. As Hesse (1974) has pointed out, even with sufficient variation of factor intensities within industries, the factor proportions theory can explain this relative growth of intra-industry trade over time only if relative factor endowments among the industrialized countries that engage in this trade have become less similar over time. This seems to be quite the opposite of what has happened in the post-war period.[35]

If the factor proportions theory cannot adequately explain intra-industry trade, one might ask whether a Ricardian model could do so. Again the answer is yes, if relative labor requirements differ among products within an industry. Petri (1980) provides just such a model and shows that it behaves exactly like the Armington model that I will discuss below. However this explanation too can account for the relative growth of intra-industry trade only if, for some reason, random differences in technology increase over time.

I conclude, therefore, more from its growth than from its level, that intra-industry trade is an empirical phenomenon that is not fully explained by traditional theories.

6.1.3. Ease of adjustment of trade liberalization

Both the Ricardian and Heckscher–Ohlin models suggest that movement towards freer trade should entail substantial relocation of factors of production and therefore very likely a difficult period of adjustment. However, this does not appear to have been the case in actual instances where trade has been liberalized. Since World War II there have been successive rounds of multilateral tariff reductions by the industrialized countries, plus the formation of free trade areas in Europe and elsewhere, all of these leading to substantial growth in the volume of world trade. Nonetheless, Balassa (1966) in his study of the EEC and Hufbauer and Chilas (1974) in a broader study of industrial countries both find no evidence of increased specialization over this period. Instead, trade among industrialized countries has grown in a fairly balanced manner at the industry level.[36]

6.1.4. Country size and export shares

A final fact also deserves mentioning since its inconsistency with traditional models is not often noted: the fraction of trade in GNP is lower in large countries than in small countries. This may seem both obvious and appropriate, since in a two-country model any given trade between them will of course constitute a larger fraction of the smaller country's GNP. But consider the trade of different size, but

---

[35] To a considerable extent, aggregation combines products at different stages of processing in a single industry. If these stages use different factor proportions, then growth of intra-industry trade can be accounted for by the growth of multinational corporations, which rationalize the locations of these stages.

[36] Incomes also grew rapidly over this period and this too must have eased the adjustment. However, income growth would not cause import competing sectors to *expand* even as trade barriers are being lowered.

otherwise identical, countries in a many-country world. As Arad and Hirsch (1981) have pointed out, the usual assumptions of constant returns to scale and homothetic preferences then imply that the two countries will trade identical fractions of their outputs. Thus this familiar characteristic of international trade is not explainable in the Heckscher–Ohlin model, and in this respect the Ricardian model is no different.

6.2. Gravity-type models of bilateral trade flows

Early attempts to account for some of these phenomena were not theoretical but instead provided more formal empirical analyses of some of the phenomena just described. Based on ad hoc but intuitive theorizing, Tinbergen (1962) and Pöyhönen (1963) independently developed the first in a series of econometric models of bilateral trade flows. This model explained the bilateral trade between two countries in terms of their GNPs, Y, and the distance between them, D, as follows:

$$X_{ij} = cc_i c_j \frac{(Y_i)^a (Y_j)^b}{(1 + eD_{ij})^f}, \tag{6.1}$$

where X_{ij} is total exports from country i to country j and the lower case letters are all constants to be estimated. In view of the similarity between this equation and the law of gravity in physics, models of this sort have come to be called "gravity models."

The simple model of (6.1) was elaborated by Linnemann (1966). He added a population variable to the equation, reflecting the role of scale economies, and also discussed in some detail the reasons for including some variables in the equation and excluding others. He even showed how something like the gravity equation can be derived theoretically from a quasi-Walrasian general equilibrium model. Crucial to this derivation, however, is an assumption of separate demand functions for imports from each trading partner. This assumption is not really justified by Linnemann himself, though it bears an obvious resemblance to the more recent work on product differentiation in international trade that will be the subject of Section 6.5 below.[37]

In spite of their somewhat dubious theoretical heritage, gravity models have been extremely successful empirically. Linnemann's (1966) equation, for example,

---

[37]An alternative derivation is provided by Leamer and Stern (1970, ch. 6) using a probability model of international transactions. Anderson (1979) has also recently suggested a theoretical foundation for the equation in terms of a Cobb–Douglas expenditure system with, again, goods differentiated by country of origin.

fitted to the trade of 80 countries, explained some 80 percent of the variance in the data. Such models have also proved extremely useful as the basis for tests of other propositions. Aitken (1973), for example, estimated a gravity model that included dummy variables for common membership in a free trade area, and thus was able to estimate the trade creation and diversion effects of the EEC and EFTA. In quite a different context, Leamer (1974) used the framework of a gravity model as the structure within which to incorporate and test the importance of factor endowments and other country characteristics as they affect international trade.[38]

The reason for the empirical success of the gravity equation is surely its ability to incorporate most of the empirical phenomena noted in the preceding subsection. Eq. (6.1) applies directly to intra-industry trade, since X_{ij} is gross trade in one direction rather than net trade. Also, if the parameters a and b are fractions less than one and sum to more than one, then the share of trade in GNP will decline with country size, while at the same time pairs of large countries will trade proportionately more than pairs of small countries, as observed in the first of the paradoxes listed earlier. With the addition of population as another explanatory variable as done by Linnemann (1966), this last result relates to differences in per capita incomes, even more accurately reflecting what has been observed.

It seems clear, then, that the gravity equation (6.1), and elaborations of it, tell us something important about what happens in international trade, even if they do not tell us why. The empirical success of equations like (6.1) should be added to our list of phenomena to be explained, and should not be regarded as testing an alternative *theory* of trade. It remains to be seen whether alternative theories that have been proposed can explain the success of the gravity equation.

6.3. The Linder hypothesis

One prominent alternative to the Ricardian and Heckscher–Ohlin models was proposed by Linder (1961). He hypothesized that trade in manufactured products arises not so much from differences in supply as from similarities in demand. The idea is that manufactured goods are produced where they are most demanded, and only then are available for export. But of course they will be exported only to countries where they are also demanded in some amount. Therefore countries with similar demand conditions will end up producing a similar range of goods and will trade them with each other. Countries with dissimilar demands on the other hand will each produce little that is of interest to the other and will trade little.

---

[38]Leamer extended the gravity model by including tariffs as well as distance among his "trade resistance" variables.

Linder's thesis is so far only loosely formulated in theoretical terms. Linder himself sketched his model in terms of scale economies and differentiated products. He also stressed the idea, later used by Vernon (1966), that producers must be close to their markets. However, no one has yet put all of these elements together in a formal model,[39] and the enduring attention given to Linder's hypothesis owes mainly to its intuitive appeal.

Empirical tests of the hypothesis have usually focused on the following particular implication of it: if demands vary with per capita incomes, then Linder's hypothesis would suggest that countries will trade disproportionately with countries of similar per capita incomes. Linder himself tested this implication by calculating bilateral average propensities to import and graphing them, for a given exporter, opposite the per capita incomes of the importers. His graphs showed a tendency to peak near the per capita income of the exporter, providing some support for the hypothesis. Others have since repeated this test using more formal methods of analysis, and the evidence is now clear that many countries do indeed trade disproportionately large amounts with countries of similar per capita income.

The problem with these tests, however, is that countries with similar per capita incomes also tend to be clustered geographically close together. Thus the large trade between them may be accounted for solely by transportation costs, and, if so, provides no evidence in support of Linder. This objection was raised most cogently by Hoftyzer (1975) and was repeated more recently by Kennedy and McHugh (1980) who also provide references to much of this empirical literature. The latter authors tried a test based on *changes* in trade and per capita incomes over time, so as to neutralize distance as a factor, and failed to find support for Linder's hypothesis. Another way to control for distance in a test of the Linder hypothesis is to include per capita income difference as an additional explanatory variable in a gravity model like the one discussed above in Section 6.2. This has been done for cross sections of bilateral industry trade by Gruber and Vernon (1970) and Hirsch and Lev (1973) with no clear support for the Linder hypothesis.[40]

Other authors have tested a variety of other implications of the Linder hypothesis, again with mixed results. On the positive side, Kohlhagen (1977)

---

[39] Gray (1980) presents some ideas that are suggestive of a theory. He relies on unspecified "specific inputs" that alter supplies and demands and are distributed across countries leading to trade. Also, Krugman's (1980) model includes an analysis of differences in demand for differentiated products that goes a long way towards formalizing Linder's ideas.

[40] Gruber and Vernon (1970) find trade to depend *positively* (though not usually significantly) on per capita income differences in most industries, directly contradicting Linder. Hirsch and Lev (1973) find the opposite, and they criticize Gruber and Vernon for including both per capita income levels and differences in their regressions. I do not find their objection compelling. Also, in a later study, Hirsch (1977) reports results that disagree with the Linder hypothesis.

found a positive effect on bilateral trade due to the overlap in the trading countries' income distributions, though again without controlling for distance the significance of this result is unclear. Davies (1975) compared unit values of U.K. trade with the U.S. and EEC, inferring that quality differences in trade correspond with income differences. Finally, Arad and Hirsch (1981) identified "Linder goods" by looking at product differentiation and found that these goods are traded with a smaller range of countries than are other goods. On the negative side, Hufbauer (1970) looked at the commodity composition of exports and imports – which ought according to Linder to be similar for similar countries – and found instead that the similarity of trade composition rises with per capita income *levels* independently of their difference. In a similar vein, Michaely (1981) calculated the "income levels of traded goods"[41] for exports and imports and found these to be negatively correlated, contrary to what one would expect from the Linder hypothesis.

In sum, for a theory that seems to have been motivated originally mostly by casual empiricism, the Linder hypothesis has found solid empirical support to be remarkably elusive. It is possible that a more rigorous theoretical foundation for the hypothesis, were it to be developed, could suggest improved methods of testing that would be more uniformly successful. But for the moment I am doubtful that it will ever take its intended place as a complement to the Heckscher–Ohlin theory.

6.4. *Homogeneous-product explanations of intra-industry trade*

Theoretical explanations of intra-industry trade were divided by Grubel (1967) into two categories: those dealing with homogeneous products and those dealing with differentiated products. The latter will be dealt with in the next subsection. Here I will just briefly mention four suggestions that have been made as to why countries sometimes both export and import identical products.

6.4.1. *Border trade*

Perhaps the most obvious explanation of intra-industry trade is border trade. If a country is geographically large enough and transport costs for a particular good are high enough, then depending on where the resources needed for its production happen to be located it is rather obvious that it might be imported across one section of the border and exported across another. The standard example of such border trade is trade in sand, stone and gravel across the long border between the

---

[41] Defined as the average per capita income of the countries that trade them, weighted by shares in trade.

U.S. and Canada. As reported by Grubel and Lloyd (1975), this trade is nearly balanced between the two countries.

6.4.2. Re-export trade

While border trade may involve goods that are homogeneous in all respects except location, it does not involve a particular unit of a good being both imported and exported. Yet in a small number of countries that have specialized in providing the services of international trade, this does happen in the form of entrepot and re-export trade. Countries like Hong Kong and Singapore take advantage of their locations and other facilities essentially to be the international traders for their regions of the globe. As a result they import many goods only to re-export them to other countries with or without a minimal amount of processing within their borders.

6.4.3. Cyclical trade

As explained nicely by Grubel (1967), for some products there are natural cycles over time for either supply or demand. If these cycles are out of phase between two countries and if storage costs are large relative to transportation costs they can give rise to intra-industry trade. Thus certain agricultural products are traded between the hemispheres in opposite directions at different times of the year, to take advantage of the different growing seasons. Similarly, electricity may be traded in different directions at different times of the day between countries in different time zones, since demand fluctuates predictably over the day.

6.4.4. Strategic trade

The final example of intra-industry trade in homogeneous products emerged from the recently growing literature on trade with imperfect competition. Brander (1981) proposed a model in which monopolists in two countries open to trade and become a binational duopoly. Brander shows that in a Cournot equilibrium with positive transport costs, each firm exports to the other's market. Such behavior is certainly an intriguing theoretical possibility. Whether in fact it occurs in the real world has not to my knowledge been tested.

6.5. Product differentiation

Confrontations with reality in international trade have increasingly suggested the possibility of some form of product differentiation between domestic and imported goods. Those who seek to explain intra-industry trade tend to place more importance on product differentiation than on the homogeneous-product explanations just outlined. Linder, too, made some mention of product differentiation in formulating his theory, and in at least one interpretation, that of Arad and Hirsch (1981), product differentiation is the distinguishing characteristic of the kinds of goods that the Linder hypothesis is about. Even the gravity models, as motivated by Linnemann (1966), depended upon product differentiation.

In this subsection I will deal with contributions to the literature that have dealt more directly with product differentiation as their primary focus. These are of two types. The first views products as differentiated by country of origin and permits perfect competition to prevail among producers in a given country. The second views products as differentiated by firm and inevitably involves a departure from perfect competition. The second form will therefore be dealt with together with the more general topic of imperfect competition in international trade.

6.5.1. Differentiation by country of origin

The pioneering paper in the theoretical literature on this subject was by Armington (1969). His assumption, that demanders view otherwise identical goods produced in different countries as different, has therefore been called the Armington assumption, though the same assumption has long been implicit in much of the empirical work estimating elasticities of substitution and demand in world trade.[42] Indeed it is precisely this empirical literature that has seemed to make such an assumption necessary. As discussed for example in Deardorff and Stern (1982), estimated elasticities of demand for imports and exports are too low to be consistent with the more traditional assumption that all goods that enter international trade are perfect substitutes.

The implications of this assumption have been further explored theoretically by deMelo and Robinson (1981). In addition, they and others have used the assumption in constructing computable, empirically-based models of trade for policy analysis.[43] The assumption serves well to make the bilateral pattern of trade determinate and to make the models consistent with the empirical fact of intra-industry trade. It also tends to insulate countries somewhat from one another, making a country's domestic prices and outputs less sensitive to changes abroad and to trade policies than they would otherwise be.

However well the Armington assumption works in such contexts, however, the fact remains that it is not inherently very plausible for more than a few industries on a priori grounds. One can imagine certain products, such as wine, where differences in soil and climate make one country's products impossible to duplicate exactly abroad. But such cases are very unusual. Somewhat more generally,

---

[42] See Hickman and Lau (1973), who use the assumption explicitly.
[43] See Chapter 12.

there are other products where uncertainty about differences in quality among producers might lead consumers to look at country of origin as a signal of average quality. Already, however, this involves substantial departures from other standard assumptions about market structure. Therefore I do not regard the Armington assumption as inherently a very desirable basis for a theory of international trade.

On the other hand, more plausible assumptions do lead inevitably to departures from perfect competition and therefore to complications, both theoretical and empirical, that make fruitful analysis difficult. The Armington assumption provides a very useful way of confronting some aspects of reality with an otherwise competitive model. Until more progress is made in generalizing and applying models of imperfect competition, the Armington assumption may be the best we have.

6.5.2. *Differentiation by firm and imperfect competition*

Product differentiation at the level of the firm implies that firms have some degree of market power. The smallest departure from perfect competition that would permit such product differentiation is the model of monopolistic competition. Yet despite the apparent importance of both product differentiation and imperfect competition for many internationally traded goods, little has appeared on these subjects in the trade literature. Johnson (1967) explained this lacuna by noting the need in international trade theory for general equilibrium models, which at that time had not successfully incorporated monopolistic competition. Since then several preliminary attempts have been made to model product differentiation in international trade,[44] but only since about 1980 have models appeared that successfully reconcile monopolistic competition with the general equilibrium requirements of trade theory.

These models have used two slightly different approaches and are described fully in Chapter 7. The two approaches have been used to explain intra-industry trade in Lancaster (1980), Krugman (1981), and Helpman (1981). Both models serve well to provide a formal theoretical basis for many of the arguments made by Grubel and Lloyd (1975) and others about intra-industry trade, and may provide guidance for further empirical work on intra-industry trade in the future as well. In Chapter 7, for example, Helpman shows that a gravity equation can be derived from one such model. I suspect that as these models are refined, all of the topics in this chapter may be brought together within a common theoretical framework.

These models are too new to have led on their own to empirical testing. In more general terms, however, there has been some empirical work on the interaction

[44]See Gray (1973) and Barker (1977).

between imperfect competition and international trade and this has been nicely reviewed by Jacquemin (1982). He notes that there is empirical support for two propositions: that trade reduces monopolistic distortions, and that trade permits expansion of outputs and lowered costs through economies of scale. On the other hand, Jacquemin notes that both theory and empirical evidence give mixed results concerning whether trade, through intra-industry trade, makes a greater variety of products available to consumers.

On the latter point, Caves (1981) has made the interesting observation that product differentiation does not necessarily lead to greater intra-industry trade. One the one hand, if product differentiation is inherent in an industry due to the complexity of the characteristics of its product, then this should stimulate intra-industry trade as firms in different countries can specialize in products with different combinations of characteristics. On the other hand, if product differentiation has a strong informational component, requiring substantial advertising by the firm in order to inform customers of its product's uniqueness, then language and cultural barriers to advertising in a foreign country may make product differentiation a hindrance to intra-industry trade. As far as I can see, it is only the first of these aspects of product differentiation that operates in the theoretical models of Lancaster, Krugman and others.

6.6. Scale economies and country size

Economies of scale are a necessary part of monopolistic-competition models of differentiated product industries, and therefore play an important role in the newly-developed trade models just discussed. However, economies of scale alone have long been regarded as a separate reason for trade as well as a determinant of the pattern of trade. Operationally, this old argument leads, less than inevitably, to absolute country size as a determinant of trade patterns. In addition, as long as I am on the subject of country size, I will also mention in this subsection an argument by Jacques Drèze linking country size to both scale economies and product differentiation.

The various ways that scale economies can enter an economic model, and the ways that they in turn affect international trade, are amply discussed in Chapter 7. The old argument for how scale economies might determine the pattern of trade, however, is much simpler and less rigorous than these models suggest: large countries will have large industries in autarky and therefore other things being equal will have relatively low autarky prices in those industries where economies of scale are most pronounced. It follows that large countries will have a comparative advantage in, and export from, industries with significant economies of scale.

A problem with this argument is that, strictly speaking, the large markets which give large countries their comparative advantage are no longer relevant once trade is free and all countries share the same world markets. The pattern of free trade is really indeterminant here, though perhaps one could make a dynamic argument that would preclude the world ever reaching any equilibrium other than the one described above. More usefully, though, the introduction once again of transport costs should salvage this result even in a static context, since the size of the domestic market would then retain its importance even with trade.

Empirical work on the importance of scale economies for the pattern of international trade has had mixed results. Hufbauer (1970) found a positive correlation between the importance of scale economies in export industries and measures of country size. Baldwin (1971) on the other hand failed to identify a scale economies variable as a significant determinant of U.S. trade. Finally, Katrak (1973) found strong support for scale economies as a determinant of the relative export performance of the U.S. and U.K., though I find it hard to accept his argument that inclusion of relative industry size in the measure of scale economies does not bias his result. Indeed, the difficulty of agreeing on a suitable measure of scale economies makes the mixed results of all of these studies unsurprising.

Drèze (1961) carried the above simple argument about the importance of scale economies one step further. He argued that as product differentiation segments a given market, a larger total market will be needed to permit producers in particular product lines to exhaust the benefits of economies of scale. It then follows that large countries will have an advantage in differentiated products while small countries will have to specialize in more standardized products. Drèze found this a useful hypothesis for explaining Belgian trade in the EEC, but I am not aware of other work that has been done to test it further.

7. Conclusion

Obviously a good deal of effort over the years has gone into testing trade theories. While the tests have seldom been conclusive, many have certainly been suggestive, and they have been successful in any case in stimulating the further development of trade theory in directions more consistent with empirical reality. However, it is desirable to end this survey with a sense of what specifically this literature has told us about the importance and usefulness of existing alternative theories of international trade. I will describe what I believe *I* have learned, with the full understanding that others might draw different conclusions from this often confusing literature.

There are three levels on which the empirical work might be expected to support or contradict theories of international trade. First and most specifically, one can ask which of several suggested *determinates* of trade are most successful in explaining the trade of a particular country, such as the U.S. Second, one can ask, among several *groups* of these determinants that are the subject of alternative theories, which are most successful in explaining the trade of the countries of the world more generally. And third, one can ask what *model* of the international economy, perhaps incorporating elements of several separate theories, does the evidence suggest as most useful for us to use, if it exists, or for us to work toward developing, if it does not. I will discuss each of these questions in turn.

As is clear from the results reported in this chapter, much of the empirical work has tried to explain only U.S. trade. Leontief's (1954) finding that capital intensity seems *not* to be the determinant of U.S. exports led to a search among alternatives that were suggested either by a generalized factor proportions theory of trade or by one of the technology theories. The search led to a group of knowledge-related variables that appear to be the most important determinants of U.S. exports: human capital, labor skills, research and development expenditures, and the employment of scientists and engineers. It is now quite clear that U.S. comparative advantage derives from the knowledge possessed by its workers or its firms. Beyond that I do not see any way of choosing among these separate variables, or the theories that suggest them, based on the evidence now available. As for the role of capital, which originally motivated this entire literature, it seems to have shifted over time to become positively related to U.S. net exports in recent years.

The next question is whether any particular trade theory is most successful in explaining the pattern of trade generally, not just in the U.S. I believe that the accumulated evidence clearly favors the generalized factor proportions theory – allowing for human capital as well as physical capital and labor as separate factors, and perhaps also including certain natural resources. The Ricardian theory generally lacks independent empirical support, while the technology theories find their greatest and most uniformly successful support in the importance of research and development. This variable is too closely related to human capital for it to provide a convincing case for technology over factor proportions as the basis for trade. It is true that there exist features of the trade data that the factor proportions theory cannot accommodate, and there exist examples of trade in particular industries for which a technology explanation is clearly the most appropriate. But as a general approach to understanding trade, the factor proportions theory has stood up remarkably well to empirical scrutiny, especially considering the inauspicious beginning of this scrutiny under Leontief.

This does not mean, however, that the factor proportions model as it now stands is necessarily a satisfactory description of the world economy. It does reasonably well at explaining the commodity composition of trade, but beyond that it is fairly helpless. We need something more, or different, even to address issues of the bilateral pattern and volume of trade. If we wish our model to be consistent with the empirical observations discussed in Section 6, a more radical departure from the competitive model may be called for. I am particularly encouraged by the recent theoretical developments incorporating monopolistic competition into trade theory. I can imagine that the new orthodoxy may center on a model in which industries differ in factor intensities and look from the outside more or less like the factor proportions model, but inside consist of monopolistically competitive firms. Such models are beginning to appear, most notably in the work of Krugman (1981). I am hopeful that further developments along these lines will provide us with a model in which factor proportions, scale economies, and degrees of product differentiation and imperfect competition all interact to determine how much countries trade, what they trade, and with whom.

References

Adler, F. Michael (1970), "The relationship between the income and price elasticities of demand for United States exports", Review of Economics and Statistics, 52 (August):313–319.

Aitken, Norman D. (1973), "The effect of the EEC and EFTA on European trade: A temporal cross-section analysis", American Economic Review, 63 (December):881–892.

Anderson, James E. (1979), "A theoretical foundation for the gravity equation", American Economic Review, 69 (March):106–116.

Anderson, James E. (1981), "Cross-section tests of the Heckscher–Ohlin theorem: Comment", American Economic Review, 71 (December):1037–1039.

Arad, Ruth W. and Seev Hirsch (1981), "Determination of trade flows and choice of trade partners: Reconciling the Heckscher–Ohlin and the Burenstam Linder models of international trade", Weltwirtschaftliches Archiv, 117 (2):276–297.

Armington, Paul S. (1969), "A theory of demand for products distinguished by place of production", IMF Staff Papers, 16 (March).

Balassa, B. (1963), "An empirical demonstration of classical comparative cost theory", Review of Economics and Statistics, 45 (August).

Balassa, B. (1965), "Trade liberalization and 'revealed' comparative advantage", The Manchester School, 33 (May):99–123.

Balassa, B. (1966),"Tariff reductions and trade in manufactures among the industrial countries", American Economic Review, 56 (June):466–473.

Balassa, B. (1979), "The changing pattern of comparative advantage in manufactured goods", Review of Economics and Statistics, 61 (May):259–266.

Baldwin, Robert E. (1971), "Determinants of the commodity structure of U.S. trade", American Economic Review 61, (March):126–146.

Baldwin, Robert E. (1979), "Determinants of trade and foreign investment: Further evidence", Review of Economics and Statistics, 61 (February):40–48.

Barker, Terry (1977), "International trade and economic growth: An alternative to the neoclassical approach", Cambridge Journal of Economics, 1 (June):153–172.

Bhagwati, Jagdish (1964), "The pure theory of international trade: A survey", Economic Journal, 74 (March):1–84. Reprinted with an Addendum in Bhagwati (1969).

Bhagwati, Jagdish (1969), Trade, tariffs and growth (M.I.T. Press, Cambridge, Mass.).

Bowen, Harry P. (1981), "A multicountry test of the product cycle model", paper presented to the Econometric Society Annual Meetings, Washington, D.C. (December).

Bowen, Harry P. (1982), "On the theoretical interpretation of indices of trade intensity and revealed comparative advantage", in process (April).

Bowen, Harry P. (1983), "Changes in the international distribution of resources and their impact on U.S. comparative advantage", Review of Economics and Statistics, forthcoming.

Brander, James A. (1981), "Intra-industry trade in identical commodities", Journal of International Economics, 11:1–14.

Branson, William H. (1971), "U.S. comparative advantage: Some further results", Brookings Papers on Economic Activity, (No. 3):754–759.

Branson, William H. and Helen B. Junz (1971), "Trends in U.S. trade and comparative advantage", Brookings Papers on Economic Activity, (No. 2):285–345.

Branson, William H. and Nikolaos Monoyios (1977), "Factor inputs in U.S. Trade", Journal of International Economics, 7 (May):111–131.

Brecher, Richard A. and Ehsan U. Choudhri (1982), "The Leontief paradox, continued", Journal of Political Economy, 90 (August):820–823.

Brown, Fred and John Whalley (1980), "General equilibrium evaluations of tariff-cutting proposals in the Tokyo round and comparisons to more extensive liberalization of world trade", Economic Journal, 90 (December).

Caves, Richard E. (1981), "Intra-industry trade and market structure in the industrialized countries", Oxford Economic Papers, 33 (July):203–223.

Chacholiades, Miltiades (1978), International trade theory and policy (McGraw-Hill, New York).

Davies, Robert (1975), "Product differentiation and the structure of United Kingdom trade", Bulletin of Economic Research, 27 (May):27–41.

Deardorff, Alan V. (1980), "The general validity of the law of comparative advantage", Journal of Political Economy, 88 (October):941–957.

Deardorff, Alan V. (1982), "The general validity of the Heckscher–Ohlin theorem", American Economic Review, 72 (September):683–694.

Deardorff, Alan V. and Robert M. Stern (1981), "A disaggregated model of world production and trade: An estimate of the impact of the Tokyo round", Journal of Policy Modeling, 3:127–152.

Deardorff, Alan V. and Robert M. Stern (1982), "Lessons from computer modeling of trade", in process (July).

DeMarchi, Neil (1976), "Anomaly and the development of economics: The case of the Leontief paradox", in: S. J. Latsis, ed., Method and appraisal in economics (Cambridge University Press, New York) 109–127.

deMelo, Jaime and Sherman Robinson (1981), "Trade policy and resource allocation in the presence of product differentiation", Review of Economics and Statistics, 63 (May):169–177.

Dornbusch, R., S. Fischer and P. Samuelson (1977), "Comparative advantage, trade, and payments in a Ricardian model with a continuum of goods", American Economic Review, 67 (December):823–839.

Drèze, Jacques (1961), "Les exportations intra-C.E.E. en 1958 et la position Belge", Recherchés Economiques de Louvain, 717–738.

Falvey, Rodney E. (1981a), "Commercial policy and intra-industry trade", Journal of International Economics, 11:495–511.

Falvey, Rodney E. (1981b), "Comparative advantage in a multi-factor world", International Economic Review, 22 (June):401–413.

Findlay, R. and H. Grubert (1959), "Factor intensities, technological progress and the terms of trade", Oxford Economic Papers, 5 (February):111–121.

Finger, J.M. (1975a), "A new view of the product cycle theory", Weltwirtschaftliches Archiv, 111 (March):79–99.

Finger, J.M. (1975b), "Trade overlap and intra-industry trade", Economic Inquiry, 13 (December):581–589.

Ford, J.L. (1967), "On the equivalence of the classical and the factor models in explaining international trade patterns", The Manchester School, 35 (May):185–198.

Giddy, Ian H. (1978), "The demise of the product cycle model in international business theory", Columbia Journal of World Business, 12 (Spring):90–97.

Gray, H. Peter (1973), "Two-way international trade in manufacturers: A theoretical underpinning", Weltwirtschaftliches Archiv, 109 (1):19–39.

Gray, H. Peter (1980), "The theory of international trade among industrial nations", Weltwirtschaftliches Archiv, 116 (3):447–470.

Gray, H. Peter and John P. Martin (1980), "The meaning and measurement of product differentiation in international trade", Weltwirtschaftliches Archiv, 116 (2):322–329.

Grubel, Herbert G. (1967), "Intra-industry specialization and the pattern of trade", Canadian Journal of Economics and Political Science, 33 (August):374–388.

Grubel, Herbert G. and P.J. Lloyd (1975), Intra-industry trade: The theory and measurement of international trade in differentiated products (Wiley, New York).

Gruber, William, Dileep Mehta, and Raymond Vernon (1967), "The R&D factor in international trade and international investment of United States industries", Journal of Political Economy, 75 (February):20–37.

Gruber, William, and Raymond Vernon (1970), "The technology factor in a world trade matrix", in: Raymond Vernon, ed. The technology factor in international trade (Columbia University Press, New York) 233–272.

Hamilton, Carl and Lars E.O. Svensson (1982), "Should direct or total factor intensities be used in tests of the factor proportions hypothesis in international trade theory?" Seminar Paper No. 206 (Institute for International Studies, Stockholm) (June).

Harkness, Jon (1978), "Factor abundance and comparative advantage", American Economic Review, 68 (December):784–800.

Harkness, Jon and John F. Kyle (1975), "Factors influencing United States comparative advantage", Journal of International Economics, 5 (May):153–165.

Heller, Peter S. (1976), "Factor endowment change and comparative advantage: The case of Japan, 1959–1969", Review of Economics and Statistics, 58 (August):283–292.

Helpman, Elhanan (1981), "International trade in the presence of product differentiation, economies of scale and monopolistic competition: A Chamberlin–Heckscher–Ohlin approach", Journal of International Economics, 11 (August):305–340.

Hesse, Helmut (1974), "Hypotheses for the explanation of trade between industrial countries, 1953–1970", in: Herbert Giersch, ed., The international division of labor: Problems and perspectives (J. C. B. Mohr, Tübingen) 39–59.

Hickman, B. and L. Lau (1973), "Elasticities of substitution and export demand in a world trade model", European Economic Review, 4 (December):347–380.

Hillman, Arye L. (1980), "Observations on the relation between 'revealed comparative advantage' and comparative advantage as indicated by pre-trade relative prices", Welwirtschaftliches Archiv, 116 (2):315–321.

Hilton, R. Spence (1981), "An estimatable model of the commodity version of trade, unpublished Ph.D. dissertation (University of Wisconsin, Madison).

Hirsch, Seev (1967), Location of industry and international competitiveness (Clarendon Press, Oxford).

Hirsch, Seev (1975), "The product cycle model of international trade – A multi-country cross-section analysis", Oxford Bulletin of Economics and Statistics, 37:305–317.

Hirsch, Seev (1977), Rich man's, poor man's and everyman's goods: Aspects of industrialization (J.C.B. Mohr, Tubingen).

Hirsch, Seev and Baruch Lev (1973), "Trade and per capita income differentials: A test of the Burenstam–Linder hypothesis", World development, 1 (September):11–17.

Hoftyzer, John (1975), "Empirical verification of Linder's trade thesis: Comment", Southern Economic Journal, 41 (April):694–698.

Hufbauer, G.C. (1966), Synthetic materials and the theory of international trade (London).

Hufbauer, G.C. (1970), "The impact of national characteristics and technology on the commodity composition of trade in manufactured goods", in: Raymond Vernon, ed., The technology factor in international trade (Columbia University Press, New York) 145–231.

Hufbauer, G.C. and John G. Chilas (1974), "Specialization by industrial countries: Extent and consequences", in: Herbert Giersch, ed., The international division of labour: Problems and perspectives (J.C.B. Mohr, Tübingen).

Jacquemin, Alexis (1982), "Imperfect market structure and international trade – Some recent research", Kyklos, 35 (1):75–93.

Johnson, Harry G. (1967), "International trade theory and monopolistic competition theory", in: R. Kuenne, ed., Monopolistic competition theory: Studies in impact (John Wiley, New York) 203–218.

Jones, Ronald (1956–57), "Factor proportions and the Heckscher–Ohlin model", Review of Economic Studies, 24.

Katrak, Homi (1973), "Human skills, R and D and scale economies in the exports of the United Kingdom and the United States", Oxford Economic Papers, 25 (3):337–360.

Keesing, Donald B. (1965), "Labor skills and international trade: Evaluating many trade flows with a single measuring device", Review of Economics and Statistics, 47 (August).

Keesing, Donald B. (1966), "Labor skills and comparative advantage", American Economic Review,

56 (May):249–258.

Keesing, Donald B. (1967), "The impact of research and development on United States trade", Journal of Political Economy, 75 (February):38–48.

Kenen, Peter B. (1965), "Nature, capital and trade", Journal of Political Economy, 73 (October):437–460.

Kennedy, Thomas E. and Richard McHugh (1980), "An intertemporal test and rejection of the Linder hypothesis", Southern Economic Journal, 46 (January):898–903.

Kohlhagen, Steven W. (1977), "Income distribution and 'Representative demand' in international trade flows – An empirical test of Linder's hypothesis", Southern Economic Journal, 44 (July):167–172.

Kojima, Koyoshi (1964), "The pattern of international trade among advanced countries", Hitotsubashi Journal of Economics (June):16–36.

Kravis, Irving (1956), "Availability and other influences on the commodity composition of trade", Journal of Political Economy, 64 (April).

Krueger, Anne O. (1977), "Growth, distortions, and patterns of trade among countries", Princeton studies in international finance, No. 40 (Princeton University).

Krugman, Paul R. (1979), "Increasing returns, monopolistic competition, and international trade", Journal of International Economics, 9 (November):469–479.

Krugman, Paul R. (1980), "Scale economies, product differentiation, and the pattern of trade", American Economic Review, 70 (December):950–959.

Krugman, Paul R. (1981), "Intra-industry specialization and the gains from trade", Journal of Political Economy, 89 (October):959–973.

Krugman, Paul R. (1982), "A 'technology gap' model of international trade", in process (March).

Kuznets, S. (1953), Economic Change. (W.W. Norton, New York).

Lancaster, Kelvin (1980), "Intra-industry trade under perfect monopolistic competition", Journal of International Economics, 10:151–175.

Leamer, Edward E. (1974), "The commodity composition of international trade in manufactures: An empirical analysis", Oxford Economic Papers, 350–374.

Leamer, Edward E. (1980a), "The Leontief paradox, reconsidered", Journal of Political Economy, 88 (June):495–503.

Leamer, Edward E. (1980b), "A study of comparative advantage with emphasis on labor's interest", in process (March).

Leamer, Edward E. and Harry P. Bowen (1981), "Cross-section tests of the Heckscher–Ohlin theorem: Comment", American Economic Review, 71 (December):1040–1043.

Leamer, Edward E. and Robert M. Stern (1970), Quantitative international economics (Allyn and Bacon, Boston).

Leontief, W. (1954), "Domestic production and foreign trade: The American capital position re-examined", Economia Internazionale, 7.

Leontief, W. (1956), "Factor proportions and the structure of American trade: Further theoretical and empirical analysis", Review of Economics and Statistics (November):386–407.

Linder, Staffan Burenstam (1961), An essay on trade and transformation (John Wiley and Sons, New York).

Linnemann, Hans (1966), An econometric study of international trade flows (North-Holland, Amsterdam).

Lipsey, Robert E. (1976), "Review of Grubel and Lloyd, Intra-industry trade: The theory and measurement of international trade in differentiated products", Journal of International Economics.

Lowinger, Thomas C. (1975), "The technology factor and the export performance of U.S. manufacturing industries", Economic Inquiry, 13 (June):221–236.

MacDougall, G.D.A. (1951), "British and American exports: A study suggested by the theory of comparative costs, part I", Economic Journal, 61 (December).

MacDougall, G.D.A. (1952), "British and American exports: A study suggested by the theory of comparative costs, part II", Economic Journal, 62 (September).

MacDougall, G.D.A., M. Dowley, P. Fox and S. Pugh (1962), "British and American productivity, prices and exports: An addendum", Oxford Economic Papers, 14 (October).

McGilvray, James and David Simpson (1973), "The commodity structure of Anglo-Irish trade", Review of Economics and Statistics, 55 (November):451–458.

Melvin, James (1968), "Production and trade with two factors and three goods", American Economic Review, 58 (December):1249–1268.

Michaely, Michael (1981), "Income levels and the structure of trade", in: S. Grassman and E. Lundberg, eds., The world economic order: Past and prospects (Macmillan, London):121–161.

Mitchell, Daniel J.B. (1975), "Recent changes in the labor content of U.S. international trade", Industrial and Labor Relations Review (April):355–369.

Morrall, John F. III (1972), Human capital, technology, and the role of the United States in international trade, University of Florida Social Sciences Monograph No. 46 (University of Florida Press, Gainesville).

Petri, Peter A. (1980), "A Ricardian model of market sharing", Journal of International Economics, 10:201–211.

Posner, M.V. (1961), "International trade and technical change", Oxford Economic Papers, 13:323–341.

Pöyhönen, Pentti (1963), "A tentative model for the volume of trade between countries", Welwirtschaftliches Archiv, 90 (1):93–99.

Sapir, André (1982), "Determinants of trade in services", in process.

Soete, Luc L.G. (1981), "A general test of technological gap trade theory", Welwirtschaftliches Archiv, 117 (4):638–660.

Stern, Robert M. (1962), "British and American productivity and comparative costs in international trade", Oxford Economic Papers, 14 (October).

Stern, Robert M. (1975), "Testing trade theories", in: Peter B. Kenen, ed., International trade and finance: Frontiers for research (Cambridge University Press, New York) 3–49.

Stern, Robert M. (1976), "Some evidence on the factor content of West Germany's foreign trade", Journal of Political Economy, 84 (February).

Stern, Robert M., Jonathan Francis and Bruce Schumacher (1976), Price elasticities in international trade: An annotated bibliography (Macmillan, London).

Stern, Robert M. and Keith E. Maskus (1981), "Determinants of the structure of U.S. foreign trade, 1958–76", Journal of International Economics, 11 (May):207–224.

Tinbergen, Jan (1962), Shaping the world economy: Suggestions for an international economic policy. (New York).

Travis, William P. (1964), The theory of trade and protection (Harvard University Press, Cambridge, Mass.).

Vanek, Jaroslav (1963), The natural resource content of United States foreign trade, 1870–1955. (M.I.T. Press, Cambridge, Mass.).

Vanek, Jaroslav (1968), "The factor proportions theory: The *n*-factor case", Kyklos, 4 (October):749–756.

Vernon, Raymond (1966), "International investment and international trade in the product cycle", Quarterly Journal of Economics, 80 (May):190–207.

Vernon, Raymond (1979), "The product cycle hypothesis in a new international environment", Oxford Bulletin of Economics and Statistics, 41 (November):255–267.

Wells, Louis T., Jr. (1969), "Test of a product cycle model of international trade: U.S. exports of consumer durables", Quarterly Journal of Economics, 82 (February):152–162.

Yahr, Merle I. (1968), "Human capital and factor substitution in the CES production function", in: Peter B. Kenen and Roger Lawrence, eds., The open economy: Essays on international trade and finance (Columbia University Press, New York):70–99.

Chapter 11

TRADE POLICIES IN DEVELOPING COUNTRIES

ANNE O. KRUEGER*

University of Minnesota and World Bank

Contents

1.	Trade policy, industrialization and growth	520
	1.1. Optimality of free trade	520
	1.2. Objections to free trade	521
2.	Analysis of trade policies in developing countries	527
	2.1. Export promotion and import substitution	527
	2.2. Tariffs, quotas, and exchange rate overvaluation	531
3.	Measures of protection and its effects	538
	3.1. ERPs versus DRCs	539
	3.2. Negative international value added	540
	3.3. Protection of what?	541
	3.4. Magnitude of protection	542
	3.5. The cost of protection	543
4.	Interaction with domestic distortions	548
	4.1. Behavior under distortions	548
	4.2. Analysis of policies under distortions	551
	4.3. Empirical evidence on distortions and their effects	555
5.	Terms of trade changes and export instability	557
	5.1. Secular deterioration in the terms of trade?	558
	5.2. Instability	560
	5.3. Empirical evidence on instability	564
6.	Concluding remarks	566
	References	566

*I am indebted to W.M. Corden, W. Ethier, R. Findlay, C. Hamilton and F. Ruane for helpful comments on an earlier draft of this manuscript. Much of the work was done while the author was visiting at the Institute for International Economic Studies in Stockholm. I am grateful for the stimulus, support, and facilities provided. I am grateful to Avinash Dixit for pointing out an error in the penultimate draft of subsection 4.2.1.

Handbook of International Economics, vol. I, Edited by R.W. Jones and P.B. Kenen
© *Elsevier Science Publishers B.V., 1984*

Trade policies in developing countries have been a focal point of analysis for international economists in the past several decades. A desire for rapid economic growth in developing countries raised many questions about the relationship between trade and growth. The policies adopted in many developing countries have often been widely at variance with those emanating from models of rational resource allocation and provided researchers with ample scope for analysis of their effects. Simultaneously analysts have examined the theoretical and empirical content of the rationales given for rejection of the rational resource allocation models. In addition, some developing countries reversed their trade policies in important ways, often with dramatic results. These reversals and the resulting changes in economic structure also provided stimulus for analysis of the link between trade policies and development.

Thus, the subject matter usually regarded as comprising trade and development emanates largely out of the concerns and experience of developing countries. A first section outlines the issues and their historical evolution, setting the groundwork for later sections. The second section focuses upon analysis of policies adopted under alternative trade strategies. The third section covers measures of protection and its effects in developing countries. A fourth section then introduces factor market imperfections into the analysis. The final section deals with issues of so-called "export pessimism" and instability of the international market.

1. Trade policy, industrialization and growth

Perhaps the issue central to analysis of trade policies and development is the extent to which special circumstances in developing countries vitiate the usual free trade dicta. In this section, therefore, the conditions under which free trade is optimal are first briefly stated. Then the various arguments that departures from free trade may be optimal are set forth. Thereafter, other issues raised by advocates of departures from free trade are considered.

1.1. Optimality of free trade

The case for free trade can be put in several ways: (1) it can be derived as a country's welfare-maximizing policy under a laissez-faire regime; (2) it can be defended as a world welfare-maximizing set of policies; (3) it can be defended as better than alternative policies; and (4) it can be shown to be welfare-maximizing in the context of optimal domestic policies under far less restrictive assumptions than are required for (1).

The first case was historically the basis for discussion of trade policy in developing countries. It was the one used to defend departures from free trade on the grounds that the assumptions necessary to prove the optimality of free trade were violated. It will be seen that considerations pertaining especially to (3) and (4) have emerged out of the policy debate and experience surrounding trade policies in developing countries, while the notion of world welfare maximization, as reflected in (2), has never been at issue for poor countries concerned with increasing their own levels of real output and welfare.[1]

At the time when rationales for developing countries' trade policies were first being formulated, the price-theoretic case for the optimality of free trade was based on highly restrictive assumptions which included: constant returns to scale in production with no dynamic effects, perfect competition within the domestic market for both goods and factors, and the small-country assumption under which international prices were given to the country.[2]

1.2. Objections to free trade

In the early post-war years, most developing countries' economies were relatively specialized in the production of primary commodities. Discussions of trade policy tended to center around the two-by-two comparative advantage version of the model in which fixed input coefficients were assumed. A frequent interpretation of the implications of the model for developing countries was that they should under welfare maximization and free trade continue to be producers of primary commodities, exchanging them for imports of manufactures.

Much of the rejection of the free trade argument was a rejection of this interpretation, as economists in developing countries instinctively reacted against the proposition that their continuing role in the world economy should be as specialized producers of primary commodities. A modern interpretation of the *n* commodity, *m* factor model would involve the compartmentalization of the economy into agricultural and nonagricultural sectors, within each of which a number of different production activities are possible. In such a setup, comparative advantage would lie within some activities within each sector, and would

---

[1] That countries might have monopoly power in trade was frequently used as a defense of interventionist policies, as is discussed further below.

[2] The modern statement of an optimum is couched in terms of requiring equality of marginal rates of transformation (MRT) in production domestically (for produced goods) with the MRT through trade, and the equality of both those rates with the marginal rate of substitution in consumption. See Chapter 2 for further exposition.

involve some degree of specialization both within nonagriculture (manufacturing?) and within agriculture.[3]

Rationales given for interventionist trade policies were based on the proposition that the case for free trade as it was stated in the price-competitive-equilibrium sense was violated.[4] Three classes of arguments for intervention were given: (1) that there are dynamic factors, either (a) infant industry or (b) others, which might broadly be classed as temporary externalities; (2) that developing countries are not price takers in international markets; and (3) that there are factor market imperfections in developing countries so that resource allocation under laissez-faire is nonoptimal.[5]

1.2.1. The infant industry argument

Many defenses of departures from free trade, and especially of protection to domestic industry, were based on the infant industry argument, and on presumed externalities and "dynamic effects" emanating from the development of a manufacturing sector. The infant industry argument is the oldest and best known rationale for intervention. Economists since Mill and Bastable have stated that infant industry considerations might constitute a legitimate exception to the case for free trade (from the viewpoint of the individual country and the world).[6] The argument essentially posits that some industries have initially high costs but may, in the long run, have a comparative advantage after a temporary period of development.[7] In order for it to be valid, several conditions must be met: (1) there

[3]See Krueger (1977) for an elaboration of the two-sector, many commodity model. Underlying any variant of this model must be the notion that, in the short run at least, there is a specific factor in one of the two sectors (such as land in agriculture). See Jones (1971) for the general two-commodity, three-factor model on which this, and other, sectoral interpretations of the comparative advantage model are based.

[4]It is an open question whether the alleged departures were discussed because policy-makers were determined to institute protectionist measures and sought a rationalization or whether the conviction that the free trade argument did not apply was the motivating force. Either way, the arguments constituted the basis for much of the research on trade and development, and are therefore the motivation for much of the discussion that follows.

[5]For an excellent analysis of these issues as they were perceived in the early 1960s, see Chenery (1961).

[6]Non-economic objectives, such as national defense, have also been recognized as a basis for departures, although questions have sometimes been raised as to whether in fact protectionist measures (e.g. American oil quotas) in any sense served their avowed purpose. There are also alternative means, such as stockpiling and stand-by ready-to-use factories, which might meet these objectives at lower cost.

[7]See Chapter 4. for an exposition of optimal interventions when "experience" as reflected in cumulated output is an argument of the manufacturing production function but external to the firm. Bardhan (1970, ch. 7) develops such a model.

must be an industry, currently uneconomic, which, if developed, would experience a sufficient decrease in costs, or generate sufficient externalities , so that the initial excess costs of the industry would be repaid with a rate of return equal to that earned on other investments; (2) some part of the decrease in costs would have to consist of externalities generated by firms in the industry or the entire industrial sector, since otherwise private producers would themselves be willing to incur the costs in order to reap the benefits (on the assumption that the industry would be genuinely economic to develop), and (3) the protection would in fact be temporary (i.e. vested interests to maintain protection would not be created). The validity of the infant industry argument as a case for a departure from free trade thus rests on the assumed short-term nature of the cost disadvantage the industry suffers from, on noncapturable externalities, and on the temporary nature of protection.[8]

Thus, both the presence of externalities and the presumed increase in efficiency of an industry over time are necessary, but not sufficient, to indicate that free trade might not be optimal. Even if a departure from free trade were warranted, it is not at all clear in theory that a trade intervention would be optimal, and it might not even improve welfare as contrasted with free trade. As is discussed in Section 4.2., a production subsidy to the producers (or equivalently, a tariff and a consumption subsidy in like amount) can provide the same benefits at lower consumption cost over the period during which the infant becomes efficient [see Johnson (1965)]. There are, however, other considerations which suggest that protection, or a production subsidy, may be an inefficient means of promoting an industry even when externalities and time effects are present.

Baldwin (1969) analyzed the possible underlying sources of externalities and the extent to which tariff protection (or a production subsidy) might move resource allocation in the right direction. In effect, four possible sources of dynamic changes in cost which might generate externalities external to the firm have been discussed. These are: new industries must acquire some knowledge and technical know-how, and these may not be appropriable by the firm or firms paying for it; new industries must bear the costs of training workers, and, once trained, new firms can bid away the skilled workers so that the costs of training can never be recouped;[9] static and continuing externalities; and, finally, market

---

[8] There is an interesting question as to whether the externalities occur in one industry or across all manufacturing industries. If externalities accrue to other industries, it is not apparent how temporary protection of the infant will help. For a careful discussion of externalities in relation to the infant industry argument, see Corden (1974 ch. 9).

[9] This argument implicitly assumes that there is a minimum or subsistence wage that must be paid during the training period which plus the cost of training exceeds the worker's marginal product during that period. Once training was completed, other firms could bid up wages to the level of worker's marginal products, and hence firms would never recoup their initial losses.

imperfections, either in information or in the capital market, such that risks are overestimated and individual firms will not undertake socially profitable activities.

Each of these considerations provides a basis for the supposition that there is an allocation of resources that could improve welfare contrasted with a laissez-faire outcome. But there are grounds on which to question whether temporary protection through a tariff would do so. Consider the case of a firm which must invest in technical know-how which will become freely available to other firms after the initial investment. As Baldwin pointed out:

> A duty raises the domestic price of a product, and from the viewpoint of the domestic industry as a whole, makes some investments in knowledge more profitable. But the individual entrepreneur still faces the same externality problem as before, namely, the risk that other firms in the same industry will copy, without cost to themselves, any new technology discovered by the firm and will then drive the product's price or factor prices to levels at which the initial firm will be unable to recover the costs of acquiring knowledge [Baldwin (1969, p. 298)].

The same sorts of considerations pertain to the other three classes of cases: when workers must be trained, protection does not provide assurance to existing firms that there will not be new entrants once training costs have been incurred by the initial group; static externalities are ongoing and do not constitute a case for temporary protection and, in addition, a tariff may not be an efficient instrument for correcting the externality; and, in the case of imperfect information or an imperfect capital market, investment in acquiring the information cannot be recaptured even in the presence of a tariff if the initial entrant demonstrates to other firms that risks have been overestimated. Even the proposition that comparative advantage will change over time and that entrepreneurs maximizing according to static considerations will make the "wrong" decisions is an argument for provision of additional information and forecasts. It is not apparent that imposition of tariffs will induce the economy along the path of comparative advantage.

These and other arguments against infant industry protection may take one of two forms. On the one hand, they may be a special case of the general proposition that a first-best intervention should be directed to the source of the distortion (see Chapter 2 and Section 4.2). In this form, it is conceded that protection would improve welfare, but demonstrated that an alternative intervention would improve welfare more. Alternatively, the stronger case can be made, as was done by Baldwin, that tariff protection may not at all represent a welfare improvement contrasted with laissez-faire because it does not induce behavior to capture the externality and thus imposes costs without correcting at all the source of the distortion. Thus, even when the proposition that there are externalities and that costs will fall over time is correct, it is not entirely clear that intervention via trade policy will improve welfare contrasted with laissez-faire, much less that a tariff or production subsidy will induce an optimal level of activity in the industry.

One other point should be noted with regard to the infant industry argument: quite aside from the question of the optimal instruments to employ to encourage the growth of infant industries, there is a question as to the range of infants. Two interpretations are possible: one, that infants, if any, must be relatively few, and that infant industry considerations imply selective growth of new industries, possibly in sequence, over time; the other is that the manufacturing sector of most developing countries is itself the infant, that externalities emanate from the sector as a whole regardless of which industries are producing. On this latter interpretation, uniform incentives (which implies a uniform rate of effective protection – see Section 3.1) to all manufacturing activities would presumably be warranted.

To date, most economists have pointed to the fact that high levels of protection have persisted for long periods as evidence that protection in developing countries generally has not been justified on infant-industry grounds. To this author's knowledge, only one attempt has been made ex-post to examine the pattern of decline in costs accompanying protection. Krueger and Tuncer (1982) showed that in the case of Turkey there was no evidence to suggest that more protected industries experienced a higher rate of decline in costs than less protected industries. There is a paucity of empirical evidence, however.

It will be seen below that the trade policies of most developing countries, even when rationalized by an appeal to infant-industry considerations, have not generally followed patterns that one would a priori expect to accord with infant industry notions. High levels of protection have continued long after what might reasonably have been regarded as a temporary learning period ended; and there is no evidence that higher rates of protection have been accorded to industries with greater externalities or dynamic factors associated with them.

1.2.2. *Terms of trade*

While the infant industry argument provided the intellectual underpinning for advocacy of restricting imports (especially of manufactures), "export pessimism" and skepticism about the reliability of the international market buttressed the case. In all its variants, the "export pessimism" proposition was essentially that export earnings of developing countries could grow only slowly, if at all, while economic growth would lead to rapidly rising demand for import-type goods. The argument was often carried one step further with the assertion that the terms of trade would inevitably turn against exports (of primary commodities) from developing countries if their supply was expanded, and hence that efforts to expand export earnings would be self-defeating.[10]

A second stated reason for skepticism regarding reliance upon the international market focused upon presumed instability in some dimension of exports: prices, quantities, or earnings. Here, the argument was that instability in these variables damaged the growth prospects of the domestic economy. These arguments have brought forth considerable research. A first line of inquiry centers around the issue of whether export prices and earnings are highly volatile (due presumably to relatively low demand or supply elasticities). A second issue is whether developing countries' terms of trade have in fact turned against them over time. Those issues are the subject of Section 5.

1.2.3. Factor market imperfections

An early rationale given for intervention in trade was that factor markets in developing countries were obviously imperfect, and that factor prices failed to reflect the opportunity costs of various factors of production. One early argument was that high wages were paid in manufacturing in developing countries, and that protection might offset some of the nonoptimal resource allocation that would result from these distorted wages. Others analyzed credit rationing (as inducing overly capital-intensive techniques and activities), minimum wage legislation, and other presumed distortions.

This set of questions focuses on the issue of the state of factor markets in developing countries, and the degree to which appropriate policy interventions can improve resource allocation in their presence. Three lines of research have resulted. First, attention has been devoted to policy rankings (from most to least attainable improvement in welfare) in the presence of unremovable distortions. Second, considerable attention has been paid to analyzing the determinants of "shadow prices" of factors of production, both to devise criteria to evaluate the outcomes of existing patterns of resource allocation in the presence of distortions, and to guide public sector investment decisions when market prices do not appropriately reflect opportunity cost. Finally, research has been undertaken on the orders of magnitude of domestic factor market distortions and their impact. These issues are covered in Section 4.

This brief description provides an overview of the issues that comprise the subject matter of trade and development. They have given much of the motivation for research in the area, to which we now turn, in order: alternative trade policies; analysis of protective structures and their effects; analysis of factor market

---

[10]It should be noted that without further assumptions, that argument would not, even if factually correct, constitute a case for protection: market forces should provide for reallocation toward import-competing production over time.

imperfections and alternative policies in their presence; and examination of commodity markets, their behavior over time, and the scope for welfare-improving intervention under alternative structures of those markets.

2. Analysis of trade policies in developing countries

What distinguishes protectionist policies in developing countries from those in developed countries is the height of protection and the degree of intervention in various markets. Therefore, the basic analytical tools used to analyze instruments of trade policy are much the same for all. However, the pervasiveness of intervention in developing countries raises to the forefront a set of issues which can, for purposes of applied analysis, generally be set aside in developed countries. These pertain to subventions of trade policy (such as illegal activities) which become more profitable as restrictions become higher, the interactions between domestic market interventions and trade instruments, and to the previously-mentioned imperfections in factor markets.

In this section, an effort is made to sketch the various analyses that have been undertaken in connection with trade regimes in developing countries, leaving aside empirical findings and the complications that arise because of domestic interventions and factor market imperfections. It will remain for Section 3 to cover issues of measurement of protection and for Section 4 to introduce domestic distortions into the analysis.

2.1. Export promotion and import substitution

As already indicated, under optimal resource allocation the marginal rate of transformation (MRT) between pairs of commodities in domestic production will equal the MRT through trade. In itself, this dictum gives no insight into the optimal allocation of new resources between import-competing and exportable industries during the process of resource accumulation. One can well imagine different countries, with different resource endowments, sizes, and locations relative to major international markets, which might consequently experience very different optimal marginal allocations of resources to exportable and import-competing industries during the growth process. In a neoclassical world of capital accumulation and a rising capital–labor endowment, one could after the fact examine the ratio of trade to GNP which would reflect the joint outcome of optimal resource allocation and consumer expenditure patterns with rising levels of income. Almost certainly, there would be some industries which were economic as import-competing and others that developed as export industries.[11]

With a few exceptions, analysis of trade policy in developed countries is typically based upon the assumption that departures from the optimum are relatively small, with "excess" incentives to some import-competing and some exportable industries. In developing countries, however, there has been an effort to guide resource allocation through trade policy and other measures, and policy makers have perceived their choices as being either "import substitution" (IS) or export promotion.[12]

The policy instruments employed to encourage the development of domestic industry were so all-pervasive, and employed to such a degree, that policy regimes were genuinely dichotomous: the height of protection has been so great in most IS regimes that development of economic new export industries (and even expansion of existing ones) was largely choked off.

Import substitution was the predominant choice in the 1950s and early 1960s. Policy instruments were chosen to provide protection to domestic industries as they were established. These consisted of various combinations of: tariffs, whose height was often increased automatically as domestic production started; restrictions or prohibitions on imports if domestic production was available, with a consequent comprehensive import licensing system necessary for enforcement; provisions for duty-free imports of capital equipment and, often, intermediate goods employed in the production of import-competing goods; domestic content requirements for domestic assemblers (to promote the local production of components); and a variety of domestic incentives, the most important of which was very frequently the provision of credit at low, if not negative, real rates of interest. A first step in analyzing such regimes was therefore to work out the links and interrelationships of tariffs (and other charges on imports), quotas, import prohibitions, credit rationing, and other instruments associated with the trade regime. These commercial policy measures are the subject of analysis in Section 2.2. below.

---

[11]In practice, even the concept of "industry" is too broad, and in two ways. First, the variety of products produced in a modern industrial society is enormous, and the term "industry" evokes the notion of a single homogeneous product such as steel, rather than metal fasteners, metal shapes, industrial hardware, and so on. Secondly, even within the same industry, some firms may prove to be efficient and others not.

[12]All countries, especially those adopting import substitution policies, have measures which are termed "export promotion". Very often, the inducements to export are really offsets to part of the incentives for import-substitution industries. In some countries, firms have been required to export part of their output in return for receipt of privileges in the domestic market. These policies can be distinguished from the regimes which are generally oriented toward exports by an estimate of the bias of the regime, discussed below. Many "export promotion" policies are really nothing more than partial offsets to the overall bias of the regime toward IS, and are often aimed at inducing the IS industries to export part of their output.

Before turning to that task, however, two related issues need attention. First, there is the question as to how conceptually one defines an IS or an EP regime. Second, as already mentioned, under IS regimes export growth was stunted, and that gave rise to a phenomenon referred to as "foreign exchange shortage", which was analyzed in the context of a "two-gap" model.

2.1.1. The "bias" of a trade regime

In a trade regime with varying levels of protection to different industries, any measure of the overall orientation of the regime must of necessity imply aggregation of the individual protective rates. In a two-commodity world, the bias of a regime (i.e. the degree to which the incentives it conveys for exporting and for import-competing production depart from those that would prevail at free trade) is intuitively straightforward: it is the ratio of the domestic relative price of import-competing to exportable goods to the international relative price of importables relative to exportables. The concept generalizes, so that it becomes:

$$B = \frac{\sum_i W_i (P_{mi}/Q_{mi})}{\sum_j W_j (P_{xj}/Q_{xj})}, \qquad (2.1)$$

where B is the measure of bias, w's are weights, P's are domestic prices, Q's are international prices, i an index of import-competing commodities, and j an index of exportable commodities. Thus, the bias of the regime expresses the extent to which domestic price incentives depart from those that would be faced at free trade.[13] An export-oriented regime would generally have a B of less than unity, while import substitution regimes have been calculated to have B's of two and even more. There are both a priori and empirical grounds for believing that departures from uniform incentives for exportable and import-competing production may be much greater under import-substitution than under export-promotion regimes.

A major question with regard to the measure of bias, as in any estimation of protection rates to individual commodities, is the choice of appropriate weights. In some sense, the ideal weights would be the value of trade foregone by virtue of import restrictions. However, that is not observable. For trade regimes that

---

[13] In addition to the weighting problem discussed in the text, the measure of bias is also subject to some qualifications with regard to whether it should be estimated with output prices or with value added prices. There has been no serious consideration given to this question in the literature. It is at least in principle possible that one regime might be found to have a greater bias under the value added definition of prices while another would be shown to have the greater bias under output prices. At any event, the costs of misallocation of resources need not be associated one to one with the divergence of bias from unity.

prohibit imports of goods domestically produced, it seems clear that weighting different commodities or industries by the value of imports would fail to capture the bias of the regime toward imports, and that production weights might be preferable for imports. For exportables, however, the converse argument can be made: some commodities may have large domestic consumption and only minor export value while others may be oriented toward the export market. Use of domestic production weights may then be inappropriate if the intent is to capture the incentive effects of the regime.[14]

Given conceptual (value-added versus output prices; choice of weights; and aggregation) and measurement difficulties, one cannot place too great a reliance upon the precision with which B and other measures of protection are estimated.[15] Nonetheless, in practice, the height of protection has been so great in most IS regimes that there has been little question of the direction of the bias: countries seem either to have relatively strong biases toward IS or to have biases within the range of 0.9 to 1.1.[16]

2.1.2. The "two-gap model"

When, during the 1950s and 1960s, most developing countries had adopted IS policies, almost all of them found themselves confronted with periodic "foreign exchange shortages". Export earnings grew relatively slowly as new resources were channeled heavily into IS industries and ambitious investment and development plans generated considerable inflationary pressure at fixed exchange rates which decreased the profitability of exports. Simultaneously, demand for foreign exchange, even with protection for the newly established industries, rose rapidly (because the heavy investment programs were import-intensive and because the import-competing industries were more import using than anticipated).[17]

Periodic "foreign exchange crises" then forced countries to alter their trade and payments regimes, and led to periods of slow growth following bursts of investment and imports.[18]

---

[14]Especially in the context of the complex trade regimes found in some developing countries, there is even a conceptual problem of defining a criterion for determining which industries belong in the import-competing, and which in the export, category. For a discussion of this, and other, measurement problems, see Krueger, Lary et al. (1981, ch. 1).

[15]South Korea reversed trade policies from IS to export promotion in the early 1960s and experienced extremely rapid growth after that change. The trade policies employed have therefore been of great interest. To this date, however, there remains an argument as to whether those policies were successful because they were really free trade policies or whether instead the Korean incentive structure was somewhat biassed toward exports. Either way, it is generally agreed that the bias did not diverge substantially from unity.

[16]These numbers are based on Krueger (1978, table 6.2).

[17]See Diaz–Alejandro (1965) for a discussion of this phenomenon.

[18]See Diaz–Alejandro (1975) for a discussion of the influence of "stop-go" policies on Colombia's economic growth. The Colombian case was in many respects typical of this phenomenon.

This led many economists to view the foreign trade sector as a separate constraint on growth. This was formalized by Chenery and Strout (1966), as they modelled a developing country in which the growth rate was determined by investment, which in turn could not be greater than permitted either by the community's savings (plus resource transfers from abroad) or by the available foreign exchange (determined by an exogenously given, and presumably binding, rate of growth of foreign exchange earnings). The model was widely used as a representation of developing countries' economies, but, as McKinnon (1966) pointed out, it assumed that exports were insensitive to relative prices and thus reflected the export pessimism discussed in Section 1. The experience of the countries that have altered trade policies (or even altered their exchange rates) has been fairly convincing evidence that sluggish growth of export earnings was at least in part a consequence of trade policies and not an exogenous phenomenon beyond countries' control.[19]

2.2. Tariffs, quotas, and exchange rate overvaluation

2.2.1. Tariff-quota equivalence and non-equivalence

In a partial equilibrium setting, the analysis of the effect of a tariff is straightforward.[20] A first question is how tariffs and import licensing systems interact.

A starting point is the analysis of quotas. In partial equilibrium analysis, it is conventional to start by analyzing the tariff-equivalent of the quota. The equivalence can be seen in Figure 2.1(a). Suppose the world price of a particular commodity at a given exchange rate is p_w, with domestic demand for the commodity represented by the schedule DD, and domestic supply by SS. At free trade, the domestic price would equal the world price, oa would be produced domestically, ad would be imported, and domestic consumption would be od.

If, instead, a tariff were placed (and enforced) upon the importation of a commodity, say in the amount represented by the ratio of $p_w(1+t)/p_w$, the

---

[19] This is not to deny that countries can have a more difficult time increasing their export earnings under some circumstances than others. Quite clearly, phenomena such as the oil price increase of the 1970s created major difficulties for oil-importing developing countries.

[20] Surcharges on imports can be analyzed by estimating the additional costs they impose upon importers as a percentage of c.i.f. price and adding those charges to the ad valorem tariff. For example, many countries have required importers to deposit, for an import license, funds equal to some fraction or multiple of the value of the license interest-free in the Central Bank, the sum being returned only after the import transaction is completed. These deposits, usually termed "guarantee deposits", place an additional cost on importation equal to the cost of borrowing the necessary sum over the required internal. That cost, as a percentage of the c.i.f. price, can be added to the tariff and other charges to estimate the total cost of tariff-like charges. [See Krueger (1974a, p. 278) for an example of such computations.]

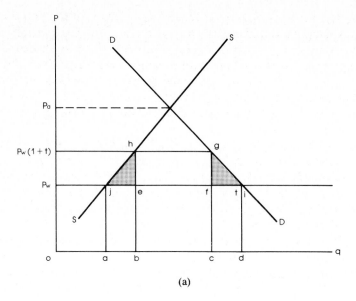

(a)

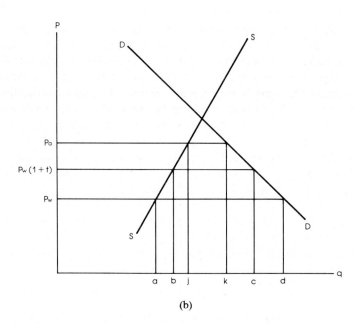

(b)

Figure 2.1

domestic price would be $p_w(1+t)$, domestic production would increase to *ob*, domestic consumption would decline to *oc*, and imports would be *bc*. The welfare losses associated with the tariff would clearly be the two shaded triangles, representing "production cost" and "consumption cost" respectively. Production cost in this case represents the additional (international) value of goods and services that could be available for society's consumption were there free trade and the resources diverted by the tariff into this industry reallocated to their best alternative uses.

For present purposes, the essential point is somewhat different. That is, the domestic outcome would be the same, given the postulated demand and supply curves, if instead of a tariff, imports were restricted by licensing to an amount *bc*. This is the fundamental tariff-quota equivalence proposition [see Bhagwati (1965)]. For purposes of analyzing the structure of protection of a country at a point in time, the analyst can start by estimating this tariff equivalent and proceed as if it were the tariff. To be sure, such an estimate requires knowledge of domestic prices which in practice are much more difficult to ascertain than are tariff rates. Nonetheless, in principle, the tariff-quota equivalence theorem provides a useful empirical tool for analyzing the static effects of a trade regime which relies on both tariffs and quotas.

There are, however, several qualifications to tariff quota equivalence. If either domestic or international market structures are not competitive, the imposition of a quota may affect the buyer or seller's degree of monopoly power, and hence, supply or demand curve, differently than it would under a tariff [see Bhagwati (1978)]. Perhaps even more important is the consideration that a tariff, unless changed, confers the same proportionate degree of nominal protection to an industry over time and domestic prices can be expected to change with changes in world prices. By contrast, a quota (unless changed) normally confers a different rate of nominal protection over time, as fluctuations in world prices are not reflected in the domestic market. Thus, shifts in domestic demand can alter the degree of nominal protection unless quotas are deliberately altered by the authorities. Likewise, technical change in either industry domestically destroys the equivalence. Therefore, under quotas domestic prices change only in response to shifts in domestic demand and supply while under tariffs, domestic prices change only in response to changes in the world price.[21] One can therefore distinguish the degree of insulation provided to domestic producers by the two alternative instruments.

---

[21] It has been pointed out by Fishelson and Flatters (1975) that this difference may be of importance under conditions of uncertainty. Depending on the source of uncertainty and who is risk averse, tariffs and quotas can have different allocational effects, even in static analysis, when risk considerations are taken into account.

2.2.2. Rent seeking

There is another major difference between tariffs and quotas. It concerns possible differences in the allocational and distributional consequences of the treatment of the rectangle *efgh* in Figure 2.1(a). With a tariff, government revenues will be equal in amount to that rectangle (the height of the tariff times the volume of imports). With a quota the rectangle is not government revenue but instead represents the value of import licenses issued by the government. Depending upon the mechanism used for allocating those licenses and upon behavior with respect to government expenditures and revenues, there can be a variety of effects in addition to those originating from the tariff equivalent of the quota.

In practice, there are often *both* tariffs and quotas on importation of particular commodities. If the quota is not binding (i.e. if the individuals can buy all they wish to at the tariff inclusive price), it is irrelevant to further analysis except as it might become binding at some future date or with shifts in underlying conditions. If it is binding, the situation may be as depicted in Figure 2.1(b).[22] All symbols retain their meaning from Figure 2.1(a). Suppose then, that with a tariff in the amount sufficient- to raise the domestic price to $p_w(1 + t)$, which would induce imports in the amount bc, the authorities restrict import licenses to an amount jk. The domestic price will rise to p_a, while the landed cost of the import will be the tariff-inclusive price. The difference is referred to as the "premium" or the "rent" on the import license.[23]

Depending upon the mechanism by which import licenses are allocated to alternative claimants, the allocation of premiums can have differing, and significant, effects upon resource allocation. In effect, recipients of import licenses receive a valuable property right. When there are ways in which they can "earn" the property right, they attempt to do so. The class of mechanisms under which potential license recipients attempt to influence the amount they are allotted is termed "rent-seeking" behavior, conveying the notion that the premium on the import license, while a rent, may be sought after in ways that use resources. When that happens, resources are allocated to obtaining a thing which is in fixed supply; those resources are, at least in the sense that they do not expand the supply, effectively wasted.

---

[22]When the exchange rate is overvalued, empirical estimates of protection via tariffs and the tariff-equivalent of quotas must be adjusted to reflect that overvaluation.

[23]It should be noted that there will, in all circumstances in which distribution is not costless, be a difference between landed cost and the wholesale or retail price of an imported commodity. The notion of a premium is straightforward: usually estimates of the value of the premium are complicated by the need to make allowance for normal distribution mark-ups. If some commodities were subject only to tariffs while others had binding quotas, one might as a first approximation take the ratio of the observed wholesale price to landed cost of the tariff-only commodities, and subtract that fraction of landed cost from observed domestic prices for quota-restricted commodities in arriving at an estimate of the premium.

Examples of rent-seeking behavior abound. A simple, and frequently-encountered, one occurs when individual firms in a manufacturing activity requiring an imported raw material or intermediate good as an input are allocated import licenses in proportion to their share of the industry's capacity.[24] In that instance, firms may be expected to add to their capacity, even when they are not utilizing existing capacity, if the expected value of the additional import license premia they will receive exceeds or equals the prevailing rate of return on alternative investments. As such, the rent-seeking associated with import licenses may go far to explain the observed high levels of excess capacity in manufacturing industries in some developing countries. One would expect to observe higher equilibrium levels of excess capacity in industries in which the premium was relatively high and where imported inputs constituted a sizeable fraction of costs.

Other examples of rent-seeking behavior may be found when businessmen and their representatives spend time and resources in attempting to obtain licenses; when small retail shops operate at uneconomically small scales because the profit earned per item is sufficient to warrant their remaining in business; and when individuals remain unemployed seeking jobs in high-wage sectors of the economy while eschewing opportunities available to them in other sectors.[25]

Recently, Bhagwati and Srinivasan (1980) have attempted to extend the concept of rent seeking. They have argued that the possibility of imposing tariffs in itself creates the possibility of tariff revenue, and that there will be "revenue-seeking" in much the same way as individuals attempt to obtain import licenses. While there is some question as to whether there is or is not a problem of appropriability of public expenditures without a free rider problem, it seems clear that lobbyists can and do expend resources attempting to influence the height and structure of tariffs and that the concept of rent-seeking generalizes to areas pertinent to all trade policies in developing and developed countries (as well as to some non-trade phenomena).

2.2.3. Illegal activities

The fact that tariffs and quotas are so highly protective in some developing countries has frequently created sizable rewards for those who can evade regulations. Many forms of subversion are illegal or evasive, and have become sufficiently widespread as to warrant analysis. Although rent-seeking may take legal or illegal forms, it is generally analyzed without regard to the legality of the undertakings which constitute it. By contrast, a separate body of literature has emerged with regard to under- and over-invoicing of exports and imports, black markets, smuggling, and other illegal activities. Interestingly, if a quantitative restriction is

---

[24]See Bhagwati and Srinivasan (1976) for the description of such a mechanism in India.
[25]See Krueger (1974b) for a discussion of rent seeking, and Section 4 for a discussion of behavior when unemployment ensues as described here.

in place and rent-seeking occurs, the activity uses up resources and there is a presumption that welfare diminishes regardless of the legality of rent-seeking. By contrast, illegal activities such as smuggling and black markets have a much greater likelihood of improving welfare.

By its nature, direct evidence about illegal activities is difficult to come by, although there may be inferential evidence. Baldwin (1976), for example, regressed the domestic Philippine price of importables against the world price and the tariff rate. He found that, above tariff rates of about 50 percent, the domestic price failed to increase significantly with increases in the tariff rate, suggestive the smuggling may have become important at about that tariff height.

Theorizing about illegal activities has proceeded along several lines. One has focussed on the relationship between the black market exchange rate and the legal exchange rate. As Sheikh (1974) has pointed out there must be legal restrictions on exchange of money in order for there to be a black market in foreign exchange. A major question about black market exchange rates has been the inferences that may be drawn from the behavior of their ratio to the legal exchange rate.[26] In general, few predictions can be made for two reasons. The black market may cover only certain kinds of transactions for which the costs of illegality are low (such as a market for currency and not for other forms of money). Secondly, there can be various sources of demand for black market foreign exchange: (1) it may be usable to purchase foreign goods for smuggling into the country (in which case tariffs are avoided and the foreign-exchange owner captures the equivalent of both the tariff and the tariff-equivalent of the quota on any imports less, of course, the costs of smuggling); (2) it may be usable to purchase additional imports which may be legally importable if there is underinvoicing of imports; and (3) it may be usable as a store of value abroad.

In the last case, the demand for black market foreign exchange is a stock demand, as foreign exchange is sought because it in turn is required to purchase assets denominated in other currencies. In the first two cases, the demand for black market foreign exchange is a flow demand, based upon the purchaser's ability to profit by importing additional goods and selling them at a higher price domestically.

Pitt (1981a) has modelled the demand and supply for black market foreign exchange in these circumstances under the assumption that the risks of detection, and therefore the costs of over-invoicing and under-invoicing, increase with the differential between the actual price and the faked price. In his model, a liberalization of the trade regime and reduction in export taxes may even lead to an increase in the black market exchange rate. This could happen if the supply of black market foreign exchange diminished because the incentive to underinvoice exports, selling the proceeds on the black market, is reduced. The consequent

---

[26] See the classic analysis of Michaely (1954); see Sheikh (1976) for a recent analysis. In addition to this line of research, there have been several models developed in which the black market for foreign exchange is a dual market in which illegal transactions may be undertaken costlessly. See Blejer (1978) and de Macedo (1980).

downward shift in the supply of black market foreign exchange raises the equilibrium black market rate in the presence of a constant tariff structure (which in turn implies an increased absolute margin for profitable under-invoicing of imports).

Moving from illegal transactions in currency to illegal trade in goods, there are questions about the circumstances under which over-invoicing or under-invoicing of imports and exports might be profitable. Over-invoicing of exports is more profitable the greater the premium on black market foreign exchange (when exporters resell abroad) or the greater the profitability of using export proceeds to purchase additional goods to be imported under license when licenses are specified in value terms and imports can be under-invoiced. For imports, under-invoicing becomes more profitable the higher is the duty rate [and therefore the smaller the duty that must be paid as the price of the import is increasingly understated – see Bhagwati (1974)]. For all these reasons, recorded trade statistics may fail to reflect the actual transactions undertaken, either in terms of volume or value.

In addition to the black market and faked invoicing, there is the additional phenomenon of smuggling. The motive for smuggling is evident enough: if the price differential between the domestic market and the international market is sufficiently wide (due either to a tariff or to a legally-binding quota), smuggling may be profitable. Bhagwati and Hansen (1973) modeled smuggling as an alternative trade technology for obtaining a good. It is assumed inferior, in the sense that resources are used up in the act of smuggling, whereas trade through legal channels does not require those resources (but the importer must pay the tariff). Smuggling can occur only if there is a barrier to free trade and the cost of smuggling per unit of the good imported is less than the legal cost of hurdling the barrier.

In their base case, Bhagwati and Hansen assume non-prohibitive tariffs, constant costs of smuggling at a rate less than the tariff, and competitive smuggling activities. Since smuggling uses resources that would otherwise produce goods and services, it has two effects of opposite sign on welfare: (1) it increases welfare insofar as additional quantities of the imported good are made available; and (2) it reduces welfare by using up additional resources in the process of obtaining the good. Hence, smuggling cannot be unequivocally evaluated in terms of its welfare effects under normal welfare criteria. In general, because of the constant cost assumption, one would expect to observe either smuggling or legal trade in the Bhagwati–Hansen model but not both. In the unlikely case that smuggling and legal trade coexisted, then one could conclude that smuggling was inferior: the excess costs of smuggling could clearly be avoided through legal importation with no loss in consumer welfare.

An alternative specification of smuggling, as first suggested by Sheikh (1974) is one in which smuggling uses up domestic resources, rather than using up tradables. As such, it shifts the domestic transformation curve inward. Smuggling can therefore affect domestic production levels even if the domestic price is the tariff-inclusive price. Legal and illegal trade could coexist, and nonetheless improve welfare.

Both the Bhagwati–Hansen and the Sheikh models assume that when smuggling lowers the domestic price of a commodity below the price at which it can legally be imported, no legal trade will occur. Pitt (1981b) noted that in Indonesia, where smuggling was very prevalent for a substantial time period, the domestic price of the exportable commodity frequently exceeded the legal export price. He proposed an alternative smuggling model to take the coexistence of legal and illegal trade into account. The crucial assumption is that smugglers engage in some legal trade to camouflage their illegal activities. In essence, some fraction of the importer's goods are illegally imported, the fraction reflecting the amount of under-invoicing, misweighing, and misrepresentation at customs. The higher the fraction underreported, the greater the likelihood of detection. Thus, legal trade is an input into the smuggling activity. The two activities coexist and the observed domestic price of an exportable can exceed the legal export price at which some transactions are undertaken.

3. Measures of protection and its effects

Tariff schedules are inadequate guides to nominal protection levels when quotas, and not tariffs, are the binding instrument of trade policy. As implied by tariff-quota equivalence, a first step in measuring the height of protection is to obtain direct price comparisons.

There are a number of problems in obtaining price comparisons, quite aside from the fact that data collection itself is difficult. There are questions as to product categories, stability of price over time, representativeness of price observations, and matching price observations with production data to obtain corresponding input coefficients. In addition, there is the enormous problem of finding ways of estimating the comparable international price, especially in cases where quotas take the form of import prohibitions and no import prices are observable.

The fact that price comparisons are difficult does not render the task any less important, however. Nor does it raise conceptual, as contrasted with empirical, problems. Once the best available price comparisons are obtained from which nominal tariff equivalents can be calculated, it is standard practice for empirical workers to use them, combined with estimates of production coefficients, to compute effective rates of protection. In this section, the task is threefold. First, use of effective rate of protection (ERP) estimates is contrasted with use of domestic resource cost (DRC) measures. Second, attention must be given to some of the peculiar problems that arise in estimation and interpretation in restrictive trade regimes. Finally, some representative estimates of heights of effective protection are presented.

3.1. ERPs versus DRCs

Early application of effective protection measures was to estimate the height of tariff barriers in developed countries. Not only was it natural and reasonable to derive estimates of the height of protection from tariff schedules, but there was good reason to believe the ERP estimates correctly reflected protection to value added.

In developing countries, there were a number of grounds for believing that ERPs might not so straightforwardly indicate this. First, observers noted that factor prices often failed to reflect opportunity cost, due to the presence of subsidies to inputs of capital, labor market imperfections, minimum wage legislation, and so on. The effects of such imperfections on analysis of the impact of trade policies is deferred until Section 4 below. For present purposes, it suffices to note that in the presence of inappropriate factor costs, the net direction of resource pulls (as contrasted with free trade) will be influenced both by the height of protection and by the degree to which factor prices diverge from those that would be observed in a well-functioning competitive market.

Second, it was a frequent observation that there were few firms producing any single commodity in many of the developing countries. This gave rise to opportunities for exploitation of monopoly power in a sheltered domestic market. To the extent that protection resulted in monopoly profits and not in resource pulls, the effects were clearly different. In particular, the extent of protection to value added as reflected in the ERP measure would overstate (to the extent of monopoly profits) and misstate (to the extent factors were implicitly subsidized or taxed) the additional domestic resources employed per unit of value added or output in the protected industries. For this reason, some analysts of developing countries' policies converted their effective protection estimates into estimates of domestic resource cost. This was done by adjusting estimates of inputs of primary factors of production (usually capital and labor) to reflect "shadow prices" (see Section 11.4), rather than market prices.

The domestic resource cost formula is:

$$\text{DRC}_i = \sum_j s_j V_{ji} / \text{IVA}_i, \tag{3.1}$$

where DRC is the domestic resource cost, s_j is the shadow price, or opportunity cost, of the jth domestic factor of production, V_{ji} is the amount of the jth factor used per unit of output of i, and IVA_i is the international value added in the ith activity.[27]

If factor markets functioned well, DRC estimates would be identical with ERP estimates plus one, since the ERP measure essentially gives the excess domestic value added as a fraction of international value added while the DRC measure gives total value added as a fraction of international value added. Divergences arise when there are differential ratios of excess production costs to monopoly profits in different industries, and when shadow prices differ substantially from market prices. This latter is empirically important for capital services.

DRCs are still used, along with ERPs, in estimates of the height of protection in developing countries. Usually, they are used when the intention is to infer the cost of the protective structure directly from the estimates.[28] Usually, ERPs give a better indication of the incentives created by the trade regime while DRCs provide a better estimate of the cost of the regime. In recent years, new programming and general equilibrium techniques have shifted attention away from DRCs and ERPs as proxies for the costs and effects of protection, although both types of estimates continue to be made and to provide an indication of the nature of the trade regime in various developing countries (see Table 3.1 below).

3.2. Negative international value added

The concept of effective protection is well behaved when domestic and international value added are both positive. This is the case that an economist would naturally expect. In fact, negative numerators and negative denominators have both been observed empirically. Each gives rise to an estimated negative rate of effective protection, but the interpretation attached to the estimate must be quite different.

Recall that the effective protection formula is:

$$\text{ERP}_j = \left(T_j - \sum_i T_i a_{ji}\right) \bigg/ \left(1 - \sum_i a_{ji}\right), \tag{3.2}$$

where ERP_j is the effective rate of protection, world prices of all inputs and outputs are assumed to be normalized at unity, T_i is the nominal tariff on the ith commodity and a_{ji} is the (fixed coefficients) input of i per unit of output at j, valued at world prices.

---

[27]The original DRC estimates sometimes included an adjustment to international value added to reflect the fraction that was attributable to domestic factors of production. This procedure essentially netted out payments to foreign capital from international value added. See Krueger (1972) for a discussion.

[28]See, for example, Monson and Pursell (1979) and Savasini (1978) for some recent applications.

The numerator expresses domestic value added. It is evident that it could be negative when the weighted average nominal tariff rate on inputs exceeds the nominal tariff rate on output. This interpretation is quite natural, and a negative ERP originating in higher protection on inputs than on outputs clearly confers less protection than a zero level of effective protection. Thus, the ERP measure is well behaved with respect to changes in sign in the numerator.

More puzzling, at least at first sight, is the occasional observation of a negative ERP derived from a negative denominator. One would anticipate that market forces would result in observation of positive international value added only. In fact, negative denominators can arise for several reasons: (1) choice of a poor location may imply that transport costs absorb the entire value added margin earned by firms in economic locations; (2) inefficient use of materials may lead to sufficient wastage, especially behind a high wall of tariff protection, so that material input costs in fact exceed the world price of the product; and (3) the value added margin internationally may be sufficiently low that, with very high levels of protection, small errors in observation may yield a negative sign on international value added, when in fact the number is small but positive.

In an economic sense, a negative ERP attributable to a true negative international value added is higher than a high, positive ERP. For this reason, the ERP measure is not conceptually well-behaved. In practice, it is straightforward to annotate tables of empirical results in ways that carefully distinguish negative international value added cases from negative protection cases.

A somewhat more difficult problem is the fact that coefficients in developing countries appear to be more unstable than in developed countries.[29] This is true both of the a_{ij} coefficients and of implicit tariff rates derived from price comparison data. Much of the difficulty stems from the fact that levels of protection are so high in developing countries that observed value-added margins are indeed low. Small percentage changes in world prices of either inputs or outputs can make a large change in the ERP estimate because a small absolute change in an already-small denominator has a large effect.

3.3.   Protection of what?

In developed countries, it is normally straightforward to interpret tariff data: tariffs are an instrument discriminating against exports and in favor of import-competing activities in all product categories. In developing countries, the same commodity may be subject to different levels of protection under different circumstances. Thus, it can often be necessary to distinguish between the ERP for sale on the home market and for sale abroad. Many developing countries have

[29]See Yeats (1976b) for a full analysis.

Table 3.1
Mean and range of effective protective
rates for manufacturing industries in some
developing countries

Country	Year	Average ERP in manufac- turing	Range of ERPs
Brazil	1958	106	17 to 502
	1963	184	60 to 687
	1967	63	4 to 252
Chile	1967	175	−23 to 1140
Colombia	1969	19	−8 to 140
Indonesia	1971	119	−19 to 5400
Ivory Coast	1973	41	−25 to 278
Pakistan	1963/64	356	−6 to 595
	1970/71	200	36 to 595
South Korea	1968	−1	−15 to 82
Thailand	1973	27	−43 to 236
Tunisia	1972	250	1 to 737
Uruguay	1965	384	17 to 1014

Source: Krueger (1983, table 3.1). The estimates are based on research undertaken by individual country authors in the N.B.E.R. Project on Alternative Trade Strategies and Employment. The individual estimates may be found in the country study chapters.

special regimes for manufactured exports which imply that domestic producers receive a different price for the same commodity than the world price in both their domestic sales and in their exports. In the case of some extremely outer-oriented trade regimes, there have been instances where effective protection to a particular industry for export was higher than the ERP when a good was sold domestically. There have also been instances when firms with sufficiently high export volumes have been eligible for favorable treatment not available to other firms. In such instances, the same commodity may be subject to different protective rates depending not only on its destination but also on the categorization of the firm producing it.

3.4. *Magnitude of protection*

Table 3.1 reproduces some estimates of the average rates of effective protection and their spread for a number of developing countries' manufacturing sectors.[30]

---

[30] For other estimates for a variety of countries, see Balassa (1982) and Little, Scitovsky, and Scott (1970).

These rates are not adjusted for any exchange-rate overvaluation, but nonetheless are representative of the sorts of levels and heights of effective protection found in developing countries. Even allowing for this lack of adjustment, it is apparent that the spread of rates within countries, and the variation between countries, is sizable. Although there are undoubtedly measurement errors and significant changes in effective rates over time, they are nonetheless indicative of both the extent to which trade regimes discriminate against exports (as reflected by the average effective rate) and confer varying heights of protection to individual industries.[31]

Trade policies in individual countries obviously affect these heights and variances. In Brazil, for example, the period from 1964 to 1967 was one during which the government was attempting to alter its trade strategy and reduce protection. This is reflected in the lower average and range of ERPs for 1967 than for earlier years in that country. ERP estimates are also sensitive to the degree of aggregation in the input–output table (from which input coefficients are usually derived), and also to the aggregation in the underlying price data or tariff schedules used to estimate nominal tariff rates.

3.5. The cost of protection

Empirical estimates of costs of protection in developing countries have been made using a variety of techniques and models. Until the 1970s, most estimates were "partial equilibrium" in nature. More recently, alternative means of estimating the costs and effects of protection have been developed. In this section, the traditional "production cost" and "consumption cost" measures are briefly reviewed. Thereafter, alternative approaches are examined. These include: (1) attribution of deadweight costs, in addition to production and consumption costs, to the total cost of protection (still in partial equilibrium context), (2) programming models, (3) log-linear general equilibrium systems, and (4) computable general equilibrium models.

3.5.1. Partial equilibrium measures

Both ERP estimates and DRCs in principle measure protection per unit. An estimate of the effects of protection and its costs requires using one or the other of these measures in conjunction with some estimate of the quantity affected.

---

[31]See Corden (1975, p. 57) for a discussion of the interpretation of average effective protective rate and its dispersion.

The traditional analysis is based on Johnson's formulation, in which the production cost and consumption cost of a tariff (or its DRC counterpart) can be separately estimated. The measure is illustrated in Figure 2.1(a), which abstracts from intermediate goods and treats output and value added as synonymous. There, the lines DD and SS represent domestic demand and supply, respectively, for a particular imported commodity. The line p_w represents the world price, which would prevail in the domestic market in the absence of a tariff. A tariff which raised the domestic price to the height $p_w(1+t)$ would result in a reduction in imports from the level ad to bc, and a reduction in consumption from od to oc.

The production cost of the tariff is represented by the triangle hej, which represents the value, at world prices, of resources pulled into the industry. The consumption cost is the triangle fgi, representing the loss of consumer welfare when consumers substitute away from the protected commodity. The rectangle $efgh$ represents government revenue, and is thus treated as a transfer, without economic loss. Production cost estimates of welfare losses have been used in a number of studies. These permit the use of available information for individual commodities and sectors and to analyze particular situations.

3.5.2. *Deadweight loss estimates*

In developing countries where protection is simultaneously high, pervasive, and variable, a number of economists have expressed unease because of the small size of the estimates of the cost of protection. One attempt to grapple with this issue has focused upon the deadweight costs of tariffs and quantitative restrictions. Rent-seeking is one such possibility. As seen above, rent-seeking converts much or all of the rectangle from transfer payment to deadweight loss. Another form of deadweight loss, which might or might not be rent-seeking, focuses upon inefficiencies in production which arise due to protection. Bergsman (1974) pointed out that there appeared to be a class of industries which, under protection, experienced high costs. These same industries, however, were able to lower their costs and sell competitively once tariffs were reduced or eliminated. He interpreted this phenomenon to imply that industries could, when forced, become efficient, but that protection permitted "X-inefficiency" of the sort first discussed by Leibenstein (1966). As pointed out by Corden (1974, 224–231), if managerial effort increases to lower other cost, the "inefficiency" may be in the combination of inputs, rather than in using more of all inputs.

Thus, a reduction in tariff levels might be expected to result in a downward shift in industry supply curves. The welfare cost of protection would then consist of the conventional production cost, plus an inefficiency cost and possibly a monopoly cost. For Brazil, Bergsman estimated a total cost of protection of 7.1 percent of GNP, contrasted with a "conventional" production-and-consumption cost estimate of 0.3 percent of GNP (p. 419).

3.5.3. Programming models

One means of simulating the behavior of an economy is to form a programming problem which can be solved under alternative specifications. These specifications can include varying levels of protection.

For example, one might develop a programming model in which the objective was to maximize the product of prices and outputs subject to materials balance constraints and production relations. Different price vectors could then be used, representing different levels of protection, and the differences in attained levels of international value added could be interpreted as the difference in real output levels associated with different tariff structures.

Early uses of this methodology were for developed countries [Lage (1970) for Japan and Evans (1971) for Australia]. The first application to a developing country was apparently that of Baysan (1972). His estimate of the cost of protection for Turkey was substantially higher than would have been indicated by partial equilibrium methods.

Programming models which assume a fixed-coefficients production technology are subject to the difficulty that there will generally be no more tradable goods produced than there are primary factors of production in the model. In the Baysan model (as also in other programming models of this type), this problem was handled by placing upper and lower bound capacity constraints on each production activity.

More recently, Henderson (1982) developed a non-linear programming model in which a Cobb–Douglas production function (taking observed shares from the input output table) was used to represent the technology between primary inputs. This model allows for estimation of both the loss in international value added associated with tariff-ridden, rather than free-trade, prices and for an estimate of the change in relative factor prices that would be associated with the shift in production. Even with nonlinearity in the production structure, however, upper and lower bounds must be placed upon production levels to prevent extreme corner solutions.

3.5.4. Log-linear and computable general equilibrium systems

The third and fourth departures from the production-and-consumption cost approach both attempt to set forth and solve the underlying general equilibrium model. Estimates are based upon full specification of an underlying structure of production, factor supply, consumer demand, and trade possibilities. The fact that there are so many possible specifications of underlying factor market conditions (e.g. perfectly elastic labor supply to the urban sector at a given real wage; upward sloping labor supply curve; different wages paid to different groups of workers; differentiation of skill groups), production technology (e.g. substitution possibilities limited in the short run, fixed coefficients between intermediate goods and final product, differing numbers of factors of production), and trading possibilities (e.g. small country, less than perfectly elastic demand for the country's exports, imperfect substitution between imports and domestic production) makes comparison and evaluation of different models exceptionally difficult.

The best-known of the log-linear specifications as applied to a developing country is probably that of Taylor and Black (1974). Using a 35-sector model of the Chilean economy, they assumed decreasing returns to labor. They classified sectors as imports noncompetitive with domestic production, competitively imported goods, exports, and nontraded goods. Taking tariff and export subsidy changes as exogenous, they solve their system for changes in competitive imports, exports and production levels.

Taylor and Black focused upon the question of the divergence between partial and general equilibrium estimates of the resource pulls of ERP structures. On theoretical grounds, it is possible that the ERP estimates may not prove good general equilibrium indicators of the direction in which resources move in response to tariffs. An important question is how realistic this possibility is in practice.

They proceeded to estimate the effects of two alternative tariff cuts: a ten percent cut in all Chilean tariffs and subsidies; and a ten percent cut in all tariffs less than 100 percent combined with a 20 percent cut in all tariffs exceeding 100 percent initially. They assumed full employment and alternative specifications of the production structure. These were: (1) a Cobb–Douglas production function in both intermediate inputs and value added; (2) a Cobb–Douglas production function for value added but with fixed intermediate input coefficients; and (3) a C.E.S. production function for value added with fixed intermediate input coefficients.

When substitution was possible between intermediate inputs and labor, the predictions of output responses generated by the model diverged substantially from those which would have been derived based on "partial equilibrium" considerations (the proportionate change in value added price times the sector's supply elasticity). Their estimates of the overall change in consumption (which can be regarded as a measure of welfare cost) were relatively small: the highest increase was 0.84 percent under a CES specification in value added and fixed intermediate input coefficients. To be sure, the assumed tariff cut itself was not "large", given the magnitude of some of the initial tariffs. In addition, the log-linear specification is a satisfactory general equilibrium representation only within a small neighborhood of equilibrium.

These drawbacks of the log-linear method led to the application of computable general equilibrium (CGE) models to the problem. Here, the underlying producer and consumer optimization problems are explicitly formulated, and demand and supply relations are explicitly derived from the underlying utility and production functions. Obviously, results depend upon the assumed formed of those functions, but sensitivity analysis is possible. The resulting "computable general equilibrium" model is one for which an explicit numerical solution can be found, generally using various computer-based iterative procedures. To analyze the effects of a particular set of commercial (or other) policies singly or in combination, the same model is solved for different values of the various policy instruments.

De Melo (1978a) modeled the Colombian economy, based on assumed linear homogeneous production functions and demand relations based on a Cobb–Douglas utility function. To date, one of the limitations of CGE models has been the number of sectors which can simultaneously be included. In the De Melo model, there are fifteen sectors altogether: coffee, agriculture, mining, eight manufacturing industries producing tradable goods, and four non-tradable goods sectors, including a "light domestic industry" sector.

He found, like Taylor and Black, that if the Colombian ERPs were "properly adjusted" to reflect currency overvaluation, their use correctly reflected the direction of change in output in response to a large tariff cut in the short run. There was a high rank correlation between physical output changes and the height of ERPs. However, the Taylor and Black finding that partial equilibrium predictions of the magnitude of output changes were closely correlated with general equilibrium estimates did not carry over to large changes. Thus, while it may be a reasonable inference that highly protected sectors will contract in response to a move to free trade, use of the supply elasticities derived from partial equilibrium estimates does not appear to provide a reliable guide to the magnitude of those changes. This result seemed to be a consequence of relatively large changes in both the prices of home goods relative to tradables and sizeable changes in relative factor prices.

De Melo (1978b) used much the same model to investigate the properties of estimates of costs of protection derived from the Johnson production cost, partial equilibrium, approach with the costs estimated from a general equilibrium model. Interpretation of the De Melo results is complicated by the fact that he assumed a price elasticity of demand for Colombian coffee of minus 1.5. "Free trade" results therefore reflected both gains from resource reallocation among other sectors of the economy, and welfare losses resulting from the removal of Colombia's tax on coffee of about 44 percent (contrasted with De Melo's estimated optimal tax of about 83 percent). Allowing mobility of factors but assuming a quota on coffee exports, De Melo estimated that welfare would increase by 3.8 percent. (With an optimal tax on coffee exports, the gain would have been 11.0 percent.) If, instead of assuming an upward sloping labor supply, the model was solved with a constant real wage (assuming thus the equivalent of Lewis's unlimited supply of labor model), the gain was 5.8 percent for free trade with the same coffee quota and 15.8 percent for free trade and an optimal coffee tax.[32]

---

[32] CGE models have also been used to analyze both causes and effects of devaluation in a developing country. See especially Dervis (1980).

4. Interaction with domestic distortions

When prices correctly reflect opportunity costs and decision makers maximize subject to those prices, the equilibrium of the economy can be described relatively straightforwardly, and analysis of the economy's response to various exogenous shocks (such as the imposition of a tariff or quota) follows conventional lines. When domestic prices do not correctly reflect opportunity cost and decision-makers respond to those inappropriate prices, however, the situation changes entirely.

There are then two tasks. A first is to analyze the positive aspects of economic behavior when prices are "distorted" in one way or another. The second is to analyze the welfare effects of various instruments of trade policy when those instruments are employed in the context of domestic distortions. Once those are accomplished, there remains the question of the empirical relevance of domestic distortions and their effects. In this section, each of these three topics is dealt with in turn.

4.1. Behavior under distortions

Perhaps the major lesson that emerges from consideration of various distortions and their effect on the economy is that each particular distortion has its own associated resource pulls. Not all can be analyzed within one framework. And, almost anything can happen in response to any stimulus, depending upon the nature of the distortion.

To cover the essentials, it suffices to consider two possible distortions. In the first, there is always full employment of all factors of production (as in the neoclassical model) but one factor receives a higher return in one sector than in the other (due, perhaps, to an institutional constraint, such as minimum wage legislation affecting industrial but not rural workers, or to the existence of union power within one sector of the economy). In the second situation, the wage to one factor is constrained to be above the full employment level and there is open unemployment in equilibrium.

Consider first the full employment distortion. There, the model is formally the same as the Heckscher–Ohlin–Samuelson two-by-two model, except that, for one of the two factors of production, say labor, the wage (w) in sector x differs from the wage in sector y by a proportion a:

$$w_x = (1 + a)w_y. \tag{4.1}$$

Full employment prevails, and the usual price-equals-marginal cost conditions hold in each industry.[33] Under these conditions it is possible that the commodity physically intensive in the use of labor may not be the commodity with a higher share. When that happens, it is apparent that some of the usual theorems do not hold: in particular, it is clear that if the price of the commodity with the higher labor share rises, full employment cannot be restored by bidding up the price of labor and expanding output in the high-labor-share industry. Jones (1971a) and Magee (1976) concluded that price-output responses might be perverse, in that increasing the price of a commodity might lead to a fall in its output. More recently, Neary (1978) showed that under a variety of plausible adjustment mechanisms, a small open economy would necessarily be unstable in a region in which value and physical rankings were reversed. Thus, one would be more likely to observe specialization (perhaps in the "wrong" commodity) in such an economy than to observe production of both commodities. An equilibrium observed under conditions of a factor market distortion of the Jones type will necessarily be Pareto-inferior to some alternatives achievable through policy intervention.

There is some basis for believing that some developing countries' labor markets are characterized by something similar to the Jones–Magee–Neary distortion. Harris and Todaro (1970) modeled such a situation in the context of a closed economy. In their model, a high floor under urban real wages coexists with a rural sector in which the wage is free to fluctuate. The equilibrium rural wage is below the urban wage. Given the wage differential, some rural workers migrate to urban areas seeking higher-paying urban jobs. Thus, unemployment is the variable that equilibrates the labor market: the urban wage times the probability of employment equals the rural wage in equilibrium. For purposes of analyzing trade policies, the assumption of a constant urban-rural differential requires replacement with the assumption of a fixed urban wage.

Bhagwati and Srinivasan (1974) modelled this situation. Their results are depicted in Figure 4.2. There, the DE locus represents the transformation curve under efficient resource allocation with full employment, with outputs of two commodities, X_m and X_a. It is assumed that A is the labor intensive sector so that the real wage falls as production shifts toward M along the transformation curve. Given international prices represented by the slope of the SS line, full employment would prevail at Q' if there were no wage restriction. With an urban real wage set at a higher real wage than that associated with Q', attainment of full employment is infeasible. Instead, open unemployment in the urban sector ensues, so that the economy reaches an equilibrium at a point such as Q, where the real wage determines the level of the urban employment (given international prices) and the remainder of the labor force is allocated between the A sector and unemployment. Were the urban real wage to be increased, the level of output in

---

[33] The analysis here follows that of Jones (1971a).

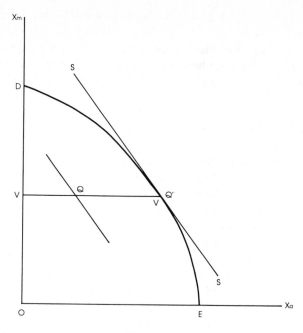

Figure 4.2

the *M* sector would decline with the *VV* line shifting downward, and the equilibrium level of unemployment would rise.

Corden and Findlay (1975) extended the model to the case where capital is mobile between sectors, and hence the return on capital is equated. In general, the Harris–Todaro results may follow in this case, but more orthodox outcomes are possible.

In general, the effects of various policy instruments may be quite different in the presence of a Harris–Todaro-type labor market than in a neoclassical labor market. Bhagwati and Srinivasan (1974) showed that the optimal policy in such a circumstance was to subsidize the employment of labor in both agriculture and industry.[34] This policy, of course, might not be politically feasible. Other policy alternatives which could improve welfare would be a subsidy to the agricultural wage and, if capital is sector-specific, a subsidy to agricultural output. Interestingly, a tariff upon imports of the urban good might well lower the international value of output, as an increase in urban output would be accompanied by a fall in

[34]Harris and Todaro (1970) originally proposed an urban wage subsidy combined with a restriction upon urban inmigration. This would achieve a first-best solution but at the cost of a differential in living standards between rural and urban areas. There is also a question as to the source of tax revenue to finance the subsidy.

agricultural output, and it might be accompanied by an increase in urban unemployment.

In Section 4.3, the available evidence about the empirical magnitudes of the types of distortions discussed here is examined. Before that, however, the subject of shadow prices as it relates to trade policies must be considered.

4.2. *Analysis of policies under distortions*

Analysis of the welfare effects of alternative trade (and other) policies becomes exceedingly complex when it is assumed that not all distortions can be removed. When attention is focused on the effects of varying one policy instrument, holding distortions elsewhere in the system in place, the general theory of the second-best indicates that anything can happen.

Three lines of analysis have been employed to tackle the issues, of which two require attention here. First, there is a sizable literature on choice of policy instruments when first-best policies are infeasible. Secondly, techniques of cost–benefit analysis, discussed fully in Chapter 2 and therefore not covered here, have been used. In connection with those techniques, a great deal of attention has been devoted to the problem of identifying appropriate shadow prices to use in project evaluation. Since there are some interesting specialized results pertaining to trade policy in the midst of the vast literature on choosing shadow prices, that topic is discussed in Section 4.2.2.

4.2.1. *Ranking of alternative policy instruments*

Obviously, in the presence of any single distortion, optimal policy would consist of its removal. If, for example, legislation set a high urban minimum real wage (in the spirit of the Harris–Todaro model), optimal policy would consist of removal of that legislation or in the imposition of other taxes and subsidies which completely offset the effect of the minimum wage.

The question arises, however, as to whether there are policy instruments which, while failing to mitigate completely the effects of the distortion, may nonetheless improve welfare (by the usual Pareto-optimality criterion) as contrasted with failure to intervene at all.

Interestingly, the main thrust of the policy ranking literature has been to show that a trade policy instrument employed to intervene in the presence of a domestic distortion will almost always be second, or even third, best contrasted with a domestic instrument. This line of research, pioneered by Fishlow and David (1961), Johnson (1965), and Ramaswami and Bhagwati (1963), led to a series of analyses of particular situations, and a ranking of policy instruments in each situation. If, for example, the urban wage is too high to permit full employment at free trade prices, first-best policy would involve removal of the wage constraint. Second-best policy would entail subsidizing employment of labor in the urban sector while third-best policy would involve subsidizing production of urban goods.[35] Only in the event that all of these policy instruments were unavailable would trade policy (imposition of protection to the urban good) improve welfare as contrasted with laissez-faire.

Bhagwati (1971) synthesized the various cases of distortion and the associated ranking of policy instruments. Since an optimal situation is one in which $DMRT = IMRT = DMRS$, there are distortions which break each of these equalities (including a tariff which imposes both a consumption cost and a production cost) and, in addition, a distortion (in factor markets) which moves the economy inside the production possibility frontier. There are endogenous distortions (such as the presence of externalities in production or consumption) which require intervention for achieving an optimum, and policy-imposed distortions which be partly offset by second-best intervention when they cannot be directly removed.

In all cases, an intervention which is addressed directly to the inequality in question is optimal. When it is not feasible, a second-best intervention is one which entails breaking the remaining equality (with a small welfare loss) while simultaneously reducing the magnitude of the initial inequality (with a large welfare gain). Optimal intervention with a second (or third) best policy instrument is achieved when the incremental gain from reducing the magnitude of the distortion with a second-best policy instrument is equal to the incremental loss associated with increasing the size of the inequality between the initially equated rates of substitution.

Figure 4.3 illustrates the proposition graphically for the case of a policy-imposed, and therefore, distorting, subsidy on the use of capital in the capital-intensive industry (the import-competing industry). It is assumed that capital and labor are the only factors of production, that they are in perfectly inelastic supply to the economy as a whole, and that there are two produced commodities. For ease of exposition, it is assumed that subsidies can be financed without imposing distortions. *OA* represents the attainable level of welfare that could be achieved in the absence of the subsidy (so that laissez-faire would be Pareto-optimal). A first-best policy would be to remove the subsidy. The line *CD* represents the attainable level of welfare as the rate of subsidy decreases. At a zero rate of subsidy, attainable welfare would be *OA*. If the subsidy became a tax, attainable welfare would be somewhat lower, decreasing beyond *OB*.

It should be noted that, under the assumption of perfectly inelastic supply of capital, imposing a subsidy on the use of capital in the export industry would

[35] In each of these cases, there would be a combination of taxes and subsidies to achieve the correct relative prices that would leave net government revenues unchanged. See Chapter 2 for a full discussion.

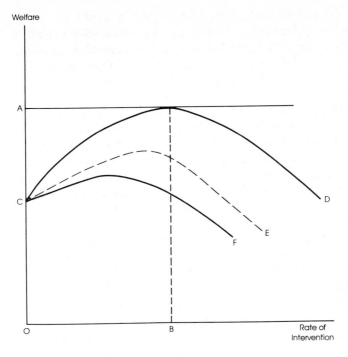

Figure 4.3

achieve the same results as would removal of the subsidy on the import-competing industry.

If these policies were infeasible, welfare could be improved (contrasted with
laissez-faire) by the imposition of a production tax on the capital-intensive good.
The line *CE* represents the attainable welfare level with variations in the rate of
production tax. It should be noted that a given rate of labor or capital tax or
subsidy is not equivalent to the same rate of production tax. As can be seen,
welfare with a production tax could never attain the full-optimum level because
the MRS between labor and capital would differ between industries. For any
given rate of subsidy, welfare would be less than with a first-best instrument, and
welfare would peak at a lower rate of intervention (because of the welfare loss
associated with transferring capital and labor from the labor-intensive industry
which would not occur with a labor tax).

If both first- and second-best options were infeasible, imposition of an export
subsidy could improve welfare as contrasted with laissez-faire, at the rate indicated by the *CF* line. The improvement would be smaller than with a production
tax, however, because of the consumption cost of the tariff (which would be

absent with the production tax). The attainable level of welfare would be lower, and would be achieved with a lower rate of intervention than with a production tax. Finally, it should be noted that the rate of intervention could be so high as to diminish welfare as contrasted with laissez-faire: it is not correct to state that any level of intervention will improve welfare.

4.2.2. Shadow prices

The problem of determining what prices appropriately reflect social opportunity cost in the presence of distortions is complex. It transcends the field of trade policy, and indeed, is virtually a specialized field in itself. However, for developing countries, the importance of the international market is so great that a great deal of attention has been paid to the appropriate shadow prices to use when tariffs, import prohibitions, unrealistic exchange rates, and other distortions pervade the system. Early manuals on project evaluation, such as that of Little and Mirrlees (1969), advocated the use of "border", or international prices, rather than tariff- or quota-influenced domestic prices, for valuing outputs in project evaluation. While there remains agreement that international prices, rather than domestic relative prices of tradables should be used in project evaluation, modern theory is complicated by the recognition that government behavior may be systematically nonoptimal in ways that may be altered by selection of particular projects. This is especially troublesome if prices of nontradables diverge systematically from their opportunity costs.[36]

From the viewpoint of trade theory, an interesting question arises with respect to the appropriate shadow prices of labor and capital to be used in project evaluation. Findlay and Wellisz (1976) analyzed this problem in the context of a simple programming problem for a small country, faced with given international prices, when there are only two factors of production (capital and labor). Initially, the country's economy can be described as having maximized $V = p_1 X_1 + p_2 X_2$ subject to $a_{11} X_1 + a_{12} X_2 \le K$, and $a_{21} X_1 + a_{22} X_2 \le L$, where p's are international prices, X's are output levels of goods 1 and 2, and a_{ij}'s are input coefficients corresponding to the factor proportions chosen by producers in the initial situation. These coefficients, in turn, are determined by producers who maximize subject to distorted prices (which are the world prices times one plus the rate of domestic intervention).

In evaluating alternative projects, it is clearly appropriate for planners to use the shadow prices of labor and capital associated with the dual solution of the primal system V. Whether or not to undertake a project would then be decided on the criterion of whether or not the international price of some third commodity

---

[36] For a modern treatment of the general theory of shadow pricing, see Blitzer, Dasgupta and Stiglitz (1981). See Chapter 2 of this volume for a fuller discussion of the issues pertaining to trade.

exceeded or fell short of the input coefficients associated with it (when minimizing costs subject to shadow factor prices).[37] Those shadow prices, in turn, clearly reflect the lost international value of production that would occur as resources were drawn out of the first or second industry into the new project.

Srinivasan and Bhagwati (1978) extended the Findlay–Wellisz analysis by noting the interesting result that one could, by their own reasoning, even have a negative shadow price for one factor of production (despite full employment). This result can be most readily understood intuitively by recognizing that a new project might pull resources out of either existing activity. If resources were pulled out of a highly protected industry into one that would require less protection, the international value of output would increase. If, however, resources would be pulled out of the relatively unprotected industry, the international value of output could decrease. Using the Rybczynski theorem, it follows that if the project under consideration was labor intensive, it would draw resources from the relatively more labor intensive of the two existing industries. Whether the project would on net add to the international value of output would depend on the relationship of the price ratios of the goods compared with the slope of the Rybczynski line indicating the path of contraction or expansion as one factor is withdrawn from an industry. In effect, if the Rybczynski line associated with removal of labor from the economy is less steep than the international price line, the shadow price of labor will be negative, as removal of labor from the economy would induce resources to move to the other industry, with an associated increase in the international value of output.[38]

4.3. Empirical evidence on distortions and their effects

Despite the importance of distortions in theory, relatively little empirical work has been undertaken to estimate their magnitude or their effects. There are, however, several pieces of evidence which suggest that, while distortions matter, they do not usually bring about "reversals" of the kind discussed in Section 4.1.[39]

First of all, there is considerable evidence that substitution possibilities between primary inputs are substantial. Behrman (1982) recently undertook systematic

---

[37] It should be noted that this procedure is not the same as selecting those projects which would be viable at free trade, except in the case where the same input coefficients would be chosen regardless of factor prices.

[38] Srinivasan and Bhagwati note that use of domestic resource costs as a criterion will be appropriate for project evaluation if the second-best shadow prices are appropriately derived from the existing, distorted situation.

[39] An interesting exception was the finding of Carvalho and Haddad (1981) that the composition of Brazil's exports (evaluated at either initial or terminal labor–capital ratios) shifted from capital- to labor-intensive from 1959 to 1970 as the Brazilian incentive structure switched from import-substitution to export promotion.

Table 4.1
Percentage estimated distortion in capital and labor
costs from various sources

Country	Year	Percentage increase in labor costs	Percentage reduction in capital costs due to:				Percentage increase in wage–rental
			Trade	Credit	Other	Total	
Argentina	1973	15	8	9	n.a.	17	38
Brazil	1968	27	0	4	n.a.	4	31
Chile	1966–68	n.a.	37	n.a.	n.a.	37	37
Hong Kong	1973	0	0	0	0	0	0
Ivory Coast	1971	23	0	3	12	15	45
Pakistan	1961–64	0	38	53	10	76	316
South Korea	1969	0	0	8	2	10	11
Tunisia	1972	20	30	6	n.a.	36	87

Source: Krueger (1983, table 7.1).

cross-sectional analysis among developing countries' individual manufacturing industries. His findings support econometric evidence from the developed countries: elasticities of substitution between primary factors of production do not appear to be significantly different from unity. Careful work on individual countries, such as that of Corbo and Meller (1982) on Chile, provides further support for a relatively high substitution elasticity.

There is much less direct evidence on the effects of distortions. About the only piece of relatively systematic evidence is from twelve countries covered in the National Bureau Project on Alternative Trade Strategies and Employment. For those countries, with the already-noted exception of Brazil, interventions did not appear to reverse predicted factor proportions in trade.[40] However, many did have interventions which were, by most standards, sizable. For example, Guisinger (1981) estimated that, for Pakistan, the cost of capital services to firms in the modern protected sector of the economy was about one-fourth of what it would have been in the absence of distortions.

Table 4.1 summarizes some of the findings with respect to the magnitude of distortions of countries covered in the Bureau project. These estimates are estimates of the proportionate differential in the wage–rental ratio between the modern, protected, sector and the rest of the economy [see Krueger (1983) for details].

As can be seen, Pakistan and Tunisia appear to have had very great differentials, with Pakistan's originating in credit rationing and investment incentives,

---

[40] For Chile, intra-Latin American trade predominated, and Chilean exports as a whole were capital-intensive. However, as would be expected, Chile's exports to developed countries were labor-intensive while those to other Latin American countries were capital-intensive. See Corbo and Meller (1981).

while Tunisia's resulted from the interaction of trade regime, credit rationing, and labor market interventions. An interesting question, on which there is to date no evidence, is how great distortions must be to be judged "significant". Evaluation of whether Argentina's estimated 38 percent differential is quantitatively significant or not would require substantially more analysis and evidence than is thus far available. Efforts to simulate what might have happened in the absence of distortions resulted in estimated increases in labor coefficients of 10 percent in Argentina, 15 percent in Brazil, and 271 percent (i.e. increasing labor almost threefold) in Pakistan.[41]

It would appear, therefore, that distortions and their effects are sufficiently important that further research on both their magnitude and their effects is warranted. It is likely that this is a topic on which considerable new light will be shed in the near future.

5. Terms of trade changes and export instability[42]

As Ronald Findlay (1980, p. 425) has so cogently put it: "The determination of the terms of trade is, at one and the same time, an esoteric technical problem in the pure theory of international trade and a highly charged emotional issue in world politics." In the context of trade policies related to development, two separate aspects of terms of trade determinants have been hotly debated. One set of issues pertains to the belief that there has been a secular deterioration in the terms of trade against primary commodities, the exporters of which typically have been identified with developing countries. The other set of issues centers around a presumed instability in some aspect of price, quantity, or volume of exports in developing countries which adversely affects their development prospects.

The two sets are logically distinct, their only connections being that they both focus upon aspects of terms of trade determination, and that both have been used as a basis to justify intervention with market outcomes. There is no reason why secular deterioration in the terms of trade should be related to instability, and conversely.[43] Moreover, one or both of the two could in principle be correct, and it would not automatically follow that intervention would per se improve welfare (under the usual criteria) as contrasted with a free-trade outcome.

---

[41] See Krueger (1983, table 8.10).

[42] I am deeply indebted to Peter Svedberg of the Institute of International Economic Studies, Stockholm University, for many helpful discussions and suggestions on the subject of this section.

[43] The terms of trade deterioration has been used as a rationale for intervention with free trade, and in particular for protection against imports. That issue is not dealt with here, although it should be noted that it is not immediately obvious why private markets will not anticipate future terms of trade movements.

Interestingly, whether there has been secular deterioration in the terms of trade of some or all developing countries is almost entirely an empirical question. The underlying theory is straightforward, and can be derived from Mill, if not earlier authors: if the terms of trade are deteriorating secularly, that deterioration represents a transfer of income from developing to developed countries (in the sense that the developing countries earlier enjoyed larger gains from trade), and by the usual welfare criteria developing countries would be worse off with each deterioration than they would be with constant terms of trade. Section 5.1 contains a brief review of the theory and empirical evidence.

By contrast, the question of instability is theoretically more complex, and there is no straightforward empirical test that can be made independently of an underlying rationale as to why instability should matter. In Section 5.2, the theoretical and empirical underpinnings to the instability question are examined. Section 5.3, finally, gives a brief review of some of the empirical findings, despite the lack of a satisfactory analytical foundation.

5.1. Secular deterioration in the terms of trade?

In theory, one can predict any secular trend in the terms of trade depending on the underlying model. If one takes Sir Arthur Lewis's view that the population growth of labor-surplus countries will proceed at a rate that maintains a subsistence wage while private foreign investment is freely available, that assures a perfectly elastic supply of tropical agricultural products. A rising real wage in developed countries would simultaneously imply an increasing price of manufactured output, and deterioration in the terms of trade would inevitably follow. If, instead, it were thought that there were "limits to growth" because of a relatively inelastic supply of primary commodities, the terms of trade might be expected secularly to move in favor of primary commodity exporters. Whichever path occurred, the welfare conclusions would be evident.

In practice, debate over the secular tendency in the terms of trade has been until recently almost entirely empirical.[44] In the late 1940s, Prebisch (1950) and Singer (1950) both put forward the view that the terms of trade had deteriorated against developing countries in the period from 1870 to the 1930s. Prebisch based his evidence on the British net barter terms of trade over the period, associating British imports with primary commodities and British exports with manufactured commodities.

---

[44] I ignore the issue of "fairness" in the terms of trade (both their level and their rate of change). See Michaely (1982) for a discussion.

That launched a series of analyses of various components of his evidence that cast considerable doubt on his findings. Quite aside from the reliability of the statistics (including whether quality improvements were adequately taken into account), there were issues concerning whether British net barter terms of trade adequately reflected those of manufacturing exporters relative to primary commodity producers, whether inclusion of all primary commodities (some of which are exported by developed countries) biassed the results, and so on.

Fortunately, Spraos (1980) has recently surveyed the voluminous evidence. Noting that many ambiguities and statistical problems in attempting to evaluate the evidence, he concluded that: (1) the data are not adequate to form a definitive judgment; (2) Prebisch probably overstated the extent of the terms of trade deterioration experienced by Britain – "at worst by a factor of more than three" (p. 126); (3) but nonetheless there probably was some secular deterioration in the terms of trade against primary products over the interval considered by Prebisch; however, finally (4) if one takes the longer interval and includes the postwar period in the analysis, it is doubtful whether there has been any deterioration.

Indeed, cyclical fluctuations in the terms of trade dominate whatever secular changes there may have been. Any analysis of the question of the long-run trend in the terms of trade between primary commodities and manufactures is therefore subject to a wide margin of error because choice of initial and terminal periods for the analysis is so crucial. Given that the quality of data is also open to question (because of conceptual differences between statistics available for different time intervals, as well as basic problems of reliability), it seems doubtful whether further empirical analysis can shed additional light on the issue. A reasonable conclusion would appear to be that whatever overall trends there may have been between primary commodities and manufactures were relatively small in magnitude. Individual countries, however, may have experienced relatively more favorable or unfavorable trends, depending on their particular basket of traded goods.

Michaely (1982) has recently put this point forcefully by noting that there are numerous problems in identifying which commodities are exported by poor countries, and which countries are poor and which rich. These issues must be satisfactorily resolved before any empirical analysis can be undertaken. Michaely proposes an index of the income level of a particular export commodity, $^{x}y_i$, as:

$$^{x}y_i = \sum_j y_j \left[X_{ij}/X_i \right],$$

where X_{ij} is the exports of good i by country j, X_i is total world exports of good i and y_j is an index of the income of country j, defined as a ratio of j's income per capita to that of American income per capita. The index of the income level of a particular import commodity is analogously defined.

He then calculated income levels associated with three-digit commodities for the years 1952, 1955, 1960, 1965, 1970 and 1973. Combining those indices with price data on the same commodities, (a set covering about 75 percent of world trade), he was able to examine the relationship between the price increase of exports of the rich countries to the price increase of exports of the poor countries, a similar ratio for imports of the two groups, and the ratio of the two ratios, which comes closest to identifying the terms of trade between rich and poor.

Michaely found that the price of exports of the poor countries rose more than that of the rich; the price of imports of the rich countries rose more than that of the price of the poor; and the ratio of the two moved in favor of the poor countries. Hence, the terms of trade had necessarily moved in favor of the poor over the period covered by his data. He then proceeded to show that using the conventional measure of manufactured goods prices relative to primary commodity prices provided the "orthodox" Prebisch–Singer result even for the postwar period. He concluded that:

"The main message of this study is that verification of the theses suggested for terms-of-trade movements requires an adequate conceptual approach to the estimate. Such an approach is suggested here. That it leads to inferences which are radically different from those yielded by conventional, traditional methods of evaluation only serves to demonstrate the significance and concreteness of the issue". (p. 28)

5.2. Instability

The instability issue centers crucially upon what it is that may be unstable, and why instability matters. Much of the discussion has been based upon the implicit premise that fluctuations in one or more aspects of exports of developing countries have adversely affected their potential gains from the international economy, and therefore their growth prospects.

A first question therefore must pertain to what sort of fluctuations might have harmful consequences. Although the list of candidates is endless, most of the discussion has centered upon alleged instability in prices or volume of export commodities or in export earnings of developing countries. The issue is complicated because it is not always true that stabilizing one of these magnitudes will result in the stabilization of others. For example, if price fluctuations arise only because of variations in supply (due, perhaps to weather), then a price stabilization scheme would entail an increase in the fluctuations in producer earnings. Even narrowing the focus to price, quantity, or earnings is not sufficient, however, because the nature of the instability which matters depends crucially upon the way in which it adversely affects welfare. And, depending on that mechanism, that empirical measure of instability can and will change.

5.2.1. Welfare effects of instability

There have been two distinct analytical approaches to the question of instability. The first has used a partial equilibrium approach to examine the potential welfare effects of various types of fluctuations. The second has assumed that there is a non-costless means of perfectly offsetting fluctuations (such as buffer stocks or holding of foreign exchange reserves at a lower real rate of return than that available in alternative instruments), and examined the likely costs of fluctuations in that light. Each of these approaches is here reviewed briefly in turn, although a full exposition would entail a complete chapter in and of itself.[45]

Waugh (1944) and Oi (1961) originated the analysis by examining, respectively, the effects on consumer and producer surplus of price fluctuations. When price fluctuations to consumers originate from supply curve shifts, consumers are clearly better off if they are permitted to choose quantities under variable prices than if instead they are always confronted with the mean of the distribution. This[46] follows directly from assuming convex indirect utility functions for consumers, for with a constant mean price they would necessarily be better off with a fluctuating price than with a stable one. Oi's analysis independently showed the same result for producers when demand shifts account for variability.

It remained for Massell (1969) to combine the producer and consumer aspects of the argument. He showed the crucial importance of the source of the disturbance for analysis. Thus, if there are disturbances in supply which cause price fluctuations, producers will clearly be worse off with price stabilization than without (income is subject to increased variance because price fluctuations cannot partially offset changes in quantities produced). However, in general Massell found that consumers and producers could jointly gain from stabilization with appropriate redistribution. This clearly has important ramifications for international trade, as producer interests and consumer interests are typically differentially represented between countries.[47]

These results are sufficient to cast some doubt on the assumption that fluctuations are inherently undesirable. Further analysis of instability has proceeded by applying the modern theory of uncertainty to it. Newbery and Stiglitz (1979) have summarized some of the problems associated with the early analysis (and especially its basic assumption that demand and supply curves are linear) and in addition have analyzed commodity price stabilization schemes in terms of reducing the mean-quantity preserving spreads.

---

[45] The interested reader is referred to Newbery and Stiglitz (1979), Turnovsky (1978), and Wilson for surveys of various aspects of the literature.

[46] It will be noted below that the Waugh–Oi–Massell results hinge crucially on the assumption that demand and supply curves are linear. The results reported here do not hold in general for all specifications of the underlying utility and supply relations.

[47] See Hueth and Schmitz (1972) who extended the Massell analysis to an open economy context.

Criticisms of the earlier approach include: (1) the assumption that disturbances are additive is unrealistic (especially if they are weather-induced); (2) price stabilization at the mean is infeasible if they are not additive; (3) it is generally unrealistic to contrast no stabilization with perfect stabilization (which is generally infeasible without an infinite stock); and (4) if price stabilization changes average returns to producers, that is likely to affect supply responses over time. Obviously, a general theory of price, earnings, or quantity stabilization must take account of these phenomena, and conclusions may legitimately differ depending on underlying conditions.

In the Newbery–Stiglitz model, a mean quantity-preserving decrease in price dispersion is the central concept of stabilization. In the simplest case, "the benefits of price stabilisation are simply the benefits of arbitrage, that is, of moving consumption from dates of low value (low price) to dates of high value. If this could be achieved costlessly, then perfect stabilisation is desirable, but since it is both costly and ultimately infeasible, perfect stabilisation is neither desirable nor possible" (p. 805). However, considerations such as changing supply in response to stabilization can alter the conclusion and in the more general case the benefits to partially buffering fluctuations can be positive or negative to either producers or consumers and long-run and short-run impacts may even be of opposite sign.

A procedure alternative to that considered above is to specify the costs of the alternative to incurring fluctuations. The best such model, developed by Gelb (1979), treats instability as a variation measure on a filtered stochastic process using spectral analysis techniques. Fluctuations can be classified according to their amplitude and according to their frequency. Very high frequency fluctuations are those of duration less than a year; high frequency fluctuations last between a year and two years; medium frequency are defined as those lasting between two and five years; while low frequency fluctuations have a duration greater than five years. Gelb showed that most existing indices of instability emphasize high and very high frequency fluctuations. These appear to be inappropriate because those are the ones that probably have relatively low costs, because buffering costs decrease as the duration of cycles shortens.

Gelb analyzed the relationship between frequency and costs per time period. His results are illustrated with the help of Figure 5.1. The line AA' is presumed to represent the mean cost incurred per period of time by assuming complete resource reallocation in response to fluctuations. Obviously, the costs increase with the frequency. The BB' line indicates the costs of non-adjustment while the CC' line indicates the costs of complete buffering under an assumed policy of complete stockholding. Buffering costs are naturally inversely proportional to the frequency, but directly in proportion to the amplitude (assumed constant) of fluctuations. As can be seen from Figure 5.1, the line $AMNC'$ indicates the maximal costs of fluctuations, as with very low frequencies complete adjustment

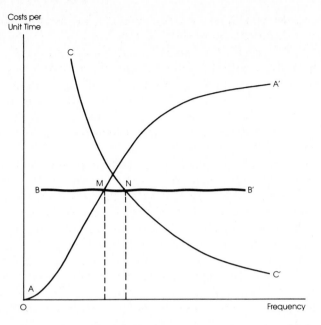

Figure 5.1.   Relationship between frequency and costs per time period.

would be optimal, for medium frequencies no adjustment would be optimal, and for high frequencies complete buffering would be optimal. Obviously, consideration of intermediate strategies (partial adjustment and partial stockholding, for example) would smooth the $AMNC'$ line.

The export instability indices usually constructed are based on relatively short (10–25 years) time periods. They are usually constructed by regressing a predetermined trend form on time and using a statistic based on deviations from trend, possibly normalized, as an indicator of instability. But this technique gives greatest weight to high frequencies, and the relatively short time series available inevitably give less weight to low frequency fluctuations.[48]

5.2.2.   *Effects of instability on exporters' economies*

Despite the considerable attention devoted to fluctuations in export prices and earnings, there are few systematic analyses of the ways in which those fluctuations might have an adverse impact on developing countries' economies. The simplest

---

[48] See Gelb (1979, p. 153), for the argument spelled out in detail.

mechanism would be a Keynesian multiplier model, in which fluctuations in export earnings induced a proportionately greater impact on developing countries' domestic real incomes. MacBean's (1965) pioneering work first implicitly examined this mechanism by empirically testing the relationship between fluctuations in export earnings and fluctuations in income. MacBean found little relationship between the two. The mechanism was further spelled out and then tested by Mathieson and McKinnon (1974). They concluded that the empirical evidence did not support the notion that developing countries' fluctuations in real GNP had been transmitted through trade.

There have been some attempts to link fluctuations in export earnings with variables presumably influencing the rate of economic growth. Kenen and Voivodas (1972), following MacBean, found little overall evidence of harmful links between fluctuations in export earnings and developing countries' overall economic performance, but they did find a link between the level of investment and export earnings.[49] Lim (1976) attempted a more careful specification of models earlier used, and showed how sensitive results are to the particular specification. Among other things, he took the finding of Voivodas (1974), that export instability had adversely affected growth, and, specifying the linkages more precisely, found the opposite. It seems reasonable to conclude that, if there are negative feedbacks from instability to growth, they are sufficiently small in magnitude relative to other factors contributing to growth that it is difficult to find robust empirical tests that detect them.

An alternative procedure is to develop an econometric model of a developing country and then to proceed to simulate the outcome of fluctuations in export prices and/or earnings. This was done by Adams, Behrman, and Roldan (1979) for coffee in Brazil. Their simulation results suggested that, for Brazil, multiplier-type effects on demand of higher coffee output or coffee export earnings existed and that, in addition, the rate of capital formation appeared to be higher with larger coffee output and exports, although the demand effect dominated.[50]

5.3. Empirical evidence on instability

As the preceeding discussion has indicated, empirical work on the degree of instability has generally been marred by the absence of an explicit analytical framework relating the particular type of instability to the loss function. Gelb (1979) noted that at least sixteen distinct indices of instability can be found in the literature and, as already noted, demonstrated that most of them emphasize high

---

[49] In principle, there could exist potentially damaging relationships between fluctuations and growth which could nonetheless be offset by governmental policies (such as holding foreign exchange reserves). In that case, the damage caused by fluctuations would be limited to the cost of holding additional reserves.

[50] See also the cross-country empirical analysis of Rangarajan and Sundararajan (1976).

frequency, low duration fluctuations as contrasted with the more costly, low frequency, long duration variety.

For reasons already indicated, there would be little purpose served in reviewing the many alternative measures of instability and the findings with regard to its empirical magnitude. All that needs to be noted here is that the empirical evidence so far available is sufficiently contradictory and inconclusive as to provide probable justification for the conclusion that the phenomenon, if it exists at all, is of far smaller magnitude than is generally thought.

The pioneering work in this regard was that of MacBean (1966). Until his study, instability had been assumed in most analyses. MacBean proceeded to take data available as of the mid-1960s, and to subject them to careful statistical examination on both a time series and a cross section basis. His richly-documented conclusion was that:

> The chief conclusion...is that probably the importance of short-term export instability to underdeveloped countries has been exaggerated ....Comparison of instability in exports of underdeveloped countries and industrial nations, of primary products and of manufacturers reveal a much greater overlap and much smaller differences than most economic analysts have assumed....For most underdeveloped countries, variations in the supply of exports seem to have been more important than fluctuations in demand [MacBean, (1965, pp. 339–340)].

Subsequent analyses have sought either to reinforce or to refute Macbean's findings. Although some analysts have reached contrary conclusions most have tended to reinforce them. Glezakos (1973) confirmed them separately for export prices, quantities and proceeds, as did Naya (1973) for quantities and earnings. Brundell, Horn and Svedberg (1980) found that, once oil-exporting countries (whose instability markedly increased in the 1970s) were excluded, there was no significant difference in the export instability of developed and developing countries, thus reinforcing the MacBean results. They further noted that highly protectionist countries appeared to have experience greater instability than did countries pursuing outer oriented trade policies, suggesting that instability might partly reflect internal policies. Another strand of literature has investigated the trend in the degree of instability over time, and found it generally to be declining.[51]

It would thus appear reasonable to conclude that there is little basis in casual empiricism or crude cuts of the statistics to indicate that instability in export earnings, prices, or quantities have prime facie been a problem. Clearly, more careful theoretical work will be necessary if understanding of the instability phenomenon is to increase. Perhaps, however, the available theory and evidence

---

[51]See Wilson, part 2, for a survey of the evidence.

are sufficient to indicate that the phenomenon has received much greater attention than its probable size and costs warrant.

6. Concluding remarks

At the outset, it was noted that the central tension in the "trade and development" literature has been between neoclassical theory and those who believed that "dynamic", or other, factors justify departures from free trade.

By and large, theory and empirical evidence have combined to reassert the proposition that a trade intervention is seldom optimal, even in the presence of market imperfections. It might even worsen the situation as contrasted with laissez-faire, especially if the intervention is too highly protectionist.

But, as the limitations of trade policy as a means of offsetting domestic distortions have become better understood, new questions have arisen. These could not be covered in this survey, but will surely be focal points of concern for future researchers. At issue is the question of how, starting from a highly distorted situation (in both the domestic economy *and* the trade regime), an economy may be optimally moved to a less distortion-ridden situation. Recent experience in Argentina and Uruguay, especially, suggest that the problem is complex, especially in the context of considerable international capital mobility. A survey of the trade-and-development literature ten years hence will surely focus more on the properties of transition paths, and less on considering the welfare implications of protection, than is currently possible.

References

Adams, F.G., J.R. Behrman and R.A. Roldan (1979), "Measuring the impact of primary commodity fluctuations on economic development: coffee and Brazil", American Economic Review, 69:164–168.
Balassa, B. (1982), Development strategies in semi-industrial economies (Johns Hopkins University Press, Baltimore).
Baldwin, R.E. (1969), "The case against infant-industry protection", Journal of Political Economy, 77:295–305.
Baldwin, R.E. (1976), Foreign trade regimes and economic development: The Philippines, (Columbia University Press, New York).
Baldwin, R.E. et al. (1965), Trade, growth and the balance of payments (Rand McNally, Chicago).
Bardhan, P.K. (1970), Economic growth, development, and foreign trade (Wiley, New York).
Baysan, T. (1972), Economic effects of Turkish entry into the Common Market, Ph.D. dissertation, University of Minnesota, Minneapolis.
Behrman, J.R. (1982), "Country and sectoral variations in manufacturing elasticities of substitution between capital and labor", in: A.O. Krueger, ed., Trade and employment in developing countries, Vol. 2, Factor Supply and Substitution, (Chicago University Press, Chicago) 159–192.
Bergsman, (1974), "Commercial policy, allocative and 'X-efficiency'", Quarterly Journal of Economics, 88:409–433.
Bhagwati, J.N. (1965), "On the equivalence of tariffs and quotas", in: Baldwin et al. (1965) 53–67.
Bhagwati, J.N. (1974), "On the underinvoicing of imports", in: J.N. Bhagwati, ed., Illegal transactions in international trade: Theory and measurement (North-Holland, Amsterdam).

Bhagwati, J.N. (1978), Foreign trade regimes and economic development: Anatomy and consequences of exchange control regimes (Ballinger for the National Bureau of Economic Research, Lexington).

Bhagwati, J.N. (1971), "The generalized theory of distortions and welfare", in: J.N. Bhagwati, R.W. Jones et al., Trade, balance of payments, and growth (North-Holland, Amsterdam) 69–90.

Bhagwati, J.N. (1968), "Immiserizing growth: A geometrical note", in: R.E. Caves and H.G. Johnson, A.E.A. Readings in international economics (Richard D. Irwin, Homewood, Illinois) 300–305.

Bhagwati, J.N. and B. Hansen (1973), "A theoretical analysis of smuggling", Quarterly Journal of Economics, 87:172–187.

Bhagwati, J.N. and Srinivasan, T.N. (1976), Foreign trade regimes and economic development: India (Columbia University Press for the National Bureau of Economic Research, New York).

Bhagwati, J.N. and Srinivasan (1980), T.N. (1974), "On reanalyzing the Harris–Todaro model: Policy rankings in the case of sector-specific sticky wages", American Economic Review, 66:502–514.

Bhagwati, J.N. and T.N. Srinivasan, "Revenue-seeking: A generalization of the theory of tariffs", Journal of Political Economy, 88:1069–1087.

Blejer, M.I. (1978), "Exchange restrictions and the monetary approach to the balance of payments", in: J. Frenkel and H.G. Johnson, eds., Economics of exchange rates: Selected studies (Addison-Wesley, Reading).

Blitzer, C., Dasgupta, P., and Stiglitz, J. (1981), "Project appraisal and foreign exchange constraints", Economic Journal, 91:58–74.

Brundell, P. Horn, H., and Svedberg, P. (1980), "On the causes of instability in export earnings", Oxford Bulletin of Economics and Statistics, 301–313.

Carvalho, J.S. and Haddad, C.L.S. (1981), "Foreign trade strategies and employment in Brazil", in: A.O. Krueger, H.B. Lary et al., Trade and employment in developing countries: 1. Individual studies (Chicago University Press, Chicago) 29–82.

Chenery, H.B. (1961), "Comparative advantage and development policy", American Economic Review, 51:18–51.

Chenery, H.B. and Strout, A.M. (1966), "Foreign assistance and economic development", American Economic Review, 56:679–733.

Corbo, V. and Meller, P. (1981), "Alternative trade strategies and employment implications: Chile", in: A.O. Krueger, H.B. Lary et al., Trade and employment in developing countries: 1. Individual studies (Chicago University Press, Chicago) 83–134.

Corden, W.M. (1975), "The costs and consequences of protection", in: P.B. Kenen, ed., International trade and finance (Cambridge University Press, New York) 51–91.

Corden, W.M. (1974), Trade policy and economic welfare (Clarendon Press, Oxford).

Corden, W.M. and R. Findlay (1975), "Urban unemployment, intersectoral capital mobility, and development policy", Economica, 42:59–78.

de Macedo, J.B. (1980), "Exchange rate behavior with currency inconvertibility", Princeton, mimeo.

deMelo, J.A.P. and Dervis, K. (1977), "Modelling the effects of protection in a dynamic framework", Journal of Development Economics, 4:149–172.

deMelo, J.A.P. (1978b), "Estimating the costs of protection: A general equilibrium approach", Quarterly Journal of Economics, 92:209–226.

deMelo, J.A.P. (1980), "Tariffs and resource allocation in partial and in general equilibrium", Weltwirtschaftliches Archiv, 116:114–30.

deMelo, J.A.P. (1978a), "Protection and resource allocation in a Walrasian trade model", International Economic Review, 19:25–44.

deMelo, J.A.P., and Robinson, S. (1981), "Trade policy and resource allocation in the presence of product differentiation", Review of Economics and Statistics, 63:169–177.

Dervis, K.A. (1980), "Analyzing the resource pull effect of devaluation under exchange control", Journal of Development Economics, 7:23–48.

Diaz-Alejandro, C. (1965), "On the import intensity of import substitution", Kyklos, 18:495–509.

Diaz-Alejandro, C. (1975), Foreign trade regimes and economic development: Colombia (Columbia University Press for the NBER, New York).

Evans, H.D. (1971), "Effects of protection in a general equilibrium framework", Review of Economics and Statistics, 53:147–156.

Findlay, R. (1980), "The fundamental determinants of the terms of trade", in: S. Grassman and E. Lundberg, eds., The world economic order: Past and prospects (St. Martin's Press, London) 425–457.

Findlay, R. and Wellisz, S. (1976), "Project evaluation, shadow prices, and trade policy", Journal of Political Economy, 84:543–552.

Fishelson, G. and Flatters, F. (1975), "The (non)-equivalence of optimal tariffs and quotas under uncertainty", Journal of International Economics, 5:385–393.

Fishlow, A. and David, P. (1961), "Optimal resource allocation in an imperfect market setting", Journal of Political Economy 69:529–546.

Gelb, A.H. (1979), "On the definition and measurement of instability and the costs of buffering export fluctuations", Review of Economic Studies, 46:149–162.

Glezakos, C. (1973), "Export instability and economic growth: A statistical verification", Economic Development and Cultural Change, 21:422–35.

Guisinger, S.P. (1981), "Trade policies and employment: the case of Pakistan", in: A.O. Krueger, H.B. Lary et al., Trade and employment in developing countries, 1. Individual Studies (Chicago University Press, Chicago) 291–340.

Harris, J.R. and M.P. Todaro (1970), "Migration, unemployment, and development: A two-sector analysis", American Economic Review, 60:126–42.

Henderson, J.M. (1982), "Optimal factor allocation for thirteen countries", in: A.O. Krueger, ed., Trade and employment in developing countries: 2. Factor supply and substitution (Chicago University Press, Chicago) 1–82.

Hueth, D. and Schmitz, A. (1972), "International trade in intermediate and final goods: Some welfare implications of destabilized prices", Quarterly Journal of Economics, 86:351–365.

Johnson, H.G. (1960), "The cost of protection and the scientific tariff", Journal of Political Economy, 68:327–345.

Johnson, H.G. (1965), "Optimal trade intervention in the presence of domestic distortions", in: Baldwin et al. (1965) 3–34.

Jones, R.W. (1971b), "A three-factor model in theory, trade, and history", in J.N. Bhagwati, R.W. Jones, et al., Trade, balance of payments, and growth (North-Holland, Amsterdam) 3–21.

Jones, R.W. (1971a), "Distortions in factor markets and the general equilibrium model of production", Journal of Political Economy, 79:437–59.

Kenen, P.B. and Voivodas, C.S. (1972), "Export instability and economic growth", Kyklos, 25:791–804.

Krueger, A.O. (1983), Alternative trade strategies and employment, Vol. 3: Synthesis and conclusions (Chicago University Press for the National Bureau of Economic Research, Chicago).

Krueger, A.O. (1972), "Evaluating restrictionist trade regimes: Theory and measurement", Journal of Political Economy, 80:48–62.

Krueger, A.O. (1974a), Foreign trade regimes and economic development: Turkey (Columbia University Press for the National Bureau of Economic Research, New York).

Krueger, A.O. (1974b), "The political economy of the rent-seeking society", American Economic Review, 64:291–303.

Krueger, A.O. (1977), Growth, factor market distortions and patterns of trade among many countries, Princeton Studies in International Finance, No. 40 (Princeton University Press, Princeton).

Krueger, A.O. (1978), Foreign trade regimes and economic development: Liberalization attempts and consequences (Ballinger Publishing Co. for the National Bureau of Economic Research).

Krueger, A.O., Lary, H.B., Monson, T. and Akrasanee, N., eds. (1981), Trade and employment in developing countries, Vol. 1: Individual studies (University of Chicago Press for the National Bureau of Economic Research, Chicago).

Krueger, A.O. and B. Tuncer (1982), "An empirical test of the infant industry argument", American Economic Review, 72:1142–52.

Lage, G.M. (1970), "A linear programming analysis of tariff protection", Western Economic Journal, 8:167–85.

Leibenstein, H. (1966), "Allocative efficiency vs. 'X-efficiency'", American Economic Review, 56:392–415.

Lim, D. (1976), "Export instability and economic growth: a return to fundamentals", Oxford Bulletin of Economics and Statistics, 38:4.

Little, I.M.D. and Mirrlees, J.A. (1969), Manual of industrial project analysis in developing countries (O.E.C.D., Paris).

Little, I.M.D., T. Scitovsky and M. Scott (1970), Industry and trade in some developing countries (Oxford University Press for O.E.C.D.).

MacBean, A.I. (1966), Export instability and economic development (Harvard, Cambridge).

Magee, S.P. (1976), International trade and distortions in factor markets (Dekker, New York).

Massell, B.F. (1969), "Price stabilization and welfare", Quarterly Journal of Economics, 83:284–298.

Mathieson, D.J., and McKinnon, R.I. (1974), "Instability in underdeveloped countries: the impact of the international economy", in: P. David and M. Reder, eds., Nations and households in economic growth (Academic Press, New York).

Michaely, M. (1954), "A geometric analysis of black market behavior", American Economic Review, 627–637.

Michaely, M. (1982), "The terms of trade between poor and rich nations", Hoover Institution, mimeo.

McKinnon, R.I. (1966), "Foreign-exchange constraints in economic development and efficient aid allocation", Economic Journal, 76:170–71.

Monson, T. and Pursell, G. (1979), "Use of DRCs to evaluate indigenization programs: The case of the Ivory Coast", Journal of Development Economics, 6:119–139.

Naya, S. (1973), "Fluctuations in export earnings and economic patterns of Asian countries", Economic Development and Cultural Change, 21:629–41.

Neary, J.P. (1978), "Dynamic stability and the theory of factor market distortions", American Economic Review, 68:671–682.

Newbery, D.M.G. and J.E. Stiglitz (1979), "The theory of commodity price stabilization rules: Welfare impacts and supply responses", Economic Journal, 89:799–817.

Oi, W. (1961), "The desirability of price instability under perfect competition", Econometrica, 29:58–64.

Pitt, M.M. (1981a), "Smuggling and price disparity", Journal of International Economics, 11:447–458.

Pitt, M.M. (1981b), "Smuggling and the blackmarket for foreign exchange", mimeo.

Prebisch, R. (1950), "The economic development of Latin America and its principal problems", Economic bulletin for Latin America, 7:1–22.

Ramaswami, V.K., and Bhagwati, J.N. (1963), "Domestic distortions, tariffs, and the theory of optimal subsidy", Journal of Political Economy, 71:44–50.

Rangarajan, C. and Sundararajan, V. (1976), "Impact of export fluctuations on income: A cross country analysis", Review of Economics and Statistics, 58:368–71.

Rhee, Y.W., and Westphal, L.A., "A micro, econometric investigation of choice of technology", Journal of Development Economics 4:205–37.

Savasini, A.A. (1978), Domestic resource cost of foreign exchange, in his Export Promotion: The case of Brazil (Praeger, New York) 53–94.

Sheikh, M.A. (1976), "Black market for foreign exchange, capital flows, and smuggling", Journal of Development Economics, 3:9–26.

Sheikh, M.A. (1974), "Smuggling, protection and welfare", Journal of International Economics, 4:355–364.

Singer, H. (1950), "The distribution of gains between investing and borrowing countries", American Economic Review, 40:473–85.

Spraos, J. (1980), "The statistical debate on the net barter terms of trade between primary commodities and manufactures", Economic Journal, 90:197–128.

Srinivasan, T.N. and J.N. Bhagwati (1978), "Shadow prices for project selection in the presence of distortions: Effective rates of protection and domestic resource costs", Journal of Political Economy, 86:97–116.

Taylor, L. and Black, S.L. (1974), "Practical general equilibrium estimation of resource pulls under trade liberalization", Journal of International Economics, 4:37–55.

Turnovsky, S. (1978), "The distribution of welfare gains from price stabilization: A survey of some theoretical issues", in: F.G. Adams and S. Klein, Stabilizing world commodity prices (Heath-Lexington, Lexington).

Voivodas, C.S. (1974), "The effect of foreign exchange instability on growth", Review of Economics and Statistics, 56:410–412.

Waugh, F.V. (1944), "Does the consumer benefit from price stabilization?", Quarterly Journal of Economics, 58:602–614.

Wilson, P.R.D. (n.d.), "Export instability and economic development: A survey", Parts 1 and 2, Warwick Economic Research Papers.

Yeats, Alexander J. (1976a), "An analysis of the effect of production process changes on effective protection estimates", Review of Economics and Statistics, 58:81–85.

Yeats, Alexander J. (1976b), "A sensitivity analysis of the effective protection estimate", Journal of Development Economics, 3:367–376.

Chapter 12

TRADE POLICIES IN DEVELOPED COUNTRIES

ROBERT E. BALDWIN*

University of Wisconsin – Madison

Contents

1.	The political economy of protection	572
	1.1. The nature of the political decision-making process	573
	1.2. Alternative models and key industry characteristics	574
	1.3. Empirical tests: Results and appraisal	580
2.	Analyses of the effects of trade liberalization	582
	2.1. General liberalization	582
	2.2. Sectoral studies	590
3.	Adjusting to increased imports	590
	3.1. The concept of social adjustment costs	591
	3.2. Estimates of adjustment costs	593
	3.3. The effectiveness of trade adjustment assistance programs	594
4.	Estimating the impact of foreign trade on employment	595
5.	Customs unions and other preferential trading arrangements	597
	5.1. Customs unions	597
	5.2. Tariff preferences and other trade policies affecting the LDCs	598
6.	Specific non-tariff trade measures	600
	6.1. Quantitative restrictions (QRs)	600
	6.2. Preferential government purchasing policies	602
	6.3. Export and domestic subsidies	604
	6.4. Dumping	605
	6.5. Border tax adjustments	607
	6.6. Offshore assembly provisions (OAPs) and domestic content protection	608
7.	Current and prospective trade-policy issues	608
	7.1. Selectivity, reciprocity, and graduation	609
	7.2. Trade in services and trade-related investment issues	610
	7.3. Institutional reforms	611
References		612

*I am very grateful to W.M. Corden, A.V. Deardorff, P.B. Dixon, C. Hamilton, P.B. Kenen, A.O. Krueger, P.J. Lloyd, R. McCulloch, D.R. Richardson, A. Sapir, R.M. Stern, and J. Whalley for their comments on an earlier version of this chapter.

Handbook of International Economics, vol. I, Edited by R.W. Jones and P.B. Kenen
© *Elsevier Science Publishers B.V., 1984*

Modern policy-oriented analysis of trade issues in developed countries focuses mainly on five sets of questions. First, how can the differences in levels of protection among industries be explained? Secondly, what are the industry and economywide effects of trade liberalization (or increased protection) on economic welfare, trade, output, employment and the distribution of income, and how effective are government policies introduced for the purpose of assisting the economic adjustment to increased imports? Thirdly, what are the economic effects of discriminatory tariff arrangements such as customs unions and the Generalized System of Preferences? Fourthly, what is the economic impact of specific non-tariff measures such as quantitative restrictions, preferential government purchasing policies, export and domestic subsidies and countervailing duties, dumping and antidumping duties, and domestic content requirements? Finally, what institutional arrangements and policies best maintain order in the international trading system and in the management of trade-policy conflicts?

This chapter surveys recent empirical and policy studies by economists who have addressed these five sets of questions. No attempt is made to cover all important contributions in these fields. Instead, representative studies will be cited with a view to establishing the main research results and suggesting issues on which further research is needed.

1. The political economy of protection

Since the early 1970s a growing body of literature has emerged that attempts to explain the differences across industries in both levels of protection and the extent of tariff reductions undertaken by governments in GATT-sponsored multilateral trade negotiations. Two factors have been particularly important in accounting for this increased interest in the structure of protection: the development of public choice theory and the burst of detailed studies measuring protection stimulated by the formulation of the concept of effective rates of protection [Johnson (1965), Corden (1966)].

Early writers in the public choice field [e.g. Downs (1957) and Buchanan and Tulloch (1962)] often referred to the level and structure of tariffs in illustrating the importance of the free-rider problem or the existence of imperfect information in shaping the nature of decisions on public goods. However, until estimates of nominal and effective protective rates at a detailed industry level became available [e.g. Balassa (1965), Basevi (1966)], economists were unable to test rigorously for the significance of such factors by regressing protection rates on various economic and political characteristics of industries.

Although much has been written on the subject, there is still widespread disagreement as to which of the various competing hypotheses best explains the structure of protection within industrial democracies. Disagreement exists at three different levels of analysis. There is, first, a lack of consensus concerning the nature of the political decision-making process. Secondly, authors differ widely with respect to what they believe are the key political-economic characteristics that enable an industry to obtain greater protection or successfully to resist duty cuts. Lastly, there is a significant divergence in views over which economic variables are the best proxies for a particular political-economic characteristic. These three differences are explored in more detail below.

1.1. The nature of the political decision-making process

Two extreme positions exist concerning the manner in which political decisions are reached. One treats government officials simply as intermediaries who balance the conflicting interests of various groups in society in order to maximize their likelihood of remaining in power. According to this view [typified by Olson (1965) and Brock and Magee (1978)], the nature of political decisions depends upon the preferences of voters and various interest groups, with the state having little independent influence. A quite different position regards the state as being largely autonomous in the decision-making process. Although writers explicitly propounding this position, e.g. Nordlinger (1981), recognized that there are societal constraints on autonomous actions by the state, e.g. elections, they stress the ability of the government to use its power to circumvent these constraints.

Most authors adopt an intermediate position between these two positions. However, those closer to the first view devote considerable time to explaining just how a particular individualistic or social objective associated with protection is actually translated into political action. Those who put more emphasis on the autonomy of the state tend, by contrast, to test for the empirical relevance of a particular social goal without dwelling upon the political process by which it is implemented.

Authors favoring the intermediation view of government differ among themselves with regard to the extent that they assume that the actors in society are motivated by short-run or long-run economic interests and by altruistic or ethical concerns toward others. Those emphasizing the importance of short-run individualistic economic interests focus upon the ability of individuals benefitting directly and immediately from protection to exert their power through voting and group pressures. However, by taking a longer-run view of self-interest or by introducing altruistic or ethical attitudes on the part of the various political actors in the economy, it is possible to account for the willingness of individuals not directly affected by the level of economic activity in a particular industry to grant protection for that industry. For example, supporting protection for an import-injured industry as a form of social insurance is political behavior [see Eaton and Grossman (1981)] consistent with the notion that individuals are motivated by long-run economic interest. And, of course, the willingness of individuals to support temporary protection for the industry even though they know the cost of the industry's products will rise somewhat is easily explained if the utility level of those individuals is related positively to the utility level of employees in the injured industry or simply if ethical considerations prompt this support. These various points are more fully discussed in Baldwin (1982a).

1.2. Alternative models and key industry characteristics

The differences among writers in the field become most evident, however, when they describe the political behavior-process that leads to protection for an industry and then select the economic characteristics of the industry that reflect this behavior. At least seven distinct (though not necessarily incompatible) models or hypotheses of political behavior can be discerned in the literature. There are several more that deal with protection for particular sectors such as national defense industries. All receive some empirical support. Unfortunately, however, there is no general agreement on just which models (or group of models) performs best.

The seven models and the key political-economic characteristic of an industry that each one stresses as being the main determinant of the industry's ability to secure protection are as follows.

(1) The common-interest or pressure group model – the ability of an industry to organize as a political pressure group;

(2) The adding-machine model – the voting strength of an industry;

(3) The adjustment assistance model – the ability of workers to adjust to greater import competition;

(4) The equity-concern model – the income and skill levels of workers;

(5) The comparative-costs model – the international competitive strength of an industry;

(6) The international-bargaining model – the bargaining ability and political importance of the countries from which competing imports are supplied;

(7) The status-quo (or historical-influences) model – the historical level of an industry's protection.

The interest-group model is probably the best known of the different hypotheses directed at explaining the structure of a country's industrial protection. Writers who formulated this model [Olson (1965), Pincus (1975), Brock and Magee (1978)] stress that the actual political outcome in a democracy may not reflect the views of a majority of the country's citizens because of imperfect knowledge as well as costs of redistributing income and undertaking political action. For example, for a country facing fixed terms of trade, a policy of free trade is welfare-superior to a protectionist policy in the sense that it is possible in a world of costless income-redistribution to make everyone better off than they would be under protection. However, because of the existence of redistribution, knowledge-acquisition, and political-action costs, this free-trade policy may not be implemented in the political process. What may occur instead, according to the interest-group hypothesis, is that industries benefiting from protection organize into political pressure groups and succeed in obtaining protection against competitive imports.

Whether groups with a common economic interest do in fact organize depends upon the gains and costs expected by their members. As Mancur Olson (1965) points out, tariff protection for an industry is a collective benefit (the tariff protects all firms in the industry) and industry efforts to exert political influence are financed by voluntary contributions on the part of its members. Therefore, the free-rider problem hampers efforts to organize for political purposes. An individual firm has an incentive to withhold its contribution and enjoy the benefits of the protection secured by the rest of the industry. The outcome may be that the industry does not organize at all, even though it is in the interests of all its members to do so. Olson reasons that the voluntary formation of pressure groups is more likely if the group is small and the benefits are unevenly distributed, since individual members or at least a group of members has more at stake.[1] While some industries may be small enough in terms of the number of firms or sufficiently concentrated to organize, he maintains that consumers generally are unable to do so. Pincus (1975) further argues that an industry's lobbying efforts will be greater the more geographically concentrated it is, since this improves its ability to coordinate and monitor these activities.

In testing these different relationships, a seller concentration ratio, e.g. the share of industry shipments accounted for by the largest four firms, and the number of establishments in an industry are usually used to capture Olson's hypotheses about group size and the distribution of benefits, whereas a geographic concentration ratio is utilized to reflect Pincus's argument. A positive correlation between the level of protection (or changes in the level of protection) and seller and geographic concentration ratios is expected and a negative one between the number of firms and the protective level. Since purchasers of goods for intermediate-input purposes are thought to be more effective opponents of protection than final consumers (for the preceding reasons stated by Olson and Pincus), a measure of the extent to which an industry's sales go to other industries rather than final consumers is often introduced to measure the resistance by others to protection. One also expects greater resistance to protectionist pressures in sectors with extensive exports and foreign direct investments because of the fear of foreign retaliation.

---

[1] Olson points out, however, that even if an industry does not meet these criteria it may succeed in organizing if it produces a private good, e.g. a journal that provides useful technical information to its members, and collects funds for lobbying by selling this good.

Olson (1982) has argued that the ability of a group to organize is influenced not only by the number and size-distribution of its firm but the extent to which its common interest has been threatened. A series of repeated shocks or crises may be necessary before a group organizes or, if already organized, increases its lobbying pressures. Thus, a variable such as the growth rate in employment or output can be introduced as part of the interest-group model with the expectation that duty levels will be higher and duty cuts lower the lower the growth rate in an industry.

Those who apply the common-interest group model to explain protection generally assume that capitalists and workers in an industry share the same view about the desirability of import protection. However, on the basis of the Stolper–Samuelson theorem (1941), one would predict a conflict between the views of these two groups. If a country is relatively capital-abundant and exporting capital-intensive goods (and thus importing labor-intensive goods), labor should, according to the theorem, favor protection because its real wage will rise whereas capitalists should favor an export subsidy on the capital-intensive good.

Magee (1978) earlier tested the Stolper–Samuelson theorem by examining the congressional testimony of labor and capitalists when the Trade Act of 1974 (a tariff-liberalizing proposal) was under consideration. He found that in almost all instances labor and management in a particular industry shared the same view on liberalization versus import protection. As he points out, this result is consistent with a specific factors model. It is this framework that Findlay and Wellisz (1982) utilize in their ingenious analysis of tariff formation in the presence of opposing interest groups.

The *adding-machine model* was formulated as a separate hypothesis and so-named by Caves (1976). Like the pressure group approach this model postulates that individual consumers do not actively oppose protection because of a lack of knowledge and the high costs of individual political activity relative to the benefits. Consequently, the pattern of protection is shaped by producer interests who have more at stake in particular industries than consumers do. However, rather than focusing on the incentives that each industry has to organize and exert political pressure through campaign contributions and other forms of assistance to politicians, this model emphasizes the voting strength that an industry possesses. Since the government officials act to maximize the probability of their election, what matters in obtaining protection is the number of votes that an industry has. Caves also postulates that an industry's voting strength increases, the higher its labor-output coefficient and the more decentralized and geographically dispersed it is.

Both the interest-group and adding-machine models are, it should be noted, based on a view of the political decision-making process that considers the state to be an intermediary responding to the short-run, individualistic economic interests of producers and consumers. The remaining five models to be considered rest upon a view of the political process that considers producers and consumers as either taking a long-run view of their self-interests or being concerned about the economic welfare of others or, alternatively, that regards the state as having some scope for autonomous actions.

The *adjustment assistance* model, first stated explicitly by Cheh (1974), hypothesizes that governments aim at minimizing short-run labor adjustment costs in deciding which industries should receive the smallest duty cuts in a multilateral trade negotiation or the largest increases when injured by increased imports. Variables used to measure the ability of workers in an industry to adjust to duty cuts include the labor-output coefficient, the percentage of unskilled workers, the percentage of workers over 45 years of age, the proportion of workers in rural areas, the height of the initial duty, and the growth-rate of industry shipments. A positive relationship is hypothesized between the first four of these variables and changes in an industry's import duties on the grounds that it takes longer for unskilled, older workers living in rural areas to find new jobs than it does for other workers. Low cuts are also expected in high-duty industries, since a given percentage cut in a high-duty item tends to reduce its import price relatively more (and thus put more adjustment pressure on domestic producers) than the same percentage cut in a low-duty item. On the other hand, since rapid industry growth facilitates adjustment to duty reductions, growth rates and the extent of duty cuts are likely to be negatively correlated.

The *equity-concern model* focuses primarily upon the governmental objective of ensuring that low-income workers are not hurt by economic change. Ball (1967), Constantopoulos (1974), Fieleke (1976), and Baldwin (1981) are among the authors who have stressed its importance in explaining levels of and change in protection. They utilize such measures as average wages, the proportion of unskilled workers, and an industry's labor-output ratio in testing the model's validity.

Several investigators, e.g. Ray (1981) and Lavergne (1981), have pointed out that one would expect protective levels to be relatively high (and duty cuts comparatively low) in those industries in which a country is at a comparative-cost disadvantage. This *comparative-costs model* takes account of the obvious point that relatively low-cost domestic industries tend to be net exporters and therefore tend to oppose protective actions because of the fear of foreign retaliation. Consequently, even though an export-oriented industry may, for example, be highly concentrated or large in employment terms and thereby capable of exerting considerable protectionist pressure, it will not do so. To take account of this point in testing the interest group, adding-machine, and other models, it is therefore necessary to introduce a comparative-cost measure as a control variable. A concern by the government over excessive dependence on imports could also be the basis of high protective levels in sectors of comparative disadvantage. An industry's labor-output coefficient, average wage, and proportion of unskilled workers are often utilized as measures of comparative disadvantage in industrial countries.

The *international-bargaining model*, first proposed by Helleiner (1977), supplements the interest-group model in that it deals with the ability of one government to influence the trade policies of another government. One obvious consideration affecting a country's bargaining power is whether it is prepared to cut its own levels of protection when others reduce their trade barriers. Since the less developed countries (LDCs) have generally been unwilling to do so, Helleiner expects that duty levels in industrial countries will be higher (and duty-cuts less) on products of export interest to the LDCs than on items supplied by countries practicing reciprocity. He uses average wages and an economies-of-scale variable to indicate those manufactured products in which the LDCs have an export interest. A more direct measure that Lavergne (1981) uses to test this hypothesis is the share of LDC exports in U.S. imports.

The last model, the *status quo* or *historical influences model*, is attributable to Lavergne (1981). In his view, there are two reasons for current duty levels (and recent duty cuts) to be positively correlated with duty levels that existed several years ago. One is a desire by government officials to avoid large adjustment costs for an industry. The other is conservative respect for the *status quo* that is based either on a regard for existing property rights (even in the form of rents generated by protection) or on a cautious response to uncertainty concerning the effect of change. In his concept of the conservative social welfare function, Corden (1974, pp. 107–111) also stresses the public goal of not disturbing the economic *status quo* so much that some income groups incur significant income losses. To test the historical-influences hypothesis for the United States, Lavergne employs the tariff levels that prevailed under the 1930 Smoot–Hawley Act.

Table 1.1 summarizes the relationships expected in the various models between levels of and changes in protection and the key economic characteristics used to reflect the political behavior assumptions of the different hypotheses. The relationships usually found in empirical tests of the models are also listed in the table.

An alternative approach to analyzing the structure of protection in terms of the type of specific behavior hypotheses or control factors considered thus far has been suggested by Anderson (1978). Following the framework set forth earlier by Buchanan and Tulloch (1968) and Breton (1974), Anderson views protection as being determined in a political market in which import-competing producers are the demanders and the government is the supplier. In his view the demand for assistance is affected by factors determining both the expected benefits of favorable action to import-competing producers and the expected lobbying costs, while the supply is determined by the benefits of assistance to the government, e.g. loss of financial support and votes. All of the variables mentioned in

Table 1.1

Expected and actual relationships between key industry characteristics and levels of and changes in protection

Industry characteristic	Various models (expected relationships)							Actual empirical relationship
	Pressure group	Adding machine	Adjustment assistance	Equity concern	Comparative costs	International bargaining	Status quo	
1. Seller and geographic concentration ratios	positive	negative	–	–	–	–	–	pos. & neg.
2. Number of firms	negative	–	–	–	–	–	–	negative[a]
3. Growth rate	negative	–	negative	–	–	–	–	negative
4. Extent of foreign investment	negative	–	–	–	–	–	–	positive
5. Extent of sales to other industries	negative	–	–	–	–	–	–	negative
6. Number of workers	–	positive	–	–	–	–	–	positive[a]
7. Labor-output coefficient	–	positive	positive	positive	positive	–	–	positive[a]
8. Proportion of unskilled workers	–	–	positive	positive	positive	–	–	positive[a]
9. Age of workers	–	–	positive	–	–	–	–	positive
10. Proportion in rural areas	–	–	positive	–	–	–	–	positive[a]
11. Average wage	–	–	negative	negative	negative	–	–	negative[a]
12. Import penetration ratio	–	–	–	–	positive	–	–	positive[a]
13. Extent of imports from LDCs	–	–	–	–	–	positive	–	positive[a]
14. Historical level of protection	–	–	–	–	–	–	positive	positive[a]

[a] Indicates the relationship is usually statistically significant at the 10 percent level or less.

discussing the seven models described above (plus a few more) are listed as demand or supply variables by Anderson. Since he is more interested in predicting the structure of protection than in separating out the relative importance of demand versus supply forces, he lists several of the variables as both demand and supply determinants.[2]

1.3. Empirical tests: Results and appraisal

An impressive number of empirical tests of the various models described in the preceding section already exist, and new studies are emerging at a rapid pace. Studies include those by Pincus (1975), McPherson (1972), Cheh (1974), Fieleke (1976), Baldwin (1981), and Ray (1981) for the United States; Caves (1976), Helleiner (1977), and Saunders (1980) for Canada; Anderson (1978) and Conybeare (1978) for Australia; Tharakan (1980) for Belgium; Shouda (1980) for Japan; Cable and Rebelo (1980) for the United Kingdom; Lundberg (1981) for Sweden; and Riedel (1977) and Glismann and Weiss (1980) for Germany.

One of the first issues to be settled in any empirical analysis is whether to measure protection in terms of nominal or effective rates. At a conceptual level effective rates are preferable, since these rather than nominal duties indicate the benefits from protection to the factors employed in an industry. However, industries may in fact focus mainly on nominal (output) rates because of a desire to avoid political conflicts with other industries. It is also necessary in some cases to utilize nominal rates because effective rate estimates are out-of-date or too aggregative to capture the desired level of detail. Fortunately, the entire issue is not very important as a practical matter, since there is generally a high degree of correlation between nominal and effective rates.

A more serious matter concerns the absence – in other than the Australian, West Germany (1980), Japanese, and U.S. (1974) studies – of measures of protection that take account of other forms of industry assistance besides tariffs. If subsidies or quotas, for example, are substitutes for tariffs, regression results based only on tariffs can be misleading. In the United States industries with high tariffs are also highly protected by non-tariff measures, so that the problem may not be serious in practice, but it is not known whether this relationship also exists in other industrial countries.

Problems of interpreting the results from the regression analyses also arise because of the high degree of correlation among some of the independent variables, e.g. average wages, the labor-output coefficients, and the proportion of unskilled workers. An additional problem is the likely existence of two-way causal

---

[2] Baldwin (1981) undertakes two-stage regression analysis in an effort to determine the relative importance of demand versus supply forces.

relationships between some of the variables. For example, even if (potentially) high import-penetration levels lead to high levels of protection, there may be no statistically significant relationship across industries at a given point in time between duty levels and the actual ratio of imports to consumption because high duty levels reduce the ratio of imports to consumption.

As can be seen from the last column in Table 1.1, the various empirical tests indicate that industries receiving the greatest protection (and the lowest duty cuts during multilateral trade negotiations) are ones in which the workers tend to be unskilled, low-paid, older, and live in rural areas. These industries are also characterized by a large number of workers, a high labor-output coefficient, a small number of firms, slow growth, a high import penetration ratio, and historically high levels of protection. It is difficult at this stage of the empirical testing to determine the relative explanatory power of the different models, since the same independent variables are employed to test several of the hypotheses. To do so, it is necessary to find economic variables that delineate the various models more sharply and thereby reduce the overlap that now exists.

Consider, for example, the common-interest or pressure-group hypothesis. This model assumes that, if an industry organizes into a pressure group, it will secure higher levels of protection. However, the failure of the concentration variables to be significantly related to protection may be due either to the fact that industries with low concentration ratios also organize and secure protection or alternatively, that while only concentrated industries tend to organize into common-interest groups, these pressure groups are not effective in securing protection. It is this latter relationship, i.e. whether those industries that organize into pressure groups – a directly observable relationship – do in fact succeed in obtaining protection, that is of more interest than the characteristics of those industries that organize. Consequently, we need to relate direct measures of political pressures across industries to protectionist result in these sectors. Although there is no single ideal index of political pressure and difficult data collection problems exist in the field, regressing tariff levels or duty cuts on such indicators of active political pressure as the size of lobbying expenditures and political contributions by an industry, the extent to which members of an industry make their view known to government officials through letters or personal visits (this also provides evidence on the adding-machine model), the volume of testimony and public statements in favor of the industry's position, etc. would seem to be a better way of testing the model than relating tariff levels to such variables as concentration ratios and the number of firms.

There are also more direct measures available for testing most of the other models. As Bale (1977) has shown, the actual magnitude of adjustment costs (in terms of foregone income) associated with a given reduction in protection can be estimated for each industry. Similarly, instead of using partial and imperfect indicators of comparative costs such as average wages and the proportion of unskilled workers, it is possible to utilize estimates of revealed comparative costs based either directly on a country's trade performance or on differences in factor prices inferred from this performance [see Hilton (1981)]. Furthermore, the willingness of other nations to offer trading concessions in return for concessions granted by others could be measured directly on a sector-by-sector basis by examining the "offers" of the various participants in a trade negotiation.

While collection of the data needed to come up with these kinds of direct measures of the behavior characterizing the various models is a formidable task, such an effort seems to be required if we are to make significant further progress in understanding the political-economic determinants of the structure of protection. Presently we are able to predict this structure reasonably well from various industry characteristics, but we do not understand what type of political and economic behavior these variables reflect.

2. Analyses of the effects of trade liberalization

A major traditional concern of empirical studies of trade policies in developed countries has been the effect of trade liberalization (or increased protectionism) on such variables as economic welfare, the volume and balance of trade, output, employment, and the distribution of income. Investigators have estimated these effects both for the economy as a whole and for specific sectors.

2.1. General liberalization

In recent years significant improvements have been made in analyzing the economywide effects of general trade-liberalizing efforts both through the presentation of much greater industry detail and, more importantly, by the development of models that capture more of the general equilibrium effects of changes in protective levels. At the time of Corden's (1975) excellent survey of the topic, the studies by Basevi (1968) and Magee (1972) typified the best work in the mainstream of trade-policy research. Basevi's analysis of the welfare effects of removing U.S. tariffs is noteworthy in that it takes into account the exchange-rate change needed to eliminate the trade deficit resulting from a unilateral tariff reduction. However, no industry detail is provided. Magee, on the other hand, while not considering the pressure for a change in the exchange rate, does provide some sectoral detail and also takes into account quantitative import restrictions.[3] Furthermore, following the approach developed by Baldwin and Mutti (1973), Magee not only

---

[3] For his measures of the ad valorem equivalents of quantitative restrictions, Magee relied on studies of specific sectors by Bergsten (1972) and Mintz (1974).

estimates the static welfare gains in the usual manner but includes a measure of the social costs associated with the temporary unemployment caused by reductions in protection.

By the early 1970s general equilibrium models were also beginning to be used to explore the consequences of protection. It was fully appreciated by then that a ranking of effective rates of protection (calculated in the usual partial equilibrium manner) in a multi-commodity world will not in general correspond to the pattern of resource shifts caused by changes in protective levels. To determine these shifts, it is necessary to utilize a general equilibrium framework. The initial efforts along these lines, e.g. Lage (1970) and Evans (1971), applied linear programming models to obtain numerical solutions to the effects of protection.

2.1.1. Recent models

Two more recent studies that provide much greater industry and country detail are by Baldwin (1976), Baldwin and Lewis (1978), and Baldwin, Mutti, and Richardson (1980) and by Cline, Kawanabe, Kronsjo, and Williams (1978a, 1978b). Baldwin et al. analyze the direct and indirect effects (assuming fixed input–output coefficients) in 367 U.S. sectors (of which roughly 300 engage in international trade) of a 50 percent multilateral tariff reduction. They assume that an industry's exports are identical to the production that it sells at home but that imports are imperfect substitutes for domestic production in the same industry. However, imports in each industry are assumed to be want-independent of all domestic goods in other industries, i.e. real-income compensated cross-price elasticities are assumed to be zero. Taxes are assumed to increase in a non-distorting manner to offset the decline in tariff revenue (all other government activity remaining unchanged), so that the country's increased spending on imports is exactly equal to the reduced spending on domestically produced import substitutes. Slack labor conditions and underutilized capital capacity are also assumed to exist both before and after the multilateral liberalization. A related key assumption is that not only are import supply curves infinitely elastic but that the prices of domestically produced goods, wage rates, and, therefore residually, returns to capital remain constant over the adjustment period. Because of these various assumptions, the total initial impact on the economy is simply the sum of the partial equilibrium effects in each industry. The final impact is then determined by taking into account the sectoral effects of allowing the exchange rate to change so as to restore the initial trade balance.

Cline et al. utilize a similar analytical framework but estimate the economic effects of a 60 percent multilateral duty cut, not just in the United States but for 11 industrial countries or country groups plus the developing countries as a whole. In their analysis these authors also take into account the trade diversion effects of a multilateral tariff cut for members of a free trade bloc, e.g. the EEC, and include an estimate of some dynamic as well as static welfare gains of liberalization. As a necessary cost of the country detail, however, their industry breakdown is less detailed (about 21 sectors) and they are unable to estimate indirect effects for most countries.

Beginning with Taylor and Black (1974), who in turn based their model upon the earlier work of Johansen (1960), a number of economists have in recent years formulated estimable non-linear general equilibrium models of international trade. Some, e.g. Taylor and Black (1974), Staelin (1976), de Melo (1978), de Melo and Dervis (1977), utilize the models for investigating the effects of trade restrictions in a particular developing country, while others, e.g. Boadway and Treddenick (1978), Cook (1981), Deardorff and Stern (1979, 1981a), Dixon et al. (1977), Dixon et al. (1982), and Brown and Whalley (1980) focus on either a specific developed country or the interactions among several such countries when trade is liberalized. Only the second group of models is considered in this chapter, since those making up the first set are described in Chapter 11, Section 3.5. It should be noted, however, that except for the assumption made by the first group [and also Boadway and Treddenick (1978)] of perfect substitution between imports and domestic output in both consumption and production, the general structure of the models is quite similar.

In all the models, explicit demand and supply functions are derived from utility and profit-maximization behavior on the part of a country's consumers and producers, assuming explicit utility and production functions and purely competitive conditions. In those that are concerned with only one economy, e.g. Dixon et al. (1977), Boadway and Treddenick (1978), and Cook (1981), the demand and supply curves derived for traded commodities are matched against exogenously given export demand and import supply curves to determine the prices of internationally traded commodities. However, in multi-country, general-equilibrium models such as those by Deardorff and Stern (1981a) and Brown and Whalley (1980), the individual country demand and supply curves for traded goods interact at the world level to determine prices and clear international commodity markets. These equilibrium prices then feed back into the individual countries to obtain values for other country-specific variables. Both fixed and flexible exchange rate regimes are analyzed by most authors, although in the case of Brown and Whalley (1980), it follows from the long-run assumptions of the model that the choice of exchange rate regime makes no difference to the characteristics of equilibrium in the model.

On the production side, industries combine in a least-cost fashion primary factors (usually only labor and capital) together with imported and domestically produced goods (regarded as imperfect substitutes) needed as intermediate inputs. Inputs from each sector are usually required in fixed proportions but substitution can take place between imports (either as a whole or by country source) and domestic production within each sector. Similarly, although primary factors as a whole are required in fixed proportions for each product, substitution between primary factors occurs. Constant elasticity of substitution (CES) production functions are usually specified both between home and imported inputs and between capital and labor.

Although all the models assume that households maximize an explicit utility function, they differ among each other as to the nature of the function. By specifying Cobb–Douglas and CES utility functions, Deardorff and Stern (1981a) and Brown and Whalley (1980) assume that expenditure elasticities of demand are unity. Dixon et al. (1977) and Cook (1981) postulate additive utility functions that do not necessarily involve this assumption. Substitutions on the part of consumers takes place at two levels: between imports (as a whole or by country source) and domestic output within a particular product sector (constant elasticities are assumed for this substitution) and among composite goods from different industries. In order to abstract from macro-stabilization issues, the models usually hold real domestic absorption constant when examining the effects of tariff changes.

Since the number of variables in the models exceeds the number of equations, some variables must be specified exogenously in order to close the models. The authors utilize existing studies to fix the required demand and supply elasticity parameters as well as the input–output coefficients and take the needed data on trade, production, employment, tariffs, other taxes, etc. from published sources for some benchmark period. The choice of the remaining variables that must be determined exogenously is what distinguishes the models most from each other. Deardorff and Stern (1981a), for example, usually postulate both that the capital stock in each sector is fixed and that slack labor conditions exist with a fixed money wage. Dixon et al. (1977), and Cook (1981) adopt the same short-run assumptions for some of their simulations of the effects of tariff cuts. In addition, Dixon et al. (1977) explore the consequences of liberalization when capital is sector-specific but labor is fully employed and perfectly mobile among a country's industries. The wage rate becomes endogenous under these circumstances. Brown and Whalley (1980) adopt a longer-run perspective by dropping the assumption of sector-specific capital stocks and allowing both capital and labor (in given total amounts) to shift among a country's industries. As they point out, these assumptions make their model an empirical counterpart of the Heckscher–Ohlin trade model. A variation analyzed by Cook (1981) is to permit a given amount of capital to shift among industries but to hold the money wage rate fixed.

Following Johansen (1960) all the models except Brown and Whalley's (1980) are solved by logarithmic differentiation of the structural equations to yield a set of simultaneous equations that are linear in percentage changes. Brown and Whalley (1980) do not linearize their system and solve it by a Newton method that utilizes information on excess demands and government budget inbalances. Their model has the advantage of being valid even for larger changes. There is, on the other hand, no guarantee of uniqueness of the computed equilibrium.

2.1.2. *A comparison of estimated effects*

Table 2.1 compares estimates of the static welfare gains (or losses) from trade liberalization for those studies that attempted to measure these effects. The major conclusion emerging from all of these investigations, which is consistent with the results of earlier studies, is that the static welfare effects of trade liberalization in developed countries are very small. For example, the net welfare benefits to the world economy from the average duty reduction of about 30 percent in the Tokyo Round of multilateral trade negotiation are estimated by Deardorff and Stern (1979) to equal only about one-half of 1 percent of the GNP of the participants, while Whalley and Wigle (1982) placed the world welfare gains of a 50 percent multilateral tariff cut at about one-third of 1 percent of world income. The efforts to reduce trade barriers are clearly very much worthwhile in benefit–cost terms, but it is evident that such efforts result in only marginal static gains in real world income. Some estimates of the dynamic benefits from liberalization are consider-ably larger, e.g. Cline et al. (1978) argue that the anti-inflationary benefits of a 60 percent cut would amount to a 1 percent increase in real GNP, but the theoretical underpinnings of such dynamic estimates are much less firm than those for static welfare gains.

Although the estimates in Table 2.1 of the gains in welfare are all quite small absolutely, the relative differences among them are considerable. For example, with a comparable multilateral tariff cut Baldwin's estimates of U.S. welfare gains equal about one-half of Cline's and only one-fifth of those by Deardorff and Stern (1979). Whalley and Wigle (1982) estimate that are same multilateral cut actually reduces U.S. welfare by one-half of 1 percent because of a terms-of-trade deterioration of seven-tenths of 1 percent. Differences in both model specification and estimates of the key elasticity parameters apparently account for these variations.

Table 2.1 brings out a point emphasized earlier by Magee (1972), namely, the relative importance of non-tariff trade barriers. Cline et al. estimate that the gains from a 60 percent cut in just agricultural barriers would be greater than those from a 60 percent reduction in all tariffs. Deardorff and Stern (1979) also find that the reduction in NTBs in the Tokyo Round amount to a significant part of the total welfare gains.

Estimates of the job losses caused by general trade-liberalizing negotiations are also very small. Both Baldwin et al. (1980) and Cline et al. (1978) estimate the job displacement from a 50–60 percent multilateral cut to amount to less than 0.2 percent of the U.S. labor force. Moreover, this figure does not take into considera-

Table 2.1
Comparisons of static welfare gains from trade liberalization

Study	Nature of measurement	Annual static welfare gain (in millions of $)	Annual gain as a percentage of GNP
Baldwin et al. (1980)	Effects on the U.S. of a 50 percent multilateral cut in tariffs of the industrial countries, 1967 base.	101	0.01
Cline et al. (1978)	Effect in the U.S., Canada, Japan, and the EEC of 60 percent tariff cut, 1974 base	1681	0.06
	60 percent cut in agricultural NTB's in countries listed above, 1974 base.	2029	0.05
	Effect of 60 percent multilateral tariff cut on the United States, 1974 base.	490	0.03
Deardorff and Stern (1979)	Effect of Tokyo Round tariff cuts (about 30 percent) in 18 industrial nations, 1976 base.	2592	0.06
	NTB reductions in Tokyo Round in 18 industrial countries, 1976.	4774	0.11
	Effect of Tokyo Round tariff cuts on the United States, 1976 base.	710	0.04
Whalley and Wigle (1982)	Effect of a 50 percent multilateral tariff cut on the EEC, the U.S., Japan, and the Rest of the World, 1977 base.	1300	0.03
	Effect of a 50 percent multilateral tariff cut on the United States, 1977 base.	−1070	−0.05

tion the new jobs created in export-oriented sectors. The net U.S. employment change (the figures are roughly the same for other countries) calculated by these authors as well as by Deardorff and Stern (1979) is essentially zero. This overall figure should, however, not obscure the fact that employment in several industries significantly decreases, e.g. footwear, food utensils and pottery, and cutlery, or increases, e.g. semiconductors and computing machines, from a significant multi-lateral tariff cut.

That the most interesting results of the various models relate to intersectoral differences rather than aggregative effects is further evident from the impact of liberalization on the demand for various types of labor. Baldwin and Lewis (1978a) estimate, for example, that a multilateral duty reduction tends to increase the demand in the United States for those engaged in research and development activities, other professional and technical workers, and farmers and to reduce the demand for semi-skilled and unskilled workers and for craftsmen. Dixon et al. (1977) also find that a unilateral duty reduction in Australia favors professional and rural workers.

Some insight into the effect of the various assumptions of the different models on the estimated variables is given in the study by Cook (1981) of the impact in the United States of the unilateral elimination of all tariffs. He considers three imperfect-substitute models: one that utilizes the Baldwin–Cline assumptions, one that follows the Deardorff–Stern assumptions, and one that postulates a fixed money wage with a given capital stock that is not sector specific. As would be expected, the Deardorff–Stern model with its less-than-completely-elastic supply curves produces a smaller change in output than the Baldwin–Cline model. The unweighted average of the percentage output changes in the 80 input–output sectors he analyzes (Cook does not give a total change) is −0.67 percent in the Deardorff–Stern model and −1.08 percent under the Baldwin–Cline assumptions. Moreover, as would also be expected, when intersectoral capital mobility is added to the fixed money wage assumption, the resulting average sectoral output declines, namely −0.91 percent, lies between the changes under the other two models.

2.1.3. Needed further research

While the improvements over the last few years in modeling the effects of general trade liberalization have been very impressive, there are some fairly obvious areas in which more research is needed. One concerns the quality of the data that is being utilized in existing models. For example, since estimates of various neces-sary parameters such as substitution elasticities and input–output coefficients are available only for a few of the larger countries, investigators are forced to apply these estimates in other countries for which no reliable measures exist. Even the estimates of such relationships that are available are often based on a much broader commodity classification than the investigator desires. Thus, much work is needed to obtain more detailed measures of the key parameters needed for existing models.

The long-standing appeal for models that take into account such factors as economies of scale and various dynamic externalities is also as relevant as ever. Most empirically oriented trade economists believe that the static gains from liberalization significantly underestimate the real income benefits of an open trade policy. However, the main reason for their inability to estimate these effects in a rigorous fashion is the lack of adequate theoretical modeling that is amenable to empirical implementation. Existing levels of understanding of the various relationships is still primitive. The theoretical developments in modeling increasing returns and imperfect competition reported in Chapter 7 open up one promising line of research, but much more effort is needed in analyzing and measuring the effects of such factors as the greater competition that is usually associated with increased trade liberalization.

While trade models incorporating more "general-equilibrium" effects clearly improve our understanding of what happens as a consequence of trade policy changes, it does not follow that simpler "impact" models are no longer useful. Policymakers are not interested only in the final net resource shifts brought about, for example, by a tariff cut but also in the intensity of the immediate pressures for adjustment and especially in the time path of the income redistributions caused by the cuts. In other words, they would like trade economists to develop dynamic empirical models that trace the detailed effects of policy changes from their immediate impact through the period of long-run adjustment. In doing so, model builders should specify more carefully the effects of financial variables such as exchange rates on real variables, such as the trade balance and employment. Clearly, financial variables can influence the magnitude of real variables in a short-run, general equilibrium model because of the rigidity of a number of nominal variables in the short run. Why and how this occurs, however, and how the relationships change as the rigidities disappear in the long run need to be spelled out better.

Another matter on which some comment is warranted concerns the small size of the general equilibrium effects produced by relevant trade policy changes. As the results reported by Cook (1981) indicate, modifying the nature of the model can bring about fairly significant percentage changes in the effects of a particular policy. However, the changes occur in magnitudes that tend to be quite small in absolute terms. In view of this, the question arises as to whether the information gained from "more general" models is sufficiently useful to justify the much greater efforts required to construct them. Differences among investigators in the sets of key parameters selected also seem to make as much difference in the empirical results as the degree of "generality" of the model.

This is by no means a new issue for trade economists. They have long pioneered in the development of empirical policy models, even though they have usually shown that the consequences of relevant trade policy shifts tend to be very small from the national viewpoint. Fortunately, the models they develop usually can also be utilized to analyze changes in exchange rates, domestic tax rates, world commodity prices, etc. where the magnitude of relevant policy changes are more significant. From the viewpoint of the economic profession as a whole, the much more significant differences in outcomes with respect to these policy changes presumably justify the development to the more elaborate models. But there is also a need for trade economists to devote more attention both to improving parameter estimates for existing models and to studying key (rather than all) sectors in greater detail.

2.2. Sectoral studies

Fortunately there have been several excellent recent studies of the consequences of protection for specific industries, e.g. Jenkins (1981) on Canada's clothing sector; Hamilton (1981b) on Sweden's textile and clothing industry; Morkre and Tarr (1980) on citizen band transreceivers; color television, sugar, non-rubber footwear, and textiles; Keesing and Wolf (1980) and Pelzman (1981) on textiles; Bale and Mutti (1980) and Pearson (1981) on footwear; Crandall (1981) and Walter (1982) on steel; Cohen (1982) on autos; and Hillman (1978) on agriculture. The advantage of such studies is that they usually not only come up with a measure of the welfare losses or employment gains associated with protection but also analyze the various reasons why the industry faces international competitive problems, what previous governmental programs have been undertaken, and what the prospects are for successful adjustment. In other words, one sees from these studies the complexity of the protectionist problem and gains a much better understanding of the possibilities (in both economic and political terms) for successful adjustment in the industry.

3. Adjusting to increased imports

The static welfare estimates reported in Table 2.1 do not include any measure of the social costs of adjusting to increased imports. However, because of the increase in empirical knowledge about the adjustment process that has come from studies of trade-displaced workers, a number of the recent studies of liberalization include estimates of these costs. This section first considers the concept of social adjustment costs and the empirical estimates of these costs, and then evaluates the available evidence on the effectiveness of worker adjustment assistance programs.

3.1. The concept of social adjustment costs

If perfect competition is coupled with flexible factor and product prices in an economy, adjusting to increased import competition will not involve any social welfare costs. However, as the theory of economic distortions and welfare indicates, e.g. Bhagwati (1971), if distortions such as wage rigidities exist, the shift of resources associated with greater import competition will entail certain social production costs that must be balanced against the welfare gains to consumers. These points can be illustrated with the following simple partial equilibrium model.

Suppose that imports and domestic output are imperfect substitutes and that imports in each industry are want-independent of all domestic goods in other industries. Furthermore, assume that the import supply curve as well as the supply curve of the domestic substitute are perfectly elastic. The line P_dS_d in Figure 3.1 is the supply curve of the domestic substitute based on the initial fixed set of factor prices that exists in the industry. The initial demand curve is D_d and equilibrium output is OA.

Now assume that the supply price of imports (not shown) falls due to a reduction in the tariff. This will cause the demand curve for the domestic substitute to decline, e.g. to D_d', as consumers substitute the imported item for the domestic version of the product. Suppose that workers are able to transfer to other industries and earn the same wage as exists initially in this industry, but that this shift involves the loss of employment for a short period because, for example, of the time involved in moving to another geographic area. If capital is sector-specific and wages are flexible, the industry's short-run supply curve will be vertical between the initial unit costs (and price), oP_d, and the lower unit costs, oP_d', that reflect the reduced wage at which workers are indifferent between

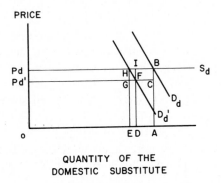

Figure 3.1

remaining at their jobs and accepting (say) a two weeks' pay loss (the time involved in transferring to other jobs) and obtaining the initial wage thereafter.[4]

Since the demand for the domestic substitute declines sufficiently to bring about an outflow of labor from the domestic industry, output falls to oD even though the price declines to oP_d'. As consumption of the domestic good declines by AD after the price falls to oP_d', consumer spending on the good declines by $FDAC$. Taking account of their adjustment costs, the released resources that had been producing AD of the domestic substitute now produce in alternative activities an output value equal to $FDAC$. However, the income of the released factors has fallen by $IFCB$, while the factors still employed in producing the good incur an income loss equal to $P_d P_d' FI$. But the drop in the price of the good means that the sum of these two areas, $P_d P_d' CB$, simply represents a transfer of income to consumers. Since in comparison with the situation at the initial price of oP_d the sum spent on the domestic good declines by $P_d P_d' CB$, consumers are able to purchase other goods that yield utility equivalent to this area. Consequently, others in the economy recoup dollar-for-dollar what factor owners in this sector lose.

The consumer surplus gain associated with lower-priced imports is the economy's net gain from the increased import competition. Of course, if there were no adjustment costs and workers released from producing the domestic substitute were immediately reemployed, the value of alternative production would have been higher. But the point is that the adjustment costs do not cause any economic distortion when factor prices are flexible and, therefore, are not associated with a social welfare loss.

Social welfare costs do, however, emerge from greater import competition if factor prices are rigid. When demand falls to D_d', output will decline by a greater quantity than in the flexible wage case, namely, by AE rather than AD. Because there is no decline in the price of the domestic good, the reduction in consumer spending on AE of this good is $HEAB$. However, assuming the same adjustment costs as in the flexible wage case, the released resources will only produce a value of other products equal to $GEAC$. In other words, since the price of the domestic good does not decline, the loss of income to these released resources, $HGCB$, will no longer be matched by an equivalent gain to consumers. Consequently, there is a welfare loss of $HGCB$ which must be compared with the consumer surplus gain in the import market. In particular, the discounted value of the temporary loss of income to workers who move out of the affected domestic sector must be

---

[4] The supply curve, $P_d'C$, would gradually rise as workers retire or leave for other reasons and as capital depreciates, since it is necessary to pay newly hired factors at the initial rates of return. Furthermore, if some factor owners are already on the margin of indifference between remaining in their present jobs and incurring the costs of moving, the BC segment of the short-run supply curve will have a finite positive slope.

subtracted from the discounted value of the net consumer surplus gain in the import market – a gain that continues indefinitely into the future.

3.2.   Estimates of adjustment costs

Investigators making estimates of the social costs of adjusting to increased import competition rely heavily upon information obtained from various surveys of trade-displaced workers, e.g. Bale (1973), McCarthy (1975), Jacobson (1978), Neumann (1978), Jenkins et al. (1978), and Corson et al. (1979). The U.S. surveys reveal that trade-displaced workers are typically older, less educated, more stable in their employment history, more likely to be female, minority status, and head of the household than the average unemployed worker. However, the average prelayoff earnings of these workers, especially in recent years with workers in such high-paying industries as steel and autos receiving trade adjustment assistance (TAA), are higher than other displaced workers. The average duration of unemployment (no matter what the cause) is greater if the workers are female or members of a minority group. In some surveys age is also positively correlated with duration of unemployment, but in the most recent study (Corson et al.) age turns out to be negatively related to the period of unemployment.

Estimates of the adjustment costs have been made for both specific industries, e.g. Bale (1977), Mutti (1977), and Jenkins and Montmarquette (1979), and for manufacturing as a whole. Mutti, for example, compares the social adjustment costs resulting from unilaterally eliminating tariffs in the following U.S. industries: industrial chemicals, iron and steel, machine tools, electrical machinery, and motor vehicles. The present value of the static welfare benefits from the duty cuts amount to $1788 million, whereas the discounted social adjustment costs come to $1382 million, i.e. a ratio of 1.3 to 1. The gain is positive for all sectors except steel.

Baldwin et al. (1980), Cline et al. (1978b), and Whalley and Wigle (1982) make the same type of calculations in their studies of the effects of multilateral tariff-cutting negotiations. The results differ considerably. Baldwin et al. estimate the adjustment costs associated with the *net* change in the pool of unemployed labor, i.e. the labor displaced by increased imports less the employment provided by the increase in exports, whereas Cline et al. use just the labor displaced by imports in making their calculations. In the Whalley model, full employment exists initially as well as in the long run after the tariff cuts. Consequently, Whalley and Wigle measure the income temporarily lost by all those who shift from one industry to another. The estimated ratio for the United States of the present value of the static welfare gains (using a 10 percent discount rate) to the labor adjustment costs is 28 to 1 for Baldwin et al., 8 to 1 for Cline et al., and − 5 to 1 for Whalley and Wigle. The negative ratio from Whalley's general equilibrium model results from the fact that the U.S. suffers nearly a 1 percent terms-of-trade loss that more than offsets the welfare-increasing effects of the tariff reductions (the present value of the annual welfare loss from a 50 percent cut is $11 billion even before taking into account labor adjustment costs). The magnitude of these divergences indicates the need for further work to isolate the exact reason for the differences, e.g. different model specification versus differences in the size of the relevant parameters.

3.3. The effectiveness of trade adjustment assistance programs

As Richardson (1982a) points out, there are three main purposes of trade adjustment assistance programs: (1) to compensate those who are injured by a government trade policy undertaken to increase general social welfare; (2) to promote inter-sectoral adjustment of resources in a manner that increases economic efficiency; and (3) to "buy off" pressure groups that could block socially desirable trade policies. Programs introduced in the United States and Canada try to accomplish these objectives by increasing both the level and duration of unemployment benefits for workers and by providing financial and technical assistance to eligible firms.[5]

Most of the surveys indicate that the better unemployment benefits received by trade-displaced workers act to lengthen the duration of the first spell of unemployment.[6] Furthermore, the most recent survey – unlike earlier ones – revealed that a recipient assisted under the U.S. Trade Adjustment Assistance (TAA) program who was identical to a regular unemployment insurance recipient (UI) in age, experience, socioeconomic status, etc. would earn about 1 percent less per week three years after being displaced than a regular UI recipient [see Richardson (1982a), and Aho and Bayard (1982)]. Other indications of the unfavorable adjustment effects stemming from the U.S. program are the preliminary findings by Utgoff (1982) that TAA compensation, which is neither taxed nor experience-related (unlike employment insurance), increased the labor supply in industries with a high incidence of TAA certification and increased layoffs in such industries. Because of such findings, Neumann (1979) argues that the present scheme should be replaced by a wage-subsidy program coupled with regular unemployment insurance benefits. Specifically, any firm hiring a certified trade-displaced worker would receive a subsidy for a period of three years equal to 20 percent of the individual's wage.

It could still be argued, however, that those receiving special benefits under the TAA program deserve them because of the greater risks they face by being

---

[5] European governments have shunned special trade-related adjustment programs.
[6] The period between subsequent jobs may be shortened, however.

employed in industries subject to possible intense import competition. Moreover, had it not been for the program, the political pressures from injured industries might have blocked such welfare-increasing negotiations as the Tokyo Round and led to even more restrictive import policies than have been introduced in steel, autos, and footwear. Unfortunately, in view of both the different weights placed by different individuals upon the three goals mentioned earlier, and the lack of solid information concerning the political efficacy of the TAA program, it will remain difficult to obtain wide agreement concerning the long-run desirability of special aid programs for workers and firms injured by increased import competition.

4. Estimating the impact of foreign trade on employment

As discussed in Section 2, the most common method of analyzing the effects of a particular trade policy change or of a shift in some exogenous variable is to simulate the outcome by using a general or partial equilibrium model in which values for the required parameters are estimated empirically from historical data. A quite different approach is to relate observed changes in the economic variable of interest to other variables that can be linked to the first variable on the basis of some accounting identity.[7] Recently several investigators, e.g. Cable (1977), Frank (1977), Krueger (1980), and Wolter (1977), have utilized this "accounting-identity" technique in analyzing the contribution of changes in the degree of import competition to employment changes in an industry.

The basis of their analyses are the two accounting identities:

$$C_{it} \equiv Q_{it} - X_{it} + M_{it},$$

(4.1)

and

$$\frac{Q_{it}}{L_{it}} \equiv a_{it},$$

(4.2)

where C_{it} = domestic consumption of the ith industry in time period t; Q is domestic output; X and M are exports and imports, respectively; L is employment; and a is the average productivity of labor. Defining s_{it} as the ratio of domestic output to consumption in industry i, Q_{it}/C_{it}, and substituting for Q_{it} in

---

[7]The "constant-market share" analysis of export growth [see Leamer and Stern (1970) and Richardson (1971)], which "explains" actual changes in the growth rate of a country's exports on the basis of shifts in the commodity and market composition of its trade and a residual "competitive" effect, is a well-known example of the use of this technique.

eq. (2) yields the identity:

$$L_{it} \equiv \frac{s_{it}C_{it}}{a_{it}}. \tag{4.3}$$

By assuming that the domestic share, s_{it}, labor productivity, a_{it}, and consumption, C_{it}, all grow at constant continuous rates, the growth rates of these variables can be related to the growth rate of labor in the following manner:

$$\hat{L} = \hat{C} + \hat{s} - \hat{a}, \tag{4.4}$$

where the "hats" denote rates of growth.

The empirical implementation involves obtaining growth rates in these variables over a particular time period for the set of industries one wishes to study. The results obtained by the authors cited above generally indicate that the contribution of changes in $\hat{s}$ (which inversely reflect changes in the import penetration ratio) to the observed declines in employment are very small in comparison with the contributions of demand and labor-productivity growth. Although all the authors of such studies note that demand and labor-productivity growth may not be exogenous to changes in the degree of import competition, they tend to minimize the interrelationship among the variables and thereby conclude that growing import competition (as reflected in changes in domestic shares) has not been an important explanatory factor in most sectors where employment growth has been sluggish or actually negative.

Critics of the analyses stress the interrelations among the variables. Martin (1981) for example, stresses that domestic producers will react to greater actual or threatened import competition by taking steps to raise labor productivity. Consequently, part of the employment losses ascribed to productivity gains may be due indirectly to increased import competition. He notes that this relationship may involve lags and, therefore, that changes in import competition in previous periods should also be brought into the analysis. Grossman (1982a) points out that the investigators tend to interpret the productivity variable as reflecting just technological progress. However, if factor substitution in production is permitted, labor productivity in an industry will change in response to changes in factor and product prices. Illustrating with a CES production function, he demonstrates how a reduction in an industry's output price due to increased import competition tends to lead to increased labor productivity, quite aside from any effects on the rate of technological progress. Grossman (1982b) also points out that the inverse of the import penetration ratio, s_{it}, changes not only with shifts in the foreign supply curve but also with changes in supply conditions in the domestic industry.

It is evident that the economic models behind the interpretations that investigators using the accounting procedure give to their results involve some highly restrictive assumptions, e.g. fixed-coefficient technology and completely inelastic product demands. A more satisfactory method of analyzing the effects on employment of increased import competition in a particular industry is to utilize the type of general equilibrium models described in Section 2 [see Deardorff and Stern (1980)]. The increase in demand caused by lower-priced imports is, for example, taken into account in these models as are both price-induced substitution effects that change labor productivity and exchange-rate induced changes in exports. (However, these models do not include a relationship between changes in import penetration ratios and changes in rates of technological progress, largely because of the absence of any clearly demonstrated causal empirical connection between these variables). Of course, reliable factor-substitution or consumption substitution relationships may not be available at the desired level of industry detail, but for those sectors for which adequate information does exist an effort to analyze the import penetration problem with existing general equilibrium models seems very worthwhile. It would indicate whether observed change in import penetration ratios can or cannot account for a significant proportion of the observed changes in employment in specific industries.

5.   Customs unions and other preferential trading arrangements

5.1.   Customs unions

Although there has been a renewal of interest in customs union theory (see Chapter 2, Section 11), comparatively few recent empirical studies of the welfare effects of the formation of customs unions and free trade areas have been undertaken in recent years. This has probably been due both to the existence by the mid-1970s of a number of detailed investigations of the two major trading blocs among the market-oriented industrial countries, namely, the European Community (EC) and the European Free Trade Area (EFTA) [see Balassa (1974) for an appraisal of these studies] and to the generally disappointing results from efforts to introduce similar arrangements among developing countries. Nevertheless, interest in the economic effects of enlarging the EC as well as in such proposals as integrating the North American market have stimulated some new empirical research.

One especially interesting study is the general equilibrium analysis by Miller and Spencer (1977) of the static economic effects of the United Kingdom joining the European Community. Their general equilibrium model is quite similar to the ones described in Section 2, i.e. goods are imperfect substitutes among countries, production is represented by Cobb–Douglas functions, and nested CES utility functions are employed. Furthermore, capital and labor are assumed to be mobile within each country but not internationally. The authors find that entry into the

Common Market will result in a loss to the United Kingdom equal to 1.8 percent of its national income. This is largely due to the net transfer of tariff revenue to other Community members that occurs because of the Common Agricultural Policy.

In another study, Kreinin (1981) estimates the trade consequences of both enlarging the EC to nine members and introducing free trade between the EC and the non-acceding members of EFTA. In doing so, he uses the change in the ratio of total imports to consumption for the United States, Canada, and Japan combined as a proxy for what the change in this ratio would have been in the EC and EFTA in the absence of integration. Multiplying the difference between the actual post-integration ratio and this hypothetical ratio by the level of post-integration consumption, he estimates the annual trade created by the enlarge-ment. To measure the extent of the trade diverted by the enlargement, he assumes that in the absence of the enlargement the ratio of external imports to consump-tion in the EC (and EFTA) would have grown in the same proportion as the two blocs' ratio of total imports to consumption. Multiplying post-integration con-sumption by the difference between this hypothetical ratio of external imports to consumption and the actual current ratio yields a measure of the trade diverted from non-member nations.

These calculations produce an estimate of $28 billion for the annual trade from EC enlargement between 1970–71 and 1977–78 and a figure of $5 billion for the extent of trade diversion. This is only one of the several techniques commonly used to measure trade creation and trade diversion [see Corden (1975) for a critique of the different techniques], but the relative magnitudes of the estimates are quite consistent with earlier results.

Recent theoretical contributions based upon a 3-country–3-good model rather than the traditional 3-country–2-good framework would seem to open up promis-ing new lines of empirical research in the customs union field. One such study by Petith (1977) concludes that an improvement in the terms of trade was perhaps the major economic benefit of European integration.

5.2. Tariff preferences and other trade policies affecting the LDCs

Preferential tariff arrangements have long existed between some of the more developed industrial countries and their former political dependencies. However, it was not until the major developed countries began in the early 1970s to grant zero-duty treatment to imports of manufactured goods from the developing nations as a group under the Generalized System of Preferences (GSP) that a significant number of empirical articles on the subject started to appear.

Because of the absence of sufficient data on the behavior of trade under GSP, most of the early studies, e.g. Cooper (1972), Baldwin and Murray (1977), and Ahmad (1978), simulated the operation of the preference arrangements on the basis of a simple model. For example, using the imperfect substitutes model of Baldwin et al. (1980) described in Section 2, Baldwin and Murray estimate the increased imports into the developed countries as a result of reducing tariffs to zero by applying available import demand elasticities to the value and tariff levels of eligible imports in the standard manner. For the crucial estimates of the trade diverted from non-beneficiaries they assume that the substitutability between a developing country product and a similar product produced in a non-beneficiary nation is the same as the substitutability between a developing country's product and a similar item produced in the donor country. This implies that trade diversion equals trade creation multiplied by the ratio of donor country's total imports of the product to the value of its domestic production of the item. On the basis of this methodology, the net trade increase resulting from the preference schemes of the United States, the European Community, and Japan amounts to 27 percent of the preference imports of these countries. Pelzman and Rousslang (1982) also utilize this approach to estimate the possible trade and employment effects in the United States of the elimination of U.S. tariffs against imports from countries of the Caribbean Basin. They conclude that the impact would be extremely small.

Fortunately, the gradual accumulation of trade data under the various preference arrangements now permits ex post evaluations of the trade benefits of preferences to the developing countries. Aitken and Obutelewicz (1976), Sapir (1981), and Weston, Cable, and Hewitt (1980) have evaluated the operation of the EC's preference arrangements. Aitken and Obutelewicz as well as Sapir utilize a cross-sectional gravity model in which a dummy variable reflecting preference group membership is introduced. Weston et al. compare growth rates of LDC exports to the EC with LDC exports of the same products to non-preference-granting industrial countries. All three studies of the EC's program support the view that preferences have stimulated exports from developing countries.[8] Aitken and Obutelewicz estimate that exports to the EC from the African countries benefitting from the Yaounde Conventions of 1963 and 1969 increased by 26 percent by 1971 as a result of EC preferences, whereas Sapir estimates that developing-country exports to the EC rose 24 percent by 1971 as a result of the EC's Generalized System of Preferences.

The study of U.S. preference by Sapir and Lundberg (1982) reinforces the conclusion of the earlier studies that the GSP has increased exports from developing countries. On the basis of cross-country and cross-product regressions that include as independent variables the actual preference margin (the difference between the most-favored-nation duty and the GSP rate, by country or product), indicators of relative factor endowments, and measures of initial supply conditions, they find that a beneficiary country or an eligible product are more likely to

---

[8]Either approach can estimate only gross trade creation, i.e. they cannot separate the increased trade into newly created and diverted trade.

gain in market-share terms the larger the preference margin and the larger the pre-GSP share in the U.S. market. Badgett (1978) has analyzed the effect of the U.S. preferences granted to the Philippines on Philippine exports. He concludes that the U.S. scheme not only shifted Philippine exports toward the United States during the period 1900 to 1940 but accounted for the development of a considerable part of the coconut oil and refined sugar sectors in the Philippines. Analyses of the effects of preferences, in particular the GSP, on production and employment in other developing countries are very much needed.

6. Specific non-tariff trade measures

Besides a continuing concern with such traditional issues as the effects of tariff liberalization and the consequences of the formation of customs unions, trade economists have demonstrated a growing theoretical and empirical interest in the various non-tariff measures that countries utilize to change their trade patterns. Not only have these measures become more visible as tariffs have declined significantly through successive multilateral trade negotiations but they have been used more extensively by governments to attain the protectionist goals formerly achieved with tariffs. This section briefly surveys some of the recent work in this area.

6.1. Quantitative restrictions (QRs)

One of the most important developments in the trade-policy field is the spread of discriminatory QRs in the form of voluntary export restraints (VERs). Under these arrangements one or more exporting countries or industries "voluntarily" agree to restrict the quantity of their shipments of particular goods to another country, usually under the threat that even more severe mandatory import quotas will be introduced if they do not do so. Such agreements are made outside of the framework of the GATT, since the basic most-favored-nation (MFN) principle of this organization rules out such selective measures.

Several of the key ways in which the effects of QRs differ from those of tariffs are discussed in Chapter 11. Furthermore, some recent studies that estimate the trade and welfare effects of these restrictions were briefly described in Section 2.2. However, one aspect of QRs has not been considered and is important for developed-country trade policy. It concerns the consequences of these restrictions for the quality-mix of imports. As Falvey (1979) points out, there will be a difference between the effects of a tariff and QR if – as is usually the case – the restriction applies to a product that is not homogeneous but instead is differentiated in quality terms, e.g. automobiles. Suppose, for example, that there are high and low quality versions of a particular product (reflected by high and low prices) and that the sums of the own and cross-price import-demand elasticities for each grade are the same. With infinitely elastic import supply curves and competitive market conditions, the imposition of an ad valorem tariff raises the prices of the high and low quality versions of the product by the same percentages and (because of the elasticity assumptions) reduces the quantities of imports by the same percentages. With imposition of a quota, by contrast, there will be a smaller percentage increase in the price of the high quality item than the low quality version because competition will cause the price of a license to import one unit of the product to be the same whether the item is expensive (high quality) or inexpensive (low quality). Thus there will be a smaller percentage fall in imports of the high quality item. In other words, QRs have the same effect as the introduction of a specific tariff and, therefore, under the elasticity conditions assumed above tend to shift the composition of imports in favor of higher quality items. Falvey (1979) also shows that similar results tend to hold even if the exporter is a monopolist. Since the value of imports declines less than the quantity of imports, the increase in the value of domestic production and in domestic employment is not as large under QRs as under ad valorem tariffs. Feenstra (1982) found, for example, that two-thirds of the rise in the price of imported Japanese cars relative to U.S. cars resulting from the VERs in this sector was attributable to quality improvements and, therefore, did not lead consumers to substitute toward U.S. autos.

A shift in quality-mix tends to occur whether QRs are implemented on an MFN or discriminatory basis. However, another aspect of discriminatory or selective QRs is that third-market diversion effects can weaken their effectiveness. Suppose, for example, that a particular foreign supplier of shoes (assumed to be identical in quality for all suppliers) agrees to limit its exports of shoes to the United States. In Figure 6.1 let S_B be this country's export supply curve and S_{RW} be the export supply curve of the rest of the world, where $S_W = S_B + S_{RW}$. Also, let the import demand curve of the United States be D_{US} and the import demand curve of the rest of the world be D_{RW}, where $D_{US} + D_{RW} = D_W$. Ignoring differences in transport costs, the world price under free trade conditions will be *op* and the volume of trade in shoes will be *oc*.

As long as the international supply at the free-trade price from all countries other than country B plus the maximum quantity of exports permitted from country B equals or exceeds the U.S. import demand at the free-trade price, the quantitative restriction on shoes will have no effect on the price of shoes in the United States. If U.S. consumers are purchasing more shoes from country B initially than the permitted amount under the VER, they simply shift to other foreign suppliers. Even if the United States purchased *ob* units of shoes from country B initially, the QR will have no price effect provided it is not less than *ab* units.

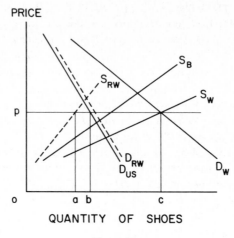

Figure 6.1

The same figure can be used to indicate the conditions under which an export quota or embargo against a particular country will be ineffective. Suppose that country B will not supply more than *ab* units of shoes to the United States. Since this quantity plus the free trade supply from the rest of the world is as large as the free trade import demand of the United States, the export quota will not raise the price of shoes in the United States. A redistribution among consuming countries of the world's traded supplies of shoes takes place to offset any price-increasing pressures.

The preceding analysis of discriminatory import and export quotas assumes that output supplied by each foreign producer is not only homogeneous but perfectly substitutable for domestic output. If – as is often the case – the output of each supplier is differentiated from that produced by others, the simple relationships indicated in Figure 6.1 that determine the effectiveness of these policies will no longer hold. However, there will still be a tendency for substitution among suppliers to offset the effectiveness of discriminatory import or export policies. Baldwin (1982b) discusses other supply and demand responses that tend to offset the intended purpose of protective measures, e.g. importing products in more or less processed form, shifting to a substitute product, and smuggling.

6.2. *Preferential government purchasing policies*

It has been a long-standing practice of governments to give preferential treatment to domestic suppliers when purchasing non-military supplies. The new government procurement code negotiated in the Tokyo Round of multilateral trade negotiations declares that governments should no longer discriminate in this manner, but its provisions apply thus far only to a selected list of products and government agencies. Consequently, there is still considerable interest on the part of trade officials in determining the economic effects of preferential government purchasing policies.

If imports are perfectly substitutable for domestic output, the effects of such policies can also be seen in Figure 6.1. Suppose D_{US} is the government's demand curve for shoes, D_{RW} is the demand for shoes by private U.S. consumers, and D_W is the total demand for shoes by the United States. Furthermore, let S_B be the supply curve of U.S. shoe producers, S_{RW} the import supply curve of foreign producers, and S_W the total supply curve for the United States. The free trade price of shoes in the United States is *op* and the total shoe purchases are *oc*. If the government refused to buy any shoes at all from foreign suppliers, the price would still remain at the free trade level, since the government's demand at the free trade price is less than the supply available at that price from domestic suppliers [see Baldwin and Richardson (1973)]. The tendency for the price to rise as the government shifts its purchases entirely to domestic suppliers will be offset by a corresponding switch by private consumers to the purchase of imported shoes. However, if S_{RW} is the domestic supply curve and S_B the foreign import supply curve, the price received by domestic producers will rise to the intersection point of S_{RW} and D_{US}, while the price to private consumers will fall to the intersection point of D_{RW} and S_B.

Since government purchases of most non-military items represent only a fraction of the domestic supply of these items, the preceding analysis suggests that government preferential purchasing policies are generally ineffective in raising the price received by domestic suppliers. Nor will they affect domestic employment, production, profits, or growth. Again, however, if imports are imperfect substitutes for domestic production or domestic producers act monopolistically in dealing with the government, this conclusion may be attenuated.

One procedure followed by some investigators, e.g. Baldwin (1970), Lowinger (1976), Cline et al. (1978), and Deardorff and Stern (1979), in empirically estimating the import effects of preferential government purchasing policies is to compare actual government purchases with what they would be if the import propensity of the government and the private sector were the same. Baldwin (1970) and Lowinger (1976) estimate that without a preferential purchasing policy imports by the U.S. government would have been between six and seven times greater than their actual level in the mid-1960s. Deardorff and Stern (1979) find the welfare gains from liberalizing government procurement policies in the Tokyo Round to be actually greater for the industrial participants than the gains from tariff liberalization. However, a drawback with the procedure is that the private import propensity will have already been affected by a shift to import substitutes as a result of the government's preferential purchasing policy, and this offsetting influence will not be captured by this empirical approach.

6.3. Export and domestic subsidies

In discussing domestic or international rules relating to foreign production or export subsidization, economists are inclined to question why any country should prevent another from providing the first country with imports that are cheaper than they would be without foreign subsidies. However, in the absence of actual compensation schemes that make all individuals in the country receiving the subsidized goods better off than before the subsidies, most people appear to weigh what they consider to be the "unfair" domestic distributional effects of foreign subsidization more heavily than they do the national real income benefits from this subsidization. In any event, whether they reflect the wishes of the majority or not, almost all countries have enacted laws condemning foreign subsidization and permitting countervailing actions against them.

The GATT has also recently strengthened its rules against subsidies. The new Subsidies Code negotiated in the Tokyo Round reaffirms the GATT ban on export subsidization (except for certain primary products) and recognizes that domestic subsidies, while important instruments for promoting social and economic policy objectives, may cause injury to a domestic industry of another country, may seriously prejudice this other country's interest, or may impair its benefits accruing under the GATT. The code signatories agreed to seek to avoid causing such effects through the use of subsidies. The United States also agreed to make its own anti-subsidy law consistent with GATT rules by requiring a finding of "material injury" to a domestic industry before imposing countervailing duties. However, despite these recent developments in providing international guidelines designed to limit the adverse trade effects of subsidies, there is still widespread disagreement within and among nations concerning the effects and legitimacy of various forms of subsidies. Since the effects of different subsidies under both first-best and distorted market conditions are quite well understood analytically (see Chapter 2), this disagreement seems to be due both to differences among individuals and nations in judgments about equity and to a lack of knowledge about the economic consequences of actual subsidy schemes.

Various investigators have estimated intercountry differences in subsidization in broad terms, e.g. Mutti (1982) and McCulloch (1978), and undertaken detailed studies of subsidization in particular industries or activities, e.g. Hamilton (1981a) for shipbuilding and Fleisig and Hill (1982) for export credits, but there is comparatively little formal analysis exploring – as in the case of import barriers – the trade, employment, and welfare implications of subsidization. However, one such study is by Hamilton (1981b), who estimates the employment and domestic price effects of subsidies to the Swedish textile and clothing industry.

Another subsidizing arrangement that has been studied to some extent in this manner is the U.S. Domestic International Sales Corporation (DISC) legislation, which is aimed at stimulating exports by reducing the effective rate of taxation on export income. Utilizing a partial-equilibrium approach in which export products are divided into four categories and assigned export demand and supply elasticities, the U.S. Treasury (1981) has estimated that as of 1979 the increase in exports resulting from DISC amounted to between 4.5 and 7.0 percent. More recently, Mutti and Grubel (1982), using a general equilibrium model estimate the net export increase to be only 2 percent. Their simulations also indicate a net real income loss for the country as a whole that involves a favorable income shift for skilled workers but an unfavorable one for unskilled labor.

An effort to trace through the intercountry market effects of subsidies to a particular industry is illustrated by Mutti's (1982) analysis of the impact of foreign government aid programs to the steel and automobile industries on U.S. producers. Employing the assumption that products from different countries are imperfect substitutes and using estimates made by others for the demand and substitution elasticities required under this approach, he solves for the interdependent industry price changes in the United States, the rest of the world, and the subsidizing countries brought about by the subsidies. He concludes that in the case of steel, for example, British and French governmental aid programs increase U.S. imports by 3 percent and decrease U.S. output by 1 percent.

While studies of the type mentioned above add considerably to our understanding of the effects of subsidies, there is a definite need for much more empirical work in this field. For example, it would seem that the trade, employment, and welfare effects of the export-credit subsidies provided by all the major industrial nations could be analyzed using the multi-country general equilibrium models described earlier in Section 2.2. Further general equilibrium studies – such as those by Melvin (1975), Deardorff and Stein (1981b), and Whalley (1980b) – of the trade effects resulting from various domestic tax and subsidy policies countries use to stimulate investment are also needed. It is also important that a greater number of detailed investigations of the effects of subsidization in particular industries be undertaken.

6.4. Dumping

Like the subsidies to production or export, foreign dumping is also viewed by most countries as an unfair trade practice that should be prevented despite the theoretical possibility that everyone in a country receiving the dumped goods could be made better off than before the dumping. GATT rules permit countries to impose anti-dumping duties if the dumping causes material injury to a domestic industry.

Economists have generally confined their attention to the theoretical aspects of dumping, and the extent of even this type of analysis has been quite limited in the post-World War II period. However, recent theoretical contributions by Ethier (1982), Brander (1981), Davies and McGuinness (1982), and Brander and Krugman (1980) indicate a revived interest in the subject. Ethier defines dumping as selling abroad (and at home) at below the cost of production (rather than the traditional definition of selling abroad at a lower price than at home) and then considers how this form of dumping might take place during recessionary periods of the business cycle. His definition has not only long been used by many businessmen but was formally adopted as an additional standard of dumping under the U.S. 1974 Trade Act.

In Ethier's model competitive firms producing an internationally traded good face two alternative states of the world – each with a probability of one-half of occurrence – characterized by either a fixed high or low world price for their output. Key assumptions are that the two factors used in the constant-returns-to-scale production process are sector-specific and that factor prices are inflexible over the two states. Furthermore, while one of the factors (laborers) can be laid off once the state of the world is known, the other (managers) cannot. Since expected profits are driven to zero over the two states, the combination of inflexible factor prices and the inability to adjust both factors means that firms will sell traded goods below cost in bad times and above cost in good times. By adding another country with similar constraints but different supply and demand conditions, it can be shown that whichever country exports the good will be dumping it when its international price is the lower of its two levels.

Brander (1981) is mainly concerned with explaining how intra-industry trade in identical products is possible when two firms in an industry, one at home and one abroad, behave in non-cooperative manner. However, he also shows that the firms in both countries may engage in reciprocal dumping even if market demand curves are the same in both countries. The Brander–Krugman (1980) paper elaborates upon this possibility.

Some empirical work on dumping has also been undertaken in recent years. For example, Tarr (1979) asks whether steel producers in the United States, the European Community, and Japan engaged in cyclical dumping during the period 1957–1976, that is, priced exports cyclically while maintaining a stable price in their home markets. His conclusion is that they did not. Eichengreen (1982) estimates that the efficiency losses resulting from the Trigger Price Mechanism introduced to prevent the dumping of steel in U.S. markets range from $18 to $43 million. Pursuing a very different set of issues, Finger (1980) analyzes the pattern of "less-than-fair-value" complaints and affirmative findings under U.S. anti-dumping and countervailing duty laws between 1975 and mid-1979. He found that the mere filing of less-than-fair-value complaints (quite aside from whether the Treasury decided in favor of the filer) had a negative effect on import growth rates. He also showed that economic and political power of an industry, as measured, for example, by industry size and concentration, is positively related to the extent of complaints, but it was negatively correlated with affirmative less-than-fair-value findings. Finger's interpretation of this result is that the major effect of political clout is to gain access to the President or legislative action by the Congress.

Like the subject of subsidization, dumping is a promising area for useful further research. The application of recent theoretical developments to a subject that has received very little analytical attention since the 1930s should produce a much better understanding of this widely followed practice. The increase in the number of dumping (and countervailing duty) cases in recent years also makes research in this field highly relevant from a policy viewpoint. Faced with growing foreign competition and disappointing results in trying to obtain protection through the safeguards mechanism, more and more domestic producers are seeking import relief on grounds of "unfair" competition by foreign producers [see Lloyd (1977)].

6.5. Border tax adjustments

Private traders and government officials in countries relying mainly on direct taxes for revenue often criticize the GATT border-tax-adjustment rules on the grounds that they give an unfair competitive advantage to countries utilizing indirect taxes for raising a significant part of their revenues. Under these rules, when goods subject to indirect taxes are exported, the taxes are rebated at the border. Likewise, imported goods are taxed at the same rate as comparable domestically produced and consumed goods. This "destination principle" contrasts with the "origin principle" under which no adjustments at the border are made. Thus, a country levying a uniform value-added or general sales tax on all goods can rebate the tax on any goods it exports, whereas countries using an income tax to raise the same revenue cannot.

Economists have for many years pointed out that it makes no difference to the equilibrium pattern of trade whether the destination or origin principle is applied in the case of uniform indirect taxes, provided factor and goods prices (or exchange rates) are flexible. However, Grossman (1980) has shown that when trade in intermediate goods occurs, this conclusion must be modified somewhat. With flexible prices a "stages-of-processing" value-added tax is trade-neutral whether the destination or origin principle is followed, but a uniform general sales tax will distort trade if the origin principle is adopted.

Indirect taxes imposed selectively on domestically produced goods distort trade under both principles [see Baldwin (1978b)]. This follows from the well-known point from distortions theory that an international measure (the border-tax-adjustment policy) cannot entirely offset the distorting effects of a domestic measure such as a selective indirect tax. Another consequence of this point is that countervailing duties equal to the rate of selective foreign subsidization of production will not completely offset the trade-distorting effects of this subsidization. Ruffin (1979) derives the general equilibrium relationships for determining the effects of various border tax adjustments designed to offset changes in foreign taxes and subsidies. As Floyd (1977) has shown, border tax adjustments for direct taxes, e.g. capital taxes, also cannot fully neutralize any distortions or trade disadvantages induced by these taxes.

6.6. *Offshore assembly provisions (OAPs) and domestic content protection*

Another type of border tax adjustment that has led to considerable controversy is the policy followed by most industrial countries of imposing import duties only on the foreign value-added when domestically produced components are assembled abroad. In a pioneering theoretical and empirical analysis of the effects of these OAPs, Finger (1976) concluded that if the United States repealed the OAPs, the reduction in the domestic production of components would more than offset the increase in domestic assembly so that there would be a slight net reduction in real domestic economic activity. The recent theoretical elaborations by Grossman (1982c) of the various effects of OAPs on the structure of protection suggest that there is further scope for empirical research into this policy.

Producers favoring the abolition of OAPs believe that the domestic production of components will not decline as much as domestic assembly activities will increase if the total value of imports is subject to import duties regardless of the components used to produce these goods. However, when domestic producers observe foreign producers capturing both components production and the assembly activities, they often urge enactment of laws requiring that a certain minimum percentage of domestic components be embodied in domestically consumed final goods. In extending the earlier work of Johnson (1971) and Corden (1971), Grossman (1981) demonstrates that this policy can be regarded as the equivalent of tariff protection for intermediates coupled with a subsidy to final goods producers. Furthermore, he shows that because the degree of protection is variable and difficult to predict, content protection may fail to achieve the protective objectives motivating this policy. Unfortunately, there do not appear to be any recent detailed studies of the effects of domestic content schemes.

7. Current and prospective trade-policy issues

As in all applied fields, there is often a considerable lag between the time when a trade-policy issue is first actively discussed in the private and public sectors and when trade economists begin to analyze the issue thoroughly in theoretical and empirical terms. This final section briefly considers some current and prospective policy issues where this lag seems to exist and thus on which future research is likely.

7.1. Selectivity, reciprocity, and graduation

The biggest disappointment of the Tokyo Round of multilateral trade negotiations for most trade officials was the failure to agree upon a new Safeguards Code. While all agreed that the increasing use of orderly marketing agreements and voluntary export restraints as means of coping with injurious imports was seriously weakening the structure of international rules that guide trade behavior among nations, it proved impossible to reach an acceptable compromise. Some of the large industrial trading groups, e.g. the European Community, favored the so-called "selectivity" principle under which it is permissible to impose import restrictions on only those exporting nations that are the prime source of the import injury. However, the developing nations and many small industrial countries strongly opposed this principle.

The case for selectivity can be made on several grounds [see Wolff, (1982)], e.g. that it makes little sense to cling to the most-favored-nation principle in view of the widespread use of discriminatory arrangements such as customs unions and the generalized system of preferences, or that the acceptance of selectivity coupled with strict rules limiting its use is the only politically realistic way of halting the drift toward the complete collapse of the structure of world trading rules. Opponents, on the other hand, argue that not being required to raise protective barriers against all suppliers removes an important restraint that will not only result in greater and more economically inefficient protectionism but protectionism directed unfairly at the developing countries and small industrial nations. They also point out that selective import controls are not likely to accomplish their intended purpose for the same reasons mentioned in the discussion of selective quantitative restrictions in Section 6.1.

Under selectivity increased import protection would be introduced in a discriminatory fashion and for a limited group of products only after it has been established that a rise in imports has caused serious injury to a domestic industry. However, under the principle of the "new reciprocity", as the term is now being used in the United States, a country could impose higher protection for all products from a particular country that did not grant (or agree to grant) U.S. access to its domestic markets comparable to the access granted by the United States. The "new reciprocity" would change the fundamental principle of unconditional most-favored-nation treatment followed by the United States since 1923 and by most European nations since the third quarter of the last century. Nevertheless, because of the difficulties that U.S. exporters face in selling their products in certain countries, most notably Japan, there is considerable support in Congress for making this change.

The proponents of the "new reciprocity" argue that its adoption not only will improve the "fairness" of world trade but, through the threat of retaliation by the United States, lead to a lower general level of barriers to world trade. Opponents such as Cline (1982) fear that counter-retaliation will result in increased protection and reduced welfare on all sides. It would be useful to explore the consequences of various trade scenarios using the computable general equilibrium models previously described. However, political as well as economic analyses are very much needed on this subject, as well as on the selectivity topic.

A proposed policy that moves in the direction of less – rather than more – discrimination is "graduation", the gradual phasing out for the more economically advanced less developed countries (LDCs) of the preferential treatment granted them under the GSP. At the same time, these countries would be expected to gradually align their own trade policies with the rules of the GATT.

As might be expected the advanced LDCs strongly oppose "graduation" and claim that they still need special and differential treatment from advanced countries in order to maintain their growth momentum. Those favoring the policy, e.g. Frank (1979), usually emphasize that an orderly withdrawal of preferential treatment for the LDCs is much better than the arbitrary and chaotic pattern of elimination of this treatment that is likely to take place in the absence of an international agreement.

7.2. Trade in services and trade-related investment issues

The significant decline in tariff levels over the last two decades has not only directed attention at the impeding effects of non-tariff measures on the flow of goods among countries but also on trade in services. Although the Organization for Economic Cooperation and Development (OECD) adopted a Code of Liberalization of Current Invisible Operations in the early 1960s, the code has achieved little actual liberalization because of the many exceptions it allows. Consequently, in view of the growing importance of trade in such services as insurance, banking, construction, design and engineering, tourism, transportation, and entertainment, there is considerable interest, especially on the part of the United States, in negotiating multilateral agreements within the GATT covering services trade. However, as such writers on the subject as Sapir and Lutz (1981), Shelp (1981), and Diebold and Stalson (1982) point out, much more research is needed to formulate sound new international rules on services trade. Our knowledge is still very incomplete concerning the extent of trade distortions in this area as well as their economic effects. Work at the analytical level is also needed, since conditions under which this trade takes place and the nature of the impediments to it differ considerably from commodity trade.

Trade-related investment issues are also receiving greater attention by governments of nations that are major foreign investors, since both developing and many developed countries appear to be introducing more measures to both regulate and attract foreign direct investment [see McCulloch and Owen (1983)]. These include trade-related performance requirements such as minimum export or maximum import targets, requirements for technology transfers and job maintenance, exceptions to non-discriminatory treatment for foreign investors with regard to taxes, subsidies, and access to finance, and the closing of certain sectors to foreign investors.

There is even less information about the extent and economic effects of distorting measures in this area than in services trade, because companies are often reluctant to report on them for fear of retaliatory action. Since sensitive aspects of sovereignty are involved, it is also very difficult to establish international rules on these matters. As Safarian (1982) points out, alternative policy approaches involve concentrating on trade-related issues within the framework of the GATT or dealing with both trade and the whole range of policies toward multinational corporations within the OECD.

7.3. Institutional reforms

Most trade-related institutional proposals made by economists are aimed either at extending existing international rules to new or uncovered forms of trade or at preventing the objectives of these rules from being undermined by public or private actions in closely related economic fields. For example, the suggestions of the preceding section for introducing international rules to cover trade in services and trade-related investment performance requirements, for negotiating a new safeguards code fit into the first category. The periodic proposal to increase the degree of regulation over private trading practices by formulating GATT-type rules and disputes-settlement procedures that cover restrictive business practices as well as the suggestions for dealing with the practices of State trading corporations [Kostecki (1982)] are other institutional suggestions along the same lines.

Corden's (1981) analysis of exchange-rate protection (by means of undervalued exchange rates), as well as the papers by Bergsten and Williamson (1982) and Richardson (1982b), pointing out how prolonged deviations of exchange rates from fundamental equilibrium can and do generate protectionist pressures, have led to the second category of institutional proposals. In order to minimize exchange-rate-related protectionist pressure, Bergsten and Williamson recommend that closer coordinating relationships be established not only between trade and monetary officials within individual countries but between GATT and IMF officials. The recognition that both excessive subsidization and regulation of foreign investment can distort world trading patterns has also resulted in proposals by some economists, e.g. Goldberg and Kindleberger (1970), for GATT-type international rules covering direct foreign investment.

As the degree of economic interdependence among countries continues to increase, there is likely to be more and more pressure to establish international "rules of good behavior" in policy areas traditionally regarded as mainly domestic in nature [see Blackhurst (1981)]. These include not only monetary and tax policies but various aspects of social welfare programs. Policies concerning the movement of labor across national borders also significantly affect the pattern of world trade. However, at the present time most countries do not regard immigration and emigration policies as appropriate matters for international agreements and negotiations.

Proposals dealing with the mechanisms for reaching and implementing international agreements on trade and trade-related issues have tended to come mainly from legal scholars, e.g. Hudec (1980) and Jackson (1982). However, one aspect of this subject area that is receiving increasing attention by economists is the process by which a few key countries reach agreement in trade negotiations [see Mayer (1981) and Jensen and Thursby (1981)]. These writers use bargaining and game theory to analyze the range of likely outcomes of, for example, tariff negotiations. Research of this type may eventually provide information useful for structuring negotiations to increase the benefits of all participants.

References

Aho, C.M. and T.O. Bayard (1982), "Cost and benefits of trade adjustment assistance", paper presented at National Bureau of Economic Research conference on The Structure and Evolution of Recent U.S. Trade Policy, Cambridge, Mass., 3–4 December 1982.

Aitken, N.D. and R.S. Obutelewicz (1976), "A cross-section study of EEC trade with the association of African countries", The Review of Economics and Statistics, 425–433.

Ahmad, J. (1978), "Tokyo Round of trade negotiations and the generalized system of preferences", Economic Journal, 88:285–295.

Anderson, K. (1978), "Politico-economic factors affecting structural change and adjustment" in: C. Aislabie and C. Tisdell, eds., Institute of Industrial Economics Conference Series no. 5 (University of Newcastle, Australia).

Badgett, L.D. (1978), "Preferential tariff reductions: The Philippine response, 1900–1940", Journal of International Economics, 8:79–92.

Balassa, B. (1974), "Trade creation and trade diversion in the European Common Market: An appraisal of the evidence", The Manchester School, 93–135.

Balassa, B. (1965), "Tariff protection in industrial countries: An evaluation", Journal of Political Economy, 73:573–594.

Baldwin, R.E. (1982a), "The political economy of protection" in: J. Bhagwati, ed., Import competition and response (University of Chicago, Chicago) 263–286.

Baldwin, R.E. (1982b), The inefficacy of trade policy, Essays in international finance, No. 150, International Finance Section, Department of Economics, Princeton University.

Baldwin, R.E. (1981), "The political economy of U.S. import policy", unpublished manuscript.

Baldwin, R.E. (1978b), "The economics of the GATT" in: P. Oppenheimer, ed., Issues in international economics (Oriel Press, Stocksfield, England).

Baldwin, R.E. (1976), "Trade employment effects in the United States of multilateral tariff reduction", American Economic Review, 66:142–148.

Baldwin, R.E. (1970), Nontariff distortions of international trade (Brookings Institution, Washington, D.C.) ch. 3.

Baldwin, R.E. and W. Lewis (1978a), "U.S. tariff effects on trade and employment in detailed SIC industries" in: W.G. Dewald, ed., The impact of international trade and investment on employment (U.S. Department of Labor, Washington, D.C.) 241–259.

Baldwin, R.E. and T. Murray (1977), "MFN tariff reductions and developing country trade benefits under the GSP", Economic Journal, 87:30–46.

Baldwin, R.E., J. Mutti and J.D. Richardson (1980), "Welfare effects on the United States of a significant multilateral tariff reduction", Journal of International Economics, 10:405–423.

Baldwin, R.E. and J.D. Richardson (1973), "Government purchasing policies, other NTBs, and the international monetary crisis", Fourth Pacific Trade and Development Conference, Ottawa.

Baldwin, R.E. and J.D. Richardson (1973), "Government purchasing policies, other NTBs, and the international monetary crisis", Fourth Pacific Trade and Development Conference, Ottawa.

Bale, M.D. (1973), "Adjustment to free trade: An analysis of the adjustment assistance provisions of the Trade Expansion Act of 1962", Ph.D. thesis, University of Wisconsin and Report no. DLMA 91-55-73-05-1 of the National Technical Information Service (Springfield, Virginia).

Bale, M.D. (1977), "United States concessions in the Kennedy Round and short-run labor adjustment costs: Further evidence", Journal of International Economics, 2:145–148.

Bale, M.D. and J. Mutti (1980), "Output and employment changes in a 'trade sensitive' sector: Adjustment in the U.S. footwear industry", World Bank Staff Working Papers, No. 430, Washington, D.C.

Ball, D.S. (1967), "United States effective tariffs and labor's share", Journal of Political Economy, 75:183–187.

Basevi, G. (1968), "The restrictive effect of the U.S. tariff and its welfare value", American Economic Review, 58:840–852.

Basevi, G. (1966), "The United States tariff structure: Estimates of effective protection of United States industries and industrial labor", Review of Economics and Statistics, 48:147–160.

Bergsten, C.F. (1972), "The cost of import restrictions to American consumers" (American Importers Association, New York) 2–16.

Bergsten, C.F. and J. Williamson (1982), "Exchange rates and trade policy", paper presented at a conference on Trade Policy in the Eighties, June 23–25, Institute for International Economics, Washington, D.C.

Bhagwati, J.N. (1971), "The generalized theory of distortions and welfare" in: J.N. Bhagwati, R.W. Jones, R.A. Mundell and J. Vanek, eds., Trade, balance of payment and growth (North-Holland, Amsterdam).

Blackhurst, R. (1981), "The twilight of domestic economic policies", The World Economy, 4:357–373.

Boadway, R. and J.M. Treddenick (1978), "A general equilibrium computation of the effects of the Canadian tariff structure", Canadian Journal of Economics, 11:424–446.

Brander, J. (1981), "Intra-industry trade in identical commodities", Journal of International Economics, 1:1–14.

Brander, J. and P. Krugman (1980), "A 'reciprocal dumping' model of international trade", Department of Economics, Massachusetts Institute of Technology.

Breton, A. (1974), The economic theory of representative government (Aldine, Chicago).

Brock, W.A. and S.P. Magee (1978), "The economics of special interest politics: The case of tariffs", American Economic Review, 68:246–250.

Brown, F. and J. Whalley (1980), "General equilibrium evaluations of tariff-cutting proposals in the Tokyo Round and comparisons with more extensive liberalization of world trade", Economic Journal, 90:838–866.

Buchanan, J.M. and G. Tulloch (1968), The demand and supply of public goods (Rand McNally, Chicago).

Buchanan, J.M. and G. Tulloch (1962), The calculus of consent (University of Michigan Press, Ann Arbor).

Cable, C. (1977), "British protectionism and LDC imports", ODI Review, 2:29–48.

Cable, V. and I. Rebelo (1980), "Britain's pattern of specialization in manufactured goods with developing countries and trade protection", World Bank Staff Working Papers, No. 425, Washington, D.C.).

Cairnes, J.E. (1974), Some leading principles of political economy (Macmillan, London).

Caves, R.E. (1976), "Economic models of political choice: Canada's tariff structure", Canadian Journal of Economics, 9:278–300.

Cheh, J.H. (1974), "United States concessions in the Kennedy Round and short-run labor adjustment costs", Journal of International Economics, 4:323–340.

Cline, W. (1982), "Reciprocity": A new approach to world trade policy?", Policy Analyses in International Economics, No. 2, Institute for International Economics, Washington, D.C.

Cline, W., N. Kawanabe, T.O.M. Kronsjo, and T. Williams (1978a), "Multilateral effects of tariff negotiations in the Tokyo Round", in: W.G. Dewald, ed., The impact of international trade and investment on employment (U.S. Department of Labor, Washington, D.C.) 265–285.

Cline, W., N. Kawanabe, T.O.M. Kronsjo, and T. Williams (1978b), "Trade negotiations in the Tokyo Round: A quantitative assessment (Brookings Institution, Washington, D.C.).

Cohen, R.B. (1982), "The prospects for trade and protection in the auto industry", paper presented at a conference on Trade Policy in the Eighties, Institute for International Economics, Washington, D.C. 23–25 June 1982.

Collier, P. (1979), "The welfare effects of customs union: An anatomy", Economic Journal, 89:84–95.

Constantopoulos, M. (1974), "Labour protection in Western Europe", European Economic Review, 5:31–318.

Conybeare, J. (1978), "Public policy and the Australian tariff structure", Australian Journal of Management, 3:49–63.

Cook, L.H. (1981), "The effects of U.S. tariffs on production, prices, employment and trade: Numerical results under alternative model structures", School of Economics, LaTrobe University, Melbourne.

Cooper, R.N. (1972), "The European Community system of generalized preferences: A critique", Journal of Development Studies, 379–394.

Corden, W.M. (1981), "Exchange rate protection" in: R.N. Cooper et al., eds., The international monetary system under flexible exchange rates (Ballenger Publishing, Cambridge, Mass.).

Corden, W.M. (1975), "The costs and consequences of protection: A survey of empirical work", in: P.B. Kenen, ed., International trade and finance: Frontiers for research (Cambridge University Press, Cambridge) 51–91.

Corden, W.M. (1974), Trade policy and economic welfare (Oxford University Press, London).

Corden, W.M. (1971), The theory of protection (Oxford University Press, London), 45–50.

Corden, W.M. (1966), "The structure of a tariff system and the effective rate of protection", Journal of Political Economy, 74:221–237.

Corson, W., W. Nicholson, and D. Richardson (1979), "Final report; survey of trade adjustment assistance recipients", report by Mathematica Policy Research, Inc. (Princeton, New Jersey), to the U.S. Department of Labor, Bureau of International Labor Affairs, Office of Foreign Economic Research.

Crandall, R.W. (1981), The U.S. steel industry in recurrent crisis (The Brookings Institution, Washington, D.C.).

Davies, S.W. and A.J. McGuinness (1982), "Dumping at less than marginal cost", Journal of International Economics, 12:169–182.

Deardorff, A.V. and R.M. Stern (1981a), "A disaggregated model of world production and trade: An estimate of the impact of the Tokyo Round", Journal of Policy Modeling.

Deardorff, A.V. and R.M. Stern (1981b), "The effects of domestic tax/subsidies and import tariffs on the structure of protection in the United States, United Kingdom, and Japan", paper presented to International Economic Study Group, Sixth Annual Conference, Sussex, U.K., 18–20 September 1981.

Deardorff, A.V. and R.M. Stern (1980), "Changes in trade and employment in industrialized countries, 1970–76", Sixth World Congress of the International Economic Association, Mexico City, 4–8 August 1980.

Deardorff, A.V. and R.M. Stern (1979), "An economic analysis of the effects of the Tokyo Round of multilateral trade negotiations on the United States and other major industrial countries", MTN Studies 5, Committee on Finance, U.S. Senate (U.S. Government Printing Office, Washington, D.C.).

de Melo, J.A.P. (1978), "Estimating the costs of protection: A general equilibrium approach", Quarterly Journal of Economics, 2:209–226.

de Melo, J.A.P., and K. Dervis (1977), "Modelling the effects of protection in a dynamic framework", Journal of International Economics, 4:149–172.

Diebold, W., Jr. and H. Stalson (1982), "Negotiating issues in international services transactions", paper presented at conference on Trade Policy in the Eighties, 23–25 June 1982, Institute for International Economics, Washington, D.C.

Dixon, P.B., B.R. Parmenter, G.J. Ryland and J.M. Sutton (1977), ORANI, a general equilibrium model of the Australian economy: Current specification and illustrations of use for policy analysis, First Progress Report of the Impact Project, Vol. 2 (Australian Government Publishing Service, Canberra).

Dixon, P.B., B.R. Parmenter, J. Sutton and D.P. Vincent (1982), "ORANI: A multi-sectoral model of the Australian economy" (North-Holland, Amsterdam).

Downs, A. (1957), An economic theory of democracy (Harper Row, New York).

Eaton, J. and G. Grossman (1981), "Tariffs as insurance: Optimal commercial policy when domestic markets are incomplete", Discussion Papers in Economics, No. 18, Woodrow Wilson School, Princeton University, Princeton, N.J.

Eichengreen, B.J. (1982), "U.S. antidumping policies: The case of steel", paper presented at National Bureau of Economic Research conference on The Structure and Evolution of Recent U.S. Trade Policy, Cambridge, Mass., 3–4 December 1982.

Ethier, W.J. (1982), "Dumping", Journal of Political Economy, 90:487–506.

Evans, H.D. (1971), "Effects of protection in a general equilibrium framework", Review of Economics and Statistics, 53:147–156.

Falvey, R.E. (1979), "The composition of trade within import-restricted product categories", Journal of Political Economy, 87:1105–1114.

Feenstra, R. (1982), "Voluntary export restraints in U.S. autos, 1980–81: Quality, employment, welfare effects", paper presented at National Bureau of Economic Research conference on The Structure and Evolution of Recent U.S. Trade Policy, Cambridge, Mass., 3–4 December 1982.

Fieleke, N. (1976), "The tariff structure for manufacturing industries in the United States: A test of some traditional explanations", Columbia Journal of World Business, 11:98–104.

Findlay, R. and S. Wellisz (1982), "Endogenous tariffs, the political economy of trade restrictions, and welfare", in: J. Bhagwati, ed., Import competition and response (University of Chicago Press, Chicago).

Finger, J.M. (1980), "The industry-country incidence of 'less than fair value' cases in United States import trade", presented at NBER-FIPE conference on Trade Prospects Among the Americas: Latin American export diversification and the new protectionism, Sao Paulo, Brazil, 23–26 March 1980.

Finger, J.M. (1976), "Trade and domestic effects of offshore assembly provision in the U.S. tariff code", American Economic Review, 66:598–611.

Fleisig, H. and C. Hill (1982), "The benefit and cost of official export credit programs", paper presented at National Bureau of Economic Research conference on The Structure and Evolution of Recent U.S. Trade Policy, Cambridge, Mass., 3–4 December 1982.

Floyd, R.H. (1977), "Some long-run implications of border taxes for factor taxes", Quarterly Journal of Economics, 91:555–578.

Frank, C. Jr. (1977), Foreign trade and domestic aid (Brookings Institution, Washington, D.C.) ch. 3.

Frank, I. (1979), "The 'graduation' issue in trade policy toward LDCs", World Bank Staff Working Papers No. 334 (World Bank, Washington, D.C.).

Glismann, H.H. and F.D. Weiss (1980), "Evidence on the political economy of protection in Germany", World Bank Staff Working Papers, No. 427, Washington, D.C.

Goldberg, P.M. and C.P. Kindleberger (1970), "Toward a GATT for investment: A proposal for supervision of the international corporation", Law and Policy in International Business, Georgetown Law Center, 295–325.

Grossman, G.M. (1982a), "On measuring the employment effects of import competition" in: J. Bhagwati, ed., Import competition and response (University of Chicago Press for the National Bureau of Economic Research, Chicago).

Grossman, G.M. (1982b), "The employment and wage effects of import competition in the United States", Discussion Papers in Economics, No. 35, Woodrow Wilson School, Princeton University, Princeton, N.J.

Grossman, G.M. (1982c), "Offshore assembly provisions and the structure of trade", Journal of International Economics, 12:301–312.

Grossman, G.M. (1981), "The theory of domestic content protection", Quarterly Journal of Economics, 96:583–603.

Grossman, G.M. (1980), "Border tax adjustments: Do they distort trade?", Journal of International Economics, 10:117–128.

Hamilton, C. (1981a), "Public subsidies to industry: The case of Sweden and its shipbuilding industry", Institute for International Economic Studies, University of Stockholm, Seminar Paper No. 174.

Hamilton, C. (1981b), "A new approach to estimation of the effects of non-tariff barriers to trade: An application to the Swedish textile and clothing industry", Weltwirtschaftliches Archiv, 117:298–325.

Helleiner, G.K. (1977), "The political economy of Canada's tariff structure: An alternative model", Canadian Journal of Economics, 4:318–326.

Hillman, J.S. (1978), Non-tariff agricultural barriers (University of Nebraska Press, Lincoln).

Hilton, R.S. (1981), "An estimatable model of the commodity version of trade", unpublished Ph.D. thesis, University of Wisconsin-Madison.

Hudec, R. (1980), "GATT dispute settlement after the Tokyo Round: An unfinished business", Cornell International Law Journal, 13:221–237.

Hughes, H. and A. Krueger (1982), "Effects of protection in developed countries on developing countries' exports of manufactures", paper presented at National Bureau of Economic Research conference on The Structure and Evolution of Recent U.S. Trade Policy, Cambridge, Mass., 3–4 December 1982.

Jackson, J.H. (1982), "GATT machinery and the Tokyo Round agreements", paper presented at a conference on Trade Policy in the Eighties, 23–25 June, Institute for International Economics, Washington, D.C.

Jacobson, L.S. (1978), "Earnings losses of workers displaced from manufacturing industries" in: W. Dewald, ed., The impact of international trade and investment on employment (U.S. Department of Labor, U.S. Government Printing Office, Washington, D.C.).

Jenkins, G.P. (1981), "Costs and consequences of the new protectionism: The case of Canada's clothing sector" in: Canada in a developing world: Trade or protection (Oxford University, New York).

Jenkins, G.P., G. Glenday, J.C. Evans, and C. Montmarquette (1978), Trade adjustment assistance: The costs of adjustment and policy proposals, report by Econanalysis Incorporated to the Department of Industry, Trade, and Employment, Canada.

Jenkins, G.P. and C. Montmarquette (1979), "Estimating the private and social opportunity cost of displaced workers", Review of Economics and Statistics, 61:342–353.

Jensen, M. and M. Thursby (1981), "A conjectural variation approach to strategic tariff equilibria", Department of Economics, Ohio State University.

Johansen, L. (1960), A multi-sectional study of economic growth (North-Holland, Amsterdam).

Johnson, H.G. (1971), Aspects of the theory of tariffs (Harvard University Press, 1972) ch. 11.

Johnson, H.G. (1965), "The theory of tariff structure with special reference to world trade and development" in: H.G. Johnson and P. Kenen, eds., Trade and development (Librairie Droz, Geneva).

Keesing, D.B. and M. Wolf (1980), Textile quotas against developing countries (Trade Policy Research Centre, Thames Essay no. 3, London).

Kemp, M. and H.Y. Wan (1976), "An elementary proposition concerning the formation of customs unions", Journal of International Economics, 6:95–97.

Kostecki, M.M. (ed.) (1982), State trading in international markets (Macmillan, London).

Kreinin, M. (1981), "Static effect of E.C. enlargement on trade flows in manufactured products", Kyklos, 34:60–71.

Krueger, A. (1980), "Impact of foreign trade on employment in United States industry" in: J. Black and B. Hindley, eds., Current issues in commercial policy and diplomacy (Macmillan Press, London).

Lage, G.M. (1970), "A linear programming analysis of tariff protection", Western Economic Journal, 53:147–156.

Lavergne, R.P. (1981), "The political economy of U.S. tariffs", unpublished Ph.D. thesis, University of Toronto.

Leamer, E. and R.M. Stern (1970), Quantitative international economies (Allyn and Bacon, Boston).

Lloyd, P.J. (1977), Antidumping actions and the GATT system, Thames Essays, No. 9 (Trade Policy Research Centre, London).

Lowinger, T. (1976), "Discrimination in government procurement of foreign goods in the U.S. and Western Europe", Southern Economic Journal, 42:451–460.

Lundberg, L. (1981), "Patterns of barriers to trade in Sweden: A study in the theory of protection", World Bank Staff Working Papers, No. 494, Washington, D.C.

Magee, S.P. (1978), "Three simple tests of the Stolper–Samuelson theorem", in: P. Oppenheimer, ed., Issues in international economics (Oriel Press, London) 138–153.

Magee, S.P. (1972), "The welfare effects of restrictions on U.S. trade", Brookings Papers on Economic Activity, 3:645–707.

Martin, J.P. and J.M. Evans (1981), "Notes on measuring the employment displacement effects of trade by the accounting procedure", Oxford Economic Papers, 33:154–164.

Mayer, W. (1981), "Theoretical considerations on negotiated tariff adjustments", Oxford Economic Papers, 33:135–153.

McCarthy, J.E. (1975), Trade adjustment assistance: A case study of the shoe industry in Massachusetts, Research Report no. 58 (Federal Reserve Bank of Boston, Boston).

McCulloch, R. (1978), Research and development as a determinant of international competitiveness (National Planning Association, Washington, D.C.).

McCulloch, R. and R. Owen (1983), "Linking negotiations on trade and foreign investment", in: C.P. Kindleberger and D.B. Audretsch, eds., The multinational corporation in the 1980s (M.I.T. Press, forthcoming).

McPherson, C.P. (1972), "Tariff structures and political exchange", Unpublished Ph.D. thesis, University of Chicago.

Melvin, J.R. (1975), The tax structure and Canadian trade (Economic Council of Canada, Ottawa).

Miller, M.H. and J.E. Spencer (1977), "The static effects of the UK joining the Common Market: A general equilibrium approach", The Review of Economic Studies, 41:71–94.

Mintz, S. (1974), U.S. import quotas: Costs and consequences (American Enterprise Institute, Washington, D.C.).

Morkre, M.E. and D.G. Tarr (1980), Staff report on effects of restrictions on United States imports: Five case studies and theory (Federal Trade Commission, U.S. Government Printing Office, Washington, D.C.).

Mutti, J. (1982), Taxes, subsidies and competitiveness internationally (National Planning Association, Washington, D.C.).

Mutti, J. (1977), "Aspects of unilateral trade policy and factor adjustment costs", Review of Economics and Statistics, 60:102–110.

Mutti, J. and H. Grubert (1982), "D.I.S.C. and its effects", paper presented for a National Bureau of Economic Research conference on The Structure and Evolution of Recent U.S. Trade Policy, Cambridge, Mass., 3–4 December 1982.

Neumann, G. (1979), "Adjustment assistance for trade-displaced workers" in: D.B.H. Denoon, ed., The new international economic order: A U.S. response (New York University Press, New York).

Neumann, G. (1978), "The direct labor market effects of the trade adjustment assistance program: The evidence from the TAA survey" in: W. Dewald, ed., The impact of international trade and investment on employment (U.S. Department of Labor, U.S. Government Printing Office, Washington, D.C.).

Nordlinger, E. (1981), On the autonomy of the democratic state (Harvard University Press).

Olson, M. (1982), The rise and decline of nations: Economic growth, stagflation, and social rigidities (Yale University, New Haven).

Olson, M. (1965), The logic of collective action: Public goods and the theory of groups (Harvard

University: Cambridge).

Pearson, C. (1981), "Discriminatory trade restraints: OMAs on rubber footwear", School of Advanced International Studies, The Johns Hopkins University, Washington, D.C.

Pelzman, J. (1981), "Economic costs of tariffs and quotas on textile and apparel products imported into the United States", paper presented for a conference on Crisis Industries and the Safeguards Provisions of the GATT sponsored by the Trade Policy Centre, London.

Pelzman, J. and D. Rousslang (1982), Effects on U.S. trade and employment of tariff elimination among the countries of North America and the Caribbean basin, Office of Foreign Economic Research, U.S. Department of Labor.

Petith, H. (1977), "European integration and the terms of trade", Economic Journal, 87:262–272.

Pincus, J. (1975), "Pressure groups and the pattern of tariffs", Journal of Political Economy, 83:757–778.

Ray, E.J. (1981), "The determinants of tariff and non-tariff trade restrictions in the United States", Journal of Political Economy, 89:105–121.

Richardson, J.D. (1982a), "Trade adjustment assistance under the United States Trade Act of 1974: An analytical examination and worker survey", in: J. Bhagwati, ed., Import competition and response (University of Chicago Press for the National Bureau of Economic Research, Chicago).

Richardson, J.D. (1982b), "New nexes among trade, industrial, and balance-of-payments policies", paper presented at a conference on The Future of the International Monetary System, 7–8 October, New York University.

Richardson, J.D. (1971), "Some sensitivity tests for a 'constant-market-shares' analysis of export growth", Review of Economics and Statistics, 53:300–304.

Riedel, J. (1977), "Tariff concessions in the Kennedy Round and the structure of protection in West Germany: An econometric assessment", Journal of Political Economy, 7:133–143.

Ruffin, R.J. (1979), "Border tax adjustments and countervailing duties", Weltwirtschaftliches Archiv, 115:351–355.

Safarian, A.E. (1982), "Trade-related investment issues", paper presented at conference on Trade Policy in the Eighties, 23–25 June 1982, Institute for International Economics, Washington, D.C.

Sapir, A. (1981), "Trade benefits under the EEC generalized system of preferences", European Economic Review, 15:339–355.

Sapir, A. and L. Lundberg, "The U.S. generalized system of preferences and its impact", paper presented for a National Bureau of Economic Research conference on The Structure and Evolution of Recent U.S. Trade Policy, Cambridge, Mass., 3–4 December 1982.

Sapir, A. and E. Lutz (1981), "Trade in services: Economic determinants and development-related issues", World Bank Staff Working Papers, No. 480, Washington, D.C.

Saunders, R.S. (1980), "The political economy of effective protection in Canada's manufacturing sector", Canadian Journal of Economics, 13:340–348.

Shelp, R.K. (1981), Beyond industrialization (Praeger, New York).

Shouda, Y. (1980), "A quantitative analysis of protection in Japan", Japan Economic Research Center, mimeo.

Staelin, C.P. (1976), "A general equilibrium model of tariffs in a non-competitive economy", Journal of International Economics, 6:39–63.

Stolper, W. and P.A. Samuelson (1941), "Protection and real wages", Review of Economic Studies, 9:58–73.

Tarr, D.G. (1979), "Cyclical dumping: The case of steel products", Journal of International Economics, 9:57–63.

Taylor, L. and S.L. Black (1974), "Practical general equilibrium estimation of resource pulls under trade liberalization", Journal of International Economics, 4:37–58.

Tharakan, P.X.M. (1980), "Political economy of protection in Belgium", World Bank Staff Working Papers, no. 431, Washington, D.C.

U.S. Department of Treasury (1961), The operation and effect of the Domestic International Sales Corporation legislation: 1979 annual report (U.S. Government Printing Office, Washington, D.C.).

Utgoff, K.C. (1982), Reduction of adjustment costs associated with trade (Public Research Institute of the Center for Naval Analyses, Washington, D.C.).

Walter, I. (1982), "Structural adjustment and trade policy in the eighties", paper presented at a conference on Trade Policy in the Eighties, Institute for International Economics, Washington, D.C.

Warr, P.G. and P.J. Lloyd (1982), "Do Australian trade policies discriminate against less developed countries?", Centre for Economic Policy Research Discussion Papers, no. 50, Australian National University, Canberra.

Weston, A., V. Cable and A. Hewitt (1980), The EEC's generalized system of preferences (Overseas Development Institute, London).

Whalley, J. (1980a), "An evaluation of the recent Tokyo Round trade agreement through a general equilibrium model of world trade involving major trading areas", Working Paper 8009, Centre for the Study of International Economic Relations, Department of Economics, University of Western Ontario, London, Canada.

Whalley, J. (1980b), "Discriminatory features of domestic factor tax systems in a good mobile-factors immobile trade model: An empirical general equilibrium approach", Journal of Political Economy, 88:1177–1202.

Whalley, J. and R. Wigle (1982), "Price and quantity rigidities in adjustment to trade policy changes: Alternative formulation and initial calculations", paper presented at International Economics Association Conference on Structural Adjustment in Trade Dependent Advanced Economies, Stockholm, 2–6 August 1982.

Wolff, A. (1982), "The need for new GATT rules for safeguard actions", paper presented at a conference on Trade Policy in the Eighties, 23–25 June, Institute for International Economics, Washington, D.C.

Wolter, F. (1977), "Adjusting to imports from developing countries" in: H. Giersch, ed., Reshaping the world economic order (Mohr, Tubingen).

Young, L. and S.P. Magee, "A prisoners' dilemma theory of tariffs", paper presented at Econometric Society Meetings, New York, 29 December 1982.

INDEX

Absolute advantage, 12, 318
Adding machine model, 574, 576–577
Adjustment assistance mode, 574, 577
Aggregation problem, 501
Anti-Heckscher–Ohlin theory, 370, 388
Austrian model, 34, 211, 315

Balance of payments, 81, 211, 227, 278–279
Baldwin envelope, 71
Bias of trade regime, 529–530
Borderline goods, 140, 147
Border trade, 506
By-product distortions, 88–89, 93–94

Capital mobility, 211, 228, 240, 246–249, 254,
      257, 265, 269, 273–274, 278–279, 296, 453,
      566
Capital movements, see capital mobility
Cartel, 405–406, 411–412
Center, 187, 191, 221
Chipman flat, 276–278
Classical paradigm, 4, 31, 37, 52–53
Common external tariff, 118–120
Comparative advantage, 3, 11, 18, 41, 49, 52,
      181, 186, 190, 205, 206, 222, 248, 269, 272,
      470–471, 474–475, 480–481, 483, 487, 494,
      496, 510, 521–524
Comparative-cost model, 574, 577–578
Comparative dynamics, 290, 302, 311
Computable general equilibrium models,
      546–547
Contingent commodity, 437, 440–441, 449
Continuum of goods, 13–14, 28, 36, 204
Cost–benefit analysis, 65, 105
Cost of protection, 101–103, 118
Cross-hauling, 40, 247
Customs union, 69, 112, 114–115, 120–123, 597,
      600
Cyclical trade, 507

Degree of monopoly, 357–358, 533
Dependency, 187, 191
Development, 186–187, 212–215, 218, 221–223,
      232, 527
Differentiated products, 355, 359

Direct investment, 240, 245, 248
Directly-unproductive activities (DUP), 104
Domestic distortions theory, 86, 96, 98, 548
Domestic resource cost, 538–540, 543
Dual economy, 218–219, 310
Dumping, 605
Dutch disease, 6, 25, 41
Dynamic trade models, 186

Economies of scale, see increasing returns
Effective rate of protection (ERP), 32–34, 82,
      101–102, 106, 108, 114, 538–543, 546–547,
      580, 583
EFTA, 597–598
Enclave sector, 258
Equity concern model, 575, 577
European Community, 597–599
Ex-ante trade, 422, 426, 431, 447
Exchange rate, 81, 211
Exhaustible resources, 36, 369–370, 377, 388,
      393, 406, 414
Export pessimism, 520, 525
Export promotion, 212, 527–528
Ex-post trade, 422, 426, 431–432, 435, 447
External balance, 81
Externalities, 91–92, 523–524

Factoral value added, 333–334, 338
Factor content of trade, 175, 177, 479–483, 492
Factor endowment, 14–15, 20, 38, 132–133, 141,
      144–147, 152–155, 157, 160–162, 168–173,
      177, 179, 263–268, 274, 342, 348, 381–382,
      386, 388, 480–482, 492, 500–504
Factor intensity, 26, 140–151, 158, 163–164,
      167, 174, 177, 181, 300–311, 314, 317, 370,
      479, 486, 491, 513
Factor-intensity reversal, 146–147, 151, 174,
      177, 350, 440, 442, 446
Factor-market distortion, 46, 72, 424, 549
Factor-prize equalization, 15–16, 23, 140, 142,
      147, 162, 166, 177–180, 261, 266, 282, 299,
      302, 315, 346, 350, 352, 369, 377, 385–386,
      481
Factor prize frontier, 143, 220
First best, 86–100, 106, 110–111, 124

Foreign aid, 217
Foreign capital, 39, 203, 279–280, 284
Foreign exchange isoquant, 204
Foreign investment, 43, 51, 187, 198, 203, 232,
    240, 247–248, 254, 278, 280, 284, 326, 558,
    575
Free economic zones, 123–124
Free trade, 3, 8, 70–77, 87, 101, 116, 121, 132,
    135–139, 142, 161–162, 177, 190–191, 231,
    283, 293, 295, 304–306, 319, 440, 442,
    446–452, 520–523, 537, 547, 566

Gains from growth, 186
Gains from trade, 69, 71–74, 77, 118, 175–176,
    186, 190, 290, 295, 305, 319, 326, 332,
    335–337, 341, 345–346, 352–354, 361, 426,
    428, 449
GATT, 572, 600, 604, 607, 610
General equilibrium, 2, 4, 30, 39, 48–51, 102,
    111, 420, 473, 509, 583, 589
Global univalence, 140, 150, 160
Golden rule, 206–207, 228, 293
Gravity type models, 503
Growth, 186–187, 193, 203, 206, 208, 211–212,
    215, 219, 223–224, 232

Harris–Todaro model, 550
Heckscher–Ohlin, 2, 4, 14–30, 34, 37–40, 42,
    45–53, 72, 110, 132, 141, 145–147, 160,
    173–174, 181, 190, 205, 261, 265–270, 274,
    282–286, 292, 297, 299, 302, 306, 310, 316,
    318, 338, 346, 351, 359, 361, 368–377, 383,
    388, 393, 398, 427, 436–440, 443, 446–448,
    453, 468–469
Heteroscedasticity, 487
Hicks neutrality, 196, 199
Hotelling factor, 369, 377, 385, 388
Human capital, 482–484, 490, 492, 512

Illegal activities in trade, 535–538
Immiserizing growth, 10, 111, 187, 198–99
Imperfect competition, 50, 589
Implicit contract theory, 457–459
Implicit tariff, 108
Import substitution, 212, 220, 527–528
Income distribution, 14, 31, 33, 70, 73, 87,
    97–99, 259, 262
Incomplete markets, 422, 437–438, 459
Increasing returns, 48–53, 72–76, 123, 222,
    326–349, 357–358, 360, 510
Infant industry argument, 91, 522, 524
Instability, 560–565

Interest group model, 574–576
Interest rate, 34, 39, 250, 253–257, 279, 292,
    294, 299, 311–315, 372, 381, 384, 389, 396,
    407–409
Inter-industry trade, 49, 52
Intermediate goods, 5, 29, 33–34, 52, 316, 368,
    468
Internal balance, 81
International bargaining model, 574, 578
International factor mobility, 226, 238
Intertemporal trade, 290, 293, *see also* time
    preference
Intra-industry trade, 28, 49, 52, 330, 339,
    354–361, 487, 501–510, 606

Joint production, 5, 30–31, 440

Labor mobility, 238, 258
Learning-by-doing, 43, 213
Leontief paradox, 37, 132, 480–493
Lerner symmetry theorem, 78, 83
Limited entry, 348
Linder hypothesis, 504–505, 508
Logit analysis, 490

Magnification effect, 16, 30, 267, 270, 275, 440
Marginal cost pricing, 331
Marshall–Lerner condition, 7, 194
Marshall plan, 240
Middle products, 27, 34–36, 360
Minkowski matrix, 154–155, 157
Monopolistic competition, 53, 326, 355, 469,
    509
Multilevel trade, 31, 37, 315
Multinational firm, 42, 51, 245–248, 439, 460,
    494
Multiplicative randomness, 438, 442–447

National expenditure function, 134
National product formation, 133
Natural resources, 31, 36–37
Natural wage, 187–190
Neo-Marxist models, 318–319
Neo-Ricardian models, 74, 229, 313–320
Non-traded factors, 179–180
Non-traded goods, 5–6, 8, 20, 81, 290, 454, 468
North–South models, 37, 187, 193, 221–223,
    229

OECD, 106, 610
OLS regression, 473–475

OPEC, 240
Optimal tariff, 82–95, 100, 105, 120, 203, 269, 283–285, 424, 449. *See also* tariff
Optimal tax theory, 98

Pareto efficiency, 67, 69
Pattern of trade, 3, 28–92, 339–352, 368, 405, 470–472, 492, 494, 510–511
Periphery, 187, 190–191, 221
Preferential trade arrangements, 122
Price stabilization, 453–455
Profit analysis, 473–474, 490
Product cycle, 43, 495–496
Product differentiation, 76, 507, 511, 513
Programming models, 545
Protectionism, *see* tariff

Quota, 79–81, 85, 101–107, 456, 531–538, 554, 600, 602

Rate of extraction, 381–382, 386, 388, 393–394
Rate of profit, 186, 189, 191, 193, 220
Rational expectations, 80, 297, 450
Real exchange rate, 6
Real rewards, 165, 347–348
Reciprocity, 5, 25, 134
Re-export trade, 507
Rent-seeking activities, 104, 534–536, 544
Resource replacement, 397
Ricardian trade model, 2–6, 10–11, 14, 19, 21, 25, 28, 31, 36, 38, 51, 72, 137, 187–192, 269–272, 338, 351, 369, 377, 379, 381n, 383–387, 393, 468–469, 472–478, 494, 499, 502, 504
Risk pooling, 428–429
Rybcyznski theorem, 15–18, 38, 141, 145–153, 167, 169, 172, 180, 190, 195–202, 207–208, 274, 283, 299, 306, 316, 346, 348, 369, 375, 387, 389, 445–446, 555

Second best, 89, 92–93, 96, 105, 110, 121, 202–203, 306, 319, 423, 453, 552
Shadow prices, 109, 526, 554
Social adjustment costs, 591
Social welfare function, 68, 72
Specialization, 12, 25, 29, 47, 245, 276, 301, 341n, 342, 350, 392, 394, 397, 405, 476, 502, 522
Specie-flow mechanism, 81
Specific factors, 4, 21–28, 33, 39–40, 47, 110–111, 148–149, 173, 180, 190, 203, 248, 261–262

Status quo model, 574, 578
Steady state, 203, 294, 297, 300–312, 317, 319
Stolper–Samuelson theorem, 15–18, 29, 37, 48, 140, 144, 147, 152–155, 163, 169, 172, 174, 180, 190, 267, 270, 282, 299, 312–316, 346–348, 361, 369, 376, 383, 387, 389, 575
Strategic trade, 507
Subsidies, 73–74, 86–97, 102, 105, 110, 213, 215, 523, 525, 604

Tariff, 9–10, 27–38, 45, 73–86, 91, 93–96, 101–116, 121–122, 186, 199, 213, 425, 452–456, 473, 524–525, 531–540, 544, 554, 557, 580–588, 593, 600, 612
Technical progress, 196, 198, 220, 270, 494
Technology transfer, 42–43, 232
Terms of trade, 6–14, 27–28, 47, 65, 82, 85, 108, 116–121, 135, 186–187, 191–199, 211, 214, 218–231, 274, 279, 283, 285, 296, 310, 319, 326, 372, 376, 381–386, 389, 394–395, 398, 433–434, 448–453, 488, 525, 557–559, 598
Testing trade theory, 468
Third best, 92, 552
Time intensity reversal, 316
Time preference, 308–309, 316–317, 384
Trade adjustment assistance, 594–595
Trade creation, 115–117
Trade distortions, 92–93
Trade diversion, 115–117
Trade-diverting union, 113
Trade in securities, 43–44, 74, *see also* uncertainty
Trade in technology, 42
Trade liberalization, 582
Transfer of technology, 42
Transfer problem, 8–9, 246–247
Transportation cost, 470, 472, 511
Turnpike theorem, 209
Two-gap models, 187, 215–216, 530
Twoness, 161, 166, 178

Ultra-optimal tariff, 84
Uncertainty, 420, 423–424, 435, 437, 446–461, 509, 561
Unequal exchange, 187, 192–193, 319
UNIDO, 106, 111

Vinerian effects, 113
Voluntary export restraints, 600–601

Wage fund, 188–190, 229
Walrasian models, 421–422, 426, 435, 450